CU00662841

TINSLEYS' MAGAZINE.

LONDON
ROBSON AND SONS, PRINTERS, PANCRAS ROAD, N.W

NSLEYS' MAGAZINE.

.

VOL. XXVIII.

From January to June 1881.

244627

LONDON:

TINSLEY BROTHERS,

8 CATHERINE STREET, STRAND, W.C.

Tinsley's Magazine, Volume 28

Edmund Hodgson Yates, William
Tinsley, William Croft, Edmund Downey

CONTENTS.

TINSLEYS' MAGAZINE.

January 1881.

STRAWBERRY LEAVES.

BY RICHARD DOWLING,

AUTHOR OF 'THE MYSTERY OF KILLARD,' 'THE WEIRD SISTERS,'
'UNDER ST. PAUL'S,' ETC.

Part the First.

THE DUKE OF LONGACRE.

CHAPTER IV.

A TOWN STORY.

'IT is the fifty-second chapter,' said the Duke of Longacre. 'You will remember, May,' his Grace continued, as he turned over the proof-slips in his hand,—'you will remember, May, that, in the chapter before this, Antony Belmore had been out of employment for two months, and that he was at his wits' end to know how to get even bread.'

'Yes, and he had a broken pane of glass to let in the cold wind; and that there was a wide gaping fireplace to let down more cold; and that he had—got rid of his violoncello; and that his landlord was pressing him horribly—'

'For one pound eighteen and sixpence, rent.'

'But, Charlie, what is the good of writing uncomfortable stories, that have no pious object, like a Sunday-school tale?'

'My dear May, the public won't have anything but groans and tears. If you can manage yells for them, all the better. Gladiators don't fight now in the arena. Gentle creatures like you, darling, have no chance of voting violent death to a man by holding down your thumbs in the Colosseum. The modern novel is the portable arena of to-day; and gentle darlings like you, May, must be permitted to view the death-agony of men and women, or you would not patronise the libraries.'

'Charlie, if you dare to say any more such horrible untruths, I'll go down to the kitchen, put on an apron, and make the pastry for to-morrow.'

'If you do that, I'll go down and eat up all the nasty indigestible dough; and then what will you say at the inquest?'

'Take your arm away, sir; I won't stay here another minute. You have, I think, made up your mind to be disagreeable.'

'Well, run away now, if you like.'

'But you are holding me, and I can't stir.'

'And I mean to hold you if you

will not sit still while I read the chapter.'

'O dear, you are a horrible tease! There, let me go. I promise not to run away.'

'Very well. Now don't stir.'

The Duke of Longacre and Marion Durrant, his sweetheart, were seated in one of the smallest conservatories in London. This conservatory was situated at the back of Miss Traynor's house in Knightsbridge. The house and all that it contained, with the exception of Marion's aunt, the owner, were small. Two people could not possibly walk abreast in the hall, nor up the stairs. It was a saying of the Duke's that one of those days he should get wedged in that hall, and would have to be extracted from it by violent means. There was a tiny front drawing-room and a tiny back drawing-room, and between them a pair of folding-doors which always stood open. At the rear of the back drawing-room was the little conservatory in which Marion and the Duke were seated. The conservatory was as wide as the room, and three feet deep. Owing to shelves at the ends and sides for flowerpots, the absolute dimensions of the place were much reduced, and it was impossible for two people to sit at the same side; so when the Duke held Marion he was standing beside her. He had risen from his chair opposite her a few minutes before. The conservatory was separated from the back drawing-room by a glass door opening into the room. At the outer end of the conservatory was a glass door yielding outwards on a little wooden landing, which, by means of a flight of wooden steps, communicated with the very small garden below.

Now this being one of the fairest days of June, the door opening outwards on the landing, and the door opening inwards on the back-

drawing-room, were open. It was one of those days which make the old young, the young poetical, and love the sweetest pastime for those who have any one to love. The day was in the fresh warm youth of the year. All the asperities of winter and spring had passed away, and the time had not yet been fatigued with summer heats. The air was moist and full of the scent of young leaves. In the dustiest street of all London there was some faint suggestion of the forest. According to the calendar it was summer; but really it was the summer end of spring, when the land is heaviest with leaves, and the air is thickest with the songs of birds. There was a savour of resin in the breeze which made those who had been country-born, and were now penned in the city, raise in unguarded moments their heads, and listen for the murmur of the brittle pine-leaves.

'With your kind permission, or rather, having plainly shown you that I do not want your permission, kind or otherwise, I will now read to you the fifty-second chapter.

"His tall thin form had now shrunken almost to a skeleton. Privation and sorrow had at length broken down his health and spirits. Although he had scarcely reached his fiftieth year, he was already an old man. His eyes were dim; his cheeks had fallen in; his hands were emaciated and tremulous. His eyes were deep-sunken and unnaturally bright.

"All the clothes he possessed were on him, with the exception of one shirt, a pair of socks, and three or four dilapidated collars. His elbows were through his coat; his trousers were frayed at the edges; the uppers and soles of his boots had, in more than one place, parted company.

"He lived in a back attic off Cursitor-street, near Chancery-lane.

There he had contracted to pay four shillings a week for an unfurnished room. One part of the contract had been fulfilled, for it might almost be said with literal truth that the room was unfurnished. It contained one chair, which had been cane-seated once, but which was now a skeleton. Across the framework of this seat had been placed a board. On this board were now placed a cup and saucer and small black crockery-ware teapot, a knife and fork, and a common delft plate. These, with the exception of a tin candlestick and a battered old quart tin kettle, were all the articles connected with the kitchen or table which could be seen in the place. In a corner farthest from the skylight lay a wretched stretcher, and by the side of the stretcher a common soap-box, which served as a seat, while the board across the chair answered as a table. Under the broken pane in the skylight stood a basin, and on the chimneypiece were a piece of soap, a worn-out comb and brush, a towel, and two small jugs.

" Beyond the things mentioned above there was absolutely nothing in the room, except the most wretched of things all—Antony Belmore himself. He was sitting on the box at the head of his miserable stretcher, when a knock came to the door.

'Come in,' said Belmore. Only two people ever called on him now—his landlord and his friend Valentine de Montmorency.

"Mr. Jeremiah Watkins entered. He was a stout prosperous-looking man of about the same age as Belmore. 'Well,' said Mr. Jeremiah Watkins, the landlord, coming into the room, ' got any money for me, Mr. Belmore?'

" The musician raised his head and shook it sadly. 'Nothing yet, nothing yet.'

'It is Saturday, you know, and I'm blowed if I don't think I've had plenty of patience. One eighteen six is no joke, you know.'

"Again Belmore shook his head. 'I have earned nothing for months. Nothing.'

'I know that. It's bad for you; but it's bad for me also. What am I to do about my money?'

'I can only ask you to wait—to wait until I get something to do; then I'll pay you. How am I to pay you when I am idle, and have been idle for months?'

'I own it's hard on you; but then, you see, this is harder on me. You are out of situation, and therefore you get no money, which is natural and proper, as I say; but here is my room in situation, as I may say, and it gets no wages. Now that's not fair or reasonable, I say.'

'I cannot answer you, Mr. Watkins. I am as sorry as you can be that I am not able to pay. What can I do?—tell me what can I do.'

"Mr. Watkins owned three houses in this alley. Each one was let in tenements, and in all he had sixteen tenants. But in Antony Belmore he knew he had a tenant far superior in mind and manners to any of his other lodgers. And yet, although he was not by nature a hard man, and although he knew he was dealing with a gentleman, and although he would not do anything harsh to poor old Belmore for a much larger sum, yet he could not be importunate with graciousness. He had one of those hard, blunt, direct natures which can never step out of the routine manner, no matter how much their minds may be out of the routine course. Said he,

'But what I look at is this, how are you ever going to pay? You're out of situation; you see no chance of getting a situation. You've sold or pawned all you could sell or pawn. Even your old fiddle is gone—'

'It is,' said Belmore, with laconic sadness.

'Then how, in the name of all that's black and blue, are you ever going to get any money if that old fiddle is up the spout? That's what's the puzzle to me.'

"Belmore rose, and clasping his long, knotty, emaciated hands in front of him, said,

'I cannot say more than that I am very sorry I cannot pay you, Mr. Watkins. If you wish it, I am willing to go. If I go, I have my choice of two things—the work-house or the river—'

'And you would choose the river?'

'And I would choose the river.'

'That is the way always with you—' Mr. Watkins paused. Belmore waited for him. 'With all you fools,' said Mr. Watkins, using the most tender word his nature would allow, instead of the most offensive, as he had intended when he had set out with the sentence.

'I will go if you wish it,' said Belmore meekly, making a motion first to an old battered hat that lay on the floor, and then towards the door.

'Who asked you to go?' said Watkins doggedly.

'No one has asked me,' answered Belmore; 'but of course you have a perfect right to ask me to go if you wish.'

'I didn't ask you to go, and I don't ask you to go, and it's manners to wait to be asked,' said Watkins ungraciously. 'You may stay another week. At the end of a week I hope you will have got some employment.'

'Mr. Watkins, I should be deceiving you if I led you to suppose I shall have got anything to do in a week. This is the dull season,' said the poor gentleman, dropping both his hands and looking hopelessly at his landlord.

'Now, Mr. Belmore,' said Watkins, 'don't you think it a little rough on me to take me so cool? I tell you, who owe me rent, you may stay another week, and I say I hope you may get something to do in the mean time; and you then round on me, and tell me there is no use in my hoping you'll be able to get anything to do. I say it's downright rough on me. It's like telling me I'm a fool for trusting you any further.'

'Indeed I did not mean to imply anything of the kind,' said the poor gentleman, in a tone of deep concern. 'But if I told you I hoped to be able to get anything to do in a week, it would be a lie.'

'But I am a business man, and I like to be dealt with in a business way; and a business man would never say there was no chance of his getting employment in a week.'

'Unfortunately, I am not a business man. I never have been one.'

'More's the pity. You see, if you were only a business man you would have a much better chance of getting something to do, and you would not make such unreasonable answers. But there, there; don't say any more about it. I am only wasting my time talking to you.'

'I am very sorry it should be so,' said the poor gentleman; 'very sorry. If I had any property—' He paused, and looked at the dilapidated chair, the box, and the stretcher.

'Bah!' cried the landlord; 'I'm not going to touch. I'm a business man and no fool, but I'm not a wild-beast. Do your best now this week, and try and get something to do.'

'I am sure I am very grateful to you, Mr. Watkins.'

'Grateful! grateful! What's the good of being grateful? Be business-like. That's the main thing. Next week you'll owe me more than two pounds, so stir yourself and get something to do.'

"Without another word Mr. Jeremiah Watkins left the room, closing the door softly after him.

"When the landlord had gone, Belmore took a few feeble steps across the room, and then staggered back again to his old place by the head of the bed. No fire burned in the huge yawning grate, on the bottom bars of which the cold gray light of winter afternoon fell through the chimneypot above. Through the skylight nothing could be seen but the leaden November sky. It was cold and raw and damp and dismal.

"Belmore dropped his head on his hands and rested his elbows on knees. Thus he sat in thought for a long while without moving. At last he raised his head and shook it gravely, smiled sadly, and whispered,

'It is more than likely I shall have proved myself, according to his idea, a fool; for a gentleman—' at this word he drew himself together, paused for a moment, and then finished—'for a gentleman cannot afford to die of starvation in a garret.'

"Then his head fell once more. Once more he dropped his face into the hollow of his hands, and resting his elbows on his knees, sat motionless.

"So deeply absorbed was he in his thought he did not hear a brisk step on the stairs or a faint knock at the door. The knock was repeated. Belmore heard it now. He raised his head slowly, compressed his lips for a moment, and then whispered, 'If he says another word about the rent I will not look at to-morrow.' He arose, and having steadied himself by holding the chimneypiece for a second, crossed the room with an air of

dignity and breeding in pathetic contrast with the mean attire and squallid surroundings of the poor gentleman.

"He opened the door and exclaimed, holding out his hand, 'Ah, De Montmorency, is it you? I am delighted to see you. Come in.'

"All at once the firmness died out of his manner, and he uttered a sob. Of this the visitor took no notice, but, walking to the middle of the room where stood the chair with the board across it, he began humming a lively air as he put down on the board a few parcels. When he had given Belmore a few minutes to recover himself, he faced round briskly and said gaily,

'Any good news about yourself, Belmore?'

'No.'

'I'm sorry. But, if your luck is bad, mine has been good. I have come into money. What do you think of that, Belmore?'

'I am sincerely glad to hear it. You did not expect it, did you?'

'I had no more expectation of coming into money than you have. Blessed are those who expect nothing. I have run through three fortunes; and no man I ever met had a chance of running through more than three fortunes. Who ever heard of any other fellow having had four fortunes?'

'Is it much?'

'Half a crown.'

'What!'

'Half a crown.'

'It's a poor joke, De Montmorency; a poor joke.'

'I think it's a capital joke. Now, if, as I came along the street, I lost the half a crown, I'd consider it a poor joke. I was looking over an old waistcoat, when, hey presto! out drops half a crown. I'd like to know what you'd call that, if not a good joke.'

"The speaker was a short little

man, with dark eyes and hair, and a swarthy Southern complexion.

'Ah, De Montmorency, if I had only such spirits as yours!'

'It isn't the best, at all, Belmore. It's only a quartern of London gin. Please observe this is no joke. No; look here, Belmore, you mustn't be offended if I have taken a liberty. I have long been wishing you would dine with me; but I've been so cruelly hard up I couldn't do the thing decently at an outside place. But, as we are both Bohemians, I've ventured to order the rag-and-bone merchant in the Lane to send over a peck of coals and a bundle of wood. I waited to see the boy start with the coal and wood before I left the place; and then I ran off and got a few little things. So I'm going—if you will not think it a liberty—to light up a fire here and cook a bit of luncheon, and ask you to have a bit with me, Belmore. You are not offended?'

'If, De Montmorency, it were any one but you—'

'Ah, that is right, my dear Belmore; that is right! That young scamp must have stopped to play with other boys. Ah, here he is! You young scamp! Put it there on the hearthstone, and, look you, here's a penny for yourself. Now vanish! Well, my dear Belmore, I don't think much of our coal merchant. When I am Comptroller of the Household I shall not give him the contract. I shall be very corrupt in those days. I shall take bribes—when I can. Now there is a piece of undesirable slate. If either of us had young children that slate might be useful in forming their young minds and making them familiar with figures.'

'Thank Heaven we have no children.'

'Ay, ay, ay! Have it as you will, have it as you will. No doubt

you are right. Now you don't happen to have a frying-pan?'

'No, I have nothing of the kind.'

'Never mind, we'll toast the rashers, and fortunately a toasting-fork is within reach.'

'There is not one in this place.'

'I will make a capital one out of three pieces of this wood with the aid of a piece of string. I think this fire will light now. It is beautifully designed and excellently built. I am a connoisseur in fires. I have been accused of resorting to bludgeon tactics. But I don't care what they may call my tactics, they always succeed. First you get a few pieces of paper—if they are greasy, all so much the better; and you roll them up loosely, as I did the piece that came round the rashers. Then you put on as much wood as you judge sufficient, taking care to cross-hatch the pieces, as an artist would say. Then put on more wood loosely until you think there is too much. After that put on more wood until you are perfectly sure there is too much. When you have done this, lay on eight pieces of coal neither larger nor smaller than a bantam's egg, and upon these eight lay three pieces as big as a turkey's egg. After that set fire to your paper, as I do. I will now, while the fire is kindling and clearing, make our toasting-fork.'

"He rose from his knees before the fire, and proceeded to splice two thin pieces of firewood, one on either side of a thick piece, having first cut a slanting bit out of the ends of the thinner ones where he applied them to the thick one. These prongs he had only to sharpen.

"While De Montmorency was engaged in making his toasting-fork, Belmore, attracted by the unfamiliar blaze and glow in that chill room, drew the old box to the fire, and sat down to enjoy the heat.

"Nothing ages a man more quickly than cold and hunger; and as Belmore sat before the mounting flames he looked seventy, although it was only about fifty years since he had first seen the light in the village of Berley, in Lincolnshire.

'There is no fender,' said De Montmorency; 'but I'll tell you what we'll do. We'll put the tea-pot down on the ground, take the lid off, and put a saucer on the top of the teapot. That will make a capital gravy-dish to catch the rich nectar from the rashers.'

"All this time Belmore never moved or spoke. With his thin hands hanging down over his knees, he simply gave himself to the animal enjoyment of warmth, a pleasure he had not known for a long time.

"At last the toasting began; and now, for the first time, the attention of Belmore was withdrawn from the fire to be concentrated on the food. He had tasted food since he had felt the heat of a fire, but that food had been the simplest and the most scanty. Convicts would have mutinied if they had been kept on such a scale as the poor gentleman had been obliged to live on for a month; that is if convicts, after a month of such diet, would have had strength enough to lift up their hands in menace.

"At length the first piece of bacon was toasted. With a large pocket-knife De Montmorency cut off a slice of bread from a loaf, which had formed one of the parcels he had brought in; and having placed this on the chair-table, he removed everything else. Then he took up the saucer from the fire and put that on the table, and dropped the hissing crisp bacon into the rich straw-coloured gravy. He poured some gin out of the bottle into a cup, and added water from a jug.

'You go on and eat now,' the visitor said; 'I'll cook and serve,

and will naturally wait. I'll make a gravy-dish of a slice of bread this time. You don't object to a slice of bread soaked in red-hot dripping of toasted bacon? Of course you don't. I should like to see the man with a wholesome appetite who did. Pretend the bacon is fish, and that we have lent our fish-forks to the bishop who lives on the landing below this, and that you have to eat your fish with a fork and a piece of bread, and then all you've got to do is to fancy my knife is an old-fashioned fork, and there is nothing more to be desired.'

"As Belmore had cut off the first piece of bacon and was raising it to his lips, some one knocked at the door. Belmore put down the bit untasted, and said, in a tremulous voice, 'De Montmorency, will you ask him to leave me at peace, or tell me I must go? Ask him to spare me or send me away.'

"De Montmorency opened the door softly and looked out.

'Is Mr. Belmore in?' asked a very low voice.

'Yes,' answered De Montmorency. 'May I ask what is the nature of your business?' He kept the door partly closed, so that the man outside could not see in. 'Because Mr. Belmore is engaged at present.'

'I want to see him on very particular business indeed.'

'Of what nature?'

'Well, I am a lawyer.'

'If it is anything about the rent,' said Belmore, 'I am willing to go, but I cannot pay. Nor do I think I shall be able to pay next week.'

'As Mr. Belmore has spoken of paying rent, I may as well tell you at once that I am in a position to say he can pay it now.'

'No, no, no!' cried the poor gentleman; 'I really haven't any money.'

'But I will pay it for him, with

the greatest pleasure. I have very good news for Mr. Belmore, if I may see him.'

'Good news?' repeated De Montmorency. 'Did I understand you to say you have good news for Mr. Belmore?'

'Unquestionably. Very good news indeed.'

'As Mr. Belmore is very particularly engaged at present, would it not be better if he called upon you at your office in half an hour?'

'Yes, that will suit admirably. You are a friend of Mr. Belmore?'

'O yes; I think I may say I am.'

'Then will you allow me the privilege of a few moments' conversation with you, sir?'

'Certainly.' And De Montmorency went out on the landing and closed the door.

"He found there a tall stoutish man of middle age and very dark complexion. The stranger moved a few paces from the door, and then spoke in a very low, confidential, and friendly voice. 'My name is Jackson. I am senior partner of the firm of Jackson & Connington, Lothbury. You are a friend of Mr. Belmore?'

'Yes. I think his only friend.'

'I am glad to have this opportunity of having a little chat with you, for the news I have for him is not only good, but so astoundingly good that we must break it to him gently. I will not now trouble you further than to ask you if you can tell me who Mr. Antony Belmore's father was, and where and when was Mr. Belmore born? We know all about it. I ask the question merely to put all doubt of his identity out of the way finally.'

'Mr. Belmore, whom I have known since we were boys, and whose father I also knew, is the only son of George Belmore of Berley in Lincolnshire. I think Mr. Belmore is about fifty years of age.'

'All right, all right! You may

break to him as gently as you can that he has fallen into an exceedingly good thing. Our firm has just found out he is heir to a fine estate. You will, I trust, excuse me for having taken the liberty of bringing this with me. But we thought it possible Mr. Belmore might want a little money before he opens his own banking account to-morrow or the day after. You will, I think, find fifty in notes and fifty in gold here.'

'Thank you very much, I'm sure. It was very thoughtful of you to bring this. Would it put you to any inconvenience if we did not call upon you for a couple of hours instead of half an hour? Some of this'—he held up the money—'might in the mean time be usefully employed.'

"He touched his coat with his other hand.

'O, I understand,' said the lawyer, with a sympathetic look towards the door, behind which the poor gentleman concealed his poverty. 'Let it be two hours. That will be—let me see—five o'clock. Good-day.'

'Good-day,' said De Montmorency, dropping the money into his trousers-pocket. 'The shock of knowing he had fallen into even a hundred pounds would be too great now.'

"He reëntered the room. 'It was really good news, after all. I don't know how good yet. But anyway 'tis good enough for him to give me some money for you on account.'

'Did he give you enough to pay Watkins?'

'How much is that?'

'One pound eighteen and sixpence.'

'O yes! He gave me five pounds. Here you are. Come now, and put on your hat. You see this lawyer believes in your luck, or he wouldn't put down his money without even being asked.'

'And do you, too, believe there is some good luck in store for me?'

'Most emphatically.'

'Then I'll go and pay Watkins, and never come back again.'

'You must send for those things.'

'Those wretched things! Why should I send for them? They would only bring up many of my cruellest memories.'

'Ay, but you mustn't leave them here; you must take them away, if you only burn them. Suppose you are to turn out very lucky. Suppose you are the real King of Burmah; then, of course, these things will be bought up, and exhibited as curiosities. But come, put on your hat. We won't waste time with Watkins. Come out, and we will have something better in the form of luncheon than we were just about to eat. I have arranged with the lawyer that we need not call upon him for a couple of hours.'

"Belmore had eaten the slice of bread and the rasher. He had drunk a little of the gin too, and had already begun to revive. Casting a look down at his wretched clothes, he said,

'De Montmorency, it was very good of you to prevent that lawyer seeing how things are here. But I am not much better off now. I am scarcely in a plight to call upon this gentleman.'

'That will be all right. Suppose he gave me ten instead of five pounds for you. You can get all you want. Finish your gin, and I'll have some, and then we will go.'

"In a few minutes they were in Holborn. De Montmorency took Belmore in a ready-made clothing shop, and got him a suit of clothes, an ulster, and a hat. They came out, and then got boots and gloves. After this, De Montmorency surveyed his friend from top to toe, and muttered with a sigh.

'You'll do. Now let us go and have a good solid meal somewhere. But stay. Ask me to dine or lunch with you, Belmore; for you are the financier. I am only your agent.'

'Where shall we go, De Montmorency?'

'To the Holborn.'

'But I am afraid you have already spent more than the lawyer gave you.'

'Let us go to the Holborn, by all means. As to money, that lawyer gave me a hundred pounds, not ten; and now here is the balance in gold, notes, silver, and copper.'

'A hundred pounds! It must be good luck, indeed, when he gave you a hundred pounds! Why, this morning I should have thought ten pounds miraculous luck, and here now am I getting a hundred on account! De Montmorency, it must be wonderful luck!'

"They went to the Holborn, and had a substantial luncheon, and a bottle of burgundy between them. Belmore paid the bill, and gave the waiter half a crown. He said, 'Thank you, sir. Very much obliged, indeed;' and flew for Belmore's ulster as though Satan were at his heels.

"When they got into the street, Belmore called a hansom, and told the man to drive to Jackson & Connington, Lothbury. As soon as the cab drew up, De Montmorency said,

'I'll wait for you in the cab. I'll ask the driver to let down the glass, and I shall be all right and comfortable.'

'But won't you come up with me?'

'No, I think it better not. I am almost sure the lawyers do not want me, and I should not like to feel that, if I went up. I shall be quite comfortable. Run away now, Belmore, and hurry back and tell me you are the real King of Burmah.'

"Belmore did not care to force him against his wish; so he stepped out of the cab and walked into the house and up-stairs.

"He had been gone about half an hour, when a man dashed out of that door and rushed at the hansom crying,

'Engaged?'

'Yes, sir.'

'By whom?'

'Tall gentleman in ulster coat—gone up-stairs half an hour ago.'

'All right! You'll do! He's taken suddenly ill, and I want you to drive me for a doctor. The job is a sovereign, remember!'

'But there's a gentleman inside.'

"De Montmorency knocked at the glass, and the driver drew it up. De Montmorency said to the man on the pathway,

'Mr. Belmore ill, did you say?'

'Yes, sir; taken suddenly ill.'

"De Montmorency leaped out, crying,

'Jump in, jump in! I'll run up and see him.'

"When he reached the room where Mr. Jackson and his partner stood, he found Belmore lying on a couch deadly white.

'Mr. de Montmorency, this is my partner, Mr. Connington. Mr. Connington, this is Mr. de Montmorency, a friend of his Grace.'

'His Grace be ——!' said De Montmorency. 'I am a friend of Mr. Belmore. What's the matter with him?'

'His Grace the Duke of Fenwick has fainted upon learning the honours and wealth that have suddenly come upon him.'

'And who, in the name of Heaven, is his Grace the Duke of Fenwick?'

'The person you knew as Mr. Antony Belmore is Duke of Fenwick, with a rent-roll of ninety thousand a year.'"'

Here Cheyne finished reading, and, throwing down the proofs, said,

'Well, May, what do you think of it?'

'O, I think it very clever indeed, only—only—'

'Yes, my ungrateful and critical sweetheart?'

'Only—only—doesn't every one know who the heir to a dukedom is, like the heir to a kingdom?'

'No; every one knows nothing.'

'But doesn't the Duke himself know who his heir is? Or doesn't the House of Commons, or some one?'

'Dukes know absolutely nothing at all, and the House of Commons knows less.'

'But he isn't gone mad, is he?'

'No; I hadn't the heart to make him go mad. He'll wake up presently as right as paint.'

While Charles Cheyne was reading chapter fifty-two in the little conservatory to his darling sprightly May, the Duke of Shropshire, having voted against the detested Radicals, was returning by express train to Silverview Castle, and Edward Graham was seated in front of the Beagle Inn, Anerly, painting the peaceful valley with Anerly Church in the near middle distance.

[To be continued.]

HAMLET RE-HEARSED.

A Comical Tragedy.

SLOUGHBOROUGH was a dull sleepy town in Blankshire. Its twenty thousand unspeculative inhabitants had few sympathies beyond the borough bounds, and lived as quiet lives as isolated oysters. A bombshell in their midst could not have more astonished and alarmed them than the rumour that an amateur dramatic club was about to arise like a deadly upas over them.

Sloughborough had always looked upon Thespis as an atrocious enemy to the social system and good business-like habits, and it determined to wage war to the knife against the intolerable innovation. Deputies from the 'most potent, grave, and reverend signiors' waited upon the Bishop of Sloughborough, and passionately besought him to use whatever influence he possessed in order to save 'those misguided young men' from ruin. The Bishop, a kindly sensible old gentleman, promised he would call upon the erring ones, but at the same time he did not consider the young men or the town *in globo* would be likely to suffer much by indulging in a little harmless amusement. The deputation rose in pious horror, and most of the worthy inhabitants of Sloughborough went to church on the following Sunday quite prepared to hear a combination of Socialism and Ritualism thundered from the pulpit.

Gradually the alarm died away, and, being assured that the club intended at first to study nothing more dangerous than *Hamlet Prince of Denmark*, 'one of Shakespeare's plays,' as the Bishop explained after visiting the members, the virtuous people became more easy in their minds, and finally began to look forward with no small degree of anxiety to the production of the drama. Such a revolution was an era in history; nothing like it had been known since the passing of the Reform Act, at least in Sloughborough.

The performance was to take place in the town-hall, and here the members of the Dramatic Club spent their evenings for a full month. Nightly they rehearsed, and upon the stage arrangements squandered as much energy as would have brought Napoleon back in triumph over the Alps. The chief difficulty was the church-yard scene, but eventually the club surmounted every obstacle. At last came the eventful night. Every seat in the concert-room was filled. The front row was occupied by the Mayor and Corporation Many of the aristocratic families in Sloughborough and its neighbourhood took their places in the reserved chairs, and the shoopkeepers formed a powerful contingent in the rear. There had been a little trouble to induce the members of the Corporation to attend the performance, as Alderman Jenkins had suddenly died, and was to be buried with honours during the week. Indeed it was at first proposed to postpone the play; but a majority of the councillors, at a specially convened meeting, resolved not to spoil sport.

The Mayor, in crimson, sat in

the middle of the front row. He was stout, middle-sized, pompous-looking, and fifty-five, with a face clean-shaven save for a fringe of grizzled hair which partly framed his good-humoured countenance. On one side of 'his Worship' sat his handsome wife, 'fair, fat, and forty'-five, or thereabouts ; and on the other side a boy of eight, with long flaxen curls and a strong look of Henry VIII., 'his Worship's' only son. Next the Mayor's wife, Mr. Powell, the most prominent, popular, and influential councilman in Sloughborough, reclined, mopping his fat forehead with a colossal bandana. He was tall, stout, and well-favoured, with a countenance wherein tears and smiles struggled in vain for mastery. You could never tell whether his next facial contortion would be accompanied with a sob or with a chuckle. His age might be anything from forty-five to sixty. Had he handed you his card—it was invariably his business card—you would have found engraved upon it the following legend :

> Mr. PERCIVAL C. POWELL, T.C.
>
> 18 WILKINS STREET,
>
> SLOUGHBOROUGH.
>
> (N.B. *Funeral Arrangements conducted in the most satisfactory manner.*)

The play began. When the Prince came on, the feminine portion of the audience fell into raptures over the physique of the hero; and, indeed, Will Waterhouse—the Hamlet of the evening —was a splendid fellow. He stood six feet in his pumps, and was built in accurate proportion. Every one was enchanted, and the curtain went down on the first act amidst uproarious applause. Then a slight sensation was created in the breasts of the 'pretty girls' by the advent of half a dozen officers from the neighbouring town of Grassholm, who had lounged over 'to see the thing, you know.' As they walked up the hall, and gazed at the rows of smiling faces, the recollection of many a night of reckless gaiety in some well-nigh forgotten metropolis was wafted back. Sloughborough had been dozing for a long period, but its awakening was more astounding than a sudden eruption of Vesuvius.

'I say, James,' said Mr. Powell to his Worship, 'those youngsters reflect great credit upon their native town ; but, between you and me, I must confess I feel a little anxious about their churchyard scene. What do you say, Mrs. Catmur ?' turning to the Mayor's wife, who did not at all relish the unceremonious manner in which the undertaker persisted in addressing her husband ; but Mr. Powell was wealthy and influential, and it would be unwise to offend him, or check his familiarity. 'I may tell you in confidence, Mrs. Catmur, that I have given the lads a few professional tips about the burial of Ophelia. Of course you can't expect the young men to know all about such matters without a little advice from a person of my large and varied experience.'

'Indeed !' said Mrs. Catmur, rather haughtily, not at all anxious to pursue the gloomy subject.

No serious hitch occurred in the performance until the third act, when the Ghost stumbled over Hamlet in the Queen's apartment ; but the audience, through sympathy with the illustrious dead, applauded, and the Mayor's little son called out, in a voice of respectful admiration, 'Encore !' His Worship instantly checked the youth with an audible 'Hush !' which evidently gave a tone to the house.

Shortly after the conclusion of the fourth act, a messenger came round to the front of the reserved chairs, and said,

'If you please, Mr. Powell, would you step behind the curtain for a moment?'

The Mayor was just about to have a joke with the smiling yet tearful councilman, that he hoped it wasn't a 'job;' but ere he had time to bandy any Sloughborough witticisms, Mr. Powell stood up, his countenance the picture of terror, and exclaimed,

'Good gracious! Can anything have happened that—' And before the astonished audience could hear the remainder of the undertaker's inspired utterances, he had disappeared with a rush behind the footlights.

Various were the surmises as to the cause of Mr. Powell's mysterious disappearance.

'It must be the Ghost, pa,' said the Mayor's little boy.

'Keep quiet, child,' said his father. 'What should *you* know about such matters?'

A confused hum had already been heard from the stage; but now the undertaker's voice electrified the audience—

'Can't get him out? But you must get him out—now—at once! The hearse is already at the door!'

'Ssh! The people outside will hear you!'

'What do *I* care about the people outside? My professional reputation is at stake. That's none of your stock coffins, but best oak, and—'

'Well, we couldn't help it.'

'Couldn't help it? What's that to me, I should like to know? Out he must come, if he has to be taken away in compartments!'

'What *are* we to do?'

'Do? I don't care what you do; but the coffin must leave this place at once. I'm a ruined man if this gets wind, or if there's a moment's farther delay.'

'Get another—a duplicate coffin. No one will be the wiser. We'll see you don't lose by it.'

'But I tell you it is impossible—none of your jokes, my good fellow. How would you like to be buried alive yourself? There's no use in struggling. If any injury is done to my property I'll have every one of you locked up.'

The audience was by this time fairly terrified. What dreadful accident, or worse, had occurred? Had Laertes murdered Hamlet in earnest, and were they trying to induce Mr. Powell to bury him secretly before an inquest could be held? Or had Polonius been mortally wounded behind the arras? No surmise was wild enough. Hysterics and smelling-bottles—luxuries almost unknown in the lethargic borough—were now the rule, rather than the exception. Even the gallant military men were becoming palpably funky.

At last the Mayor, with that calm dignity which would have reflected credit upon the mother of Coriolanus, rose and said,

'Ladies and gentlemen, something wrong—decidedly wrong—seems to have occurred upon the stage. Let us hope it is nothing *very* serious or tragical; *but*' (here he paused and coughed, in order to lend additional gravity to his remarks), 'as Chief Magistrate of Sloughborough, I feel it my duty to allay the painful anxiety of my fellow-citizens by ascertaining—personally ascertaining—the extent of this unfortunate disaster.'

Then, bidding a tender farewell to his wife and child, and grinning a ghastly but re-assuring smile through his horsecollar whiskers, he stepped bravely and majestically from the hall and sought the stage-door. He was instantly admitted, and he advanced cautiously towards the stage, whence came the mysterious voices of the night. Here he beheld Councillor Powell in tears bending over Ophelia's coffin (lent for the occasion by the enterprising undertaker) in which lay the body of a man.

'I'll tell you what we can do, Waterhouse,' said Horatio. 'The pall can be put over the coffin while Ophelia is being duly consigned to the grave, and when your lines come on we can place the coffin standing on end, with your face to the audience. You could "speak your speech" in that manner. Eh?'

A general titter from the actors greeted this suggestion.

'Good Heavens! What *am* I to do?' sobbed Mr. Powell. 'Old Jenkins is to be buried in this very shell. Here, some of you, help me to lift the coffin and *shake* him out of it.'

'No, no!' from the coffin.

'Bleed him, Mr. Powell, or put him on the Tanner system,' suggested the First Gravedigger.

In the uproar and confusion his Worship's presence had not been noticed until now.

'O James,' said the injured undertaker, 'isn't this very hard lines? These young ruffians were so elated with success, that nothing would satisfy Mr. Hamlet but to squeeze himself, for a lark, into a coffin that's three sizes too small for him; and we can't get him out now, he's jammed so tightly into it. It is old Jenkins's coffin. I had the misfortune to lend it, and it should have been sent to his house to-night without fail. I'm ruined! We are *all* ruined!'

'Ring up the curtain,' cried the Mayor; 'nothing else will allay the alarm in the house.'

'No, no, for Heaven's sake don't do that!' gasped the colossal Hamlet in the coffin. 'If the audience sees me, I shall be the laughing-stock of the town.'

'There's no help for it, Waterhouse. You must suffer for the exuberance of your youthful spirits. The peace of mind of hundreds of your fellow-citizens depends upon prompt and energetic action. Personal vanity cannot for one moment be allowed to interfere in a matter of such tremendous magnitude; *and*' (here he paused), 'as Chief Magistrate of Sloughborough, I feel it my duty—I should say I am responsible for the tranquillity of the people. No, Waterhouse, I must—nay, it is my *duty* to ignore your appeal. Ring up the curtain, I say!'

And as it slowly rose the coffin was placed on end and carried towards the footlights. In the struggle Hamlet fell out and made his final exit, but not before the audience had seen his predicament and guessed the cause of the mysterious confusion.

POE: HIS LIFE AND WORK.

By G. BARNETT SMITH.

THERE is no more terribly suggestive story in literature than that of Edgar Allan Poe. A lurid light plays round the career of this brilliant genius from the moment in which his star rose above the horizon to that in which it set amidst gloom and despair. Everything about him is *bizarre*—his life, his character, his writings. Endowed with the finest faculties and the most sensitive organisation, it was his misfortune to fall into depths of degradation which caused him the keenest anguish and remorse. That he was far more unfortunate than guilty is now abundantly proved. Adopting a saying of Victor Hugo, his stories created *un frisson nouveau ;* and this same shiver overtakes us when we study his life. Yet, under whatever guise we see him, there is a fascination about this remarkable man which we cannot shake off; 'he holds us with his glittering eye,' and literary annals probably furnish no such striking example of what may be called personal magnetism. With this wayward child of genius, existence was a perpetual struggle between the divine and the animal instincts—between the evil and the good. In his best moods he had moments of exaltation such as come to but few men ; in his worst, he was plunged into excesses over which we would willingly draw a veil. His own expressed thoughts convey to us the impression of one constantly looking behind him for the evil spirit who is ever dogging his footsteps, and who is conscious that, sooner or later, his dread enemy must claim the victory. Never, surely, were such passionate exclamations addressed to high Heaven as those which were wrung from the lips of Poe— never, surely, had human soul more of those 'violent delights' which have 'violent ends,' or more of those moments of terrible despondency when the blackness of desolation envelops all.

Poe has added a new note to the gamut of sorrow and despair. He stands apart as an object of singular interest, and, notwithstanding all that has been written upon him, that interest still remains inexhaustible. He was born at Boston on the 19th of January 1809, a year which also witnessed the birth of such different personalities as Elizabeth Barrett Browning, William Ewart Gladstone, and Alfred Tennyson. The fitness of things is seen in an exceptional birth resulting from an exceptional union. Poe's father was of good birth, but of a roving and excitable disposition. He took to the stage, and married a talented actress named Elizabeth Arnold. From the paternal side Poe inherited a strange mixture of French, Italian, and Irish blood ; but the intellectual endowment came, as it most frequently does in the case of men of genius, from the mother's side. Mrs. Poe appears to have excelled both as an artist and an actress. The future poet being left an orphan very early, he was adopted by his godfather, John Allan, a wealthy Scotch merchant, who had settled down and married

in the State of Virginia. It was
unfortunate for Poe that, at an age
when few children have abandoned
their leading-strings, he was left to
the guidance of his own will, and
became virtually master of his own
actions. In one of an imaginative
and easily excitable temperament,
such license, as he himself has remarked, naturally became, in time,
a cause of serious disquietude to
his friends, and of positive injury
to himself. Poe came to Europe
with the Allans ; and in the year
1816 was placed at school at Stoke
Newington. While here, his cleverness attracted attention ; but it
was also observed that he had been
spoilt by his adoptive parents.
Mr. Allan was largely responsible
for the after consequences ; for he
appears to have been changeable
and fitful in his treatment of Poe,
whose temperament he was perfectly unable to understand. Recalled to America in 1821, we find
the youthful poet busy construct-
ing imaginative pieces at the age
of fourteen. For three or four years
he was a scholar in a well-known
academy at Richmond, Virginia.
It was in this city that he met his
first and last love, Elmira Royster,
who afterwards became Mrs. Shel-
ton. One year Poe passed at the
University of Virginia ; and it is
admitted, by his warmest admirers,
that his conduct here was far from
exemplary, though he was not that
hardened, intemperate, and reckless being he has been frequently
represented.

Fortunately for the memory of
Poe, the world is at length supplied
with an antidote to the slanders of
Griswold and others, in the shape
of a perfectly trustworthy and most
interesting account of his career.*

* The biography by Mr. John H. Ingram,
entitled *Edgar Allan Poe : his Life, Letters, and Opinions*, which throws a new
light upon many passages in Poe's career,
and disposes of many hitherto unrefuted
statements.

It is to this work we are indebted
for many of the biographical facts
which it is necessary briefly to re-
capitulate in order to a right understanding of the poet's character.
Poe was always being inspired by
a passion of some kind, either Platonic or otherwise. In the former
category we must class his admiration for Mrs. Helen Stannard,
which he has described as ' the
one idolatrous and purely ideal
love' of his ill-starred boyhood, and
which gave rise to those exceptionally beautiful stanzas, beginning,
' Helen, thy beauty is to me.' His
regret for this lady was deep and
lasting ; and one who knew him
later finds in it a key to much that
seemed strange and abnormal in
his after life. In 1827, Poe's first
volume appeared, *Tamerlane, and
other Poems*. We look back to
this volume now chiefly because it
set forth the author's indestructible
belief in his own powers. Some
of his numbers, even in this early
volume, were by no means con-
temptible, either on the score of
sentiment or rhythm ; but the
whole conveys the impression of
being a jumble of passion and ambition. There was some power of
song, certainly ; but as yet it was
quite possible for it to have died
without ripening. The book was
suppressed; and shortly afterwards,
if we are to believe what was confidently stated by Poe's friends, and
never contradicted by himself, he
came to Europe in order to offer
his services to the Greeks against
their Turkish tyrants. Hannay
loved to think of Poe in the Mediterranean ; but that he ever reached
there is more than questionable ;
and it is asserted that it was an
elder brother—also a poet, and a
dissipated one into the bargain—
who was fired, like Byron, by the
Greek struggle for independence.
During Poe's absence in Europe
Mrs. Allan died ; and on his re-

turn, in 1829, he does not appear to have got on well with her surviving husband, his guardian. Poe probably exasperated him in many ways; and Mr. Allan had not the pleasantest manner of his own, so that a rupture ensued. For two years we find the poet residing with his aunt, Mrs. Clemm of Baltimore; but, before this, he had been a cadet at West Point Military Academy, from which he had been expelled for certain breaches of the regulations; and he had also gone through a variety of experiences in the pursuit of literature. Mrs. Clemm had an only child, Virginia, a very beautiful girl of fourteen; and with her, of course, the susceptible Edgar immediately fell in love. She reciprocated his affection, and eventually became his child-wife, loving him and clinging to him through all the painful vicissitudes of his subsequent career, until her untimely death. Poe was married in the year 1836; and from this date forward we constantly find him, as he once wrote to John P. Kennedy, the novelist, falling into 'a little temporary difficulty.' Still for some time there was no shadow over his domestic happiness. He was happy in his home and happy in his wife, while composing such strangely self-revealing works as the *Narrative of Arthur Gordon Pym.* In 1838 he removed to Philadelphia, having the whole burden of the household upon his shoulders. He appears, in all earnestness, to have sought literary work, and to have struggled manfully to live as a man ought. It was now that he wrote the weird tale of 'Ligeia' for the *American Museum.* This story, which was suggested by a dream, had for its motto a quotation from the *Essays of Joseph Glanvill:* ' Man doth not yield himself to the angels, nor unto death utterly, save only through the weakness of his feeble will.' Such a theme exactly suited the imperious defiant spirit of Poe, who sometimes carried his estimation of his own powers to a sublime excess. For example, a friend records that, upon one occasion, when he got into a discussion with the poet upon the subject of Pantheism, Poe was at first very quiet, but, slowly changing as he went on, at last a look of scornful pride worthy of Milton's Satan flashed over his pale delicate face and broad brow; a strange thrill nerved and dilated for an instant his slight figure, as he exclaimed, ' My whole nature utterly revolts at the idea that there is any being in the universe superior to myself !' There was an extraordinary and unconscionable egotism in Poe which was not held in check either by any intellectual or social restraint. At times this egotism, or conceit, borders on the ridiculous; and its amazing strength is but another lamentable proof of the absence of those wholesome checks which such natures absolutely require in their boyhood.

The years 1841-42 were years of rapid production with Poe, many of his best-known tales being at this period published in *Graham's Magazine,* a periodical whose sale enormously increased on account of his efforts. In April of the last-named year, however, he resigned the editorship of the magazine for reasons which are partially veiled in obscurity. Even with the aid of Mr. Ingram's biography, we are unable to understand many of the episodes in Poe's career. There always seems to be something in the background, something for which no adequate explanation is forthcoming—certainly none that is to the credit of the poet. ' Nervous restlessness' is no doubt a very uncomfortable thing to suffer from, but it does not compel a man to throw away his best chances;

and it is greatly to be feared that moral irregularities must account for the frequent lapses of Poe, and his failures to preserve his occupations and his friendships. He gave way periodically to intoxication, but never without bitterly lamenting his fall afterwards. But, while thus blameworthy, every one must pity the man. Hear him unbosom himself in this sad autobiographic fragment:

'Six years ago,' he said, writing to a correspondent in 1848, 'a wife, whom I loved as no man ever loved before, ruptured a blood-vessel in singing. Her life was despaired of. I took leave of her for ever, and underwent all the agonies of her death. She recovered partially, and I again hoped. At the end of a year the vessel broke again. I went through precisely the same scene. Then again—again, and even once again, at varying intervals. Each time I felt all the agonies of her death, and at each accession of the disorder I loved her more dearly, and clung to her life with more desperate pertinacity. But I am constitutionally sensitive—nervous in a very unusual degree. I became insane, with long intervals of horrible sanity. During these fits of absolute unconsciousness, I drank—God only knows how often or how much. As a matter of course, my enemies referred the insanity to the drink, rather than the drink to the insanity. I had, indeed, nearly abandoned all hope of a permanent cure, when I found one in the *death* of my wife. This I can and do endure as becomes a man. It was the horrible never-ending oscillation between hope and despair which I could not longer have endured, without total loss of reason. In the death of what was my life, then, I receive a new, but—O God !—how melancholy an existence !'

There is the stamp of truth in this confession, which disarms criticism and inspires commiseration ; but Poe's contemporaries were scarcely likely to put the best complexion upon the affair, especially when he had attacked many of them in their works with extraordinary bitterness. He undoubtedly purified American literature of many excrescences by his bold and fearless method of criticism, but this only made him a marked man in certain quarters. That he was ardently attached to his young wife admits of no doubt ; Mrs. Osgood, who knew them both intimately, testifies strongly to that ; but when he lost her it was but too apparent that he had no solid and sterling basis of moral principle to fall back upon for his support. His imagination was the strongest thing about him, and when the waves and billows of trouble buffet a man, he needs a stronger staying-power than that.

The ever-recurring necessity of writing for bread was very galling to Poe, while the illness of his wife unfitted him for literary work. It is said that, powerless to provide for the necessities of home, 'he would steal out of his house at night, and go off and wander about the streets for hours, proud, heartsick, despairing, not knowing which way to turn, or what to do, while Mrs. Clemm (his wife's mother) would endure the anxiety at home as long as she could, and then start off in search of him.' What a picture of domestic life this furnishes ! At one time he attempted, but unsuccessfully, to obtain a government post, which should at least lift him above want and complete dependence. He was again driven to ply his pen with renewed vigour. It would have been well for Poe could his life at Richmond, Virginia, when he wrote for the *Southern Literary Messenger*, have continued. His singularly clever story of the *MS. found in a Bottle* had made him many literary friends, and work promised to be profitable and abundant. But these days were long over. He now became acquainted with a Philadelphia publisher, by whose aid he hoped to launch *The Stylus*, a magazine over which he had long brooded; but the scheme fell through. In 1843 he obtained a prize of one hundred dollars for his story of 'The Gold Bug;' but by this time he was in very low water pecuniarily. And yet, under the continual stress of poverty, he wrote many of his best critical articles. There was one upon Horne's *Orion*, which led to a correspondence between the two poets. In 1844 Poe perpetrated a startling hoax upon the New York world through the medium of the *Sun* newspaper. Our Yankee cousins are fond of a good rattling sensation, and they certainly got it on this occasion. We can fancy the readers of the *Sun* rubbing their eyes as they pondered the following piece of very special intelligence: 'Astounding news by express, *via* Norfolk! The Atlantic crossed in three days! Signal triumph of Mr. Monck Mason's flying machine! Arrival at Sullivan's Island, near Charleston, S.C., of Mr. Mason, Mr. Robert Holland, Mr. Henson, Mr. Harrison Ainsworth, and four others, in the steering balloon Victoria, after a passage of seventy-five hours from land to land! Full particulars of the voyage!' There was, of course, a rush for the sole paper containing such news, and the trick was a great success; but, like many of Theodore Hook's, it would not bear repeating. Towards the close of this year the *New Mirror*, a periodical to which Poe had been a frequent contributor, collapsed; and leaving Philadelphia, he resolved upon trying his fortunes in New York once more. The following year was the most

brilliant in his literary career. Towards the close of January the first published version of his poetic masterpiece, 'The Raven,' appeared in the *Evening Mirror*, edited by N. P. Willis. The publication was from advance sheets of the *American Review*, and in describing the poem Willis affirmed that it was 'the most effective single example of fugitive poetry ever published in this country, and unsurpassed in English poetry for subtle conception, masterly ingenuity of versification, and consistent sustaining of imaginative lift.' It certainly made Poe famous, and has kept his name famous ever since. 'No single fugitive poem,' says his biographer, 'ever caused such a *furore*. In the course of a few weeks it spread over the whole of the United States, calling into existence parodies and imitations innumerable, and indeed creating quite a literature of its own.' Yet for 'this masterpiece of genius— this poem which has probably done more for the renown of American letters than any other single work —it is alleged that Poe, then in the heyday of his intellect and reputation, received the sum of ten dollars!' We can neither subscribe to the dictum as to the value of 'The Raven' transcending anything else in American letters, nor express much surprise at the remuneration paid for it. Certainly Longfellow in poetry, and Hawthorne by his *Scarlet Letter*, have done as much for the mere renown of American letters, while the editor who accepted Poe's poem would naturally plead that at the time he published it he could not possibly foresee the *furore* that would attach to it. For the poem itself, however, in common with thousands, we have nothing but admiration, and it is worth while to look into the genesis of a thing which may be fairly said to have acquired a universal fame. It is matter of speculation where its first root-idea came from. Poe described to Buchanan Read the whole process of the construction of his wonderful lyric, and declared that the suggestion of it arose from a line in Mrs. Browning's poem, 'Lady Geraldine's Courtship.' The line in question is, 'With a murmurous stir uncertain, in the air the purple curtain ;' and there is certainly a very close resemblance between this and a line in 'The Raven.' But there was a still more remarkable coincidence in connection with a poem entitled 'Isadore,' by an American writer, Mr. Albert Pike, and published some time before Poe's. As Mr. Ingram states, both write a poem lamenting a lost love, when, in point of fact, neither one nor the other had lost his 'Isadore' or his 'Lenore,' save in imagination. But the coincidence extends to subject, refrain, and the word selected for the refrain. Poe has two immense and towering advantages, however, over the other writer. He is a consummate artist, in the first place ; and in the second, by his fine imagination, he is able to invest his work with a meaning and a power which shall appeal to the great mass of mankind. Nevertheless, two stanzas from Mr. Pike's poem will show that Poe must not only have seen it, but been strongly impressed by it :

'Thou art lost to me for ever—I have lost thee, Isadore ;
Thy head will never rest upon my loyal bosom more.
Thy tender eyes will never more gaze fondly into mine,
Nor thine arms around me lovingly and trustingly entwine.
Thou art lost to me for ever, Isadore.

My footsteps through the rooms resound all sadly and forlore ;
The garish sun shines flauntingly upon the unswept floor ;
The mocking-bird still sits and sings a melancholy strain ;
For my heart is like a heavy cloud that overflows with rain.
Thou art lost to me for ever, Isadore.'

Dickens's raven in *Barnaby Rudge* appears to have given Poe the idea for the melancholy bird which plays so striking and so weird a part in his immortal poem. In fact, calling attention previously to a point which Dickens had failed to make with his raven, the poet remarked that the bird 'might have been made more than we now see it, a portion of the conception of the fantastic Barnaby. Its croakings might have been prophetically heard in the course of the drama. Its character might have performed, in regard to that of the idiot, much the same part as does, in music, the accompaniment in respect to the air.' Other curious, but less important, facts might be cited proving that 'The Raven' was by no means a totally unassisted work of the imagination.

We now see Poe once more with the ball at his feet. Another chance is given to him, such as falls to the lot of but few literary men. In 1845-46 he is in New York, mingling in the best society, charming every one by the fascination of his manners and the brilliancy of his conversational powers. He is, in fact, idolised for his genius. Mrs. Whitman has recorded the interest taken in the poet by the literary society of New York, and how he was regarded as something fresh and novel. Whether right or wrong, he was always terribly in earnest, and, like De Quincey, 'he never *supposed* anything, he always knew.' It was at this time that Poe became intimately acquainted with Mrs. Frances Sargent Osgood, a lady of considerable poetic gifts. Describing her first interview with him, she says, ' I shall never forget the morning when I was summoned to the drawing-room by Mr. Willis to receive him. With his proud and beautiful head erect, his dark eyes flashing with the electric light of feeling and thought, a peculiar, an inimitable blending of sweetness and hauteur in his expression and manner, he greeted me calmly, gravely, almost coldly; yet with so marked an earnestness that I could not help being deeply impressed by it. From that moment until his death we were friends.' Rebutting the calumnies of his enemies, Mrs. Osgood asserts that Poe had always the strictest reverence for women. While blameless, however, he allowed himself to be drawn into entanglements which furnished food for scandal. His better judgment also forsook him occasionally in literary matters, as in the controversy with an obscure writer named English, which Mr. Ingram relates at length. Poe's treatment of the man was clever and sarcastic, but the play was not worth the candle. But there is also something in the poet's attacks upon far abler and better men of letters which leaves a suspicion of jealousy. It may not have been so, but the manner of Poe's criticism certainly creates that unfortunate impression. He was frequently too stinted in his praise of some of the finest literary spirits of America.

Early in 1846 Poe removed with his wife and Mrs. Clemm to a little cottage at Fordham. Here life for some time was perfectly unclouded, and all that it should be. Mrs. Gove-Nichols, who visited the Poe family at this place, has pictured the scene of domestic content and happiness. In writing and receiving letters the poet was perfectly content. He had been especially delighted on receiving a letter from Mrs. Browning, telling him that his 'poem of "The Raven" had awakened a fit of horror in England.' The narrator throws a strong side-light upon the character of Poe when she adds, 'This was what he loved to do. To make the flesh creep, to make one shudder and freeze with horror, was more to his relish (I cannot say more to his mind or heart) than to touch the tenderest chords of sympathy or sadness.' This is the great point of his tales, and the idiosyncrasy was an unfortunate one for the author. Being reminded on one occasion by Mrs. Gove-Nichols of a previous conversation in which he had said that he despised fame, Poe exclaimed energetically and almost fiercely, 'It was false; I love fame. I dote on it; I idolise it; I would drink to the very dregs the glorious intoxication. I would have incense ascend in my honour from every hill and hamlet, from every town and city on this earth. Fame! glory! they are life-giving breath and living blood. No man lives unless he is famous. How bitterly I belied my nature, and my aspirations, when I said I did not desire fame, and that I despised it!' Such talk may appear wild exaggeration, but it is confessions like these which give us an insight into the man's nature. His soul, which was more often intoxicated than his body, was as ambitious in its way as that of a Napoleon Bonaparte.

While at Fordham the youthful Mrs. Poe was attacked by consumption, and sank rapidly. The household was very poor. Mrs. Gove-Nichols, on visiting the invalid, found that 'there was no clothing on the bed, which was only straw, but a snow-white counterpane and sheets. The weather was cold, and the sick lady had the dreadful chills that accompany the hectic fever of consumption. She lay on the straw bed, wrapped in her husband's greatcoat, with a large tortoiseshell cat in her bosom. The wonderful cat seemed conscious of her great usefulness. The coat and the cat were the sufferer's only means of warmth, except as her husband held her hands, and her mother her feet.' These painful facts having been made known to a benevolent lady named Mrs. Shew (afterwards Houghton), she not only headed a private subscription, but from that moment watched over the suffering family as a mother. But the end could not be averted. Death came for the young wife, and the day of the funeral seems to have been a desolate dreary day—'The skies they were ashen and sober'—and the bereaved husband 'was forced to assume his old military cloak, which Mrs. Shew had been at pains to hide out of sight, fearing the memories it must arouse, it having, erstwhile, and in the days of their greatest tribulation, served as a covering for Virginia's bed.' When all was over the poet gave way, and fell into a kind of apathetic stupor, but Mrs. Shew still continued to befriend him. He recovered somewhat, but soon afterwards suffered a relapse; and amongst those who came to his aid were General Scott and 'Stella' (Mrs. Lewis), the author of 'Sappho.' Amongst other peculiarities of Poe, of which we are reminded by his correspondence with a New-England lady, he had a habit of unburdening himself of his very heart's secrets to any one who would listen to him; and, further, he was always deeply enraptured by his newest friend, whomsoever it might be. These things were due to the quicksilver nature of his temperament. How he came to be grossly misunderstood is shown clearly by these sentences from one of his own letters: ' My habits are rigorously abstemious, and I omit nothing of the natural regimen requisite for health, *i.e.* I rise early, eat moderately, drink nothing but water, and take abundant and regular exercise in the open air. The desire for society comes upon me only when I have been excited by drink. Then *only* I go—that is, at these times only I have been in the practice of going among my friends, who seldom, or in fact never, having seen me unless excited, take it for granted that I am always so. Those who *really* know me know better.' Poe was as active as ever in 1848 over his great scheme of the *Stylus* magazine. For some time he could write and speak of nothing else. To further it, he gave a lecture on ' The Universe,' but very few of those who had the honour to be included in the universe attended. He was brilliant as usual, but he had scarcely mastered the great secret he was determined to unriddle. His theory is explained at length in his work entitled *Eureka*. That he was not a scientist this effusion clearly proves, and of course only an intellect trained in scientific learning and method could be expected to grapple with such a theme in a fit and worthy manner. Poe himself appears in the end to have been convinced of this, and wished his work to be taken only for what it is, a prose poem. The Universe would doubtless be an attractive theme for one possessing a daring imagination like Poe, but its secrets were, and are, such as utterly to defy a reasonable exposition from merely vague generalisations. In *Eureka*, Poe demonstrated that, if he held firmly any theory at all concerning the relations of life and the universe, it was a Pantheistic one. In all his writings we perceive one great defect—the absence of humour. Of invective he had enough and to spare, when wasted upon nobodies and busybodies, but of that quality which would have enabled him to cast off despair he had none. Humour is the enemy of settled gloom, and it would have been well for

Poe as a man if he had been endowed with it. The only approach to it recorded in conversation was when he was once speaking of the Jesuit fathers at Fordham College —'They were highly - cultivated gentlemen and scholars,' he said; 'smoked, drank, and played cards like gentlemen, and never said a word about religion !'

Poe took an intense interest in his *Eureka*, and there is something approaching the ludicrous in Mr. Putnam's account of the fierce earnestness with which he regarded the book. ' Newton's discovery of gravitation,' he assured the publisher, ' was a mere incident compared with the discoveries revealed in this book. It would at once command such unusual and intense interest, that the publisher might give up all other enterprises, and make this one book the business of his lifetime. An edition of fifty thousand copies might be sufficient to begin with, but it would be but a small beginning. No other scientific event in the history of the world approached in importance the original developments of the book.' Mr. Putnam scarcely saw his way to the relinquishment of all other engagements, in order to make room for the *Eureka*, but he had no objection to begin the revolution in a small way; so, instead of beginning with fifty thousand copies, he ventured upon five hundred. It was quite as well he did so; for although there is a certain grandeur in Poe's ideas, yet Poe himself has gone, and the secrets of the universe still remain unravelle I. So that, grand and majestic as may have been Poe's speculations, it would doubtless be very inconvenient for Messrs. Putnam to be burdened with them in a concrete form, in the shape of forty-nine thousand five hundred volumes, upon their shelves.

Turning from this gigantic theme,

which was stated and expounded in a modest little volume of 144 pages, dedicated to Baron von Humboldt, we follow the poet in his wanderings, destined, alas, now to be very brief on this grief-stricken planet. He appeared at Richmond again, renewing old and making new acquaintances,and still pushing his scheme for a magazine. Then he returned to Fordham, where he was employed writing for the magazines, rarely leaving home now. At the residence of Mrs. Shew, however, he wrote the first rough draft of ' The Bells,' amongst the most melodious of poems. Here again one of his best-known effusions arose out of the simplest circumstances. Coming in one day, he said that he had to write a poem, and had no feeling, no inspiration. Church-bells were ringing in the distance. Mrs. Shew handed him paper, but he declined it, saying, ' I so dislike the noise of bells to-night. I cannot write; I have no subject—I am exhausted.' The lady took up the pen, and, pretending to mimic his style, wrote, ' The Bells, by E. A. Poe,' and added, in mere sportiveness, ' The bells, the little silver bells,' Poe finishing off the stanza. She suggested, for the next verse, ' The heavy iron bells,' and this Poe also worked out into a stanza. Thus the poem grew. The poet was not well; and when he had finished the work retired to rest, sleeping for twelve hours. Next day he could hardly recall the evening's work. 'This showed his mind was injured,' Mrs. Shew observes, ' nearly gone out for want of food, and from disappointment. He had not been drinking, and had only been a few hours from home. Evidently his vitality was low, and he was nearly insane.' It was probably a reaction, such as the taking of opium frequently brings. But Poe was certainly now in a very weak and debilitated condition. Mr. Ingram says that, at times, his contempt for the ordinary conventionalities of life rendered it difficult for his friends to maintain their relations with him. The observation is vague, and we are left to fill in its details as best we may. Whatever Poe's faults were, nevertheless, they were such as to alienate from him the very friend who had so long befriended him. He wrote to Mrs. Shew a passionate and fervid appeal, in which he described himself as 'a lost soul' (a figure of speech); but she must have seen that it was hopeless longer to attempt to guide him, and the two never met again. But there was another lady with whom he had become acquainted, the well-known poetess, Mrs. Helen Whitman. With her he appears to have instantly fallen in love, and some idea of the fervent nature of his letters to her may be gathered from this extract: 'All thoughts, all passions seem now merged in that one consuming desire—the mere wish to make you comprehend—to make you see *that* for which there is no human voice, the unutterable fervour of my love for you; for so well do I know your poet nature, that I feel sure if you could but look down *now* into the depths of my soul with your spiritual eyes, you *could* not refuse to speak to me what, alas, you still leave, resolutely leave, unspoken. You would *love* me, if only for the greatness of my love. Is it not something, in this cold dreary world, *to be loved?* O, if I could but burn into your spirit the deep, the *true* meaning which I attach to those three syllables underlined! But, alas, the effort is all in vain, and " I live and die unheard."'

The poet's soul seemed to be constantly exhausting itself in italics and dashes. This and other pass-

ages are very typical of the chronically disturbed state of his heart. In another letter he asks to be allowed to comfort her, to tranquillise her, or, if Fate so wills it, to go down into the grave with her. In a third of these passionate love epistles there is a solemn asseveration which it is of great importance to note as bearing upon his career. 'By the God who reigns in heaven,' he exclaims, ' I swear to you that my soul is incapable of dishonour ; that, with the exception of occasional follies and excesses, which I bitterly lament, but to which I have been driven by intolerable sorrow, and which are hourly committed by others without attracting any notice whatever, I can call to mind no act of my life which would bring a blush to my cheek—or to yours.' He continued to plead with her, until at length she sent him a brief and indecisive note which perplexed him. Poe then wrote that he would be at Providence, where Mrs. Whitman resided, on the following evening. He went ; but instead of going to the lady's house, he returned in a dreadfully depressed state, and, by an abortive attempt at suicide, 'reduced himself to a truly deplorable condition.' Poe still gave the lady no peace, and one morning called upon her in a state of delirious excitement, imploring her to save him from some terrible impending doom. She was afraid to speak the word he wished, viz. that she would marry him, for she had been warned by others against doing so. The poet prevailed in the end, however, and Mrs. Whitman ' permitted him to extract from her a promise that she would become his wife, upon condition that he never touched intoxicants again, declaring that nothing, save his own infirmity, should cause her to recede from her plighted troth.' The preparations for the marriage were now pushed forward, but the union never took place. Information was conveyed to Mrs. Whitman and to her relatives, that during his absence he had violated the solemn pledge of abstinence so recently given. This might possibly have been the work of some enemy; but Mrs. Whitman, though she observed no trace of the infringement of his promise in his appearance, was impelled afterwards to write the following account of their separation: 'I was at last convinced that it would be in vain longer to hope against hope. I knew that he had irrevocably lost the power of self-recovery. Gathering together some papers which he had intrusted to my keeping, I placed them in his hands without a word of explanation or reproach, and, utterly worn out and exhausted by the mental conflicts and anxieties and responsibilities of the last few days, I drenched my handkerchief with ether and threw myself on a sofa, hoping to lose myself in utter unconsciousness. Sinking on his knees beside me, he entreated me to speak to him—to speak *one* word, but one word. At last I responded, almost inaudibly, "What can I say?" "Say that you love me, Helen." "*I love you.*" These were the last words I ever spoke to him.' A melodramatic situation, surely, but one of terrible import to Poe.

The last tragic scene in the poet's ill-starred career reminds us in its naked horror of the death of a still greater man of genius, Christopher Marlowe. The rupture of the engagement with Mrs. Whitman gave rise to scandalous reports, and Poe, in regard to this and other matters, was undoubtedly greatly maligned; but still, there is one passage in his most friendly biographer's account which is indirectly damaging to his character. 'Mrs. Osgood, Mrs. Shew, and Mrs. Whitman attempted, as has been seen, more or less to befriend the helpless poet; but as they one after the other deemed it necessary to let him go his ways, he sank deeper and deeper into the "Slough of Despond."' Why did they deem it necessary to let him go his ways, unless they had discovered that the work of reformation was hopeless? But we may well feel with them, while strongly blaming the poet, that there is room enough for pity. There were few who could understand such a nature as Poe's, or gauge the depth and strength of the struggles which he made after a higher and nobler life. Poe died at Baltimore, and from Mr. Ingram's narrative we quote the passage in which the end is depicted: 'Early in October, on the 2d apparently, Poe left Richmond for New York. He proceeded by boat to Baltimore, which city he reached safely on the morning following his departure. Upon his arrival he gave his trunk to a porter to convey it, it is stated, to the cars which were timed to leave in an hour or so for Philadelphia, whilst he sought some refreshment. What now happened is still shrouded in mystery. Before leaving Richmond the poet had complained of indisposition, of chilliness, and of exhaustion, and it is just possible that the increase of these symptoms may have enticed him into breaking his pledge, or into resorting to some deleterious drug. Be the cause whatever it may, it now appears to have become the fixed belief of the Baltimoreans that the unfortunate poet, while in a state of temporary mania or stupor, fell into the hands of a gang of ruffians who were scouring the streets in search of victims. Wednesday, the 3d of October, was election-day for members of Congress in the State of Maryland, and it is the general supposition that Poe was captured by an electioneering band, " cooped," drugged, dragged to the polls, and then, after having voted the ticket placed in his hand, was ruthlessly left in the street to die. For the truth of this terrible tale there appears to be too great a probability.' Dr. Moran, physician of the Washington University Hospital, Baltimore, states that the poet was brought into that institution on the 7th of October, in a state of insensibility. He had been discovered in that condition, lying on a bench by a wharf, and having been recognised by a passer-by, had been put into a conveyance and taken to the hospital. Poe's cousin, Judge Neilson Poe, visited him in hospital, and did everything for his comfort, but in vain. The poet recovered consciousness for a time; but 'the horror and misery of his condition, combined with the effects of exposure, produced such a shock to the nervous system that he never recovered, and about midnight on the 7th of October 1849, his poor tortured spirit passed away.' Mr. Moncure Conway says he has heard it related that when, near the close of his life, Poe was found by one searching for him in a low public-house in Baltimore, he raised his tipsy head and exclaimed, *Sic transit gloria mundi !* But whatever may have been the precise manner of his death, it was a painful and ignominious one. The vital spark was extinguished as the result of stupor and excess. That vivid imagination was overwhelmed in gloom—gone were those glorious visions of beauty which he had been able to call up at will! Those many-coloured brilliant lights of existence which illumined his path —for, notwithstanding his excesses, Poe was able to create a very phantasmagoria of physical and nervous enjoyment—were all dead, gone down into utter darkness! The teeming brain, the flashing eye, the throbbing heart, all were alike cold and silent, for 'the silver cord was loosed, and the golden bowl was broken at the cistern.'

What of the character of this extraordinary man ? If it be the truth—and there seems no possibility of evading it—that his career was cut short by his excesses, let the truth be spoken. Pity and sympathy may come in at their proper place, but *after* the confession, not before; they cannot do away with the facts; yet these divine sentiments may help us to make all possible allowances for the very strong temptations to which Poe was subjected. It is peculiarly a case in which we should emulate the spirit of Him 'who makes allowance for us all.' Still, Poe drank heavily to drown bitter memories and feelings well-nigh unbearable ; but he drank consciously. He knew why he drank, and the object of it ; and nothing is gained by endeavouring to deny or explain away the fact. His sufferings were no doubt great, and his anguish at certain periods intensely keen ; with all this we can sympathise, while we at the same time regret the absence of that will which, instead of allowing him to sink beneath himself, would have led him into the path of a noble and manly endurance. To endeavour to divest Poe of responsibility would be to set up a false and dangerous standard in morals. Baudelaire has an extraordinary theory in regard to this matter, which he connects with the writings of Poe : ' Je crois que, dans beaucoup de cas, non pas certainement dans tous, l'ivrognerie de Poe était un moyen mnémonique, une méthode de travail, méthode énergique et mortelle, mais appropriée à sa nature passionnée. Le poëte avait appris à boire, comme un littérateur soigneux s'exerce à faire des cahiers de notes. Il ne pouvait résister au désir de retrouver les

visions merveilleuses ou effray-
antes, les conceptions subtile qu'il
avait rencontrées dans une tempête
précédente ; c étaient de vieilles
connaissances qui l'attiraient im-
pérativement, et pour renouer avec
elles, il prenait le chemin le plus
dangereux, mais le plus direct.
Une partie de ce qui fait aujour-
d'hui notre jouissance est ce qui
l'a tué.' This is certainly the most
extraordinary defence or palliation
of the conduct of Poe which has
ever been put forward. And it is
as dangerous as it is extraordinary.
The spectacle of a number of poets
rushing about the world, and seeking by means of intoxication to recall certain methods of composition, would be as inconvenient and
immoral as it is novel. We are
afraid that Baudelaire's hypothesis
must be dismissed as having little
to do with the actual facts in the
poet's case. There are grounds,
however, for forming another hypothesis in connection with the poet,
and that is that he took opium.
The symptoms from which he suffered were certainly those which
would be produced by a use of
the drug ; and it is not a little singular that, in referring to De Quincey's *Confessions of an Opium-Eater*,
Poe himself said that there was
'yet room for a book on opium-
eating, which should be the most
profoundly interesting volume ever
penned.' Now, unless there was
some special reason founded upon
experience, it seems scarcely likely
that a man would venture to speak
with authority upon such a painful
subject as that dealt with in De
Quincey's work.

However, we will now pass from
the dark side of Poe's character,
and consider its best. If there were
strong shadows in him, they were
only the more apparent because
there were also strong lights. His
natural affections were very deep ;
he was honourable and chivalrous ;

his bearing had usually the refinement and delicacy of a gentleman;
he had strong self-reliance in regard
to those things over which he was
a master ; and he deserves every
credit for the manly fight he made
to live entirely by literature, when
such a resolve implied self-abnegation and much hard work. In personal appearance Poe must have
been very attractive—a man to
captivate the female sex, and to
interest deeply his own. Professor
Valentine speaks of the profound
impression made by the poet's
recitations, especially by his rendering of Hood's ' Bridge of Sighs ;'
and he thus refers to his general
appearance : ' His brow was fine
and expressive; his eye dark and
restless ; in the mouth firmness,
mingled with an element of scorn
and discontent. His gait was firm
and erect, but his manner nervous
and emphatic. He was of fine
address, and cordial in his intercourse with his friends, but looked
as though he rarely smiled from
joy, to which he seemed to be a
stranger ; that might be partly attributed to the great struggle for
self-control, in which he seemed to
be constantly engaged. There was
little variation and much sadness
in the intonation of his voice ; yet
this very sadness was so completely
in harmony with his history as to
excite on the part of this community a deep interest in him, both
as a lecturer and a reader.' Mr.
E. C. Stedman, the American critic,
speaking of Poe in his best period,
as recalled by Halpin's engraving,
remarks that we see one ' slight,
but erect of figure, athletic, and
well moulded ; of middle height,
but so proportioned as to seem
every inch a man ; his head finely
modelled, with a forehead and
temples large, and not unlike those
of Bonaparte ; his hands fair as a
woman's ; in all a well-dressed gentleman ; one, even in the garb of

poverty, " with gentleman written all over him." We see the handsome intellectual face, the dark and clustering hair, the clear and sad gray-violet eyes—large, lustrous, glowing with expression; the mouth, whose smile at least was sweet and winning.   We imagine the soft musical voice (a delicate thing in man or woman), the easy quiet movement, the bearing that no failure could humble.   And this man had not only the gift of beauty, but the passionate love of beauty—either of which may be as great a blessing or peril as can befall a human being stretched upon the rack of this tough world.'   So much for one picture; now look upon this, as reflected from some daguerreotype taken shortly before his death : ' It is like an inauspicious mirror, that shows all too clearly the ravage made by a vexed spirit within, and loses the qualities which only a living artist could feel and capture.   Here is the dramatic defiant bearing, but with it the bitterness of scorn.   The disdain of an habitual sneer has found an abode on the mouth, yet scarcely can hide the tremor of irresolution. In Bendann's likeness, indubitably faithful, we find those hardened lines of the chin and neck that are often visible in ·men who have gambled heavily—which Poe did not in mature years—or who have lived loosely and slept ill.   The face tells of battling, of conquering external enemies, of many a defeat, when the man was at war with his meaner self.'   There is great truth in these psychological readings from the outward presentment of the man.

Poe's genius was volcanic; it did not burn with a pure, steady, lambent flame, but seemed to gather its forces in secret, and then burst in lurid and fitful gleams upon the world.   And this peculiarity was in harmony with his character.

Never, perhaps, was poet's nature so mirrored in his work as in Poe's case.   Through all there beams a glowing appreciation of beauty; but this cannot bring him happiness in his desperate struggle against Fate, while beneath all there is a deep and unfathomable undercurrent of sadness.   The music and the misery of ' The Raven' are alike typical of Poe.   His soul has found a theme congenial with itself.   In metrical and unconventional form the poem stands alone. Nor is this work, and others of the poet, distinguished for genius alone. We see in almost all that he has written consummate art; such art as we are apt to associate with the ancient Greeks, and which sprang from their all-consuming love of beauty.   The Southern Celtic blood of Poe had much to do with moulding his genius after this type. Music, art, passion, beauty; all these may be discovered in this versatile writer; nay, are so inextricably blended with all that he has done as to be perceptible to the most casual reader.   Time may demolish much of what he has written; but there are some things which are safe from his destroying hand, immortal and indestructible. Every poet of his own age has been impressed by his original force, and a not inapt comparison has been drawn between him and the great dramatist whom we have already mentioned, Marlowe.

We shall not linger over poems whose fame is now contemporaneous with the English language. But there are some which are not so universally known that seem to us stamped even more strongly with Poe's peculiar individuality. Of such poems is ' The Conqueror Worm,' whose note of hopeless melancholy strikes deeper than that of ' The Raven,' and almost makes the flesh to creep.   The poet pictures himself in a theatre upon a gala night, and he sees amid the mimic rout a crawling shape intrude. It is the victorious worm, which fastens upon its victims :

'Out, out are the lights—out all!
  And over each quivering form
The curtain, a funeral pall,
  Comes down with the rush of a storm;
And the angels all pallid and wan,
  Uprising, unveiling, affirm
That the play is the tragedy "Man,"
  And its hero the Conquering Worm.'

How strangely poetic, though widely differing in subject and treatment, are 'The Sleeper' and 'The City in the Sea'! Rich music is the predominant quality in 'Annabel Lee' and 'Eulalie,' though we would not forget the graceful fancy in both; but it is in that wonderful dirge 'Ulalume' that the 'absolute perfection' of rhythm is attained. The poem itself is autobiographical, and, by its evident spontaneity, reminds us of the improvisations of the French and Italian poets. The midnight walk, described in this monody, and the sharp transitions of experience, hope treading upon the heels of despair, were, we are told, the exact experiences of Poe himself. The memory is haunted by such strains as these, while there is a magical force in the alliteration and the repetition of the ideas and the most striking words :

' The skies they were ashen and sober,
  The leaves they were crispèd and sere,—
  The leaves they were withering and sere;
It was night in the lonesome October
  Of my most immemorial year;
It was hard by the dim lake of Auber,
  In the misty mid-region of Weir,—
It was down by the dark tarn of Auber,
  In the ghoul-haunted woodland of Weir.'

This too is surely exquisite versification :

' And now, as the night was senescent,
  And star-dials pointed to morn,—
  As the star-dials hinted of morn,
At the end of our path a liquescent
  And nebulous lustre was born,
Out of which a miraculous crescent
  Arose with a duplicate horn,—
Astarté's bediamonded crescent
  Distinct with its duplicate horn.'

Of our own poet Coleridge we are forcibly reminded by such stanzas as these, from 'The Haunted Palace,' and their melody is not unworthy of the writer of 'The Ancient Mariner' himself :

' In the greenest of our valleys,
  By good angels tenanted,
Once a fair and stately palace,
  Radiant palace, reared its head.
In the Monarch Thought's dominion
  It stood there:
Never seraph spread a pinion
  Over fabric half so fair!

Banners—yellow, glorious, golden—
  On its roof did float and flow
(This, all this, was in the olden
  Time long ago);
And every gentle air that dallied,
  In that sweet day,
Along the ramparts plumed and pallid,
  A wingèd odour went away.'

Of that class of poems showing the unrest of the poet may be taken 'A Dream within a Dream;' while the exquisite verses 'To Helen' and 'Israfel' speak of happier and healthier moods. The last-named poem is worthy of ranking with Poe's very best work. It has a beautiful lilt, and is very noticeable both for its melody and its poetic aspiration :

' In heaven a spirit doth dwell
    "Whose heart-strings are a lute:"
None sing so wildly well
As the angel Israfel ;
And the giddy stars (so legends tell),
Ceasing their hymns, attend the spell
    Of his voice, all mute.
      *   *   *   *
If I could dwell
Where Israfel
    Hath dwelt, and he where I,
He might not sing so wildly well
    A mortal melody ; .
While a bolder note than his might swell
    From my lyre within the sky.'

Real poetry, then, we may find in abundance in Poe—lyrical poetry of a high order. It is not invested with any deep moral significance, neither has it much to tell us of the great questions of the age, philosophical or otherwise. Poe sang because he must, as the birds do. It was his vocation to make music, and from this point of view he has rarely been excelled.

As to the niche he will occupy amongst the world's writers, that is another matter. He certainly does not belong to the first order of poets—those in whom are blended, in equal degree, melody, reflectiveness, and dramatic strength. It is as a lyric poet he must be judged ; and if his range be narrow, we must remember that a perfect cameo is finer than the most towering inartistic statue. Taking his poems altogether, twenty pages would more than cover, perhaps, all that he will be remembered by ; but how many poets of the past have bequeathed us twenty pages even which are immortal ? From the simplest elements, as by a touch from the wand of an enchanter, he has constructed one or two poems whose matchless music will continue to ring in the ears of generations yet unborn.

In England, at least, with most persons, the reputation of Poe will chiefly rest upon his poems ; yet some of his prose 'Tales' are no whit below these in original and graphic power. Wild and fantastic creations many of them are, but powerful notwithstanding. Griswold, though he has done more harm perhaps than any other person to the memory of Poe, was not far wrong when he thus observed with regard to these weird prose compositions : 'His realm was on the shadowy confines of human experience, among the abodes of crime, gloom, and horror; and there he delighted to surround himself with images of beauty and of terror, to raise his solemn palaces and towers and spires in a night upon which should rise no sun. His minuteness of detail, refinement of reasoning, and propriety and power of language, the perfect keeping and apparent good faith with which he managed the evocation and exhibition of his strange and spectral and revolting

creations, gave him an astonishing mastery over his readers, so that his books were closed as one would lay aside nightmare or the spells of opium.'

Yet so cleverly were these tales constructed—take, for example, 'The Facts in the Case of M. Valdemar'—that they fairly puzzled people by their psychological problems, and experts even were at a loss to comprehend them. There was a curious mixture of the real and the manifestly unreal in these stories, which made them both tantalising and fascinating. They defy analysis, as they were probably intended to do, for it was Poe's supreme delight to startle people by the grotesque and the supernatural. Such pieces as 'The Murders in the Rue Morgue,' 'The Mystery of Marie Roget,' 'The Man of the Crowd,' 'Hans Pfaall,' 'The Gold Bug,' and 'The Descent into the Maelstrom,' have no exact parallel in literature. Their qualities are such as we find developed now in Hoffman, now in Balzac, and now in Fouqué. On the author's side they were *bonâ-fide* attempts to pierce the mysteries of the invisible world, for it was Poe's burning desire to get to the secret heart of things. Beaten back in his quest, he returned to it again and again, and his *Eureka* shows with what tenacity he clung to his hope and expectation of solving the secrets of the Universe. But the tales in which lyrics are introduced—and of these 'The Fall of the House of Usher' may be mentioned as being of the highest type—'are full of complex beauty, the choicest products of his genius. They are the offspring of yearnings that lifted him so far above himself as to make us forget his failings, and think of him only as a creative artist—a man of noble gifts.' Poe's tales have naturally suggested to the critics a comparison with those of Hawthorne; but the latter are far superior to Poe's in literary finish, while the spiritual tones in them are finer and more subtle. The soul of one was capable of finer issues, of nobler and purer suggestions, than that of the other. There is the crashing of the storm in Poe; there is the music of the Æolian harp in Hawthorne.

Such, then, was this Transatlantic poet—this man of intense, if somewhat restricted, genius. He fulfils some of Carlyle's requisites of a true poet, though not all. 'As the first and indispensable condition of good poets,' says the author of *Sartor Resartus,* ' they are wise and good men; much they have seen and suffered, and they have conquered all this, and made it all their own; they have known life in its heights and depths, and mastered it in both, and can teach others what it is, and how to lead it rightly. Their minds are as a mirror to us, where the perplexed image of our own being is reflected back in soft and clear interpretation. Here mirth and gravity are blended together; wit rests on deep devout wisdom, as the greensward with its flowers must rest on the rock, whose foundations reach downward to the centre. In a word, they are believers; but their faith is no sallow plant of darkness; it is green and flowery, for it grows in the sunlight.' It is only the Shakespeares and the Goethes of mankind who attain this height of development, men of the infinite eye and of profound heart. But in the forests of Nature there are trees as beautiful, though not so majestic and noble, as the oak. So the realm of poetry is divided. He who has sway over the highest gifts is poet, philosopher, and singer in one; yet he who is singer only claims our admiration in proportion to the sweetness and melody

of his utterances. We do not go to Poe for deep thought, for that searching wisdom which penetrates to the heart of things; but we go to him for his genuine inspiration —an inspiration that gives him high rank in the brotherhood of song. In the same sense—though not in the same degree—he is a poet as Shelley is; and both 'learnt in suffering what they taught in song.' Poe lacks the high ideality and the deep spirituality of the English poet; but his ear was almost as musical and as finely attuned. As to the question whether the world is the better for his living in it, we must unhesitatingly answer yes. He who adds but one note of joy, or pleasure, or happiness to the sum of human life, has not lived in vain. His own existence is mortal, and it may have been marred by many imperfections. All these have but a short space to live, and perish with his humanity; but his song lives for ever — it is passed on from generation to generation, to give exquisite delight to thousands who may know nothing of the singer. Such is the reward of genius. It creates immortality for its possessor, and none can trace the bounds of its influence.

It is extraordinary that Poe, with his highly sensitive organisation, his melodious endowments, his noble aspirations, and his poetic gifts, should have sunk into the depths which he has himself depicted. One more illustration the poet furnishes that a man may be near the earth and yet nearer to the highest heaven of thought and feeling at the same time. We remember the description of the idol whose head was of gold and his feet of clay. Such a one was Poe. Torn by the conflicting forces of good and evil, at times he was able to rise to the true height of his being, and to tread down the baser elements which struggled for the mastery. But he lacked that commanding moral energy which would alone have insured him complete victory. Cut off at an age when his faculties had begun to ripen, it is impossible to say what he might not have achieved had he been able to conquer and bring into subjection those passions which were to him what the chariot of the sun was to Phaeton. Yet literature presents fewer names commanding at once so strong and so genuine an interest. We may not accept the theory, that if he had been a better and a wiser man his poetry must necessarily have been of an inferior type. Yet, as we have observed, never was man's work more incontestably stamped by the individuality of character than his. Whatever there was of gloom, of spiritual exaltation, of moral weakness, of beauty, or of grandeur in that character, all was reflected in his writings. Hence, this suffering, sinning, aspiring, and chivalrous soul, buffeted and tempest-tossed, with so much of our common humanity in him, and so much also that was far above our common humanity, extorts from the world sympathy with his sublime yearnings, pity for his Titanic struggles, and admiration for his unique genius.

SCEPTRE AND RING.

BY B. H. BUXTON,

AUTHOR OF 'JENNIE OF "THE PRINCE'S,"' 'FROM THE WINGS,' ETC.

Part the First.

CHAPTER IV.

A PROLONGED HONEYMOON.

SCENE: a bright airy room, high up in one of the substantial old houses of Great George-street, Westminster. It is a back room; but it has a large window facing north, and as Mr. Cuthbert Strange pursues the profession of an artist, this north light is a *sine quâ non* to him. He has taken the apartment he now inhabits from a friend of his, an engineer, whose work has called him abroad for a time; and Cuthbert has established himself here, because he is within ten minutes' walk of his wife's dreary home in Sydney-street. He has given her a latch-key, he calls her 'sister,' and he accounts for her frequent visits by the statement that she sits to him as a model. This fact is corroborated by the hasty sketch of her lovely head upon the easel in the studio; but, though that sketch was satisfactorily accomplished in one morning, it is not followed up by any larger painting.

'How can a man settle to work during his honeymoon?' Cuthbert says, laughing, as his anxious young wife repeatedly urges him to try and make some progress. 'If we were like an ordinary married couple, and had gone abroad together and got tired of one another's company, it would be different—I should rejoice in settling to my work and forgetting you for a time; but, as it is, I spend the

morning waiting, watching for you, hoping you will come, fearing you will not, and then rejoicing that it is afternoon, and that you cannot possibly tarry much longer. Don't scold me, wife; rejoice in the prospect that, as soon as we have a little home entirely our own, I shall be always at work for *your* sake. Now do let me enjoy a little rest and peace.'

'But how about money, Bertie?' she asks wistfully. 'I know if my father neglects his work, purse and larder are very soon empty.'

'No wonder you are anxious, my darling,' says he, smiling. 'But, you see, I have not been extravagant, and I don't gamble or drink; so I have a reserve fund, a little account at my banker's, and a cheque-book. There's a pleasing revelation for you, you mercenary little woman! And now I have re-assured you as to the state of my finances, I hope you will never vex me again by refusing a little aid to your housekeeping fund. Don't you understand, wife, that all that is mine is yours also?'

'I do understand that you are the best, the kindest, and the most considerate of men, my true love!' she says, her eyes filling with grateful tears, and her sweet voice trembling with the fervour of her emotion.

'Don't get sentimental,' says Cuthbert lightly, 'or I shall never progress with my work. Try a new position, Olga, with your head a little more turned from me. I think a bit of black lace thrown over the back of your fair hair would look well. Let us try the effect.'

Cuthbert rises to fetch some artistic 'properties' out of an old cabinet in the adjoining room, and then he amuses himself by decking his lovely bride out in ribbons, laces, and flowers.

'But, Bertie, this is not painting,' says she, with much gravity.

He laughs aloud.

'I will begin at once,' he says, and seizes his palette and brushes. 'Attention!'

But her thoughts have wandered away now, and, with a dreamy look in her eyes, she says,

'Husband! do you know that we have been married eight weeks to-day—eight whole weeks, very nearly two calendar months?'

'Is it possible? It seems more like eight happy days to me. What a benevolent fairy you are, Olga, to make the dark weary winter days disappear with such delightful rapidity!'

'And you really are so much happier, Cuthbert, so much better pleased with your life and your work since I have begun to take up so much of your time?'

Mr. Strange raises his eyes from the canvas on which he is sketching, and gives his fair model a look of the most perfect love and content.

'I don't think I knew the real meaning of the verb "to live" until your presence began to brighten my days,' he says, smiling; 'and as for "to love," you and you only have enabled me to understand those sweet words to my entire satisfaction. You are a witch, Olga, or rather an elfin queen. "When the elves at noon do pass," eh?'

He hums the air as he glances wistfully at her from whom he heard it first.

'I suppose you do miss me from the old house?' he asks; 'though we saw so little of one another while I was there.'

'It still seems very strange to me to pass your room, to see the door standing open, and to remember that you live there no longer.'

'And do you suppose that I do not miss the sound of your light footstep on the stair, child, and that it is not hard for me to part from you day after day, knowing that, though you are mine, your home is not my home yet?'

'Yes, it is hard; but for father's sake I am sure it is best so, for a time at least. And I don't want to disturb him just now, for he has been kinder and less—less thoughtless ever since that fatal night, when—you know, Cuthbert—'

O yes; Cuthbert is never likely to forget that night!

'Father believes you left your lodging in our house on account of *his* conduct,' says Olga, 'and he feels ashamed, I know. Poor father!'

Cuthbert suppresses the impatient protest that rises to his lips. It shocks him to hear his gentle wife expressing love and pity for the 'unmitigated ruffian' who is now his father-in-law.

'It was certainly the most prudent course to take for your sake, darling,' Cuthbert continues his explanations. 'If I had remained in the same house with you after you were my wife I should certainly have committed some imprudence—called you Mrs. Strange, or I don't know what—and then that loquacious maid-of-all-work would have had something to talk about indeed.'

He laughs, but Olga looks reproachfully at him.

'I am grieved to think that you will persist in doubting and misjudging my good old Patty,' she says. 'Remember I have known her for many years; and, faithfully as she served my poor mother, she will always serve me; that I am sure of. She is true as steel, Cuthbert, and if you had allowed me to take her into our confidence she might have helped us in many ways, and she would most certainly never have betrayed our secret.'

Cuthbert shakes his head dubiously. 'I never knew but one woman who could keep a secret,' he says, 'and she *is* as true as steel. I have tried her. She is the one woman in the world to me, and I gave my heart into her keeping more than a year ago.'

'A year ago, Cuthbert?' cries Olga, amazed. 'Why, you have only known me for seven months —seven months and three days. It was on the 24th of June that you came to lodge in Sydney-street.'

'But it was not in the month of June that I saw you first.'

'O, tell me!' she pleads eagerly. 'I always knew there was some mystery about you, and about it all. And I shall continue to believe that you had something to do with that tall man in the fur coat, whose face was muffled up, and who—'

'"When the elves at noon do pass,"' sings he; and then he laughs and holds out his arms to her.

She hides her sweet face on his shoulder.

'You were that Russian prince, I do believe, Cuthbert,' she says, blushing vividly. 'But I have never seen the wonderful fur coat since, and yet I felt that you and the mysterious stranger had something in common; for my luck, which was indeed at a low ebb that night, changed from the moment I saw him, or you. Which was it? Won't you tell me, dearest? Surely you can have no secrets from me now; and O, how I should like to hear all about that romance! There is some romance, and you are a prince in disguise after all. Trust me, and tell me all now.'

'You patient little darling, I know you have wanted to ask me a thousand questions about all those events which you call romantic, and yet your discretion has invariably conquered your curiosity and sealed your pretty lips. O Olga, how unlike you are to the rest of your inquisitive, chattering, hare-brained sex!'

'Don't abuse them, husband, since you have found a wife among them,' she says, smiling.

'Ah, you may well look triumphant,' he says, and he laughs. 'The night I met you first, a girl had so enraged me by her deceit and her effrontery that I had vowed to remain a bachelor for the rest of my life.'

'Is this part of my romance, Cuthbert?'

'It is. And now you shall have the recital in categorical order. I shall not do any more work to-day, but will sit on this stool at your feet, and tell you stories as long as you like to listen.'

'I am afraid I interfere with your painting, and make you idle the daylight hours away,' says she, with compunction.

He laughs. 'A bride complaining of her lord's devotion!' he says. 'Let us be idle and happy while we can, darling. Make hay while the sun shines; tell stories by the fireside. We are not going to starve, I can promise you. I have a reserve fund to draw upon, and painting, after all, is more an amusement than a profession for me.'

'But I thought you were entirely dependent on your pictures and your teaching for your living, Cuthbert?'

'My teaching—ah, yes; but not entirely, child. There is that banker's account, as I told you;

but it was as well not to mention the fact to papa-in-law !'

She covers her face with her hands. This is a most painful subject for her, poor child.

'You are forgetting all about *our* romance, Ollie,' says he. 'It is a pretty little story of course, since you are the heroine.'

Cuthbert puts his palette and his brushes down. *If* he depends on the result of his artistic labours for daily bread, the chances are in favour of imminent starvation; for since his marriage he has accomplished nothing more satisfactory than the crude commencement of various sketches of Olga's lovely head and shoulders. He tells her that these slight studies are always necessary before a *real* picture is commenced, and she believes him implicitly in this as in all else. That he has painted her 'beautifully' there is no doubt. Her admiring eyes can see that on the canvas, which stands before him day after day, but shows such slight signs of advancement from week to week.

He now draws a large cushion close to the fire, and, flinging himself leisurely down upon it, rests at his young wife's feet, looking into her face as he tells her the promised story.

'It was on a bitterly cold afternoon last February; the east wind that was blowing chilled the very marrow in my bones, and I hated the exigences of *society*, which necessitated my turning out of my cosy study and presenting myself at the house of some very wealthy people living — in Brook-street, Grosvenor-square.'

'Pupils were they?'

'No, not exactly pupils. I should rather describe them as patrons,' says Cuthbert, and a curious smile passes over his handsome face. 'Well, there was one young lady present at this juvenile festivity,

who, I suppose, came in the *rôle* of *chaperon* to her little sisters; for she could hardly lay claim to be considered a child herself. She was remarkably dressed, and her manners matched her obtrusive costume. She twice asked me to dance with her, and, during a waltz, she deliberately made me an offer of marriage.'

'Cuthbert, how can you !' cried Olga, aghast.

'How can *I*, my dear? How could she, you mean. I am telling you the simple truth, startling and incredible as it may appear to you. Such things do happen in real life, though if we read them in books we declare them impossible, forgetting that our daily experience teaches us how much stranger truth is than fiction.'

'And she was a *lady* ?' asks Olga, who is still at a loss to reconcile certain facts in her mind.

'A lady by birth and education certainly,' says Cuthbert; 'but that does not always involve the natural instinct of one. This Miss Isabel —we won't mention other names ; you might meet her one day, and it would prejudice you—had seen me twice before, but we had scarcely exchanged a dozen sentences. She was a dark girl, with a high colour and a loud voice; the sort of person I always feel inclined to run away from. When I fully understood the nature of her startling proposition (at first I really thought it had reference to a dance or charade, or other games of that sort) I declined the honour delicately and with all courtesy, I think, but most decidedly; of that I am sure.'

'What a horrid girl !' says Olga sharply.

'Ah, worse remains behind, my dear,' says Cuthbert, laughing ruefully. 'Judge of my dismay when I discovered that Miss Isabel had been telling the story of the pro-

posal—*her* version of it, that is—
right and left all over the room;
and presently the audacious girl's
mother, a manœuvring old general
in petticoats, called me to task
very sharply for "trifling" with her
innocent child's affection.... I
scented a breach-of-promise case
with all its attendant horrors of
newspaper publicity, and I bolted
out of the house. I had had one
previous experience of the machin-
ations of a girl of the period; but
this last attempt at landing me was
a sharper lesson than I ever expected, and I ran out in the teeth
of the bitter wind, cursing like a
trooper, and making all sorts of
mental resolutions anent your
brazen sex, my wife. I vowed to
abjure society for the future; it
certainly had not done much that
was pleasant or profitable for me,
and I was more than ever determined to remain a bachelor to the
end of my misanthropic days.

'And as I was walking furiously
along Park-lane, I was suddenly
arrested by the sound of a young
fresh voice singing—'

'Ah, I know, Cuthbert, "When
the elves at noon do pass." Was
that the song?'

'It was, my darling. Shall I tell
you more?'

'Of course,' she says eagerly.
'You know all this is news to me;
but even you cannot guess how interesting it is.'

'Well, I stopped a while, listening for the end of that wonderful
song, and then an irresistible desire took possession of me. I felt
I must see the face of that gentle
songstress, and hear her speak. I
crossed the road warily, and went
up to the further corner, where a
young girl was standing, her slight
figure wrapped in a large plaid
shawl, her lovely face lifted to the
brilliantly-lighted windows of the
mansion, before which she was
singing her weird appeal. I knew

there was something tragic and
exceptional in that girl's sad history, and I determined not to ob-
trude upon what I felt was a false,
an embarrassing position for a lady.
Still, she was certainly singing for
money. That fact was undoubted;
and I marvelled what adverse fortune could have exposed her to so
cruel an ordeal. I drew up the
fur collar of my coat, slouched my
hat down over my eyes, and approached her as though I were addressing a duchess. Her simple
dignity inspired me with awe, I
assure you, and when I asked,
"Will you allow me to offer you—"
I positively trembled.'

'And you spoke with a foreign
accent, Cuthbert,' says Olga
eagerly.

'I fancied the impertinence of
offering a lady money would be
less startling in a foreigner,' says
he gently; 'and knowing the Germans were music-mad, I made that
an excuse for—'

'For the amazing gift of a sovereign,' she says hurriedly. 'O, if you
had but known how much those
twenty shillings did for me, how
much they saved me from, Cuthbert!'

He takes her little hands closely
in his, and kisses them tenderly.
'My darling, my poor precious
darling!' he says. 'But how is it
that in all these months you have
never told me anything about that
miserable experience of yours?
What can have induced you to go
and sing in the streets?'

'Great hardship, you may be
sure, dear,' she says sadly. 'I
only tried it that one evening. I
had had a most wretched day.
Father and I had—had disagreed
about something. He wanted me
to appear in some play—a burlesque, I think it was called—at
the Temple Theatre. The manager
had seen me walking with father,
and told him I might go on the
stage with the rest of the girls

there; but I would not do that. Father left me in great anger. I had no money, none at all. And I was really very hungry. Then I knew I must get something ready for his supper when he came back in the evening, and how to buy without money is an art I have never learnt.' She smiles; but the misery of her retrospection has taken all sunshine out of her sweet face. 'I have had a good deal of trouble one way or another,' she says; 'but I have tried to look my difficulties in the face, and then I have not found them so very hard to conquer after all. But that day I was in a wicked despairing mood. My father's anger had hurt and depressed me, and he—I mean *we*—owed poor Patty some money, which we had borrowed of her, and I was determined that I would earn some before I went to bed that night. There was no fire in the grate, no food in the cupboard; what could I do?

'Just as I had come to the wretched conclusion that I could do *nothing*, a poor creature out in the street, who was, perhaps, still worse off than I was, set up a plaintive quavering little song. The sound seemed an answer to my fervent prayer for guidance and help. I saw a little girl run out of the house opposite, and give something to that shivering old singer; and then I thought, " I can go out and sing too; I can do better than that." My darling mother had taught me several of her favourite songs, and there was one from the *Amber Witch* which was a special favourite of hers and mine. I knew it well, every word, every note, every little turn and flourish. I prayed God to protect me; I wrapped my old plaid shawl closely about me, and I walked right away to Eaton-square. I was ambitious, you see, Cuthbert; but pride oft gets a fall. Mine did,

and soon, too; for I had scarcely finished the first verse of my ditty, and was feeling rather pleased with the sound of my voice in the clear frosty air, when a tall footman, with powdered hair, walked statelily out of one of the houses, and bade me move on. I moved at once, a little discouraged, but not much. In Chester-square I was far more successful. An old gentleman stepped out of a brougham, and instead of walking straight up the steps, over which a carpet had been spread ready for the expected guests, he came to the edge of the kerb, stared at me for a moment, lifted his hat, and said, "Take care of that voice, my dear; you possess a treasure, though no one seems to have told you of the fact yet." Then he gave me half-a-crown, and went away muttering, "Good God! What a voice! what a voice!"

'I at once refreshed myself with some milk at a dairy. It was cold, but fresh and sweet. I drank two glasses, and, still possessed of what seemed a fortune at the moment, I walked on and on—up Park-lane, and into a certain square, where a foreigner very much muffled up bestowed the marvellous gift of a sovereign upon me. Was not that truly generous, Cuthbert?'

'*Cela dépend*, my child! I believe the spell of the *Amber Witch* was upon him. He was fascinated, enslaved by the sound of your voice. Perhaps he gave his heart into your safe keeping as well as his gold.'

'O Cuthbert, you don't mean to say you thought anything about me then?'

He springs to his feet, and, in clear glad tones, sings,

'" I then gave my heart to that singer's keeping.
The sov'reign was dross; but my love is pure gold.
And the stars shall fall, and the angels be weeping,
Ere I cease to love *thee*, my queen, my queen!"

New version, Olga. It was a case of love at first sight with me, was it not, my queen?'

'It is so beautiful, dearest, that it all seems too good to me still,' she answers, rising also; and she links her hands on his arm, and they walk to and fro together, up and down, up and down. The rooms Cuthbert has taken for himself now are far more spacious and comfortable than the wretched lodging he occupied in Sydney-street; and when Olga comes in for her daily 'sittings,' the artist's simple home seems like paradise to the happy young couple. Never was honeymoon sweeter and brighter than theirs; and the notion of taking Mr. Layton into their confidence now was equally distasteful to both. He knew of no change at home; for Olga was more devoted than ever since she felt so much happier, and Cuthbert's assistance made housekeeping a much easier matter for her since she had some money to spend. Mr. Layton asked no questions as to the supplies. It was their absence at which he grumbled readily enough; but as his daughter never showed him money, and refused him when he asked her for any, he contented himself with the belief that she was an excellent manager, and that she contrived to make the few shillings he gave her out of his salary go farther now than she formerly did.

'Tell me the rest of your adventures that evening, Cuthbert,' says Olga presently. 'Did you come to lodge in Sydney-street by chance?'

'Quite by chance on purpose like, as the schoolboys say,' answers he, laughing. 'That song of the *Amber Witch* certainly exercised some occult spell upon me. I was very much afraid of the proud young singer; but most determined to find out who she was and where

she came from; so I bided my time, and when she walked away I followed her on the other side of the way. I kept well out of sight myself; but I watched her anxiously enough, and, close to the corner of Sloane-street, I rushed to the rescue when a ruffianly soldier—'

'O, then that *was* my gallant foreigner again!' cries Olga, in great excitement. 'I thought there could not be two fur-coated tall men in the street that night; but you spoke English, and you said bad words, and were in such a passion with that coward, that I thought I must be mistaken; you were not my generous friend from Grosvenor-square, but you were a second and a most gallant benefactor also. Is this the end of the romance in which I so unexpectedly find myself a heroine, Cuthbert?'

'No,' says he. 'Perhaps the *dénouement*, of which you know very little, will surprise you more. 'I followed my Amber Witch all the way to Sydney-street. I saw her open the door of a house there with a latch-key, and presently I perceived a light which appeared in the front windows of the second-floor. Then I went away satisfied for that night. But next day I returned to her house, and finding that I could hire a room there, I did so at once, and within a week I took up my abode under the same roof with *my queen.*'

'She lived in a very shabby palace,' says Olga. 'Do you mean to tell me that you chose that lodging entirely on my account?'

'Most decidedly, child. You cannot suppose that I selected it for its beauty or comfort.'

'O Bertie, how strange!' says she, and she pauses in her walk by his side, and confronts him. 'All for *my* sake!' she repeats, wondering.

'For my own also,' he answers promptly. 'I was determined to find out all about you. You interested, you preoccupied me—indeed there is no other explanation possible, you had *bewitched* me.

'Before many days were over I had learnt my queen's sad story. I soon found out all about Mr. Layton. I discovered that my queen lived in a miserable home and in wretched poverty. I knew before many days were over that I loved her, and that it was true honest love, and not witchcraft, which possessed me. I knew that my darling led a most miserable life, that she had a wicked degraded father, and yet kept herself bright and pure as one of God's angels, bless her!'

'O, hush, Bertie dearest!' cries Olga, laying her hand on her husband's lips. 'I cannot listen to such praises. You happened to hear these good things of me, and you believed them right away; but you little dream how many bad things remain for you to find out yet.'

'I am quite content to wait,' he replies cheerfully; 'the year is young, and I have a lifetime before me to learn to know you better still.'

'The year *is* young,' she says, with a frightened glance at the clock; 'but the day is waning, and I must hurry back, or father may get in before I do, and then—'

'Nonsense, child!' interposes Cuthbert, persuasive at first, but impressive and earnest as he sees her inclined to rebel. 'It is *not* time for you to go home. I shall take care to send you off before your absence is either remarked or commented on. It is not five yet; you did not come until two—'

'But my going out at all is quite an event, I assure you, and I know the people in the house talk and wonder.'

'Let them—they know nothing.'

'No; but they might suspect a great deal. Formerly—before—before I was your wife, Bertie, I hardly ever went out at all—never more than for five or ten minutes, to do our little bit of marketing.'

'And now you are out for two or three hours every day? Very much better for your health, my dear, I assure you. Being cooped up in those stuffy lodgings took all the brightness out of your sweet face. Then you looked like a fading lily, now you seem like a blooming rose. Delicious!'

To prove his approbation Cuthbert kisses the blushing cheeks of his wife, and thinks of her again, as he has thought of her any time these last three months, as the loveliest and the most lovable being on God's earth.

'Don't run away yet, my darling,' he pleads, as he holds both her hands.

'But I am always so afraid of arousing suspicion,' she replies, alarmed still.

'What matters if you do?' he asks hastily.

'I thought *you* objected now, Bertie?'

'O, that is all over,' he answers, with decision. 'Your alarm was contagious, my poor child. I think we have both got over the nervous stage now, and I shall certainly tell your father of our marriage before long.'

'I begin to wish you would, husband; indeed I often think he ought to be told the truth now, but I so dread a scene. He has been so much quieter and nicer lately, and I can't bear the thought of his flying into a passion.'

'You shall not be troubled, my love. One morning, when you come round here, I will write him a letter which he will get with his dinner, or I will go straight to him and tell him that you are my wife.'

'He will be furious, I know.'

'I think not; but if he is, that will not matter to me in the least. Who cares for the futile anger of a—'

Her look of entreaty silences him.

'O Bertie, my love,' she says, with a sudden outbreak of long-pent-up emotion, 'I *do* wish, I do hope you will soon, very soon make a point of telling my father the truth.'

If the loving young husband could have seen the expression of the sweet frightened face she hides on his shoulder, he would not have tarried a day with the revelation which would have freed his wife from the growing misery, the repeated violence to which her absolute dependence on her drunken parent exposed her. But Olga so revels in the innocent happiness of the brief blissful hours she spends with her husband now, that she is resolved not to betray the increasing wretchedness of her existence at home; and while she plays and laughs with Cuthbert, and teases him about his idleness, and makes abortive attempts to stand very still as a model, she sedulously strives to hide all her cares, her doubts and fears, from him. If he knew all she has to endure, he would be unhappy, and his anxiety would cast a gloom over the sunny vista of their newly-wedded contented existence. Olga has had so sad a life hitherto, that she wishes to concentrate the sunshine of the glorious present, and, as far as she is concerned, no cloud shall mar its perfect brightness. Experience has long since taught her to suffer in patience, and she has taught herself to bear all her troubles in silence. Thus she gains steadily in moral strength, and becomes possessed of the proud courage which appertains to a noble mind.

CHAPTER V.

DIANA AT HOME.

'YES, Sir Gilbert, Miss Hartley is still at home.'

It has been Miss Hartley's custom to be 'at home' to her particular friends on Sunday afternoons for so many years past, that the inquiry becomes an empty formula to those who enjoy the proud privilege of considering themselves among Miss Hartley's intimates. These she welcomes cordially once a week, and, in the course of time, they have formed a sort of coterie, which their hostess calls 'a meeting of the elect.' Outsiders rarely commit the indiscretion of asking for admission on Sundays; they are aware that the less select Thursday afternoons are set apart for their entertainment. And Luke Day, the white-haired, wizen-faced butler, who has lived in the service of Miss Diana's family ever since she herself was a baby, is quite a master in the art of selection where visitors are concerned. He knows very well whom to admit, and whom his mistress would wish to exclude, and he very seldom makes a mistake. He never ushers in the wrong people on Sundays, and he welcomes the right ones with genuine cordiality; for he considers that Miss Hartley's friends are his friends, and all those on whom she smiles graciously he also is ready to receive with the utmost courtesy.

The Sunday coterie was a very large one during the season, and Miss Hartley's enemies declared it to be very *mixed* always. It certainly was varied; but there were a few visitors whose attendance was regular.

First and foremost among these was Sir Gilbert Clive, who for many years had been Miss Hartley's most devoted admirer, and the patient slave of her caprices. His son,

Cyril Clive, of the 100th Hussars, presented himself at 'the Cottage,' in Regency-terrace, almost as frequently as his white-headed young-hearted parent; and Campo Maestro, the celebrated *impresario*, was never absent either on Thursdays or Sundays. The 'mixed' atmosphere which he gratefully inhaled at the house of *questa amabile Signorina Diana* suited his Bohemian tastes exactly, for he found a *varied* society far more congenial than an exclusive one, and the signorina certainly had the talent of making her guests feel quite at home and thoroughly at their ease always.

Frank Allonby was a Sunday visitor: his week-days gave him little spare time, for he was junior and working partner in the firm of Allonby, Bidewell, & Allonby, the eminent Pall Mall publishers.

The youthful Marchese Rialto, *attaché* to the Italian Embassy, was another frequent visitor at the Cottage, and Miss Hartley patronised him with a pretty affectation of maternal indulgence. He was the only son of a very old flame of hers, and the sight of the picturesque oval face, with its wondrous black eyes and waving dark locks, recalled the face of the noble old father, who once adored the English signorina, and would have made a Venetian marchioness of her, had she not preferred her maidenly independence to an old husband with a title.

Another favourite guest at the Cottage was Achille Lafont, the famous French tenor, whose voice had such exceeding sweetness and power that he was nicknamed 'Il flauto magico' in musical circles. Indeed, to hear him was to follow him; and he effected many social triumphs by his subtle rendering of certain French *romances*.

Old General Carteret, now an octogenarian, had known Miss Diana ever since she was a precocious coquette in very short petticoats and a proportionately wide sash; he had stood godfather, in fact, to the only child of his late comrade in arms, and he had loved and petted her ever since, with a fervour of constancy which did not characterise his domestic affections, for he cared very little for his old wife and his daughters, who were not particularly young or beautiful either. His answer to remonstrances on the head of his *absurd* devotion to Diana Hartley became a formula, oft repeated, impressively delivered, 'She is my only godchild; Dick Hartley, her father, was my only and beloved friend for more than fifty years; she is an orphan, and needs my care and affection far more than those who are surrounded by officious relatives.'

Such were the most conspicuous of Miss Hartley's men friends, and the female element admitted on her Sundays was decidedly more varied still; for the simple reason that Diana Hartley eschewed the society of her own sex, when it did not minister directly to her amusement, and this very few women could do.

Little Lady Furnival, who had the ugliest face, the best figure, and the wittiest tongue of any woman in London, was mostly to be found at the Cottage on Sundays; but for this intimacy there was a special reason. Lady Furnival was supposed to be all-powerful with George Horrocks, and George Horrocks was a theatrical critic. If, side by side with this fact, you place that of Miss Hartley's ambition as a dramatic author, the *raison d'être* of her attentions to Lady Furnival appears at once.

A strange contrast to her reckless clever ladyship was presented by poor, stiff, stupid, old Mrs. Carteret, the General's wife. She was a prominent member of a certain Low Church set, and she looked quite as ill at ease as she felt among the uncongenial society by which she was surrounded in Miss Hartley's reception-room. Why, then, did this eccentric old lady insist on presenting herself where she certainly was not wanted?

Her visits had two reasons. In the first place, she really was as fond of, and as much attracted by, clever Diana as the old General himself, though this affection was never avowed; and, secondly, she liked to be quite sure how often her husband went to the Cottage, how long he stayed there, and, more than all that, whether he talked too much to Miss Susie Delane of the Melpomene Theatre, whose beautiful eyes and ingenuous 'baby manner' had made a profound impression upon the aged warrior.

Miss Susie's pretty face and excellent acting had contributed not a little to the success of Miss Hartley's 'much admired comedy' (thus the *Era* described her dramatic effort) *On the Brink*. The piece had been played twice at experimental afternoon performances, and its undoubted success was, in a great measure, due to the spirited rendering which Miss Delane gave of the heroine's contradictory character.

Miss Hartley was well aware of this fact, and appreciated the young actress's talents accordingly. A feeling of mutual admiration sprang up between authoress and actress after that first performance, which promised to mature into something like lasting friendship.

On this dubious intimacy, Mrs. Carteret could not withhold her anxious remonstrances; and the bigoted old lady spent many a weary hour in *arguing* the compro-mising matter with her husband's reckless godchild.

'I am assured, on indisputable authority, my dear Diana,' protested the General's wife on one occasion, 'that Miss Delane has been much talked about already.'

'So have most of my friends, and a good many of yours, dear Mum,' replied Diana, laughing.

'Mum' was the name she had bestowed, in her childhood, on her oldest friend.

'But what can induce you, my dearest Diana, to seek fresh acquaintance with a woman who is certainly not of your own class, and who, according to general impression, is not quite above either reproach or suspicion?'

'The same remark, without any hesitation, applies most decidedly to your acquaintance with the fast and fat Duchess of Blankshire, dear Mum,' replied Miss Hartley composedly; 'and I should advise you, in the moral interest of your daughters and yourself, to object to her Grace's acquaintance.'

'But she is the most distinguished member of our congregation,' said Mrs. Carteret hastily; 'and I hope to get her to subscribe her name as leading patroness of my new scheme for the supply of crochet-hooks to the children of the poor. I also believe most sincerely that the uncharitable things which are whispered against her Grace are quite without foundation.'

'Exactly my sentiments about dear little Susie,' said Diana briefly.

Thus ended Mrs. Carteret's last abortive attempt to interfere with Miss Hartley's visiting-list; and thenceforth she contented herself with gathering up the skirt of her Sunday black silk with an ominous frown whenever she approached Miss Delane.

'That solemn old lady evidently thinks I bring an epidemic from the theatre,' said Susie, laughing, as she mentioned this fact to her affectionate patroness.

'It is your former connection with "that sink of perdition" the Kaleidoscope Theatre which a-larms poor old Mum,' said Diana. 'Never mind her, my child; her growl is far worse than her *heart.* She is not a bad old lady, though she looks it; but her daughters, giants in body, pigmies in spirit, are odious; and as they occasion-ally honour me with their patronis-ing presence on Thursdays, it is as well for you to keep out of the way then, as they might shock you.'

'As much as I should certainly shock them,' laughed Susie good-naturedly.

But she took the hint, and never presented herself on the Thurs-days.

Besides this oddly assorted trio of lady-visitors there was old Ma-dame Strozzi, a great character in her way, and one of Diana's many governesses; but if the weather was bad (and it mostly was bad on Sundays), Madame Strozzi, who was infirm, could not come all the way across the Park unless Campo Maestro called for her in his brougham.

If any of the favoured visitors desired a private consultation with Miss Hartley, the cue was to come at three or at six. At three the guests had not commenced to ar-rive; at six they had all departed.

But it was nearly seven on the Sunday evening when Sir Gilbert Clive rapped at the door of the Cottage, and inquired if Miss Hart-ley were *still* at home. He feared she might be going out to dine.

Luke's affirmative reassured the Baronet.

'And is she alone?' he again asked eagerly.

'Quite alone, Sir Gilbert; yes, sir.'

'Thank Heaven!' muttered the intending visitor, with a sigh of re-lief; and he brushed past Luke and hurried up-stairs.

The butler disappeared. There was no need for him to announce Sir Gilbert Clive, who went in and out of the house as he pleased, and who was certainly always a wel-come guest.

CHAPTER VI.

SOME OF DIANA'S SECRETS.

WHEN Sir Gilbert hurriedly, but noiselessly, enters the drawing-room, he finds Miss Hartley stretched wearily in a low arm-chair that is almost a lounge. She holds a fan of peacock-feathers in her jewelled hand, to shade her face from the scorching rays of the huge glowing fire. Before she rises to receive her late but wel-come guest, let us regard her at-tentively, and seek, if possible, to fathom the mysterious secret of that power of fascination which she undoubtedly exercises over all who come in contact with her. She certainly possesses some spe-cial charm; and it is not that of beauty, though its attraction is as potent, and more lasting; for it has survived her youth, and yet it is essentially youthful. With the announcement of the startling fact that Miss Diana Hartley has now reached the mature age of thirty-eight, I fear the interest of some readers in this heroine may cease.

A heroine of thirty-eight! Well, it does seem absurd. A heroine, moreover, who had never been beau-tiful, and who yet is, as she has al-ways been, a formidable rival to the youngest and fairest of her sex.

Diana Hartley had *lived* every hour of her life; and she had en-joyed the passing hours to the ut-termost, as only such natures as hers can enjoy. She possessed a keen sense of pleasure, and appreciated every detail that could minister to her enjoyment. She delighted in the simplest pastimes, as she revelled in more piquant pleasures. She had seen and done more adventurous deeds than commonly fall to the lot of women to hear of. And, as yet, she was tired of nothing. The damning shadow of boredom had never crept over her. She had loved much and many; but she had never felt the sad satiety of wasted affection. Where others wept, she mostly contrived to laugh; and laughter is the privilege of youth.

What kept her as young and fresh in appearance as in ideas no one could positively define. Perhaps it was the variety, the constant change of her interests and occupations; for her life was full of both. She was a successful dramatist; she had written one startling and indisputably clever novel, which took society by storm, and rapidly passed through three editions. She was a much-desired and eagerly-welcomed guest in houses to which the *entrée* was both coveted and difficult; and her busy brain and clever fingers dabbled in many a scheme philanthropic or diplomatic. These constant alternations of earnest work, with exhilarating play, probably kept her mind and body fresh, vigorous, and on the alert.

She had her hours of despondency, of course, and was now and then oppressed by a spell of low spirits; but these are characteristics of all highly-strung, nervous, impressionable natures; and Diana certainly managed to recover her mental equilibrium very quickly. She allowed nothing to mar her enjoyment of life and its good things permanently.

It is a common mistake to suppose that a succession of vivid excitements wear life out and age the rapid livers prematurely. No-thing ages so much as monotony, which eats into the vital fibre like rust, and consumes it sluggishly but surely, as rust destroys iron itself in time.

Miss Hartley might have been fifty-five, as her enemies declared, or thirty, as she herself admitted; she certainly looked young for either age.

Rose-tinted lamps illumine the pretty inner room, to which she has withdrawn as soon as her last guest departed; and the logs of ship-wood which fill the ample fireplace cast rainbow hues upon the dainty cretonne-covered furniture and the still daintier mistress of the bijou home. She is clad in silver-gray brocade, looped here and there with knots of rose-coloured ribbon; and the dress fits its shapely wearer like a Parisian glove. Her *élancé* figure suggests youth and energy; so do the large hazel eyes, sparkling with mirth and intelligence. Not a silver thread is visible in the waving black hair, which for the most part is coiled closely about her head, and only falls in artistic disorder upon the broad brow—to hide her wrinkles, she explains, laughing. But if that be so, it seems odd that Time should have left no trace of his passage on the rest of the pure smooth face.

Who, looking at Diana Hartley in this roseate flickering light, could deem her other than youthful still? Decidedly young—and most attractive.

Sir Gilbert, who has been scanning the admired face attentively as he takes his hostess's shapely hands into his, thinks her as charming as ever, and tells her so with more earnestness than the occasion seems to warrant. But Sir Gilbert is a diplomatist, and he seldom misses a chance of furthering his promotion either in his private or his public career.

Having described Miss Hartley as she appears to her visitor to-day, a brief glimpse into her eventful past history may interest the reader.

Miss Hartley's father was a soldier, and he died in Spain while actively engaged in the service of his king and country.

Diana was born on the day her father died, and this fact may account for her being reared without discipline of any sort to hedge her in. She was so marvellously like that much-loved dead father, that his devoted heart-broken widow could not bring herself to thwart the child in any way. If she cried, it seemed as though the feelings of the dear departed were outraged; and prohibition and contradiction were unknown quantities in the lively tale of Diana's juvenile experiences.

So she grew up, wildly worshipped—a very *rara avis* in her mother's eyes, who continued to pet and spoil her until she reached an age when severity and remonstrance were equally unavailing to stem or divert the wild current of self-will with which haughty Di now swept over all threatened barriers or natural obstacles. Fortunately, the child was endowed with a good disposition and a sweet temper; and though the petted baby and passionate schoolgirl developed into a somewhat masterful young woman, she always treated her timid little mother *en très bonne princesse*, coaxing, scolding, and petting her alternately; but never heeding her warnings, or obeying her gentle commands. Kind, easy-going, weak-minded Mrs. Hartley was certainly never fitted to cope with so strong and wilful a child as was this daughter of hers; and by the time Miss Diana had completed her eighteenth year, she was not only

mistress of her own actions, but she ruled the household generally by the sway of her indomitable will, combined with the utmost fascination of manner whenever she chose to display it.

Many seriously contemplative hours did poor Mrs. Hartley pass in unavailing regret over the past; often and often she ventured to express a futile wish that Diana had been differently brought up. 'If only she were more like girls in general!' This was her plaint to her most confidential friends. But as Sir Gilbert Clive and General Carteret ranked foremost among these, and both thought Diana infinitely charming, Mrs. Hartley received little sympathy or encouragement in her meek fault-finding.

Diana, who had very decided opinions about society and its constituent parts, gave her adhesion to its male members from the first, and had no hesitation in declaring this preference. This seemed in itself shocking presumption for a girl in her teens. Twenty years ago the girl of the period had not arrived at the stage of independence which they all with one accord assume as soon as they leave their schoolroom now. Advanced opinions and the discussion of grave social questions were deemed heinous offences against all laws of decorum by simple-minded Mrs. Hartley. But her bold daughter knew nothing of maidenly reticence; so she did just as she pleased, and said all that came into her mind without the slightest hesitation.

Was she a genius or merely an *enfant terrible?*

On this question there were divided opinions between the friends of mother and daughter.

Variety is always charming, and Diana was too original not to possess great attractions for admiring minds. She had several excellent offers of marriage, and certainly might have gratified her mother's most ambitious hopes had she chosen to accept one of her first suitors.

' But, alas,' to quote Mrs. Hartley's constant complaint, ' Di most persistently and wilfully stood in her own light. She had not the least idea of accommodating herself to circumstances !'

This, being interpreted, meant that Diana was too proud and high-spirited to take the yoke of marriage willingly upon her young shoulders; and when an excellent offer was made her by a very rich but a very old widower, she rejected it with all the indignation of rash youth. This hasty action on wilful Diana's part caused her mother such acute grief, and brought so many painful discussions into their erst peaceful home, that both resolved to go abroad for a time, and seek such distraction as Paris would afford them. To Paris they went, and were soon very comfortably established there in a charming *appartement* in the most fashionable quarter of the gay city.

But the spirit of rebellion nascent in Diana soon sought fresh vent in novel adventure. She, who had shrunk from matrimonial fetters in horror and loathing, now plunged with all the zest of a novice into romantic love-affairs. They were only flirtations, none of them likely to lead to any satisfactory result, and the first the most desperate and the least desirable at the same time.

Paris, the gay chattering world there, soon rang with the exciting details of the passionate attachment evinced by the beautiful and eccentric Miss Diana for her Italian singing-master.

Mrs. Hartley was now reduced to a condition of absolute despair, and humbly implored the immediate aid of General Carteret, who was her daughter's guardian. *Il maestro* Lorenzo Martelli was appealed to, his sense of chivalry was earnestly invoked, but all in vain. But, though moral pressure failed to have the desired effect, a more satisfactory result attended the practical experiment of an extravagant bribe. The *maestro* left Paris without a word of explanation to the girl, who manifestly adored him; and no one knew whither he had fled. To his numerous creditors this circumstance was very exasperating.

Diana was carried off to Spa to get over her infatuation; but, instead of conquering it, she was laid low by a wasting fever, the results of which were so serious that her life for a time was despaired of. And when she at length recovered, it was to hear that Il Signor Martelli was a married man; that his young wife, tired of awaiting his return in Naples, had followed him to Paris; and that they had now departed to America together, to try their luck in the new country.

This intelligence, instead of further crushing, roused and fortified Diana. She laughed heartily at her *grande passion* and its unworthy object; and at Ostend she consoled herself by a new flirtation with the handsome young Graf von Stolzfels, the son of a German ambassador. The toying with love here again merged into something like earnestness; but Graf Otto was already engaged to the daughter of his father's best friend; and the old nobleman appeared in person to frustrate his young son's new plans, and insist on his keeping his solemnly-pledged word to Fräulein Friedegonda. So arbitrary was this stern parent, that he carried his foolish boy—a boy of five-and-twenty—off bodily, whereupon

Mrs. Hartley left Ostend with poor Diana; and both returned to Paris wiser, but not happier, for their six months' absence.

By this time Mademoiselle Diane had come to be a great deal talked about, and this at a period when notoriety was not considered desirable for young ladies. And Mrs. Hartley's handsome daughter was already declared to be too eccentric even for *une Anglaise.* It was about this time that the young Marquis of Dagenham fell madly in love with capricious fascinating Diana; but she had already become so notorious by her eccentricities, that his friends moved heaven and earth to save him from what they deemed snares and pitfalls. The Duchess was urgently written to by an old friend of the family; and Diana's happiness (she was now formally engaged to the Marquis) was once more imperilled. He was desperately in love, and might, perhaps, have defied parents and friends for the sake of the dear adored one, had she but played her cards with a little more care. But she was as reckless as ever, and, tempted by the attentions of a more interesting, but less eligible, adorer, she turned to the latter, and neglected her affianced cruelly.

Jealousy acts as a stimulant to some natures, and as an extinguisher on others. With Dagenham the latter was the effect. He was very much in love with Diana, but still more in love with himself. His vanity was hurt; he grew sulky; and Diana at once became restive.

Poor Mrs. Hartley all this while walked upon thorny paths of anxiety and distress. She longed to see her darling happily married and comfortably settled; and it was not likely that such a chance as Lord Dagenham offered her would ever come again; so she implored Diana to be more patient, more gentle, more considerate. Lord Dagenham saw through the anxious mother's simple manœuvres, and was perfectly aware, too, of the irritability her enforced self-restraint was causing poor Diana, who was daily growing more and more tired of him, and turning with a rebound of fresh affection to another man. The new-comer was a clever young author, who had been twice imprisoned for his rashly avowed political opinions, and who lived in hourly expectation of outlawry and exile.

The devotion of a patriot and hero, such as Alphonse de Nîmes was considered in certain circles, conferred more distinction upon Mademoiselle Diane, she thought, than the attachment of a dozen insignificant young Dagenhams, who was a nonentity in the intellectual society, where fame was superior rank. The inclination of the moment always outweighed all prudential considerations where impulsive Diana was concerned; and when the reckless girl felt that she was in love she neither stayed to look backward nor forward. She lived essentially in the fleeting joy of the present, and revelled in the pleasure that lay nearest at hand.

One evening at a grand ball she threw over the peer for the republican, and the following morning the offended Marquis left Paris for England.

'Thank Heaven for having rid us of the dear old bore!' cried Diana, clapping her hands gleefully, when she perceived her erst adorer's P.P.C. card upon her mother's table. And poor Mrs. Hartley was fain to rejoice also; for she was well-nigh worn out with anxiety and suspense. Even the worst certainty was better than such prolonged doubt.

'After all, my poor darling might not have been happy with him,' was the afterthought with which she consoled herself. 'He was certainly rather a heavy tiresome sort of young man, and might have grown worse as time went on.'

But gentle conciliatory Mrs. Hartley's regrets and consolations were very soon merged in a new and growing anxiety; for she now lived in hourly fear of hearing that her wilful daughter had thrown herself away upon that wild rebel young De Nîmes.

Mrs. Hartley's fears, fortunately for all concerned, no doubt, were not fulfilled. While heedless Diana was confined to her room by a sore throat, the result of careless exposure to the night air at the open window of a ballroom, Monsieur de Nîmes was peremptorily ordered to leave France, and had to decamp at a few hours' notice. It was now Mrs. Hartley's turn to thank Heaven for ridding them of this dangerous incubus, and her gratitude for the relief was sincere and profound. It was at this period of her eventful career that proud Diana first sought a refuge and a reprieve from her love-sorrows in literary work. She conceived the notion of confiding her love and her suffering for the rebel De Nîmes to paper, and actually wrote five acts of a tragedy in blank verse, of which Alphonse was the gallant hero. The work was never printed, and its fair author some years later destroyed the ambitious MSS. with much sarcastic laughter. But the fact of her settling to work at all had most desirable effects. It roused her mental activity, and revived her energetic spirit. Having discovered a new pleasure in active occupation, she now resolved to try her hand at a three-volume novel, and set to work with tremendous enthusiasm. But her hope and energy were suddenly nipped in the fresh bud of their

new promise. For Diana was now confronted by her first real sorrow, and it threatened to overwhelm her. To facilitate the publication of her novel, first in serial and then in volume form, Diana desired to return to London, and to this new scheme her mother readily consented. It would be delightful to have a home of her own again instead of the regulation flat in the high house in Paris. Both mother and daughter began to pine for their dear familiar old London again; and they found a house exactly to suit them in Regency-terrace, S.W. 'The Cottage' was really a miniature mansion, and as in those days the south-western suburb still boasted of lanes and fields, these fortunate tenants were able to secure a considerable piece of ground in addition to their new and charming residence. Mrs. Hartley was a rich woman, and she judiciously invested a part of her capital in the purchase of the Cottage and the surrounding gardens. But no sooner were mother and daughter comfortably settled in their new and congenial abode than the former fell suddenly ill, and died after a few days of intense suffering.

This was indeed a terrible blow to Diana. Her love-sorrows had not been unalloyed griefs; there was the spice of adventure, the possibility of better days, to carry her through those disappointments. They were fraught with sentimental luxury, and gave the zest of feverish excitement to her life. But the loss of her gentle mother filled the proud girl with passionate grief, and she mourned her indulgent parent with a lasting despair, which amazed all who knew her. Who could have believed that the rash wilful daughter cared so much for the feeble and rather querulous little woman, over whom she had ruthlessly tyrannised for so many years?

Which of our neighbours, who even of those nearest and dearest to us, is able to gauge the true measure of our griefs and our joys?

What outsider can presume to tell how much remorse mingles with our lamentations for those who have gone from us to that unknown land whence no traveller returns?

How seldom do we appreciate the love and tenderness lavished upon us until we are deprived of those accustomed outward signs of a profound and lasting affection!

Mrs. Hartley's death marked the first grave epoch in her child's careless life. Diana was never quite the same reckless girl after she had confronted a trouble she could neither laugh at nor forget. Sorrow is a crucial test, and ofttimes it develops latent qualities which, without such exciting cause, might have remained dormant. Not that any remarkable transformation took place in Diana's appearance or her mode of life; but her jubilant nature had received a poignant shock, and its effects were, in some sort, lasting.

> 'The world goes up, and the world goes
>   down,
>   And the sunshine follows the rain;
> But yesterday's smile and yesterday's frown
>   Can never come back again.'

After Mrs. Hartley's death, Diana soon assumed a position of absolute independence; and though, for the sake of her anxious friends, she went through the experiment of taking a lady chaperon or companion to live in her house, the plan was very soon given up as an evident and egregious failure. Diana had never been able to get on with any one but her mother, she declared, and it was quite impossible to change her manner of life now.

The anxious friends shrugged their shoulders and sighed. Mrs. Grundy shook her head in fierce deprecation; but Diana heeded neither warning nor expostulation. She was quite old enough to live by herself and to take care of herself, she affirmed; and Luke Day, the butler, and Mrs. Day, the housekeeper, cordially approved the decision of the mistress both had known and faithfully served since her childhood.

'I shall devote myself entirely to a literary career,' declared Diana, with reviving energy. And her intense application was followed by surprisingly successful results. 'Art gives life its best reprieves,' had been said to her as an encouragement, and she seized upon the idea with avidity. Her novel. *On the Brink*, on which she subsequently founded the successful comedy, cost her a couple of years of earnest thought and constant labour; but she was more than rewarded for her trouble and perseverance by the cordial approbation her work received when it at last made its appearance in public.

The novel was published by Messrs. Allonby, Bidewell, & Allonby, and it was from that time that Diana's great friendship with handsome Frank, the junior partner, dated—a friendship that soon ripened into intimacy, and was of decided importance to the young authoress in her newly-adopted professional career. For Diana did not at all approve of amateur workmanship, and was as much in earnest over her writing now as though her daily bread literally depended upon the success of her labours.

But her friendship for young Frank, innocent and pleasant as it was to them both, brought down unmitigated wrath and sharp reproach upon Diana's proud head. People said that she had turned the poor young man's handsome head, and that she would never rest until she had got him completely into her

toils. Her influence was so deleterious that it had already made
him dissatisfied with his position in
the business, his home, and his poor
wife. Until Miss Hartley unsettled
him by her subtle flatteries he had
felt quite contented with the pretty
little fool he had married while
both he and she were still infants
in the eyes of the law. But that
wicked Diana was successfully
pointing out his past errors to him
now, and Mrs. Frank grew daily
more fractious and disagreeable.

'Your precious godchild is
beginning to flirt as recklessly as
ever again,' said Mrs. Carteret
viciously, as she came home one
day full of the latest scandal
apropos of her husband's pet. And
then she corroborated her statement by declaring that Frank Allonby had been seen to enter the
gates of the Cottage four times during the past week, and that he was
actually there again this afternoon.
Mrs. Rivers, who had lived in the
long terrace known as 'Regency,'
was Mrs. Carteret's informant, and
Mrs. Rivers was well known to
have little occupation beyond that
of watching her neighbours.

'But Allonby goes on business,'
pleaded the old General in extenua-
tion of his favourite.

'That's rubbish!' replied his wife
sharply. 'Publishers do not run
about after their contributors, any
more than solicitors run after their
clients—unless there is some special
attraction offered them. It really
is too bad of Diana to worry her
friends by these wild vagaries. She
is surely quite old enough to know
better now. Look at our girls!'
Mrs. Carteret tossed her head and
paused; the excitement and wrath
combined made her breathless.

The General, whose long life had
taught him the value of the soft
answer, cheerily replied,

'Poor little Di has no mother to
look after her, my dear. Do not

forget the inestimable advantage
our daughters have in you!'

Mrs. Carteret was mollified,
though not convinced; and her
husband walked away laughing his
odd little laugh.

In spite of all personal scandal
and petty tittle-tattle, Miss Hartley's novel scored a decided success with the public, and so did
her comedy. But the charming
and talented authoress failed to
continue the work begun with such
amazing energy but a few years
ago. The literary fever died out,
and some new interest preoccupied
her now to the exclusion of all
others. She did not follow up
her first novel by any other, and
the nine days' wonder about the
promising author of *On the Brink*
was already supplanted by some
fresh question of social interest.

When her friends twitted her
about her sudden change of purpose, her unfulfilled promises, and
her seeming laziness, she answered
them somewhat impatiently. She
was not in the mood for any fresh
enterprise, she said wearily, and
her wonted energy certainly seemed
to be failing her. Those who loved
her grieved about this perplexing
change, and those who envied or
disliked her rejoiced at it. But
neither her friends nor her enemies
suspected the true cause of her altered spirit and purpose. She alone
knew and deplored both cause and
effect. And yet the absorbing
study of a certain portrait, a pale
face with light-brown deep-set eyes
and thick black hair that fell over
the low brow, was her secret consolation and her lasting joy. While
she was looking at that face, and
thinking of its fascinating owner,
she felt tranquil, if not happy; but
her interest in aught else had ceased
to exist. She was in a restless and
irritable frame of mind, but her
dissatisfied condition was not that
which finds comfort in mental oc-

cupation. She could not abstract her thoughts from *him*. She wondered why he never came now; she thought drearily of his prolonged unaccountable absence. Where was he? What was he doing all this time? She felt miserable, and her heart was sick with the poignant *regret a'un absent*. Once he came to her house every day; he talked to her on every conceivable subject; he confided in her; he asked for her help and advice in all his affairs; and she fondly believed that not a thought of his was hidden from her. But a change had come over him of late. Something or somebody was dividing them. He gave her neither clue nor hint to explain the ominous shadow which had fallen over their friendship; and she had no right to be inquisitorial.

'How the women who are jealous of me, and the men I have been cruel to, would triumph and rejoice if they could read the thoughts in my dejected soul now!'

This was the thought in her mind as she threw herself wearily back into the lounging-chair in her pretty boudoir, and covered her face with the fan of peacocks' feathers. It is long past the visiting-hour now, and he has stayed away again.

There is a sharp rap at the door. She starts to her feet:

'Cyril—at last!'

[To be continued.]

A LESSON IN ANATOMY.

A New and Original Sketch from the French.

BY JOHN AUGUSTUS O'SHEA.

In one of the old noisome narrow streets which still crouch at the bottom of certain nooks in the Latin Quarter of Paris there was, in 1871, an obscure *crêmerie*, surnamed by the customers who frequented it, 'The Refuge of the Destitute.'

It was there I took my meals during the Commune.

At that period very few customers came to 'The Refuge of the Destitute;' for the destitute were too busily occupied fighting.

Every evening at dinner-hour the patron wiped the marble tables, as a matter of routine, and perfunctorily arranged his service of humpbacked dish-covers, thick glasses, large heavy plates, and diminutive light decanters. Apart from two or three chance guests, we were seldom more than five who came to the place regularly—two elderly workmen, one of whom was infirm, a little ironmonger of the neighbourhood, a student, and myself.

The two workmen always sat at the same table; they bore themselves with a contemptuous air towards the ironmonger, who took a seat by himself at the entrance of the *salle*, and read the *Bien Public* as he munched his meals. They used to speak of him in an undertone as 'Old Chucklehead.' From time to time, as the affairs of the Commune appeared to go on swimmingly, they treated themselves to a *chopine* or a *demi-setier* of the blue wine, by way of rejoicing.

On those days they were gay, and made no concealment of their gaiety, breaking out into the chorus of an old workman's rhyme familiar to their apprenticeship. These two worthy fellows, the ironmonger and I, naturally entered the house by the street-door. The fifth customer, the student, always came in by the kitchen-door. As seven o'clock neared, he was to be seen close to the cooking-stove, where the patron kept his soup warm. At first he used to drink a large glass of water with avidity. Then he dined very slowly; his repast always being the same—lentil soup, an underdone omelette, a fried sole, a morsel of cheese, and an apple. When he had finished, he leant back in his chair, shut his eyes, and seemed to doze for half an hour, like a boa-constrictor in the act of digestion. When the clock over the counter struck eight, he rose, and left by the kitchen, as he had entered, without taking notice of anybody.

He had a singular head. A bushy growth of black, curly, snake-like hair fell over and shadowed his forehead. A few rebel locks, disengaged from the mass, stood up here and there like spikes. His beard, on the contrary, was extremely fine and regular. From the midst of the sombre framework of his dark hair shone out brightly two large limpid eyes, almost expressionless by reason of their gentle unsettled look. His face, of a livid white, was illuminated, now and again, by their wandering light.

As to the body which was surmounted by this curious head, it was that of a child, weak, meagre, and ungainly.

This original being, his manners and appearance suggestive of the monomaniac, and his impenetrable silence, vividly piqued my curiosity. What class of student could he be? Was he really a student at all? I had certainly overheard the two workmen call him by the name; but that proved nothing. I could restrain myself no longer, and plumply questioned the patron on the subject.

'That's Monsieur Féru,' he said. 'He's well known in the Quarter.'

'What occupation does he follow?'

'He's a medical student, and attends a great many poor people for nothing. He's a good sort, and no question about it; only, you see, the poor lad is a little queer.'

'So it struck me. His extraordinary behaviour interested me from the first day I saw him. That's why I asked you what he was. What whimsical habits he has!'

The patron was enchanted at the opportunity of gossiping a little with anybody, and did not need pressing to continue.

'Ah, you see,' he said, with a knowing shrug, 'there's quite a romance about him!'

And bending close to my ear, he added,

'He's a philosopher. He has a bee in his bonnet, a tile off, a brick loose in the upper story, you know.'

'You don't mean it?'

'Fact; true as I am here, I assure you. No wonder he is touched in the head. He works too hard. He never comes down-stairs except to his meals. O, I know what I am talking about, for he lodges in the house, and my wife tidies up his room! If you were only to see

it; it's a regular lumber-box. Nothing but books, bones, and sheets of paper. He writes like one possessed. I almost believe he makes verses.'

'I see nothing in all that to prove that a man is mad—'

'O, but I do! It is not natural for a young fellow of five-and-twenty to be poring over dusty volumes like that all day long. He has never been on a "spree" once in his life, I do think. Did you remark how he eats?'

'Yes, always the same articles of food.'

'Well, that's done intentionally, on principle.'

'On principle?'

'Precisely. I have often told him he would end by making himself ill, if he never altered his diet. Then he explained to me why he would not alter it. Just listen. A man must be very far gone when he has such ideas. He says there are machines in eggs and cheese that are good for the nerves, queer-sounding words in *en* and *ine*.'

'Albumen and caseine, perhaps?'

'Yes, that's just it. But the funniest part of it is, that he pretends there is a lot of that match-stuff—how do you call it?—ay, ay, phosphorus, in fish and apples, and that they feed the brain, and that lentils make his mind clearer.'

At the thought of anything clarifying poor Féru's mind, the patron could not help chuckling.

'I don't mean to say, you know,' he continued as he recovered, 'that he is not clever. On the contrary, it appears that he is full of knowledge. He won a medical prize somewhere, and they say he once had an article printed in a newspaper.'

'You don't know which?'

'Yes, the one he gets regularly, the *Revue positive.*'

At this moment the half hour after seven struck, and Féru came in by the kitchen-door. As soon as he had sat down, the patron approached him and whispered something. What stupidity was the idiot committing? Could he be speaking of me? I had no doubt of it, when I saw the young man lift his head and fix his regard upon me. I was somewhat embarrassed by his steady gaze, and did not well know how to relieve myself from the awkward position, when Féru himself came over and said to me, in a voice of much sweetness,

'Is it true, monsieur, that you feel interested in me?'

'I ask your pardon for the indiscretion—'

'No necessity. It is a compliment. It is the first time anybody paid me the compliment to feel interested in me.'

I was astonished at his ease and affability. This eccentric was most amiable. I rose and reconducted him to his table, where I sat opposite to him, and we entered into a conversation upon literature, out of which grew that quick frank friendship which springs up spontaneously among young people who have tastes in common.

After a few days had passed we were closely intimate. Every evening we conversed for a good hour. By a happy hazard our ideas ran in grooves on many points of art and philosophy. But expansive as Féru was when the subject was the *belles-lettres*, he was reserved and self-contained when I endeavoured to lead him on to the discussion of certain great philosophical problems. I could divine that he was a materialist; but I never could elicit from him on what grounds he justified his belief, or rather his want of belief. He uniformly evaded the topic. At last I point-blank asked him why he never spoke of medicine, and did not dare to descend to the bottom of

what I believed to be the source of his atheism.

'I don't speak to you of medicine,' he said, 'because you are not a doctor, and I hate to talk shop. The advertisement of one's acquaintance with a science before a person who is ignorant of it savours too much of charlatanism.'

'I am not a doctor, it is true, but neither am I ignorant of your science. My father is a doctor, and I have learned something from him. You may be certain, therefore, that I shall listen to you with sincerity and without afterthought.'

As he held his peace, and did not give any token of becoming communicative, I bluntly told him I suspected some hidden cause for his reserve; and that, most probably, was a want of confidence in me.

'At all events,' he said, 'I beg of you not to believe that.'

'What am I to think, then? May it be,' I added, smiling, 'that you are not sure of your doctrine? Are you, perchance, one of those superficial philosophers who take up a system without caring for it, as one drinks a glass of beer without feeling thirst? Are you afraid you may have to stop *en route* in the attempt to sound the depths of your idea?'

'*Parbleu!*' he replied; 'that is a pleasant notion. I afraid to sound the depths of my idea! I a superficial philosopher! You do not know me, my dear friend. Learn that, for now almost ten years, I study, I think, I search. Ay, and so little have I succeeded in exhausting my head that some of my comrades believe it is empty. As to my idea, I have adopted the habit of keeping it to myself and of avoiding every question which might lay it bare. I do not like to pass for an idiot. I prefer to pass for an eccentric.'

'Your idea, then, is very strange?'

'No; it is very simple.'

'In that case, you may surely make it known to me. I hope you do not confound me with those fools who jest at everything. I appreciate you when you talk of literature. May I not be equally capable of understanding your idea?'

'Now that I reflect, why not? Stay, I have a great esteem for you; I mean to treat you as a true friend, and make a candid and complete avowal. But you must not expect anything gigantic or monstrous; do not stare by anticipation. What you are about to hear is a platitude, nothing more.'

He rested his elbows on the table, passed his hand over his face, and, settling his cloudy glance upon me, thus calmly began:

'I am a materialist, as you have guessed. That is to say, I recognise in this world but one substance—matter. All phenomena are, therefore, material phenomena. When I say therefore, I am wrong: it is precisely this therefore which must be made evident. So far no one has succeeded in that. Every physiological, physical, and chemical phenomenon has been perfectly shown to be reducible to the laws of matter; but no one has yet established the connection with them of intellectual phenomena. By that I mean that no experimentalist has yet caught matter *in flagrante delicto* of thought. That must be sought out, and that it is which I hope to find. You must own that all this is natural.'

'But the practical method of arriving at the proof? I own I do not see that.'

'There is nothing more easy: it is but to analyse, to dissect, to hold under one's fingers a thinking brain. Evidently one would seize the thought, one would perceive, one would touch it, as one seizes, perceives, and touches an electrical phenomenon, for example.'

'But how can you hope that such a thing is possible—to study a thinking brain?'

'Assuredly that is the difficult point. Nevertheless, I have already determined to make an experiment which is an approach to it, and which will lead me to the desired end. I propose to dissect a living being.'

'A living being?'

'Yes; and since I have confided to you my idea, I may as well tell you the wild visions it has given birth to. The dream of my ambition is to make my studies upon men.'

'What you say is frightful! Do you mean to tell me that you would kill men for yourself, for your own pleasure?'

'No, not for my pleasure. I would kill men for the good of mankind.'

His face, at this instant, was singularly changed. His eyes, from restless, became set and almost haggard; a hectic spot burned on his white cheeks, as if he were struck with fever. He stood motionless in front of me, his chin supported on his clenched hands. He was like a man in an ecstasy. Of a truth, he was more powerfully dominated by his idea than any person ought to be who was merely enunciating a theory. I understood at once that there was here something more than a mere tension of the intellectual faculty. His idea was a rooted, immutable, rigid one—strongly imbedded in his nature. The unfortunate creature was tainted with monomania. I bitterly reproached myself for having brought on the conversation, and led Féru over a field of speculation he had shrunk from, no doubt, because conscious that he lost himself when he ventured upon it. I did not know how to bring him back to the reality.

He recovered of his own accord after a few minutes, and rapidly shook his head, as if he were irritated by an insect. The colour suddenly left his cheeks, and he became deadly pale.

'What's the matter with you?' I asked. 'Are you ill?'

'No, no,' he answered, rising to leave. When he was near the door he slowly turned, as if he had forgotten something. 'O!' said he suddenly, 'I recollect. I wanted to tell you to speak to me no more of that. You'll promise me?'

He did not need to make the request twice. From that moment I would have infinitely preferred to have turned his thoughts away from such a subject than to have led him into conversation upon it. We were satisfied afterwards to discuss art and poetry.

Moreover, he was less familiar with me. Sometimes he seemed embarrassed, and often he left me to indulge in dissertations to myself. By degrees his silence almost took the form of a rebuff. I felt I was considered importunate, and we became distant with one another.

He took up his former corner anew, and sat with his back to the *salle.* I moved nearer to the workmen, whose gossip was now the only accompaniment to the clatter of knives and forks.

Some eight days after our definite separation came the agony of the Commune.

On Wednesday, the 24th of May, I entered the *crêmerie* in the afternoon, driven from my own chambers by the fight. I had eaten nothing since the previous day, and called for breakfast. In the neighbouring streets the combat was raging some five minutes before at farthest. Rifle-shots could be heard in muffled ping, like the crack of a whip in a padded room. The reports sometimes came quite close, and again receded.

The ironmonger turned up soon after me.

'I came round to you on purpose, patron,' he said. 'I have shut up my shop, and I prefer being here to stopping at home. The affair is getting along gaily, do you know? We'll have the Line here to-morrow, for certain; and a good job too.'

And he poured out his abuse, his insults, and his prophecies after the fact, with all the glibness of a poltroon vomiting his ill-humour on a vanquished foe.

'Don't speak so loudly,' said I; 'there may be Federals in the street.'

He turned towards the door terrified, as if he felt himself already in their gripe. His knees trembled under him. The fit of trepidation calmed his fit of anger, and for a moment he held his tongue.

'You are right,' he said. 'Anyhow, those two drunkards who come here every evening will be sure to drop in before long. I saw the tall old fellow pass a while ago. I would take my oath he is going to make believe to fight, and by and by he will return to report himself. Only think of fighting at his age! The old rascal will never see seventy again.'

He was proceeding with his sneers, when we heard a loud crash of broken panes in the kitchen, which was covered with a glass roof. It sounded as if a body had fallen through. The patron and I ran in; while the ironmonger, almost fainting, crept under the table, and cried,

'O, it's a shell! It's going to burst!'

It was Féru.

He lay on the ground, on his stomach, perfectly naked. His sides were furrowed with long scarlet gashes, made by the sharp edges of the fractured glass, which had cut into him like a razor.

Our first instinct was to take him under the arms to lift him. But hardly had we turned him when we let him fall upon his back, such was the fearsome surprise that seized upon us. The unfortunate wretch had his breast flayed, the palpitating flesh exposed to the quick, and that not from the effect of the glass, but in consequence of an operation. He had been dissected! The white nerves, the blue arteries, the red muscles, the grayish aponeuroses, were laid bare in hideous excoriation; and the skin, peeled off in great square flap, fell upon his stomach like a rose-coloured apron.

At length I mustered courage to stoop and turn back this raw tissue of epidermis over his butchered chest, and we carried the body into the front room.

The ironmonger was still motionless, and did not dare to look around him. He gave us no help.

The coldness of the marble table on which we laid him having revived Féru, I leant over him.

'It's frightful, isn't it?' he said to me, in a very low voice. 'This is all because of my idea.'

I prayed him not to excite himself by trying to speak.

'No, no, listen to me,' he answered. 'I shall die within a quarter of an hour. That's positive as fate. I had an attack of madness. I determined to make a living dissection upon myself. I felt no pain while I was at work. Of a sudden I recovered my senses, and then I suffered so much that I flung myself out of the window. Ah, what a misfortune to have to go without having made my discovery! My anatomical preparation was skilful, eh?'

Here he tried to raise his head so as to view his breast.

'No matter,' he resumed; 'it is a grand idea which dies with me. To dissect the living—to study a thinking brain!'

The sinister pauses which punctuated his words were filled with the crepitation of the fusillade coming near and nearer.

'What! fighting still! I took advantage of the opportunity to work while everybody else was fighting. Sly, wasn't it?—But why are they fighting? To kill! Why kill? For nothing!—I would have killed all these creatures if they wished, but for some good at least. —To dissect the living!'

At this moment the door was violently thrown open, and the old workman hobbled in, supported by two comrades. There were blood-stains on his clothes.

'Hallo!' he said, on seeing Féru stretched on a table. 'There's already a wounded man here.'

'No,' replied the patron, 'it is Monsieur Féru, who has made an attempt to commit suicide.'

'To commit suicide!' said the workman. 'He must be a d—d coward, then, to kill himself for nothing, when one has the chance of dying for a good cause.'

Féru struggled to rise, no doubt with the intention of making a rejoinder. But life exhausted itself in this supreme effort, and he fell back dead upon the table.

The workman kept on talking.

'Peace!' I said. 'Do you not see he is dead?'

'What of that! I shall be dead myself by and by. I have the right to say what I think. I, at least, I die for—'

I interrupted him by uncovering the breast of Féru, and saying,

'He died for science!'

The workman and his friends were struck dumb, as if petrified by horror. They could hardly have understood what they saw, or have heard what I said, so appalled were they by the shocking spectacle before them. Suddenly, it seemed as if one of them took in the meaning of the sight, and his look of intelligence enlightening the others, all three respectfully removed their *képis.*

Meanwhile, the ironmonger took advantage of a cessation in the firing to save himself by the back-door. As he passed by me I could overhear him muttering between his teeth, 'Good God! Everybody is going stark mad!'

THE LAST VENTURE.

It is many a weary year ago,
    Since before the April gale
I sent my fairy bark to sea,
Over waves that sparkled and danced in glee,
With her gay flag fluttering merrily,
    And the sunlight on her sail.

Alas and alas for my bonnie boat,
    Did she leak 'neath the water-line?
Did her timbers rot, spite red, white, and blue?
Was the rudder flawed, though it looked so true?
Ask the ocean the fate that I never knew
    Of that first fair venture of mine.

And, ah, since then I have launched in hope
    Brave boats by three, by four;
But nor wind nor wave would keep their faith,
Sharp reefs would nestle soft foam beneath,
There was doom in each wild north-easter's breath—
    They never came back to shore.

And now, with weak weary fingers,
    I have launched my last and best;
Her sails were woven by Love's own hand,
By Prayer and Faith she was nobly manned,
Each rope by my prescient care was scanned,
    Ere I gave her to ocean's breast.

All alone on the wind-swept beach,
    All alone in my dread I stand;
Fancying storm in the south wind's sighs,
Dreaming of presage in calm gray skies,
Wrenching Nature to omens and prophecies,
    Seeking solace from sea and land.

A steadier head than mine for the helm,
    A stronger hand for the sheet,
A truer heart? Nay, my love, my love,
If fond prayers can reach to the Throne above,
A fairer voyage than thine will prove,
    No ship ever sailed to meet.

SUSAN K. PHILLIPS.

DRAMATIC CRITICS AS ACTORS.

By HAL LOUTHER.

'O, how the world would open its eyes
Would critics act and actors criticise!'—LORD BYRON.

OURS was a large northern city, possessed of more than one important theatre, and celebrated for the severity of its dramatic critics. All who sought its sock and buskin atmosphere approached cautiously. Old actors, whose very names seemed built on pedestals of press opinions manufactured in other towns, fronted our journalists with anything but their usual self-possession, and very often the balloon of their vanity was punctured. But woe betide the aspirant who, with heels unaccustomed to histrionic spurs, dared to enter the lists of criticism and, as it were, break a lance with these knights of the pen, who were known to scatter ink as savagely as ever crusader's sword did Saracen blood!

Well, it seems, for some purpose or another, this brotherhood of dramatic censors needed a large sum of money, and so a meeting was convened and solemn council held as to how the money was to be raised; but when an hour or so had been spent in deliberation, they found the problem was not so easy to solve as they had imagined. 'How could it be done?' was the oft-repeated question.

Beards were twitched in vain, chins were reflectively stroked, bald heads rubbed fiercely, while spectacles and eye-glasses, under a fever of irritation, and with the aid of pocket-handkerchiefs, were subjected to perpetual friction; and still the paper, prepared to receive their rules and resolutions, remained as pure and unsullied as when the sages first sat down.

Public appeal was out of the question, private subscription impossible; yet the money *must* be had, and out of the *public* too, but how—how? O that confounded conundrum again, with everybody giving it up!

At length one of the critics, a fledgling on the outskirts of that bewildered council, suggested, 'Let us act a play!'

The notion was seized upon at once, but the young man was elbowed further away on the outskirts than ever.

'Act a play!' they said; 'the very thing.' And each one suddenly remembered that he was just about to propose the idea when that impertinent scribbler for the evening halfpenny interrupted. Here was an unexpected way out of the dilemma!

Besides, what an opportunity to air their vanity by trying histrionic woods and pastures new! and then for a *charity*, that proverbial cloak which is supposed to cover a multitude of sins!

It was glorious.

Not that they knew anything about the art *practically*, but what did that signify? Nothing whatever; had they not dissected plays and cut up actors enough to warrant them knowing all about it? Pshaw! had they not seen performances till they *felt* they were histrions of the highest order? So it was duly settled that the play was the thing. A piece was chosen and cast, a theatre was placed at their disposal, professional ladies engaged, and an afternoon performance advertised. Splendid! and each member, who had *so nearly* suggested the idea, shook hands with himself in the heartiest manner. In due time bills were circulated, announcing *The Two Polts* and *Still Waters Run Deep*.

The news travelled like wildfire among the professionals; the members of the company belonging to the theatre where the performance was to take place would have a welcome holiday, which they would spend, as actors mostly do, in the theatre.

How they gloated over the chance!

'Ha, ha, ha!' laughed the heavy man, who had been often scathed by the local *Thunderer's* bolts, 'now we shall see if *he* is fitted to sustain *his rôle.*'

'The *Evening Growler* cannot see any fun in my low comedy,' said another. 'I shall be there, prepared to split my sides at his.'

'The *Morning Wasp* calls me a woollen actor,' cried the handsome light comedian, the son of a well-known actor, 'and says that I am not a chip of the old block. Now we shall see what stuff he is made of.'

'But what are they all to the *Impartial Observer!*' groaned the leading man. 'The others will praise you *sometimes;* and if they do cut you up, it is done with the skilful keenness of a polished lancet; but the *Impartial* hacks you with the blunt edge of a rusty cutlass.'

'Well, I don't know,' interrupted the flippant walking gentleman, 'so much about him. I think he is about the best in the bunch. Ah, you may laugh; all I know is, he has always been most kind *to me.*'

'Then your mind's eye must be short-sighted indeed!' retorted the leading man. 'True, he *has* praised you at the beginning of his com-

ments about you; but it was always done on the principle of ninepins—he placed you up to show his skill in knocking you down again! Gentlemen, *I* shall keep my eye on the *Impartial Observer.'*

The only silent member of the company was the one who had suffered most. He was the useful man; that is to say, he must be always ready to play any part, old or young. One of the critics had taken a set dislike to him, and made a sort of victim of him. When he could discover nothing else in the performance to complain about, he was sure to find a blood-let for his satire in the poor butt referred to. The critic, I think, would have been less severe had he known how the poor fellow's wife and family suffered through his witticisms. A heavy blow had fallen upon them; for the manager, influenced, no doubt, by these constant raids, had given the unfortunate 'useful man' his notice! Yet he was silent; but the reproaches lay in those dull wistful eyes and the mournful paleness of his sunken cheeks.

Knowing the circumstances, it will be readily understood that all the power which our local press could bring to bear upon the coming event was set in full motion; in fact, for days all the papers teemed with the performance. It literally flavoured your morning coffee; it fringed your political leader; it pervaded every advertisement column; it brightened the bankruptcy list; it fluttered timidly about the police news, bleared the foreign policy, seasoned the newest and most diabolical case of wife murder, and finally made suicide appear more culpable than ever for daring to brave the mystery of eternity without waiting for the promised joys of this grand performance.

The critics had rehearsals without end, long drawn out, but minus the linked sweetness, for each one, being conscious of his own power, wished everything done his own particular way. At first they read their parts and treated the whole affair, from their journalistic pinnacle, with a sort of affable contempt. Rehearsals might be well enough for regular actors, but for — No, the very hint of *their* requiring such things was an insult to common egotism. By and by, however, the supercilious manner seemed to merge into apoplectic little spasms as the eventful day drew near. There was a marked contrast between the first and last rehearsal. They had begun by *teaching* the actresses, and ended by being taught! In fact, it became painfully apparent in many cases that the heart of their confidence was melting, and likely to emulate the courage of Bob Acres by seeking an ignominious outlet through their fingers' ends.

At last the night arrived.

The regular playgoers, knowing what amateurs are as a rule, were conspicuous by their absence; but others who seldom or never visited a theatre took advantage of the elastic plea of its being for ' charity,' and so the house was crowded.

The members of the stock company, acting in concert, engaged a private box, where they were screened from the audience, but could be plainly seen by all on the stage; and when the curtain rose on the farce, Peter and Tom Polt soon became conscious of the fact that the professional representatives of those humorous parts were present, for actors and critics in provincial towns soon learn to know each other, if only by sight.

The light comedian had been censured for his rendition of Tom, and by the very man who was then playing the part. How the censured one laughed as he saw the critic's feeble efforts to appear at ease! Instead of being fluent and glib of speech, the words in some instances oozed from his lips in sluggish whispers, as it were; while in others they came forth in such a sudden and jerky manner, any one might have imagined that some invisible power had taken them by the throat and literally heaved them out!

Peter, who in his critiques was a determined opponent to exaggeration, and from whom his friends expected so much, was a huge disappointment. His attempts to be funny were most pathetic, and he wriggled about the stage as if both limbs and features were troubled with spasms of acute rheumatism, solemnly watched by the low comedian, who every now and then relieved his feelings by letting off an inward cannonade of derisive little chuckles.

To sum up the farce, everybody appeared glad when it was over, even to mutual friends with the largest of magnifying eyes. So general was this impression, that the very curtain seemed to come down with a sigh of relief. Better things were expected from the play. Meanwhile the local *Thunderer* and *Evening Wasp* sought their dressing-room. The masquerade was over, at least as far as they were concerned. How different their feelings as they stripped off the dresses which but an hour or so before they had donned with so much pride!

Peter's crop-wig seemed to look at him from the dressing-table in stolid wonder, as if asking how a man like that had ever dared to wear it; his busby frowned darkly at him; and the comic regimentals, so used to roars of laughter, lay scattered about limp and prostrate with the inglorious failure; nay, even the sash, used so effectively by former Peters, appeared to have turned a deeper red, as if blushing at the insult heaped upon it. Peter knew in his heart of hearts they were right, and felt humbled.

Tom fared no better at his table. His uniform, being, as it were, of a more gentlemanly nature, simply gazed at him with all the offended dignity of proud disdain; his moustache, as it lay upon the looking-glass ledge, had all the appearance of a human lip curling at him as if in scorn; while the pigments, that were to make him appear so fascinating, looked as though they regretted the fact that their mingled blandishments had been put to such base uses.

But the climax was reached when, on leaving the room to see the rest of the performance, they were met on every side by friends who *would* drone out their sympathy, invariably ending with, ' and those confounded fellows of actors in front, too !'

I have often wondered since how those astute gentlemen felt when, in the seclusion of their chambers, they called to mind the events of that memorable night. Did any pangs of conscience trouble them as they dropped off into restless slumber? I have often wondered too, when the affair was half forgotten, whether any of the sparks struck from the anvil of their satire ever rebounded on themselves with a reproachful sting. I am afraid not. Human nature is still in the same egotistical state as when Robby Burns deplored the want of that gift which would enable us to see ourselves with other people's eyes. But the curtain is up again, so a truce to conjectures.

The play being the principal event of the evening, every one settled down as quickly as possible.

It soon became apparent to all in front of the house that the prompter would have a busy time, and, though not in the cast, he was destined to play a most important part in the performance.

As the play proceeded, the leading man found out quickly that the *Impartial Observer*, who was playing Mildmay, was not at all bad ; and he groaned louder than ever as he saw the consolation of a failure fading away gradually.

The heavy man chuckled. His terror, the local *Thunderer*, was the Captain Hawkesley, and, though well made up, he seemed to have lost all control over his voice ; in fact, his speech appeared to be of the true asinine breed : in the middle of a quiet trot it would suddenly stop dead, and no spurring on the part of the prompter could move it. But the worst of it all was, when the others, by going on, had glossed over the break, his speech would as suddenly again resume the trot just where it had left off, and so send the scene plunging about in hopeless confusion. Taking this peculiarity into consideration, it may be easily imagined what a thorn he was in the sides of Mildmay and Mrs. Sternhold.

The heavy man was in ecstasies, every now and then quoting from some of the unfortunate critic's most satirical notices. But Potter, in a porcupine wig and outrageous get-up generally, was simply idiotic; while the young visitors, Markham and Langford, made everybody uncomfortable by their painful efforts to appear at ease on the stage.

The scene arrived when Dunbilk makes his appearance. Now the Dunbilk of the night was the man who had made the poor useful actor his victim. There was a loud burst of applause, for he was very clever with his pen ; and those who did not really like him at heart dreaded him. In a self-sufficient manner he saluted Hawkesley; and all at once he paused : his eye had caught sight of the pale face of his victim, looking down upon him, more in sorrow than in anger, from the corner of his box. The prompter was hard at work again. Dunbilk paced about for a moment or two in a restless way, and at last a few lines came to his aid ; but, go where he would, those eyes seemed to fascinate. He knew the man had received his notice through him, and he had looked upon the fact as a compliment to his skill. Had the victim been angry, the critic would not have minded ; but that pale sorrowful face—he could not escape from it. In vain he tried *not* to see it; there was all the magnetism of a portrait watching you from the wall ; and his nerves failed him completely. There he stood, spellbound, with a seared look, as if through that wistful gaze the eyes of an injured wife and children looked down reproachfully into his soul. He opened his mouth, but he could not speak ; the words bubbled up to his lips, and then bubbled back again ; a rush of water seemed to inundate his ears ; and he felt, as he afterwards expressed it, as if his mind were drowning. It was impossible to go on.

The curtain was dropped, and when it rose once more the 'useful man' was reading the part.

The piece dragged its slow length wearily along till the detective Gimblet appeared.

O, he was a triumph of unconscious fun !

He was unusually tall, with a broad laughing face ; he wore a pair of short white trousers, a body coat, an old-fashioned stock and a frilled shirt, which, together with a blood-red wig and blood-red whiskers to match, caused him to look anything but like a representative from Scotland-yard on secret service.

When he appeared he gave you the idea of having drifted on from the wings mechanically. He bowed to the company, and grinned; then he bowed to the audience, and laughed and slapped his thigh, and laughed harder than ever, as though the whole thing were the most enjoyable joke. Here was a new phase of stage-fright ! He never attempted to speak ; but the more his companions glared. the more he laughed ; and by this time he had the whole audience with him. Some one took him by the coat-sleeve, walked him to the back of the stage, and sat him on a chair. It was no use, nothing could stop the laughter ; and to complete the *fiasco,* he drew from his pocket a pair of handcuffs, and, amidst one of the greatest roars I ever heard in a theatre, he insisted upon taking the hero of the piece, John Mildmay, into custody !

Those critics have never tried to don the sock and buskin since, for that night they retired to rest sadder and wiser men.

AMARANTH'S MYSTERY.

By ANNABEL GRAY,

AUTHOR OF 'MARGARET DUNBAR,' 'WAIT AND WIN,' ETC.

CHAPTER XI.

A CHILDREN'S PARTY.

AMARANTH did her utmost to forget this interview with Captain Clarence Kinnaird; she went out more than ever, rode and wrote equally hard, following that rapid current of change of scene and thought which will alone promote forgetfulness. She had no wish to fall in love with any one, above all a fickle swain, and avoided chance meetings. Amaranth had a distinct horror of anything dishonourable or mean; her affection for and gratitude to Dr. Kinnaird made her turn from the man who had destroyed his life, with that shivering aversion the very force of which has a sinister meaning.

To be sacrificed on any shrine, and this one above all others, seemed more than half absurd; but the very contrast of the Captain's pleasure-loving existence, compared with his brother's severe asceticism, imperceptibly made her linger on his memory with indeed the best intentions of consigning it to oblivion.

In losing her gift, might not the power of that old prophecy have also ceased? Why should she, of all people, be doomed to be the victim of an unrequited love? Amaranth's natural thoughtfulness, her capacity for grasping subjects requiring high intelligence and reflection, pleased Clarence Kinnaird without his scarcely knowing why. If he inspired Amaranth with un-

reasonable alarm and fear, he experienced electric convictions that she was altogether delightful; he liked women who could take things to heart, and felt 'cut to pieces' at trifles.

Hardness and incapacity for pity were excellent safeguards in steering clear of mistaken impulses; but Clarence had resolved to marry, to leave heartless riot alone—one may have too many surfeits of honey—and see whether the magic of the word 'Home,' and all its sweet simplicity, was not a better substitute for hotels and fashionable apartments. He sought in a wife's character the very opposite qualities he cherished in a mistress. What is fairly creditable at twenty is utterly discreditable at forty; and bearing in mind the excellent maxim, 'It is never too late to mend,' the brilliant cavalry officer saw the error of his ways, and concentrated all his energies in the pursuit of Amaranth. Try as we may, it is impossible to eradicate warmth of character where it once exists. People never really change; those who are idle, cold, and indifferent in youth will only be considerably more somnolent, lazy, and callous in age. The sins of really good-hearted people are very different from the sins of really bad-hearted ones, even if the effect in some instances be much the same. And with all his faults, Captain Kinnaird had some fine qualities. If he followed his inclinations, he did his best to make amends for

F

evil done : he never sneered, his generosity was limitless, and his care for others (whom he believed cared for him) was equally inexhaustible.   He wanted to be loved by a pure-minded virtuous woman whom he could respect, not a nonentity without two ideas in her head ; nor a mere animal (although he was fond of saying, *en parenthèse,* the nicest women were always the stupidest) ; and there was something attractive to him in remembering *Vanda* had run 290 nights at the Crescent, and that Amaranth's genius and versatility were above the common.   Why did she appear so startled—almost shocked —at her introduction to him ? he wondered.   Well, he should decidedly cultivate her, call at the Sylvesters', and get introductions to the various parties of the season where she was likely to be present. He was glad to have done with Nancy, for the husband's sake : he was going to reform and marry Amaranth, if she would have him.

For this soft-voiced Amaranth, with her black hair and pale face, her dazzling talents, calm purposes, and harmonious *tout ensemble,* charmed Clarence Kinnaird in a totally different way from the ordinary fashion he was moved by women.   This confessedly 'much-loved' individual, either from necessity or the nature of things, had become a sort of emotional epicure, which was singular, considering his profession.   From the very first he had seen through Mrs. Gilbert's manœuvres, which perhaps proved she was somewhat of a bungler.   But Nancy's solid beauty seemed to quench his own *surcroît* of imagination, in the same way that Amaranth's increased it ; in fact Clarence was falling into melancholy mysticism when he thought of Amaranth, and Nancy's common sense balanced his reason.   So for a time he flirted with both girls, because

he could not practise self-denial in gratifying any fancy, and the entrancement he experienced from the fascinations of the one—if somewhat blasted in its effects by the cool worldliness of the other— was very agreeable, and Clarence sedulously cultivated the 'agreeables' of life, after the fashion of the 'much loved.'   To awaken new hopes and aspirations in the mind of Amaranth, while appealing to Nancy's materialism, was decidedly exciting.   Nancy's pouts and sulkiness had charms too : while it was impossible not to be fascinated by Amaranth's fervour, Nancy piqued him by her coldness and disdain.   After some well-meaning efforts, he resolved to resign Mrs. Gilbert and marry Miss Markham.   So he went to work with practised skill, inwardly certain Amaranth would be throwing herself away in marrying him, but equally positive he looked upon her as a divinity, and that his affection would last for ever.   Every time he met the girl he was more than ever impressed by the influence she had exercised over him during their first interview, since evidenced in his indifference to Mrs. Gilbert and other pretty women of his acquaintance.   Who can describe the beautiful Nancy's gusts of rage and fury when the truth was slowly revealed ?   For women, without the slightest capacity for real love, are generally the most jealous and infuriated at a silent defeat of this kind ; and the Captain, who perfectly understood the relative advantages and disadvantages of Amaranth's timidity and Nancy's hauteur, amused himself by exercising power over both, by appealing to the imagination of the one and the self-interest of the other.   We frequently find men loth to lose the soothing flattery of feminine sympathy, even when it is of a very meretricious nature ;

and so, while not dashing all Mrs. Gilbert's hopes to the ground at one fell swoop, he devoted himself more than ever to Amaranth, looking admirably 'killing' as Nancy beseeched him to pity the drudgery of her profession and domestic lot, while all the time he was longing to listen to Amaranth's exquisite word-painting and polished elegance of style.

It was fully understood in the Sylvester family that Captain Kinnaird had intentions regarding their young guest, and fully expected after every visit he meant to propose, or else why haunt the back drawing-room and library late in the afternoon? Ladies with six marriageable daughters are essentially practical; they have no objection to feed slightly famished young men twice or even thrice a week, provided they have expectations and are making up to one of the girls.

But there was no mistaking the Captain's present intentions as far as Amaranth was concerned; to her he talked, and talked well, and, without being necessarily brilliant, a man of the world, of varied experience and ripened intelligence, can be very amusing. Amaranth felt she also was falling in love with her eyes open, and that this systematic attention and insidious homage were leading her captive; for he knew how to follow up every sign of surrender on her part, and his attacks moved the subtlest instincts of her mind, like a masterly hand sweeping the chords of a fine and complicated instrument. However, this state of affairs could not go on for ever, and to-night, being the glorious 'Twelfth-night,' a children's party had been hastily arranged at the Sylvesters'; and amongst the elders the noble Captain (self-invited with his most fascinating smiles) was expected to appear about eight o'clock in the evening.

There is something remarkably jolly in a children's party. Jealousy is generally banished from the elders' minds, and thorough *bonhomie* and kindness reign supreme. For if children on these occasions are not particularly lovable, being too excited to care for anybody but themselves, they are charmingly natural, and make pretty little pictures in their white frocks and coloured sashes, their silk stockings and long *crêpé* hair. The Captain vowed he adored children's parties; they reminded him of his youth, his infant Samuel days, &c. No one, perhaps, believed him, but it sounded very nice and unaffected; and as he patted the little girls on their shoulders, tied their sashes, admired their shoes, and danced till he was purple, performing frog-like evolutions and playing dance-music to rival Dan Godfrey's band, everybody said he was a very charming fellow indeed.

Who could believe those naughty tales rife about him, or that he had 'pinked' an adversary in Belgium, while the actress, who evoked her husband's jealousy, was dancing in green tights on stilts at the Mabille?

Amaranth confessed he had never seemed so captivating in her eyes as when carefully and conscientiously feeding a certain 'Tommy' at the sideboard (a pugnacious youth, who had knocked 'Harry,' metaphorically, into a cocked hat). The children clambered on his shoulders, and pulled his ears and close-cropped hair, till one comrade, hankering after some champagne at the sideboard, muttered, 'By Jove, Clarey, you look a regular family man!'

Of course he contrived during the evening to look 'unutterables' at Amaranth. She wore a gray-coloured silk to-night, trimmed with crimson velvet, and a ruffle of tulle at her throat (he once confessed he preferred silk to muslin), and played with the children as amiably, if not quite so energetically, as the Captain; and every now and then she caught him watching her in between the games and dances abstractedly, while he flourished a piece of mistletoe under the hall-lamp, and felt a boy again.

The innocent simplicity of the affair pleased our Captain. The ringing laughter of happy children; the stately respectability of the various matrons in moire antiques dotted about the room like autumnal dahlias; the well-trained servants; the warmth of the large crackling blazing fires; the merry girls all enjoying the romp; and, lastly, Amaranth, his future wife he hoped,—made up an enchanting scene, devoid of coarse laughter, cynical criticism, or stifling alcoholic fumes. What more winning than the buoyant spirits and pretty saucy pertness of innocence and youth?

After supper he meant to take Amaranth aside, beseech her to listen to him, and end his perplexities and torments once and for ever. He knew he had changed— that a bright home and a beloved young wife promised more enduring happiness and heartfelt peace than all the turmoil of a hollow and reckless career. His natural warmth of nature expanded at the thought of 'our home,' 'our life.' How sweet those words would sound coming from her lips in her sincere tones! 'We'—no word dearer or sadder to lose than that little monosyllable when eye and voice have once responded to the same magic unity.

He was a man who, once resolving on the attainment of any particular scheme or object, allows nothing to impede his course. And what difficulties could possibly now intervene?

He was sure Amaranth was **not** indifferent to him; he had a **fine** income to offer, and the **truest** attachment; and yet, was it **the** remembrance of the past **that** threatened his ease of **mind?** Clarence was decidedly anxious **to** hear Amaranth's answer to-**night;** conjectures were all very well, **but** slightly unsatisfactory.

So in this lover's mood of **hope** and fear he offered her his arm **for** the quadrille merrily planned **after** supper for the amusement of **the** elders; Mrs. Sylvester and **her** daughter playing a brilliant **duet,** and making as much noise on **the** grand piano as their muscles **would** permit.

Traces of Christmas decorations still lingered on the walls, **holly** embraced the heavy glass chandeliers, and Amaranth's little **wreath** of red berries, which she **wore** entwined amid her raven black locks, looked remarkably girlish and coquettish.

'I expect those poor young kids are awfully tired,' said Clarence, trifling with her fan, as he led her down the room, and slightly pressing her finger-tips; 'they've all gone home laden with little presents, from sugar-plums to wax dolls.'

'I'm sure you've exerted yourself immensely to please them,' Amaranth answered, blushing and thinking she will never forget this enchanting Twelfth-night, and that the Christmas season has peculiar attractions, which midsummer, with all its soft moons and twilight harmonies, can never possess.

'I've been waiting all the evening for the happiness of a quiet five minutes by your side,' he said, with gentle meaning, 'and the children have hitherto kept you fully occupied; but now you can give *me* the smiles I've so envied *them*. Perhaps they'll let us have a waltz by and by, before ending the most delightful evening I ever spent; for if I could not talk to you I have watched your every glance and gesture,' ended Clarence, who, though somewhat devoid of poetry, looked as enraptured as any noble specimen of our British poets, and was at last beginning to take an exaggerated view of everything.

After a glorious waltz, played by a young unknown professional, who gave his services for a supper, Clarence and Amaranth sauntered into the conservatory, which, being warmed by flues, produced no chilling effect. And Amaranth, picking an azalea to pieces, listened to the pleading of this man who had been prophesied to bring her anguish and death—listened and resolved, as many other daughters of Eve have done before her, to run the risk as she accepted him.

Long ago she had told him of her strange trance—the revelation of the dark forest, and its sinister effect. But superstition, animal magnetism, and invisible influences had ever been laughed down by the acute man of the world as stories to frighten old women and children, or merely used as pretexts to extort money from the thoughtless and the credulous.

'At any rate you exercised marvellous magnetic influence over me the very first time we met,' said Clarence delightedly, not forgetting the embraces accompanying scenes of this kind. 'I felt thoroughly electrified, by Jove! and never more hipped and wretched in all my life than when driving home from Fulham, after seeing you off, my little muse. All inspiration and kindness, are you not, dearest? and soon to be my darling wife.'

He bent his handsome head, and pressed his lips to hers in a long and passionate caress.

So now the Sylvesters were satisfied. Amaranth was engaged; and Mr. Sylvester brewed some capital punch, of which they all partook in honour of the occasion; while the Captain, smoking hard in the library after the ladies had retired, found himself after a time slightly overpowered with fatigue and emotion; for, after many noble efforts to sit upright, to the astonishment of his host and all beholders, he fell asleep on the green-leather couch, and had to be violently shaken several times, and severely appealed to, ere fully aroused.

On his return home a letter awaited him on the mantelpiece, informing him of the sudden decease of his brother, Dr. Kinnaird. Surely the grave is a great reconciler! and the eloquence of death has a tenderness that knits hearts together with truer affection, even if one must be cold and motionless; and then memory, the fond elegiac, shoots out its roots underground like the grass that grows and weeps o'er desolation.

CHAPTER XII.

THE LIVING TRIUMPHS.

AMARANTH was a good deal startled and grieved on hearing of the sudden death of Dr. Kinnaird. Of late he had seldom answered her letters, and, while never complaining of his state of health, had gradually sunk into the arms of death.

'This is the last time we shall meet; so farewell for ever on earth,' he had said, as he wrung Amaranth's hand ere they parted.

People who isolate themselves from their fellows sooner or later generally fall a prey to disease, either of mind or body; and we ought to endeavour to fight against the approach of that melancholy which often attends painful shocks and disappointments, and which a little less weakness and sensibility and more common sense would effectually disperse. Philosophy is not needed when all runs smoothly and to 'even song;' it is for those dark hours when the human barque is threatened with wreck and ruin mid frowning seas, when the hand we have weakly clung to is withdrawn, and we are left alone, isolated and trembling, to meet our destiny as best we may. Then is moral strength tested; and the man or woman rises to something grander from amid the blackened ruins, or sinks, with inert cowardice and sloth, into a being worldlings laugh at, and only the wise and thoughtful pity and understand.

Dr. Kinnaird died as thousands have done, and ever will, from cherishing disease—not casting it off. How many throw away their lives for an idea! And he died alone, uncared for, and untended, bequeathing his worldly goods to Amaranth.

When Amaranth returned to Selwood, she and Clarence investigated the dead man's papers; and the latter found a letter addressed to himself, in which the writer offered full forgiveness of the past, and even expressed a wish to see his brother once more. So he had died at peace with all his little world.

Amaranth passed several weeks with her uncle and aunt at Selwood, and Clarence returned to town alone. The worthy Mrs. Stapleton was a good deal impressed with the Captain's graceful manner and indifference to halfpence.

The Captain enjoyed his visit; for was it not delightful to contrast Amaranth with the prosy set he met at the Stapletons'? There is, after all, something soothing in sleek, well-fed, middle-class re-spectability, although the hours are early. He felt extremely good, healthy, and pious after the two Sunday services, and considered that falling in love with a charming girl, and with holy matrimony before them both, had dispersed his former impatience with life's unsatisfactoriness; for all his restlessness and cynicism had given place to that softness and repose peculiar to early youth and large faith in womankind.

If Mrs. Stapleton's devotion expressed itself in constantly brushing his hat the wrong way, or mending his coat-lining so that he could not well get his arm through the sleeve, he conscientiously reflected she meant well; and to people who mean well, like those who love well, much, we know, must be forgiven. The Captain believed these new acquaintances were impressed with his good-natured condescension; and so they may have been, for Mr. Stapleton found his political notions singularly lucid and unclouded. He listened to accounts of strategy, forts, and cannon, till he almost fancied he smelt powder, and longed to be one of the foremost in repelling a Russian invasion. He also professed himself an enlightened Whig; while Mrs. Stapleton was sure Clarence appreciated her house-proud tendencies. But, after a fortnight's self-sacrifice, he found he had had enough of it. He loved Amaranth more than ever; but he wanted to return to London. Paradise was all very well; but the ambitions and struggles of the Selwoodians wearied him ever so little. Routine began to bore him; and the suspicion of a 'hash' on the following Saturday sent him at once to his A B C Guide for relief. He talked sentiment by the yard first, and he really meant what he uttered; spoke of the 15th of May with that eccentric admiration for the future we always note in any sincere admirer who has no intention of running the gauntlet of a breach of promise in the interval.

'Do you really care for me as much as you say?' asked Amaranth, on the morning of his departure. 'Remember, you must write to me *incessantly*, and tell me any nonsense you like.'

'No man in love ever wrote sense,' cried the Captain; 'if he did, he never loved. The brain, not the heart, dictated *his* effusions.'

He drew Amaranth's dark head on his breast, and kissed the lips that quivered under his caress.

'My little girl will not forget me, I know,' he continued, looking fondly into her eyes. 'Remember, I am jealous, even of the sun that shines on your beauty, and of the waves you will watch when I am gone. But I think of the happy hours we shall pass together in a few months; the home I shall prepare for you, with every luxury and comfort—our home! Yes! Amaranth, I had to learn from you the true meaning of heartfelt joys— the consolation imparted by a deep and fervent love!'

They were almost his last words; and Amaranth, on hearing them, stared mutely at the fire in her old sad way, as if to forget the doubt this parting created, and the words that never ceased to haunt her— 'To me, death; to you, despair.'

'I will believe him,' she cried, while the tears fell on her hands. 'There was truth in his accents.'

But the silence seemed very terrible after he had departed; and the bland smiling faces surrounding her imparted a sense of loneliness. Was it the beginning of darkness? For the heart has instincts and vibrations none can fathom, and that will be aroused and shaken by a tone or dead leaf

or perfume. Amaranth carried away out of the hall a little piece of scented geranium-leaf that had fallen from the button-hole of his greatcoat, and placed it next her heart, as though to remind her she was not forgotten. But Amaranth must have an unreasonable dread, for what was there at present to disturb her perfect belief and security? Had he not said, 'I am jealous of the sun that shines on your beauty, and the waves you will watch when I am gone'?

CHAPTER XIII.

PARTED.

'True love in this differs from gold and clay,
That to divide is not to take away.'

THE next month was February; and, after November, we must consider February the least agreeable of the twelve variable sisters that visit us from birth to burial.

There were heavy falls of snow, lasting twenty-four hours; nipping east winds, that spread toothache and neuralgia far and wide; mud and slush in the roads, pathways, and pavements; and lastly, the weather began to freeze hard, and plenty of people bruised themselves and twisted their ankles in falling unexpectedly prone on the hard breast of mother earth.

Every one admits the weather has a great effect on people's spirits and temper, and, shut up for a week in a dull house, we set our wits to work to manufacture miseries for ourselves, suspecting our best friends of nefarious designs, and our most relentless enemies of covert benevolence.

Selwood was not agreeable in February. What seaside place ever is? Amaranth read and wrote herself very nearly into a fever in her desire to astonish Clarence with the amount of work she had executed in his absence, and, as a matter of course, imagined his letters were shorter, colder, and less sympathetic than they ought to have been, and wrote him rather a furious reply to one of his mildest and least sentimental effusions.

But Nancy's evil influence had been again 'at work; for she also wrote to Amaranth, and very skilfully made the most of the Captain's visits, even enclosing a little note the misguided officer had written months ago, wherein he likened her (in very bad grammar) to Diana, and himself to Endymion.

Amaranth cried and raved over this production, dashing it into the fire, and then regretting she had not enclosed it, with her kind compliments, to the Captain, &c., as a pleasant greeting for him the following morning. Amaranth's jealousy was very different from Nancy's—as a volcano differs from a torpedo—and, brooding over her disillusion, she lost her health, her enthusiasm, and her happiness. Her mind may have become somewhat warped in the conflict; for, on one particularly dreary morning towards the end of this unpleasant February, Amaranth wrote the Captain an extremely curt note, full of verbs, principally in the subjunctive mood, and broke off her engagement once and for ever.

Clarence was at breakfast when this interesting missive was brought to him, and, after swearing audibly over the hard-boiled eggs and thick toast, he tore up Amaranth's note in vicious little pieces, which he deposited in hot water in the slop-basin. His first impulse was to go down post-haste, chariot and pair —express train—anything—to Selwood; his second, to have a row with Nancy, whom he suspected of mischief-making; and the third, to make the best of the unexpected blow. True, they had quarrelled

somewhat of late in their correspondence, but he never imagined it would come to this. Are not lovers' quarrels caused by absence?

By Jove! he was awfully cut up; as any man must naturally be who, after finding an ideal of beauty and grace, and furnishing a house too in the best style for her, receives his *congé*, and a covert sneer into the bargain on mythology. The Captain forgot all about that foolish little note to Mrs. Gilbert, as he reflected Amaranth must be more than half insane to carry matters to this pass. So much for a beauty and a genius! Must he, after all, console himself with the society of the handsome Mrs. Gilbert, who loved him for herself, and presented, when he last saw her, an exhilarating picture of healthfulness and animation, in a costume of George II.'s reign?

'She'd certainly ruin me in five years,'—was Clarence's inward rumination—'but I'm so nearly tired of her class I'd give her five years, and the endless worries and vexations they involve. I thought to have found my ideal of womanly perfection in Amaranth. And there's the house taken at Kensington! carpets and curtains ordered, to say nothing of the water-colour drawings.'

Still, much as he should grieve over her loss, he knew she was not the girl to respect a man who acted any abject slavish part. He also considered himself ill-used: her letters had wounded him a good deal more than he cared to admit at the time. And so the Captain resolved to stand on his dignity, trusting chance would again throw her in his way, and that she might then relent, and both of them be happy again.

For the present he should abide by her decision, write her a manly note, slightly tinged with melan-

choly, but decidedly avoid all poet-
ising and regret.

After Amaranth had posted her
letter she inanely trusted some unaccountable error in postal delivery
might prevent its reaching him;
or if, as was only too probable, he
received it, he might come down
to Selwood by an early train, and
listen to her penitent avowals of
jealousy, ill-temper, &c. She knew
all the world must be henceforth
empty to her, a shroud of dead
hopes and designs, ' her best gone
to worst,' if Clarence accepted his
release, and took her foolish feverish words for more than they were
worth. And as, mute and tearless,
she flung herself down on her little
couch, and writhed at the conviction of her misery, she had the
additional satisfaction of thinking
she herself was alone to blame.
Why have heeded Nancy's malicious innuendoes? What is love
worth without faith?

Mrs. Stapleton grew quite anxious as she watched Amaranth's
increasing pallor; and one day,
when her niece came up to her in
the old appealing way, the good
woman drew her to her side, and
said,

'There's something worrying and
fretting your life out, child. You
don't deceive me. You've given
up eating puddings and potatoes,
and take no breakfast; bad signs
in a young creature.'

'I've quarrelled with Clarence,
auntie, and broken off the engagement. I—I thought he preferred
Nancy.'

'Nancy! our Nancy! a married
woman, brought up to say her col-
lects and catechism every Sunday,
and with no wicked modern notions in her head!' Mrs. Stapleton
paused for want of breath, and
then continued severely, ' I'm
quite surprised at you! If that's
all the good your London acquaintances and London experiences

have done you, you had better
have remained at home with us
simple folk. Nancy, indeed !'

'Auntie, don't be angry; you
don't understand—'

'No, I should hope not.'

'Nancy found William's income
had to be reduced, and so she acts
on the stage.'

'Heavens! what next, I wonder? And does this villain—this
Captain — want to entice her
away?'

'No, no, auntie, I think not;
but I'm half crazy with one thing
and another. I believe he really
loves me; and yet—'

Here Amaranth broke down altogether. Mrs. Stapleton sent out
for a copy of the *Era*, to seek for
her daughter's name as an actress.

'Nancy wishes her profession
kept a secret from her friends; and
so for the present you had better
not take any notice of it,' said
Amaranth quietly; ' when she has
obtained some triumphs, it will be
time enough to talk about them.'

'If you imagine *my* girl capable
of deceit and treachery, you may be
also under a very wrong impression
regarding *your* Captain Kinnaird,
and judge them both wrong.'

'Perhaps so. Anyway it's all
over now. He' (laughing bitterly)
' doesn't offer any opposition to my
views, but seems rather glad he is
released.'

'It's very strange how young
people sometimes seem bent on
destroying their own happiness;
and it's because they've no trust in
each other. Well, well, you're old
enough to know your own minds;
and Nancy's sensible enough to
keep out of trouble if she does go
on the stage for an honest livelihood. Dear, to think of it ! I call
it noble of her to try and keep her
husband afloat—always a poor soft
sort of fellow, *I* thought.'

'Yes; Nancy will take care of
herself; no fear of that,' said Ama-

ranth, conscious of the futility of making Mrs. Stapleton take a definite view of any situation.

She was also conscious, which perhaps imparted keener pain than anything, that her creative faculty was expiring, like the flicker of a dying flame, and that her mind was a dull mass in which no novel thoughts or lofty inspiration could find place. Yes, this was the anguish foretold, and death in its train; for she had invested her new happiness with that visionary passion which distinguishes poets; that romantic charm which survives age, and lights up the dreariest pathway with recollections that are almost living realities.

So the skein was all torn and ravelled, and the finely-spun silk in danger of destruction. Week after week passed, and Amaranth's health completely broke down. How often do we find two people warmly attached to each other drifting away in different currents, longing for reconciliation, and yet neither with the moral courage to attack the sails of some tiresome windmill of foolish misunderstandings, whirling them far apart for ever! The Captain trusted to chance, and assumed an injured air. Amaranth, whose organ of hope was small, and faith still less, sank into a state of dejection and apathy, which was decidedly foolish, considering that the man she loved, if fascinating, was somewhat commonplace. She had trusted he would come to her, and demand an explanation; but he felt she deserved punishment, and trusted her caprices had brought her suffering, but he never for one moment thought she had vanished for ever out of his life. No, they would meet again, and, after delicious reproaches, confess all was unchanged.

So he waited patiently enough, for a man whose knowledge of the meaning of love had been hitherto somewhat hazy and obscure, consoling himself with a sort of mute chivalrous belief in fortune turning, and taking in the mean time small doses of chloral—much against every one's advice—for insomnia. It was impossible, of course, for a man of the Captain's antecedents, and his peculiar training in pleasure's paths, to be hopelessly grief-worn; but he felt as much cut up as Nature would permit; found less delight in new hats and collars, and experienced a certain uncomfortable pang whenever meeting any interesting young person with raven-black hair and eager submissive eyes. How often he longed to take the train to Selwood, and hang about the beach in the hope of meeting Amaranth! It was really terrible to saunter into the house at Kensington, and look at the blue china, the water-colour drawings, and *bric-à-brac*, shaken with a doubt, that daily grew to be a certainty, that they must soon be sold off, and no young hands arrange them deftly on the various buhl cabinets and *marqueterie* tables in the drawing-rooms. He also sedulously avoided Mrs. Gilbert, to whom, by the way, he gave some advice that sank deep into Nancy's mind, and made her prize her husband more than ever. So Nancy remained a guardian spirit of the hearth, as well as a fairly successful actress, prudent enough to appreciate at his true worth that *rara avis* of all times, an excellent husband, patient and loving in sickness and in health. For if he admired her beauty when coronets or wreaths encircled her fair head, he was equally gentle and fond when that head ached, and applied eau-de-cologne to her temples till his arms were wearied. The lover, on these occasions, is apt to glide smilingly away.

CHAPTER XIV.

A MODERN GOSTANZA.

'O, my life I did not spare
To possess thy heart to-day.'

'WHAT do you say to our accepting Nancy's invitation to Fulham?' Mr. Stapleton remarked one morning towards the end of March, as they lingered over a late breakfast.

'I should like it above all things,' his wife answered, turning over the leaves of the baker's book, 'and a change will do us both good. Fortunately, Amaranth can take care of the house.'

'Rather mopish, isn't she, just now?'

'O, these young creatures take their love-affairs to heart so, and cry their eyes out when they're alone. Pity she hadn't picked up a homely man with no new-fangled notions.'

'So Captain's offended Amaranth, has he? Perhaps I'll run my eye over him in London, and take my gentleman to task! But she declares it's all her own fault. Still, I can't help thinking a jilted girl resembles damaged goods; but of course *I'm* a plain-spoken man.'

'She'd sooner have her tongue cut off than speak against any one she cares for, however bad he may have treated her; and Mary's dull enough; but they seem happy together. I shall leave home quite satisfied they will take care to lock the house up safely.'

'How long do you mean to stay in London, auntie?' Amaranth asked, on entering the room. 'I hope you'll enjoy yourself, and Nancy will take you everywhere, and show you all that's worth seeing.'

'Maybe a month, child, if your uncle likes the change. He's fond of prowling about St. Paul's, Westminster Abbey, and the Tower of London,' said Mrs. Stapleton, coyly folding the strings of a new pink bonnet that had just arrived, while Amaranth, with all the world before her, half-sickened at the sight of her aunt's content.

If all the bonnets, dresses, and jewelry of London were placed by her side, could she take pleasure in wearing them now? While this elderly matron, all wrinkles and frivolity, would peep into shop-windows in the metropolis, and try and see the effect of her mantle and back hair with the curiosity of some young bride.

'How you sigh, child!' cried Mrs. Stapleton, fully satisfied with her last inspection. 'It's really wonderful how pale pink suits me even now.'

'Yes, even now,' repeated Amaranth mechanically; 'and so it will years hence, too, no doubt, when you're getting into your dotage.'

'Ah, that's fine! Well, you'll take care of the house and the back door, as I said before; and don't let Susan's young man—*he's* the baker, of course—come and sit too late in the kitchen on Sunday nights—that we always objected to; it's a bad example to Jane, who's quite lively enough.'

'So you leave to-morrow night, auntie?'

'Yes, my dear; and I'll write as soon as we arrive, or else pop a directed envelope into some pillar-post near the railway to ease your mind. And now help me with the packing, and be sure and remember to order half a pound of cut tongue for sandwiches.'

After the worthy couple had departed the following evening in a hired fly, Amaranth felt so languid and depressed she put on her hat and ran down to the beach. Here, after all, was her one great solace—the sea. Its unchained freedom, its majestic strength, were a relief to her tired brain.

Perhaps she stayed rather too long by the waves on this evening, for dangerous fancies began to take root in her distorted mind.

Was this hankering after the sea gaining fatal ascendency over her reason, or was the *unseen influence* still at work, leading her on to extremes and defiance? There was unnatural fire in her eyes to-night, as she threw little pebbles, one by one, into the foaming water; and when an encroaching wave wetted her boots and almost swept her off her feet, she laughed a little —a wayward fitful laugh, such as may be heard sometimes on Suicide's Bridge in November, near what some of the newspapers call 'Agony Hole.' But she turned away and went straight home. Thousands of young women had gone through this sort of thing; and here was she, never resting day or night, eating little, and throwing away health and peace— all for what? Surely she despised this indifferent Clarence, who flirted with any one handy, and could never have really cared for her, or why not have refused to believe her written words, and come down to Selwood for an explanation? Was he worth all this grief? Certainly not—not the best or worst man that ever breathed was worth a woman's tears; only, alas, hero-worship is exacting, and, when not ludicrous, pathetic.

Was it not fanatical, wicked, absurd on her part to be so miserable over the inevitable? Perhaps, if Selwood were not so dull, she might have forgotten him ere this; but the thoughts accompanying brain-wearying monotony are ever persistent and fatal. Tears were worse than useless. Let her rally her courage, and endeavour to forget, perhaps hate, him, by putting him into a new play. Impossible. She was too sensitive, too delicate-minded to entertain the thought.

She had lost her power of writing. Ideas will not flow in failing health, and people who suffer have always the lurking principle of hidden disease within them, of either mind or body.

She did her best, however, to partake of some supper; but, unfortunately, we are not all like noble cattle, to be crammed at will. She drank some hot coffee, and this made her still more wakeful for a time; but it was pleasant to find the house quiet, to do as she liked, and be alone. If this were selfish, it annoyed no one else; and Amaranth, battling hard against weakness, and what some call maudlin sentimentality, sank at last into slumber by the fire.

When Amaranth woke it was dawn. She felt cold, and, placing some pieces of wood on the half-expiring fire, succeeded in keeping it alight; she threw a woollen shawl over her shoulders, and lighting her lamp endeavoured to read. No sense of hunger oppressed her, though for two days she had barely tasted food; but her thirst increased, and adding some water to the coffee in the little coffee-pot on the hob, boiled it up again and poured some into a cup. She felt as if all hope had left her, and that she was a meaningless shadow, with only the power of suffering left. Could she welcome this morn with smiles? Yes, if she had the courage to accomplish her end, and sail over the silver sea with Death at the helm!

She looked strangely wan and wasted; always pale, her complexion now assumed an unearthly grayness that only rendered the glow in her eyes more fitful and brilliant—a flame almost now exhausted and burning rapidly towards its close—the suppressed if fierce excitement of a mental tempest.

'To me, death; to you, despair;'

and later on, at least so I read destiny, 'To you, death; to me, revenge!'

Nothing but those words ringing in her ears night and day; cruel words that triumphed in their fatality, and had worked her ruin. Once or twice she rose and clasped her hands appealingly, as though entreating mercy of some one, or as if the dead mystic might even yet control her destiny. At eight o'clock she bathed her face, knotted up her hair, and ascending the stairs, entered her cousin's room. Mary stirred slightly from her sleep and held out her hand.

'Good-bye, Mary,' said Amaranth, bending over her and kissing her on the forehead. 'I am going out for a walk.'

'So early, dear?' said her cousin sleepily. 'Well, the sea air is always lovely at this hour; remember to dig for anemones for my new fern-case. Why, Amaranth, what's the matter?'

'Nothing; I'm only a little nervous, and want air,' said Amaranth, steadying herself, and fastening on her hat at the mirror. 'What a fright I look, to be sure, all gray and yellow! The morning light is certainly not flattering.'

Something in the cavernous tones of her voice startled Mary, for she said rapidly,

'It's a pity you didn't go to London with the old people, and stay with Nancy.'

'Nancy!' cried Amaranth, wheeling round. That name was the symbol of her ruin.

She hurried from the room, and, throwing a heavy cloak over her shoulders, unlocked the hall-door and went out. Mary, who was uneasy about the girl, had risen, dressed herself, and at nine o'clock was looking at the address on a letter which had just come directed to Amaranth. It was evidently from Clarence Kinnaird.

Mary, who dearly loved Amaranth, could hardly restrain her impulse to break the seal and see whether good news awaited her; but, expecting her cousin's return, she placed it on the mantelpiece and began preparing breakfast. Half-past nine, and no Amaranth. She had now been out an hour and a half, and Mary grew alarmed; she rang for the obliging Susan, and sent her in search of Amaranth, telling the servant to beg Miss Markham to return at once, and that a letter of great importance awaited her.

In the mean time, where was Amaranth? She had crept along the beach, about a mile from home, to a small cove or creek where some fishermen's little boats had been moored, and she threw herself down on the shingle, now and then touching these boats, as if at last making up her mind to some definite action. She had left no message or note behind for her lover to read after her death; she thought death a sufficiently eloquent exponent of her misery, which perhaps it was, and that he would understand. She had only brought out with her the little piece of faded geranium-leaf and his last letter, and for an hour she viewed these two reminders of her love, lifting them now and then to her lips, as she had lifted her mother's hand in her coffin the night before her burial. All the memories of early childhood, even the regrets she had felt on leaving her home for her aunt's roof, returned. Very beautiful was the ocean in this calm morning, when another victim was ready to fly to its embrace and find rest under its billows.

The very sound of these surging waters had a depth of meaning her sensitiveness too well appreciated. It seemed to embody all her scathing tears; her fine intellect and rare capacities for feeling vibrated even now at æsthetic associations of ideas; imagination here still struggled for mastery, in spite of sickness and weariness.

'Clarence, Clarence, must the prophecy be fulfilled?'

She uttered his name this time more softly; and what answered? Only the sobs of the sea, the wavelets along the beach, and the silence that echoed, 'Depart!'

Dearly had she loved the sea, and it had pleased her to think that the ripples of her strong hair resembled it. Even now she let her hands lie in the white lace-like foam. Would they soon be tangled with sea-weed, or perhaps crushed against some vessel or craft?

What a strange creature she had ever been!— caring so much for what was but an incident in most women's lives (for is not love to the greater portion of the commonplace a comedy or affair of barter?), and then letting regret, unkindness, disappointment, and that implied neglect of silence tyrannise over her till they brought dejection and then despair. But despair, like other passions, has its moments of intoxication; and this was one.

So thinking, Amaranth again read over the last letter she had received from Clarence. That beloved writing! She gazed at the words as though they were pictures—now lifeless and colourless, yet still impressed upon her brain. Yes; a hopeless case was hers indeed; and not one draught of forgetfulness had been granted her: only the sea would give her that by and by. Had she been perfected for this—only for this—when, deformed and neglected, she might have lived on to ripe old age? Old age! She smiled at the thought.

Death would not have seemed hard contemplated by such a mind as hers, had she not remembered the sweetness life must have held

with Clarence. He had compelled her to love him; every spell, every allurement, had he exerted to enslave her heart and brain. Why had he not practised his well-learnt tenets on some one else better versed in his arts, and let her escape?

And yet her own act and deed had in truth sundered them. Should she seek him again, and confess her folly? Pride forbade supplication. But the earth—its odours and richness, its sights and scenes, its beauties and joys, its men and women—maddened her. She had always held aloof from them, so to speak. So she went again to the sea for pity, as in the old dark days, when human beings moved her irony and contempt, and listened to the songs of the dear waves she had so loved in her early youth. Amaranth thought of that evening-party at the Sylvesters': the memorable Twelfth-night; that first dance with Clarence; the Christmas festivities; the shrill voices of the happy children. Even the Christmas bells, sombre and mournful in their farewell to the dying year, seemed to ring in her ears again. What joy they had ushered in with them, and with what different eyes had she drawn aside the curtains on that Christmas morning, and looked at the snow-clad landscape, pure as her love and as calm!

But was this, what some people might call aberration of mind, her own fault? If her miserable weakness and its attendant depression were not to be silenced by orthodox rules—by the efficacy of time, common sense, faith, or patience—was she solely to blame? or might she not even yet be the victim of that invisible influence to which she had succumbed in the past— claimed by the *dead* instead of the *living?* She saw the sad eyes of the mystic uplifted to hers as on the last day they parted; they seemed to be beckoning her on.

'I shall obey the prophecy,' she cried, rising quickly, and stretching out her arms for one moment to the land.

What could save her at this eleventh hour? And yet she fancied she heard the tones of a human voice, borne by the breeze over the cliffs, calling, 'Amaranth! Amaranth!' But this surely was delusive fancy: the die was already cast.

So musing, she took a boat and drifted out to sea.

CHAPTER XV.

STRONG LANGUAGE.

'Have you not found the least trace of her? Do you think she has gone to London?' cried Mary, on the return of the housemaid, who merely shook her head and looked frightened. 'You must go again in search of my cousin. I cannot rest till she is found. She spoke so oddly, and her manner seemed unnatural as she bade me good-bye. Wait; I will open this letter. She has told me everything, and surely will not mind my reading it, when she hears how alarmed I have felt at her absence.'

Mary broke the seal as the girl disappeared below, and uttered a cry of surprise at reading the following lines:

'St. James's-street, Pall Mall,
'March 187—.

'Dearest Amaranth,—I cannot rest without writing to you. Something tells me you are ill; and I must see you once more, even at the risk of your displeasure. What is the reason you have doubted and despised me? I must hear from your own dear lips the real cause of my dismissal. I have waited, in the hope Fate might throw us once more together; but hang Fate; nothing of the kind has happened. I feel I love you more madly than ever. All my future rests on the certainty of our reunion; so I shall be at Selwood at half-past ten to-morrow morning, and you can only order your servant to shut the door in my face if I'm not to be admitted. But let me plead to be forgiven— faith in your constancy still fans the flame of hope.'

'Half-past ten!' cried Mary, dropping the letter, 'and the quarter has just struck; in another fifteen minutes he will be here, and no Amaranth to meet him. What shall I do?'

And even as Miss Stapleton spoke a cab dashed up to the villa, and the Captain alighted, looking every inch a thoroughbred gentleman, with the reverse of a tragical air; for he smiled a little towards the large bow-window, as if he hoped to catch a glimpse of a form waiting for him, a face never absent from his thoughts. Certainly he appeared in the best of health and spirits, a fact which struck a colder chill than ever into Mary's heart as she ran to let him in at the hall-door, followed by Susan, who, remembering his munificent gift of half a sovereign, curtsied mournfully and looked somewhat aghast.

'I'm very sorry to alarm you, Captain Kinnaird,' said Mary hurriedly, 'but we cannot find Amaranth. She left the house two hours ago; and, as she is fond of wandering about at all hours by herself on the beach, I was not surprised at her going out so early alone. I thought she might find me some anemones; but she ought to have returned long since.'

'Ah, gone out, has she? Fishing, perhaps? Well, I've no doubt she'll soon be back. Perhaps she went to meet me at the station, and we've missed each other. People always do miss each other when they don't want to. I wrote to her, don't you know, and told her I was coming.'

'But the letter came after she had left, Captain Kinnaird. Here it is. No one has seen it but I,' said Mary restlessly, and going to the window; 'and I'm really frightened about my cousin's absence. You know she's so different from others.'

'Ah, yes; lots of imagination and that sort of thing,' said Clarence, laughing. 'Great mistake, I always think; and of course bored to death at Selwood, as who wouldn't be? That's what you mean. I haven't the least fear but what she will return very shortly. I never think of accidents and probabilities, Miss Stapleton; nothing like calmness and *laissez-aller* in this world. Your cousin has no doubt gone out in a bad temper, and found the morning air more agreeable than she expected. Why, what on earth are you going to do?'

'I am not very strong,' said Mary quietly, 'but I mean to go down to the beach, and you must help me. Believe me, I know Amaranth's nature thoroughly; she's been unhappy lately—eaten next to nothing, and so—'

Captain Kinnaird's face darkened. What could this girl hint at? Suicide? It seemed rather like it; and he felt incensed at what he thought a mixture of nervousness and stupidity.

He watched her fetch Mr. Stapleton's large sea-glass, and wondered still more.

'It may be useful,' she explained, handing it to him to carry; and there was that in her manner which conveyed a certain dread with it. But his strong organisation and naturally sanguine temperament soon reasserted themselves.

Of course they would discover Amaranth by and by on the beach, looking particularly interesting, fishing, or crab-hunting, or sketching, with her back hair down, and awfully hungry for breakfast.

They were both silent till, after wandering along the beach, they neared the little creek from which Amaranth had sailed.

'She has evidently been here,' cried Mary, picking up something on the shingle. 'See! this is the little lilac bow she wore at her neck. Give me the glass, Captain Kinnaird. What is that speck yonder in the distance—the little boat?' She grasped his arm as she pointed over the sea. 'Amaranth is in that boat,' she cried, making frantic and useless efforts for the girl to see them. 'She's now about half a mile from land. You must save her—and you can. You see I was right, after all. She hadn't the courage to take her own life; but she's there, drifting away to death, in that boat. Soon it will be too late to save her.'

The Captain had by this time divested himself of his new coat. Loosening his dark-gray necktie, he sprang into the little craft that was to convey him to Amaranth. His face was pale and set; but he appeared calm and cool as marble as he listened to Mary's terror-stricken voice. Then he turned to her, and said,

'There is not the least occasion for alarm, I assure you. Miss Markham will be with us in less than an hour. On such a morning a child might tack about near the shore in safety. So keep a good heart, Miss Stapleton, and, above all things, avoid a scene; we shall both return, and none the worse, I hope, for our adventure.'

But Mary only wrung her hands; she remembered the dark look on Amaranth's face as she fastened on her hat at the mirror; it was awful to think what she must be enduring, waiting in the silence of the morning for some wave to burst over the tiny cockle-shell in which she was seated. Mary waved her handkerchief and shouted till she was hoarse.

But by this time the Captain was nearing the unconscious Amaranth. He had rowed hard, as the swollen muscles in his hands and arms testified, and the perspiration hung in beads over his brow. He well knew the danger threatening Amaranth, and that the waves surrounding her were hungering for their prey. Yes, there she was— his love, the girl he hoped to have called wife. He was more thankful than he could well express when he had lifted her safely to his side, her clothes soaked with sea-water, and her body icy cold. She was in truth half insensible, and looked a spirit of the sea gradually assuming human form and semblance under his influence. Her exquisitely-cut features and pallid brow seemed to need the breath of another's life to evoke those finer movements of the soul that find utterance in soft sweet speech.

'You've certainly given me a deuce of a spin this fine morning!' cried the Captain characteristically, as she raised her heavy blue-veined eyelids. 'Thank God I have you safe again; but don't make a second attempt of the kind, or I shall have to tie you up at home to the leg of the table. Now, Amaranth, *why did you do it ?*'

'O, don't ask me,' sobbed Amaranth, burying her face in her hands.

To be alive, and watch him, and listen to the quick plash of the oars over the sea after her passionate anguish, brought a sense of awesome fear as well as ecstasy.

'Can you not guess what I have suffered? . . . The sea was merciful, after all.'

'Yes, but I advise you not to trust to its tender mercies again— it's rather apt to prove the fallacy of human hopes—or you'll find yourself on a lea shore gulping down salt-water by the pint. Do you think I could spare you, although you're mortally offended with me? Why, to think of the wickedness, the madness of this outbreak, makes me half inclined to use strong language.'

'Then don't, please,' said Amaranth, smiling through her tears; 'at least not now, for I couldn't stand it at present; let me have some breakfast first.'

'By Jove, and so you shall, and so will I—is that Irish? And now don't speak another word, but just drink this, darling; it's some brandy-and-water I left in my flask, and little thought you would want. It will bring colour to your lips, which are as white as my collar;' and as he spoke he bent over and kissed her brow.

It was quite evident he had forgiven her. Although essentially matter-of-fact, like most men when tired and famished, the Captain found an alarming sense of devotion instantly aroused by the action; perhaps he felt a good deal flattered and triumphant when the truth dawned upon him, although he scolded Amaranth seriously for her folly, at the same time, indulging in rose-coloured pictures of the house at Kensington. It was satisfactory to remember no sale would now be needed.

After breakfast, when these two were alone, refreshed by prawns, hot rolls, and coffee, the Captain said:

'By the way, you have yet to find out whether my taste is good for anything. I may be, and doubtless am, an utterly soulless individual unless I'm with you; but I used to think I had a pretty correct eye for harmony and design —a talent I have recently developed in furnishing rooms. I adore comfort.'

'Missed your vocation evidently,' said Amaranth, laughing; 'ought to have been an auctioneer, house-decorator, or designer of paper patterns warranted free from poisons.'

'Come, that's not bad for an invalid. Well, I must humour you to-day, I suppose; tell me, darling, have you no curiosity to judge for yourself of my house-decorating abilities? Do you ever think of the little home at Kensington waiting to shelter you?'

'Yes,' said Amaranth, resting her hands in his; 'and I'm longing to inspect the blue china and water-colour drawings.'

END OF 'AMARANTH'S MYSTERY.'

A CONTRAST.

You love a girl, who seems to me
  Like sunlight in these frosty days;
  A diamond with many rays,
But concentrated all on thee.

I love a maiden like the light
  Which floods the meads in soft July,
  When afternoon is loth to die;
A pearl which gives to all delight.

Your diamond, from mines of thought,
  Unfathomable mines, unknown,
  Saving to you and her alone,
Its hard majestic brilliance brought.

My pearl was found on Love's own shore;
  From mid the ocean's soft white foam,
  Where wondering men are wont to roam,
Its sweet mysterious gleam it bore.

ZEPHYR.

CHORISTER BOYS.

MANY people would laugh to scorn the notion that chorister boys could furnish a subject upon which a dozen lines of interesting matter could possibly be written. I am of a different opinion. I have been one myself, have mixed with them, and have ruled over them, and so have had considerable opportunity for studying their characters and dispositions.

Come now, dear lady reader, have you not walked into a cathedral, and been held spell-bound by the voice of some white-robed youngster as he sang his solo in the anthem? And have you not felt a desire to speak to the urchin when service was over, in order to see what kind of human animal it was out of whose mouth had proceeded those exquisite strains which had so elevated your soul? Of course you have.

I once saw a boy of about thirteen in a college-chapel, whose countenance struck me as being one of the most beautiful and spiritual that I had ever seen. He was singing the solo in the anthem, which was that intensely beautiful and pathetic composition of Mendelssohn—'Hear my prayer.' I will not say that it afforded me a treat: it would be almost profane to apply so commonplace a term to that which was a feast of elevated musical emotion. It seemed to me that the lad might have been found worthy at once to be translated, as he stood, into the heavenly choir. I was never more overcome by any musical experience than I was on this occasion; and ever since I have avoided hearing this hymn sung in any concert-room, lest the affectation and coquetry of some over-dressed *prima donna* should seem but a burlesque and a desecration to the memory of the ever-to-be-remembered rendering of it in the old college-chapel.

And let me here make a remark upon the singing of boys in general. When an intelligent boy of twelve or thirteen years of age is blessed with a good voice and fair perception of music, a moderate amount of careful training will suffice to prepare him to sing sacred music in a style, the equal of which for purity, simplicity of expression, and what, for the lack of a better term, we will call 'devotional feeling,' has rarely been attained by any adult female singer, even though she be the chosen pupil of the best accredited Italian master of the day.

The professional *cantatrice*, with her personal attractions (often the secret of half her popularity), and her studied and cultivated 'production,' is for the concert-room. This is the sphere in which may be also freely indulged the dearest ambition of many women—dress. In the sanctuary matters are very different. Here 'effect' counteth not; neither is there to be gained the reward towards which the highest ambition of public singers is devoted—*encores*. In the church there is no voice that finds a congenial home but that of the surpliced, childish-hearted chorister boy. I speak of course of the leading voices, the soprani: men's voices, if good, find a noble office wherever their services are required.

It is my belief that the singular charm realised in the singing of an efficient chorister boy is to be accounted for thus. As a rule a boy under fifteen is too young to be *conceited.* Moreover he is as yet uninfected with that vice most hostile to the interests of true art, the motive spirit of too many adult singers, the desire of making 'effect' their sole aim. I have heard this denunciation of mere 'effect' uttered by an eminent composer on the subject of composition. 'Let us write,' said he to me, 'from our heart, and faithfully set down what is revealed to us : "effect" is for the coquette.'

The chorister boy knows little, and cares less, about effect. He sings as the lark sings his matin-song, *naturally ;* it is performed as an act coming in the ordinary course of things. The lark sings his ravishing strains because glorious Nature has put it into his tiny heart to pour forth gladness with his voice :

' The summer air is full of sounds of mirth,
    That from a myriad throats attain their
        birth :
    The hum of insect tribes, the trill of birds,
    The lowing of the happy flocks and herds.
    The brooklet babbling on gives forth a lull
    Of tender music, faint, but wonderful.
    The trees anon, as by each zephyr stirred,
    Add the soft murmur of a breathless word,
    Too deep for utterance, save in softest
        spell,
    Of that deep mystery that trees full well
    Alone can flutter forth from out their hearts
    Of leafy love and majesty.'

Neither the lark nor the chorister boy of twelve is much trammelled with the selfish passion of ambition, hence the unsophisticated freshness and purity of the performance. Understand, kindly reader, I am speaking only of the better class of chorister boys, those gifted with musical talent. Into the heads of a large portion of the urchins of this class it is impossible to drive music, save in the way by which

you teach a parrot to mimic human speech.

But I pass from the musical qualifications of chorister boys, and proceed to relate a few experiences of them *as boys ;* as the set of romping, mischievous, light-hearted, generous fellows I have, for the most part, found them.

In the course of six or seven years some seventy or eighty lads passed through my hands, and were, for such time as their voices lasted, under my tuition and control. I am perfectly certain that amongst all this number there were not more than three bad characters. The classes of society from which my little army was from time to time recruited may be said to have been for the most part the middle class ; my boys were the sons of clergymen of small income, tradesmen of the better class, and of widows who, perchance, had seen better days.

During the greater part of the period I am now referring to I possessed a beautiful Malacca cane, sent to me by a military friend from Singapore : this cane was generally in my hand when I entered the singing-school, and when I left it ; at other times it was always quietly keeping company with my hat and gloves. At a neighbouring establishment of a similar description to my own I heard that the 'cane' and the 'birch' were almost every day the accompaniments to the preparations for singing. Never, except on one occasion, did I raise my hand to strike one of all these boys, and that was when, in a moment of extreme irritation, I gave one of the elder boys a slap on the head. I afterwards begged his pardon for losing my temper in the presence of all the other boys. This found favour in the eyes of all, and discipline never suffered a whit.

While on the subject of punishment, I cannot refrain from remarking that I have noted one fact. When I have put a particular boy in Coventry for some trifling breach of discipline—disrespect or insolence I have scarcely ever suffered at the hands of a boy—I have generally found that the punishment which has been caused by the temporary withdrawal of my countenance from him has been amply sufficient, and that a *free pardon*, after evidences of contrition, has wrought more good to the character of the boy than any amount of severity could have done.

What is the lamentable mistake that is made by so many parents but this? They warn their children that they are so many nothings, and that they (the parents) alone know what is right for them to do, and that they must not think for themselves; and having thus crushed all individuality out of the children, they expect them to act with the wisdom and circumspection of grown-up people! Parents impose the utmost responsibilities upon their children, but deny them all discretion. They exact from them the behaviour of philosophers, and when the little ones fail they punish them as idiots. Although this paper is not designed as an essay on the duties of parents towards their offspring, yet I cannot pass over the subject on which I have touched without remarking, that it is my solemn conviction that in the punishment of children the gravest responsibility rests. And to parents, as well as to schoolmasters and choirmasters, I desire to sound this one note of warning: when you punish the little ones under your charge, let it be done with all judgment, lest in the exercise of your temper the child discern that, of the two, you are the more wicked.

But now let us to the pleasanter side of our subject, the contemplation of the times when the singing-school, the schoolroom, and in fact business, is left behind, and pleasure is our occupation.

I was once for two months engaged in the fulfilment of temporary duties at a chapel in the far north. Four of my best choristers from the University shared in the engagement. The place we went to was a charming little seaside resort, lately established, and as yet for the most part unpolluted by the flaunting presence of fashion. Our duties being light, leaving us in some cases whole days wherein to disport ourselves as we chose, we had ample time for the enjoyment of all manner of pleasant and health-giving pursuits. We visited neighbouring places of interest, we fished from the rocks and from our boat, we bathed, climbed up mountains, and were nearly shipwrecked several times. When we first arrived here, I, though of mature years, could not swim. Two of my boys took me as their pupil in the art of natation, and in a fortnight I could go confidently off the gunwale of our boat into twenty fathoms, and swim a hundred yards to land.

During the latter fortnight of our stay I fell ill, and received two visits daily from the local doctor, who said that I required great care. I told him that I had four excellent nurses; and so in truth I had; for four nurses whose devoted attention and tender thoughtfulness could outdo what was displayed by these four choristers I defy any hospital in the three kingdoms to bring forward.

At our college, when at work in the singing-school, I used to sit at a harmonium, with the sixteen choristers ranged on either side of the room, in the same order in which they appeared in chapel, 'Decani and Cantoris' at their respective desks. During business, the discipline I maintained was of the most rigid description. Work over, we were friends, and I was a boy among the rest. I was Honorary Secretary and Treasurer of their Athletic and Cricket Clubs, and was referred to as umpire in all their disputes, and in all things they sought my countenance and sympathy. Sometimes I made companions of these fellows, and many were the glorious country walks we used to take in times of leisure, in a party of from four to a dozen, as the case might be. I used to delight in conversing freely with these miniature men, and in listening to their views on all manner of subjects. Their opinions were daringly honest, as a rule, and diplomacy was conspicuous by its absence.

Some of them would take me into their confidence even in the matter of their 'love affairs.' One day I was talking in the cloisters with a bright curly-haired youth of twelve years of age, who told me much about a young lady of ten, towards whom he assured me he entertained the most serious views. 'Then,' said I, 'I suppose you will some day marry this lady, if her friends consent—very soon, perhaps?' 'O, dear no, sir!' he exclaimed, 'not for at least *two years!*'

There was one fellow in my choir obviously destined by Nature to take the position of 'low comedian' in any company to which he might happen to be attached at any period of his life. He was 'a fellow of infinite jest,' with a vacant expression of countenance, and a tongue everlastingly wagging with witticisms. I liked this lad extremely; for although I was constantly obliged to check the exuberance of his spirits, I knew that he was as honest and faithful as a boy could be, and that is saying a great deal. But my desire to preserve discipline was often rendered difficult of execution by a struggle to suppress

hearty laughter at some of his grotesque expressions.

One day his passion for humour carried him beyond all bounds. I was sitting at the harmonium in the singing-school, about to teach the boys some anthem or other, when, just as I was commencing, I noticed that a suppressed tendency to laugh reigned upon the countenances of all the boys, and our commencement of the anthem met with failure. I sternly demanded to know what was the matter. No answer, but a perceptible broadening of the respective grins. Again, more sternly, I addressed them. The grins developed into a loud laugh, interrupted by the boy at the end of one rank pointing to the floor on the other side of the harmonium to where I sat, and saying half-apologetically, 'Please, sir, G—!'

I stood up, and looked over the harmonium. There sat Mr. G— with his back to the instrument, his legs sprawling over the floor, engaged in lolling his tongue out of his mouth, and wagging it at his companions in a manner the most intensely ludicrous.

It was very comical, and I all but gave way. I, however, held myself together, and said, in a subdued but significant tone, that he must instantly take his place at the desk, and added, 'I shall remember this: remain here after chapel.'

Service over, I found the comedian there, looking crestfallen and doubtful. Two or three other boys had remained, curious to know the result of his extraordinary behaviour; but these I quickly commanded to retire.

Left alone, with the culprit entirely in my power, I pointed out to him the impudence and absurdity of his conduct, to which he made no reply. I told him quietly that it was absolutely necessary that I should this time make an example of him, and punish him severely. I said,

'As I have some respect for you, in spite of your folly, I shall give you your choice of two penalties. Either you will write out three hundred lines of poetry, which I shall select; or I shall give you twelve cuts with the cane. Which shall it be?'

He replied, with submission,

'The poetry, sir.'

'There,' said I, 'I think you are wrong. The imposition will give you a great deal of trouble, and take up your play-time; while the caning will hurt you, but soon be over. Won't you choose the flogging?'

With a huge shudder (he was a slender delicate boy), and a look of abject appeal, he quietly answered,

'As you please, sir.'

I took him by the arm, his heart perceptibly palpitating (my cane lay with my hat and gloves).

'Come,' said I; 'you are a good boy, but very thoughtless. I won't punish you at all if you will promise not to be so silly again.'

He burst into a torrent of tears: gratitude overcame him. From that time forth he would any day have sold his dinner to buy me a cigar.

Before I close I must record an experience which will, I think, tend to exhibit the unreasoning, but thoroughly faithful, allegiance that boys will manifest towards one in whom they believe, and who possesses their regard.

Some years ago I was, for a time, made the victim of the convenience of the dean and chapter of a certain cathedral many miles from London. I was appointed temporary organist and choirmaster, as a stop-gap during the period that must elapse between the compulsory retirement of the then present organist and choirmaster to a distance, 'on urgent private affairs,'

and the appointment of his permanent successor.

Although fair prospects were held out to me that, in all probability, I should be that chosen one, it afterwards was revealed that their choice had already been made.

A 'show' of fair dealing was exhibited in the matter of a competition, or 'trial of skill,' in which I was mercifully permitted to imperil my reputation, as one of four, chosen from among a vast number of applicants, hailing from all parts of the country. The matter was officially decided by a committee of *one*; and the return presented my name, in brackets, with the name of the gentleman whom they subsequently appointed, and whom they had intended to appoint from the first.

At the time of the competition I had already done duty as organist and choirmaster in the cathedral for about six months; and during that time I had succeeded in gaining the entire goodwill of my subordinates.

It came to my ears, on the morning of the trial of skill, that the chorister boys had conspired among themselves, and resolved to sing *well* when I played my turn, and *badly* for the three other candidates, in the hope of 'putting them out in their playing.' 'He is *our* proper master,' they argued; 'and what do they bring strangers here for, to rob him of his place?'

I told the conspirators, in a body, that I fully appreciated their motives, but that if they attempted to spoil fair play it would pain me very much.

I heard a minor canon say afterwards, as a report of the intended conspiracy had reached his ears, 'Little bleg-gurds! they ought to have a gud flagging!'

I could not help feeling that, if the dean and chapter had but been of their nature, I should not have had to face the utter blighting of 'six good months' hope,' as I afterwards did; to say nothing of the fact that my professional prospects were, for the time, well-nigh ruined.

Now, dear reader, I believe that you will be disposed to think somewhat kindly of the little white-robed musicians, when you again see them in their antique carved-oak stalls. And should you observe, on the part of any of them, a disposition to go to sleep during the sermon, ask yourself whether it is not a matured sense of responsibility as to decorum that prevents your doing the same thing. Singing is peculiarly apt to induce sleepiness. Take them all round, chorister boys are by no means a 'bad lot.'

THE SHADOW OF THE CROSS.

THE sun sank in clouds and the gloaming came on,
As he stood in the churchyard in sadness alone,
And the mists of the evening crept up from the vale,
While the light of the moon glimmered ghastly and pale.

'My darling! my darling! I left you in scorn;
I was young, and my spirit was maddened and torn.
God help me! I knew not you loved me so well,
Till the heart that you gave me lay shattered and still.

And then fell a blight on the earth; and the sky
Grew dark, and I longed in my anguish to die.
Your face was before me by night and by day,
All around life's horizon grew ashen and gray.

I am old! I am lonely! I long for my rest;
But Death will not come with this wrong unconfessed.
O, hear me, my darling! I kneel by your grave;
But say you forgive me! 'tis all that I crave.'

The shade of the spire fell dark on the grass,
And the moonlight cast downward the form of a cross;
Did that symbol of love bring a voice from the past?
Did he know he was pardoned, long pardoned, at last?

The sky became gray, and the morn grew apace,
The sun rose in glory, night fled from his face,
And the rays of his brightness flashed golden and red
On a wild heart at rest, for the mourner lay—dead!

ROBERT NUGENT.

A STRANGE INTRODUCTION.

By JESSIE SALE LLOYD,

AUTHOR OF 'THE SILENT SHADOW,' 'RUTH EVERINGHAM,' ETC.

I MUST, I suppose, introduce myself, as I have undertaken to bring a portion of my history before the public, and shall begin by telling my name and state.

I, George Falconer, then, am one of the members of the Civil Service whom *Punch* so unfairly likened, some time since, to the fountains in Trafalgar-square, accusing us, like them, of 'playing from eleven till four daily.' But Mr. Punch was for once mistaken, and should be informed that we, who thus *civilly* serve our country, have not the easy times we are supposed to have. Having relieved my mind by which protest, I will proceed with the narration of my story.

Well, then, being tired with a heavy day's work, I walked, perhaps somewhat languidly, up Regent-street, making for my rooms in Margaret-street, where I knew I should find my dinner awaiting me. It had been a sultry August day, and London, with its slack trade time and many shuttered windows, looked like a city of the dead.

Nobody was in town, which means nobody worth knowing; and I was myself longing to get away among the grouse, or by the salt sea-waves, to inhale the briny, and blow off the London smuts and cobwebs, which gather alike on mind and body; and indeed men need this bracing up of nerves and sinews, to enable them to resist the suicidal feeling engendered by the London fogs which are to follow—thick enough to frighten the Zulus, if they could only be enveloped in them for a few hours. As I said before, I was tired, and longing to get away for a holiday. But my seniors had to be satisfied first, and I had to await my turn; and that is why I was in the great metropolis, when every one else was gone, with the exception of a few unfortunates like myself.

It was one of those days of leaden heat, when the sun does not seem to shine so brightly after all, nor to send down scorching rays; yet when the very fish in the Serpentine come to the surface and gasp; when the pavements sear your feet, and your boots feel several sizes too small; when to hold up an umbrella would be useless exertion and absurd, and it is impossible to find out which direction the wind is in, for there is not the faintest breath of air to indicate it; when the weary cab-horses loll out their parched and thirsty tongues, with scarcely the energy to whisk the tormenting flies from their harness galls; when one could drink the sea dry, if only it were not salt! I had taken a long time walking home; but I was nearly there at last: I had only to turn the corner of the street, and within a few doors I should find one which fitted my latchkey—*that* I knew—when a slight diversion occurred.

An elderly gentleman passing in a hansom cab was frantically gesticulating to *some one* near me, but to whom I could not imagine, as, on looking round, I saw no one at all likely to be the familiar acquaintance of the person in the cab, who was an aristocratic-looking old man.

One thing I felt sure about—it could not be *me* he was signalling to, as I had never set eyes on his face before; and it was a face which, if seen once, would not readily be forgotten. The cabman was drowsy, and, having received his orders where to drive, he was enjoying a sort of dog's sleep, with only half an eye open, the faithful horse chiefly guiding himself among the not very crowded traffic of the dull streets, and not troubling himself to pass any vehicle which might be said to be trotting.

I couldn't resist a half smile at the futile efforts of the gentleman to get the driver to stop, and thought for a moment of going to his rescue; but this would have entailed exertion, and that was out of the question on such a day. And, after all, what business was it of mine? The man might be a maniac for all I knew, grimacing at his own reflection in the plate-glass of the shop-windows.

I turned my corner with the full intention of putting on my slippers and a white-flannel boating-jacket, and sitting down to dinner looking more like a miller or a baker than a respectable member of society. Not that I intend for a moment to insult one trade or the other. Both are very good in their way, and we couldn't do without them; but, you see, *their* way is not *our* way, and I intended not to look like a respectable member of *our* society. But why a coat like a *miller* should be less respectable than a coat like a *waiter* is one of those things which I imagine no man can fully understand or explain. A black swallow-tail is correct—is usual—it is the custom. Yes, I know; but why?

'Well, George, old boy, how are you?' cried a hearty voice, as my footstep ascended the stairs.

'Why, old man, who ever thought of seeing you—and on such a day too? It is like living in an oven. What has brought *you* up to town, away from your shooting and country breezes? You don't find it a very good exchange, I should think, Bruce.'

'Business, George! Business, you know, must be attended to,' he replied, laughing, at the same time almost shaking my hand off, and using an energy which would have been impossible with me on such a day, and which, even second-hand, I found quite exhausting.

'Business!' I echoed. 'Why, what business have *you*, except enjoying all the goods the gods provide you with? Ah, Bruce! you are one of the few lucky fellows born with a silver spoon ready to feed you' (for my old schoolfellow and friend had well-lined pockets and a comfortable estate in prospective, as the only son of a wealthy man of good family).

'Never fear, my boy,' he answered cheerily; 'the spoon will come to *you* some day, and sooner than you think perhaps. And now I am going to carry you off to the theatre to-night. Where shall we go?'

'The theatre! Why, we should be suffocated!' I gasped.

'Not a bit of it,' he answered. 'You shall have as many ices as you please to cool you. I've only this one night in town, and I'm not to be baulked of going to the play. You Londoners don't know what it is to enjoy things as we countrymen do.'

'But why come up for so short a time? I can put you up as long as you like, and—'

'O, you'll feel more "fit" when you have had your dinner, George. By the bye, when *shall* we have it? I am deucedly hungry, I can tell you.'

'Hungry!' I murmured, looking

at my friend in astonishment. 'Well, old man, you *are* a wonder. Fancy any one being hungry to-day!'

And sure enough he was. I acknowledged the fact as I saw the breast of a chicken, followed by the wing, merry-thought, and two legs, vanish before him like summer lightning, assisted by several slices of ham, and an alarming quantity of vegetables and bread. I watched and envied him his appetite. Of course he had his way, the great big overpowering fellow! He was some years older than myself, and I had been his 'fag' at Eton. Not that he had ever *bullied* me; still, I was accustomed to follow out his wishes; and to the theatre we went. *Our Boys* was being acted, and upon that he decided. We took our places in the stalls; the curtain rose, and the piece began.

My friend Tom Bruce was instantly absorbed in the plot—ready to laugh at all the jokes, and pretty nearly to cry at the pathetic parts. Soft-hearted old fellow! I had seen *Our Boys* till I knew just when to expect the tid-bits; so I was not giving much attention to the stage. And then I saw coming towards the stalls the very same old gentleman whom I had seen in the hansom cab some hours before; and I fell to wondering whether he had managed to rouse the driver and stop his friend. I smiled as I remembered his excitement, and looked up at him. To my astonishment, I found him regarding me with a most annoyed, not to say stern, expression of face. I supposed he had seen me in the afternoon, and had noted that I was amused at him, and now was determined to resent it—a fact not likely to be particularly pleasant, as he walked up and took possession of the very next seat to the one which I occupied. I had no

wish to annoy my neighbour; so I fixed my eyes upon the stage, and tried to be interested in the actors; but all the time I was aware that the gentleman in the next seat was doing me the honour of staring intently at me, and that he was becoming very angry. And then he said, 'Edward!'

A man had taken the place on the other side of him—*that* I saw without looking. Could *he* be Edward? Yet I felt that my neighbour's face was turned towards *me*. First he had spoken in a low tone; but now he raised his voice, and said again 'Edward!' so suddenly, that it made me jump. Still I did not turn round, as it was no business of mine, and I did not wish to give my irascible neighbour any cause of offence.

'Do you hear me, sir?' he continued hotly. 'What is the use of your pretending not to see me?'

By this time Tom Bruce's attention had been attracted, and I was feeling very uncomfortable, for a violent jerking was going on at my left coat-sleeve; and the idea had returned to me that this excitable gentleman was not of sound mind, and having the distaste for being made a 'laughing-stock'—which is strong in most people—I feared lest he had singled *me* out to render me absurd in the eyes of all assembled there. A more violent tug, however, made me turn with an indignant remonstrance.

'To what am I indebted, sir, for this unusual conduct?' I asked.

'What the devil are *you* doing here at all?' he replied, in an angry tone.

('Mad,' I said inwardly. 'Mad as a hatter!')

'Sir,' I answered solemnly, 'you must be labouring under some delusion. As I have not the honour of your acquaintance, you can have no possible right to question where I should or should not be. At the same time, I feel bound to remark that this is not a proper moment for conversation, and I must beg you not to address me again ; at any rate while the acting is going on. If you have anything to say to me *afterwards* I shall be happy to hear you.'

Surely right is might, for I felt I had spoken well, and doubtless he thought so too; for though he looked at me from time to time he did not speak to me again till the curtain fell at the end of the first act. But no sooner had it touched the floor than he turned on me at once.

'And now, sir,' said he triumphantly, 'what have you to say for yourself ?'

'Nothing,' I replied; 'and if it is not disrespectful to gray hairs, sir, I beg to return the compliment.'

'Confound you,' cried the old man, springing up; 'this is too much ! A joke is a joke, but it won't do to carry it too far. I have found you out, and you should try to conciliate and not to aggravate me.'

'Sir,' I replied, 'all you say is doubtless perfectly true; but it is quite beyond my powers of comprehension.'

He put his double gold eyeglass tightly upon his nose, and looked at me long and keenly. I had risen too, and stood facing him. At last he said, with a sad resentment,

'Edward, is this the right way for a son to treat a father ?'

'You are labouring under some mistake,' I answered gently, for there was a moist look about the old man's eyes suggestive of tears. 'I *have* no father; I only wish I had.'

There was silence between us, and Tom stood regarding us both curiously.

At length my strange acquaintance broke out again.

'Nonsense, boy ! Do you think I don't know my own son ?'

'But surely, sir,' I replied, 'you do not suppose *me* to be he !'

'It would be strange indeed if I could mistake my own child,' he answered, with a plaintive smile. 'Edward, you have carried this folly far enough, indeed too far.'

What was I to do ? what to say ? How was I to convince this gentleman, whom I supposed to be wandering in his mind, that he had made a ludicrous blunder in mistaking me for his son ? Here my honest friend Tom came to my rescue.

'If you are really serious, sir, in what you say, I can relieve any anxiety you may feel on the subject. That gentleman and I have been friends since we were boys together at Eton; and even in *those* days he had *no father*.'

The people were now again taking their places, and the opening of the second act put a stop to further conversation ; but I felt that my would-be relation scarcely removed his eyes from my face; still he never spoke again until the play was entirely finished, and I was showing signs of leaving the theatre. He then placed his hand kindly on my arm.

'My boy,' he said, 'I will forgive you if only you will acknowledge that you have been wrong to play such a trick on your father. You should not have left your work when you knew how much I wished you to pass your examination well; but now that you *are* so near home, you must not return to Cambridge without a look at your mother. I am going down by the last train, and you will go with me.'

'My dear sir,' I exclaimed, 'I will do anything you wish. I see you believe what you say ; but indeed not only am I not your son, but I have never had the pleasure of seeing you before.'

A smile was lurking round the old man's mouth.

'Well, well, you will come home with me, at any rate.'

'Certainly, if it will ease your mind;' then suddenly remembering Tom Bruce, 'that is, if my friend will excuse me for a few hours; I must be back very early in the morning. Where is it we are going?'

'Where, but to Richmond?' he answered impatiently; 'you know we do not leave there for some weeks yet.'

'Never mind me,' exclaimed Tom good-naturedly; 'give me the latch-key, that is all;' this aloud, and then, in a whisper, 'Who knows, George, but you may find the silver spoon at the bottom of this; you had better go and see it out.'

I meekly handed him the key, and we went out of the theatre together. I made one more protest, but it was useless; my old new father placed his hand within my arm and drew me into a 'four-wheeler,' as though fearing I should escape from a hansom. We drove to Waterloo, and were soon in the train. A handsome carriage and pair met us at Richmond Station, and I had to follow my new-made acquaintance into it. I began to feel most uncomfortable. Here was I, a perfect stranger, driving up to the house of—I did not know whom, and supposed to be a member of the family. What was to become of me? I had come out of sheer good-nature, entirely because of the dewy look in the old man's eyes; and now I saw what a fool I was likely to make of myself. I had no means of getting back to London that night, and I had not even a razor or a night-shirt—not even a clean collar for the morrow; and, what was worse still, I should have to go up in my dress-clothes. These reflections were not very comforting; but it was of no use to show my vexation to my peculiar friend.

At length the silence was broken by the carriage stopping suddenly.

'Here we are!' he cried, eagerly preparing to get out.

'I beg your pardon,' I said, detaining him; 'but I should be obliged if you would tell me your name; it is awkward not knowing.'

He burst out laughing.

'Come, drop that nonsense, Teddy; it is too absurd!'

The carriage-door flew open, and I followed my companion out.

'Good-night, Mr. Edward,' said the footman.

'Glad to see you, sir!' exclaimed the butler. 'This is an *on*expected pleasure; thought as how you were at Cambridge still, Mr. Edward.'

My strange acquaintance looked at me triumphantly.

'Where is your mistress, Johnson? Is she up still?'

'O yes, sir, and Miss Ida too; they both said as how they would wait for you, sir.'

It did not take us long to relieve ourselves of our hats, &c., and then I found myself following my host and the butler up some broad softly-carpeted stairs. The man threw open a door, and I could see before me a drawing-room of large proportions, beautifully furnished, and two ladies advancing to meet us with outstretched arms.

'Here is an unexpected pleasure for you, mamma!' said my companion blithely.

'O Edward, my darling!' exclaimed the elder lady, throwing her arms about my neck and hugging me heartily. 'But how *did* you get away at the present time, my dear boy?'

'Come! leave a little piece of him for me, mother,' cried the girl, kissing me affectionately.

And then, as though in that kiss

she had found me out, she started, and looked at me keenly, but said nothing. As for me, I felt like a traitor and a villain. Here was I —not willingly, to be sure, but still none the less certainly—in this house, sailing under false colours, receiving welcomes and greetings, which were decidedly never intended for *me*. I was too utterly bewildered to guess even at what it could mean. No doubt it was some curious and most unfortunate mistake. Ida's lips were the sweetest I had ever touched, and I was sorely tempted to give her kiss for kiss. Perhaps my omitting to do so caused her to look at me so strangely. They were all crowding round me with questions and kindly words, and I felt I could bear it no longer.

'My dear sir,' I exclaimed impatiently, 'you are placing me in a very painful position. What *can* I do to convince you that I am a stranger to you?'

Ida changed colour, from white to red, and from red to white. The elder lady looked from one of us to the other for an explanation of my words.

'Is it not absurd?' said the old gentleman. 'I have brought him home almost by force, protesting to the last that he has never seen me before; but now he is carrying the joke too far.'

Ida (how pretty and graceful she was!) walked quietly up to a reading-lamp, which stood on a table at some distance off, and raised it to my face.

'O papa!' she exclaimed, 'this is not Teddy. What *is* to be done? Don't you remember *he* has a scar across his right eyebrow which this gentleman has not?'

It was difficult to convince him even then; but the mamma disowned me at once.

'Only to think that *I* should for a moment have been deceived!'

she said apologetically. 'But, indeed, the likeness is marvellous!'

Ida said but little; and whenever our eyes met she blushed, remembering, doubtless, how warmly she had embraced me.

I soon found out that my host was a Mr. Bayley, who almost overpowered me with apologies for his mistake.

They insisted upon my sleeping there, and I accepted, on condition that they would let me depart before they were down in the morning, that I might escape the observation my dress-clothes would call upon me from the very *gamins* in the London streets; and also I was really anxious to see my friend Tom Bruce, and explain to him the curious events of the evening.

To this they agreed, exacting from me a promise that I would come down again before they left Richmond for the sea. 'An acquaintance so strangely begun,' they said, 'must not be allowed to fall through.'

And Mr. Bayley even now found it hard to believe his mistake, and could scarcely take his eyes off my face, which so curiously resembled his own son's.

The next morning an early breakfast was brought to me in my room, and I was *en route* to London before my new friends were awake. I escaped the jeers of the street arabs by jumping into a hansom, and whirling home as fast as the horse could carry me.

Tom was still asleep, but roused up when I opened his bedroom-door, and called loudly for me to come in.

'Holloa! who is that? O George, my boy, it is you, is it? Come and tell me all about it. Have you found the silver spoon, eh?'

'I have found the prettiest girl I ever saw in my life,' I replied, with a smile.

'O, it's *that sort of spoon*, is it?' cried he, with a loud guffaw. 'Well, George, I didn't expect that of you, and you so many years my junior; but I forgive you, my boy, and will be best man. When is it to be?'

'My dear Bruce, what are you driving at? I tell you I have met a pretty girl, and you ask when it's to be? You and my new friend, Mr. Bayley, might run in a curricle for two lunatics, I really think,' I answered impatiently.

'Whew!' cried Tom; 'bad as all that, are you? Well, well, it's what we all come to sooner or later; it's a complaint it is better to have young. Now, George, what's she like?'

'Who?' I replied resentfully. 'Do you mean Miss Ida Bayley?'

'Yes, to be sure, if that is her name.'

'Well, then, Miss Bayley is the prettiest girl I ever saw,' I answered enthusiastically.

'Yes, I know,' replied he calmly; 'you mentioned that before.'

'Why, Bruce, old man, you don't expect me to describe every feature, do you, like a cheap Jack at a fair? and if I would, I couldn't. How do I know the colour of her eyes?—but I know how they look. What does it matter to me whether her mouth is the shape of Cupid's bow or not?—I know how it smiles. Ida Bayley is not the girl you could criticise as you talk to her; you *feel* she is there—that if she is *not* beautiful, beauty cannot be worth having.'

I looked up at my friend, who was regarding me fairly open-mouthed.

'Do you understand?' I asked.

'Quite,' he replied, with an honest smile, 'and I congratulate you; and now, George, tell me—has Miss Ida a sister? If so, I think I will accompany you to Richmond.'

Well, of course, I went down into Surrey again; and, odd as it may seem, I became quite a favourite with all the Bayley family. It was my strange resemblance to the absent Edward, no doubt, which endeared me to them; but, whatever the reason may have been, the loop-line Waterloo Station ticket-clerk soon grew familiar with my destination, and gave me my ticket for Richmond as a matter of course when my face appeared looking through the pigeon-hole at him.

The Bayleys were going to the Isle of Wight, and, strange to say, I found *I* was going there too; though I fully believed myself to have made up my mind to have a good month's sport among the birds with Tom Bruce over his father's well-preserved acres. But I discovered now, for the first time, that I didn't care much for shooting; and the prospect of some trips with the Bayleys in their yacht was a delightful anticipation to me, outweighing all other counterbalancing influences.

We all went down together, and a happy time indeed we had of it. Too many others have described the beautiful island to need any word of mine to echo its praises; and there are few who have not seen the fairy-like isle for themselves; but I must say, as we first beheld it on that bright autumn day, with the sun glinting upon its pretty houses, and lighting up the green of its verdure, while the sky and clouds were reflected on the water, lending it their violet and azure shades, blended and softened, and the white sails of the yachts skimmed butterfly-like upon its surface, I thought I had never seen anything more softly lovely. One felt as though it were a sort of dreamland, from which it would be terrible to awake to life's stern realities; and I think Ida felt it so too, for she was silent, and her eyes had a far-off look in them, as if she were seeing visions which were hid from others. Yes; certainly that holiday of mine was one of the happiest periods of my life! I shall never, never forget it. I do not know how it came about; but somehow I found I had told Ida of my love. It must have been owing to the beauty of the scene surely, and her own loveliness; for though I had loved her from that first night when her dear lips had met mine, I never intended to have let her know my secret, fearing so greatly to lose all while grasping at more. But I had done it in a moment of unrestrainable feeling and agitation, and how glad I am I did! for, poor match as I am for her, my Ida gave me all her dear love when I asked for it; and, indeed, she acknowledged, with a sweet warm blush, that it had been mine before I asked it at all.

What Ida wished every one wished; so Mr. and Mrs. Bayley were kind and good to me. But of course they felt they must not let me have her without a little tantalisation; so we were to wait till Christmas before we were to be considered actually engaged, as our acquaintance had been so short a one. It only made me love her the more to have my happiness retarded; and I looked forward to that Christmas-day as I have never done before, and never shall do again.

It came at last, and my darling was ready to fly into the arms that were eagerly outstretched to clasp her. And before I had half made up my mind to release her, the door suddenly opened, and, looking quickly round, I was never so astonished in my life; for I saw my shadow—no, not shadow, for that is lifeless, but what appeared to be my very *self*—walking across the room. Ida stood by with a smile to watch the meeting, and we two men gazed steadily at one another, and then burst into uncontrollable fits of laughter.

'It *is* absurd!' we both remarked, in a breath.

And so it was, for even our voices were similar.

Edward Bayley and I became great friends; and many a trick have we played successfully in consequence of our strange likeness to each other—a fact I have never ceased to be thankful for, for did it not gain me my wife?

Ida says she does not think we are so much alike as we were; but having been some years married, she, doubtless, knows my face as others do not, and has found out in it beauties for herself which are invisible to other eyes, and which none but hers would have discovered.

FEMININE FORCES.

By ELLEN CRUMP.

—◆—

Sisters.

By which term reference is not made to that domestic relationship which in some families means everything which is gentle, kind, thoughtful, and unselfish; while in others it is synonymous with nagging, teasing, and all that is disagreeable; I refer rather to those devoted women who band themselves together for good and unselfish purposes, with the knowledge that in 'union there is strength,' whom we meet constantly in the streets of our great city—sometimes pale, patient, and middle-aged; sometimes young, rosy, and cheerful—going busily about the work they have to do, dressed in the long cloaks and white caps that everywhere mark their calling, and never fail to obtain them a quiet passage through even the noisiest crowds. Years ago the term 'sister' was applied almost entirely to Roman Catholic Sisters of Mercy; and ignorant and narrow-minded people nowadays look upon a *Sœur de Charité* as a sort of Jesuit in disguise, to be carefully shunned, and kept out of one's house at any cost. Many of them, doubtless, do belong to Roman Catholic communities, and have done much good and noble work amongst the very poor. The term 'sister' is, at the present day, in general use amongst all denominations of women who are banded together for work, whether paid or unpaid, amongst the sick ; and there is no work too humble for their hands to do, no sorrow too heartrending for them to witness and try to alleviate.

The range of their labours is immense, and extends from acting as paid nurses in the houses of the wealthy to begging from door to door for the broken food that the careless ones of the earth would cast away, but which *they* make into soups and stews for the destitute. Their lives are full of self-sacrifice and devotion to others. They have to put far from them the thoughts of home ties and home joys, so dear to the hearts of all true women, and throw themselves into the joys and troubles of those around them ; and there have always been women unselfish enough to do it. As far back as the apostolic age, there were women authorised to undertake certain duties analogous to the duties of a deacon ; and these received the name of deaconesses, and are still represented amongst us, each individual member of the body being always designated as 'sister.'

There are at present in England several deaconesses' institutions in active working order. The principal one has (or had) its home in Burton-crescent, and was founded in the year 1861 as ' a training college for parochial deaconesses, who are to go forth, with episcopal canction guaranteeing their fitness, to work under the parochial clergy in all that an educated woman can do with propriety and efficiency for the cause of God and His Church.' This is a Church of England institution, and is under the patronage of the Archbishop of Canterbury, and is visited by the

Bishop of London. It consists of a central home, where candidates are trained and sent forth into various works. There are wards in the house, where a limited number of cases are taken and nursed by the sisters. The deaconesses also have under their care a school for girls in St. Jude's, Gray's-inn-road, where their probationers are trained for teaching. Some few years ago, when I paid a visit to this institution, it was not in a condition to support its working members, and candidates had to pay 50*l.* a year towards the general expenses, besides giving all their time and labour, which necessarily greatly limited the number of applicants for admission to the community. There are many wealthy women who might, if they would, give money; and there are many earnest women who have no money, but would gladly give time and labour. For these latter, however, there is another deaconesses' institution at Tottenham, founded by a German Protestant pastor, and supported entirely by voluntary contributions. Sisters desirous of joining in the good works carried on are accepted from all ranks, neither wealth nor poverty proving a barrier to their admission, provided their hearts are in the work. The institution becomes, for the time being, the true home of the members, where they receive food, clothing, shelter, and pocket-money. If they become ill, they are loved and cared for; and even if they become confirmed invalids, it is as if they were at home. They have given their labour, and it is not forgotten. They are not bound to remain in the work; but unless required by their parents, or, as the German head-sister expressed it in her pretty quaint English, 'called for marriage,' it is expected they will remain in their vocation, before

entering which they always undergo a year's probation. No sister must ever refuse to do any work, however menial, that comes to her hand, though, at the same time, if she has any accomplishments that in leisure moments can cheer and amuse the others, so much the better. When I visited the house a piano was being played merrily in a comfortable homely room, looking on to a quiet old-fashioned garden, where the children and convalescents were enjoying the summer breezes on the smooth-shaven lawn, under the cool shadow of great gnarled trees; whilst in another part of the building other sisters were taking their turn in tending the sick poor, who are received and cared for free of all charge. There was a surgery, in which the sisters learned to make up medicines, and from which numerous out-patients received aid; and a dissecting room, where they were taught such surgical knowledge as should make them good and efficient nurses.

Perhaps there is no work more peculiarly suited to a woman's character and abilities than that of nursing the sick. It is work which requires no great amount of intellect or originality, but a considerable amount of patience, tenderness, cheerfulness, and large-hearted sympathy, united with quickness of thought in emergencies. Some women seem to know instinctively how best to shake up a pillow, or place a patient with the least fatigue in the most comfortable position; how also to move about a sick-room so quietly as not to disturb the most sensitive, yet without that stealthy step which irritates even the least nervous. Sisters who have chosen their vocation from real love of the work are often endowed with this knack of nursing,—for it is not often that people really like and choose work they are incapable of doing,—and it is they who will have the most control over their patients; even the delirious will yield to their firmness, whilst soothed by their gentleness; and the invalid's recovery may be greatly aided by the true bright cheerfulness that is so frequently a characteristic of those who devote themselves to the busy, useful, unselfish life of the convent or hospital.

At St. Thomas's Hospital, Albert Embankment, a number of nurses are trained, free of all cost, under the Nightingale Fund, founded by Florence Nightingale. Of these the major part are from the working classes; and a comparatively small proportion are ladies, who are termed 'sisters,' and after completing their training take the superintendence of the wards; but they all live under the same rule, and have meals at the same table. They are taken first for a month on trial; and if that trial is satisfactory, they are entered for a year as probationers, four years being the complete term of training. The probationers are lodged in the Nightingale Home, adjoining the quarters of the matron of the hospital, and have each a separate bedroom, and joint use of a large handsome apartment where they take their meals, and sit when not occupied in the hospital. The matron, Mrs. Wardroper, courteously took me to see the children's ward, where many of the nurses were engaged in alleviating the sufferings and supplying the wants of the poor little occupants of the numerous iron cots, which, covered with white quilts, were ranged down both sides of the long ward. It was a big lofty room with dark oak floor, and two large bright stoves reflected the dancing flames and sent forth a pleasant warmth. Over each little bed hung a bright-coloured picture; and

across the top of the cot a polished wooden tray was placed, on which were toys for the infant invalids. Two or three beds were empty, and their late occupants—up and dressed—were running from cot to cot, laughing and talking with their less fortunate fellows. Some flowers stood about the room, and everything was redolent of cheerfulness and kindness. As we passed out, the door of the sister's room which adjoined the ward, and had a window overlooking it, opened to receive two small children, and I looked curiously in; whereupon the matron begged permission for me to enter. A pretty sight greeted me—a pleasant-faced sister, in her dark dress and white cap, stood just preparing to open a pot of jam which she held in her hand. A small round table, covered with a white cloth, held tea-things, bread-and-butter, and plum-cake; three or four convalescent children were seated on the floor, playing with some toys, and watching the preparations for tea with great interest; whilst behind the door on the sister's bed sat a small child, who had evidently been brought down in a blanket from his bed to share in the fun, and who was brimming over with glee and the spirits of returning health. This was the head-sister of the children's ward, who had kindly organised a small treat for some of the little ones, and was entering heartily and unselfishly into their childish glee.

So far—to the passing visitor at least—all seemed bright and cheerful in the lives of these devoted sisters; and even in the male surgical ward everything looked cheery and almost home-like. It was just tea-time, and the tea was being drawn from a bright urn in the little kitchen adjoining the ward, and passed through a window to the patients, accompanied by white plates of bread-and-butter. The first bed was occupied by a poor delicate-looking lad of about fifteen, by whose side sat his mother, vainly striving to restrain her tears, which reminded me that, bright and pleasant as everything looked, there must be many heartrending partings of dear friends to soothe, many sickening operations to witness, which would at times try hearts and nerves to the utmost.

In a large well-ordered public building like a hospital, the work is necessarily less trying than it is under other circumstances. There are rigid rules laid down as to the number of hours each nurse is to be on duty; there are stated hours for sleep and for exercise; and as it is to the advantage of a hospital to keep its nurses in good health and strength, they are well fed, healthily lodged, and a proper amount of sleep and exercise enforced. And where there is a large staff of nurses and sisters, this can be done satisfactorily; but in private cases, which the sisters often undertake, even though the same rules are bargained for, they are not often properly carried out. A conscientious nurse cannot leave her patient if there is no one at hand to take her place, and say, 'It is time for me to go out now,' or 'to go and lie down.' She is obliged to adapt herself to circumstances, which in private houses are often very uncertain, and mostly very trying. Many people think, when they have once established a 'sister' by a sick bed, they have done all that is necessary, and relieved themselves of all further responsibility. That the said sister should sometimes require a little rest and relaxation does not occur to them : they would as soon think of the invalid-chair desiring a change of scene. But what must it be for those sisters—often ladies brought up with delicacy and refinement—who go bravely to nurse the sick poor in their own homes, which are, alas, sometimes terrible dens of darkness and dirt? What is the work in the clean, light, airy, well-ordered hospital, where every necessary appliance is ready to your hand, or in the wealthy well-furnished house of the most trying patient, compared with what has to be encountered in some of the terrible courts hidden away in our midst, where dirt, disease, and poverty wrestle for the mastery? Yet there are women—many of them *ladies* in every sense of the word —who undertake this Christ-like work unflinchingly, and who, ministering humbly in obscurity and discomfort to the needs of the suffering and indigent, are faithful disciples of their Great Master.

TINSLEYS' MAGAZINE.

February 1881.

~~~

SCEPTRE AND RING.

By B. H. BUXTON,

AUTHOR OF 'JENNIE OF "THE PRINCE'S,"' 'FROM THE WINGS,' ETC.

Part the First.

CHAPTER VII.

THE GREATEST SECRET OF ALL.

MISS HARTLEY is too thorough a woman of the world, and too completely mistress of herself also, to permit any trace of disappointment to be visible on the smiling face with which she turns towards her guest. She had been put on her guard by that sharp knock at her hospitable door, and she has gone through a preparatory pantomime of sinking gracefully back into her chair (after a rapid survey of her face in the glass), while her late visitor has mounted the stairs. By the time he enters she is quite prepared to receive him, whoever he may be, and her face betrays nothing but pleasure now.

'How very, very good of you to come after all!' she cries, with more than her wonted *empressement*. 'I began to think that even you were going to make yourself conspicuous by your absence to-day, traitor!'

She lifts her hand with a pretty gesture of deprecation, and, as her eyes meet those of her most faithful, most devoted friend, she sees that there is trouble in them.

He has not come solely to see her to-day; he wants her advice, her help, perhaps. For whom?

Her heart gives a throb, so sudden and violent that she lifts her hand to her side with a gesture of pain.

'Are you not well, Diana? you do look tired and pale!' he cries, in sudden alarm; and he strives to possess himself of her hand. But she hastily moves a step backwards.

'It is *you*, on the contrary, who look pale and worried,' she says eagerly. 'I am perfectly well, and in the best possible spirits; but you are in trouble. What has happened? Can I help you in any way?'

The gallant old Baronet certainly does appear anxious, and his manner is far more preoccupied than he himself would consider complimentary to the lady in whose society he finds himself. But she understands him; she is too sensible a woman to heed such trifles as a careless manner when she knows how absolute is her sway over his every thought and action. She will put her clever finger on the key-stone of his present trouble as soon as he hints its nature to her. On that point he is confident.

'Have you seen Cyril?' he asks, and his voice betrays as much anxiety as does the dejected air with which he flings himself into a chair at his hostess's side.

'No; he has not been here at all this week,' she answers, and it is with difficulty she speaks quietly.

'I thought he would be likely to look in here on his way to Waterloo. He has little time for any adieux; but of course he would not leave without seeing you.'

'Leave! Where is he going?'

Never has Diana found it so hard to control herself before. She feels as if she must rush at her hesitating informant, and shake the truth out of him by sheer physical force.

'He is off to India; it's quite sudden. Ah, I see you have not heard?'

'To India—to *India!*' she stammers, as one who cannot believe in the sound of the words she utters.

'Of course you are surprised. Have you not heard of young Downes' sudden death?'

'I have heard *nothing!*' she says, with an odd contortion of the lips, which is certainly quite unlike a smile; and she clasps her hands and wrings them until she presses the rings she wears deep into the firm white flesh.

'Ah, you may well be surprised, then,' he answers abstractedly; and he lifts the tongs from the fender, and gently replaces a bit of burning wood upon the fire with them. 'Young Downes was to accompany Lord Greatacre on his diplomatic mission, and all was settled for an immediate start, when the poor boy (his heart was weak, they

say) fell down in a fit and died on the spot. He had excited himself too much over this hurry-flurry business, no doubt. All things are being done far too rapidly in these days to have good results.'

'But Cyril—what has this to do with Cyril?' she asks.

'Everything,' says Sir Gilbert, in his usual decisive manner. 'Young Downes' place had to be filled at an hour's notice. Cyril was proposed, I was telegraphed for, and, to make a long story short, the boy has resolved to do his duty—accept the appointment and go. He starts for Southampton to-night. They sail to-morrow. It is a case of a word and a blow. Not an hour's delay possible anywhere.'

'To-night—to-morrow?' Miss Hartley repeats the words inquiringly, as though she fails to understand their meaning. 'I cannot follow you; I do not make it out,' she says helplessly.

But his startled look at her face suddenly recalls her to herself. This is the very last man in all the world whom she can permit to guess at her secret. She forces herself to smile, and, with that effort, her fleeting wits return to her. Suddenly she grasps the situation, and, with intense eagerness, cries,

'On Thursday you told me that Cyril was going out of town for three days, and you seemed vexed because he refused to accompany you to Rivermead, and yet gave you no reason for his sudden journey, nor even hinted at his destination. Mr. Downes died last night. And Cyril was away—no one knew where. How could he accept this sudden appointment? Who offered it to him? You say it was a word and a blow. It seems to me as though the blow had preceded the explanation in this case.'

'Perhaps you are right. Great-acre telegraphed for me, and made the proposition to me, and of course I—'

'You accepted for your son? O, then he is furious, naturally! I wonder he did not throw the whole thing up on the spur of the moment.'

'I hope my son knows his duty as a gentleman too well to appear a *coward*,' says the Baronet, in hot haste. 'Fighting is imminent. There is a chance of a further brush with those accursed hill tribes. No Clive has ever shrunk from facing danger yet.'

Miss Hartley does not speak; but the sudden snap that follows Sir Gilbert's words betrays the fact that she has broken the ivory handle of the peacock fan she holds. Like most women possessed of nervous energy, she is more apt to express agitation by her hands than by her lips.

'I cannot say that Cyril likes what I have done, or the prospect before him,' resumes Sir Gilbert, a little nervous in his turn. 'But we all have to do things we don't like. That is discipline, and wholesome accordingly.'

A sudden thought flashes across Miss Hartley's active brain. She springs to her feet, and confronts her startled visitor with a threatening aspect.

'You *asked* for this appointment for your son, Sir Gilbert. Do not attempt to deny it.'

'My dear Di—'

'O you cruel, unnatural father!' she cries, and a stifled sob chokes her utterance.

'My dear child—my dear Di—' he resumes; but she will not listen.

'You are sending your son away from his home, and from all who love him, away into danger—perhaps into death!'

She cannot suppress the rising sob any longer, but breaks into a wild fit of weeping.

'Diana, my dear, my dear child, be calm. Listen to reason. I do not know you like this. You cannot suppose that I require to be taught how to love my dear boy —my only child? He is dearer to me than all the rest of the world —save one, perhaps.'

Sir Gilbert's look, and the sudden pressure of his hand on hers, once more recall Diana to a true sense of her position and her duty.

'Why, it is my love for Cyril that is influencing me now, of course,' said Sir Gilbert, thankful to see her more composed. 'I cannot allow things to go on as they have been going. There are graver dangers to be met with than a man finds in the jungle or on the field of battle. There are separations which are worse than death itself. Cyril has gradually withdrawn himself from all his friends, from all his former companions. He is never at his club, he has deserted his home entirely. When his brother-officers want him, he is nowhere to be heard of, never to be found. He has been lost to his friends and his relations as entirely as though thousands of miles separated him from us all. What does he do with himself? I will not play the spy upon my son; and he has refused all account of himself point blank. I don't mind confessing to you, Diana, that this anxiety about the boy leaves me neither rest nor peace. It is maddening! He has some secret, some undermining, preoccupying secret which weighs upon him night and day. He is sad, silent, and morose—he who was once so gay, frank, and open-hearted! I am utterly at a loss to understand this change in him. Would that I possessed some clue to the miserable mystery!' Sir Gilbert rises in his impatience, and commences to pace to and fro restlessly. 'There is a woman at the bottom of it—that, of course. And it is some woman he cannot present to me, or he would not have refused me all explanation of his mysterious conduct.'

' He may have desired to *spare* you,' says Miss Hartley.

' No, no! It is nothing low, nothing bad. Of that I am positive,' replies Sir Gilbert hotly. ' My son would never condescend to—'

' His *liaison* is certainly with one he has no reason to be proud of,' says Diana decisively, ' or he would have confessed the truth to you or —to me.'

Sir Gilbert has stood, lost in thought. This woman's lightest word never fails to make a deep impression on him.

' You think me harsh and unkind because I have resolved to send my boy off at a few hours' notice,' he says. ' You would not blame me, if you knew how I have suffered lately. I shall really be thankful for anything, even for Cyril's absence, if that serves to break through the bonds of the mysterious entanglement that holds him. I thought you would rejoice at the prospect with me, since you have certainly been as much perplexed and troubled by the change in our boy as I have.'

Diana is silent. She cannot bring herself to say that she rejoices in Cyril's departure. True, her heart has been torn by jealous anxiety for months past; but will the absence of the man she adores alter this grievous state of things? Will it not rather complicate them? If he loves the woman who has stepped between him and all his former friends and pursuits, who can tell what may happen now?

Perhaps the *creature* (how bitter are the promptings of jealous rage!) will insist on following her lover to India; or this rash decision of his father's may have the disastrous effect of forcing Cyril's hand. He may be rendered desperate by Sir Gilbert's precipitancy and throw up his commission, or commit some other act of irremediable folly.

But surely, surely, whatever has happened, or is about to happen, he will not leave London without seeing her and bidding her farewell? She is as much in the dark concerning his movements as his father is. Indeed, the late mystery shrouding his hitherto straightforward course of life has been frequently discussed between his anxious elders of late.

If she had but a gleam of light to guide her into the dark labyrinth in which the young man seems to have lost himself of late!

Is there anything she would refuse to do, if she thought she might be of use to him? Where would she not go to help, serve, or save him whom she loves with all the concentrated passion of matured womanhood? Tumultuous thoughts are agitating her as Cyril's father paces the room, in evident perturbation on his part also. She makes no further outward sign of the trouble that is racking her brain; but it tries her sorely to control herself.

Could she but know all! Any certainty must be preferable to this maddening perplexity and doubt. And yet, would it not be even worse to be assured of the fact that Cyril had given his heart to another, than to live on in the faint hope that, as yet, he had pledged himself to no woman? Suspense was horribly trying; but some certainties must be even worse to endure than prolonged doubt.

Miss Hartley was in a condition of nervous irritability that was painful to behold; for, with all her self-command, she failed to hide the restlessness that possessed her, the feverish anxiety gnawing at her heart.

Sir Gilbert had admired and loved this fascinating woman for years now; and he knew her various moods well, and mostly managed to adapt himself amiably to her caprices. But to-day she baffled him. A look of painful perplexity furrowed her broad brow, her eyes had the feverish look that betrays unshed tears. With all her strength of will, Diana had too little self-restraint to act an uncongenial part. She could not—as so many women can—smile in the face of the present lover while her heart was aching for the absent one. Her forced spirits, the seeming gaiety with which she had received her visitor, deserted her as her thoughts about Cyril became all-absorbing, and the drift of them became apparent, as she suddenly cried, with fresh animation in her tone and look,

'If the climate does not suit Cyril he will come back at once, of course.'

'O, the climate is right enough,' answered Sir Gilbert cheerfully. 'Greatacre has been out there for fifteen years, and he is as strong and hearty as possible. They live up in the hills, you know, and don't get the trying heat.'

'And he positively goes to-night?' asks Diana wistfully.

'Most certainly. He has everything packed and settled by this time, no doubt. If he should not look in upon you during the next hour, pray come up to Dover-street and give him his last cup of tea.'

'But surely he *will* come to me?' she cries; and her eyes fill with tears.

Sir Gilbert sighs impatiently.

'You could not put yourself out more, my dear, if the boy were your own. Good-night!'

'Thank Heaven he has gone at last!' mutters Diana, as the front door closes on her retreating visitor. 'I could not have borne it any longer. I should have cried aloud or fainted. O my love, my love—my last, best, fondest loved darling!'

She flings herself, face downwards, upon the sofa, and sobs as if her heart would break.

CHAPTER VIII.

CONFIDENCE AND JEALOUSY.

HALF an hour later, Luke, the butler, observant and discreet, entered the room on tiptoe, and quietly arranged the long-neglected fire. He placed fresh coals upon it, one at a time, with the tongs, avoiding the fuss and clatter in which ordinary domestics, who wantonly rejoice in noise, are apt to indulge.

Luke was surprised to see his mistress sitting moodily upon the sofa, and concluded that her visitors had tired her out. 'They do worry her so, poor dear, and she is far too indulging to them,' was his mental comment as he noticed the strange pallor of her face.

'I shall not want any dinner to-night,' she said, with a sigh; 'ask Mrs. Day to make me a good cup of coffee instead. I have a headache, and will not come down at all this evening.'

'Your dinner will not be ready for another half-hour, ma'am,' replied Luke, glancing at the clock on the mantelshelf. 'By that time I hope, for your health's sake, you may feel inclined to eat a bit. I will countermand the cutlets; but poulet marengo is a thing that mostly tempts you; and, indeed, you ought not to starve yourself, ma'am. Just think of the many fatigues that you have in the course of a day.'

'Very well, Luke, do as you

body

like,' says Miss Hartley, with a very faint smile. She is too weary to argue the point with Luke, who is certainly master in the house as far as domestic details are concerned.

'Something has put her out dreadful, poor dear; I don't know when I have seen her look so worried,' mutters the faithful servant, as he wends his way down-stairs. 'Most like it is some trouble about Master Cyril again. She do love him as though he were her own son.'

Luke has no sympathy with any perversion of the laws of nature. Personally he still regards Miss Diana as almost a child. That is for old association sake; but he is quite aware of the fact that his revered mistress is 'Master' Cyril's senior by more than fifteen years; and to suppose that she regards him with aught but a parent's love would be to asperse that dignity and good sense for which she is distinguished. While Luke is informing his wife that the mistress seems quite out of sorts, and requires a cup of coffee to rouse her a bit, a hansom drives rapidly through the outer gates of the Cottage garden, and an impatient knock at the door summons the old man up-stairs again.

This *is* 'Master Cyril.'

'Has Miss Hartley gone up to dress yet?' asks the visitor eagerly.

'No, sir, the mistress is in the drawing-room still; but she *do* seem that tired—'

Cyril Clive has no time to listen to any explanations. He is halfway up-stairs already.

'O Cyril, how thankful I am that you have come to me!' exclaims Diana, and she extends both hands in welcome as she rises to receive him. 'You would not start without seeing me; I felt sure you would not!'

She watches his face as she speaks, and her tone vibrates with

tenderness; but she always addresses him in that voice, and he knows that she loves him as a mother or a fond elder sister.

'Of course I should come to you, Di,' he answers impetuously, 'if it were only to tell you how shamefully, how cruelly I have been treated. My father seems to have forgotten that I am no longer a child, a schoolboy, and he orders me about in the most ruthless manner. I feel inclined to defy him even now, to teach him by a practical example that a man of three-and-twenty will not submit to be ordered about like a child of thirteen. Do you know what he has done, and how he has done it?'

'I know, I know it all, Cyril,' cries Diana, and tears course down her cheeks as she speaks. 'I feared your father had made a grave mistake when he told me of his precipitate action.'

'Had it not been for the imminent chance of a farther fray in Afghanistan, I should have thrown up the appointment *in toto*,' answers Cyril hotly. 'As matters stand now, however, honour necessitates my going. But the day this fresh bother about the frontier is finally settled I shall come back; that I am quite resolved upon, and then—'

'And then—' echoes Diana wistfully. She gazes straight into his clear brown eyes, and sees a strange look of trouble and tenderness melt in them that almost suggests tears.

He is silent for a while; but her inquiring glance seems to recall some fleeting thought. He holds his hand out for hers, and when she gives it to him—

'Diana, I believe, I feel sure that I may trust you implicitly,' he says, with intense earnestness, and he lingers on the last syllable as though to give it all the importance it deserves. What is to be said between them next?

Miss Hartley is hysterical to-day. The colour comes and goes in her smooth cheek, her heart beats loud and fast, although she has been standing still, watching, waiting; she is breathless. What hope throws that expectant gleam into her hungry eyes?

'Indeed, yes, you may trust me, Cyril,' she answers, and her tone is as earnest as his was. 'Believe me, I deserve your most implicit confidence.'

'I am about to ask you to do something for me, which I consider of the utmost importance,' he says; 'but before I add another word, I must insist on your faithful promise to tell no one of the service you have undertaken to render me.'

'Tell me what you expect of me,' she replies hurriedly. If she hoped for a secret which it would please her to hear, she knows already that she is doomed to disappointment.

'It is this,' he says, drawing a letter from his breast-pocket, and holding it lingeringly in his hand, as though loth to part from it. 'I want you to register this letter for me, and to post it before two o'clock to-morrow afternoon; then it will be delivered early in the evening. If I post it to-night it would reach its destination to-morrow morning, and that must not happen for several reasons. This is a matter of vital importance to me. I could not trust a servant with it, on account of the money contained in the letter, which renders registration necessary—and—and—without explaining the matter further, I would a thousand times rather confide this trust to you than to any one else I know.'

Miss Hartley receives the important letter in silence; she simply bows her head in token of assent. This is to *her*, she thinks, and her heart is filled with the bitterness of

passionate revolt. The clock upon the landing chimes eight with its clear silver bells.

'Good God, I must be off!' cries Cyril, springing to his feet, and moving hastily towards the door.

'O Cyril,' cries Diana, laying her hands eagerly upon his arm, 'don't go, don't leave me like this; you have not been here ten minutes, and it is the last time!'

Her own words sound so terrible to her, the vision of her future desolation seems so overwhelming, that she utterly breaks down. Hiding her face on his shoulder, she sobs aloud. He presses his lips gently on her soft black hair.

'My dear, kind, patient friend, I am so sorry to leave you suddenly like this,' he says.

'It would not seem so hard, Cyril, had we not been estranged of late. You have been separated from all your friends for so long now, and from me also; what has come between us? Is it from any fault of mine that I have lost your confidence?'

She has lifted her head, and is looking into his face with her tear-dimmed, anxious eyes. He turns away for a moment, but then suddenly confronting her again—

'You are my *true* friend, Di, are you not?' he says.

'Can you doubt that?' she answers reproachfully.

'I do not,' he says, 'and therefore I am resolved to tell you the whole truth—'

'Sir Gilbert Clive!' cries old Luke Day, throwing the door wide, as he ushers in the Baronet, whom for the first time he considers a troublesome guest; 'as if the poor mistress had not had enough of his visitings for one day!' grumbles the faithful servant. 'It was he who upset her before with his troublesome talk; and she has been crying over Master Cyril now, and here's more bother for her !'

'Time is up, my boy !' says Cyril's father, in a peremptory manner; 'I have brought your luggage on a cab, and the brougham is waiting for us. Come !'

The sudden and cruel parting was over. Miss Hartley was a-lone once more—alone with the crushing sense of her trouble upon her. She felt that it was greater than she could bear. Never before had she been so heart-broken, so utterly despairing, as now. This was her conviction. She was one of the women (and their number is legion) who persuade themselves that their last passion is their first. Her keen vitality enabled her to live entirely in the present; and it was this vigour of concentration which kept her youthful and fresh beyond her years. She neither looked backwards nor forwards, but enjoyed the moments as they passed thoroughly; and her emotions were as lively and keen to-day as. on that other day, so many years ago, when she first met and fell desperately in love with Lorenzo Martelli, the fascinating singing-master in Paris, who had for the time being forgotten the matrimonial ties which had held him in Naples. Highly imaginative, emotional women are apt to ignore the law of limitation as regards both evil and good. The present constitutes their all-absorbing interest. This was exactly Diana's condition, and she felt that she could never, never get over the present sorrow of losing Cyril. Never ! It is a little word, and yet it sometimes means much; but Diana's eventful past history might surely have taught her that *never* was a word that had no meaning as regarded the events chronicled in the dictionary of her

capricious career. The burden of her new grief seemed intolerable now; but the time would surely come (and it was not far distant perhaps) when she would feel able to toss this crushing weight aside as lightly as all her preceding love-troubles. Her genuine sorrow for the loss of her mother did not come under this more frivolous head. That was a true grief, and—it was tinged with remorse—therefore it stood apart from those other capricious troubles which ended in laughter.

Diana's character was certainly not one that profited by experience. She loved gaiety; she revelled in the pleasantness of life. Disappointment and sorrow were hateful, unendurable. She chafed under them as though the suffering they entailed was physical. They were as mental scalds and wounds, and she nervously shrank from and vigorously rebelled against all pain.

For more than an hour after Sir Gilbert and his son had left the Cottage, Miss Hartley paced to and fro in her pretty rose-lighted room. She was like a caged animal pierced by a well-aimed arrow.

The poisoned shaft of Cyril's sudden departure had wounded her to the quick, and she could only wail and moan, and swing her hands in helpless agony.

Poor Luke, venturing to announce that dinner was waiting, the fish 'hot and tempting,' was summarily dismissed.

'I told you I should want no dinner. I wish to be alone, undisturbed. Cannot you leave me in peace ? Go !'

The passion of grief which possessed her found a momentary relief in the sudden wrath with which she turned upon her faithful servant. And when he gently closed the door after him, she was sufficiently roused to think. She strove to collect her ideas now. She flung herself back in her chair, weary of weeping.

How short a time Cyril stayed with her! How pale and preoccupied he looked! How nervous he seemed! How utterly different from the easy-going young soldier, who had assumed an indolent manner and a low way of speaking since he joined his regiment a couple of years ago! To-day he was eager to restlessness. And that letter!

Diana sprang up, and seized it where he had laid it face downwards upon the edge of the mantelshelf.

'Remember my letter!' were the very last words he had whispered, as he pressed her hands to his lips. But until this moment she had forgotten it. Now she seized the mysterious packet.

The clue to the secret he had so carefully kept from them all was in her hands at last. For the moment her grief was ignored in the fresh fever of excitement possessing her. The letter was sealed with a large red seal. It was heavy. What were its contents? Those she could not know. But to whom was it addressed? He had been on the point of telling her 'the whole truth.' He certainly would have confided the name of the mysterious person to whom that important document was addressed.

She held the letter in her hands now, and she trembled in every limb. When she turned it over, the very legible address seemed to dance about upon the paper. But presently she read: 'Miss Olga Layton, 12 Sydney-street, Westminster.'

With a gesture of rage and despair she flung the hateful packet from her, and, worn out by the conflicting emotions of the last hours, she sank back into the armchair Sir Gilbert had left before the fire. She felt faint, very faint, very sick, very weary. If she could close her eyes for ten minutes and forget all, she would be better. Better able to understand, better able to think.

'O, do let me put you to bed, ma'am; pray do. Luke was so anxious about you having no dinner, and not answering him when he spoke to you just now. He sent me up, and I really thought you had fainted, you was so white and still. O dear Miss Diana, do let me put you to bed and get you some tea or some brandy. You are regular worn out, I'm sure!'

Motherly Mrs. Day was leaning over her mistress, when the latter opened her eyes. She felt bewildered, scarcely awake. Had she fainted, or been asleep? What had given her this terrible headache, this feeling of oppression? And her eyelids were so heavy too! Had she been crying? Yes, she had cried about Cyril—and Cyril's letter.

'I was very tired, and I must have fallen asleep, Mary,' she says, with a weary little smile; 'that is all. I am not faint; but my head aches. Go and make me some tea, strong and refreshing; you know how I like it.'

Mrs. Day nods acquiescence, and hastily departs to fulfil the welcome order.

Cyril's letter! What had she done with that letter?

As Mrs. Day leaves the room her mistress starts up from the lounging-chair.

Where is that letter? Has any one else seen it? Surely she took it from the mantelshelf, and held it in her hands when she sat upon the sofa. Yes; she had drawn the lamp closer, because she could not read the address at first.

'Miss Olga Layton.'

The name is graven in her memory now in indelible letters.

And the address?

Westminster. But what street? One quite unknown to her. And where is the letter itself? She turns the sofa pillows over; she kneels and looks below the furniture. Not a scrap of paper lies upon the carpet, and only her fan and handkerchief are on the armchair on which she has last been resting.

Then she returns to the mantelshelf. It is not there. It seems to have disappeared by witchcraft. And yet she distinctly remembers having held it in her hand. And she flung it from her, as she conjured up a vision of *Miss* Olga Layton, and pictured to herself the sort of creature for whom Cyril— *her* Cyril—had neglected all his friends. Some low-bred vulgar girl, of course. Sir Gilbert was mistaken when he thought his son could never stoop. Sydney-street, yes; that was the name. Who ever heard of Sydney-street, Westminster? It must be some out-of-the-way slum, just the place for a *Miss* Layton. Olga?—a theatrical name. Ah, a ballet-girl, no doubt. One of those shameless hussies from the Kaleidoscope or the Temple Theatre. Susie Delane would know of her, perhaps. But, meanwhile, where was that letter? It had money in it, no doubt. It was to be registered, he had said. And how earnest and impressive he was about it all! how strangely moved! O Cyril, cruel Cyril!

Miss Hartley moans and shivers. She is ill, she feels so cold. The fire has burnt very low; it is down at the third bar. Luke feared to stir it when he came in last and found her sleeping.

What is that?

She starts up, attracted by a white gleam of something in the ash-pan. It is a folded paper. Cinders lie upon it. They have evidently fallen out of the fire red-hot, and quietly, but surely, eaten their way through to letter, banknotes, and all.

Diana seizes the partly charred scraps. Yes, his writing is upon them. She reads *darling* on one, and *my own* on another. Nothing more is intelligible. The letter must have been composed of these mawkish terms of endearment, since on the only bits remaining such words stand forth as though to mock her with their cruelly tender significance. For a moment a fresh access of jealousy overwhelms her, and then a revulsion sets in. She is frightened. What has she done? What trouble and suffering will her frantic jealousy, her recklessness, cause? That letter was intended to explain his abrupt departure to the lost girl he left behind him. The money was sent to console her.

Console *her?*

Wretch that she was! Why should chaste Diana give her a thought? Was she worth it? She had tempted him, led him astray, kept him away from all his friends. Meet punishment for her if she did suffer now. She had caused more than enough misery to others already. Olga Layton!

Miss Hartley repeated the name aloud over and over again, as if to impress it upon her memory.

'Olga Layton, I hate you!' she cried at last. 'And if you have a heart, I hope that it may be broken by his absence, as mine is broken to-night. Vile, treacherous, deceitful adventuress!'

When Mrs. Day returned with a light meal temptingly set out upon a little tray, she was fairly amazed at the change in her mistress. Certainly there never had been such a one for ups and downs as Miss Diana! She had left her white, cold, almost inanimate. She found her now with flushed cheeks and sparkling eyes, eager, alert, ready to accept the meal previously disdained, grateful for the substitution of a pint of champagne for the cup of tea.

'Luke made you bring that, I know. Thank dear old Luke for me !' cries Miss Hartley, laughing. 'And here is to the health of Mr. and Mrs. Day!' she adds gaily, and lifts her glass above her head, much as the excitable Traviata does in the banquet-scene of the opera.

There certainly never was such a wonderful woman as her handsome mistress! thought meek little Mrs. Day, watching Miss Hartley with evident admiration.

From Malta, Cyril despatched a few brief lines to his old friend, and from Cairo he wrote at greater length; but in neither letter did he allude to the trust he had bestowed on her. Perhaps he feared that the letter might be read by Sir Gilbert; perhaps he did not desire to allude any further to the mystery of which he certainly at one moment intended to give his old friend the clue.

Ah, if he could but have told her all then! She must have granted whatever he desired when he was in such despair. But now the silence of estrangement had fallen between them again, and it was likely to harden during his absence. He had turned to her in his perplexity because he had none other to confide in, to trust. But his old allegiance, the perfect confidence, the strong affection he had once given her, were taken from her now. Olga Layton had come between them; Olga Layton had robbed her of those most precious gifts; and if the girl suffered from his absence and probable silence, she was righteously punished.

He had showed some anxiety about the hour in which his letter should arrive in Sydney-street. There was some one living with the girl, some parent, guardian, or employer, who had to be outwitted and deceived.

So much the better. That would restrict Cyril's inclination to write folios of endearment in future. He would never compromise any one; he would rather abstain from any correspondence, than run the risk of getting the girl he loved into trouble.

Loved?

What manner of woman was this who had so far entangled Cyril in the meshes of her fascinations as to estrange him from his parent and his friends?

Miss Hartley was suddenly possessed by an irresistible desire to see this mysterious Olga with her own eyes. She would go to Sydney-street, look about her, perhaps inquire.

She had been unable to recall the number of the house; but the dwellings there were all much alike, no doubt, and the name she should never forget!

It was about six weeks after Cyril's departure before Miss Hartley carried out her determination to reconnoitre the purlieus of Westminster. She had been lunching with a friend, a Mrs. Chapman, who lived in Albert Mansions, and had dismissed her brougham as it deposited her at her destination.

The luncheon-party at an end, Diana set forth on foot, bent on her journey of exploration.

The people of whom she inquired for Sydney-street told her to go to Chelsea; there was such a place there, but in Westminster, no.

As she was wandering up one street and down another, idly

musing on the squalor of the old slums, that seemed to be elbowed out of place by the fine new and almost palatial buildings, her thoughts travelled back to the days when Cyril probably walked over these very pavements, around these perplexing turnings, bent on visiting his *innamorata*.

'No wonder he was lost to us,' she pondered dreamily. 'No wonder he was ashamed to show his handsome troubled face to me, when he had been passing his time among such gutter-folk. The girl who lived here could only have been a *figurante* at a theatre, and that sufficiently accounts for her romantic name.'

A pretty romance indeed!

A tall elegant girl, simply dressed in a plain but well-fitting gown and jacket, passed Miss Hartley at this moment. She led a child by the hand.

'Sissy, why doesn't that nice gentleman come to see you now, who took us to the theatre and gave me a 'alf-a-crown?' the child asked eagerly.

The sister answered sharply:

'Do have done botherin'! He's off to India, I tell you. Bad luck go with him! He weren't no good to you, nor to me neither, with all his theatres and fine words and 'alf-crowns. He'll never come back no more.'

That is Olga Layton. Miss Hartley feels that Fortune has so far favoured her. The treacherous goddess has brought her face to face with her rival.

She hurries on, overtakes the girl, and addresses her. She is undeniably handsome. Bold, dark-eyed, coarse; but a typical *fine woman*. The sort of girl likely to attract young men, as presenting so thorough a contrast to the ladies with whom they are wont to associate in their mothers' houses.

'Can you direct me to Sydney-street?' asks Miss Hartley, in her most courteous tone.

'It's pulled down. We lived there a month ago. Now the railway people have bought it all up. They didn't consider the houses good enough, I s'pose, so they've destroyed the lot.'

'Thank you,' says Miss Hartley, and she bows her head and passes on.

That *was* Olga Layton. Not a doubt of it. And Sydney-street is pulled down. That demolition will account, if account be ever necessary, for the non-delivery of Cyril's letter. And of course no succeeding one can ever reach the girl now!

It is a reprieve.

Miss Hartley was an accomplished clever woman, but no logician. Few women are. She jumped at conclusions with almost incredible rapidity, and yet she was so convinced of the justice of her inferences that she would at this moment have staked a large sum of money upon their truth. That coarse handsome girl, with the fine eyes, and the cockney twang in her speech, could be no other than Olga Layton. And according to her own admission she had lived in Sydney-street until a month ago. ''Twas confirmation strong as Holy Writ.'

Miss Hartley had promised to return and dine with Mrs. Chapman. And that lady, who had known Diana for many years, was a little alarmed at her guest's unusual excitability and vehemence.

Mr. Chapman also listened in meek wonder; for he was a quiet man, who held strong-minded women in fear and abhorrence, and Diana held forth with startling eloquence to-day on many subjects which, by common consent, are left for smoking-room discussion. One dubious topic seemed to preoccupy the irate lady beyond all others, and to this she reverted again and again. She inveighed with a bitterness akin to passion against the women who make it their business to entangle young men in their toils.

'To hear Diana talk, one would think she had sons of her own whom she had to protect against flattering syrens,' remarked Mrs. Chapman to her husband when their loquacious guest had departed. 'I am quite thankful we were alone, my dear; Diana's wild talk would have shocked most people; but then we know her so well!'

Mr. Chapman smiled, and his smile was peculiar.

'Possibly her manifest anxiety is for somebody else's son,' he said; but he utterly refused to elucidate this ambiguous speech.

'I sincerely hope that Diana has outlived all nonsense of that kind,' said Mrs. Chapman, with emphasis. 'She has surely sown all her wild oats years ago.'

'She has contrived to manage a longer spell at flirtation and folly for herself than most *young* ladies, that's very certain,' replied Mr. Chapman; and both he and his wife laughed.

This was the way in which Miss Hartley's friends and acquaintances spoke of the grand passions which formed the most absorbing interest of her life.

If we could see ourselves as others see us! A wholesome profitable experience possibly, but hardly a pleasant one.

After that expedition in search of the mysterious Sydney-street, every spark of remorse in Diana's mind was extinguished. She not only justified her breach of trust to herself, but very soon came to the satisfactory conclusion that she was doing what was wisest and best for the man she adored in not acquainting him with the untoward

fate of his letter. The coarseness of that bold-eyed girl, whom she had so promptly taken for Olga Layton, shocked Miss Hartley's susceptibilities. She thought she could have borne it better had she found her rival endowed with unsurpassed attractions. It was degrading to find that she had been superseded by so common and vulgar a girl. It gave additional poignancy to her jealous grief and disappointment.

Had Olga, the Olga who had stolen Cyril's affections from all those who loved him, been a rustic Venus, Diana, who prided herself on her resemblance to the *casta diva*, fancied she could have borne the blow better. A youthful embodiment of grace and loveliness might have attractions likely to enslave a young man's fancy. But such a creature!

Thus it was Miss Hartley pondered day after day, night after night, and wildly argued the question of Cyril's infatuation. But it never occurred to her to doubt the identity of the loud-voiced girl whom she had seen in Westminster with the intended recipient of Cyril's letter. Sometimes she contrived to comfort herself with the belief that the import of that epistle was to break off the degrading *liaison* in which the young soldier had been entangled. But in that case he would have been delighted at the prospect of leaving England. And he, on the contrary, was so low-spirited, troubled, dejected.

Surmises were quite as useless now, however, as regrets. What was done could not be undone; the only possible course was to make the best of it. That girl had said, 'He's off to India, and bad luck go with him! He'll never come back.' *She* was evidently resigned to his absence, and did not even regret it. 'Bad luck go with him!'

The wretch! How could she be so cold-hearted, so cruel?

No matter; time and absence must irrevocably sever the ties that neither Diana's love nor Sir Gilbert's persuasions could loosen.

––––––––

CHAPTER IX.

DESERTED.

IT was a clear, bright, bitterly cold January evening. The sky overhead looked purple, the moon white, frozen, and the myriad shimmering stars sparkled like bright watchful eyes above; but they did not seem to smile upon the seething, angry, jostling crowd that pushed its noisy way through the populous thoroughfare known as Tottenham Court-road.

As Patty Bray emerged from the general dealer's shop, where she had just laid in some second-rate provisions, she shivered with cold, and drew her shawl closer around her shoulders.

'O my, it is a cutting wind!' she muttered: 'and I've got no money left to buy either tea or ginger; nothing to comfort my poor weak darlint. It's awful, that it is. Poor dear Miss Olga, she has to do without a power of things now. I do think we are even worse off than we were in the old days, when Miss Olga was just Miss Olga. We knew no troubles then but wanting money and that drunken old wretch her father. The unchristianlike brute, to turn his own flesh and blood out into the streets! It was summer then; St. James's Park wasn't such a bad place to sleep in, after all. But poor Miss Olga's shame and throuble! O dear, O dear! "I'm married, Patty, I'm a true wedded wife," she kept saying again and again. And how she sobbed that night! As if I ever

had a doubt about that! But, O my, what sort of a husband did she put her trust in, worse luck? Men are deceivers ever. It was that lardy-dardy soft-eyed swell; of course it was. Is her name Mrs. Strange, I wonder? She won't say, and I daren't ask again. She gets to look so wild and scared if I do. My darlint, my poor darlint! And the old brute's house has been bought away right from over his head, and now the whole lot is pulled down. Pride must have a fall. Serve him right too! Turning that angel out of doors, to roam about the streets and starve, for all he knew or cared! Well, can't you look out, you brat?' This is the exclamation which ends Patty's rambling soliloquy, as a little vulgar boy cannons up against her. 'D'ye mean to say you didn't see me?'

'I might have done, you're ugly enough,' shouts the boy, and runs off with a whistle and a yell.

'This is not a fit place for Miss Olga to live in, or to die in either,' thinks poor Patty, and tears begin to roll over her cheeks. '*Dyin*', that's what she'll be doing next, and then there will be an end of all things. A nasty low ragamuffin place I call it; and she such a real lady. But there, beggars can't be choosers, and with all the jobs I manage to get I can't scrape more than ten shillings a week together. If we was to be partickler as to our lodging now, they'd starve, both of them, the poor sick mother and the blessed baby too. O dear, O dear!'

Patty's old buoyant spirit seemed quelled. A series of sharp struggles with troubles of all kinds, want and penury preëminent among them, had robbed the faithful girl of the saucy cheerfulness which was at one time her chief characteristic. She had reached her own door now; the miserable, sun-blistered, scratched, stained portal to a most wretched home, situated in one of the narrow courts of the most poverty-stricken part of the West-Central district. Olga, her child, and the devoted Patty had been forced into this slum by impecuniosity a month ago. When first Michael Layton turned his daughter adrift with a volley of terrible curses, she, who had some money in reserve, took a modest but clean and comfortable lodging for Patty and herself. There the baby was born, and by degrees the reserve stock of money diminished and dwindled, and for the last three months Patty had managed to support the entire family by her own unremitting exertions. This was no easy matter; but its difficulties did not alarm the brave girl, and so carefully had she managed their financial arrangements, that as yet poor Olga had never known absolute want. But the wolf was approaching the door now, with silent and awful rapidity. Patty felt that her earnings were no longer proof against the gnawing teeth of threatened starvation, and to-night she mounted the steep filthy stairs to the back attic in St. Giles's-passage with a very heavy heart, an empty purse, and the final stock of cheapened provisions just purchased; on these her last penny had been expended. After the removal from their first commodious lodging, Olga had had a relapse, and the baby had almost died. Troubles never come alone, and in this instance they succeeded one another so rapidly that Patty really began to despair of their ever coming to an end. This evening she thought the culminating point had been reached at last, for this was Saturday, no more money could be earned until Monday, and the slender exchequer was empty, as were tea-caddy, coal-scuttle, and cupboard.

Never before had Patty Bray felt so heavy-hearted, so hopeless, as she did this night. Things were looking black indeed, and there seemed no ray of light anywhere. It was all very well for Miss Olga to say she was getting stronger, and would very soon be able to work. What work was the delicate darlint to undertake? She could neither scrub a floor nor cook a dinner. She could cut out and make her own clothes; but she was no dressmaker, and to please others required skill and experience. People would not pay for second-rate work. She talked of seeking an engagement in one of the grand West-end shops. But who would engage a young lady whose clothes were patched and darned in order to keep them together? And if Miss Olga should get a situation and go out by the day, what in the world would become of that unfortunate baby?

'You're a blessed darlint, in course!' exclaimed Patty, as she heard the little one within the room set up a lusty scream; 'but I ofttimes wish, my deary, that you had never been born. That would have been better for *her*, and me too perhaps.'

But though Patty grumbled, she smiled too. She loved the baby, and its cry brought a gleam of the old brightness back into her homely face, which changed to a look of alarm, as she opened the door of the attic, and saw her young mistress standing by the grimy window with her hat and cloak on.

'Halloo!' cries Patty, 'what is the meaning of this? You're never going out, my deary, are you?'

'Yes, Patty, I am.'

'Why, my darlint? Whatever are you a-thinking of doin' of now?'

Patty speaks in a tone of protest that rises to the pathos of entreaty.

'I feel so much stronger and braver to-night, Patty, that I am determined to go out and try to make some money. Baby and I have had a long sleep this afternoon that has refreshed me, and I had the most wonderful dream too, Patty!'

'I knew something had done you good, for certain sure, Miss Olga; I saw it in your eyes,' says Patty, looking at her mistress with fond admiration.

Olga is very beautiful now. Mental sorrow and physical suffering have transformed the gentle yielding girl into a proud self-possessed woman. Grief has not crushed, but it has matured, strengthened her. The small kissable mouth, that erst looked childish and pouting, is compressed with an air of decision. The well-shaped head is carried higher, the little chin raised almost defiantly. The oval face is very pale now; even the faint blush-rose hue has died out of it, leaving it white almost to transparency.

No wonder Patty had such grave doubts as to her mistress surviving her troubles. If it had not been for her child's sake she would probably have succumbed, and fretted herself into her grave. But the mother's instinct beat strong and true in her brave young heart, and, for the sake of her little daughter, Olga clung to life with the energy of despair.

She looked very lovely at this time, and yet so ethereal that her faithful servant's expression, 'She do but want wings to carry her out of this miserable world,' seemed warranted. But the tears that had washed the blue depths of her eyes had intensified their colour, and not dimmed them. For her baby's sake the brave girl resolved to conquer her trouble, and once she had fairly met it face to face, her courage revived—a phœnix of

fresh enterprise arising from the bitter ashes of dead hopes.

'Now do 'ee tell me what your dream was about, Miss Olga,' asks Patty, after a long silence. 'Maybe it'll make me feel brighter, too; I always did have a kind of belief in dreams. They often comes true when they're good ones, you know.'

Olga answers with increased animation now, and a hopeful smile lights up her face.

'I dreamt that I stood before a crowd of people—fine people, such as sit in boxes at theatres, you know, Patty. I had been singing—I know which songs they were—and I heard the people clapping their hands. That made me feel very glad. And then I made my curtsy, and a tall handsome lady dressed in red velvet came towards me, carrying a golden crown in her hands. "That is for you, Olga," she said. "You have won it, and you shall wear it; *nil desperandum!*" That means never despair, Patty. And I will not despair. That was more than a dream. I know it, I feel it. Our Father in heaven, who is merciful to the least of His children, has sent me a vision to rouse and to comfort me, and I will accept the warning, and act upon it!'

She speaks and looks as one inspired. There is a new brightness in her eyes, and her voice has a ring in it which thrills even Patty with renewed hope.

'And whatever is it you are going to do, mistress darlint?' she asks eagerly.

'To sing in the streets, as I did once before,' says Olga promptly; but there is no indication of a happy mystery in her face now. Patty remembers the evening distinctly on which Olga once before alluded to her singing in the street.

How strangely excited, how

bright and glad, her poor mistress seemed then! It was on the dreadful night when she (Patty) had been sent out of the way to pawn the shawl, and that wicked designing Mr. Strange had stayed talking so long with Miss Olga. And by and by Michael Layton had lifted his hand against his daughter (the brute!).

Yes, that was the beginning of all the secret troubles, thought Patty sadly, and where and when would they reach the end of them?

'But it is a bitter bad night for you to set off singing in the streets, my darlint!' exclaims Patty suddenly, reverting to the present, as the bundle of red flannel upon the bed moves, stretches, and cries aloud. 'You are not strong enough to walk about that way yet. Indeed you are not. Who knows what may happen to you, deary?'

'I do,' answers Olga quite cheerfully. 'All sorts of good things will happen now. I shall bring home heaps of money for you and our baby, my one good faithful friend.'

She moves towards the door, afraid of being detained at this last moment.

'Take care of my blessing,' she cries, lifting the bundle from the bed, and kissing its small face tenderly before she hands it to Patty.

A minute later she has left the dingy house, and is out in the bright noisy street, bent on setting forth upon her new and perilous enterprise as speedily and hopefully as may be.

It was nearly eight months ago now since Michael Layton had turned his daughter out of his house, to roam the streets or starve, for aught he cared. This was the view indignant Patty took of his harsh conduct. And he

was sober when he insisted on Olga's instant departure from the poor shelter of such a home as he had given her. This unwonted condition of his made the ejectment the more terrible, as it seemed irrevocable, and the unhappy girl did not even seek to combat his rash and cruel decision. But before that final degradation fell upon her, Olga's heart was well-nigh broken, and she had come to such a pass of misery that it seemed as if nothing worse could possibly happen to her.

There is a climax to agony which, once reached, deadens the feeling of the sufferer. After the anguish Olga had endured for her husband's sake, all other troublous burdens must seem easy, and a merciful Providence sheltered her broken spirit in a cloud of indifference. For a time she ceased to feel acutely. Grief had petrified her vitality; she took little heed of what went on about her. Nothing could hurt her much now; no pain could ever surpass the pain her heart's lord had caused her.

She had gone to him in Great George-street as usual one morning, and had spent some hours in his studio with him, posing as his model for that sketchy picture which advanced so slowly, chatting, reading, working, and perfectly happy, as his presence always made her. It was Friday, the first Friday in November.

'I shall have to say good-bye to my darling until Monday,' he told her. 'I am going out of town on business and—on pleasure. The business has to do with money matters; if I can settle certain things as I hope to do, I shall be in so satisfactory a position that I can tell your father about our marriage at once, and feel sure of his approval beforehand.'

'And the pleasure?' Olga asked wistfully.

'The pleasure is to look at a dear little country cottage that belongs to a friend of mine, and which I believe he will let us have furnished for a year. There you can fit up a couple of rooms for your father, and we will keep him quiet and out of the way of temptation. If the place is what I hope and expect, I shall take you down next week to see it; so you will have to find some excuse for staying away all day.'

The idea of parting from her husband for three days was very terrible to Olga; but she acquiesced in his decision without question or protest. She believed in him implicitly, and she felt fully satisfied that his decrees were always right and just. Besides, he was going to hasten matters, so that her father might soon learn the truth about her marriage now; and if Cuthbert could arrange everything as satisfactorily as he said, what a bright happy future was in store for them all!

'If by any chance I cannot get back on Monday morning,' were his last words, 'you shall have a letter that afternoon, giving you a full account of myself, of what I have done and purpose doing; and on Tuesday you will be with me as soon as you can slip out, won't you, my darling?'

'Be sure to write to me on Monday,' pleads Olga; 'but pray be careful to send your letter off so that it reaches me when father is not at home. Six o'clock in the evening is always safe, you know.'

She was very impressive, poor child; for her father's violence had increased of late, and he kept her in a state of perpetual terror; but of this she told her husband nothing.

'Of course I will be careful for your sake, my precious one,' was Cuthbert's prompt assurance. 'A letter at six on Monday, and our next merry meeting here on Tuesday as near eleven as you can manage to come. Trust me, my wife, and all will be well.'

Of course she trusted him entirely. When she was preparing to take her leave—

'I have just received a banknote,' he said, 'and I want you to take care of it for me, wife. It is not safe to travel about with so much money in one's purse.' And then he handed her a note for twenty pounds.

She had made a little silk bag, in which she wore her 'talisman' (her dead mother's thin old wedding-ring) and her own new massive one. Now she added the crisp bank-note to these treasures.

No letter came by the six-o'clock post on Monday.

It was a little disappointment; but he had been too busy to write. He would be back to-morrow, and then he could tell her all, and to listen to his dear voice would be better than reading any letter, even his.

Since her marriage Olga had never spent an entire day without seeing her husband; and now they had been separated almost a hundred hours! A weary, weary time.

Next morning she counted the chimes and the striking of Westminster clock with quite a feverish impatience.

Would her father never go away and leave her free?

At last Michael Layton departed in no very amiable mood. But what did that matter? What did anything matter, since all would so soon be made right and clear? This trying separation would be amply atoned for by the news Cuthbert was going to bring her. The news that all was so far satisfactorily arranged, and that Michael Layton himself could not possibly object when he heard of her clandestine marriage.

This glad intelligence Cuthbert had promised to bring her; and, of course, all would be well.

With a beating heart and very light feet, she danced forth from her dingy lodging, crossed the dismal old street, and was soon on the broad stairs that led to her now happy home.

He had returned, of course! She had used the latch-key below; and when she reached the door of the 'studio' she tapped with trembling fingers.

In another moment she would be in her husband's arms!

There was no response to her hurried knock.

She waited anxiously; but she was not impatient. It was only a question of minutes, of course; and he had never failed her. Never been absent on her arrival.

The minutes grew into an hour. 'Something has detained him; I will come back this afternoon,' she thought, and went her way a little sorrowfully; but she did not go far.

She paced the street up and down, backwards and forwards. She could not tear herself away, when any moment might bring *him* in view. How many times did her expectant fancy imagine it was he who turned the corner of the street hurriedly, walking towards her with quick eager steps! But when the individual she was thus watching came nearer, how different was he from the man she admired above all others! A sickening feeling of disappointment possessed her as the great Westminster clock boomed *one*. She must leave without seeing her husband. Duty called her back to Sydney-street. Her father might return at any moment, and she must be at home to receive him.

Well, she would come back in the afternoon. And so she did, poor girl; but this time the housekeeper met her in the hall.

'Is Mr. Strange out of town?' inquired the matron, eyeing the visitor's troubled face, with suspicion upon her own.

'He left on Friday, but promised to be here this morning, and asked me to come as usual.'

'O, he did, did he? Well, it's no use your going up-stairs; for he ain't there now, and what's more, he ain't coming back here at all.'

'What do you mean?' asked Olga.

'This,' said the matron, 'which I received from Mr. Urquhart this morning. I know nothing about your Mr. Strange, nor I don't want. He's a mysterious gent, and he has never said a word to me, although all the other gentlemen as has chambers here is always most polite.'

'Please let me see,' asked Olga, holding her hand for the telegram, which the stout matron had at last managed to extricate from the depths of her pocket, and was smoothing between her plump hands.

'You seem to be in a mighty hurry,' she said, glad to show her disapproval to the girl who had never stayed to chat on her daily journeys up and down stairs.

'Pray let me see!' cried Olga, and held out her hands again eagerly.

'Tis from Mr. Urquhart, who lent his rooms to *that* Mr. Strange,' said the matron; 'and this is the message:

"Get my rooms ready for this day week. My friend's things will remain. He has left England."'

'Give it to me! Let me see!' cried Olga, and she snatched the pink paper out of the astonished woman's hands.

Thereupon followed a volley of long pent-up abuse from the irate matron. She said terrible things to frighten Olga, and, suddenly seizing the bewildered girl's arm, forcibly ejected her from the house, the ''igh-class respectability' of which was endangered by her presence.

Such was the housekeeper's verdict. Instinct, the instinct of the hunted animal, rather than the reasoning powers of a woman, led Olga safely home. She went through the day automatically.

'Wake up, girl; are you drunk?' her father cried brutally.

But she was past rousing.

'I am ill to-day; let me be,' she said quietly; and something in her voice or in her haggard face checked the coarse words that came so readily to Michael Layton's lips.

'You are always ill now. What ails you, girl?' he asked again, after a few weary days had been lived through, she scarcely knew how.

'I shall soon be better, father dear; be patient with me for a little while,' she had answered; and she looked so wofully like her dead mother that Michael was awed into silence, and for some time to come he brought home his salary, and bade Olga feed herself up better.

'I do believe I've been starving you,' he said, with totally unexpected contrition.

The anxious days of doubt and perplexity lengthen into weeks, the weeks into a month, and no solution has been offered to poor Olga for the miserable enigma that bewilders her, and leaves her no rest night or day.

'Meine Ruh' ist hin; mein Herz ist schwer,
Ich finde sie nimmer und nimmer mehr.'

Her mother had often sung poor Gretchen's pathetic lamentation when Olga was still a child; but the memory of love is strangely retentive, and the sad phrases echoed in the deserted girl's brain now with cruel iteration. Her parents had spent two years in Berlin on their return from Russia, and Olga had attended a good German school during that time. She was a bright intelligent girl, and learnt with pleasure and ease. She so thoroughly mastered the language, too (conversationally), that she never forgot it afterwards; and as her mother loved to sing Schubert's songs, Olga had the opportunity of improving her knowledge, and those favourite songs took root in her mind.

One evening Michael Layton, who happened to be sober, heard Gretchen's plaint uttered in his daughter's thrilling voice.

'Sing out, my girl! Let me hear that!' he cried. 'You'll do. You'll make your *début* one of these fine days, and electrify some of them yet, I can tell you. Sing out!'

Olga stood up and obeyed. She did sing out. Her secret, her suffering, her bitter grief, all were poured forth in the lamentation of that erring, heart-broken sister of hers, Goethe's Gretchen.

'By the powers that be!' shouted old Michael, in whom the fire of the musician was not quite extinguished by drink, 'you've electrified me, my girl; and there's the stuff for success in you. You've got your poor mother's own sweet powerful voice—a clear delicious soprano—ringing, true. And you have twice her stamina. You're full-chested, strong, like me. Your poor mother was pigeon-breasted, always delicate, always ailing. Such a trial for me, you know!'

But there was something apart from his daughter's voice and her charming rendering of the eloquent words of the song that arrested old Michael's attention as she stood before him. He began to watch her curiously, as he had never watched before. When he was sober he bade her sing again and again, night after night; and when he was drunk he also insisted on hearing her songs, and drowned them in hideous clamour of glasses and fists, with which he knocked the table in deafening applause.

Patty also watched her sweet mistress in growing anxiety. She saw the lines which haggard care was drawing upon the lovely young face; she noted the cloud of despair which settled upon the now lowly-bent head; and she noted the continued absence of Mr. Strange with surprise, and, after a while, with dismay.

And all this time Olga never doubted her husband's loyalty and truth. Something had happened. Some business of vast importance to him, and of which he had not been able to tell her the details, had suddenly called him abroad. He was prevented from writing to her, and of course he had not telegraphed to her, fearing to compromise her with her suspicious violent parent. There were surely valid reasons for his silence, if only she took the trouble to regard the affair from *his* point of view. One of these days—to-day, to-morrow, or next week—he would return, surely, surely, unless—and this was the deepest and really crushing anxiety for the poor young wife—unless he had met with some accident. She could ask no one, she knew naught of his family or friends. He had never alluded to either. And she had no means of finding anything out for herself.

Something had happened!

Each passing day increased the strength of that conviction, and soon it became firmly rooted in Olga's mind. At last her husband's absolute silence led her to the fatal inference that he was dead. And she could consult no one in this miserable perplexity. There was none to whom she could turn for sympathy, advice, or consolation. Once she so far did violence to her feelings as to return to Great George-street, bent on an interview with the housekeeper, and subsequently, perhaps, with her husband's friend, the owner of the rooms on the second floor.

'You dare to show your face here again, you shameless hussy!' cried the indignant matron, as she came to the door in answer to poor Olga's modest summons.

'I should be so thankful if you would allow me to see Mr. Urquhart for five minutes,' pleaded the girl, with great earnestness.

'I shall be thankful if you will hand over Mr. Urquhart's latch-key this moment, or I'll get a policeman to make you.'

This was the housekeeper's ultimatum; and Olga, handing over the latch-key, felt that she gave away the last link of the happy chain that had connected her with the glad days of that past honeymoon.

Sometimes the necessity of confiding all her troubles to some one tempted the wretched girl to unbosom herself to Patty, that faithful friend of her own and her dead mother. Her mother! She herself would be a mother some day; and then—

Cuthbert's intense dislike to Patty had sealed his wife's lips in the first instance, for her love had taken the form of blind faith and unquestioning obedience; and now a sense of shame, and a shrinking from the exposure of her heart's deepest secret, kept her silent.

Nobody knew of her marriage. Cuthbert had taken out a license, and arranged all the details with the registrar, who had obligingly provided witnesses for the ceremony.

'We don't profess to do this part of the business,' the official had said doubtfully; 'but a bank-note is apt to overcome technical objections where the recipient, though honest, is poor, and knows that no question of law or morality is involved.

Patty had certainly suspected that the 'young swell,' of whom she so thoroughly disapproved, was paying his court (keeping company, she called it) to Miss Olga. But though the girl was rough and uncouth in her manners, she had a natural delicacy of feeling, and had long before this ascertained that her revered mistress was not one who liked chaff. So, with a forbearance that many of her superiors would do well to imitate, she abstained from all allusion to the 'sweethearting,' which she more than suspected. She asked no question, made no comment; and Olga was deeply grateful for this discretion.

But after that evening when she came back from her charing and found Miss Olga looking like a ghost, and seeming so strangely indifferent to all around her, Patty felt sure something was very wrong. Then, in a month or two, Olga began to sing to her father, and her voice thrilled Patty with the strangest emotion.

'How scared Miss Olga looked, how quiet and indifferent she seemed!' thought simple Patty, wondering and anxious. 'And that Mr. Strange—what had become of him?'

Long after he left his back room in Sydney-street he used to return to the house in the evening to have a chat with Miss Layton. But for more than two months he stayed away altogether, and then Miss Olga ceased to mention his name. At one time it was constantly on her lips, and it was always pronounced with a smile and a blush. But after he ceased to pay his regular visits, Olga never alluded to him at all.

And then—one night Patty knew the worst, and all her secret fears were suddenly defined and realised. Her mistress rushed into the maid's little attic after she had laid down on her miserable truckle-bed, and said, in a frightened whisper,

'O Patty, take me away, take me away; hide me, save me! My father has turned me out of his home for ever! He has cursed me, Patty, cursed me, and disowned me! But I am married, Patty. I am a truly wedded wife, and my poor husband is—dead!'

She felt that she spoke the truth as she uttered the word at last that had haunted her for months. And Patty, seeing her frenzied state, forbore to ask questions. She would know all in good time, no doubt.

A period of much suffering and countless hardships followed the expulsion of Olga from her father's home. But, when things were at the worst, she reluctantly handed the bank-note her husband had given her to take care of to faithful Patty. With replenished funds, a modest but comfortable lodging was taken in Camden Town; and there the baby was born.

In obedience to her mistress, Patty went back to Sydney-street once a week to inquire for letters; but there were none; and the fourth time the faithful maid was despatched on her errand she found the old tumble-down houses razed to the ground, and no one knew what had become of the impecunious landlord or his disreputable lodger, Layton. Patty now had more than enough to do in looking after her mistress and the precious baby, besides earning as many shillings as her willing hands could obtain.

The baby was a bright good-tempered little creature. She was stout and healthy, had fine limbs and sound lungs, and soon became the delight and idol of the two women, who watched her with jealous eyes and loving care.

Olga had been ailing for a long time after the birth of her child, and even now was still very delicate. The twenty pounds, though rigorously economised, had dwindled down to nothing in the course of six weary months. And when Patty spent her hardly-earned wages at that second-rate provision-shop in the neighbourhood of Tottenham Court-road, she really was at a loss how to raise the shilling which certainly would be necessary for the support of her mistress and herself until the following Monday. It was at this crisis that Olga asserted herself, and courageously declared her intention of setting forth once again on the ambiguous errand of singing in the street, and thus earning the absolutely necessary money for the morrow's bread.

CHAPTER X.

NOT DESPAIRING.

THE district known as West Central certainly does not offer facilities to those requiring an attentive audience; and this is what Olga seeks, as she wends her way westwards as briskly as her scant strength permits. In a quiet side street leading out of Regent-street she manages to obtain a hearing and—a shilling.

She has stood before a lodging-house, and two heads have looked out from behind the drawing-room blinds—the curly head of a girl and the sleeker one of a tall man. Presently the girl has opened the house-door, and, beckoning to Olga, has given her the money, hastily and without a word. Olga's voice sounds weak and trembling to herself; but, as she commences the second verse of her old favourite air from the *Amber Witch*, it rises clear and thrilling. She gains

courage, too; and she is determined not to think. Thinking would cause her to break down, of course. She wends her way still further west, into a street that abuts on Park-lane, and there she once more commences, 'When the elves at noon do pass.'

'You're to drink this, miss, it'll warm you; it's good old port. My missis sends it to you; and here's a sandwich; and then please to move on. Your singing is trembly-like, and it makes all uncomfortable.' The speaker is an old man-servant; and he waits while the shivering girl drinks the glass of wine his good-natured mistress has sent from her own dessert-table. Then he hurries back into the dining-room, and reports that the poor creature was all of a tremble with cold, and that she seemed very thankful, and also that she has now moved on.

The wine stimulates poor Olga's failing strength. She walks away with brisker steps, and the exercise warms her. With her reviving circulation her thoughts become animated also. She recalls the names of the streets she passes. She recognises Park-lane; but she refrains from going up to Grosvenor-square again. That would bring her first meeting with her husband too vividly back to her. Tears fill her eyes at the mere sight of the turning down which she hurried that bleak February evening nearly two years ago.

And he had watched her and followed her. Dear much-loved husband!

But these thoughts bring more tears; and this is no time for weeping. She must be brave, and forget all her trouble, and sing, sing merrily for her hungry child's sake.

She takes up her position before some houses that front the main road beyond Hyde Park Corner.

She receives a few coppers from passers-by and sixpence which a footman brings her. But she is told rather gruffly to move on by a stern-looking policeman; and this behest frightens her. She walks along the main road, and gets into a line with handsome shops, and there she tries her luck once more. In various instalments she receives another shilling, all in coppers. But the high-road is no fit place for her. Some of the men passing jeer at her, others pay her coarse would-be compliments, which alarm her far more than their ribald jokes. One man persistently addresses her; he stands beside her, and lays his hand upon her shoulder.

'You're far too young and pretty for this sort of squalling, my dear,' he says; and he tries to draw her hand within his arm. 'You just come along o' me,' he adds, and thinks she is coming. But she breaks away from his detaining hand with a frightened cry, and runs swiftly away down the street. 'Well, here is a go!' shouts the man, with a curse.

Olga hears him, and runs panting on and on. She has quite forgotten how far from her wretched lodging she has already strayed; and she is determined to find some quiet respectable street where she can sing one song from beginning to end without any unwelcome interruption. She has set herself a task. She will earn five shillings before she goes back to Patty. She set forth with that determination; and she has the moral fibre which is strengthened by difficulties, and resists them.

It is quite dark now, and bitterly cold still. The glow previously imparted to her delicate frame by the old wine has left her chiller than ever now. Ah, this is the sort of street she has been seeking. The houses look cosy, homelike. They are detached, and they have gardens with gates to them. Dare she enter one of those gates? Why not? There are no people in the road, and there is no echoing sound of the heavy policeman's tread. She does not feel like singing 'When the elves at noon do pass' now. Her heart is very heavy within her, and the song from the *Amber Witch* must be rendered lightly, trippingly.

She pushes a white gate back; it swings to again with a jerk, and closes behind her with a click. She is in the garden now. At the worst she can but be told to get out or move on. For a moment her pride rises in revolt at the thought of the indignity to which she exposes herself. To be ordered off like a trespasser or a beggar! She, who has lived among ladies, whose mother was truly a lady by birth and breeding; that she should have come to so pitiable a pass! But it is all for her baby's precious sake. And it shall be done.

She draws her thin shawl closely around her slender form; she straightens herself; she lifts her pretty head; she walks a few steps forward and stands close against the balustrade of the stone stairs that lead to the front door, above which a bright light is shining. The shutters of the room on the ground-floor are closed; but through the chinks a gleam penetrates. Perhaps there are people dining within. They will like a merry song; she must try!

'When the elves at noon do pass.'

There is perfect silence in the road and in the garden. Her voice rises pure, sweet, clear, and melodious.

It is for baby's sake.

She sings, and feels that she is singing well. No sign is made from the house before which she stands. Are they deaf, or indifferent, heartless, or—what? She felt so sure she should be successful here. But no; she has moved no one. Their doors, their purses, their hearts all are hard, all are cruelly closed against the outcast, the beggar. 'Meine Ruh' ist hin; mein Herz ist schwer.'

The pent-up passion of her love, her sorrow, her suffering, all are embodied in the glorious and most pathetic melody. Her heart was heavy and full to breaking; but she has found a vent in the song which seems written for her, so truly does it convey her misery, her longing and despair. And she sings it to-night as she has never sung before. For baby's sake. Suddenly the front door at the head of the broad stone steps is opened. 'The servant will throw me money or bid me get out—which?'

This is the thought in her mind, and it is followed by a swift regret that she should have sung so well to such callous listeners. But no; nothing is thrown to her; she is not ordered away. The servant descends the steps quickly, as one obeying orders with alacrity.

'Walk this way, if you please,' he says politely. 'A lady wishes to speak to you.'

And he leads the way back into the house, Olga following, wondering. She is ushered into a large comfortable dining-room. The furniture is of ebony inlaid with silver. The walls have peacock's feathers upon them, the dado is composed of twining lilies. The lamps shed a rosy gleam over everything. Bright crystal, red and white flowers ornament the dining-table, on which the dessert is laid in wondrous dishes.

Olga looks at it all, and it seems like a set-scene on the stage to her bewildered eyes.

The effect is heightened, the situation becomes more romantic still, as a lady rises from the dining-table and comes towards the singer.

The lady is tall, and her figure is elegant. She has shining dark hair, and its wavy masses fall prettily over her brow. Her eyes are bright, full of intelligence and animation. She wears a close-fitting pale-gray satin dress, and at her throat nestles a crimson rose.

Olga is fascinated, and for a time does not perceive the other occupant of the room; but presently he addresses her as Mees, and then she looks up and discovers a little man with olive complexion, a wrinkled face, and most vivacious manner.

'Who teach you to sing like zat, mees?' he cries, gesticulating fiercely.

'Don't frighten the poor child, Campo,' says the lady, and her voice sounds sweet in Olga's appreciative ears.

'You will not mind my asking you to come in, my dear,' she continues, the lady taking Olga's hand in hers and speaking very kindly. 'This gentleman is a judge of music, and he thinks that you have a marvellous voice.'

'I do not *sink*, but I do know,' says the foreigner promptly. 'And mees must tell me who teach her so well, and what next she will do with her voice. *Cielo!* but it *is* a voice!'

'You look very weary; are you tired—or—hungry?' asks the lady, with accents of tender compassion.

'I want money; I must have five shillings for the rent, and Patty, and my poor baby. O, please give me the money for my baby!' cries Olga, in sudden and almost feverish excitement. She lifts her hands in pitiful entreaty. She is overwrought. Her long fast and the heat and the scent of hothouse flowers are bewildering her senses. 'I must go home, my darling wants me; don't keep me; please don't keep me!'

As she looks up into the lady's compassionate face, her wandering glance is attracted by something above that shapely, well-poised head.

It is a picture, hanging above the mantelshelf, the life-size portrait of a boy with curling hair and round merry face and sturdy limbs. Why does her heart give that sudden throb?

She puts her hand to her side. Surely that is the picture of her own little May. It is the same round merry face. How strange! Is she dreaming, or are cold, hunger, and fatigue robbing her of her senses?

She no longer hears what they are saying to her. . . . There is a rushing sound in her bewildered ears. The lights seem dancing. . . . The lady with the crimson rose at her throat sways to and fro before her dazzled vision. Then she vanishes; there is a black cloud in her place, on which the crimson rose appears to float, and there—above—is the child's face in the picture, smiling and nodding. . . .

Olga stretches her arms upwards. The child is beckoning to her.

'I am coming, I am coming to my baby May!' she cries, tottering forward, and then falls senseless into the eagerly-extended arms of the compassionate lady.

[To be continued.]

MUSAM QUÆRIT AMATOR.

Is there no Muse
 For a lover's song?
Must he berhyme—
 And in vain—so long?

Let his beloved
 Be the fairest born,
Is there no balm
 For his soul forlorn?

How is it so
 That he least can write
Sweetest and best
 When his love's most bright?

How without song
 Can my Maud be won?
Lackaday! where
 Are the Muses gone?

       W. C. B.

THE TWO FLAGS.

A Reminiscence of Algeria.

By JOHN AUGUSTUS O'SHEA.

I.

'NOTHING yet,' said the Colonel, searching the horizon with a longing eye. 'Nothing! What can this delay mean?'

He looked again, but not a pillar of dust, the most slender, was to be seen.

'What do you think of it, Captain Fabert?' he added, addressing one of the two officers who had followed him to the mamelon —a grizzled veteran with figure full of energy, but face seamed with wrinkles and scars.

'The worst, my Colonel. Either our detachment of chasseurs was surprised on the road yesterday, and not a trooper got into Algiers, or the reinforcement we're expecting has been attacked *en route*. There's no other supposition to make.'

The Colonel shrugged his shoulders, pressed his hand on the pommel of his sword, but made no comment.

He was young for his rank, only thirty years of age, the Colonel, but he had inherited a name illustrious in France; to that accident he owed his rapid promotion. His signal personal courage and his great military skill had warded off the natural envy that dogs the spoiled child of Fortune. He was adored by the privates, and he had not an enemy even amongst the clan of old officers, the sworn detractors of the Restoration and all its belongings.

The scene narrated took place six weeks after the capitulation of Algiers, that is to say, on the 17th of August 1830, at seven in the morning. At the time the characters in our little story were ignorant of the events which had recently happened in Paris.

'*Vive Dieu!* Here we are in the middle of the mess, with nothing to hope for! So much the better! The men are biting their nails with rage and disappointment. We must only start the old tune over again, and that without losing a minute.'

The speaker was the Chevalier de Valade, a youth whose lips were hardly yet conscious of down; but he had an epaulette on his left shoulder, and a double band of gold on his képi.

'Is that your opinion, Fabert?' asked the Colonel.

'I think the game is up, and we have no resource but to turn on our heels.'

'What!' shouted De Valade indignantly.

'Tell me your reasons, Captain?'

'My reasons, Colonel, are the same that made you decide yesterday to stop the assault. This pretended biscuit-box can only be taken by artillery. *Morbleu!* Whose is the fault?' continued Fabert. 'The Marshal was badly served by his spies, that's all. A battalion is sent on the service with five-and-twenty chasseurs, and not even a rocket-tube! It was too much and too little. They thought we had nothing but a pigeon-house to smash in; and here we are, staring at an infernal fortress that a *tobdji* could defend against an army without cannon. Success was impossible.'

'Impossible !' echoed De Valade. 'I have heard it said that in the time of the Emperor nothing was impossible.'

Fabert looked at him, and in his calmest voice said,

'A mistake, Monsieur le Chevalier. In the time of the Emperor there was one thing impossible, that a raw recruit should try to teach his business to an old soldier.'

De Valade grew purple with anger, and was about to reply ; but a glance from the Colonel closed his mouth.

'You forget, gentlemen, that we are in front of the enemy !'

This simple reminder, short and severe, stopped altercation. They rested yet a little while on the rock, from whose summit they could command a vast spread of country, a succession of arid plains and parched ridges, and the blue background of the Mediterranean, on which gleamed whitely in the sun the domes and minarets of the barbaric city. On a plateau at a short distance off bivouacked the battalion. Farther back came out in relief on the sky the Arab *bordj*, whose guns protruded, their muzzles painted red—the colour of their messages of blood—from the grim black embrasures. Surrounded by fantastic crags, there was but one access to this redoubtable fort, through a narrow gorge enfiladed by the cross-fire of ordnance rising in tiers.

From time to time the outline of a caftan or an embroidered vest could be caught glancing past a loophole, or the steel of a gun-barrel glimmered in the sunshine. Giant vultures, with dusky-gray wings, circled slowly round in the silent heavens.

The French camp was out of range of fire, in a dip of the ground. Near the tents the arms were piled ; the soldiers gossipped, or slept in the shade, their pocket-handkerchiefs over their faces, or busied themselves with one duty or another. Here and there could be detected the silhouette of a watchful sentinel. The affair of the previous day can have been no child's play, to judge by the number of bandaged heads and arms in slings in the camp.

As the three officers prepared to leave their post of observation, a sudden noise arrested them. It seemed as if it were the far echo of a trumpet-blast.

'At last,' cried De Valade, 'here come our artillerymen.'

They listened attentively, but the noise was not repeated ; and they began to think they had been the dupes of their senses, as travellers in mid-ocean often fancy they hear the music of church-bells. All at once the lieutenant extended his hand.

'My God !' he muttered. 'What is that ?'

He pointed to a hill on which could be distinguished white masses, like snow-flakes, moving about, gathering, spreading, and shortly, when the whole crest was covered by them, sweeping down like an avalanche.

'Humph !' growled the veteran, 'instead of Grouchy, it is Blucher.'

A wild tumult of trumpets, flutes, and drums, and an outburst of savage yells announced the approach of the enemy.

In an instant the officers had got back to the camp. Their men were already in order of battle. Every post was assigned, and all the dispositions for defence taken. From the walls of the *bordj* hurrahs and reiterated discharges saluted the unexpected aid from without. The French battalion was in a most hazardous situation—enclosed between two fires, entirely blockaded on a plateau, frowned upon by sheer pathless precipices.

———

II.

THE Bedouins halted, and their main body, in which some discipline seemed to prevail, took up ground on the surrounding heights. Although they shrieked like demons, and brandished their long matchlocks as if they were spears, they made no appearance of attacking. By and by this show of bravado ceased, and two horsemen, detaching themselves from the host, were noticed riding towards the plateau: the one waved a white handkerchief; the other, who preceded him, blew a trumpet-call.

'A *parlementaire!*' said an officer, laughing. 'Do these beggars take themselves for a civilised people?'

'They must be the tribes of the Bey of Tittery,' conjectured the Colonel; 'they are commanded by a French renegade.'

'It's just as you think, my Colonel. I know their phizzes. I saw them near Sidi-Ferruch. Look, below there, that fellow in the blue burnous, that's El Hadji Ali.'

'What the devil can the rascal have to say to us?'

The *parlementaire* was led before the staff. In a French variegated with Italian, and in a formula where Oriental affectation jostled Occidental platitude, he signified that, before the combat, the magnanimous and most illustrious Khaliph El Hadji Ali desired an interview with the commander of the French.

The Colonel came to the conclusion that he was justified in acceding to the request. A *marabout* about half way between both forces was the spot appointed for the meeting, and the two chiefs,

on horseback and without escort, proceeded thither.

The Colonel regarded this El Hadji Ali with some curiosity; for strange stories had been current in the army touching his romantic career. Rightly or wrongly, it was said that the name disguised a former officer of rank under the Empire, who had been erased from the rolls of the army after the Hundred Days, and had been cast by the whirligig of Fate amid the corsairs of Algeria, whose religion and mode of life he had adopted. The Colonel saw a large and robust patriarch, very gracefully draped in a rich burnous, and managing with consummate ease a thoroughbred charger. His countenance was cold, diplomatic, impenetrable. His thick ebon eyelashes, his piercing eye peeping from under a half-closed lid, and his swarthy complexion contrasted with the snowy beard, which fell fanlike upon his bosom.

After an interchange of salutes of the ceremonious order, the Khaliph began, in grave accents,

'Colonel, I shall not insist upon the situation. You see the overwhelming superiority of our forces. Expect no help from Algiers. The bones of your chasseurs are bleaching by the roadside. You can assure yourself of that fact by casting your eyes over some of the horses mounted by my men. Under these circumstances I come to offer you the chance of avoiding a disproportioned struggle, the issue of which cannot for a moment be—'

'Halt, sir! I have heard that you are French. Can I believe it?' interrupted the Colonel disdainfully.

The Khaliph replied, without any token of offence,

'Doubtless I have not made myself well understood, and you make a mistake as to my proposal. Yes, I am French; and I will prove to you that I do not forget it. Can my sentiments be questioned the day I welcome, after so many years, those noble colours, that glorious flag, so bitterly regretted, for which my blood was freely shed on every battlefield of Europe?'

In thus speaking, in a tone almost theatrical, but perfectly self-possessed, the Khaliph fixed a scrutinising regard upon the features of the Colonel, as if to divine the impression his words created.

'I don't understand you,' exclaimed the Colonel, stupefied.

The other paused a few instants, and then, giving way to a gesture of astonishment, demanded,

'Is it possible, Colonel, you have not heard of the news from France which arrived yesterday?'

'What the devil business of yours is it, sir?'

'Ah, I understand,' replied El Hadji Ali impassively, 'it is not my province to inform you: that should be done officially. Hearken!'

A loud and multiplied report came echoing from the distance in the still hot air. It was repeated in repercussions from the mountains like rolls of thunder, volleying in quick succession from every side. It was the cannon of Algiers.

Was there a revolt in the city?

Silence came again. Then a second concussion shook the atmosphere and made the earth quiver. A third and a fourth discharge succeeded, always at precise intervals.

What could be passing?

The Khaliph spurred his horse towards the other side of the *marabout*, from which the ramparts of Algiers could be discovered.

'If you wish the explanation of what we hear, Colonel, just turn this way, and you can read it as plainly as in the columns of the *Moniteur.*'

The Colonel did as he was asked. El Hadji Ali stretched out his arm without uttering a word, and the young officer could not restrain a cry of surprise and grief.

He was witness to something unheard of, impossible.

It was no longer the flag of Henry IV. which floated from the summit of the Kasbah of Algiers. To his amazed vision the banner which was now shaken out over the nest of pirates, which had been captured, to the shouts of 'Live the King!' was—the flag of the Revolution and the Empire—the tricolor.

'The Bourbons are dethroned,' quietly said the renegade, letting each word fall upon his listener like the stroke of a sledge-hammer. 'Charles X. has recrossed the English Channel. The ministers are in the hands of the people, who are preparing to cut off their heads. The Empire, with Napoleon II., is reëstablished.'

Never was man more suddenly or cruelly smitten to the heart. His Royalist devotedness, his dearest affections—family, country, the past and the future—all swam in misty confusion before his stunned vision. Pale, with a haggard gaze, trembling with emotion, he was the picture of one menaced by an apparition.

El Hadji Ali stood rigid as a statue, gloating on the poor officer's pitiable state, but still pointing with inexorable finger to the standard on the Kasbah.

'Now,' he said coldly at length, —'now you know why the guns of the army and the fleet are firing a salute!'

———

III.

In the horrid whirlwind of feeling which enveloped and choked him, the Colonel suddenly recollected that there was one there, a wretch who was scrutinising him, who feasted on his astonishment, his anguish, and his feebleness. By a superhuman effort of will he freed himself from the thrall of his senses, breathed more like a man, resumed the command of his faculties, and, with an admirable assumption of composure, addressed El Hadji Ali.

'It seems to me, monsieur, that this is not exactly the question that we two have met to discuss. Let us return, if you please, to our own proper affairs. What have you to propose to me?'

El Hadji Ali bowed.

'The digression was not of my seeking, Colonel,' he murmured. 'As to my proposal, here it is: we shall withdraw on condition of your withdrawing likewise. That's all. I leave you the road to Algiers uninterrupted.'

For a moment the Colonel was perplexed. Could this unexpected offer be genuine, or did it hide some deep designing plot? The conditions were so absurd on the part of the Mussulman chief that the Frenchman could not bring himself to believe in their sincerity.

The Mussulman, perceiving that some explanation was yet required, continued,

'We hope that the successor of Monsieur de Bourmont will understand better than *he* has shown himself competent to—up to this —what are the true interests of France. A formidable enemy, the Bey Bou Megraz, may become a valuable and faithful ally. I am authorised to ask you to take this message to your new General.'

The Colonel held his tongue, not that he had the faintest hesitation as to the line of conduct he should pursue, but he wished to get at the secret springs of this man's behaviour. He was anxious to ascertain the peculiar snare that was hidden under his outward benignity.

'Supposing that I accept,' he said, 'what guarantees of good faith can you offer me?'

As he spoke the words, he imagined he could catch a flash of triumph in the eyes of El Hadji Ali. The latter nevertheless answered him in a tone of almost reproachful candour.

'Ah, Colonel, so you will not trust yourself to the word of a Mussulman—prejudice of race and religion. Amongst us the word of a Christian has not a much higher value. Be it so. Exact hostages. I myself am ready to march unarmed by your side to the very gates of the town.'

As the Colonel did not answer, he added, with an ironical smile,

'Does my good faith still appear doubtful to you, Colonel?'

'It would not matter much if it did, as I am not going to put it to the test,' responded the Frenchman. 'I decline to accept your proposal.'

El Hadji Ali could not keep himself from shuddering.

'I have received, in the name of the King, orders to take that *bordj*. I intend to carry them out. My intention is the stronger and firmer, as you can quite comprehend, that it is only too probable that this is the last commission of the kind I may have the chance of being intrusted with for a long while to come.'

'Have you seriously reflected, Colonel?'

'*Ma foi*, no! This is not a thing that demands much thinking over. Pardon me, monsieur; but if you have no other overtures to make, our interview must close.'

'Colonel,' said the renegade, with a fibre of profound emotion in his voice, 'at least you will render me the justice to admit that I have done all that honour would allow to avert the combat which appears to be inevitable.'

'Can the old scoundrel have

been sincere?' thought the Colonel to himself, as he quitted the rendezvous. But he had not perseverance to try to solve the problem, so overshadowed was his mind with other preoccupations. His King was no longer on the throne. What had become of France, of his family? Who could read the future? The terrible catastrophe to the dynasty called up a thousand phantoms round him. What was his own transient difficulty, a mere routine portion of the soldier's lot, compared with this evil? To drive away gloomy bodings at a crisis when action was needful, he put his barb to a full gallop; but all of a sudden he reined up, pulling the spirited animal almost on its haunches, as he noticed, with surprise, the change in the appearance of the troops he had left behind him drawn up in steady phalanx.

IV.

THE ranks were broken as if the 'dismiss' had been sounded. Officers and privates, mixed pell-mell, were looking in the direction of Algiers. The ruling expression on their features was consternation. In fact the regiment was composed for the most part of Bretons devoted body and soul to the cause of Legitimacy.

It was a melancholy spectacle, that of those old *soldats du Roi*, the wrecks of the legendary bands of the Chouannerie, gazing at the new flag. They stood as if transformed to stone, their hands convulsively gripping their gun-barrels, despair imprinted on their rough visages framed in gray hairs. The younger men were bewildered; they turned from the flag to the veterans in mute but sullen questioning. Some had thrown away their arms. Lads of sixteen lay on the ground, and wept with their heads in their hands.

An awesome silence reigned in the crowd.

But, at the other extremity of the plateau, a group of about a hundred men presented an aspect widely different. They were drunk with joy; they held aloft their shakoes on the muzzles of their muskets; they laughed, burst into acclamations, jumped, embraced each other, and acted altogether like delighted schoolboys. They had gone mad with enthusiasm. Now and again they fixed a threatening frown on their Royalist comrades, and on the white flag sprinkled with golden lilies which was borne unfurled by the *porte-drapeau.*

The Colonel took in at a glance the meaning of the whole scene. He had there before him a tableau of the moral condition of the entire French army, the divisions which tore it asunder, the anarchy which was imminent.

Clapping his hand to his forehead, it seemed as if a ray of light had dawned on his brain.

Had he accepted El Hadji Ali's proposal, the retreat of the Royalist battalion would have been attributed to the spirit of faction; his honour as a soldier would have been compromised; every circumstance would have told against him; suspicion would have smeared · with its taint himself, his men, and all who shared their convictions; they would have become the butt of every odious accusation; and, in the midst of the general excitement, a frightful outbreak might have been provoked in Algiers which would have led to the virtual ruin of the expeditionary army.

The depth of the ambuscade was now plain to him; he penetrated the dark Machiavellianism of the renegade. The resolve he had taken was the true, the only one open to him. A fight, even though without the slightest chance of success, was an absolute necessity.

He ordered the 'assembly' to be sounded, explained the situation in a few words to his officers, and with the brevity of a man of deeds, not words, issued his orders.

The Bedouins had already opened fire. Their bullets began dropping on the surrounding boulders.

As Fabert took up his post, he approached De Valade and offered him his hand.

'Lieutenant,' he said, 'I was wrong a while ago. Will you pardon me my heat of temper?'

The loyal hand of the old Captain was grasped with as warm a cordiality as it had been proffered.

'I, too, owe you an apology, my Captain,' answered De Valade. 'I hope to pay off the score before the day is done.'

The voice of the Colonel was heard. With a proud and defiant gesture the gallant officer pointed with his naked sword to the white standard, which displayed its folds —for the last time perhaps—under the deep blue of the African sky.

''Tis the regimental flag, my lads, the same that was at Castel-Terzot, at Gaen, at the Trocadero, at Staouëli! Everywhere we carried it we held it aloft in honour. There are no stains on it but bloodstains. It was given us by France. We are not going to surrender it to any enemy. Close up your ranks, and forward!'

This short manly speech lifted the soldiers off their feet. Like a mighty blast of wind, it blew away all angry passions, all lurking differences; a flame of patriotic fervour blazed from every front.

The ancients of the Chouannerie, who had fought side by side at Corsley and Andiqués, raised their war-cry of *Vive le Roi!*

Those who were of contrary opinions held silence. Their attitude was not less determined than that of their comrades, but a smile of irony played about the corners of their mouths as they heard the *vivats.*

Captain Fabert did not like that smile. He scowled, and plucked at his *barbiche.*

The enemy drew nearer; their balls, better aimed at the shorter range, knocked over a man here and there. The ensign, with his white flag, was struck down, mortally wounded.

Fabert whispered a few words to the Colonel, called over an old *sous-officier* with a skull hard and bald as his own, gently removed the flag from under the corpse, and placing it in the hands of the veteran, cried out, in a voice that dominated all the tumult of the fusilade:

''Tis a soldier of Eylau that will carry it now! To-day let us have but one cry, my children: *Vive la France!*'

It was evening, and the great red disc of the setting sun could be discovered sinking in the west as the screen of smoke rose; it was evening, and for eleven hours a desperate combat had been waged, furious charge succeeding to charge, and bayonet parrying sword in a series of Homeric hand-to-hand duels, before the appearance of the head of a column of relief, advancing from Algiers, put El Hadji and his legions to flight. The French were masters of the battlefield; but at what a price! The battalion had lost the majority of its officers and one-third of its men. The Colonel had fallen amongst the earliest, his breast pierced through and through by a *flissa.* The body of the young leader, piously covered with his cloak, reposed behind a rock, sheltered from the bullets.

The other superior officers having been placed *hors de combat*, the command devolved upon Captain Fabert.

De Valade had also been slain. The raw recruit had fought like a veteran, had died like a hero.

The column of relief reached the plateau as the defenders of the *bordj* attempted a last despairing sortie; they were repulsed, and the French entered the fortress at the tail of the baffled Arabs.

A few instants afterwards a scene that is memorable was enacted amid the unanimous cheers of the troops.

The standard of the deposed King was hoisted by the soldier of Eylau; the standard of the *régime* that came after, the standard brought out from Algiers, was hoisted by a Breton. The two flags, the white and the tricolor, for the first and only time floated victoriously, side by side, 'in an amity cemented by blood, on the walls of the Bordj-el-Djebel.

A MORNING DREAM.

ABOVE the brackish shallows of the shore
My thoughts, like sea-birds, hover.　The bass roar
Of the unfettered breakers I can hear,
And view their surf with inward eye and ear.
Fate drew me inland from the mighty sea;
But dreams have power to cheat necessity.
Behold! I spread the ocean on the land,
I shut my eyes and pace a lonely strand.
See yonder crimson chaos in the west—
Mark how each billow rears its radiant crest!
How soon the furnace cools! A barren glare
Of saffron floods the blue ethereal air.

Anon the moon slips up the dim sea-line,
Shedding a ray like light through amber wine;
The sea-wind strengthens as the dark grows strong,
And louder rings the sea's triumphant song.
If sweet is ocean, sweet the lonely shore:
Love adds its sum of sweetness to their store.
My loved one comes to meet me, her bright hair
Flung o'er one shoulder by the freshening air.
Though sweet the sea, and sweet the lonely shore,
O loved one, add thy sweetness to their store!
Adieu, my dream! The ocean is withdrawn,
My casement shows the first faint light of dawn.

RICHARD DOWNEY.

AN IDYL OF THE WHITE RANCHE.

A Californian Sketch.

By IZA DUFFUS HARDY.

———◆———

I.

JOSIAH P. JONES, of Jonesville, California, was a proud and happy man. He had, perhaps, better reason for pride and happiness in general than any other man in the neighbourhood. Jonesville was a flourishing town; there were not many failures there, but few such successes as his. Had he not the most fertile lands, the finest ranche, the most stalwart sons, and the fairest daughters of any man for miles around? Had not the *Daily Occidental*—the local paper—dubbed him 'The Big Bug of our Happy Valley'?—a compliment of which he was sincerely proud. He had owned nearly the whole of the said Happy Valley, and was reported to have made a fortune out of what he sold, as well as reaped a fortune out of what he kept. He had bought and settled on the land when his ranche was the only human habitation in sight. Jonesville had arisen on his ground; he had planned the streets, and marked out the lots himself, and had watched the settlement grow up from one wooden shed into a thriving town. Of course that first shed had been a bar, where execrable liquors were sold to the travellers who passed that way; it developed into a saloon, and finally into the Grand Central Hotel. The second building had been a grocery store, and the third a meeting-house and school in one, while the gaol was the *last* public building to be erected.

Josiah P. Jones loved the town which had grown under his own eye, born of his own land, as he loved his children. Jonesville had been by general vote christened after him, in which respect it differed from his own offspring. There was not a Josiah among them. He was dissatisfied with his own name. He used to say he did not see, while there were classic names to choose from, why a parent should afflict his child with such a baptismal burden as Josiah. Accordingly his own sons were christened Coriolanus, Placidus, Lycurgus, and Antonius, and his daughters Virginia, Imogen, and Cassandra. Nor had he the faintest perception of the ludicrous in the juxtaposition of these appellations with his own patronymic.

They were a fine family; and, as I observed before, for his happiness in general he had very good ground.

This season especially his crops had prospered; and on this particular day, as he tooled his favourite team of dapple-grays at a brisk trot through the main street of Jonesville, he was proud and happy to be conducting to his ranche the guest who sat beside him.

Miss Clara Seyton, 'of London,' as she was characterised in the Hotel Registers and Social Notes, was a distant cousin of the Jones family, although they had scarcely been aware of each other's existence until Virginia Jones, being in San Francisco for a few weeks' society and shopping, met Miss

Seyton, and discovered their relationship. The two made friends rapidly, although there was not much in common between the Californian girl and her new-found English cousin, except that they both sang, and found their voices harmonise in duets, and both enjoyed with the zest of youth the gaieties of the gay Golden City.

Even here they 'wore their roses with a difference.' While society and admiration were as the wine of life to both, Virginia had tasted so little thereof that she quaffed it eagerly, all palpitating with childish pleasure, and anxious lest a drop of the sweet cup should be spilt, while her English friend enjoyed it as an every-day draught.

To Virginia it was fresh, sparkling, and effervescing; to Miss Seyton it was pleasant, but somewhat flat. She had gone through three London seasons, and one in New York; had been reported as 'the dazzling English blonde' at Saratoga, and taken her degree in flirtation there. Society was to her a necessity of life, admiration as the very air she breathed, although occasionally moods of reaction and world-weariness came upon her, in which she vaguely longed for something beyond it all —she knew not what; and thought of rest and peace and love as, after all, the sweet things of life, and sickened at the whirl of the world in its mad dazzling round of pleasure. Such moods were all unknown to bright light-hearted Virginia, frank and gay, though honestly weary sometimes of the quiet life at the White Ranche, and revelling with childish joy in her rare visits to the city.

When Mr. Jones came to fetch his daughter home he was as delighted as she was with their new-found 'cousin,' as they chose to call her, although the connection was but a very distant one. Their

cordial invitation to her to visit them at Jonesville was seconded by an equally cordial letter from good Mrs. Jones; and so it happened that Miss Seyton, who was getting a little fatigued with late hours and dancing, and surfeited with the devotion of one or two San Franciscan admirers, sat this day in Mr. Jones's buggy, behind his favourite grays, on their way from the railway-station, some five miles off, to the White Ranche.

Having passed through the town, they slackened pace on a road like a strip of new-ploughed field, over which they bumped at as solemn a step as if going to a funeral. Miss Seyton was just wondering if all the roads in the neighbourhood resembled this, when Mr. Jones caressed the near horse's ear with his long whip, and observed,

'G'lang, old fellow; we're getting home now. See, Miss Clara, there's our goal!'

'*Which* is the Ranche?' she inquired, looking in the direction indicated, some distance ahead, and surveying a large group of buildings, mostly painted white, scattered, with liberal spaces between them, over a considerable tract of ground.

'Why, *that!*' he replied, waving his whip comprehensively; 'it's *all* the Ranche.'

'But—it looks like a village,' Miss Seyton said, glancing from roof to roof of the many cottage-like edifices.

'Ha, ha!' laughed Mr. Jones, with an explosion of delighted mirth. 'So all strangers say!' And, indeed, the collection of buildings might have put in a very fair claim to be entitled a 'city' in the Far West. 'This is my avenue,' the lord of the land observed presently, introducing a long stretch of smooth sunny road, bordered by sapling trees carefully planted out in boxes. 'Eucalyptus all these; and those are our native acacia. We have to enclose them, you see, because of the gophers. They eat the roots away. They've killed that one, you see, in spite of all my care; the root's quite gone. It was a fine young tree!'

Mr. Jones heaved a regretful sigh, and then, as the dapple-grays trotted briskly round a turning, and through the outlying 'village' of the Ranche, he proceeded to introduce the various edifices as they passed them.

'This is our water-work tower. The well's sixty feet deep. My boy Coriolanus dug it, and Lycurgus built the mill. He's a born engineer is Lycurgus. Pretty piece of architecture, isn't it? That's the blacksmith's shed. Lycurgus put up the forge too. That's the coach-house; and there's the granary—our new granary; Coriolanus and Antonius built it. There's the old one; we use it as a lumber-shed now. See those three gables?—that's the barn. Coriolanus's work, those gables.'

'But really did they do all that work themselves? with their own hands?'

'With their own hands, and tools,' Mr. Jones replied literally; 'how else? I made *my* way, Miss Clara, with my own hands, and my boys must do the same.'

'Not quite the same; for they start with the advantage of their father's success,' she said, smiling.

'And where would my success have been if I hadn't worked for it?' he rejoined. 'If I'd gone in for keeping my hands white when I came out here, I shouldn't have stood where I am to-day.'

They now arrived at a great wall of *adobe*, or sun-dried brick, which looks exactly like solidified London mud. An archway in the wall, wherein swung a rude wooden gate, admitted them to the court-yard. The square was bounded on one side by the house, on two others by kitchens and outhouses, and on the fourth by a long *adobe* building, which, like the wall, was a relic of the early Spanish days of California.

Miss Seyton looked at the house, and her countenance unconsciously elongated a little. She had expected the Jones dwelling, the centre of so much outlying architecture, to be a handsome residence. But lo! here was a long low wooden 'frame-house,' very plain, very much weather-beaten, with narrow slits of windows cut up into little lattice-panes. It reminded her instantly and unpleasantly of the bailiff's cottage on her uncle's estate at home—only the bailiff's cottage was in rather better condition. Mr. Jones drew up at his door with a flourish and a satisfied smile. *He* thought his home a palace; and so, in truth, it was to him—a palace wherein all his household gods were throned.

'Here, Imogen, Virginia, Cassie! —here we are!—here she is!' he exclaimed, as the door was flung hospitably wide, and the whole family—at least all the female members thereof—swarmed out to give Miss Seyton affectionate welcome. Here was Mrs. Jones, kind, faded, and careworn; here were Virginia and Imogen, fresh and bright as morning; here was shrill-voiced, apple-cheeked little Cassandra, *ætate* twelve; here also were two or three farm-labourers, two China-men in blouse and pigtail, and a half-breed Indian with a huge ragged hat and bare feet. Miss Seyton surveyed these domestics with approbation. To Chinese attendants she was well accustomed; but the Indian was quite in keeping with her ideal of *ranche* life: she only wished there had been more of him!

She looked round the Jones family, and liked them all. She also charmed them—not that this was anything very new to her, who was used to charming. Her beauty rendered her way in life an easy one, seconded as it was by her animated sweetness of manner, lightened up by flashes of bewitching sauciness, and occasionally sinking into a pensiveness which had done unaccountable execution amongst the stronger sex.

Virginia and Imogen conducted her over the house, their three voices blending in a babble of girlish chat and laughter. The parlour was handsomely furnished, albeit the ceiling was low and the windows small. Miss Seyton noted with pleasure the Steinway piano, the pile of music, the goodly array of literature of every class, from Darwin and Gibbon down to the last number of her old friend *Punch.* The dining-room was an immense barn of a room — unceiled, uncarpeted, unpapered, but every foot of smooth-planed timbers clean as a fresh sheet of note-paper; with a few chromos, mostly taken from the illustrated papers, ornamenting the wooden walls; with a liberal supply of luxurious rocking-chairs; with a huge old-fashioned fireplace big enough to be used as a room, a mountainous pile of logs blazing on the hearthstone; a long table at which a regiment might dine, and on which the cloth laid for the very respectable number of the Jones family looked like an oasis in a desert.

The dinner, cooked by Wong Lee, and served by Sing Hi, was the usual American meal—a lavish procession of dishes, admirably stewed, boiled, baked, and fried, with never a roast among them.

'And where are your sons?' the guest inquired, observing the absence of the young gentlemen with the classic cognomens.

'O, they are out with the plough,' was the reply. 'They won't appear to-night; they don't get in till late, and they come home tired out.'

II.

LIFE at the White Ranche was a pleasing novelty to Clara Seyton; indeed, what novelty is not pleasing to a woman of her type? In the mornings, as they kept no female servant, Mrs. Jones and her daughters were always busy with the house-work. Not that female help was impossible to get; but they had never yet succeeded in getting the female help to stay, and they disliked the idea of having a Chinaman as chambermaid. Thus Miss Seyton had generally the morning to herself, and spent it either in roaming about the wilderness called a garden, or helping Cassie to feed the poultry; or more often sitting by the crackling wood-fire with Mr. Jones, who delighted in her company. She would sing to him, read to him, or, what he liked better still, listen while he read aloud to her. Mr. Jones often preferred reading aloud to talking. Habitually taciturn, albeit of sanguine temper, and with no shade of melancholy, he seldom talked much, except when stirred by any special subject; but he kept in his heart a love that was almost a passion for poetry and music. He was happy reading Tennyson and Byron. Jealously hoarded away, he preserved certain effusions of his own composition, never to be shown to mortal eye. He found in Clara Seyton a sympathetic listener, which in his own family he lacked. They listened with respectful admiration, but no thrill of sympathy and delight. Clara Seyton delighted in all that was beautiful, and her eyes seemed to look far away down vistas of beauty beyond earth when she listened to any lines that appealed to her easily-stirred, super-ficially-emotional nature. But her keen perception of the humorous never left her, and in her frequent moods of exuberant mirth no laughter rang more hilariously and contagiously than hers.

It was mid-winter, and yet the gardens were green as summer. Geraniums, fuchsias, and myrtle were blooming still, although more sparsely than in the floral season. The forest-trees had not a russet tinge among their evergreen leaves, whose dark hues contrasted with the tender bluish-green of the young eucalyptus or 'blue gum.' Only the grove of willows by the river betrayed the season by their bare boughs.

For the first few days Clara Seyton saw nothing of 'the boys' except the youngest one, Placidus, aged fifteen, who occasionally made his appearance at dinner. No places were ever laid for the three elder ones. It appeared that they did not even abide under the general roof, but inhabited three little houses of their own looking on the courtyard. They were up at daybreak to their work at the plough, and only returned in time to go to bed at night, so that Clara saw no sign of their presence; and although she heard them alluded to occasionally, she began almost to regard their existence as mythical. Until one evening Virginia announced gleefully,

'The boys are coming in to-night.'

Accordingly Miss Seyton was looking out anticipatorily, when, some time after dinner, there was heard a great shuffling outside the door. It opened wide, and admitted what appeared at first sight to be quite an overwhelming irruption of youthful manhood, although it presently resolved itself into three young men—all tall, all dark, all big and broad-chested, and

herding together shoulder to shoulder.

Imogen jumped up, and, seizing the foremost one by the hand, pulled him towards their guest.

'This is Clara!' she exclaimed. 'Clara, here's Lycurgus.'

'Miss Seyton,' amended Mrs. Jones.

'Eldest first, it should be!' cried Virginia, drawing the next brother forward. 'Clara, this is Coriolanus.'

'You're leaving me to introduce myself to Miss Seyton,' observed the third, and apparently the most at his ease of the three.

'There's no need for any introduction to tell that you are one of the family,' Clara replied. 'Mr. Antonius, I presume. Why, what a likeness between you all!' she added, glancing from one to another. 'Mrs. Jones, how do you ever tell them apart?'

'Why, they are not a bit alike!' exclaimed Virginia.

'Not an atom,' agreed Imogen. 'If you saw them by daylight you couldn't think they were. It's this stupid dim old lamp!'

'Why,' struck in Cassie eagerly, 'Antony is ever so much the shortest; and Lycurgus's eyes are blue' (Lycurgus here retired with alacrity into the background); 'and if you just look at Coriolanus's nose,' pursued the *enfant terrible*—whereat Coriolanus also endeavoured to efface himself, and retreated behind his brother.

'Mr. Coriolanus has evidently no intention of allowing his features to be inspected,' Clara observed demurely. 'But I have no doubt, Cassie, I shall learn to distinguish them in time. Do you know, I was beginning to regard you as mythical beings,' she added, turning to Antonius; 'I thought you were only *names*.'

'O, we're solid substantial facts enough,' he responded, smiling.

'No doubt of their solidity,' observed Mr. Jones, bringing his hand down with a sounding slap on his son's stalwart shoulder by way of corroboration.

Clara at first found Antonius the most approachable and easiest to get on with of the three; but the two elder presently waxed conversational, and before the end of the evening the last vestige of ice was completely thawed, and the rafters resounded to ringing laughter, from Cassie's shrill treble down to the bass chorus of the 'boys,' whose high-sounding appellations were, in the bosom of their family, abbreviated into Lanus, Tony, and Curgus, while Placidus was irreverently contracted into *Patch.*

The next morning at breakfast, however, no boys appeared; at luncheon ditto. Clara began to think their first appearance was also to be their last one; but in the afternoon, as she was wandering in the grounds, while Virginia and Imogen were dressing for a drive, she came face to face with one of the brothers.

'Good-evening, Miss Clara,' he said.

'Good-evening, Mr. Jones,' she replied, with sweet gravity. 'You call it evening here directly it ceases to be morning, don't you?' with an inquiring smile.

'Isn't it right?' he rejoined.

'Whatever *is*, is right,' she quoted gaily. 'Have you been at work to-day?'

'Yes, but I left off early. I'm going to town this afternoon.'

'And your brothers?'

'They're still at the plough. There they are—don't you see them?'

Miss Seyton gazed in the direction indicated, and took up a dainty eye-glass to aid her to distinguish more clearly, in a distant field, two lofty ploughs, each drawn by four horses, and, perched high up on each, a young man in the rough garb of a day-labourer.

'Yes, I see them,' she said. 'And now—you'll think I'm very short-sighted—but which are you, may I ask?'

'I'm Coriolanus.'

Miss Seyton stifled, with a hard struggle, an outburst of unseemly mirth. The perfect gravity of his reply was too much for her, with her sense of humour, to stand.

'Have you seen the little pigs?' he inquired, unconscious of her amusement, and with the directness habitual to him.

'No, not yet. Cassie was telling me about them.'

'Yes, Cassie's wild about them,' he rejoined. 'They're cunning little things. Will you come and see them?'

'I should like it,' she answered, walking willingly by his side, conscious that he was regarding her appreciatively.

She admired the nine little pigs and their fat black mother with due gravity; and Coriolanus appeared pleased with her sympathetic society, and observed, with a perceptible tone of regret, that the vehicle to take her and his sisters for their drive was ready at the door.

The girls took their drive, and paid their visits in the neighbourhood; and on their homeward way, calling for letters, fell in with Coriolanus at the Jonesville post-office. It happened that Virginia had hospitably invited two young ladies to return to the Ranche and spend the evening; and to take them both in the rockaway, which Virginia was driving, would be rather close packing. Coriolanus had his light buggy, with room for two; and his sister was about to suggest that he might drive one of the Misses Leslie, when the young man somewhat hastily put in his own suggestion.

'Won't you drive back in the

buggy?' he inquired, addressing Miss Seyton. 'Yes? Say, Virginia, I'll drive Miss Clara.'

'You won't be afraid of Lanus's horse, Clara?' suggested Imogen; 'he's kind of lively, but there's no harm in him.'

'She's not afraid of anything, I'm sure,' Coriolanus answered for her, and offered his hand to help her up into the vehicle.

They were not a very talkative pair. Coriolanus attended to his horse, glanced admiringly now and then at Clara's delicately blooming face—set off by the most becoming and coquettish of hats—and looked, and was, in a mood of perfect contentment with things in general. So was Miss Seyton. There was a man by her side—a handsome one, a young one, and one who had the good taste to appreciate her charms.

The sun was setting, and at a curve in the road she suggested that they should pull up for a minute to enjoy the view.

Walled in by the high mountains on either side, the wide valley stretched away before them into dim distance. Near at hand lay the willow-wood—all pale hues of gold and brown and russet—and the white walls of the outlying buildings of the ranche; and beyond these the steel-blue gleam of the river. The sun had sunk in a flaming bed. The western mountains lay in a cold purple shadow, their dark outline icy clear against the golden fire of the sky; but all the eastern range was bathed in a wonderful luminous haze of rose and gold, and above those transfigured hills sailed slowly up a great white moon. Thus half the landscape lay in shadow deep and cold as the darkest blue of the glacier's heart—half in a flood of warm light and colour, the last glow of the dying day behind the opposite hills. It was a contrast, an effect of colouring such as can only be realised to perfection in a Californian atmosphere.

Clara looked upon the scene with a dreamy delight in her eyes. Her artist soul thrilled and expanded in this air of beauty. Her look spoke more than her words, for all she said was, with a sigh of almost painful pleasure,

'It's *too* beautiful!'

Coriolanus was silent. He *felt* the loveliness of the hour and place; but all he could have *said* would have been to echo her words.

'I suppose you are used to it?' she observed, finding he made no response.

'Yes, we have it every day.'

'One soon ceases to appreciate the beauty one sees every day,' she said.

'Does one? I shouldn't think so,' he replied, looking into her uplifted eyes. 'I wonder,' he added, 'how long you'll be getting tired of this?'

'I shall not give myself time to get tired of it,' she answered; and added laughingly, 'I fear the inference of that speech is not quite polite.'

'I don't like politeness,' said Coriolanus, 'and I hate society.'

'But did you ever go into any?' Clara inquired innocently and wickedly.

'I don't know what you would call society,' he said. '*We* call the Jonesville parties and the hops at the "Central" society. We do have such things; we're not quite savages here.'

Clara looked up in his face with her sweetest archest smile, as she queried demurely,

'No?'

She was already perfectly aware not only that she should get on with Coriolanus, but that her way with him, being *her* way, could not offend, and was the surest thing to attract him. But she scarcely anticipated the sudden sunshine that lit up his face at her words—the frank smile of sympathetic mirth on his lips, and in his eyes the light of ardent honest admiration, tender as if a lovely bird had lit upon his hand.

After this evening the hopeful male scions of the Jones family again lapsed out of sight, and for some days Clara saw no more of them, except an occasional glimpse of a manly form mounted on a plough in the distance. Then one evening all the 'boys' again trooped into the parlour together, with the old overwhelming effect of numbers, though they were but three. The parlour-lamp had not improved, and by its dim and flickering rays Clara mistook Lycurgus for Coriolanus, and gave a cordial hand-pressure and an especially sweet smile to the wrong brother. Lanus did not assert his rightful claim to the welcome then, but, later in the evening, he observed abruptly,

'So you didn't know me?'

'How could any one know any one by this light?' she replied.

'Well, do you know now which am I?' he demanded, looking in her face.

'You are—*Patch!*' she said innocently; whereat Patch, aged fifteen and hobbledehoyish, roared delightedly, and Lanus, who was easily amused, laughed too, but softly. It was rarely that the elder Jones boys laughed loud or raised their voices, their gentle even-toned Western voices, which Clara at least never from first to last heard elevated. But then she did not accompany them on their daily round of duties.

'If you forget me again,' Lanus said, with his clumsy pleasantry—he had not a light hand at badinage—'I'll upset you the next time I drive you.'

'If there *is* a next time,' she suggested.

'There shall be,' he rejoined, a trifle more decisively.

And there was; and another, and another.

III.

THE hard work of the ploughing season was now nearly over; the young Joneses had leisure hours more and more often, and took to spending these hours in the house. They generally whiled away the evening with music. And those were happy evenings, when the curtains were drawn, the huge logs blazing cheerily on the hearth, the whole family assembled round the piano, and sometimes, absorbed in song, sitting up until what were deemed unholy hours at the White Ranche, where the usual time of retiring was nine o'clock at latest.

When the thoughts of the Jones boys wandered from their main interest of crops and cattle, they one and all stooped to the lure of music as readily as their father did to that of poetry. When Mr. Jones read Tennyson aloud his sons sat silent, respectfully bored; when Virginia and Clara sang, they hung around the piano like bees around a honey-pot; and Lycurgus, who had a fine baritone, consented to step from the ranks of the audience into that of a performer. But even Clara could not induce them to appreciate Tennyson. They one and all admired Miss Seyton exceedingly; but Coriolanus retained his post in the van of her friendship, and his sisters were delighted to see Lanus, who was considered reserved, diffident, and even misogynic, 'getting along so well and so much at home with dear Clara.'

'I wish you would show me the inside of your house,' Clara said to Coriolanus one morning, when she and Cassie were scattering grain to a gobbling turkey and a flock of excited hens in the court-yard; 'I'm tired of contemplating the outside. Imogen and I tried to get in yesterday.'

'But he always keeps it locked; they all do,' cried Cassie. 'O Lanus, do let us go in now!'

'There's nothing to see in my house,' said Lanus, but not de-murringly; on the contrary, taking a big key out of his pocket and turning towards the door.

His abode was a snug, neat, wooden outhouse, about the size of a cabin on board an Atlantic steamer, and exactly the shape of a dog-kennel. The door being opened, disclosed a narrow bed covered with a patchwork quilt, a small old-fashioned bureau, a back-less chair, and an old Saratoga trunk, which completely filled up the limited space of Coriolanus's quarters.

'Nothing to see?' repeated Clara, standing on the threshold and peering in daintily, apprehen-sive of dust, and gathering her garments from contact with the walls. 'Well, there is a remark-ably good show of *boots*, and also of deadly weapons!' She glanced at two pairs of topboots (one ap-parently meant to be worn *outside* the other, it was so much bigger, and both evidently nearly waist-high when put to their proper use, though now lopping limply down), at the rifle hanging over the bed, and the revolver on the shelf, which, by economy of space, served as table, bookcase, and washhand-stand. 'What can you want with such a supply of fire-arms? Are they loaded?'

'Rather,' he replied dryly. 'It wouldn't be much use keeping them if they were *not*. You see,' he added, polishing the Derringer tenderly as if he loved it, 'one might want them in a hurry.'

'*Please* don't touch it!' pleaded Clara, shrinking prettily. 'I can't bear firearms.'

He put it down, but looked at her with an incredulous smile.

'You know you are not *really* afraid of my handling it,' he said.

'The boots interest me more than anything else,' she observed, her attention returning to those ar-ticles. '*These* originally belonged to a giant! How did you come by them? Are you a descendant of Jack the Giant-killer?'

'They're my field-boots. Would you like to try them on?'

'They would be too small,' she objected. 'But really they have a dejected air, a kind of droop, like a rabbit's ears! They are the kind of boot that would look tru-culent and belligerent—brigand-ish—*on*, but they have a depressed and ignominious look *off*. Now this pair at least *can* stand almost upright; it looks quite alert and lively by comparison.'

She transferred her critical gaze to the walls, papered with cuttings from the illustrated journals, and then to the literature on the shelf, the *Farmer's Manual, Practical Agriculture, Willis on the Cow,* &c.

'Thank Heaven, here is some-thing at last that is not agricul-tural!' she observed, unearthing Irving's *Life of Washington.*

'Why do you object to agricul-ture?' said Coriolanus, slightly ag-grieved. 'We live by it.'

'But you needn't live *for* it and for nothing else.'

'Do you think I don't live for anything else?' he asked, looking at her most earnestly.

Clara innocently turned her eyes away in a final glance of inspec-tion, and gaily changed the sub-ject.

'Yes, I can congratulate you on your collection of coats, boots, firearms, art, and literature; but I cannot help remarking a trifling deficiency of *hats*,' she added, with a glance at the one on his head, which indeed was startling to eyes accustomed to a whole and sound headgear.

'I have another one,' he said.

'It is to be hoped so,' she rejoined.

'Why?' he inquired, taking off the hat and surveying it. 'Is this so very bad?'

It had been a fine Panama once; but now it was torn and discoloured, the brim curiously jagged, and in one place looking as if a dog had bitten a piece out.

'I should say it had seen its best days,' Clara replied gravely. 'Come, put it on again!' she added, laughing. 'It isn't unbecoming to you, after all!'

Nor was it. Coriolanus's dark well-featured face looked very handsome with the wide shady brim tilted forward over his brow.

'Do I tease you past all bearing?' she asked, looking up, with a half-caressing smile, as frank as if he had been a great Newfoundland dog.

He smiled too. He had a singularly sweet soft smile, and Clara liked to call it up.

'You *never* tease me,' he said.

They then proceeded to view the quarters of Tony and Curgus.

'Why don't you have the *adobe* for your house?' asked Clara, indicating the old mud-walled building which nearly filled up one side of the courtyard.

One of its two rooms was employed as a storeroom; the other had once been used as a dormitory for the farm-hands, but now had fallen into disuse, and contained only a side of bacon and a sack of apples. The adobe walls, adobe roof, and mud floor were innocent of carpet, ceiling, panel, or paper; the walls, two feet thick, were only pierced with two unglazed holes about a foot square, for windows,

so that the place was dingy, not to say dark, although the door, which would not shut, also admitted its contribution of daylight.

Clara looked round this promising apartment appraisingly.

'Somehow, I like this old place,' she remarked. 'It's a relic of the old days of Spanish chivalry; that's interesting. And I like these thick walls and loophole windows. It wouldn't make a bad room at all if it were properly fitted up. Fancy it with a nice rich carpet and a few rocking-chairs, glazed with stained glass, making a coloured twilight, and at night a shaded lamp and a big fire. I presume that corner was meant for a hearth? Don't you think it might be made very comfortable?' she appealed to Coriolanus animatedly.

He seemed to be thinking of something else, and only gave a brief and half-absent assent.

'It must be nearly time to go and dress now,' she suggested. 'We are going to town this afternoon to get that *Tannhäuser* March as a duet, you know; we ordered it at Smith's. We'll have it to-night; we'll get up quite a concert. You will come?'

'Yes,' he agreed. 'But Virginia won't be ready for half an hour yet. Come and look at the horses.'

'O yes; let us take Prince his carrot!' she exclaimed.

'And you haven't been into the Water Tower yet, and we have always been just going,' observed Coriolanus, as they took their way towards the stables, Cassie lingering behind in the courtyard to chase a frightened stray chicken.

Coriolanus, who had dug the well, and was proud of his work, reminded Clara of it as they entered the Water Tower; and she was inclined to appreciate the achievement then, if never before, as she looked down the deep black well. Although he had left the door ajar to admit a little light and air, the lower chamber of the tower was still nearly as dark as midnight, close, damp, and with a faint stifling dungeon smell.

Here was the well, above which a shaft and a frail ladder led into the upper chamber.

'Pretty dark down there, ain't it?' observed Coriolanus. 'When we go down to clean up the shaft, it's just the reverse of warm and cheerful, I tell you.'

'*Do* you go down *there?*' she asked.

'Why, yes; Curgus or I, when the works want looking to.'

Clara moved forward to the brink, and gazed straight down into the dark grim mouth of the pit, black as Erebus, and silent as night, with not the faintest gurgle or gleam to betray the sullen still water deep down below. She had stepped so close to the edge that Coriolanus hastily put his arm round her waist—lightly, respectfully—simply to hold her safe. The black yawning abyss looked so ghastly, she shrank back, swayed close to his side with a little shudder, a little feminine gesture of clinging appeal. For a moment his arm trembled round her waist, he half pressed her to his side, then suddenly released her.

'Don't,' he said abruptly, impetuously drawing her back from the well. 'Let's get out of this.'

She looked at him as they emerged into the daylight, and saw that his bronzed cheek had turned pale as she had never seen it yet. But on hers there glowed a lovely rose.

'Say, Lanus!' exclaimed Lycurgus, suddenly emerging from a gate near at hand, with a gun over his shoulder, and three dogs at his heels, and Patch following, 'there's been a coon down to the poultry-yard, and we're going for him. There's three young turkey-chicks missing, and we're on the track of the coon. You coming along with us?'

IV.

CLARA sat in the aromatic odorous shade of the biggest of the Australian gum-trees in that portion of the ranche ground which was dignified by the name of the garden. She had in her lap the letters that morning's mail had brought her; she was looking at them without re-reading them— having perused them twice already —thinking of the writers, and of the writers of other similar effusions in bygone days. Clara Seyton never forgot. One thing was always linked with another in her mind. She did not, as some women do, take life piecemeal, making it a patchwork of detached episodes. Rather, she 'dragged a lengthening chain' of memories and associations. She preserved her love-letters—not all of them, but a selection. She would probably preserve the two specimens now in her hand.

One was from a handsome young Southerner, whose face unluckily was his fortune, and began, 'My fairest Princess?' The other was from a San Francisco millionaire, and began more formally, 'My dear Miss Seyton.' One of the victims was in a more advanced stage than the other. 'Give him an inch and he'll take an ell,' meditated his princess calmly. 'A little cold water must be judiciously thrown on his ardour?' She did not want to marry either of the two; but she did not wish to repulse them decisively. Clara's moral attitude was frequently that of a dog with his paw on a bone, which he cannot eat himself and will not allow another to carry off.

Now, even with these two effusions in her lap, and an admirer close at hand—for although she was uncertain as to the degree of Coriolanus's admiration, she was perfectly clear as to the fact that he did admire her—she was thinking of 'the others.' Of poor Tom Bruce, who went out to India and died there of jungle-fever, with a dream undispelled, believing in her love; of George Bellasys, who, after many episodes of love and anger and jealousy and reconciliation, finally married another, and just after his marriage came into the Bellasys baronetcy and estate. Clara always sighed as she reflected how badly Fate had used her in not giving her a prophetic hint or warning that his uncle was going to die so soon. How different things would have been if she had only known that old Sir Luke's days were numbered! And she thought too of Jack Randolph, who unluckily took to drink and went altogether to the dogs. His mother declared that it was all Miss Seyton's doing; but *that*, Miss Seyton said impatiently, was nonsense.

She was aroused from this train of thought by the sight of Coriolanus Jones coming across the wet dewy grass. Encouraged by her greeting, he took a seat on the garden-bench beside her at a respectful distance.

'So you've got some letters this morning? Love-letters?' he conjectured lightly.

'You have hit it; *two!*' she answered. 'An *embarras de richesses*, isn't it?'

'How?' gravely inquired Lanus, who did not understand French.

'O—well—too much riches,' Clara explained literally.

Lanus paused, and then inquired, 'Are they really?'

'Are they really—what?' she laughed—'love-letters or riches?

Well, they *are* the former. As to their value—'

A careless shrug of the shoulder intimated that she held them lightly enough.

'Both from the same fellow?' he questioned, still unsmiling and openly interested.

'No. Even the ardour of *my* admirers doesn't go so far as to prompt them to write twice by the same mail!'

Clara had been a girl of rather delicate reserve in her first season; but a good deal of this delicacy had been rubbed off by much flirtation. She played a bold stroke now, and said gaily and confidentially,

'Are you interested in my love-affairs? Yes? Then come. You shall be my father confessor. *This* man'—touching one of the letters—'is decidedly what we wicked worldlings call "a good match;" indeed I might go even further than that and say he is a *catch*, being a shade more desirable than a match. *But*, I don't like him at all! This one'—indicating the other—' is neither match nor catch—a detrimental! Must I explain what that means to your unsophisticated mind?'

'I think that even I can understand,' he replied.

'It is a curious thing,' Clara pursued meditatively, 'that detrimentals almost invariably have all the attractions to themselves. Between the wealthy bores and the attractive detrimentals a girl has a hard task in making up her mind and managing things satisfactorily.' She heaved a comical little sigh. 'I daresay you could give me some good advice,' she continued, 'but good advice is a thing I never take.'

'The question doesn't seem to me a difficult one,' said Coriolanus; 'but then I am, as you say, a kind of wild man of the woods. As to advice, I don't know whether mine would be good or bad, but it would be simple enough at least. I should say, "Marry the man you love."'

'But,' she objected frankly, 'I don't love any man.'

'Not *any* one?' he questioned, looking her suddenly straight in the face.

'Not any one.'

'Is that really true?'

But at this interesting stage of the interview Cassie and Patch came racing across the garden in high excitement and delight, Cassie hugging in her arms the body of a murdered crane, a huge gray bird almost as big as herself.

'Wong just shot it!' she exclaimed. 'He shot it down by the river. And I'm to have its wings; look, aren't they splendid?'

'Don't touch me with it, Cassie dear, pray!' pleaded Clara, shrinking away from the great dead bird's stiffening wings.

'Take it away, Cassie! Miss Clara doesn't like it,' said Lanus, a shade less gently than he was in the habit of speaking to his sisters.

Miss Seyton's visit was now nearly at an end. Much to the regret of the whole family, she was to leave them the next day, under a promise to return in the spring and spend a longer time. On this last day they all hovered round her, and made so much of her that she saw comparatively little of Coriolanus. She sent for him to lock and strap her portmanteau, however, and amiably insisted on kneeling on the top of it meanwhile, to render that task the easier.

'I'm sorry you're going,' he said, jerking the information at her with a brusqueness that did not add either sentiment or impressiveness to the commonplace words.

'*Are* you? you don't say so! What, sorry I'm going?' she echoed merrily.

He laughed reluctantly.

'Clara, Clara! the carriage is ready,' cried Imogen.

'Well, good-bye,' said Clara, standing up, and holding out her hand.

He held the slender ungloved hand in his own big bronzed one, and wasted the last few moments in silence, as we are all apt, under such circumstances, to waste, and afterwards to regret, them. Only just at the last he said hurriedly, in a lowered voice,

'You'll come back—you *will* come back to us, Miss Clara? Life won't be the same thing until you come again.'

V.

WHEN spring was smiling on the valley, when the willow woods were just breaking into tender green, and the wild-flowers beginning to blossom on the plains, Clara Seyton returned to the White Ranche, to pay her promised second visit. Her uncle and aunt, with whom she was residing in San Francisco, had gone on a short trip to Honolulu; and as Clara was a wretched sailor, and the trip was to comprise more sea than land, she did not accompany them, and chose to spend the period of their absence at Jonesville.

Mr. Jones, jovial, smiling, monosyllabic as ever, met her at the station as before; and in the courtyard this time all the family, male as well as female, swarmed out to give her welcome. The boys now appeared, 'clothed and in their right mind,' in broadcloth and linen, with their boots for once *inside* their nether garments. Coriolanus was brief and reserved in his greeting; he seemed to have gone back to the diffidence and distance of the first hour of their acquaintance. Virginia and Imogen were full of gossip; Tony had taken to visiting very frequently at Judge Leslie's, and Letty Leslie was growing a very pretty girl. Lanus and Lycurgus had been talking of buying a ranche of their own up in Sonoma county; and Sheriff Brown called *very* often at the Ranche—here Imogen blushed, and told Virginia to 'hush up.' Lycurgus, it appeared, had an attraction over in Silver City; but there was no gossip about Lanus.

He and Clara soon fell into their old intimacy; and Clara speedily perceived that, in his case at least, 'absence had made the heart grow fonder.' He was more enthralled than ever.

'We've got the sunshine back,' he said one morning, when they were alone on the verandah, waiting for Imogen and Cassie to join them in a ramble.

'It *is* a glorious day,' Clara assented.

'I don't mean *that* sunshine; we have had plenty of that all the time you've been away.'

'O? Was it a metaphor?' she rejoined. 'You really mustn't think me obtuse for not grasping it at once; but I never heard you wax metaphorical before!' Then she added more softly, 'So you missed me a little, did you?'

'So much,' he answered, 'that sometimes I wished you had never come.'

Another morning, when Mrs. Jones and Imogen were in the dairy, and Virginia holding a consultation with Wong Lee, Clara was wandering aimlessly round the courtyard, flinging bits of bread to the poultry, and occasionally aiming a stray crust at the fat cat which lay asleep in the sunshine; when Coriolanus, perceiving her from the glazed slit in his house that he dignified by the name of a window, hastened to join her. A pig, which was roving, apparently as aimlessly as the young lady, followed him, grunting an inquiry as to whether he carried about any provisions in his pockets.

'Is that one of the litter we used to go and see?' asked Clara; 'you remember, on the first day of our acquaintance, when you couldn't think of anything to show me but pigs?'

'No; *this* is one of Lady Margaret's; *those* were the Queen of Sheba's. I remember taking you to see the litter. I think I remember everything about that day —the first day I knew you.'

'What a good memory you must have!'

'I tell you one thing I remember very well,' he observed presently, standing on the threshold of the old *adobe* building. 'Do you recollect saying this wouldn't make a bad room? I've thought of it often.'

'Well, with a good deal of alteration and touching up, it certainly would make a cosy den,' she said, peeping into the dark and dingy place.

'I've come in here,' he continued, 'and looked round, and tried to picture it as—as you said it might be. I've seemed to see you sitting here with your needlework—'

'Not a characteristic aspect of mine, I fear,' she interposed.

'Why, I have seen you work,' he rejoined, with his usual literal matter-of-fact.

'O yes — embroidery; but I don't think you ever saw me do anything useful and domestic.'

This was true. Lanus could not contradict it. But he was sure that Clara Seyton *could* do anything she set her mind to accomplish, domestic or otherwise.

'Won't you come for a walk?' he suggested. 'It will be nice and shady in the wood.'

Clara assented, forgetting, or not caring, that Virginia had promised to join her in the courtyard in a few minutes.

The sky was such a fleckless vault of burning blue as England never knows: the mountains stood out in the clear air in sharp and strong relief that annihilated distance, and made them seem within a stone's throw; the field by the wood, thick with yellow wildflowers, was verily the 'field of the cloth of gold.' Under the budding willows Coriolanus and Clara went their way by pleasant shady paths towards the broad blue river.

They were not talkatively inclined. Clara threw the ball of conversation in vain; he let it drop time after time, until at last she observed,

'Do you know, my friend, that you are not lively company to-day?'

'I know I'm not,' he answered, more morosely than he had ever spoken to her.

She looked up at him with a questioning smile, and met his eyes. Her own sank before his look.

'Why are you so silent?' she asked, with a pretty playful feint of petulance, glancing aside from him.

Then he burst out abruptly,

'I can't talk to you because I'm thinking too much of you. Say, Clara, *could* you be happy here? or, when I get a ranche of my own —in *my* home—with *me?*'

Clara knew very well that she never could. It was not in her nature to be happy, save for a brief restful holiday, out of the whirl of life in great cities. For the matter of that, her morbidly restless, excitement-craving nature was never likely to be perfectly happy anywhere; and certainly the last place in the world for her to endure existence in was a Californian ranche. But she did not wish to

put her victim out of pain too quickly. She liked him too much to lose him. And he was so strong! and Clara worshipped strength. He had the muscles of a gladiator, and, withal, the gentleness of a woman. He had just that mingling of power and tenderness—force unexpressed, and tenderness unspoken—that, belonging only to pure and thorough manhood, is most enthralling to womankind. No; he was too good to lose!

So first she 'smiling put the question by,' as she had good practice in doing; then she evaded, fenced, temporised. He urged his love with the rough eloquence, or rather lack of eloquence, of real passion, yet with all the chivalrous gentleness of his nature and his race. She listened and drank in the full sweetness of conquest. Coriolanus had a limited insight into Clara's nature—limited, but correct enough, so far as it went. There was a vein of truth in her, deep down. Truth perceives truth, as only purity knows purity; and he recognised what was true in her surely enough to feel that her downright 'Yes,' or downright 'No,' would be honest. But he did not know her well enough to see that either the 'Yes' or the 'No' was exactly the decisive word she would not say. As soon as she began to fear it was possible he might lead her to one or the other, she discovered it was very late, and they must return immediately—discovered, also, Tony and Patch by the riverside, who, she declared, were no doubt looking for them.

'Stay—stay a moment!' he urged. 'Don't hurry on, Clara; won't you—won't you—let me—give me one kiss?'

She looked round to see that they were well out of sight of Tony and Patch; and then cast a shy fleeting glance up in his face, and said,

'No—no; please let go my hand!'

Somewhat contrary to her anticipation, Coriolanus did let it go, and also apologised for his 'roughness' in having detained it. Whereupon Clara, who had only been experimentalising as to how far she might go in encouragement, and how little repulse would suffice, relented, and let him take just the one kiss he craved.

Looking back upon the interview afterwards, she reflected that he had borne himself very well. Certainly it is the best of a man that always shows in his wooing. Clara knew that; but she also knew that the qualities that are not there cannot manifest themselves. It is the cream of the nature that rises on such occasions; but the cream is there to rise. Coriolanus had come out well, so well that she sighed more than once as she lived the interview over again. There was something in his earnest abandonment that reminded her of poor Tom Bruce. He was one of the few men who, even in urging his love and pressing his cause, had seemed to think more of her than of himself. If only he had been of the world and in the world, *her* world, instead of buried alive here on a country ranche, and, still worse, content to be so buried, she could have liked him well. As things were, of course it was not to be thought of seriously. The idea of the name was enough. 'Mrs. Coriolanus Jones!' The San Francisco millionaire was still at her feet; but he was coarse and common, and she hated him, although she smiled at him. The Southern detrimental she had been constrained to dismiss when he insisted on an answer. One piece of news which she had quite accidentally discovered in an old English newspaper during the winter had, perhaps, partially influenced her in her course of conduct with these two—was influencing her now in regard to Coriolanus. It was merely a brief announcement of the death of 'the infant daughter of Sir George and the late Lady Bellasys.' The *late!* So George's wife was dead, and he was free. She had never cared much for George Bellasys. Man for man, she liked Coriolanus better. But her heart had bounded when she read that Lady Bellasys was no more; and she resolved that she would, at least, keep herself free until her return to England in the coming summer. But she did not tell her latest lover this.

They were now of course on changed terms. Across the old frank friendliness a shade of consciousness, of distance, had fallen. In private, Lanus held the position still professedly of a friend, really of a lover not discouraged, yet not accepted. In public, he was supposed to be merely a friend and brother. But he could not adapt himself to the supposition as easily as she. He had not such practice in histrionics. The family observed the change in him, put their own constructions upon it, and, as they had one and all a strong affection for and an unshaken belief in Clara, they rejoiced; Virginia and Imogen watched sympathetically, and said,

'If only Lanus and Clara would make up their minds, how lovely it would be!'

And Antonius, when Lycurgus expressed a similar sentiment to him in fraternal confidence, responded,

'Bully!'

But, with an innate delicacy never learned in society nor drilled in by rule, the family refrained from any allusion, either jocular or sentimental, to the attachment which, with their natural fond pride in son and brother, they did not imagine was likely to be otherwise than mutual. Now Clara's heart was not altogether adamant; and the more she saw of Coriolanus in the light of a lover, the more and more she liked him. She began to compare him less with his predecessors, to forget the past in the present. Sometimes when she saw his dark handsome face light up as she drew near—when she listened to his deep gentle voice speaking 'words sweet to say and hear'—she forgot that he was roughly nurtured and countrybred, that he was utterly and blissfully ignorant of the literature of the day, that the Fleshly School, Æsthetics, and pre-Raphaelitism were unknown to him even by name, and that his highest ambition was to live on his own ranche, and raise his own crops, and rear his own beef and mutton. She sang her sweetest songs to him, and he was entranced; she walked by sunset and starlight with him, and he was in paradise; and even she, between flattered vanity and growing affection, her heart beating high with triumph of conquest, and melting fast beneath the tender fire of his love, was happier then than she thought herself to be.

And little by little his influence over her increased, and she yielded more and more to the sweetness of the present, and thought less and less of the future—though still neither for him nor for any other man would she have sacrificed that 'future,' which to her meant only a shining place in the gay world for which she lived, and which yet did not content her ever-unsatisfied soul.

'And are you really going to leave us next week?' he asked one day.

'I must, you know. I must be in San Francisco, ready to receive uncle Horace on his return.'

'The time flies,' he said. 'And yet it seems to me I've lived a lifetime in this little while that you have been here. But now, next week will be upon us before we know it. Miss Clara, you'll give me an answer before you go?'

She was silent.

'I have not pressed you,' he pursued. 'I have tried not to be impatient. But suspense is very hard to bear. You will not leave me in this uncertainty?'

'Would you rather be certain, then, at once?' she asked.

'Yes!' he exclaimed impetuously. 'Give me your answer, Clara, now, whatever it may be. I'd rather know the best or worst at once. If you feel you can never care for me, tell me so now!'

'But I—I,' she murmured, faltering and flushing with an emotion that was partly sympathetic sentiment and the pleasing sense of a crisis, partly genuine feeling—'I cannot—cannot say I don't care for you!'

'You—you *do* care for me, Clara?' he asked under his breath, his cheek pale, and voice a little shaken.

'Am I made of marble?' she answered, turning her eyes away. 'You have been so good to me, how could I help caring for you—a little?'

'Only a little? But, Clara, Clara! won't that little grow to much? I love you so, I think you must love me in time!'

'In time,' she repeated. 'O Lanus,' she had seldom before called him by that familiar name, 'give me time.'

Her voice was tender and tremulous, and she laid her slim fingers softly on his broad brown hand.

'Take what time you like, my darling,' he replied, clasping her in his arms and kissing her, unforbidden and unrepulsed. 'My own! my love, my life! take whatever time you will, so that you are mine at last!'

VI.

CORIOLANUS was happy in his fool's paradise. Life seemed all pure sunshine to him now. He built castles in the air. What earthly castles ever tower so grand and glorious as those ethereal ones of our own architecture! Earth and sky and sea furnish no colours so bright as those we paint them with. In his dreams of love and Clara—nay, the two were one, for love to him meant only Clara—he soared up into a higher heaven than he would ever know in his after hours on earth.

He said nothing about his happiness to his family, as Clara wished their understanding kept a secret, and to honest unsuspicious Coriolanus this wish of hers was law. He felt he could never be thankful enough for God's goodness to him—could never do enough for this angel who had as good as promised to come down to share and bless his life. All day he thought of what he could do to please her. He would fit up the old adobe for her just as she had planned it; it should be 'Clara's Bower,' and ready for her to come home to, if he had not a ranche of his own by that happy time. And Clara, if she did not talk of the future herself, let him talk, and listened, and smiled, and sometimes sighed, he knew not why.

Meanwhile the only cloud upon his horizon was that she was going back to the city at the end of the next week. Next week seemed so near! these golden hours flew so fast! He did not know that he was too happy for it to endure. But before the too near 'next week' opened, it happened that one day the post brought a letter to Miss Seyton.

It was from Sir George Bellasys. He dated, to her astonishment, from Chicago. He was, it appeared, making the fashionable tour round the world. He was coming over-land to San Francisco, where he contemplated making some stay, and where he hoped to have the pleasure of seeing *her*. There was not a word of love in the letter, nor any allusion to his recent widower-hood. But Clara read between the lines, and knew that what they meant was that he had not forgotten her; that now that he was free, his thoughts at least must have turned to her again. If the old love were altogether a thing of the past, if no flame lingered in the ashes, would George Bellasys have written to her at all? She remembered his fiery love and anger in their long-ago quarrels, the ardour of their reconciliations. Could such love as his had been be extinguished and forgotten? She remembered, too, the sternness of his last farewell; the bitter resolve with which he had spoken his last words, 'No, Clara; no. *You fool me no more!*' She wondered, would Coriolanus be as stern and bitter with her now? How would he take it, when she should tell him?

For with the sight of Sir George's handwriting, Clara awoke as from a dream. It was not love that stirred her, but the shining chance of the high place she desired in the world she loved.

The next morning her answering letter went to San Francisco. She gave it to Lanus himself to take to the post-office, and smiled, and let him kiss her as he took it, with something the same feeling that had prompted her when a child to thrust her finger in the flame 'to see how much she could bear.' For she had never liked Coriolanus so well as now that she had made up her mind to leave him.

She walked in the avenue that evening, at the most beautiful hour of the beautiful day. She had often and often seen the valley as it looked now, half dusky in the cold purple shadows of evening, half flooded in the golden and rosy light of the last flame of the dying day. But it seemed that she had never realised so fully before either its beauty or its desolation. She felt it would be madness to stay, and yet that it would cost her a bitter wrench of the heart to go. But Clara Seyton never shrank from carrying out a purpose because it hurt her a little more or less.

Virginia, who came presently to join her, found her rather a silent companion. Virginia was full of the latest news of the floods up in Sonoma county; and when Lycurgus came in sight, hailed him with an eager inquiry, ' How was the river?' It was a question Clara had heard put pretty frequently for the last day or two, but which she heard without any anxiety, knowing nothing of the hazards of flood and field in those regions.

' O, the river's all right,' Lycurgus said ; ' only just up to high-water mark.'

' It isn't often as much as that,' observed Virginia thoughtfully.

'Don't you go making Miss Clara nervous,' said Lycurgus. ' Our river hasn't overflowed in our day yet ; and I don't see why we should be alarmed about it now.'

' I shouldn't be alarmed if it was going to overflow to-day,' said Clara ; ' I should look upon it as rather an interesting episode in Californian life.'

' Rather *too* interesting for us natives,' remarked Virginia dryly.

Later in the evening, some of the young people went out for a ramble, as was frequently their habit ; and Coriolanus and Clara paired off, also a frequent occurrence. The wind was rising; a few dark clouds were floating up from behind the mountains ; and the willows, waving their long arms in the starlight, looked eerie and spectral.

' It is a ghostly kind of night,' observed Clara, sighing.

' Why,' said Coriolanus the practical, ' it's a fine night enough, although it looks as if it was blowing up for a storm presently. I hope it won't blow the river up our way. I shouldn't like you to have a scare just your last few days here.'

' Why not?' she rejoined. ' My last few days here might as well be eventful ones. And—about that —there's something I wanted to say to you. I leave here on Wednesday, you know—'

' But soon to come back to us?'

' I think not,' she answered steadily ; ' I think it would be better not.'

' Not to come back to us?' he repeated, startled. ' Clara darling, what do you mean?'

' We have been a little mad,' she said ; ' and it is time we came to our senses now. I am going, and—'

Even Clara hesitated, paused a moment.

He looked at her, waited for her to continue ; then, as she still paused, he said, in a strangely altered voice,

' And you will not come back?'

' You will forget me,' she responded. ' You have only known me three months.'

' Why is this?' he demanded, like one half-stunned. ' What have I done that you should throw me over in this way?'

' *You* have done nothing. But *I* have been thinking. It would never do. We were mad to dream of—of such a thing. Two people more utterly and radically unsuited to each other than you and I never came together. *I* could never make *you* happy, nor *you* me.'

' You throw me over like this?' he repeated.

' If you choose to put it so, *yes !* But I had rather say that I ask you to release me from an understanding into which I was foolish ever to enter.'

'Release you?' he echoed impetuously, in a tone of feeling so bitterly wounded as to lose all anger in pain and astonishment. 'Good God! as if a man could hold a woman against her will! Release! Why, at the very altar you would be free if you spoke but one word to me as—as you have spoken now!'

Clara was silent. Her heart was fluttering fast, but her resolve was unshaken.

He added suddenly, with a burst of passionate incredulity,

'But I can't believe it, Clara! You do not really mean it? You are only trying me? Tell me, Clara, is it true, or are you only trying me?'

But his question was not to receive its answer that night. A horse's hoofs beat quick upon the road behind them; the rider, drawing rein as he came up with them, hailed Coriolanus.

'Say, Jones, the boys are going down to Smith's Ferry to look to the bank thar. They're kinder anxious about it. Tony sent me after you. Will you join us?'

To such a question a man could not say nay. He hastened to take Clara back to his sisters, and went off with his neighbour hot-foot to the scene of anxiety.

They sat up at the Ranche to await the return of the three brothers, Mrs. Jones periodically shaking her head, Virginia relating horrible stories of floods; while Mr. Jones improved the occasion by reading aloud, 'High Tide on the Coast of Lincolnshire,' which made little Cassie cry, and Imogen put her fingers in her ears, while Clara observed sceptically that she did not suppose anything so romantic or exciting was going to happen here. The boys returned with the report that the bank had

certainly been in a bad way, but there were a dozen men at work upon-it; they had been lending a hand, and they guessed it would hold out.

'If it doesn't,' observed Coriolanus, 'it's Smith's that will get it first.'

Then they all went to bed reassured, and slept peacefully.

The next morning at breakfast none of the male members of the family appeared. Mr. Jones and Lanus were down by the riverside, superintending and assisting in the removal of the contents of a row of sheds, which stood too near the river for safety in the present aspect of things. Tony was 'down at Smith's,' and Lycurgus had gone off to the town to inquire what was the prevalent opinion there, and what precautions were being taken at the bend of the river. For alarming reports came in that morning from the neighbourhood, and a rise of the river appeared probable; although to Clara, looking on the sunny landscape—for through the dark drifting clouds the sun burst out, shining in a rift of glorious blue—any serious apprehensions seemed absurd. She went with Virginia to look at the river. It was rushing more furiously than usual, surging higher up the banks; and broken branches, and even now and then a whole tree, went swirling past in the current.

'I daresay we're perfectly safe,' observed Virginia; 'but for all that I shall be very glad when the water's down to its old mark. You see how much higher it is than yesterday.'

As the day wore on, they all seemed incapable of resting indoors. The river drew them by an irresistible fascination. Hour by hour its rush grew more fast and furious. Hour by hour it encroached upon the lower curves of the shore. By the evening even Mr. Jones's jovial face was grave.

'I hope you're not very tired to-day, Clara,' said Imogen, 'because the chances are we shall none of us go to bed to-night; we shall sit up and watch.'

At sunset they were all out of doors. The aspect of things, as even Clara could perceive now, was such as to justify some apprehension. The river was now a raging flood, and as they watched they saw a whole cottage, with one side smashed in, swept by.

'Poor souls, where are they to-night?' wondered Mrs. Jones.

'O, they've probably got shelter somewhere,' said Lycurgus cheerfully. 'I hope we sha'n't share their fate. If this bank goes—' He finished by a significant pause.

'This bank *won't* go,' asserted Mr. Jones, ever sanguine.

It was a wonderful sunset—such as Clara in all her travels through Europe and America had never chanced to see before—such as even the most deadly practical and unimaginative of the spectators could scarcely look upon without a thrill. All across the western sky from north to south there hung a huge black pall of cloud, shot through and through with flaming scarlet, as if through rents in the inky mass the lurid tongues of blood-red fire reached out. And above this stormy splendour there seemed to writhe a great serpent of glowing gold and purple light, undulating along the upper line of the midnight blackness, in hues more vivid and varied than those of the fabled dolphin's death.

The gorgeous gloom of the skies struck home to Clara's heart with a strange thrill she would never forget. If ever in life she should see such a sunset again, this hour and this place would come back to her, not as a dream, but as a living reality that should make all life besides seem the dream.

This night it seemed somehow in keeping with her feelings. She seemed to be living only in the conflict of the present hour.

The field wherein they were standing stretched between the river and the so-called 'garden' of the Ranche. The ground whereon the house was built lay low, being only about level with the ordinary high-water mark of the river. The field sloped slightly upward to the river-banks. Thus the banks here were their only protection. But the stream had never overflowed these boundaries in the Jones day, which was so far reassuring.

It seemed to them that the earth trembled a little; or was it only that the dizzy deafening rush of the torrent filled their ears and brain? Two or three of the party stepped close to the brink to watch the white river boiling past. Clara stepped a little closer than the rest—lingered when the rest had retired. She was standing watching it in a kind of dream, when a sharp shriek of terror calling her name, 'Clara! Clara!' smote her ear.

Startled, frightened, she turned, and saw between her and the rest of the party *a crack opening in the ground*—a crack which widened as she looked, while the ground trembled beneath her feet, and the hoarse roar of the river seemed suddenly strangely near.

Paralysed with horror, she turned giddy as she gazed on the gaping crack, and, in spite of the cry, 'Come back! *Back!*' she stood as if rooted to the spot, her tongue cleaving to the roof of her mouth, the sky and earth whirling darkly before her eyes. It was but the affair of a moment. For only one ghastly moment they saw her stand like a statue on the dreadful brink. Then she might have shaken off the paralysis of the shock, but might have recovered herself too late, when Coriolanus rushed upon the scene.

Before they could utter a word or stretch a hand to detain him he had leapt across the crack to Clara's side. He caught her round the waist, and was about to drag her back; but even as he flung his arm around her the opening gulf yawned wide, the ground shuddered and sank beneath them with a rushing rumbling sound, and the seething water surged up through the chasm. The whole bank, long insidiously undermined by the river, gave way suddenly at last.

Lifting Clara like a child, Coriolanus made one desperate bound for safety; but too late! The ground sliding from under his feet made him reel as he sprang. He felt himself sucked down by the current, and, with a supreme effort, threw Clara from him to the brink, where Lycurgus, rushing forward at infinite peril to himself, succeeded in seizing and drawing her into safety, while the torrent bore her rescuer away.

Clara, dizzy and half-fainting, scarcely comprehending what had happened, clinging blindly to Lycurgus, heard the agonised shriek of the mother and sisters. She turned, and saw for one instant, tossed above the foam, a hand— the strong kind hand she knew so well. Powerful swimmer though he was, he was swept away like a reed by the torrent. She saw, and, with a wild sobbing cry, fell insensible at Lycurgus's feet.

A little way down the river, it happened that a tangle of timber, drifting along on the waves, had caught on some jutting rocks and lodged there, piled up and wedged, and acting as a kind of dam against the shoreward current which eddied round it. The flood, instead of sweeping Coriolanus past this obstruction, dashed him against it. The eager watchers saw him strike and cling to it. They flew to the spot; they reached him just as his failing grasp was giving way. Lycurgus found a precarious footing along the slippery ridge of rock and timber. For a few moments of awful suspense his life also was in jeopardy, as he swung himself down close to the raging flood. Then he reached the senseless or lifeless body of his brother, grasped and dragged him to the shore.

They had left Clara in Imogen's care. They all crowded round him as he lay. They could not tell what injuries he had received, or whether he was mortally hurt. They lifted his right arm, which was doubled under him, and found it broken. He was terribly bruised, and bleeding from a wound on the head where he had been dashed violently against the jagged timbers.

They were feeling for a sign of life at his heart, when Clara, pale as he, came among them and knelt at his side.

'Is he dead?' she asked, not weeping now, but calm with the high-strung tense calmness of passionate feeling.

'No, no! His heart beats—he breathes!' exclaimed Lycurgus. 'There, don't you all cry now. He'll come-to all right.'

'We must get him to the house,' sobbed Mrs. Jones.

'Not to the house,' Lycurgus said. 'Why, mother, the house won't stand the night through!'

That evening, while the rapid semi-tropical night fell fast, the Joneses transferred themselves and their belongings to the abode of their nearest neighbour, who had built on a higher level and at a safe distance, and who bade them all 'come right over and stay.' They carried all their portable valuables out of the house, collecting the last batch by lantern-light, while the waters gurgled and splashed outside. Clara, pale and silent, was self-possessed enough to pack up her best dresses and jewels.

No one slept that night. They listened and looked out into the darkness, heard the river's rush and roar, and wondered what was happening out there in the night.

In the morning, where their home had stood, the swift flood rolled. The waters were calming; they had done their work, and would rise no higher. But of the White Ranche not a sign reared up above the rapid rolling current.

Clara sat by Coriolanus's side, as he lay in the deep sleep of exhaustion on the impromptu couch their hostess's neighbourly hands had made up in the back-parlour. Virginia had been keeping vigil by him in sisterly tenderness; and now Clara was taking her turn, watching for his awakening with a sickly suspense that dreaded and yet longed to hasten to meet his first look in her face—the first words he would say. She knew well what they would be!

All night her soul had tossed in as passionate a tempest as that which was raging outside. If she had never loved him before, it was something surely nearly akin to love that shook and stormed her spirit now. Freely and gallantly he had risked, and all but lost, his life for her. And could she now reward him by leaving him? Could she strike such a blow home to the brave heart that loved her so dearly, that for her sake had been so nearly stilled for ever?

'Ah,' she moaned to herself, restlessly twisting her hands together, 'what woman could do it?'

Then the vanity which, after all, was the master-passion of her nature—deeper than mere pride of face and form—came to her assistance, and she said,

'If other women could not do it, *I* can—I *will!*'

She stood, she knew, at the cross-roads of her future. Sir George Bellasys might even then be awaiting her in San Francisco. Should she, Clara Seyton, stoop to a weakness she despised? Let weaker women's hearts relent; *she* would stand firm. It must be done sooner or later. Why not now? Why put it off? If it hurt her, if it cost a heart-ache, what then?

The impulse of testing herself—of trying, probing, torturing herself—was strong in her, as it is ever found in women of her temperament. Now that to wound herself she must strike through him, should that hold back her hand?

Long before he woke the conflict in her heart was over.

He woke, and saw her sitting by his side.

'What was it, Clara, you were saying to me — that night?' he asked. 'Did I dream it? or— what did you tell me?'

Then she spoke. She repeated her resolution clearly, plainly, in tones more marble-hard and cold than if the iron had not entered into her heart. She left no doubt, no hope. She had been mistaken in dreaming for a day that she could ever be happy with him.

'All must be over between us,' she said.

His haggard altered face smote her, but her voice never shook.

'Then all *is* over,' he said, and turned his face to the wall.

She waited a while, and then spoke, half incredulously, half impatiently,

'Have you—have you nothing more to say to me?'

'What should I say?' he muttered hoarsely. 'If all is over— what more's to be said?'

'Are you not going to utter one word of reproach?' she said. 'Say something bitter to me, that I may remember when I have gone away.'

Her tone was urgent; the thought underlying it was, 'If he does not reproach me, how can I ever forget him? if he forgives me, how can I ever forgive myself?'

'Bitter?' he repeated, looking round. 'Why, Clara, it's not your fault if you can't love me.'

She smiled—a pale bitter smile —and wrung her hands together, till they were red with the pressure, as she said slowly, clearly,

'No, it is not my fault!' After a while she added—and they were the last words she spoke alone to Coriolanus, spoken slowly, truthfully, from soul to soul, as a last farewell—'In time you will forget me; but I shall never forget *you*. In leaving you, I think I leave the truest love that will ever be offered me—the truest heart I have ever known!'

'But you leave me!' he said drearily; for he knew *then*—knew well—that though her hand was clasping his hand, and her eyes meeting his, from out of his life and hope and future she was already gone.

A few months after, when the new ranche was built, and Mr. Jones, hopeful and energetic, was laying out his new land, Coriolanus one day visited the spot where the old White Ranche had stood. Nothing was left to tell of it now, save a low crumbling heap where the adobe walls had been. A ruined trunk or two lay where the tall eucalyptus‑trees had reared their evergreen heads. The waters had gone back to their old bed : their part was played. Coriolanus had a letter in his hand, signed 'Clara Bellasys.' It announced her marriage, of which she had resolved he should only hear from herself. Clara liked nothing to be left incomplete. She always put *finis* at the end of all her stories. It was rather from instinct than conscious sentiment that Coriolanus had brought her letter here. The golden morning mist veiled the valley just as in the days when she was by his side; the river shone in the sunshine just as before it had swept his home away. He tore the letter slowly into pieces, and let the fragments fall into the water.

'There's nothing left of it now!' he said to himself, as the white flecks floated away.

And the river at his feet seemed to murmur, 'Nothing left!'

THE PLIMSOLL ACT.

By AN EX-SHIPOWNER,

———

THAT a necessity for some maritime reform existed at the period the late Merchant Shipping Act was passed few will attempt to deny; but that a still greater necessity for reform exists to-day, and that the Act of 1873 has done an incalculable injury to a not unimportant portion of commercial Great Britain, I will venture to assert. I shall confine myself chiefly in this article to an examination of the working of the Act among shipping destined for the coasting or 'home' trade.

Every one will recollect the excitement created some years ago by Mr. Samuel Plimsoll's energetic proceedings both in the House of Commons and outside it, and it will also be remembered that what is generally termed 'the Plimsoll Act' was hurriedly made law rather on account of the dramatic action of the Sailor's Friend than as the outcome of calm and reasonable deliberation. I do not mean for a moment to set up a defence for those who sent 'coffin ships' to sea; but I should like to prove that the coffin ship was not the rule, but the exception; that it would not pay an ordinary shipowner to be the deliberate scoundrel which thousands believed him to be; that there are many necessary reforms entirely overlooked or ignored; and that the working of the Act itself savours in many instances of injustice, not to say corruption.

To build a schooner, say, of two hundred tons dead weight, so that she could be classed A1 at Lloyd's for twelve years, would cost about two thousand pounds. When a vessel of this description had 'run off her class' she would probably be valued at five to six hundred pounds, and would be converted into a coasting schooner or collier. If she were lucky, avoided accidents, and made rapid voyages, she might, perhaps, earn two hundred a year. This, no doubt, seems a large annual return for a small outlay, but 'look you now what follows.' Twenty-five per cent on the outlay would represent the depreciation in value and ordinary 'wear and tear,' and ten to twelve per cent the insurance premium, so that the margin for actual profit would be reduced to a minimum. As a rule the owner of this class of ship was compelled to make his profit in the dual character of owner and underwriter. He sends the ship to sea uninsured, or insured for a sum which in no way represents his risk, and so saves fifty to sixty pounds a year. Then comes the truly lively period in the life of the shipowner. If the weather is boisterous, his nights are passed under the same load of anxiety and dread which is usually accorded to the melodramatic murderer. There is no music for him in the sighing of the winds. He is reflecting that canvas is so much a yard, and oakum so much a pound, and very likely he has a dim vision of picking the latter article of merchandise in the character of a condemned trafficker in seamen's lives. When the tall pines bend and sway in the forests, he can fancy the masts of his argosies are being carried overboard to leeward. A fog has for him terrors unknown even to a winter resident of London. A balmy summer's day brings him no 'respite, however brief.' He fears it is a dead calm at sea, that his property is tumbling helplessly about, shaking cordage to pieces; or, worse still, drifting towards some hated rock which is waiting to gore the sides of his gallant barque. I defy the powers that be to invent weather which could have a soothing effect upon the uninsured shipowner. The load upon his shoulders was heavy indeed before the passing of the Plimsoll Act; but when the Act was put into violent operation the load became greater than mortal man could bear, and drove him into despair, the Bankruptcy Court, or the county gaol. In addition to his weather terrors, he had now the dread, if not the actual experience, of fine and imprisonment, and the knowledge that his fellow-men gazed upon him with a glare of contempt and abhorrence, that he was branded by them a low cunning schemer who traded upon the lives of unfortunate romantic sailors, and that in their heart of hearts they considered he was deserving of no better treatment than is meted out to a professional garrotter.

Every one appeared to overlook the fact that the majority of unclassed ships were either wholly uninsured, or else insured for a trifling sum, and therefore by no possibility could the owners of such ships profit by sending them to sea in an unsafe condition. It was their interest to keep them alive, not to send them to the bottom; to see that their hulls and equipments would render them seaworthy, 'having' (as the Act of 1873 says) 'regard for the nature

of the voyage or employment for which they may be intended.' But the Plimsoll Act took little or no account of the nature of the voyage or employment for which the coasting craft was intended. It wanted every ship to be equal to one classed A1 at Lloyd's, and from a commercial and reasonable point of view it will be seen that this would be an utter impossibility. Shipowners are not invariably wealthy philanthropists, but men of business with a keen sense of the value of pounds, shillings, and pence; and to invest 2000*l.* in a speculation which would (taking depreciation of value, &c., into account) infallibly cause a loss of some hundreds a year would be a thing 'no fellow could understand.' It will, perhaps, astonish landsmen to learn that the number of 'coffin ships' which actually *founder* round our coasts is and was so small that it would be scarcely worth while making a record of it. Ships are lost chiefly by getting ashore, by collision, by capsizing, by being pooped in a gale, by bad seamanship, and in some cases—though not so frequently as might be supposed—through overloading. It need scarcely be said that no matter how 'tight, staunch, and strong' a vessel may be, these accidents fall without distinction to her lot, whether she be classed or unclassed. Old Boreas is no discriminator of persons or property. He has the same sovereign contempt for the hulls which are certified by Lloyd's or the Board of Trade as for the hulls which bear no certificate. He drives them on a lee shore, rock, or sandbank without stopping to inquire if they are sound or unsound, shapely or deformed, classed or unclassed. When a steamboat runs over a schooner at night, the man on the look-out—should he happen to be awake—does not ask if 'the damned schooner' (the usual nominative of address with steamer folk) is old or young. So much the better if she is out of her teens, for there is seldom much of a row kicked up over an elderly victim.

Bad seamanship is a fruitful source of disasters on Neptune's highway, and the present loose system of shipping sailors in the coasting trade is utterly ignored by the powers that be. In the foreign trade a seaman is shipped and signs his articles before a shipping-master, but it is not easy to extend this custom to home-trade ships. The voyages are too short, and crews are employed and discharged so frequently that it would be almost impossible to bring them before a shipping-master on every occasion. However, there is no reason why the apprenticeship system should be allowed to fall into disuse. There is as much necessity for serving an apprenticeship to the sea as for being bound to a trade ashore. No man is born with an accurate knowledge of the devious workings of main braces or topsail-sheets; and few infants are taught to box the compass in their cradles. It is usually at the expense of the shipowner that seamanship is acquired. Any man can go on board a vessel, and obtain employment as an able seaman, if he is clever enough to deceive the master into the belief that he knows how to reef and steer, though very often the only 'steer' he is acquainted with is a herd of cattle. It may be urged that the master can ascertain on the voyage if his crew are competent to perform their duties, and if not, he can, by his articles of agreement, decline to pay them their wages. But it must be borne in mind that the sailor—or would-be sailor, as the case may be—can, if any dispute with the master arises, upon his arrival in port seek a Board of Trade surveyor under the Merchant Shipping Act, and inform him that the ship is unseaworthy. The surveyor courts reports of unseaworthiness, no matter from what quarter they come. It saves him a lot of trouble. He has a certain duty to perform towards his superiors; and, like a good policeman, the more 'cases' he has on his list the more likely he is to obtain promotion to a higher sphere. He comes on board. Something is certain to be wrong with the ship. If the hull is all right, the equipments are sure to be defective, and extensive repairs are instantly ordered. It is the business of every smart surveyor to discover some weak point in every ship. Few classed or unclassed ships are without some trifling defects, which do not, in the majority of cases, make them less fit to perform the voyages for which they are intended; and the surveyor, like a dutiful servant, discovers these defects. It may be that the ventilator is a little out of gear, or that the forecastle is not scientifically white-washed, or perhaps it is a more serious or less serious error which the microscopic eye of 'the Board of Trade man' detects. At all events, his fees have to be paid, and this is the main point at issue. Some time ago a wideawake gentleman at a certain seaport hit upon rather a neat plan for earning an honest livelihood. He would go aboard a coaster—he dare not fly at higher game—on pretence of looking for work, and seek an interview with the captain. After a thoughtful survey of the ship, he would demand half-a-crown or half-a-sovereign, according as he considered circumstances would warrant. 'For what?' would be the astonished reply. 'Well, there's a very active Board of Trade man hanging about; a word from me could do you a lot of harm. Tip us a few shillings, and I'll keep it square.' The result usually was a favourable one for the ' long-shore' man; as the master well knew, no matter how staunch his little ship might be, a surveyor would be certain to have his fees—if nothing worse—should he be induced to step over the gunwale, acting upon 'information received.'

A word or two more about Board of Trade surveyors, who should, in my opinion, be models which even the Chevalier Bayard might have studied with profit, and who should, above all things, be men possessed of an accurate and thorough knowledge of ships and their requirements. ' Would you be surprised to hear' that a distinguished surveyor once informed me gravely that he considered the ' rivets' in a certain wooden ship were defective? Now a rivet has as much to do with a wooden ship as the pitch at Her Majesty's has to do with Stockholm tar. No doubt this eminent 'Board of Trade man' would have recommended anti-corrosive paint for the mainsail had I stopped to listen; but the ' rivets' were too much for me. An ostrich may be able to digest tenpenny nails, but I doubt if the healthiest bird could swallow those rivets.

A shipwright, also, if he sees that business is not likely to be very brisk, can (out of pure philanthropy) report that such and such a vessel is sadly in need of a thorough overhauling.

In fact, there is scarcely any limit to the varieties of terrorism practised upon the man who unwisely invests in floating sticks.

But to return to the question of seamanship. Is it not reasonable to expect that some measures should be taken to protect owners of coasting vessels from unseaworthy sailors? Yet the authorities do nothing to improve the present state of affairs. A ship is as much

in need of a competent crew—particularly in this economical age, when short-handed sailing is the order of the day—as a watchmaker is of competent men to make his watches. It may be said that the owner or commander of a ship has just as much right as the watchmaker to know what sort of men he employs; but, as I have attempted to show, the sailor is the master, not the servant; and will remain master of the situation so long as there is no compulsory system of apprenticeship in existence, and so long as Board of Trade surveyors attach paramount importance to his complaints. It appears strange, too, that as the law stands at present any one may take command of a coasting vessel, and style himself ' master mariner.' A modern Cincinnatus, fresh from the plough, might possibly prove an excellent statesman; but put him on the deck of a schooner, and he would most likely attempt to steer with the pump-rake. The master of a ship in the foreign trade is now compelled to pass an examination, and to satisfy his examiners that he is competent to navigate his ship in any latitude; but the master of a coasting vessel is not obliged to undergo any examination. Of course, it is the interest of the owner to see that no master mariner takes charge of his property unless he is competent; but it would be no injury to anybody if the Board of Trade insisted that every seaman should show he was possessed of a thorough knowledge of his business before he could be put in command of any craft, whether in the coasting trade or otherwise. Shipowners have often to suffer severely in consequence of the laxity of the law in this instance. The home-trade masters need not be obliged to undergo such a searching examination as their brethren in the foreign trade; but at least they might be asked to prove that they have been sufficiently long at sea to know their work. No reasonable seafaring man could object to this; and it would tend to make the position of the coasting shipmaster a more lucrative one than it is at present. A seafaring life is now the last infirmity of ignoble minds; and instead of labelling the coaster a coffin ship, it would be more accurate to term her a floating workhouse.

Measurement is another subject which sadly needs a little looking after. With trading ships the registered tonnage is usually a little less than two-thirds of the dead weight, or gross carrying powers. As all port charges, &c., are chargeable on the 'register,' it is obviously a matter of great importance to the owner to have it as low as possible. Allowances are made for enlarged crew-space and for other reasons, and this often reduces the registered to nearly half the gross tonnage; but I have seen ships which could stow away considerably more than double their certified powers. I have interrogated seafaring men as to the cause of this peculiarity. Some declared their ships were oddly constructed, or gave extraordinary accommodation to the crew, and so forth; but more than one has whispered, 'You see, a surveyor comes on board to measure or remeasure the vessel. We have a chat in the cabin about the weather or the crops. I am suddenly called on deck, and in the hurry I leave my purse on the cabin-table. When I return the purse has disappeared. I could not dream of accusing such an upright man as the surveyor of taking it—could I?'

Although every precaution is taken to prevent loss of life amongst British tars, no effort is made to secure the life of the foreign sailor. Any foreign ship, no matter in what condition are her hull and equipments, can proudly weather the gale and the Board of Trade surveyor. So long as it is not the union-jack which floats over the stern, so long is the ship exempt from interference of any kind. No doubt it would be against all principles of free-trade, freedom, or good breeding to tamper with a foreign coffin ship; but it certainly gives an extraordinary advantage to the Gaul, Scandinavian, Italian, German, or Yankee who cares to cruise in British waters. He has no surveyor's fees to dread, no felted bulkheads to look after, no compulsory ventilators to contend with. He may stow his cargo in the forecastle, eschew whitewash, and stick his side-lights over his bows, should he be so inclined. As the result of all his advantages, he is enabled to carry merchandise at a lower rate of freight than his less favoured British neighbours; and the only wonder is that the numbers of little foreign crafts that find a fat living in British waters is not largely augmented. It is a significant fact that, for the four years from 1875 to 1878, the number of British tons entered and cleared at ports in the United Kingdom shows a *decrease* of about five millions; while the number of foreign tons entered and cleared in the United Kingdom during the same period shows an *increase* of one million.

The French do not allow our ships to trade coastwise in France; but then we wish to outdo even our Gallic neighbours in mercantile politeness. The restrictions which cripple the English ship in competition with the foreigner are not, I must admit, felt so keenly at home as abroad. When the Grain Cargoes Bill was going through committee, last session, a merchant was examined, and asked what course he would be likely to pursue in case it were made compulsory with British vessels to carry grain in sacks. 'Order my agents *not* to charter a British ship,' was the gist of his reply.

And here, it may be readily seen, lies one of the worst features of the case. We are always too eager to be first at everything. We dub the Americans a 'go-ahead' people, but in reality they are not nearly so go-ahead as ourselves. We went headlong into the adoption of Free-trade, under the impression that other countries, especially France and America, would follow our lead. But France and America did not think it was time enough yet, and they determined to hold fast to the protection system until they saw how Free-trade prospered with us; and of late years they have been quietly reaping a harvest while we are struggling to ride our hobby.

The portion of the shipowning community which suffered most by the harsh provisions of the late Merchant Shipping Act consisted of poor seafaring folk, who had worked hard all their lifetime in order to put a few hundred pounds together. Their savings were then invested in some small craft, which, perhaps, had seen the best of her days, but which nevertheless was quite capable of carrying her crew and cargoes safely from one port in the British Isles to another. Not unfrequently a whole family, father and sons, would purchase a handy schooner, and sail her themselves. It would be very hard to say that these men would wilfully intrust their lives to a craft which was ut-terly unfit to make a voyage. Yet the Board of Trade surveyors evi-dently thought a suicidal mania was abroad. The vessel was stopped, repairs of an extensive nature or-dered, and no quarter given. The owners had no more money to spend; so the ship was laid up, and

the proprietors driven to begin life afresh, some of them at an age when beginning life was out of the question. Often have I heard an old salt remark, 'We ought to be thankful to the Government of our country. The Board of Trade has made up its mind that we sha'n't die at sea; so we are supplied with another Board—the Poor Law—to fall back upon for a resting-place.'

Another injustice is, that if a ship is repaired and made sea-worthy under the inspection of a Board of Trade officer, she is still liable to be detained and over-hauled at any moment on the most frivolous pretext. Perhaps the dia-meter of a bell which is never tolled, or the revolving power of a fore-castle ventilator, which is carefully 'made snug' by the inhabitants of the forecastle when the ship goes to sea, is not in exact accordance with the regulations laid down by the Merchant Shipping Act. In such a case more fees are cheerfully demanded and as cheerfully paid.

It may be said, Why do not shipowners rebel? Why do they not expose the grievances they labour under? But please bear in mind that the owners of coast-ing vessels are frequently men of limited means, who are unable to wrestle with a powerful opponent like the Board of Trade. As a matter of fact, when, smarting under some unusually stinging lash, the shipowner has rebelled and sought a court of law, he has, in most cases, worsted his enemy; but it is a question if 'the cost did not outweigh the profit.' There is no grade of life in which submission to tyranny can better be practised than in the *rôle* of a shipowner with a small capital. Not only is he compelled to stop the *leak*, but he must eat the *leek* too. Welsh-men will please excuse this joke.

Sailors were enthusiastic about the Plimsoll Act during the early stages of the agitation; but they will tell you a different tale to-day. Want of employment and semi-starvation have taken the spice out of the enthusiasm. The number of seamen employed in British sailing ships in 1878 was nearly twenty thousand less than the number employed in 1872, a falling off of about fifteen per cent. This, in the face of a rumoured reduction of hands in the navy, is not very cheering intelligence for our tars; but let us hope that the wave of returning prosperity will not reach our shores without floating Jack clear of the rocks and shoals of maritime depression.

That the vast majority of lost seamen perish through causes which no Shipping Act can cope with, or over which no Board of Trade can have control, is a fact which cannot be dwelt upon at sufficient length. Our lifeboat system, our lighthouses, our ports of refuge, and good careful seamanship have done more to preserve the life of the sailor than all the clauses which have ever been passed through a Select Committee. If the authorities would only devote their attention to lifeboats, lighthouses, efficient training for seamen, and harbours of refuge, it would be more useful than spending time and money in repressive legislation. But it would be absurd to suppose that those who know nothing, or next to nothing, of the real perils and dangers of the seas would be likely to frame good laws and regulations for the prevention of maritime disasters. Landsmen are carried away by the enthusiasm of a few philanthropists who imagine that every case of loss of life at sea is attributable to causes which poor human beings have complete power to negative. Such is unfortunately not the case. The very document which each master of a ship signs as a receipt for the

cargo intrusted to him, and as an engagement to deliver it safely at its port of destination, expressly states that 'the act of God, the Queen's enemies, fire, and all and every dangers and accidents of the sea of whatsoever kind,' must be taken into account. Those dangers and accidents, broadly speaking, are dangers and accidents which cannot be legislated for. Even ashore, where similar difficulties do not arise, we are unable to make railway travelling a perfect security; yet Mr. Plimsoll's Bill attempted to promise Jack afloat that for the future he would be quite as safe as Jack ashore—or rather more safe.

On the whole, it would not be easy to find an Act which, though it appears to be framed in as unobjectionable a manner as possible, has in it more elements of injustice; or an Act which is less likely to fulfil the intention of its promoters, namely, to rescue the sailor from a watery grave. This is no doubt chargeable, in a great measure, to those who have the executive portion of it in their hands. Let any one examine the lists which give a record of those who were lost round our coast, through the *foundering* of ships, in the years when no Plimsoll Act existed, and compare them with the lists of late years when the Act was in operation, and he will be astonished to discover that the Sailor's Friend has done little service to suffering humanity. On the other hand, let any one examine the records of the Bankruptcy Courts, or the workhouses which deal with places and people who depended upon ships and shipping for a livelihood, and he will be convinced that the Plimsoll Act has at least done an irreparable injury to one section—unimportant, perhaps, though it may be—of the British Empire.

THE BARD OF INVERALN.

By Jb. MONTEATH,

AUTHOR OF 'THE LOVES O' LANGSYNE,' 'MEN WHO HAVE FALLEN,' ETC.

I.

Mrs. Black was not a widow : her husband was ' over the sea'—somewhere. Mrs. Black had been a wife a twelvemonth and a day when, during the forenoon, Mr. Black came home from business, and intimated to the partner of his joys and sorrows that a crisis in the affairs of his firm necessitated his immediate departure for Spain. Mr. Black's firm—White, Black, & Co.—were stockbrokers. There was no 'Co.' in existence ; that was an ornamental appendage tacked to the name of the firm when Mr. White, feeling himself old and less able than in bygone years to traffic on 'Change, assumed as partner his principal clerk, Mr. Black. Leaving the management of affairs entirely to the junior partner, Mr. White sought well-earned rest in a suburban villa, visiting his office once or twice a week to advise with Mr. Black. For a time all went well with the firm; business, through the active exertions of the junior partner, increased tenfold— so at least reported Mr. Black to Mr. White, who, glancing at the cashbook and skimming the pages of the ledger, was satisfied he had taken a wise step in giving his chief clerk a large share in the concern.

The story of the rise and fall of the firm of White, Black, & Co. has no interest for us beyond the fact that, when the crash came, Mr. Black found it necessary for his personal freedom to fly to lands afar ; therefore we do not enter into the history of the transactions —'frauds and forgeries' they were at the time of their occurrence stated to be—that led to the utter ruin of old Mr. White, and to Mrs. Black being forsaken by her husband.

Mr. Black had told his wife that it might be a month or two before he could return ; but she was not to fret, for, if he did not soon reappear in New Sidon City, he would send for her. Mrs. Black was a somewhat matter-of-fact woman : sorrow did not seem to depress her, nor did joy unduly raise her spirits. When Mr. Black said he was going, she answered, ' Very well,' and hoped he would take care of himself : she did not add, ' For my sake, dear.' And, replying to her husband's promise to send for her if he did not soon return, Mrs. Black said, ' Of course you will ;' but she had no idea of adding that she could not live happily without his presence. Mrs. Black, in short, was not a woman of affectionate nature : she owned to likes and dislikes—she liked her husband much as she liked a new dress, and disliked his going away in the same fashion as she would have disliked parting with a favourite article of jewelry. When Mr. Black had said good-bye and was gone, she did not ' dissolve in tears :' her study was how, during the next few weeks, she could best amuse herself. When, on the morrow, the truth was revealed to her by Mr. White, that her husband had been guilty of serious crimes, and had brought ruin and dishonour on all connected with him,

Mrs. Black quietly said, 'Who would have thought he could have done such things!' But tears came not: she was annoyed—not grieved. And when, later in the day, Mr. Morgan, the eminent cabinet-maker, called, and, expressing regret at having an unpleasant duty to perform, intimated that only a small sum had as yet been paid of his bill for furnishing Mr. Black's mansion, and inquired whether Mrs. Black had any offer of settlement to propose, she replied, 'Well, I daresay Mr. Black did intend to pay your bill—some day; but as he is gone, and I am afraid will not be in a hurry to return, you had better take back your goods and reckon with him for the damage done thereto, should opportunity ever occur for so doing. For my part, I have no money with which to pay your account.' She did not appear to regret that even her home was involved in the wreck caused by her husband's misconduct. She opened her eyes to the inevitable, surveyed the situation calmly, and closed her eyelids sans a tear. A few days later Mr. Morgan removed *his* 'goods,' and Mrs. Black returned to that home whence, a short year ago, she emerged the wife of a successful young stockbroker, who, according to his own account, meant to realise a fortune within a few years, and afterwards devote himself to acquiring local, if not national, honours.

Time hung heavily on Mrs. Black's hands: she had no sisters at home with whom to idle hours away; and her mother was an invalid, confined to her room and in charge of a sick-nurse who permitted no 'trifling' with her patient. Mrs. Black's father and brothers were engaged in the spirit trade, and did not come home until midnight. Therefore Mrs. Black was left to the freedom of her own will: her will led her to take up a book and look at it a while, and then lay it down with air of unconcern that plainly said, 'Not in my way'—even fashionable novels for her possessed no charm. All feminine and ladylike accomplishments she had acquired, but not one of them seemed now to deserve her attention, even as a pastime, in her loneliness. Perhaps, in one sense, she was over-educated: be that as it may, she had not been trained up a true woman—full of love for a fireside and sympathy for the joys and sorrows of life.

Exteriorly, however, Mrs. Black was (as some tastes go) a lovable woman. She had a good figure, pleasant features, and an excellent manner: she was, in short, a good drawing-room ornament; and, as such, most suitable for many men, since many men study outward appearance rather than genuine worth in woman. Had Mr. Black only kept within the bounds of legal honesty, and continued successfully his rising career, some future day Mrs. Black would have made a charming chief magistrate's lady.

Time, as stated above, hung heavily on Mrs. Black's hands. Weeks passed: Mr. Black did not return to New Sidon City, nor had he written for his wife to come to him. Mrs. Black had an elderly maiden aunt residing in Inveraln, a 'sweetly pretty' village about forty miles distant from New Sidon City. Her mother (whose elder sister was the aunt alluded to) suggested that Mrs. Black ought to pay her relative a visit, to help her 'bear her sorrow patiently' until news concerning Mr. Black should arrive. The aunt was communicated with, and in due time sent an invitation to her beloved niece to come and stay as long as she liked.

———

II.

WHEN a young girl, Mrs. Black had on more than one occasion visited Inveraln. She was therefore not an absolute stranger to the beauties of the locality; but so many years had gone by since her last visit, and so much had happened during the long interval, that the scenes were in a sense all new, fresh at least, to her, and for some days she passed time pleasantly, if not profitably—now by the riverside, anon in Fernie Glen, again in 'Sweet Jerah Wood.' As with books and music and needlework, so with 'running brooks' and 'sylvan shades'—Mrs. Black soon tired of them; and she had recourse to her old aunt, into whose ear she poured a most matter-of-fact version of the story of her marriage and wedded life and of her husband's 'silly conduct,' as she mildly termed his delinquencies.

'Doubtless,' said Mrs. Black to her aunt, 'Tom has started business afresh somewhere, and he defers writing until he has arranged a home for me.'

'I hope such is the case, my dear Bella,' replied the aunt. 'It is a great pity your husband so far forgot himself as to be guilty of—of—what he did.'

'Well, it was very silly of him to write other people's names: I'm sure he could have made plenty of money without doing that.'

'I daresay he is now very sorry for his misdeeds; and of course, being his wife, you must forgive him.'

'O yes: I forgive him,' said Mrs. Black in a cheery tone.

'That's right, my dear; and I hope you'll both soon be together again and happy.'

But her aunt's hopes were after all poor consolation to the forsaken wife, who in her heart of hearts perhaps entertained serious doubts of her restoration to happiness—such happiness as her wedded life and her loveless disposition had afforded her: in truth, it was not so much happiness she sighed for, as restoration to her former position of mistress of a well-lined purse, by means of which she could gratify her every passing whim. For the present she was dependent on the bounty of her father, who, having educated her and handed her over to a husband, fancied that, so far as his daughter was concerned, his paternal mission was accomplished. In the hour of misfortune she was of course welcome to his home and heart, but his purse was closed against her.

'If,' said the aunt kindly—'if you had had a baby to engage your attention, how much happier you would have been during your husband's absence!'

'Perhaps,' replied Mrs. Black; 'but there's no baby, and there's no use thinking what I might have been with one: it is quite enough to have to think about what I am without a baby.'

'Well, well, my dear,' said the aunt tenderly, 'don't trouble yourself thinking—do the best you can here, walk about and enjoy yourself: all will come right—by and by.'

Mrs. Black's aunt now wished to indulge in her afternoon nap; and her niece, for want of better employment, betook herself to the kitchen to consult Mary, the aunt's maid-of-all-work, whether there was not one place she had not yet seen.

Mrs. Black found Mary employed washing up the dinner-things, the while 'singing like a lintie.'

'Sing on, Mary—don't stop on my account.'

'Please, ma'm, I never sing before any person.'

'What song were you singing,

Mary ? One of those silly Christy Minstrel songs ?'

'No,' answered Mary, 'not a Christy Minstrel one : not that I think the Christy songs silly, but because I prefer Scots songs.'

'Well, we'll not discuss the silliness of the Christys. I suppose it was some foolish love-song, about a Jamie or a Johnnie ?'

'No, ma'm : a love-song it was, but one about a—a lassie.'

'And doubtless her name is Mary ?'

'Yes, ma'm.'

'Those poets are all alike—they all call their heroines Mary, although I daresay their sweethearts bear less elegant names.'

'Do you think Mary a nice name, ma'm ?'

'It sounds well enough, and I daresay that is why the poets are so fond of it.'

'It's my name, ma'm.'

'Ah, so it is—I forgot that. And, because the song is addressed to a Mary and your name happens to be Mary, I suppose that while singing you were indulging a romantic dream that you were the song-heroine, as those poets term their sweethearts ?'

'I'm the Mary o' the song.'

'What !—you *the* Mary ?'

'Yes, ma'm—it's true.'

'And who may the poet be ?'

'Ah, well—maybe I've said too much already ; but it's a friend o' mine that made the song, and that's all I'll say.'

'Very good, Mary ; I'll not ask any further questions ; but perhaps you'll not object to show me the words of the song—unless indeed you'll sing them to me ?'

'And that I winna do,' replied Mary ; 'but you may read them if you like, ma'm.'

Mary opened a drawer, and from it produced a half-sheet of foolscap, on which were written, in a big round hand, three verses entitled 'Mary, Queen o' Inveraln,' and signed 'William Stuart.'

'You'll let me take the song with me to read it at my leisure ? I'll give it you back unharmed.'

'Very well, ma'm ; and I hope you'll enjoy reading it—not, however, on my account, but because the lad that made it is ane o' the best o' men—all the village folk have a good word to say o' Willie Stuart.'

———

III.

'AND so you are the Village Poet,' said Mrs. Black, addressing William Stuart, who, at Mary's request, had brought several of his pieces to show to her mistress's niece from New Sidon City. It was not that she cared for poetry that induced Mrs. Black to ask Mary to influence William Stuart to submit a few of his rhymes to her inspection : it would be something new to her to look upon and to talk to a songwriter—something to which she could give her attention, and thus agreeably pass an hour.

The Village Poet had long enjoyed the praises of his equals : now there was opportunity to hear a kind word—so dear to all poets —from one belonging to a station in life higher than his own, and that one a woman ; and therefore William Stuart gladly obeyed Mary's request to show his rhymes to Mrs. Black ; for praise from woman's lip falls sweetly on the poet-ear.

'Your song to Mary I much like,' continued Mrs. Black : ' not, however, because I care for love-songs, for, generally speaking, they are excessively foolish—the girl is made far too good, more like an angel than a human being.'

'That, madam, may arise in this way : the poetic eye sees differently from the bodily eye—a very ordinary female is thus transformed into an angelic creature; or perhaps we sing of woman as she ought to be, not what circumstances have made her.'

'Well, we will not discuss the point. Of course all your verses are not love-songs?'

'No, madam—not all love-songs.'

'Then read me one that is not a love-song.'

'Here is one entitled "A Hearty Laugh:" does the subject meet your approbation?' asked the Poet.

'An uncommon theme, I should say, among poets, who, I have always understood, are melancholy men,' remarked Mrs. Black, the faintest shadow of a smile playing on her lip. 'Yes: read it — or sing it, if you please.'

'I seldom sing—singing I leave to my friends. But I will read the verses.'

William Stuart somewhat tremulously yet distinctly read the following verses:

'Let those who will the wine-cup quaff,
    Or disagree o'er Whig and Tory:
Give me a right good hearty laugh
    O'er some rich joke or well-told story.
A hearty laugh—none dare gainsay—
    Will blunt the edge of keenest sorrow:
Help man enjoy his life to-day,
    And courage give him for the morrow.
    Let those who will the wine-cup quaff,
        Or disagree o'er Whig and Tory:
    Give me a right good hearty laugh
        O'er some rich joke or well-told story.

A hearty laugh is better far
    Than drugs some folk persist in buying:
With nature they wage constant war—
    No wonder 'tis they're always dying.
This homely hint, if you are wise,
    You'll look upon with certain favour:
The salt of life is exercise—
    A hearty laugh that salt's best savour.
    Let those who will the wine-cup quaff,
        Or disagree o'er Whig and Tory:
    Give me a right good hearty laugh
        O'er some rich joke or well-told story.'

'Very well put together,' said Mrs. Black; 'and for poetry most sensible advice. I daresay we all should be much better at times if we indulged in a hearty laugh: some of us, however, were born to

sorrow, and laughter is not in our way.'

The Poet knew that his fair critic was married, but he was not aware that Mr. Black had run away, leaving his wife to the 'cold charity' of the world: had he known her position, how his compassionate heart would have sympathised with her in her sorrow! He would have credited her with bearing a load of woe of which she herself knew nothing.

'What other subject can you recommend to my notice?' asked Mrs. Black. 'Something touching.'

'A couple of verses entitled "Isobel" may be worthy your attention.'

'Read them, please.'

'From Cherubland she came
    With us to dwell:
To her we gave the name
    Of Isobel.
But, loving not this sphere,
    She closed her eyes;
And hurried far from here—
    Beyond the skies.

"Not lost, but gone before:"
    At Glory's gates,
Upon the Shining Shore,
    For us she waits.
But, ah, the tear will start—
    Though silent, tell
How dear to soul and heart
    Was Isobel.'

'Poor little dear!' said Mrs. Black. 'Whose child was Isobel —that of some friend of yours, I suppose? for, if I mistake not, you are not married.'

'You rightly guess, madam: Isobel was the child of a friend, whose touching intimation of her decease suggested the verses.'

'I daresay you are fond of such themes—they suit your disposition, I suppose?'

'To hear of a friend's death is certain to inspire a verse or two.'

'Then you really believe you are inspired? Cannot you dash off a verse or two at a moment's notice? I have heard of poets that could do so.'

'Possibly what you have heard is true: in my case, however, the rule, if it be a rule, does not hold good. Perhaps I use a too high-sounding word when I talk of "inspiration:" be that as it may, in more homely phraseology, I feel the rhyming fit strong upon me at times, and I cannot resist stringing lines together; whilst at other times, even if I tried ever so hard, I could not produce a single line.'

'Therefore,' said Mrs. Black, 'should I wish you to make a verse or two for me, I must wait patiently until I find you in a rhyming mood?'

'Which, madam, you are not likely to do.'

'Why?'

'Because when the rhyming fit comes on I am generally in some lonely nook, where no one is likely to find me.'

'Lonely nook—ah, loneliness is the subject I should wish you to write upon for me.'

'Any particular phase of loneliness, madam? I daresay you know that loneliness is altogether a matter of taste or of disposition: once, for instance, I paid your great city a visit, and how lonely I felt among the busy crowd!'

'What! lonely in New Sidon City? Who would have thought one could feel lonely on such busy streets as those of New Sidon?'

'It was true in my case. When I am buried in some leaf-covered nook in Jerah Wood I do not feel lonely: possibly in such situation you would consider yourself not only lonely but lost. Therefore, madam, I must ask what phase of loneliness you prefer I take up on your behalf?'

'Well, in truth I never dreamt that the subject had more phases than one. What I wish is a verse or two telling of one who is—who is, say, left alone in the world: alone, that is, on account of—of—of the nearest and dearest being absent.'

'Mayhap my verses entitled "Uncle Tom" would suit you?'

'Perhaps: will you read them?'

'He grew frae boy to man,
  And moved frae place to place;
But never wi' the lasses ran,
  Nor loved a pretty face.

We all agreed that he
  No thought had o' a wife—
That Uncle Tom indeed wad be
  A bachelor through life.

And yet there came a day
  That he resolved to wed:
The fairest lass on banks o' Tay
  He to the altar led.

Their home was Love's domain—
  Their hours in pleasure sped:
None saw and markt wi' secret pain
  A dark cloud overhead.

Alas! 'twas life for life!
  A moment's joy—then gloom!
Within a year Tom's darling wife
  Was laid in silent tomb.

As e'ening creeps apace,
  The day's turmoil gone by,
Tom sits and scans his bairnie's face,
  Then looks toward the sky.'

'Uncle Tom, madam, has lost the one nearest and dearest to him—his wife: doubtless, as he looks toward the sky, he feels lonely. Does the piece meet your wish?'

'Not exactly—I did not, for one thing, have absence on account of death in view: I meant lonely because—because—well, never mind for the present. Is "Uncle Tom" a true story?'

'Founded on facts, madam. Indeed, except the name of the man and the scene of the narrative, I may say the story is a truthful record.'

Mrs. Black felt she ought to say something more about the verses on Uncle Tom — criticise them: so she remarked:

'Your verses are very charming, Mr. Stuart. I wonder you remain in this secluded village, where at most your songs can only enjoy a local popularity. You ought to

migrate to New Sidon City : there
you would soon become a great
man : there the music-publishers
would, I feel certain, readily purchase your songs, giving you a
handsome sum for them ; and in a
short time you would be a rich
man.'

'Well : I have never dreamt of
writing songs for money, nor has
my ambition ever soared so high
as appearing in print, far less of
having music composed for my
songs and their being sung at concerts. No, no—I am too humble
a poet for all that.'

'If I may express my opinion,'
said Mrs. Black, with a slight
spark of enthusiasm in her tone,
'you are as good as most, and perhaps better than some, of the verse-
makers whose songs are popular :
you may not be a Burns or a Tanna-
hill, but you are a great deal better
than those poets who provide us
with the silly "Darling Nelly Gray"
songs. Take my advice—migrate,
and become a city poet.'

'I'll think over it, madam.
Permit me to say that I am much
pleased that my songs are so highly
thought of by you.'

'They are delightful—indeed
they are ! Good-night, Mr. Stuart.
Hereafter you and your songs will
be recalled with pleasure ; and I
thank you very much for having
brought your verses to me.'

'Good-night, madam. I thank
you for your pretty compliments.'

IV.

ON the evening of the day following her interview with the Village Poet, Mrs. Black started on a
long ramble. She chose the riverside path, and intended going as far
as 'the Brig' [Bridge], a distance
of about three miles, and then returning by the highway. As she
walked along the bank of the river
her thoughts reverted to William
Stuart—not to his songs : it was
the man, not the poet, she recalled :
not even the man as a whole, only
his eyes—they were large, hazel-
coloured, and seemed to 'look one
through and through.' And she
wondered if those eyes had looked
her through, and what impression
she had made upon the man. And
it occurred to her that Mr. Black's
eyes, which she could not remember
were of any particular colour, had
never cost her a thought ; and that
she had never wondered what impression she had made on the mind
of her husband. Thus she mused
—making comparisons which lowered the stockbroker, while they
raised the songwriter, in her estimation. She also thought of Mary
the maid-of-all-work, and wondered
whether Mr. Stuart really meant to
'throw himself away upon the like
of her.' He was worth a far better
woman than Mary was or ever
would be. One other step, and she
regretted that she herself was a
wife.

'But, alas,' she thought, 'even
suppose I were still single, or for
that matter a widow, which perhaps I am, for maybe Tom is dead,
this poet is so poor that I could
not think of him as a husband. I
wonder if Tom is still alive : he
has never written—perhaps he is
dead ; but I must not think such
things : it is very silly—very wicked
perhaps. . . If Mr. Stuart were here,
how much more pleasant this walk
would be ! I wonder if he is in a
rhyming mood this evening, and
whether he is indulging his verse-
making hobby in the wood.'

As Mrs. Black walked she wondered—now her husband, now William Stuart, engaging her thoughts.
She allowed her imagination full
scope—for the first time in her
existence—man *versus* man, not
stockbroker *versus* poet, being its

theme—which theme was argued and reargued until the men changed places : she was Mrs. Stuart, not Mrs. Black.

'It is very silly—very wicked, perhaps,' thought Mrs. Black; nevertheless she turned aside from the river-bank and directed her steps toward Jerah Wood, the skirt of which was only a hundred yards distant from the river.

Had water and wood been a mile apart, Mrs. Black might have had time to reflect on her 'wickedness' and to turn back; as it was, on reaching the edge of the wood she was in imagination still Mrs. Stuart; and when her eye fell upon the Poet—who was reclining on the grass, his eye (that piercing eye of his) fixed on a wild forget-me-not—Mrs. Black exclaimed, with a fervour of tone hitherto strange to her lip, 'So, I have found you! I am so glad!'

The Poet looked up in amazement, for a moment not seeming to recognise the intruder on his sacred musing-ground. Quickly rising, however, and casting away his forget-me-not—which Mrs. Black at once picked up—Mr. Stuart apologised for his attitude of the moment, explaining that such was his favourite posture while stringing his lines together.

'In that position,' said the Poet, 'I can best from Nature look up to Nature's God.'

'Don't be silly!' remarked Mrs. Black impetuously. 'Never mind Nature—never mind poetry : are you glad to see me?'

'Certainly I am,' replied Mr. Stuart quietly; 'only I might have been more glad to see you had you delayed your arrival for half an hour.'

'Indeed! why?'

'Well : that little forget-me-not, which you were kind enough to lift from the ground, after I had heedlessly cast it away, when you arrived, was suggesting some pretty ideas, and in a half-hour's time those ideas would have taken the shape of words—'

'I'm very sorry I disturbed you; but you'll forgive me—pray do?'

'Madam, there is nothing more to forgive than a lost rhyme,' replied the Poet somewhat sternly; 'and that is forgiven.'

'Of course it is—more especially when—when—'

Mrs. Black paused and glanced toward the ground.

William Stuart fancied his reproof had offended the lady, and he begged her to excuse his rough manner, saying that he would rather toss himself in the river than hurt the feelings of any one, especially those of a woman: 'I beg pardon,' he added, 'a lady.'

'It is my turn to forgive,' said Mrs. Black, raising her eyes, to meet those of the Poet fixed upon her, 'and I forgive you. Are we now friends, Mr. Stuart?'

'Friends, madam! You, a lady—I, a common clod—friends! Madam, your servant;' and William Stuart, uncovering, bowed respectfully.

'No!' exclaimed Mrs. Black—'not servant—friend! Be my friend, Mr. Stuart.'

'Madam—'

'Do not say madam—say—say nothing !'

'Except good-evening, ma—' and, again uncovering, William Stuart turned away.

'You are not going—come back; will you not show me your favourite spots in the wood? I came here hoping to find you, and believing that you would not deny me the boon of—of seeing where you compose your songs; will you so greatly favour me? Now—this evening,' added Mrs. Black softly, 'for to-morrow I may bid adieu to—to Inveraln.'

'I will show you every nook and cranny of the wood if you wish, ma— Now what can I say—how am I to address you?'

'Call me—yes, Mrs. Black. I am Mrs. Black—you know my name?'

'Yes——Mrs. Black.'

'Come—make haste ; it will soon be dark.'

'But we have beautiful moonlight now, and—'

'We shall not be lost, like the celebrated Babes in the Wood,' interrupted Mrs. Black in a cheery voice.

'Even were it the darkest night in winter you would be safe while in my charge ; each tree is my friend, telling me where I am and how far I have still to go.'

'And so I may trust you—you will not lose me : well, let us proceed.'

————

V.

'It was very silly—very wicked, perhaps ; but—'

Mrs. Black paused: she hesitated to confess to herself the truth.

'Very silly—very wicked on my part—a married woman—to give way to—such—silliness ! But that Village Poet, as his friends at Inveraln style him, is not an everyday man ; there is something attractive about him—some attraction that one cannot resist. What is it? There is nothing uncommon about his appearance as a whole ; nor, when I endeavoured to criticise each individual feature, could I fasten upon one that deserved particular attention—except his eyes. Now what are eyes? Useful to see with. It could not be his eyes that enslaved me, and led me a willing victim to his side, ready to sacrifice *all* for him ; yet those eyes of his do look at one so—seem to send an electric shock through one's whole frame. I wonder whether his

maid-of-all-work sweetheart—that Mary whom he seems to worship —ever feels as I felt that night in the wood? Of course she has not had my experience—she is not a wife—a widow, perhaps. Wife or widow? I really wonder where Tom is—what he is doing—whether he be alive. If he were dead—if I was only certain Tom was no more—I would—yes, I would give up all for William Stuart. True, he has his Mary ; but I think, were I only free to give him the chance of having me, he would forsake that country girl and share his lot with mine. I remember— that night in the wood—when, after telling him the story of my unfortunate marriage, I placed my head on his shoulder, and confessed myself sorry I was a wife, how he started, and, fastening those big eyes of his upon me, seemed spellbound—only for a moment, though. He stepped aside and—that look of his ! "Madam," he said, "remember you are a wife—a wife is sacred to her husband, be he absent or present : do not forget your duty !" But I was not to be subdued. "Doubtless my husband is dead," I replied ; "and what duty do I owe him even if he be still alive? did not he prove himself a bad, unprincipled, wicked man— wronging his fellow-men and deserting his wife? Duty—what duty can a wife owe to such a husband?" "A wife's duty, madam," he replied ; "that is all I can say." What is my duty to Tom? To sit here, in my father's house, day after day, week after week, month after month—it is now fully six months since he went away—waiting patiently his pleasure to write to me ; is that a wife's duty? I suppose it is—so I must submit to it : only I do so unwillingly, because there lives one who I think could make me happy.'

'Madam,' said a servant—who, having twice knocked, concluded that Mrs. Black was not within, and entered to deposit on the table a letter that had just arrived by the midday post—'a letter for you.'

'A letter for me!' exclaimed Mrs. Black, who, since her 'fall,' as she termed the circumstances connected with her return to her father's house, held correspondence with no one.

The servant, not being interested in Mrs. Black's affairs, retired with a simple 'Yes, madam,' leaving Mrs. Black to meditate at leisure over the unexpected communication.

'From Inveraln,' said Mrs. Black, glancing at the postmark; 'and, I feel certain, it is from William Stuart: I only once saw his writing, and this,' continued she, carefully scanning the envelope, 'looks very like his: I wonder what he has got to say? I feel half-inclined not to open it. He was so stern—so unkind—that night in the wood: his harsh rebukes still ring in my ears! No: unopened, I shall put it in the fire. But why? What shall I do? Open it, of course—what a silly creature I am!'

'MRS. BLACK. Madam, You will be sorry to learn that Mary died a few days ago: she sleeps in "The Auld Kirkyaird." There now being no tie to bind me to Inveraln, I have resolved to follow the advice you gave me on the occasion of your visit to our village—namely, to migrate to your great city: whether I shall woo fame as a city poet or simply follow my usual avocation, I leave to Fate to determine. Trusting you will pardon this intrusion, I beg to subscribe myself, madam, your humble servant, WILLIAM STUART.'

'So, *he* is free! But I am not —perhaps. He does not ask me to reply to his letter: he does not say he will call here on his arrival.

Call here! What would papa say? He must not call here: he is too poor to be admitted under this roof. But I can write to him. Ought I to write to him? Is it part of my duty toward my absent husband to write to Mr. Stuart? I wonder whether *he* thinks it is? Would he, were I to send him a letter, bid me remember I was still a wife? Why did he write to me? Why should I learn that his Mary is dead? Why should I be informed that he has determined to migrate to this city? Can I say I am sorry that Mary is dead? Can I—dare I—say I am glad he is coming to New Sidon? Am I sorry—am I glad? William Stuart is nothing to me: he is free to come and to go—for me. Yet he writes to me—why? Because his Mary is gone, does he think the deserted wife will make up for her loss? No: I will *not* answer his letter.'

Notwithstanding her resolution not to answer the Poet's communication, Mrs. Black immediately seated herself at her desk and wrote a long letter, in which she acknowledged herself to be 'very silly and very wicked perhaps:' at the same time she charged Mr. Stuart with having been guilty of wanton cruelty toward her in so harshly rebuking her 'on that sad occasion' when she laid bare her heart to him, and chided him for writing to her, 'causing her wounds to bleed afresh.' She thanked Heaven, however, that she had overcome her 'foolish fancy,' and that she was now able to calmly intimate to him 'that further correspondence was most undesirable;' and concluded by curtly wishing him every success in his city career. 'Everything considered, the least I can do,' thought Mrs. Black, 'is to hope that he may be successful here.' She folded the letter, put it in an envelope, and—paused.

'After all, perhaps I have written unkindly to him : he does not deserve harsh words. Let me see—'

Unfolding the letter, she glanced over its contents, and saying, 'No, no : it's too bad,' she committed to the flames the story of her love and her resentment toward the Village Poet.

'But I *must* send him an answer —of some sort,' she thought.

Again seating herself at her desk, Mrs. Black quickly spoiled a half-dozen sheets of paper, saying things she ought not to say— things she did not wish to say— things she dare not say; 'for,' she argued, 'he will bid me remember I am still a wife.'

'I will not commit myself to anything,' she decided, and wrote the following note :

'MR. STUART. Sir, Please write at once, and inform me on what day you will reach New Sidon, so that I may arrange an interview— that is, if you think you require any advice from me as to your business affairs here.—Yours, &c.
'ISABELLA BLACK.'

'He cannot say that I forget I am a wife,' thought Mrs. Black as she sealed the envelope. 'No : to him I am a— Come in.'

'Please, ma'm,' said a servant, entering, 'your father desires your presence in the drawing-room.'

'My father! in the drawing-room at this time of day! What ever has brought him home so early! Something's the matter, surely! Margaret, please, would you oblige me by putting this letter in the nearest pillar-box at once? It is an answer to an intimation of the death of my aunt's servant,' added Mrs. Black, who thought it advisable to somehow—if not quite truthfully—account for her sending a letter to a gentleman. 'Those servants,' she thought, 'are so fond of scandalmongering !'

'Dear papa !' exclaimed Mrs. Black, on entering the drawing-room, 'are you unwell ?'

'No, no, child : there's nothing wrong. I've news for you—of a pleasant kind, so do not fidget and fret.'

'News for me !'

'Yes : have you not long been expecting some from—'

'Tom : of course, papa, I have been expecting to hear—'

'That he is alive and well, and has evidently turned over a new leaf : I daresay you are glad to learn that ?'

'Where is he, papa? in Spain ?'

'No, child—not in Spain, but far in the Western States of America. He has sent me a letter expressing contrition for his misdeeds, which, he says, were solely prompted by a desire to save his firm from the results of certain unfortunate speculations into which he had unwittingly entered : he hopes I will "not put the law on his track." Further, he states that he is doing well, and he asks that you should join him as early as we like to part with you. Of course, Bella, he is your husband, and as he has amended his ways you ought to go to him. There is his letter—you can read it and think over the subject. I thought it advisable to run home and break the news to you.'

'You are a good, kind, dear papa !' answered Mrs. Black.

'But, Bella, one word—tell me you are glad to hear of Tom's safety—are you ?'

'I ought to be, papa ; but, you know—well, you know there are those people who cannot readily shape their thoughts into words— I am of their number. Do not ask any more, papa—not yet : give me a little time to think and to collect my thoughts.'

Father and daughter parted : the former to return to his great city spirit-palace — the latter to her room : the father glad at heart — the daughter not sure whether to weep or to smile that she was not a widow.

VI.

'So we again meet, Mr. Stuart !'

'Yes, Mrs. Black.'

Mrs. Black, on receiving the Poet's reply to her question concerning his arrival in New Sidon City, had felt that she dare not receive him under her father's roof : therefore she had written to him, saying that on the day he purposed reaching the city she should be in town on business, and desired him to meet her in front of the Royal Exchange at four o'clock.

The street, Mrs. Black knew, was not the place for the interview she meant to have with the Poet. She was prepared, having now to 'cast the die' of her future life, to once more acknowledge herself to be 'very silly and very wicked perhaps,' but willing to forsake all and follow William Stuart. It was possible that a 'scene' would attend her confession, and therefore it was necessary that a secluded spot should be selected — 'to end the matter, one way or other,' thought Mrs. Black.

'Is your time very precious, Mr. Stuart ?' she asked quietly; 'if not, perhaps you will accompany me on a short tour southward, which business requires me to undertake. We can have a friendly chat at our journey's end.'

'Madam, I desire nothing better than a friendly chat ; my heart is sighing for a friendly word !'

'For your dead Mary rather,' said Mrs. Black in a whisper. 'I'm very sorry for you. Well, you'll come ? That is our way,' she continued, pointing across Exchange-square. 'An omnibus from the next

street will take us to our destination.'

By 'destination' Mrs. Black meant the public park on the southern extremity of New Sidon City.

Assured that at this season of the year they would have the southern hillside all to themselves — have ample scope for 'words' — Mrs. Black led the way to the battleground, confident that she would return therefrom rejoicing in a great victory, having succeeded in irrevocably enslaving 'those big eyes of his.' He could not now plead his Mary as an objection. His heart was sighing for a friendly word : she would give him more than friendship — she would bestow upon him love — could he refuse to accept it ? Doubtless he would remind her that she was still a wife : she would deny the statement — she would say intelligence had arrived of her husband's death (soothing conscience by inwardly adding, 'Dead to me'). She would propose going abroad, and there they could be married : who would know ? (Mrs. Black forgot the Recording Angel.) She was armed on every side — he must yield !

'Now that your Mary is gone,' whispered Mrs. Black, shortly after entering the park — opening fire upon the Poet with, as she thought, a well-aimed shot that would quickly bring him to her feet — 'now that no tie binds you to Inveraln, you must feel very lonely, Mr. Stuart ?'

'Yes, madam — lonely indeed ; but, like my Uncle Tom, I " look toward the sky," and — '

'Don't be silly, Mr. Stuart ! Looking toward the sky sounds very well in poetry, but surely you can find something far more pleasant than that to occupy your attention. Look toward — me, William Stuart.'

'Madam!' sternly exclaimed the Poet, fixing his great soul-orbs on Mrs. Black, who had raised her eyes to his to welcome an expected 'sweet reply.'

Eye against eye—momentary, yet severe, the struggle; the victory belonged to the Poet. Pale—trembling—speechless—weeping: Mrs. Black stood before William Stuart. In that stern face of his she read his strength of mind—in his eyes she saw the purity of his soul; she could tempt no more.

'Forgive me, William Stuart!' she cried piteously; 'forgive a sinful woman—who will sin no more! Say you forgive me!'

'Madam,' replied the Poet tenderly, 'look toward the sky: there dwelleth He whose province it is to forgive.'

Silently Mrs. Black and William Stuart returned to the park-gate.

'Madam,' said the Poet, 'return to your father's house. Farewell! Look toward the sky!'

VII.

'A SAD END.—We regret to state that as Policeman A96 was at an early hour this morning patrolling his beat, he found in a by-lane the body of a man almost covered with snow, which he at once conveyed to the Central Police Chambers, where, immediately on its arrival, every effort was made, but without success, to restore animation. From papers found on the deceased we are enabled to state, with deep regret, that the body is that of Mr. William Stuart, author of " Mary, Queen o' Inveraln," " Be Ready, Scotsmen, Ready," " The Wee Wildflowers o' Fernie Glen," and other popular Scottish songs, who has been resident in this city some six or seven years. From inquiries made we learn that during the past two years Mr. Stuart suf-

fered from lung-disease, and was therefore unable steadily to follow his occupation, and it is supposed that want, no less than disease, has brought to a sad end the life of this highly-gifted son of Song. We have been informed that, beyond an occasional copy of his songs to present to a friend, Mr. Stuart declined remuneration for his verses. Among the papers alluded to above were the two following songs in manuscript:

" FERNIE GLEN.

Farewell, sweet Glen o' Ferniehill!
  Afar frae thee I now maun hie:
Thy fragrant shades and dancing rill
  Mayhap again I'll ne'er espy.
But, wheresoe'er my lot is cast,
  Whatever fortune I may ken,
I'll often wander o'er the Past,
  And rest a while in Fernie Glen.

As Nature a' her works survey'd,
  Her grand design fain to fulfil,
She gave the word—the rocks obey'd;
  And cleft in twa was Ferniehill,
When dull wi' care, or tired wi' toil,
  Or weary o' the haunts o' men,
I'll close my e'e on life's turmoil,
  And dream I'm back in Fernie Glen."

" THE AULD KIRKYAIRD.

In a wee toun in the West
  There's an auld kirkyaird,
And my kin a' hae their rest
  In that auld kirkyaird:
Generations twa or three,
Some near and dear to me,
Frae the ills o' life a' free
  In that auld kirkyaird.

There was ae time bune the lave,
  In that auld kirkyaird,
I had sair heart by a grave
  In that auld kirkyaird:
It was when we buried ane
Wha for my love I'd taen—
My dreamt life o' bliss was gane
  In that auld kirkyaird.

Though I hae been lang awa'
  Frae that auld kirkyaird,
The thought aye bunemost a'
  Is that auld kirkyaird.
When the day comes I maun dee,
Content I'll close my e'e
If a grave be promised me
  In the Auld Kirkyaird."

We have only to add that the deceased Poet was of a retiring disposition, and had few acquaintances in the city; but those to whom he gave his confidence will long miss a worthy friend; and that to-day Scotland is called upon to mourn another untimely death added to the many that have befallen her "sweet singers."'—*New Sidon Evening Chronicle,* March 14, 18—.

A twelvemonth after William Stuart's death a letter came from 'a far country,' addressed to the Parish Minister of Inveraln: in it was enclosed a bankdraft for two hundred pounds, accompanied by a request that a portion of the money be expended on a marble tablet to be placed in the Parish Church of Inveraln to the memory of William Stuart, and the remainder to be expended in keeping his grave, wherever it might be, 'aye green.'

Reader, should you ever visit 'The Auld Kirkyaird' of Inveraln, which is one of the classic spots of Scotland, the 'minister's man,' who combines the duties of church-officer and gravedigger, will take you to a pew numbered 30, and will say, 'This was where *he* sat.' If you show yourself ignorant of who is meant by *he,* the old man beside you will look astonished but say nothing: he will point to a marble tablet on the wall over the pew at which you stand, and thereon you will read:

'*In affectionate remembrance of*
WILLIAM STUART,
THE BARD OF INVERALN.
Born March 14, 18—.
Died March 14, 18—.'

'And now, sir, if you please, we will step round to his grave,' your attendant will remark. And he will lead you to a corner of the churchyard, and say, 'That is where *he* lies, and where "Mary, Queen o' Inveraln," also lies: I buried them both. "In death they are not divided,"' he will add reverently. Then he will tell you the story of the bankdraft and the marble tablet in the church. 'But, sir,' he will continue, 'the money that was sent to keep his grave aye green is in the bank, and will be gi'en to my successor, if so be he must be paid to keep green the grave of the Bard of Inveraln.' Further, he will tell you that when the news came to the village that William Stuart was found dead on a street in New Sidon, the minister at once set off to the city and brought the remains to Inveraln. 'He wasna promised a grave here, as he hoped in one of his songs; but he had his wish fulfilled for a' that.' And he will conclude thus: 'They let him starve and die on their streets, but they dinna hae the honour of sheltering his bones. No, sir, here he lies, beside his Mary, awaiting the Great Day; and on what hand Willie Stuart and his Mary will then find a place needs no argument to determine.'

If his auditor shows a sympathetic interest in his story, the old man will offer him a tuft of grass from off the grave of the Bard of Inveraln.

STRAWBERRY LEAVES.

By RICHARD DOWLING,

AUTHOR OF 'THE MYSTERY OF KILLARD,' 'THE WEIRD SISTERS,'
'UNDER ST. PAUL'S,' ETC.

Part the First.

THE DUKE OF LONGACRE.

CHAPTER V.

UNDER ANERLY BRIDGE.

ALTHOUGH the view from the portico in front of the Beagle Inn at Anerly was very lovely, it would by no means make a good picture. It was too broad and monotonous and scattered. There was no composition in it. The pleasure derived from looking down that peaceful slope and valley was gained by glancing at it unconsciously from several points of view rather than from any particular one. If you fixed your eyes on the central or road line, no doubt you commanded Anerly Church and some fine trees and the wide plain below; but then there was no right-hand or left-hand frame to the picture, and the effect was insipid, if not distracting. If you looked through the trees you had the broad valley and the silver streak of stream; but you missed the church and the pine-clad slope which lent the romantic air to the whole scene.

Edward Graham was not a great artist. He was one of those indolent men who study art no more than the study yields pleasure. He liked painting and artists, but preferred the society of artists to that of a lonely easel, a laborious sketch-book. He was a Bohemian born, not made. He loved art for what it brought him from without more than for any divine joy it aroused

within. By fortune he was poor, and by nature idle. He did not like doing anything; but of all occupations that could bring him money he disliked painting least. Therefore he painted for his bread. If he had been rich—so much did he like the atmosphere of art, and the companionship of those who follow art—he would have painted all the same, that he might be entitled to smoke pipes and discuss pictures with better painters than he. He was one of those men who, although earning their bread by a profession, are amateurs to the last, one of those to whom talk of art is dearer than the use of artist's tools. He always wore a brown-velveteen coat, a soft hat with a broad brim, and a Cambridge-blue tie. He was about twenty-eight years of age, of medium height, lightly built, and of dark complexion, the most remarkable thing in his face being a pair of large, round, brown eyes. In manner he was cordial, enthusiastic, almost boisterous.

The morning after Edward Graham had heard the story of Stephen Goolby's temptation was bright with dew and sunshine, and sweet with spices from the pine-trees and brisk balm of the meadows. Young Graham was on a walking-tour. In his knapsack he carried two clean flannel shirts, a few collars, toilette brushes, and a comb; a couple of pair of thick knitted stockings, and a razor and strop; for Edward Graham shaved his chin and cheeks, wearing no hair on his face but a pair of moustaches. At the back of his knapsack was strapped a small rectangular japanned case, containing a large sketching-pad, three small canvases, a mahlstick, moist water-colours, oil-colours, brushes, and so on. A stout walking-stick he carried was a folded-up easel, and his knapsack served as a seat when he was painting or sketching in the open air.

On this beautiful morning in June Graham rose early, and, having filled and lighted a brier-root pipe, strolled out in front of the Beagle Inn. He took a leisurely survey of the place, drew his hat knowingly on the side of his head, as though to show the crows—the only living things in view—that Nature might be very clever in her way, but that she could not impose on him, and that he was about to probe her to the core.

He lounged indolently down the winding road that led by Anerly Church to the valley and broad stream beyond. He had his hands in the pockets of his velveteen shooting-jacket, as, with hat on one side and head on the other, and legs moving loosely and without any premeditation, he strolled down the hill.

As soon as he got near Anerly Church he paused, and, turning half round, looked up the pine-clad slope. After a careful scrutiny of a few minutes, he shook his head gloomily at it, as though he had expected and deserved much better treatment at its hands. Then, drawing his jacket tightly round his hips in a leisurely and dejected way, he continued his descent.

When he got as far as Anerly Church he paused again and looked round him. There was a slight

relaxation of his critical stare, and a glance of approval in his large brown eyes. The approval was not so much of the landscape as of the fact that he, Edward Graham, approved of himself for having found out a suitable standpoint from which to make a picture of the place. For, give Nature all her due, what was the good of setting forth fair landscapes if no one with an artistic eye and artistic skill came her way to paint them?

The aspect which the young artist selected was gentle and charming as the soul who loves peaceful England could desire. Beneath the road ran a small stream. From the right-hand side of the road, as one went down from the village, the ground sloped rapidly towards the valley below. The little stream running under the road had worn a deep narrow ravine, which expanded lower down, and over this rose a gaunt narrow bridge supporting the road. The sides of this glen were lined with mountain ash, silver beeches, splay alders, gigantic ferns, and tangles of broad-bladed grasses, and masses of mingled bush and bramble and shrub, down to the golden mosses that slept upon the dark cold rocks above the sparkling curves of falling water. And below each tiny cascade lay a level miniature swamp, with a few huge flags standing up in each green, rush-fringed, open space.

On the slope of this glen, and on the slope of the great valley, stood Anerly Church, a couple of hundred yards from the bridge. Past the church the glen opened, and the dwarf vegetation near the bridge gave way to lofty pines, whose tops made a long sombre arch over the stream. Beyond this dark arch lay a blaze of green light, and a scarf of flaming white satin, where the valley and the stream caught the full sunlight.

'This will be jolly!' said Edward Graham, as he scaled the low parapet to the approach of the bridge, and threw himself down on the slope of the glen. 'That archway is partly dry; I'll walk up in it until I get the picture focussed, and then I'll paint it. The bridge is so high there is sure to be plenty of light.'

But when he got under the arch, and had picked his way to the rear of it, he altered his mind slightly. 'By Jove!' he cried, for a moment looking at the startling effect of light and shade. 'I don't know whether Salvator Rosa or Rembrandt would have admired this the more, but I am going to paint it; and instead of using the arch merely as a means of focussing the scene, I will paint the whole blessed lot, archway and stalactites, water under the archway and all.'

The picture was striking.

By the sober light of the vault it was possible to make out with dim distinctness the outline of every object in it. This dimness did not arise from want of light, but from the fact that the floor and the sides of the vault were damp, and the outlines of damp objects in such a light are always uncertain to the eye. The archway looked north and south, and now a small portion of the western inner wall had caught a beam of the early sun, and the water in a pool at the eastern side, struck by the rays refracted by the wall, threw a blue and brown patch of trembling light on the middle of the roof. This light in return fell into another pool at the eastern side, where it made a trembling veil of orange-brown and golden-green; while all round, on the gray walls, the white roof, and the ashen stalactites, were scattered wandering hints of prismatic fire, which seemed rather to come through the stone

than to be reflected from the water below.

Thus the huge barrel formed by the bridge, with its wavering, dull, dappled, transparent lights, was connected by one patch of brightness on the western pier and vault with the foreground of blue-and-white water, and rich green and ripe yellow of the rushes and grasses and underwood in the flat light of the glen. Beyond the flat light was the gloomy tunnel formed by the pines, where the yellows turned to browns, and the greens to sad blues, and the water flowed furtively from dull olive pool to dull olive pool, until at last it sprang out, a white blaze, into the full sunlight beyond, and fell headlong in foam to join the silver scarf of stream lying across the golden meadows below.

For a long while Edward Graham paused in reverence. He was not in his essence an artist, and the impulse which would have come first to an artist came second to him.

His first distinct thought was, 'What a picture it will make!' His second, 'How beautiful it is!' Then he looked for a long time without thinking. He was gazing at the simple whole without reflection, as one may listen to a note prolonged, and be yet content, although there is no succession of anything produced in the mind, no idea suggested by the sound.

Then his mind came back suddenly, and he thought, 'By Jove, it requires no painting at all! It paints itself!' He had not been able to say 'By Jove!' as long as his form of thought was abstract. But the moment he thought of the concrete, of brushes and canvas, and tubes and palette, he fell to the level of his own mind in his studio, where came no intoxicating visions of delight, no visitings of poetry, no fine frenzy to cause the eye to roll. Of his own nature he was not capable of evolving a thought or idea worthy of any more powerful or enthusiastic form of expression than ' By Jove !' But here something new had been set before him. He felt there was poetry in the scene. He knew at a glance it would make a good picture. A second glance showed him there was poetry in it, but where he could not tell. He had no originality. He was a reflector, not a prism.

After another period of mere gazing he looked around. Yes, the place would do admirably for a painting-room. The vault ran north and south, and the back or lower end of the archway, that from which the scene should be painted, faced the north, which settled the question of light in his favour. Then the archway was quite wide enough for an easel. The legs of the easel might stand in the water, and he could make a little platform of flat stones on which to rest a seat for himself. At the back of the archway was an open green space. The place was damp. But then in summer the roof would not drip, and that was all he cared about. He should have to write up to London for a much larger canvas than any he had with him. His easel, too, he should write for. Well, he'd go back to the Beagle now and have some breakfast, and write his letters afterwards.

He clambered up out of the hollow on the northern side, and walked back to the inn much more briskly than he had come.

' I shall make sketches and studies of the place while I am waiting for the easel and the canvas,' he thought, as he went along the road.

When he arrived at the inn he ordered breakfast, and sat down to write a couple of letters while he was waiting. The first of these was to the man in London from whom he got his colours, asking him to send a canvas of the size he wanted. The second ran as follows :

' Beagle Inn, Anerly, Devonshire,
June 18—.

' MAY IT PLEASE YOUR GRACE,— I am now sojourning in Anerly, one of the most charming villages in the dominions of her who calls you Our right trusty and right entirely beloved Cousin. Everything here, including, of course, myself, is excellent, except the bread, which is beastly. The cocks and hens, the scenery, the cider, and all other things of that class, cannot be surpassed. There is a man here six feet high, twenty-three years of age, sixteen stone ten (not an ounce of which you could pinch with a steel nippers), whom I have been telling of you, and who is awfully anxious to fight you. He is by profession a carpenter. He never saws a three-inch deal, but breaks it across his knee. He says he will fight you for nothing with great pleasure. I want you to come down at once and stop with me for a week or two. I'll treat you like a prince. You shall have three full meals and as many quarts of cider. The fact is, dear old Duke, I am going to paint a picture here. It's awfully good. I'll swear to you it's the loveliest thing you ever saw. It's the real whangdoodle and no mistake. Come down and judge for yourself. And now I want you to do a thing for me. Go to my diggings (I mean the studio), get my big box of oils and my easel, and send them on here. You shall have one extra quart of cider for this job if you come. But if you don't come you shall not have a stiver. If you come I will tell you a story I heard here, and which will surely make your fortune if you write it. I am going to paint Anerly Church, and this story is about Anerly Church ; so that if you come down here, see the place, and do the story, it will be in a magnificent way writing up to my picture ; and if you get out your book by next May, if your *Romance of Anerly Church* is in the libraries, and my " Under Anerly Bridge" is on the line, we shall both be helping one another to fame and fortune. Now, whatever you do or avoid doing, you must come here. I am called for breakfast. But remember and come.—I have the honour to be, my lord Duke, your Grace's most obliged and obedient servant,　　EDWARD GRAHAM.

' To his Grace the Duke of Longacre.

' P.S. By the way, the people about whom I am to tell you the romance are namesakes of yours.
'　　　　　　' E. G.'

CHAPTER VI.

WHAT'S IN A NAME.

WHEN the Duke of Longacre got Edward Graham's letter he immediately packed off the easel and colours. He liked Graham very much, and Graham loved him. Cheyne was one of those men who are always asked to do odd jobs for friends. He was good-humoured, of active habits, and liked to be busy always.

Although he was prompt about the commission he had received, he had no intention of doing the other thing Graham asked. No inducement of an ordinary kind could drag him out of London just now. He was moderately busy for the papers and magazines to which he contributed, and he was exceedingly busy with the affairs of his heart.

There was no happier lover in all London than Charles Augustus Cheyne. He loved his love, and his love loved him, and he envied

no man's lot. She was as bright and dear a sweetheart as ever man had, and he loved her in a thoroughly comfortable common-sense way. He had written about romantic love, but he had never felt a pang of it in his private experience. Romance was a good thing in a book, for it amused one, but it was a poor stock-in-trade on which to begin matrimony. So he kept his romance for the public and his friends, and his straightforward manhood for his sweetheart. Sweetheart is the finest love-word we have in English, and she was his sweetheart—his sweetheart—his sweet heart.

He loved her simply, frankly, wholly, without any mental reservation. He never told her he wanted to die for her, or that she was blameless or perfect. He told her she was as good a girl as any man ever might hope to marry. He knew she was as well as he knew that two and two are four. He praised her face less than was reasonable. He told her she had most lovely eyes, which was a temperate and judicial way of putting the matter. He was quite sure of his girl. He did not want any one to tell him anything about her. He did not want her to tell him anything about herself. The only thing he wanted was to make her happy, and he thought he could do that. If she were happy he should be happy for three reasons—first, because he had an excellent constitution and was not soured by ill-health ; secondly, because he had a gay and cheerful nature ; thirdly, because the very sight of her happiness could not fail to be a source of abiding joy to him.

When he put his arms round her he always felt glad he was big enough and strong enough to protect her. Once while holding her a moment in his arms he said,

'I could crush you to death now, May, if I liked.'

'You great bear, don't frighten me to death first,' she said.

'Or,' he added, 'I think I could kill any man who annoyed you; of course I mean who injured you desperately.'

'Well,' she said, 'as I don't mean to be injured dreadfully by any one, as I don't want to be frightened to death or crushed to death, I don't see why you should not let me go. O dear, men are such plagues.'

Yes, Charles Augustus Cheyne was a very strong man physically; mentally he was by no means so strong. Notwithstanding the fact that he told lies by the thousand, no one ever dreamed of saying he was a dishonourable man. He made no earthly use of his lies. If he told a new acquaintance that he had the day before dined with the Marquis of Belgravia, and his listener then asked him to dinner next day, Cheyne would most certainly decline to go. If he lied he lied for his own pleasure, not for his profit, not for the injury of any one. He never said a bad word of any man he knew, and he never said a bad word of any member of the aristocracy, for had he not broken the bread of every member of it?

But of all the weak points in Cheyne's mental equipment the weakest was a dread of any allusion to his family. Any allusion to his people always made him uncomfortable; and where he could possibly manage to do so, he always changed the conversation as soon as possible. When asked point-blank who his father was, he replied in almost the same form of words, 'My father was a poor gentleman who met many reverses of fortune.' He never said anything about his mother, and those who knew him best had long ago made up their minds that he had no right to his

father's name, and that Cheyne had been his mother's name, or an assumed one. Indeed most of his friends were convinced that neither his mother nor father had borne the name of Cheyne.

He did not know much more about himself than those around him. He had never known his father or mother. His earliest recollection was of an elderly spinster who wore corkscrew curls, kept a day-school for young ladies, and took in a few boarders. He was one of these boarders, and now he always looked back on that part of his life with the deadliest hatred. Two facts connected with that establishment clung to his imagination with terrible tenacity. First, that he never got anything to eat there but bread steeped in boiled milk; secondly, that on frosty days his schoolmistress hit him on the knuckles with a lead-pencil because he did not hold his pen properly. Even now the smell of bread steeped in boiling milk made him ill.

From this school he was sent to another, a private one kept by a clergyman in Cumberland. No one ever visited him, and he never left school for holidays. He did not know who paid for him at those schools. He had a small allowance of pocket-money. At school he had displayed some taste for literature. He always took first place in essay-writing. He assumed from this that the clergyman must have suggested he should in some way be linked to literature; for when he left school, at sixteen years of age, the clergyman told him a situation had been secured for him in a publisher's office in London. The clergyman came up to town with him, introduced him to his new master, handed him a ten-pound note, saying it came from his guardian, and then took leave of him.

From the day he left that old maid's school he had never seen or heard anything of her. From the day that clergyman handed him that ten-pound note and bade him good-bye he had never seen or heard anything of him. At the time he first found himself in the publisher's office he was too young to set any inquiries on foot about himself; and as time went on and he began to know something of the world and its ways, he came to the conclusion he had no right to his father's name, and that the one he bore was his mother's. When he had grown to be a man he felt deeply the humiliation of his position, and made up his mind to inquire no further into the matter, lest what was now only matter of inference might become matter of certainty. Let sleeping dogs lie, was the motto he adopted, and he had never departed from it. To Marion Durrant he had told all he absolutely knew of himself. He had not told her anything he inferred or suspected. He had been told by the clergyman who had looked after his education that both his father and mother were dead. He had told Marion that he had never known either his father or mother, that they were both dead, that he had no memory of his childhood and youth apart from those two schools, and that as far as he knew he had no relative alive. But he had said nothing to her of his misgivings or doubts.

From all this it will be seen that Graham's allusion to the story connected with Anerly and his name would be anything but an inducement for Cheyne to leave London for that Devonshire village.

Every day he found his way out to Knightsbridge, and every day he had long sweet hours with his May.

It was afternoon on the day he got Graham's letter before he could leave home, and four o'clock had struck before he knocked at the hall-door of the little house in Knightsbridge.

When he came into the room where Marion Durrant sat hemming an apron, she said,

'What! come again to-day! In the name of wonder, what brought *you* here now?'

'You know, May, the pressure of race is ever from east to west.'

'The pressure of race! What on earth are you talking about? Don't! that hurts my hand.'

'I was slapping your hand to prevent you from fainting at the unexpected sight of your slave and master. I meant the pressure of the human race—or, more accurately, the attraction of the inhuman race —meaning yourself, sweetheart.'

'Do you know, Charlie, you always begin a conversation as if you wanted me to think you clever; and if there is one thing I hate it is cleverness in a man.'

'Do you know, Miss Durrant, you never by any means allow me to begin a conversation. Before I am fully in the room you always fly at me with some question or other.'

'But you are so slow, Charlie. You take up half an hour getting ready to say Howd'y'do; and if there is one thing more odious in a man than cleverness it is slowness.'

'But you must admit, Miss Durrant, that if when we meet I am slow of speech, I am not slow in other matters proper to our meeting.'

'Go away, sir! How dare you! I will not let you do that again. Sometimes I think you a bear, and sometimes I think you an elephant, but I think I hate you always.'

'If you say any more I'll get a divorce on the grounds of cruelty and desertion. May, let us drop this sort of thing. Run and bring me a glass of beer. I've been trotting about the whole morning, and am dying for a glass of beer.'

'You deserve to be starved, and you deserve to be thirsty, and you deserve to be—'

'I admit it all. I deserve it all, and every other thing that's awful, except to be married to you. Marion Durrant, spinster, what would you do if I cut my throat?'

'Charlie !'

'Or if I put my head under the wheel of an omnibus laden with exceedingly fat people?'

'Charlie ! Charlie !'

'Or if I threw myself over Westminster Bridge with a couple of forty-pound shot tied round my heels?'

'I'll run for the beer, Charlie.'

'Ah, I thought I'd get you to move at last. You see you can't bear to leave me even for a minute.'

'Conceited fellow !' and she tripped out of the room.

She went herself with a jug into the little cellar under the front door-steps, and drew the beer in a most elaborate and painstaking manner. She looked into three jugs before she was satisfied with one, although they were all as immaculate as human hands could make them. She looked at the glass as if it were a jewel she was thinking of buying, and the slightest flaw in it would render it valueless. She placed the jug and the tumbler and a plate of biscuits on an exceedingly slippery Japanese wooden tray, and declined to let the maid carry it up. She was proud of that polished jug, that polished glass, that polished tray. The jug and the glass and the tray were more to her than the condition of the beer. As a matter of fact, she never thought of the beer at all. It would be a pity if the beer was not in good condition; but it would be a disgrace if the

jug, glass, and tray were not in perfect order.

When she came back to the room she was meek and penitential. We are always softened towards those to whom we have done ever so slight a service. When he had taken a draught of the ale and broken a biscuit, she said plaintively,

'Charlie !'

'Well, my fire-eating she-dragon, what bloodthirsty thing have you to say to your down-trodden slave now?'

'Only that you were right when you said—'

'When I spoke about cutting my throat?'

'No, no, no ! When you said I did not like to go away from you even for a moment. Charlie, I hate going away from you, and I hate myself when you are away; for then I remember all the foolish things I have said to you, and— and I am always afraid—'

'Of my taking four pounds, apothecaries' weight, of solid opium?'

'No. Of your being angry with me some day, or of your not forgiving me.'

She was very pretty and very penitent, and he had had a long walk and a glass of beer, and he felt perfectly at rest and happy; so he put out his arms and took her into them for a moment, and when he let her go they both felt that, say what you like about love, it is the finest thing in all the world, and that there was nothing else which made people so utterly unselfish.

'I had a letter from Graham this morning,' said Cheyne, after a pause.

'Where is he now?'

'In Devonshire still, sketching at some place called Anerly. He wrote me to send him some painting materials. He is going to begin a picture down there, so

I suppose we shall not see anything of him for some time. He has asked me to run down to him for a few days.'

'And will you go?'

'Not I. I am too busy just now.'

'But you could do your work down there, and I am sure you want a run away and a little fresh air.'

'Yes; I could write there, no doubt. But then you see, May, I should not be able to come and read my MS. to you, and I should not get on very well. While I am at work at Longacre I am in a hurry to be done, in order that I may get back to you, and I am too anxious to please you to do slovenly work; so the result is that I work longer and yet have more leisure, which is a paradox, and a paradox is particularly unsuited to the understanding of women.'

'You are always saying nice and disagreeable things in the one breath; and I don't know whether to like you or to hate you.'

'To cases of this kind an infrangible rule applies. It is, when I say nice things, hate me; when I say disagreeable things, love me. This is another paradox. Paradoxes, although they are not intelligible to women, are all the more dear to them on that very account. You never yet knew a woman who thoroughly understood a man care for him. I never did.'

'But, Charlie, I think I understand you very well.'

'Rank presumption. The rankest presumption I ever heard in all my life. Know me, May! Why, you don't even know who my father and mother were!'

'You told me they were dead.'

'Yes, they are dead. But you know nothing of them. You do not know if they were felons, or shopkeepers, or gentlefolk.'

'I am sure, Charlie, they were gentlefolk.'

'Ah, you do not know. And now, May,' said he, taking her hand very tenderly and softly patting the back of it with the palm of his own, 'I must tell you a secret I ought perhaps to have told you long ago, as it might influence you in your decision of accepting or not accepting me.'

'Nothing you could have told me would have made the slightest difference in my decision, Charlie,' she said, in a very faint voice.

He ceased patting her hand, and pressed it softly between his two palms. He spoke in a low voice,

'Well, May, the fact of it is I do not know who my father and mother were. It could do no good, dear, if this fact were generally known, and I count on you for keeping it secret.'

'You may,' she whispered back, returning the pressure of his hands, and laying her disengaged hand upon the upper one of his. The action was slight and made without thought, yet he felt its import. He knew by that gesture she meant to convey to him that not only was the hand his own, but that all the faculties of her nature owed allegiance to him alone.

'Thank you, darling; I know how good you are. Every day I see you I am more and more convinced of your goodness. But you see, May, that is my only great trouble, and day by day I am afraid I may find out something very unpleasant, something disgraceful, about my father and mother.'

'But nothing you can find out will be disgraceful to you, Charlie.'

'No; logically and morally not. But then you know the sins of the parent are visited on the children, not merely by Heaven, but by the world. You know very well that if a man's father had been a hangman, or a murderer, or a forger, his son would be looked on with suspicion and dislike by the majority of the world. A man in my position is of course more alive to the discomfort of any such discovery than a man who knows about his parents. He is continually fancying all manner of horrible surprises, until the mind becomes morbidly sensitive on the subject. I confess I am morbidly sensitive on the subject; and of one thing I am quite certain—that if I made any discovery of the kind I have been speaking of, I could not stand England, London. I'd emigrate. I'd go to the United States or Australia—some place where the English language is spoken, and where I might have a chance of making a living by my pen. I am telling you all this for a purpose, May. It is all only a preface to a question. And the question is, In case anything of the kind arose, and I was about to leave for the United States or a colony, would you marry me and come with me?'

'O, how can you ask such a question! I'd go anywhere with you. What does it matter where I am so long as I am with you, Charlie?'

He thanked her and kissed her, and soon after took his leave; for he had work to do that evening.

As he walked home in the fresh bright air his step was elastic, and he carried his head thrown back. His happiness was now complete. The two great points he had reserved had been cleared up. May cared only for himself. Whatever time might unearth about his father and mother, she would not be altered by it; and if anything obliging him to leave the country did transpire, she would marry him and go with him all the same as if nothing had come to light. This was the most peaceful, contented, and joyous day of his life.

When Cheyne arrived at the house in Longacre, he found Mr. Whiteshaw, the carriage-builder, standing in his ware-room.

'Good-afternoon, Cheyne,' cried the builder cheerily.

'Good-afternoon,' said Cheyne, pausing and drawing near.

'What news?' asked the carriage-builder, rubbing his hands, as though news ever so dismal would be preferable to none.

'Not a word,' said Cheyne, stepping into the ware-room.

'Heard anything of the Duke of Shropshire since?'

'No, no. Nothing particular. Except that the Duke of Dorsetshire, in a note I got from him a day or two ago, says his Grace is awfully cut up by the way these rascally Radicals are behaving.'

'If I were at the head of affairs now, I'd pass a law treating all Radicals as working men out of situations, and I'd clap every man Jack of them into jail. That's what I'd do.'

'You'd never get a Bill like that through the Commons, although you might through the Lords.'

'Ah, I suppose not. I suppose not, Cheyne. We live in a degenerate age. But you, if you were in the House, would you vote for such a measure?'

'I am afraid it is extreme,' said Cheyne, with a good-humoured smile.

'But you, you ought to be dead against Radicals and demagogues. Your name alone—why, sir, your name alone shows you come of a great stock, the great house of Shropshire. (By the way, we weren't long putting that brougham right for his Grace. There it is, you see; and a pretty job too.) But, as I was saying, you must be a member of that family. Why, look at how few there are of the name.'

'No, no. I assure you, most sincerely, I am in no way connected with any great house. The name is common enough in England— common enough. Well, I must be off to work. I have a whole lot of stuff to get away by to-night's mail for the morning.'

With these words Cheyne walked out of the ware-room and got to the hall-door, and mounted the stairs to his own room.

'I never can understand,' thought the carriage-maker, 'why this Cheyne, who lies right and left about noblemen, should have such a strong objection to thinking he was descended from a big swell.'

When Cheyne reached his own room he sat down and thought a moment. Then he said to himself very gravely,

'I wish Whiteshaw would give up this connecting my name with that of the Duke of Shropshire. Supposing a person found a poor deserted child, would it be kinder to name it Fitzalan Howard or plain William Brown?'

And when he had put the question to himself, he fell to wondering very unpleasantly whether or not he had at one time been a poor deserted child, picked up by some passer-by, to whom had been given the high-sounding name of Charles Augustus Cheyne.

So the afternoon which had been the happiest of his life ended under a sombre cloud.

———

CHAPTER VII.

A STORY OF A CITY.

WYECHESTER is a small city in the Midlands. It does not contain more than thirty thousand people, so that it is possible for every man and woman of the middle class to know every one of the same class, or, at all events, to know everything about everybody, which is almost as good, if not better.

Wyechester is not a place of any importance now, save what it draws from its cathedral and its bishop, and the other great dignitaries around the cathedral. If the city disappeared wholly one night the world of England would hardly miss it, provided the cathedral and church dignitaries were spared. It does not manufacture anything; it has no mines near it. No one ever thought of hunting or shooting in the neighbourhood but those who lived in the neighbourhood. The fishing was poor; and the land, although fairly fertile, was not held in much esteem by farmers. It was a faded washed-out old cathedral city, surrounded on all sides by an uninteresting country.

It had one virtue, which, as it concerned only itself, did not spread its fame. It was pious. It was the most pious city in England. It could not, of course, be said with truth that there was no hypocrisy in it; but, speaking relatively, there was very little—much less than in any other city of its size.

It was pious, and it was severe. To do any wrong there was much worse than to do the same wrong in any other city or town in England. Going to church twice on Sunday regularly for thirty years entitled one to consideration. Going once a day freed one from adverse comment. Going only twice a month was looked on as bad, very bad. But not going at all made middle-class people in Wyechester think that the sooner the offender left the diocese the better.

Five-and-thirty years before the pole of the omnibus went through the door of the Duke of Shropshire's brougham, five-and-thirty years before Edward Graham decided upon painting that landscape revealed to him under the bridge at Anerly, Mrs. Mansfield, widow of the Rev. James Mansfield, lived in Wyechester. The Rev. James Mansfield died very young. He was, at the time of his death, curate to one of the city churches, and was looked upon as a very exemplary and clever young man who had a career before him. But his career may be said never to have begun ; for he died before he was thirty. He left behind him a widow and daughter, and about a hundred and fifty pounds a year from money in the Funds willed him by an aunt who had the warmest affection for him.

On this modest income, and about seventy pounds a year coming in from other sources, the widow managed to live quietly, respectably, and to give her daughter a very good education. Five-and-thirty years before what may be taken as the present time of this story, a thing occurred which horrified all Wyechester and bowed down the head of Mrs. Mansfield for ever.

At that time Harriet Mansfield was on a visit with some friends in the country. One morning Miss Mansfield left the house of the friends she was staying with and did not return. Neither did she go home. After days of anxiety a letter, in the daughter's handwriting, came from London, in which she simply said she had left her home for ever, and that there was chance whatever of her going no back.

Mrs. Mansfield was then forty-three years of age, but, with the flight of her daughter, her life may be said to have closed, although she was living at the time this story opened. She loved her daughter with all the love she was capable of. But she was a hard, cold, stern nature. To her daughter she never showed her love except in rigours, and insisting on doing her own duty by her child, without any sympathetic conception of what effect doing her own duty would have on a gentle, soft, and confiding nature like her daughter's. The result was that the mother did her duty according to her own lights. She endeavoured to bring up her daughter according to her own rigid code, and she justified herself to herself.

But the daughter had no Spartan nature. She loved pretty things and soft things to wear. She was not allowed to keep pets, or to be too familiar with other children. While in the world, and now and then coming in contact for a brief period with pleasant people and grateful things, she was under a discipline as rigid as a convent without any sustaining code ; for she did not believe it necessary to be uncomfortable in order to be good. So when love for the first time approached her, and she was from under the immediate eye of her mother, the oppressive goodness of that cathedral city, and the prospect of love and brightness and sunshine and freedom were all presented to her eyes by a man who owned the gift of erratic eloquence, and who was richer than any other man she had ever met, richer than even the bishop, she did not hesitate long. She fled with him. She knew that running away was wrong, but she underestimated the risk, or indeed did not think there was any risk at all ; for she was as simple as a child, and did willingly all things her lover told her, as all her life she had reluctantly obeyed her mother when uncongenial tasks were imposed.

In that letter from London, a letter dictated by the companion of her flight, she had said nothing about him, nothing about marriage.

It was therefore plain to the mother that the daughter was not married. So the mother cast the image of her daughter out of her heart, and shut up her heart against her child for ever. All through her widowhood this girl had been the sole source of her secret love and happiness, as far as worldly things were allowed to count in the love and happiness of any one who ruled herself by the rule of duty. Now that child had become the only source of secret and open reproach to her. Soon after she got that letter every one in the city knew all about her misfortune, and the neighbours turned up their eyes and held up their hands in virtuous shame. Her daughter had disgraced her home, had disgraced the sacred order to which she might be said to belong, had disgraced the city which had given her birth. Into the mother's heart the image of the daughter should come no more. Across the mother's threshold the foot of the daughter should never pass. It was hard to keep the image out always; but no sooner did it gain an entrance than she cast it forth with bitter reproaches against herself for her sinful weakness in holding commune with the only thing which had ever brought shame home to her.

The mother took no steps to follow the daughter. Several people came and offered help. She wanted no help. Her daughter had taken her fate into her own hands, and there matters should rest. She was inflexible. Nothing could move her in the least way. Clergymen who had been friends of her husband came and expostulated, and said that it was wrong and sinful of her not to do something to win back the fugitive. But she would not listen to them any time with patience. She told them she had done her duty by the girl, and the girl had taken herself off, and she,

the mother, could not think of taking her daughter back. They then told her this was not a Christian spirit, and that she must remember the story of the Prodigal Son. And, upon this, she grew angry with them, for it hurt her beyond endurance to hear her daughter, her only child, referred to in such a way. She told them she knew her duty as a Christian as well as any one, and that they at least knew she had been under good guidance, the guidance of her husband, for many years, and that she was much obliged to them, but that her mind was made up beyond the chance of change.

Time proved she could adhere to her resolve, for she never made the least inquiry. Nor did she ever see her child again.

Harriet Mansfield had behaved very badly. There could be no excuse for her running away as she did. She was weak by nature, and her weakness betrayed her; but her weakness was no justification. Yet her folly had not betrayed her into such a desperate position as her mother imagined. She had run away, and she had run away with a lover; but there the disgrace ended.

The people with whom Harriet Mansfield was staying when she ran away were Mr. and Mrs. Gore, old friends of Mrs. Mansfield. They were childless, and lived in very good style in a comfortable house close by an excellent trout-stream. Mr. Gore went to his office in a town close by every day, and came home to a late dinner. During most of the day Mrs. Gore was engaged about domestic affairs, and could give little of her time to her guest. This was the first time Harriet had ever been free. It was lovely weather, and she soon found out a few pleasant walks in the neighbourhood. The place was beautiful compared to the dull monotony of the scenery round Wyechester. Her favourite walk was along the banks of this trout-stream, which wound in and out through delightful shady glens and peaceful meadows.

One day by chance she met here a fine stalwart gentleman fishing. He was more impetuous than careful, and he managed to fix one of the flies of his casting-line in her dress. The hook had to be extracted at the cost of some slight injury to the dress; apologies had to be made; and by the time the apologies had been made and accepted, an acquaintance had been established. He asked if he might be permitted to know the name of the lady to whom he had caused such annoyance, and whose dress he had so shamefully injured. She told him her name, and then he in return told her his name was Cheyne.

From that day forth they met daily by the stream, and before a fortnight had gone by he had asked her to marry him, and she had consented. He was impulsive, chivalric, romantic; the man more than any other calculated to set on fire the heart of a girl who had been so repressed all her life. He obtained a complete mastery over her. She submitted herself to his word as she had submitted herself to her mother's, only one submission was voluntary, joyous—the other a task, a burden. He made passionate speeches to her, explaining how, if they got married now, it must for his sake be kept an inviolate secret. She did not understand the reasons he gave, but she understood his wish—that no word of their marriage should go abroad then, or it would injure him—and she made the necessary promise. She understood only one thing of the reason why their marriage should not be made known at present; and that was, that if it

was known he had married a poor woman now, a property worth ten thousand a year might be taken from him. Whereas under the will of his father he was in a year or so to come into more than would pay all his debts twice over.

He had told her the simple truth. If he had told her the simplest lie, it would have been just as satisfactory to her; for she did not think in any matter which concerned him. She was willing to do, to dare, to suffer anything for the love of him. So she took him at his word, and ran away with him on the understanding that they were to be married in some quiet out-of-the-way place, and that she was to say nothing of their marriage until he came into his fortune.

He brought her first to London, where she wrote that letter dictated by him. Then he took her to Anerly, where he married her. Between the time of his taking her away from the Gores' house until the ceremony at Anerly Church he treated her as though she was a foreign princess whom he was escorting to espouse a prince.

For a few months after the marriage the life of Harriet Cheyne went on like a dream of delight. Her husband was erratic; but he was kindly erratic. He never tired of inventing or devising some agreeable treat or pleasing wonder for her. They travelled much in England and on the Continent. Every place she went to was fairy-land, and he was the enchanter. He was never from her side. He told her he would rather hear her call his name than find the praise of all the world else within his ears. She was intoxicated with happiness, and could scarcely speak, her joy was so great. The black dreary past was more than a million times compensated for. When she lay down at night she dreaded to go to sleep, lest on waking she should find herself back in cold wretched Wyechester. Each waking of mornings was a new delivery from the past. She now knew how unwise her mother's treatment of her had been. But she forgave her; and now and then, when she woke at dead of night, she thought of her hard-faced stern mother at home, and a tear stole down her cheek—a tear of pity for the poor woman who had the misfortune to bring up a daughter who had acted with such perfect indifference to a mother's feelings.

But at last a sad change came. They were abroad. A letter came one day to her husband, saying that some of his enemies had got hold of the fact of his marriage, and were preparing to sell the information to his creditors. Something must be done at once. The bride and bridegroom were then at Brussels. It was essential he should set off at once for England, and under the circumstances it would be exceedingly dangerous for her to accompany him. So he left her, giving her emphatic instructions not to leave Brussels, no matter what might happen, until she saw him or heard from him. She never heard from him nor saw him afterwards.

He got to England safely, and reached Anerly, made an ineffectual attempt to bribe Goolby, left Anerly that day, and died within a couple of days. His death made a final settlement with his creditors, and whether he had married or not was no longer a matter of the least consequence to them.

At Brussels, Cheyne's child was born months afterwards. The mother, whose stock of money had by this time dwindled down to almost nothing, had saved a twenty-pound note, and this she gave to a woman whom she knew she could

trust to bring her baby-boy to Wyechester, to her mother; for she was dying, and knew it. She sent a very brief note with the boy; saying he had not been christened, that his surname was Cheyne, that she was dying, that she had been legally married, but that owing to circumstances the fact of her marriage could not be divulged. Then she appealed to her mother in very pathetic terms to be kind to the boy and provide for him, as she had no means, and had not heard of her husband for months. She also said she sent by bearer a sealed packet of letters and papers belonging to her husband, and begged her mother to keep it, and not to break the seals until some momentous occasion arose for doing so, as she was under important promises to her husband regarding certain matters, reference to which was contained in papers in the packet. Then there came a plea for forgiveness.

At first Mrs. Mansfield was filled with dismay. It was horrible to think of her daughter dying, deserted by the man who had taken her away, and dying in a foreign land too. There was of course an appeal for forgiveness in the letter; but to Mrs. Mansfield's mind the appeal came far too late, and even if it had come earlier it would have appeared an appeal to an affection of the flesh, which was in itself an offence against the spirit.

Mrs. Mansfield had tried to crush down Nature, but Nature was too strong for her; and when the messenger threw back the covering from the face of the infant, the tears, tears of the flesh, stood in her eyes, and her hand trembled. For that small, white, contented, sleeping baby-face reminded her of the time when her own infant lay in her own arms, and she speculated as to what her baby's future might be. And now here was her child's child; and the little one who had lain sleeping in her lap years ago, that seemed no farther off than yesterday, was dying in disgrace among strangers. Her own baby had come into the world sanctified, as it were, by the very atmosphere in which it was born. Its father was an exemplar of what a man and a clergyman should be. There was every reason to suppose her baby would grow up into a woman who would be spoken of as a model of all a woman should be. Now here was her child's child. It was an unholy, an unrighteous child. There was no blessing or grace about it.

Ah, it was hard to hold that babe in her arms and think of her own child, and have a proper Christian feeling towards its father.

And the grandmother, who was not yet forty-five years of age, undid the baby's hood and passed her hand over the child's beating head, and touched the little fat double chin with her bent finger, softly pinched its white cheeks, and forgot for a while all that had happened since, and was back again in the old time.

Then all at once, as though God had taken pity on her, her tears began to fall, and she became less of a rigid Christian of the poor and narrow kind, and more of a Christian in light of the Sermon on the Mount and the story of the Good Samaritan. She said, ' I'll take the boy and do my duty by him.' She said after a pause, ' I'll take the boy and do all I can for him.' At that moment she did not so much want to do her own duty as to be good to him.

But when the messenger had gone away, and she found herself alone with the baby, she receded somewhat from the advanced position she had taken. She had resolved for a few moments to keep the boy and live down the talk of idle tongues. Now that idea seem-

ed no more than a temptation to give way to vainglory, and she resolved to send the boy away as speedily as possible.

She took the boy with her to a town a hundred miles from Wyechester, and had him there baptised Charles Augustus Cheyne. Subsequently she got a nurse for him, and, having made a liberal arrangement with the nurse, she said,

' I shall come and see you and him at irregular intervals; and whenever I come and find him looking well and comfortable, I will give you a guinea in addition to what I have arranged with you for.'

By this she intended to secure the continual good treatment of the child; for though she had failed in her heroic resolve of living down the talk of the idle tongues of Wyechester, she had made up her mind to be as good to the orphan as she could.

When she got home she found news awaiting her of the death of her daughter. She put away the thought of her daughter as much as she could from her mind; and in a few years, when the boy was old enough to go to school, she went to that town again, and having requested an attorney to preserve secrecy in the matter, without giving him any reason for it, she asked the attorney to find a school for the boy. Accordingly he was sent to the school kept by the old maid, and later to a college. Subsequently he was put to business in London; but from the time he left the place where he had been brought up, he had never seen his grandmother, and the early days at his nurse's had completely faded out of his memory.

His grandmother was now a very old woman. She still lived in her old house at Wyechester. She had altered greatly in face and figure, but her nature had softened in no way with years. She was still as stiff and intellectually assured as ever she had been. She had the willing power of one hundred and fifty pounds a year; the other seventy died with her; and she had made this will in favour of Charles Augustus Cheyne of Longacre, in London. Although he had never within his memory heard her name, she had always taken care to know what he was doing, and how he was getting on.

She had even so far given way to worldliness as to read the publications to which he contributed; and as she read them, she thought of how strange it should be that his grandfather was younger than his grandson when he died, and here was she now reading what the grandson had written.

But in all that Charles Augustus Cheyne had ever written there was nothing so surprising as would have been the result of bringing together the sealed packet held by his grandmother, the registry of Anerly Church, and Charles Augustus Cheyne.

[To be continued.]

A SONG.

THERE'S a star come forth in a far-off sky,
　A guide to a wandering soul beneath;
There's a ray beams clear from a light on high,
　To shine o'er a path in the Vale of Death!

A gleam of light for the mariner's weal,
　That says to his heart mid the pitiless blast,
'Courage; have courage! Be strong and leal,
　And I will lead thee to peace at last!'

There's a hope in life, and a goal to gain,
　Something that tells of a glad surcease
To endless striving and endless pain,
　Beckoning upward to realms of peace.

It is thou, O my queen! my love so fair!
　Thou, love, the empress of this lorn breast!
Take all my heart to thy bosom's care,
　And there thou'lt hush it to endless rest!

HAMILTON CLARKE.

APOLLO AMONG THE PEOPLE.

By ELLEN CRUMP.

'Music hath charms to soothe the savage breast.'

NEXT to love, perhaps, there is nothing in our world that has so strong and so subtle an influence over the human mind as good music. It soothes like tobacco; it cheers like wine; it melts one's higher and inner nature, like the caressing touch of a fondly-loved hand; or it makes one's heart and feet dance merrily without apparent rhyme or reason:

'Music, when soft voices die,
Vibrates in the memory.'

It finds a responsive echo in the hearts of many thousands of people who technically know no note of music, but who can, nevertheless, thoroughly love and appreciate sweet sounds. Really musical sounds, in almost any form, seem to awake in us vague and indistinct memories of some far-off higher life—memories perchance of happy careless childhood, or still more dim and distant echoes of the world beyond. Who has not experienced this feeling when listening to church-bells echoing over the silent summer fields, or to the soft chimes of a distant clock in the quiet night hours?

'A feeling of sadness and longing,
That is not akin to pain,
And resembles sorrow only
As the mist resembles the rain.'

The soothing power of song upon the human soul is evidenced in the time-honoured custom, handed down from generation to generation, of singing lullabies to our babies; and many a time, when visiting in the cottages of the poor,

have people been met by the request, 'Sing me something,' from some aged or bedridden member of the family. Men returning home from such east-wind-like atmospheres as the Law Courts or the Stock Exchange are often inexpressibly soothed and refreshed by music; and in these days of universal education there are few men, excepting quite amongst the lower orders, who have neither wife nor sister, son nor daughter, capable of giving them such refreshment. On the other hand, there are perhaps few things more intensely irritating than bad music to an ear at all sensitive; the jangling of a half-worn-out street-organ, or the jingling of a third-rate piano badly played, disposes unpleasantly any one not under very high moral discipline. And yet this rasping irritating music is often all our poorer brethren have wherewith to solace themselves.

The universal power of music is acknowledged and evidenced all around us in our daily life. Nothing is complete without it. The height of luxurious living is to have music whilst we are dining; to be lulled to sleep by soft strains of distant melody, or even by a pleasant-sounding voice reading to us; to have music with our coffee after a Turkish bath, as we lie indolent on our divans. What would our flower-shows be without a band; our theatres without the accompanying orchestra; or our excursion-boats without the dulcet sounds of harp and fiddle floating over the

P

waters? Even our hairdressing must be done to the strains of a musical-box; and the Punch-and-Judy show must have its pandean-pipes and drum to attract an audience; whilst the charm of music over the smaller fry is seen by the rapid way in which games and quarrels are forsaken when a street-organ strikes up a lively tune, to which the small pattering feet may dance on the pavement. What more dismal can be imagined than a High-Church service on Good Friday, when the organ is closed, and the black-robed choristers file in to their seats silent and sad? and what can more distinctly show the popular love of song than the aspect of the crowded churches noted for their full musical services? If a wandering preacher desires an audience, he takes up his station under some sheltering tree in the park, or at a favourable street-corner, and starts a hymn, and in a very few minutes numerous other voices join in the attractive strain. A very great deal of Moody and Sankey's popularity was due to their hymn-singing; and that vast Agricultural Hall was crammed to the doors by a mixed congregation of thousands of people, some eminently respectable, some eminently ragged, some with books, some without, but all joining with intense zest and enjoyment in the lively strains of 'Shall we gather at the River?' led by Mr. Sankey's small American organ, and singing so much in time and unison as to prove very effectually how true a notion of music there is even amongst our uneducated masses. And it is a power for softening and refining our people that should be far more widely used than it is, though much more is being done now to bring music of a good class within the reach of the million than has ever been attempted before. It would surprise many who are sceptical about the people's caring for refined music to see the large congregation that assembles at the busy hour of four o'clock in the afternoon in St. Paul's Cathedral—the number that leave immediately after the anthem proving conclusively what is the principal attraction.

We are not a great musical nation. We can claim no such composers as the Germans, and we have no such singers as the Italian and the Swedish nations can boast; but we are a thoroughly *music-loving* people; and hitherto our music, like our museums and our art galleries, has been monopolised by those who have had money and leisure. For many years penny readings and concerts, supported by local amateur talent, were almost the only decent forms of cheap amusement offered to the working classes, and these were apt to degenerate principally into comic songs; because, unless the music is good of its kind, it must be amusing. Even uneducated people are often keen critics, and can appreciate a pure voice or a skilled performer very thoroughly; and if they do not get either of these they will have something amusing, unless they may take an active part in the performance themselves, when they are perfectly content to sing anything, good, bad, or indifferent. If they are to sit still and listen, it must be to something either good or amusing.

Mr. Haweis, the present Incumbent of St. James's, Westmoreland-street, when a curate in the East-end of London many years ago, started some schoolroom entertainments of a higher class for his parishioners, which were very popular and successful. Mr. Haweis is himself an accomplished violinist, and obtained the assistance of many friends in his efforts; but his was only an isolated attempt, and to do any wide good more concerted means are needed. To meet this need, Mr. Charles Bethune, some three or four years ago, started 'The People's Entertainment Society,' which, from very small beginnings, has risen, by dint of indomitable energy and perseverance on the part of Mr. Bethune, into a fairly flourishing society, with its own offices at 180 Brompton-road, and its own paid secretary, who relieves Mr. Bethune of a portion of his arduous duties. This winter the society is giving sometimes as many as six or seven concerts a week in different parts of London, but chiefly in the poorer and more crowded districts. Very often the admission is entirely free, or, at the most, but a very trifling charge is made, and that sometimes by the request of the people themselves, many of whom retain the true British spirit of independence. At these concerts, besides highly-educated amateurs, such professional artists as Madame Patey, Madame Antoinette Sterling, and others of equally high standing, occasionally give their services; thus conferring upon their audience a pleasure that people of their class could scarcely hope otherwise to enjoy, and one which lingers long and lovingly in their memories. The wealthy classes, who have their stalls whenever Patti or Nilsson sings ; the middle classes, who have their five or three shilling seats at St. James's Hall to hear the most cultivated music of the day,—can hardly realise what an era it is in the life of a working man to hear one of our great musical artists. 'You can hear any of them for a shilling at the Albert Hall,' grumbles an old curmudgeon ; but a shilling seat to a working man is more than a half-guinea stall to a rich man ; and few working men who would go to an oratorio would be so selfish as to go alone and leave wife and children at home. It is such lower pleasures as drinking and skittles that a man enjoys best without his belongings about him. Added to which the shilling seats become terribly expensive to the working classes by reason of the time that has to be wasted in securing them. Time to a working man is money, and he cannot often afford to go several hours before the performance, as many people do, and, taking a book or paper, sit and enjoy himself quietly. Last Good Friday at the Albert Hall, when the *Messiah* was performed, hundreds were turned away from the shilling seats, they being all filled up some time before the oratorio began ; and at the concerts of the Entertainment Society every available seat is always filled soon after the doors are opened. These facts prove what a grateful and kindly work is being done by those who are endeavouring to give the toiling multitude an occasional taste of the high pleasures they themselves enjoy so fully and freely. Many kind friends have aided Mr. Bethune in his labours, amongst others conspicuously Sir Coutts and Lady Lindsay, who have twice arranged amateur concerts for the benefit of the society —once in Sir Coutts's studio, once in the Grosvenor Gallery—the result on both occasions being an addition of some 200*l.* to the funds of the society, which much needs help both in the way of donations and yearly subscriptions. Last summer the society arranged for a band to play in Regent's Park ; and next summer it hopes to do still more in giving the people open-air music. A secondary feature of this particular society is that it often extends a helping hand to young professionals of promising talent, giving them the opportunity to sing in public ; bringing them at the same time under the notice perhaps of distinguished musicians, and paying them besides a guinea for their services for the evening.

Another society that is doing a good work amongst the masses is the Kyrle, the idea being originally started, I believe, by Miss Octavia Hill, who, like many other prime movers in good works, likes to stand aside in the shade and let others take the *kudos* and the sunshine. The Kyrle Society differs from the People's Entertainment Society in various ways, the first and foremost being that it has five or six different works in hand, instead of only one: 1. The organising a voluntary choir of singers to give oratorios and concerts to the poor. 2. The laying out of waste strips of ground as gardens for the poor, and the encouraging of window-gardening, &c. 3. The decoration by mural paintings, pictures, flowers, and other means, of workmen's clubs, schools, hospital-wards, mission-rooms, &c., without distinction of creed. And so on. I can only deal in this paper with their volunteer choir, which is a very large one, and has been most successful in many districts of the East-end, where they have sung such oratorios as *Elijah* and *St. Paul* in churches crammed to the doors by an eager attentive audience, composed mainly of the very riff-raff of the neighbourhood; there being no charge, and no restrictions as to admission beyond orderly conduct. Surely this is a great work. Can these listeners come out of their hard, coarse, ugly lives, and sit for an hour or two in warmth and comfort hearing perfect words set to perfect music, without gaining some dim idea of a higher and better life even here on earth? 'O, rest in the Lord; be thankful unto Him, and He shall give thee thy heart's desire.' 'Be thou faithful unto death, and I will give thee a crown of life.' Such words to their splendid music, floating down the lofty aisles, and over the hushed people, must surely make many hearts swell with a vague longing for better things, and send some at least back to their homes silent and thoughtful, with a warm feeling of new tenderness in their hearts, and such a gentle answer on the rough tongue as shall make the little ones at home wonder where father has been.

'Music's golden tongue
Flattered to tears this aged man and poor.'

Those who have daily baths as a matter of course, food daintily served in clean fresh rooms, grand pianos at home, and concerts and picture-galleries, flower-shows, theatres, and other luxuries abroad, can hardly realise what it is to the toiling grimy multitude to be lifted now and again out of the mire of their material life into a higher and purer atmosphere; or surely the wealthy ones of our land would give more freely to the societies *that* are working so steadily and patiently to help the struggling mass to rise.

TINSLEYS' MAGAZINE.

𝔐𝔞𝔯𝔠𝔥 1881.

THE ROSE OF DESTINY.

BY ANNABEL GRAY,

AUTHOR OF 'MARGARET DUNBAR,' 'AMARANTH'S MYSTERY,' ETC.

CHAPTER I.

JOAN.

'The summer flower is to the summer sweet,
Though utterly alone it live and die.'

SHE was a thorough Irish girl, no mistake about that, with dark, bright, wavy hair, and eyes that change from blue to black in anger or mirth—stormy eyes, yet, as emotion swayed their owner, revealing with instantaneous flash either the joy or sorrow of the soul.

She was called Joan Carden, and she lived with a cousin, poor as herself, at a tumble-down old mansion called Ravensdale, not more than fifty miles from Dublin. It was a wonderful old place with a history—a moat, a ghost, a chapel, and a picture-gallery. In this gallery dead and gone Challoners faced each other from panelled walls: gentlemen in doublets and brocaded waistcoats, and ladies in the costumes of Queen Anne's reign; girl-children with mournful old-world faces, and boys who looked as if they had lived centuries before the glories of cricket or football were revealed.

Little Joan, lonely herself, got into the habit of pitying these repressed-looking specimens of juvenile humanity. She would sit hour after hour among the family-portraits of the Challoners when the moon was at its full, and watch the spiral points of the fir-trees waving over the cracked skylight under which a musicians' gallery had been built. She knew a good deal of the history and legends of the Challoners, and had as a child wept over the effigy in marble of a sorrowful noseless knight in the chapel—a gentleman who had clearly ' done the State some service' in his time. 'Ah, dear people, dear people!' she would say, gazing thoughtfully at the ladies in powder and patches, and the gentlemen in those curious waistcoats, ' were you very strict, I wonder, with the sad-faced children, whose grandchildren now are quite old people? Did they ever make daisy-chains, and romp with their dogs, and feed their pets in the stable and poultry-yard, or scamper about the fields on ponies? I'm afraid, judging from the impression they made on the artist who painted them, that those melancholy kids had the reverse of a jovial time of it.'

And Joan, rejoicing that she lived in the sensible nineteenth century, would rush into the fresh air, and stumble over cones and furze-roots, and, disdaining gloves and umbrellas, wander over the mountains, revelling in the beauty of the romantic scenery of the district; Irish to the finger-tips in her physical wildness and passionate love of Nature and liberty; watching the bee on the bloom of a flower, or the skylark soaring to heaven, with the eye of an artist and the soul of a poet.

To-day Joan was in the stable-yard—a moss-grown deserted place, where only rats disported themselves, and a fine black retriever—Joan's especial dearest pet—was allowed free range. She was holding out her hands, coaxing her doves to alight on her shoulder or breast, and made a picture lovelier by far than any in the gallery, with her brilliant complexion and the wavy brown hair blown across her forehead.

' It will be hard to say good-bye to Ravensdale,' muttered Joan, glancing at its quaint turreted towers. ' I love every blade of grass, every stone and flower on the dear old place; but if it's true that Mr. Challoner means to return soon, and is selling off all his Irish lands, we shall of course have to turn out; no help for it.'

She loved the old decaying place; she cared, too, for the riotous tenants, who never thought of paying their rent, and had nearly murdered Patrick O'Grady, Mr. Challoner's agent, when he had endeavoured to collect some rents that were long overdue.

Joan was on good terms with the little babies and shoeless children squatting out in the sun, making mud-pies, and begging for apples as she passed by; even the

pig seemed to welcome her with an appreciative grunt; while the mothers, leaving their washing-tubs or lace-making for a minute, would curtsy to her at the door of their mud-cabins, and say,

' Och, thin, and shure it's plased, miss, we are to see yer shadder ; for what'll we do without yer ? And it's happy may ye be in yer life and love !'

For the Irish are nothing if not sentimental. Life and love,—life, that fades like a flower, and love, which is its breath,—when would her soul awake to a knowledge of the meaning of either?

Joan was never weary of her pleasant outdoor excursions amid the woods, fields, and forests ; the mountains were to her like dear familiar friends. Careless of all exposure to the weather, indifferent as to her personal appearance, defiant of freckles, she would climb and walk and run with the skill and patience of a mountaineer accustomed to the grandeur and sublimity of the Matterhorn.

And these blue Irish mountains set every poetical fancy at work—elevated her mind, as everything grand and infinite in Nature must ever do.

The cousin Joan had lived with from her infancy was called ' old Miss Carden,' not that she was by any means an octogenarian, but in order to distinguish her from Joan. Both were on sufferance at Ravensdale. The Challoners were an eccentric family, and the only surviving member was supposed to surpass all his predecessors in eccentricity. He was like the ' Wandering Jew'—here, there, and everywhere. Old Miss Carden had been his favourite aunt's drudge and companion ; and when his aunt died, he told her to go and live at Ravensdale. His agent called from time to time, demanded a list of her bills, and paid them, to the good woman's unutterable astonishment.

'When are we to leave?' she asked, a decade and a half ago, in writing to her patron.

'Stay and take care of Ravensdale as long as you like, only, for Heaven's sake, don't worry me,' was the answer.

Little Joan had been staying with her at the time of Mr. Challoner's relation's death, and the child, who was utterly destitute and an orphan, had remained with her ever since; and now a rumour had arisen that Mr. Challoner, disgusted at his tenants' behaviour, and averse to being made a target of himself for a stray bullet, had resolved to sell all his Irish estates. A tenantry who decline to pay their debts, preferring to murder their creditors, are not desirable people to live amongst. At one time Mr. Challoner had enjoyed the privilege of being considered 'good for nothing.' He quarrelled with his father; he pronounced himself, to that worthy gentleman's horror, an advanced Liberal; he thwarted several of the paternal schemes; he was the author of various satirical poems; and was, moreover, a fine essayist—scholarly, epigrammatic, and concise. But withal 'eccentric;' for instance, he fell in love with a beautiful peasant-girl, insisted on marrying her, but did not; he lent ridiculously large sums of money to friends, who under no possibility could ever repay him, and he got into debt. But he got out again in his usually brilliant eccentric way; turned artist, painted and sold pictures for his living, and was supposed to be nobody's enemy but his own, and a universal genius—both, as good-natured people are fond of saying, emphatic mistakes. A good hater, in comparison, would be considered wise. Joan, however, heard a very

different history of him from her cousin. There was another Guy Challoner besides the college rake so often caught *in flagrante delicto*, a man whom dogs and horses loved, and to whom women, when 'pure womanly,' were sacred; who did unknown good, while being considered a cold man-of-the-world; who helped the weak, and had given her and her cousin a home here for years. Did they not both exist to a great extent on his bounty? Her cousin might see to the farming of the lands with the sagacity and foresight of a man; the butter might be of the finest, the fruit, eggs, honey, and vegetables might be sold to the best advantage; but all this did not cover their expenses. There were the visits of Patrick O'Grady still, the lists of the bills owing, and Mr. Challoner's cheques that made everything easy.

After Joan had walked round the stables, and patted the old cob and fed him with carrots, she went into the poultry-yard, the retriever at her heels, and here she found her cousin completely surrounded with a feathered tribe. The dog rushed at old Miss Carden and nearly knocked her over, and laid his nose in the warm palm of her hand, and then, dividing his favours, jumped upon Joan's blue-serge dress, and was scolded, threatened, and played with, till he seemed on the verge of canine delirium.

'I've had an invitation for you to-night, Joan, at the rectory,' Miss Carden said, holding up an envelope with a large design, suggesting a coat-of-arms in pale mauve. (Mrs. Piggott, the Rector's wife, was the only daughter and heiress of a retired fishmonger in Liverpool; hence, was particularly anxious to prove an ancestry.) 'The girls are home for the midsummer holidays, and have set their hearts on a dance. Of course you'll go, child; you love dancing?'

'Ah, don't I, Gip?' cried Joan, pulling the retriever's ears; 'literally adore it!' and her eyes and lips instantly attest her happiness.

Old Miss Carden was a little bird-like lady, with delicate features and a withered skin. Her dress was neat, and fitted her figure perfectly. She wore mittens and an apron. She clung to a waistband. A small narrow black-velvet bandeau hovered somewhat nearer her forehead than was in accordance with æsthetic tastes; but her every gesture and tone were refined. She was more intellectual than intelligent; and she reflected deeply, and enjoyed the delights afforded her by the well-selected books in the library of Ravensdale. Some indeed thought her too natural and clear-spoken, among whom were the Piggotts; while various members of the Roman Catholic clergy—the sons of peasants—who had graduated at Maynooth, and had Fenian sympathies, shook their heads ominously when she was spoken of, and invariably called her 'that very dangerous old person.'

'I'm delighted that you should have a change, dear, seeing that you'll very likely have to be a governess after Christmas; at any rate, we must look out for a place.'

'Don't say place, cousin,' said Joan piteously; 'no, nor situation, it sounds so like an advertising housemaid out of work. Call it an engagement, if you like; there's something "elegant" in the word, as our good people here would say.'

Miss Carden shook her head.

'It comes to the same thing in the end, Joan. I wish you could marry well and escape drudgery.'

'Marry well! Yes, I've had some offers. I'm always open to an offer, you know. Young Todd,

the veterinary surgeon; and Mr. Piggott's curate; and—let me see, poor Mr. O'Brian, the widower at the Glebe, with eight children— *all* my victims; and the three joined together wouldn't make, to my fancy, a perfect man in mind, station, or anything else.'

'It may be a case one day of take what you can get, and be thankful,' suggests Miss Carden, smiling; 'but now it's about time for you to have a cup of tea, and think about your dress for the dance. By the bye, Joan, what will you wear?'

'Ah, that's the question! My wardrobe literally groans with costumes: there's the black grenadine, with the scarlet bows, two seasons old; and a white ditto, draggle-tailed and done for; a black silk that has seen better days; and all my gloves are odd ones. O cousin dear, what shall I wear?'

A look of mimic horror steals to Joan's face. It is a question millions of Eve's daughters daily ask, and few under more trying circumstances than hers.

But as Joan spoke a smile played upon her lips; she was too happy in thinking of the dance to be worried by a simple and unfashionable toilette.

The two ladies entered the house together, and Joan was soon on her knees beside an old trunk in her cousin's bedroom, which contained various odds and ends of ribbon that might replace with advantage the somewhat faded scarlet bows on the black grenadine. Miss Carden, after mature reflection, decided on this particular dress, and found some really splendid brocaded ribbon that had belonged to Mr. Challoner's favourite aunt, and, if somewhat out of date in point of pattern, was decidedly pretty. Joan had no consuming vanity; she knew they could not afford to buy more. Bridget had been despatched to the village of Ravensdale to buy a pair of new gloves, and the old gardener had sent in some beautiful flowers for Joan's hair.

It was towards the end of July, and Joan could well see to dress by daylight; for she was no West-end beauty, accustomed to three 'crushes' in one night, but a wild Irish girl, with a hundred sweet little ways only those who lived with her could appreciate. To Joan a dance was quite an event, even one so simple and impromptu as that arranged at the rectory.

Old Miss Carden stitched away at the bows, and made Bridget bring an iron with which the creases in the dress were straightened, while Joan darted off to her little room and prepared to dress her hair.

Suddenly she appeared before her cousin, holding a wicker-basket of flowers in her hand. A ray of evening sunlight fell upon her as she stood in the centre of her cousin's bedroom, her hair about her shoulders, while she tried the effect of some pale-pink roses before the looking-glass.

'Are they not lovely?' she cried, resting a crimson rose on her lips, and throwing the others aside. 'Which shall I choose, the pale roses or this?'

Miss Carden put on her spectacles, shook her head at the smaller flowers, thought they looked shaky and would all fall to pieces with the warmth of the room, and finally fastened the deep-hearted rose in her young cousin's hair with an old-fashioned diamond *aigrette*—a parting gift from Mr. Challoner's aunt.

'It matches the ribbon, dear,' she said approvingly, as Joan reappeared in her black grenadine. 'I'm afraid Bridget has bought too large gloves; but you must make the best of them.'

Joan laughed again, kissed her cousin, and ran down the stairs, humming an old Irish air under her breath; sprang into the car, and was driven rapidly along the white winding road to the rectory.

Mrs. Piggott came out to welcome her with a considerable rustle of silks and laces—all her costumes came direct from Paris, and were the envy and admiration of the whole county; then Joan was conducted up-stairs to take off her wraps, and found several young ladies had arrived.

The Misses Piggott were playing a duet—a dashing quadrille on the trichord grand—when Joan was conducted to the drawing-room by Master Piggott, a youth of fourteen, who had disfigured himself by a large white choker, which flapped under his left ear, and gave him a somewhat inebriated appearance.

Joan's heart beat quickly as a battery of eyes was turned on her; she felt her colour rise. People who stay much at home are often morbidly sensitive on these occasions; and she was only a country girl of eighteen summers, feeling painfully insignificant by the side of fashionable Mrs. Piggott in Honiton lace and heliotrope satin, and her daughters in pale-blue and cream-coloured silks.

As she took a seat—as much out of sight as she could find—she was conscious of a pair of dark eyes resting on her face—eyes with an amused look in them, that yet had for Joan a certain charm. There was an indefinable expression of interest and amusement mingled in these glances, as if by some subtle intellectuality or keen perception the person read her confusion, and understood that modest diffidence.

The man who watched Joan from his corner by the grand piano was of splendid physique, with a breadth and massiveness of form fitting him to be an army's champion; and when he spoke she could tell his voice was grave, dashed also with the slightest foreign accent; but it was also a deep and musical voice, with a strange persuasive gentleness in it.

Joan was talking and laughing with her young admirer Charlie Piggott, who played the violin, when the stranger crossed over the room and sat by her side. Then, as the Rector stooped to speak to one of his daughters at the piano, he whispered something in his ear; and Joan found herself threatened with a formal introduction.

'M. Meunier, a French artist, would like to have the pleasure of your acquaintance, Joan,' said the Rector; and Joan, flattered and pleased at having awakened interest in any one, bowed her pretty head demurely, while the introduction with M. Meunier was gone through.

The Rector then left them, and passed on to his other guests.

'Are you not going to dance, Miss Carden?' M. Meunier asked, his eyes travelling from her slender figure to the deep-red rose in her sunny hair.

'No one has asked me,' said Joan naïvely, her colour rising again; 'and then I have only just come.'

He looked half inclined to invite her himself; but, on second thoughts, preferred a *tête-à-tête*.

'Have you ever been abroad?'

'I? No. I have a great wish to travel; but there is not the slightest chance of that.'

She spoke quietly, without the faintest tinge of bitterness.

'After all, one never knows,' he said, smiling; 'the most extraordinary and unexpected things are happening every day.'

'But when one's life is in a groove, and when there is no pos-

sibility for the slightest workings of any romance of Fate?'

There was an abrupt and unexpected emotion in Joan's voice that gave him, with his fine poetic instincts and perceptions, an inkling of some inner mental struggle.

'The unforeseen resembles to my mind something like a golden empyrean, which lifts us poor mortals from earth when we least expect it; for instance, what more extraordinary and unexpected than love at first sight?'

'I don't believe in it,' said Joan, hesitating, and rather bewildered at the assertion.

'Why not? Don't entirely repudiate the sweet delusion, or else where would all our most charming fictions vanish? and, indeed, truth is stranger than fiction.'

'There were certainly Romeo and Juliet,' said Joan, longing now to talk: she had read rather more than the average girl, and she did not wish him to think her an ignoramus.

'And hosts of others. But women have a wonderfully elastic faculty of forgetting—do you not think so?—of slipping away from burdens and memories that wound.'

'I don't know,' she said nervously. 'I thought it was generally the other way—I mean that it was men who get over things.'

He smiled again, and stroked his beard. Frenchmen were considered critical over matters of the toilette. Was he secretly amused at her girlish attempt at finery? She fancied the old-fashioned ribbon bows amused him. And then he said, as she looked away,

'Do you know that I watched you in church last Sunday?'

'In church!' echoed Joan, blushing. 'O, you must be joking!'

'One has odd dreams in church, you know. I am a very visionary unpractical sort of person; and I like to see how people take a sermon. By the bye, *you* did not go to sleep.'

'I never saw you,' she said shyly.

'Miss Carden, will you not give me this dance?' asked a little timid man, leaning over the piano to address her; and Joan, looking up, saw the eligible widower with eight children, Mr. O'Brian, and, by force of contrast with M. Meunier, her little inoffensive admirer did not perhaps shine at his best.

She could not well refuse; but she regretted losing the conversation of her interesting companion. As Joan moved and took her partner's arm, the crimson-hearted rose, so carefully fastened in her hair by her cousin, slipped from the old-fashioned diamond *aigrette* on to the seat she had just vacated. M. Meunier picked it up, sniffed its delicate fragrance, and then coolly walked away with it towards the dining-room, where claret-cup and refreshments were served.

'Should it be the rose of destiny!' he muttered, touching its leaves. 'She's really a dear little girl.'

After waltzing vigorously with Mr. O'Brian, Joan and her partner entered the dining-room, and, as Joan sipped her claret, she found M. Meunier again by her side. She was half fascinated by those sombre ardent eyes and the low and *trainant* voice—so different from Mr. O'Brian's, that had a powerful dash of Paddy's brogue.

'I see you love dancing. Are you fond of sketching? Do you paint or draw?'

'A little.' (If a young lady painted as well as Rosa Bonheur, or sang like Malibran, she would always say 'a little.')

'Would you permit me the pleasure of giving you some lessons? I am an artist.'

Joan found her breath coming quicker. Watching her at church,

and now anxious to give her lessons! What would her cousin say?

She fancied there was an amused twinkle in the Rev. Temple Piggott's eyes, as he passed them; while Mr. O'Brian sighed quite volubly, and helped his hostess to the drumstick in mistake for a liver-wing, so mightily was he disturbed.

'I will ask my cousin,' said Joan shyly, her senses growing somewhat bewildered; and then she saw her rose in a glass of water at his elbow.

'But I may call to-morrow, may I not?' he pleaded. 'Mrs. Piggott shall bring me, that will be best.'

'My rose!' cried Joan, touching the *aigrette*. 'Why, *that* is it!' pointing to the flower.

'You will not take it away,' he whispered; 'there are plenty more in Ravensdale.'

After that he moved from her side, taking the flower with him; and Joan was alone.

She saw the mysterious stranger no more that night, till the car arrived and she stood cloaked and hooded on the step ready to return home.

'Good-night, Miss Carden,' he said, advancing and shaking her hand, 'or rather *au revoir!*'

When Joan returned home, she hurried to her cousin and gave her a graphic account of the evening's amusement.

'Somebody kept the rose, and somebody's going to call to-morrow, who saw me in church on Sunday! Cousin, we've actually flirted!'

'Go to bed, you silly child,' said old Miss Carden, kissing her, 'and I'll send Bridget to you with a cup of tea the first thing. Don't hurry up on any account.'

Joan flew to her little room, drew the diamond *aigrette* from her wavy tresses, and smoothed out the old-fashioned ribbon bows on her dress. What could he mean? It was wonderful—impossible! Love at first sight? She wasn't in the least like Juliet, who always had seemed rather too gushing to quite satisfy Joan, a girl who put her heart too much *en avance.*

'It's all nonsense, of course; but how handsome, how interesting, he is; a voice like music!' muttered Joan, as she laid her head on her pillow; while later on the childlike breathing that stole from her parted lips was here and there broken with vague murmurs; and in her dreams she was kissing the leaves of a rose that wandering rays of moonlight shone upon— rays that beamed also on the dark noble face of one who smiled.

CHAPTER II.

IN THE PICTURE-GALLERY.

'Belike she wakened to a thought
That lay in ambush through the night.'

M. MEUNIER was as good as his word: he called at Ravensdale the following day, accompanied by his hostess, Mrs. Piggott, whose visits to Miss Carden were generally few and far between.

They invariably differed on questions of dogma. Miss Carden mentally ticketing the Rector's wife as a good-natured hypocrite, whose outward and visible form was the embodiment of fashion, but whose inward and spiritual grace was not lit with the light of holy charity.

She swept into the drawing-room of Ravensdale in an elegant morning-dress of gray cashmere, trimmed with old lace, followed by the French artist, her guest and friend, who saluted Miss Carden with respectful interest and curiosity; and then his eyes travelled round the room in search of Joan. Mrs. Piggott plunged *in medias res* be-

fore Miss Carden could get in a word.

'I know how you and dear Joan are situated,' she said, vigorously fanning herself, with a consciousness of being ultimately bored by her visit, 'the great uncertainty of both your positions here—that is why I think she would do well to profit by M. Meunier's kind offer of instruction and assistance. Joan herself has told me that it is more than probable, after Christmas, she must seek a situation; and she really has a pretty taste for drawing. I wish Ada and Gwendoline had the same—I do indeed. You must really allow me the pleasure of purchasing those two water-colours of Joan's, representing Ravensdale by moonlight.'

M. Meunier fidgeted somewhat on his chair, smiled, admired his finger-nails, and examined a large smiling angel in terra-cotta on a cabinet. He pitied Mrs. Piggott for her want of tact and taste; he saw the colour rise in the elder lady's thin cheek.

'I do not know if Joan will part with them,' old Miss Carden said quietly; 'she values them highly. She will keep them always to remind her of Ravensdale.'

Miss Carden involuntarily glanced towards M. Meunier as she spoke, and he, glad of an opportunity to be heard, said,

'*Vraiment!* How nice of her! It is a fine sentiment to care for one's home.'

'It is not her home,' explained Miss Carden; 'we are merely taking care of it on sufferance during Mr. Challoner's absence from Ireland.'

'Indeed! Is Mr. Challoner about to return soon?'

'So they say,' here interposed Mrs. Piggott; 'and that is why I felt anxious dear Joan should profit by some good drawing-lessons: she might enter some school of art, you know, by and by, and earn her bread by painting. They say pot-boilers often bring in a good sum.'

'My cousin will be a governess: she will essay no wild flights of any kind,' said Miss Carden gravely. 'But still, I am extremely obliged to your friend for his kind offer of instruction; he might give us the benefit of his opinion regarding Joan's work.'

At that moment the door softly opened, and Joan appeared. She had awoke early, risen, and taken a long ramble by herself amid the purple mountains and flower-decked fields. There was the faint dreamy scent of midsummer in the air; birds were singing, bees flitted from flower to flower; not a leaf stirred —every fanciful imagining of her girlish brain had full scope. Joan entered with a fine colour on her cheeks and a lovely spiritual light in her eyes. Did she for a second pause to think that this man, who had so mysteriously watched her unseen in church, and talked to her the previous night with marked in-terest and subtle ardour, already viewed her with a lover's tender-ness and an artist's criticism? Their eyes met, and again her colour changed; a vague delight and sinking of the heart set her pulses beating as he retained her hand a thought longer than was necessary in his own.

'Will you let me have the plea-sure of assisting you in your paint-ing?' he asked, smiling down on Joan's shy changing face. 'You may find knowledge useful to you in after-years.'

She glanced appealingly at her cousin, who looked considerably mystified and surprised. It was like a romance already, a sort of absurd parody on the Lord of Burleigh, and everything whimsical and quixotic. Perhaps, so quick are women's instincts, she saw danger in the acquaintance for her young cousin. This was the 'some-body' who had kept the rose, and with whom Joan had confessed to flirting the previous night.

'My dear Joan, you must not encroach on M. Meunier's time; besides, you are not going to be an artist. You might show him your sketches, and have his opinion of their worth.'

'They are simply horrible,' said Joan, shrinking from the thought of exhibiting the contents of her portfolio to the critical eye of a trained artist.

'What! Ravensdale by moon-light horrible?' he asked, lifting his glass and again carelessly scan-ning the angel in terra-cotta.

'Why, how did you hear of that?' she cried, her voice slightly trem-bling.

'Through me, my dear girl,' began Mrs. Piggott, finding herself over-looked. 'I wish to purchase your sketches and hang them up in dear Temple's sanctum; the girls say they are quite lovely.'

Looking very beautiful in her hesitation and timidity, Joan at last fetched her portfolio and ex-hibited her drawings.

They were clever—he saw that at a glance—spirited, and true to Nature; but they were crude and even careless in their treatment, and yet they pleased him.

The first was a sketch of the sea: angry and rapid clouds swept over the heaving waters, the light falling here and there on a ship, disabled and dismasted, with the lifeboat in the distance pushing off to succour the crew. The chief beauty of the picture was in the movement of the heavy rolling breakers, the dark expanse of sky, and the suggestion of the storm. The ship and the lifeboat were utterly out of drawing; and the attempt to represent a corpse float-ing by the vessel ended in a failure that was almost grotesque.

'It has merit,' he said quietly, replacing it; 'but you want to work and study more. These water-colour sketches of Ravensdale are decidedly the best you have yet attempted; that moonlight on the ivy towers is excellent, one almost feels conscious of the dreamy hush of the summer night. You were in love with your subject evidently.'

'Ravensdale is to Joan what Ireland is to Paddy,' said Miss Carden rather vaguely; but more reconciled to the stranger since his last speech.

'It's a pity she will ever have to leave it.'

'Whatever is, is best,' said poor Joan, philosophically tying the strings of her case; 'but still I should like to have your advice and aid, since you are good enough to offer them. I would rather be an artist, of course, than a governess.'

'I daresay you would,' said Miss Carden rather crossly; she feared Joan might have her little head turned and be good-for-nothing ever after; 'but the idea is not to be tolerated for a moment.'

'Why not?' asked Mrs. Piggott, amused at Miss Carden's wrath.

'Why not? Because she has her bread to get, and such notions will unsettle her. Artist, indeed!'

'Well, I promise not to let the lessons interfere with common sense,' pleaded Joan. But how could she answer for that, with a vague presentiment of 'something going to happen' to her? What could it be? Suppose she had real talent, and there was no need for her to lead a drudge's life? M. Meunier, watching her with his grave ardent eyes, saw the commencement of a delightful romance, that *might*, after all, be disturbing to common sense, and convince Joan of the truth of his remarks regarding the unforeseen.

After an agitated whisper from Joan in old Miss Carden's ear, Mrs. Piggott, by dint of coaxing, reasoning, and persuading, induced her to agree to M. Meunier's proposal regarding the drawing-lessons. And then Bridget appeared with wine and glasses on an antique silver waiter, biscuits, and 'seedy' cake which no one touched. M. Meunier, however, helped himself to some Madeira, and then begged to be shown over the gardens and grounds of Ravensdale.

Pretty flower-like Joan conducted them first into the old chapel, where the noseless knight reposed, and found M. Meunier at her side when Miss Carden and Mrs. Piggott lingered to read an inscription on a marble tablet.

'We know the chapel so well,' the Rector's wife said, with a wave of her hand towards Miss Carden; 'but a foreigner like M. Meunier will no doubt find it interesting.'

There was a deepening colour on Joan's cheeks as she explained the history of the melancholy knight, in whose career the artist appeared to take a deep interest.

'In this age of fastness, slang, Americanism, and caricature it is refreshing to find oneself transplanted into the thirteenth century. After all, the Crusaders were in earnest,' he was saying, in reply to some remark of Joan's.

Mrs. Piggott found the chapel damp, coughed and sneezed, and begged to be taken to the picture-gallery.

'I remember I used to cry over him, and tell him all my troubles when I was a child,' said Joan, laughing a farewell nod at the hero; and M. Meunier gave her a strange rapid glance under his dark lashes that did not escape old Miss Carden's naturally acute observation.

As they entered the picture-gallery M. Meunier sighed.

'To me a gallery like this arouses

sad sentiments,' he murmured, conscious that Joan would understand him. 'They are all dead and gone, you know. Have you ever read over the letters of those who are dead addressed to others who have also joined the great majority? Nothing is more mournful. Well, a picture-gallery like this gives me the same impression.'

And here Mrs. Piggott's hard voice interposed,

'None of these Challoner ladies ever thought of giving sly peeps under Gainsborough hats, or postured behind huge feather fans, or nonsense like that. I don't care for the beauty we see nowadays; it's all too loud, too self-asserting, too audacious,' she said, scanning the portraits on the walls. 'These were more like what women should be, with less sham and pretence.'

M. Meunier was silent; he was looking at the cold handsome figures and faces of those who had moved and breathed amid the past. Were they loyal, honourable, and brave? Gallant gentlemen or churlish knaves? What would they think, if they could speak, of the science of modern life—the universal toleration, the deification, of so much that is coarse and vile; the languid contempt and gentle disdain of all things that mark the typical golden youth of the nineteenth century; the 'buttonholes,' the high play, the turf-ruin, and the divorce-court?

'That is the musicians' gallery,' said Joan, with gentle deference.

She had seen the shade upon his brow; she had caught the melancholy of his mood.

'Indeed!'

'It was built in Queen Anne's reign, and then it was burnt down; and when Sir Hubert Challoner—'

'Hush, hush, my dear Joan!' said Mrs. Piggott playfully. 'Don't

go into that everlasting history; you're getting as tedious as a tourist's guide or the official in the Tower; and really, let me see, it's getting dreadfully late. Temple will be expecting us to luncheon; and he's so angry, dear soul, when we're late. M. Meunier, like most Frenchmen—I'm sure that horrid chapel was damp—eats nothing at our early breakfast; he must be literally famished. Suppose we go through the terrace-gardens into the park, and do the rest of the mansion another day.'

M. Meunier stroked his beard and smiled, as if amused at Mrs. Piggott's sudden desire of an exodus.

'As you will,' he said, knowing it was useless to endeavour to change her decision, and muttered something about *les caprices des femmes;* and soon after he was bidding Joan and Miss Carden good-bye at the entrance of the park.

'To-morrow we will begin our first lesson, remember,' he whispered. 'You must not despair, or think you will be doomed for a governess. *Fi donc,* the firmness of individual resolve will work wonders. There are talent and taste to be unearthed here.'

Joan walked rather disconsolately back by her cousin's side.

'What do you think of him?' she asked, in a low voice.

'He's a gentleman evidently, but I wish he wouldn't come here, making love to you.'

'To me!' echoed Joan, half charmed with the idea, but frightened to give it form in words. 'How can you say such a thing, cousin!'

'I mean it, Joan: we old maids are not always blind as moles or bats, and perhaps the man's an arrant flirt; nearly all those Frenchmen are, they say.'

Joan said no more, but went straight to her little room in a brown study.

Was there really, after all, such a thing as love at first sight? She had always, to a certain degree, despised Juliet, as do many girls whose hearts are fancy-free; but now the love-frenzy of that luckless heroine evoked less contempt. She felt touched, softened—a sweet and pensive languor oppressed her; but her habitual self-control made her check emotion. Joan had few pleasures, few girl-friends of whom she made *confidantes*. She knew when tears forced their way that she was weak, absurd, and selfish; and yet why did his eyes confuse her senses and stir her very life? And why was she longing for the morrow?

CHAPTER III.

'I LOVE YOU.'

'I would make his home
A resting-place from each uneasy effort :
The very eagle cannot hold his weight
For ever in the sky.'

IT was not without considerable trepidation that Joan prepared to receive her first lesson; her life had been so perpetually becalmed that the smallest change in it seemed an event, and about M. Meunier was all that charm of mystery which is so fascinating and bewildering to a young mind. She knew that he was an intellectual man, a thinker, who studied life as a philosopher, and she already felt a reverence for his authority; he was so different from the material thoughtless rustic types—the careless talkers to whom she had grown accustomed, who passed hours in the open air and never touched a book. Joan had no imaginative genius; but then again she was neither frivo-

lous nor vain. She was sensitive and impressionable, and M. Meunier's quiet dignity, his *esprit*, the vein of irony that occasionally ran through his remarks, gave him an interest in her eyes that no one had ever yet awakened.

Sympathies are very strange, but they govern humanity.

M. Meunier came to-day, along the avenue leading to the old mansion, smoking a cigarette, and with De Quincey under his arm. He walked quickly; his gray-felt wideawake pushed sideways on his head, a few flowers in his hand, which he had gathered coming through the terrace-garden.

Joan, who had been watching for him at the oriel window, was conscious of that shrinking susceptibility which makes a young girl of her nature like a mimosa plant.

She rearranged her easel, drew her brushes over her fingers, and mixed some madder-brown and yellow ochre furiously together on her palette as his approaching steps were heard along the corridor.

'Good-morning, Miss Joan,' he said, holding out his hand, into which hers went with the faintest perceptible tremor. 'Well, are we going to work hard? Are we prepared to paint out that smoky-looking sky and the trees resembling those in a child's toy-box, and suggest a firmament more like heaven's own blue? Do you know, young lady, that you have been badly taught?'

He had seated himself before the picture, and, taking up a brush, went rapidly to work; Joan standing by his side and watching every movement of his hand. It was wonderful how sudden was the transformation.

'I could never paint like that if I tried all my life,' she said shyly.

'Never depreciate yourself,' he

answered; 'plenty are ready to do that for you: people take you at your own estimate. You have nice taste, and painting is such an agreeable distraction. When one dreams on some sunlit moor, or wanders about the East, or strolls by the Mediterranean or along the Riviera, see what amusement it gives one: as a matter of barter, painting is often a drudgery, and it is the same with every art.'

'Do you think I could ever paint well enough to—to make a living at it?' asked Joan earnestly. She did not wish to indulge in foolish dreams.

'Not at present, certainly; perhaps never. You see there are so many at it.'

'I know it must be difficult; but to have to go away, live with strangers, and work for them—*that* is hard. I would rather live in the tiniest garret and paint for a living, even if—'

Her voice faltered. She had hoped he would have praised her. He evidently thought very meanly of her capacities.

'You mustn't take a dislike to what may be a necessity,' he said dryly. 'Toil and bondage are the lot of all who are not born with the silver spoon in their mouths. There are thousands — hundreds of thousands—of young girls who have to earn their own living. Feminine labour is a drug in the market. If you ask me candidly, I should say, Abandon any Utopian schemes you have in your mind of being an artist. Follow your good cousin's advice, and make the best of things.'

Joan was bitterly disappointed. Mrs. Piggott and others had exalted her work and given her sweet flattery. She was accustomed to be admired and thought clever; she blushed painfully, and the tears forced their way, but were bravely beaten back. She was silent, mor-

tified, and even distressed. He watched her and saw the struggle, and then he gazed almost wistfully at the velvet lawns, the fragrant flowers, the stately trees in the old avenue, the poetry and beauty of Ravensdale, which she must leave.

'What sort of a man is this Challoner?' he asked abruptly, after a pause, still painting away to Joan's intense mystification.

'He has been very good to us; he lets us live here.'

'A character, isn't he, from all accounts?'

'I don't know about that; every one speaks well of him.'

'Even his tenants? These Irish are a cut-throat set.'

'They are misguided,' said Joan sadly; 'they have never been understood.'

'They've a lively knack of killing their creditors. I don't wonder at people preferring to live away from the place.'

He had risen and was standing at the window; a glimpse of the blue mountains just visible through the trees, the sunlight streaming on the silvery waters of the lake.

'We will work no more to-day,' he said, scanning her face. 'I have brought you a flower in return for the one I took possession of the other night. That is blooming still on my mantelpiece in a glass of water.'

He tossed her a splendid Devoniensis rose, and as Joan picked it up she forgot her disappointment; and then they talked on a variety of subjects, and he discovered that Joan loved reading and had a fair stock of information. He dazzled, bewildered, wounded, and encouraged her with his semi-mordant and cynical mood; but never had an hour flown so quickly; their glances, unknown to each, grew warmer. Joan felt under a spell, dreamy, sad, and enchanted, all in turn.

Then old Miss Carden entered, shook hands with her guest, and heard his opinion of Joan's talents. He advised her strongly to abandon all idea of earning a livelihood at art; promised to look in on them in a day or two and give her fresh hints, if she pleased ; and, after a few gentlemanly farewell remarks, withdrew.

Joan could assume a part no longer. She lifted her hands to her brow and burst into a passion of tears.

'Why, my dear child, what is the matter?' cried her cousin, startled at this extraordinary display of emotion.

'I am so miserable!' sobbed Joan. 'I had so hoped he would praise my work and encourage me ; and I would have lived in a garret, and had nothing but tea and bread-and-butter, and any substitute for meals, to have got on, and now it's all no good! I'm stupid, and have no talent, and shall have to be a governess, and fetch and carry ; and I hate the thought of it!'

'Just what I expected,' answered Miss Carden gloomily; 'that ridiculous dressed-up doll, Mrs. Piggot, puts such absurd notions into young girls' heads, and I never heard—'

At that moment a light tap came at the door, and M. Meunier, to Joan's horror, appeared, pleading guilty to the carelessness of having dropped his pocket-book and gloves, and begged to be allowed to find them.

'Never mind, my dear,' whispered Mrs. Carden to poor Joan, who drew down the blind with an angry jerk. 'He won't notice you.'

But Joan shivered and put her hands before her face, and ran out of the room, not before an amused smile of his warned her that he had caught a glimpse of her tear-stained face.

'And my complexion is simply horrid when I've been crying,' mut-

tered Joan, rushing to her room; 'it looks like mottled soap.'

M. Meunier did not appear for several days. Joan fancied he had forgotten her, and she began to feel unhappy. She was immensely lowered in her own estimation, and was quite meek and humble when Ada and Gwendoline Piggott came over to tea, and sang duets, and looked at her paintings.

'My dear, you are a genius—mother says so, and M. Meunier thinks the same, I'm sure,' said Ada, who gushed at everything.

'O no, he doesn't, Ada,' answered Joan sorrowfully; 'it's all a mistake. I'm going to give it up.'

And when Ada told M. Meunier he was wicked and cruel at disheartening Joan, and that she had lost her spirits and appetite, and didn't care what became of her, he went out of the room, put on his hat, and resolved to walk over to Ravensdale. There had been two or three more lessons given since the first, when he had slaughtered Joan's hopes, and she was decidedly improving ; but he was very chary of praise. That fair bright face, those sweet girlish ways, the pure and tender nature of the girl whom he had fallen in love with at first sight, were growing daily dearer to him. He loved her—how he loved her! Her merest glance, her lightest touch, her every gesture, thrilled him with a passion that startled him with its vehemence. And to-day he must find out if she cared for him—ever so little—if her heart reflected his image, as a lake the hues of the heaven above. If not—and no man living could better judge the meaning of a woman's looks, manners, and words than he—he would go away from her for ever, and forget the foolish dream, the pain and longing, the anguish of a hopeless love.

It was a lovely morning when he set out for Ravensdale, and under

the soft shafts of the summer sunshine it looked like a miniature
paradise, with its quaint range of
old gothic casements, its stately
avenue, the distant park, where,
deep in fern, the deer wandered
amid long grasses, or plunged into
the thicket that surrounded the
estate.

He came upon Joan in the middle of the avenue; and spite of her
resolves, a vague and unintelligible
melancholy had of late possessed
her, that gave a beseeching expression to her face, a sadness to her
young loveliness, which, glowing in
the sun's warmth, had lost the deep
rich tints of a colouring that had
been once Titian-like in its perfect
glow.

The scent of M. Meunier's strong
cigar arrested her attention. She
tried at first to steal away unnoticed;
but he was too quick for her, and
came at once to her side. A
great butterfly flew over her broad-
brimmed straw hat, and then alighted on some flowers she had just
gathered in her little basket.

'I have come to say good-bye to
you, Miss Carden,' he said, after
they had talked of the weather, and
the fruit, and the sweetbrier hedge,
a piece of which adorned his coat.
'I am going away from Ireland.'

'Are you returning to Paris?'
asked Joan, with consummate indifference. She tried to convince
herself she disliked him.

'*C'est selon,*' he answered, with
a shrug; 'but before leaving Ireland I have something to say to
you'

'Is it very important?' asked
Joan, with a brave attempt at arch-
ness, and pulling a fuchsia to
pieces

'It's about your work that I wish
to talk,' he said, with an assumed
professional severity of manner.

'Indeed! That interests you very
much, I know.'

'You think I've been unkind to

you, do you not, in throwing cold
water on your artistic efforts? I
have always disliked the mere
thought of turning art into money,'
he went on, studying her face intently. 'Try and look upon art as
a luxury, a delight, a pastime; follow
it humbly and reverently, but do
not seek for payment.'

'One must live,' said Joan a little fiercely; 'but as I have no talents
I mean to resign all attempts at
painting for a living—I shall have
to be a governess.'

He smiled, and rested his hand
on her shoulder.

'Pardon me, you have considerable talents, but you have no humbug in your nature: a little talent
and plenty of the latter would
eventually get you on; without it
you are lost. The most successful
people in this world are the hum-
bugs.'

Joan sighed, and the tears very
nearly drowned her eyes. It was
hard; he admitted, after all, that she
had talent.

'What, then, shall I do?' she
asked, with a sigh that must have
gone to the most invulnerable masculine heart.

His hand travelled from her
shoulder to her arm, and he let it
rest there; his head drooped over
her dark wavy hair; the vivid crimson darted in a flood-tide to cheek
and brow.

'There is no need for you to
do anything,' he whispered; 'no
need, believe me, for you to be
any one's slave, or to do anything
you do not like. You have but to
choose—'

His hand trembled over the
sleeve of her dainty morning-dress,
but she only looked at him with
startled bewildered eyes. Was it
a dream? He drew her towards
him; he imprisoned her little hands
and held them fast.

'I love you, my darling. I've
come to ask you to be my wife—an

artist's wife, Joan; together we will work and reverence art.'

Joan covered her face, and turned away with a sigh. Why had this man so soon become to her more than any other being on earth? She felt at a word ready to follow him to the world's end, and she sobbed from sudden utter joy.

'And if you are no genius,' he went on, smilingly, 'what then, Joan? Do you think a man cares about a woman whose fame is on every tongue, and who could set the world on fire? Such mental gunpowder is worrying. A woman with all sorts of wonderful designs, drifting through strange unknown seas, and dragging a fellow after her—what a bore she would be, what charm could she have to a man seeking rest?'

'I never thought you cared for me,' stammered Joan, enraptured, but shy; 'it's all so new—so wonderful.'

'Joan, I love you.'

Her head for a moment rested on his shoulder. He drew her nearer to him; the light from his grave ardent eyes came in tender, broken, fitful gleams—it seemed to infold her in one vast luminance, and kindle fresh beams in hers.

'What must be my answer, little one?'

She looked pale and bewildered. He was her first lover; no man had ever yet soiled her innocent lips with a kiss; new life throbbed in her veins—love was intoxicating her senses.

'My answer is—yes,' murmured Joan.

'And you are quite sure you love me?'

'I have thought of nothing else but you since the first night we met,' she faltered beneath his embrace. 'It's awful to be ruled thus; but I could have conquered it — you remember you kept the rose?'

'The dear Rose of Destiny, Joan?'

'Was it that?' smiling.

'I think so, Joan; it affected me as if I were some sentimental schoolboy; and now, my darling, will you prove your love for me by doing something to please me? I must leave you for a time—it is indispensable to our future interests. During my absence we must be engaged in secret. Can you trust me enough for this?'

'Not mention it to my cousin?' cried Joan, too *exaltée* to have yet given a thought to her romantic lover's income.

'Not till I return: we will then make our confession, and sue for forgiveness; and I think I can give a sufficiently satisfactory account of myself to relieve her of every fear—that I'm either a bigamist, an adventurer, or a bankrupt.'

'I will do what you wish,' answered Joan steadily.

'That's a dear obedient child; and I'll bring a pretty ring back with me for you from Paris—a diamond one; girls like diamonds, don't they?'

Joan glanced at the shabby little pearl ring on her finger—the only one she possessed.

'Will you give me this?' he asked.

She slipt it off her finger, and he took possession of it with a kiss on the dimpled girlish hand.

'And now, Joan, what of your scepticism as to the power of love at first sight? Remember, I fell in love with you at church.'

'The unforeseen *is* like a golden empyrean,' she muttered. 'I know it is so now. You are always right, I suppose.'

'God bless you, Joan; be true to me!' he answered, with a fond glance and a farewell embrace. 'It's hard to leave you; but I must —no help for it. Walk with me to the end of the avenue.'

When Joan returned alone she found her cousin sitting out on the lawn in her low-backed chair, the retriever by her side, and a piece of work in her hands.

'How you have idled away your morning, Joan!' old Miss Carden said a little irritably. 'This dreaming will never do; you must learn to be more practical. Why, what a colour you have! It's the sun, I suppose.'

Joan knelt down rather confusedly on the grass, and played with the dog.

'While you've been mooning about the place I've been worried. Here's a letter come from Milan, from Mr. Challoner, saying he thinks of returning to what he calls his "drowsy refuge" at Ravensdale for a few weeks, and then he means to sell it and live in England.'

But Joan gave vent to no dejected expressions, as was her wont when the possibility of Mr. Challoner's return was mooted.

She nodded at Gip with wistful indecision, as if uncertain whether to take him into her confidence, and then hung over her cousin's chair and read Mr. Challoner's letter through.

'We shall have to turn out, that's all, I suppose,' she said, blowing a soft kiss on Miss Carden's ear.

'And you will have to be a governess, Joan. I'm glad you've given up all that nonsense about painting.'

'O, there's nothing like sound common sense for getting on in this world,' cried Joan airily, 'or a little talent and plenty of humbug.'

CHAPTER IV.

THE MASTER OF RAVENSDALE.

'True conscious honour is to feel no sin ;
She's armed without that's innocent within.'

MR. CHALLONER arrived in due course, and preparations to make his drowsy 'harbour of refuge' agreeable had taken a certain spasmodic form that even Miss Carden's philosophy could not altogether control.

Although Joan was mentally pursuing the absent M. Meunier to Paris, wondering if he thought of her much, or had ever looked at the withered Rose of Destiny, she too caught this general excitement. She found herself rushing at the brown-holland covers on the Metternich suite in the drawing-room, dragging them off, heedless of the tapes that bound them ; and in uncovering the magnificent glass chandelier, that for more than fourteen years had never been revealed to the honest eyes of daylight, detached several of the wonderfully-cut lustres, and found them at her feet shivered into complete wrecks.

A professional cook was telegraphed for from Dublin, who disgusted the worthy Bridget by her strong libations of Irish whisky, and who proved herself true to the old national proverb, 'Wine to-day, water to-morrow ;' for after exerting herself to an alarming extent over soups and pastry on the day Mr. Challoner was expected, utterly collapsed on the morrow, and was found in a hopeless state of semi-inanition, from which she could only be aroused by vague promises of attending a local 'wake.'

Joan and Miss Carden were both seated in the drawing-room, wearing their best dresses, and looking rather nervously at each other from time to time, first down the avenue, and then at the surrounding magnificence of the Metternich suite.

What would he say? How would he look? Would he turn them adrift when Ravensdale was sold, or pay for their existence in lodgings?

The realities of life look very grim in certain lights. They were both penniless. They were absolutely dependent on his bounty. Both, too, were proud. Joan's manner had, however, a certain sprightliness and assurance that old Miss Carden could not fathom. Her moods had never before been so variable or so bright. She talked of 'governessing' as a charming distraction, with nothing exhaustive to youth's energies — it was more romantic than commonplace. She meant to make every one fond of her, and see nothing that was disagreeable. And still they sat watching for Mr. Challoner's arrival, while the evening twilight was melting into darkness, and Bridget had twice rushed in to say they were sure he was coming, for they distinctly heard the sound of approaching wheels.

'Suppose we have a cup of tea in the library, Joan; it's no use waiting any longer. I don't fancy he'll arrive till to-morrow,' Miss Carden was saying, as the furniture took weird invisible shapes in the gathering dusk.

'Very well, cousin; I'll go and make some. It strikes me very forcibly our patron is a capricious man. What with telegrams, letters, and all the rest of it, he's kept us in a pretty lively state of mind lately. How I wish he would come, and have done with it!'

Spite of her assumed coolness, her eyes had darkened with suppressed emotion; those glorious wild Irish eyes of hers, that were all-unconscious of their beauty and power of entrancement

Miss Carden ran to the window and listened.

'I believe I do hear something this time, Joan. It is he! Hark at the furious pace the man is driving! Guy Challoner always seemed to act like magic on everybody.'

'Yes, cousin;' and Joan clapped her hands, and danced round the room. 'What fun it will be to watch him and hear all he says! I fancy he'll be awfully gloomy, with a sort of dismal Byronic despair about him, and smoke from morning till night.'

Mr. Challoner's valet, Lowten, had by this time leapt off the box, and rung violently at the bell. Bridget opened the hall-door wide, and saw a smiling gentleman, with a good deal of brown whiskers and gold chain, standing with some furs and wraps on his arm. The worthy soul at once mistook the valet for the master, and curtsied humbly to the ground. Lowten was apparently quite used to such homage; indeed, expected it; and it was only when he turned to assist his master from the carriage that she discovered the mistake she had made.

The valet was offering his arm with studied grace to his master, who appeared a chronic invalid from his numerous wrappings and the profound air of attention with which his servant viewed him.

Miss Carden and Joan were in the hall as Mr. Challoner, on his valet's arm, ascended the steps; but they could see little of his face, it was so muffled up, and his straight gray eyebrows were slightly contracted with a frown.

'Deuce take you, Lowten,' said the master of Ravensdale, in a rather shrill *crescendo;* 'but you've mangled my foot; and if you can't be more serviceable, I shall really have to send for Gulliver back again.'

'What a horrid temper!' muttered Joan, and blessed the absent Meunier, who would save her from an unpleasant future.

'He's dreadfully changed!' whispered old Miss Carden, with a nervous quake.

She was always alarmed at the least show of temper in one of the opposite sex.

When Mr. Challoner found himself safely in the hall, and upon one of the old oaken chairs, with a griffin carved on its back, he held out his hand, and looked less grim.

'And how are you both?' he asked, scarcely glancing at Joan, who hung back a little.

Bridget had curtsied till she could bend no more; and a savage nudge from Lowten so alarmed her, she screamed, 'Ah, begorra, an' it's an impudent feller, ye are!' when the prudent valet whispered in her ear, 'Have you any boiling water ready?' which evidently suggested a purpose, and she retired to the kitchen, where the professional cook was tasting some splendid *soup de galle*, and at the same time drinking the half pint of sherry Miss Carden had poured out for the soup and pudding.

'We are quite well, sir,' answered the old lady, with an anxious glance at Joan.

Joan was so pretty and winning when she liked, why should she not conciliate their benefactor by a few pleasant words?

'And so that is your young cousin?' Mr. Challoner went on, lifting his glass. 'I left her quite a child. I verily believed she climbed a walnut-tree the last time we met. Well, Miss Joan, have you no word of welcome for me?'

Joan came forward with a steady resolve to be beautifully conventional, and speak to the purpose.

'We are very pleased, sir, to see you once more at Ravensdale;' but no colour dyed her cheek: she thought his manner heartless, and his temper 'cubbish.'

'Don't "sir" me either of you, for Heaven's sake! Am I an ogre or a monster that you begin— Deuce take that fellow Lowten, he's off with my stick, and how on earth does he expect me to hobble to the dining-room?'

'I am sorry you suffer so,' said Miss Carden, in a low grave voice. 'I regret it more than can be expressed; we know how much we owe you, your kindness for years, and your generous care for our wants.'

'Generous fiddlesticks! You owe me nothing, my dear Miss Carden; it's I who am your debtor. Fancy, both of you buried in obscurity in this God-forsaken hole, isolated, bored from morning to night— Where has that fellow gone?'

'Lean on me, Mr. Challoner,' suggested Miss Carden, 'while Joan rings for your valet. I suppose it's gout: your poor aunt was a sad martyr to that horribly painful complaint.'

Joan followed them at a discreet distance as they walked slowly towards the dining-room; Mr. Challoner leaning on her cousin's arm: she liked him better since he completely disowned their being under any obligation to him.

'It was kind, it was good taste on his part,' thought Joan, giving a fleeting glance at herself in a mirror: the vivid hue of some cardinal-coloured ribbon in her hair made her look bright as a little tropic flower or bird.

'Gout, yes; of course it's gout, and rheumatism and biliousness and heart-disease and a mixture of every ailment we poor mortals, who don't work for their living, are subject to. And it isn't as if I had not tried every mineral and medicinal spring on the face of the earth— bitter waters, sweet waters, Cheltenham, Malvern, Bath, and then

Carlsbad. I've worked like a nigger to get back my health.'

'We shall dine in a few minutes. I sent for a cook from Dublin. I hope the seasonings will be satisfactory: diet is everything, I suppose, in these cases?'

Miss Carden had again grown painfully nervous, and Mr. Challoner leant against the marble mantelpiece, taking a comprehensive glance around. Joan, entering, saw a tall man looking considerably older than she had imagined Mr. Challoner would be, with fierce bristling eyebrows and a reddish beard of unusual length, dashed here and there with gray.

He was not exactly an ugly man, but he looked decidedly cross with that deep furrow between his eyebrows. It was wonderful to think her cousin should have praised his beauty, and spoken of his personal fascination, his wide cultivation, his social attainments, and the calmness and grace that distinguished him, if this were a specimen of his manner. What a contrast to M. Meunier! But then gout was awful, and a tiresome valet tried his temper—that and a long journey combined.

'He will be better after dinner,' thought Joan, and sat down demurely in her accustomed seat, winding wools and watching Mr. Challoner.

He turned from leaning on the mantelpiece and glanced at her. Perhaps he had not been prepared, from Miss Carden's somewhat vague descriptions of her young cousin, for the beauty that met his gaze, and it was the beauty he liked best—that dark mobile loveliness which very fair women never possess, and that bore the brilliance of perfect health and vigour; the health that comes from inhaling much fresh air and taking long walks; the vigour that is constitutional, and has a supple grace of its own.

Joan was not dressed according to the modern ideas of a 'stylish girl.' She wore no tie-back; her hair was not flattened to her skull, and screwed in a hard knot behind, but waved in splendid shining masses—hair that painters love; rebellious, fluffy, flowing; it was plaited about her head, but no plaiting could make it completely smooth, or what coiffeurs are fond of calling ' dressed.' As he watched the girl, Lowten appeared, handed Mr. Challoner his stick, and informed him, with all the insinuating toadyism of a valet who has found a good berth and can sell his master's clothes with advantage, that preparations for his toilet were made, a fire had been lighted in his dressing-room, and the bitter waters unpacked.

Mr. Challoner could scarcely repress a smile; but at the appearance of Bridget, struggling under the weight of a large soup-tureen, he dismissed the obsequious Lowten, told him he was at home, and should not on this occasion dress for dinner.

Then they all sat down to dine, and soon Joan remarked a complete change in the host's manner. Not that the culinary preparations of the professional from Dublin had anything to do with it; Mr. Challoner was not a man to be subdued only through the senses, and leave off snapping like an ill-bred cur when nourished by food.

He partook of little, drank off a glass of hock with his fish; but he talked, and with the accent, the gesture, the charm of a true gentleman, a cultivated man of the world. He was gentle and deferential to them, heard Joan's enthusiastic remarks about Ravensdale without looking bored, and soon a happy light spread itself over a face that, if somewhat ugly, was altogether interesting.

'I am changed more than you,

Miss Carden,' he said, stretching his legs under his mahogany and refilling his glass. 'Do you not think so?' The thin faded cheeks flushed a little as he spoke; Miss Carden was thinking of the 'long ago' when she had been the patient drudge of a fretful woman, but her youth then had not quite flown.

'Yes, you are changed; so much so that I should never have recognised you,' she said simply and honestly, as was her wont.

Joan stole a glance at him, and thought how that great red beard disfigured him, and the bristling eyebrows evidently wanted combing straight.

'And now to sell Ravensdale,' he said, glancing at Joan under those heavy brows.

Joan sighed; a darting pain oppressed her at the words. Something seemed to catch at her throat and almost make her cry, but, trained to repress emotion, she gave no outward sign of distress.

'*Must* you sell it?' she faltered —it was like losing a beloved friend—and although her voice was low, it had a passionate ring in it which his keen ears detected.

'Must I?' smiling towards her. 'Well, Miss Joan, do you wish me to stay and be murdered? Threatening letters will be sent me. I shall be treated to a sketch of a coffin, and myself reclining full length in it, with "Prepare to die" printed on the outside. They peppered my agent pretty well; they mean to make "cold meat" of me.'

'It is awful to think they should be so misguided, so misled and infatuated,' said old Miss Carden, who was clever and had a clear meaning of politics. 'And worse still to find they have no powers of endurance, no capacity for patient toil, no thriftiness or common sense. Look at the English peasant, the German, the French. Is any more done for them? But they are noble and heroic, each of them, compared to the Irishman. Priest-ridden, you will say; but is that any excuse for the treachery of their blows? Were Ireland to be given up to them, they would all be quarrelling and fighting and murdering each other just the same; a hundred claimants would arise and struggle for possession of a particular piece of land.'

'But the mud-cabins are very dreadful,' said Joan, thinking of the little peasant babies she had nursed and the mothers who loved her.

'Everything could be improved for them if they would work and were thrifty and frugal,' said Mr. Challoner quietly. 'It is not a question of sentiment. Life is difficult, and a man must work; they are incapable of endurance and strain. Treating their friends to whisky, and rioting at wakes, and murdering their creditors, cannot improve their position. Their vanity makes them clamorous of applause. Every Irishman has the makings of an actor in him, I sometimes think.'

'It may be difficult to find a purchaser for Ravensdale,' suggested Miss Carden.

'Very; but in any case, whether I find a purchaser or no, I shall live in England.'

He had not once alluded to themselves, and Joan looked confused as he talked of England. Then, leaving the discussion of politics alone, he turned to arts and literature, and found Joan was but little acquainted with the mysteries of the modern novel, and that her knowledge of light and imaginative literature was extremely limited.

'And music,' he said, limping towards the drawing-room, 'are you fond of it? Do you sing or play?'

'Very little,' said Joan timidly. 'I—I prefer painting.'

This had been a very sore point hitherto. Miss Carden fidgeted as Joan alluded to art. Mr. Challoner, however, evinced no interest in the matter, but sat down to the grand piano and played a nocturne of Chopin.

Fascinated in spite of herself, Joan drew nearer. This ugly man with the great red beard was evidently a fine musician. The dreamy sadness of the music made Joan think of her absent lover—the romantic M. Meunier with his delightful dreaminess, his ultra-refinement, his quotations from Homer and Balzac, and rapid development of sky in water-colours. And then a sudden thought darted over her consciousness that made her pale. Suppose he was faithless and never returned, could she, expelled from Ravensdale, earn her daily bread—that terrible daily bread which forms such bitter and unsatisfactory rations for some of us? And a girl may be more clever and capable than the average, but who will buy her brains or the work of her hands?

The nocturne was now finished, and Mr. Challoner, finding old Miss Carden had left the room, smiled at Joan in a new and beaming way, as if he meant to make love to her. She did not understand this change of manner; for Joan, in her ignorance of light fictions and works of an amusing but 'naughty' tendency, had had as yet no experience of the fascinations and dangers of gentlemanly *roués*. She looked him fearlessly and straight in the eyes; she drew her little, dainty, fragrant, girlish hand away from his large one; there was no sly coyness in her ways, no attempt at 'leading on' a rich man, who could largely benefit her and load her with gifts. He saw she was honest-minded and innocent as a flower.

Then Miss Carden reappeared, and gave Joan a warning look, as much as to say,

'Ten o'clock—bed-time.'

Joan rose; she had been hurriedly turning over Chopin's Mazurkas with tremulous touch. She was angry, wounded, her face burning and her eyes half full of tears.

'Good-night, Mr. Challoner,' she said coldly, moving to the door.

She had been prepared to serve him with reverent affection, with frank true worship; but now—he had repulsed her yearning.

'Ah, good-night, Miss Joan!' he answered, reseating himself at the piano; '*dormez bien*.'

Joan hurried along to her little room, banged the door rather savagely to, and the tears fell one by one down her hot cheeks. A pain, vague and formless, had fallen upon her life. She felt confused and bewildered.

Mr. Challoner had disappointed her expectations; he was not at all the hero she had pictured him to be. Her love for the absent man seemed now more exalted and glorified. He would save her and take care of her. O, how she trusted him! How chivalrous, how noble he seemed!

It was long ere Joan composed herself sufficiently to sleep; for even when her eyelids grew heavy she could still hear that beguiling music of Chopin, and, mixed up with the darkness of her room and the general unsatisfactoriness of her thoughts, she fancied the music was like a mocking sprite, daring her to sleep and bringing discordance to her dreams.

————

CHAPTER V.

THE KEY TO THE ENIGMA.

'All thy vexations
Were but my trials of thy love, and thou
Hast strangely stood the test.'

FOR the next few days Joan saw very little of Mr. Challoner. He kept his room for days, sedulously waited on by Lowten; but sometimes, as Joan came across the lawn or passed along the shrubbery drive, she caught sight of him, in a loose dressing-gown, at one of the old oriel-windows, a book in his hand and a cigar between his teeth.

Occasionally he descended into the library; and once Joan met him face to face in the picture-gallery, and they entered into some fragmentary conversation, which yet had the effect of discomposing her and making her glad to escape. Her innocent unconsciousness and impulsive remarks decidedly amused him. He liked her to enter his room, after a nervous tap at the door, to bring him any little *souvenir* sent by an old friend, such as the rector or the village doctor, a gray-haired old man, who had called several times at Ravensdale and mixed hot toddy as they discussed the past.

Sometimes Mr. Challoner's moods varied considerably. He would be cold and ironical; and Joan, who, spite of the dulness and monotony of her life at Ravensdale, had been brought up as a loved and petted child, felt stung and wounded, worked up at times to hot fits of rebellion, at others trembling with impatient anger; and then again, grieved at his harshness, evinced symptoms of that awkward crisis in young ladies' lives of nearly bursting into tears.

The girl began to yearn for her lover's return. This fitful erratic treatment, from a man to whom she was under heavy obligations, brought keen mental distress and nervousness with it. She, who had been every one's favourite, to be tortured for mere caprice! Why did he wish to make her suffer? Perhaps to drive her away in a rage.

Joan's splendid health lost a little of its former robustness: she was pale; she had begun to dread the cold glitter in Mr. Challoner's eyes. She found she had also to disguise her aversion for him; and there was the absent man, who had never written to her, or given any sign of his existence. As weeks passed on, Joan gradually lost heart. There had, indeed, been two or three very unpleasant scenes between Mr. Challoner and Joan that perplexed old Miss Carden; and on this particular evening, Joan, pleading headache, had left the dining-room abruptly, while Mr. Challoner and her cousin were playing *bézique.*

She hated the game; Mr. Challoner had tried to teach her it, and it had ended in Joan flinging the cards under the table, and both of them losing their temper.

She now went quietly to her room: she did not mean to go to bed yet, for it was early, and she had never been a good sleeper; but she wanted to be alone.

'I never can bear it,' muttered Joan, taking down her hair and feeling in a perfect maze of bewilderment, as she thought of the future; 'nothing I ever do is right, and yet I try to please everybody. Even cousin has lately begun to scold me.'

She was sitting by the window, leaning her cheek on her hand; the moon was at its full, and its uncertain light fell on the grand old beeches in the avenue, on some birch-trees to the right, and the park-fencing, while beyond was the magnificent shadow of a mountain, and at its foot the faint outline of a valley.

'How beautiful it is!' sighed Joan; 'and how I love it all! Dear, dear Ravensdale!'

She was an Irish girl to the core, with all the passionate sentiment of the Irish for their native land; but she was also proud and brave; and in her fierce rebellion against slights and unkindness she was prepared for any struggle. That shadowy sky, the night-wind that stirred her hair, the fitful moonlight, were all emblems of her destiny. And she could understand nothing.

Meanwhile, the couple down below played *bézique*, and talked in a bright jovial way of old times and scenes. Mr. Challoner gave a brief *résumé* of his career abroad for old Miss Carden's benefit. They had evidently forgotten all about Joan. But at last he yawned, still dealing his cards with carefulness, and looking at a purple butterfly that adorned his partner's cap. Fancy a married couple, who did not care in the least about each other, sitting down to play *bézique* night after night.

'Where is Joan?' he suddenly asked, throwing away a wrong card. 'What idea has she got into her head now?'

Miss Carden was very loyal; she loved Joan; she wished him to think well of her; and as yet they had got on so badly together.

'I think she is tired, Mr. Challoner; she had a very long walk to-day.'

'O, that's all nonsense and affectation!' he said, a little sharply.

Miss Carden was silent. She sighed, and forgot to lead.

'Do you wonder why I have never married?' he asked, after a pause. He, too, was forgetting *bézique*. His hand shook a little over the head of a king.

'No,' she said, in a low voice. 'You swore never to take a wife when Hetty—'

'Poor girl! What fools men make of themselves in their extreme youth! They fall in love with any decently pretty girl at hand; when they have seen no other, it's a case of taking paste for gems; and sometimes the paste answers every ordinary purpose very well.'

'Sometimes,' assented Miss Carden. 'But Hetty was happier in her own sphere.'

'And I in mine. I used to fancy her like the girl Tennyson sings of:

"She knows but matters of the house;
But he—he knows a thousand things."

Knocking about the world removes many of our foolish illusions.'

He was playing carelessly now. Miss Carden called out 'Royal marriage!' and he threw down the cards.

'But I mean to marry,' he said, in a low grave voice, looking steadily at his partner. 'I've lately fallen into that melancholy state of mind called a love-seizure.'

She was not weak or vain enough to think he was alluding to herself, even if his eyes rested on the wing of the butterfly in her cap. She was a sensible woman, and picked up the cards very leisurely.

'Indeed,' she said, somewhat surprised at being the recipient of his confidence.

'Yes, Miss Carden, I mean to marry Joan—that is, if she will have me.'

'Joan!' repeated Miss Carden, starting up, and staring at him as if she believed he had suddenly lost his senses.

'She's a dear little thing,' he went on dreamily, taking a few hurried turns across the floor; 'rather rebellious and hot-tempered, and all that sort of thing;

but I can play the part of Petruchio—no man better.'

'Marry Joan !' echoed her cousin. 'Why, you've done nothing but quarrel ever since you met each other !'

'I've been studying her character, that's all ; and, on the whole, it pleases me. Her incivility and sulkiness have been candid, at any rate. By the bye, I suppose she's quite fancy-free, eh ? No lover lately been prowling about Ravensdale, has there ?'

Miss Carden blushed to her ears. Why at that moment did she recall the dazzling Meunier ? Not a word had Joan whispered to her of any sentiment which he might have aroused ; and yet so quick are women's instincts, even those of old maids, that she half divined Joan's secret.

Mr. Challoner had begun to look very stern, and her voice trembled when she next spoke.

'Not that I know of, certainly.'

'Then she's artful, perhaps, and has her letters sent to the village post-office.'

'O no, no, Mr. Challoner ; she's the dearest girl in the world !'

'So *I* think.'

'Only sometimes I fancy Joan may have had the least *penchant* for a guest of the Piggotts, who was staying there some time ago— an artist, a Frenchman.'

'Deuce take the fellow !'

'He gave Joan some lessons in painting.'

'Hang his impudence ! Be so good as to gratify my curiosity sufficiently by telling me his name.'

'His name was Meunier.'

'O ! So you think Joan was fascinated by this Meunier, and that I shall have a poor chance ? But then I'm wealthy, and this French artist was probably poor as a church mouse.'

'Joan can be very obstinate and self-willed when she likes. Most girls are, you know.'

'Well, I'll prove all this, and to-night. Kindly request Miss Joan to come to me here.'

Miss Carden dared not disobey, and yet she hesitated. She wanted to have time to take Joan to task —to beseech and entreat her to hear reason, and forget the absent Meunier, if indeed he had won her heart. Such a wonderful future would Joan have were she to accept Mr. Challoner !

'Do you think it's wise to disturb her to-night ? I believe she's gone to bed,' said Miss Carden hesitatingly, but still moving towards the door.

'Then let her get up again. Why, it's only eight o'clock ! No ; it's temper that sent her away.'

'And a bad headache.'

'A little conversation with me may cure it, have an electric influence on the nervous system. Kindly give Miss Joan my compliments, and beg her to come to me here ; mind, not a word of the subject I broached to you ; but I know you too well to say more.'

Miss Carden found herself out in the passage as if by a miracle, and passed quickly up the stairs to Joan's room.

The girl was still sitting at the window watching the moonlight on the mountains, her loosened hair about her shoulders. She had been crying ever so little, as girls will at difficult times in their lives, for everything lately seemed to have gone wrong with her. She rose as her cousin entered, and went to her and wreathed her arms round her as if glad to find some human presence in the room.

Miss Carden put down the candlestick on the dressing-table, and for a second stared musingly at her young cousin in a kind of stupor, her breath coming hard and fast.

'You must go down-stairs at

once, Joan, to see Mr. Challoner. He sent me for you.'

Joan saw the pleading in her eyes, but she did not understand its meaning. She pushed the candlestick, a little irritably, further back on the table.

'I hate Mr. Challoner,' she said, in a clear steady voice.

Miss Carden started to her feet.

'O my dear, don't say that! don't—don't.'

'Why?' asked Joan defiantly.

'Because he's so kind—our benefactor,' faltered Miss Carden, feeling a hypocrite for the first time in her life.

'If he orders me to come,' said Joan, shrugging her shoulders and petulantly tossing her hair about in her rage, her face crimson with anger, 'why, under the circumstances, I suppose I *must* obey; but I'm tired of being his slave. I have resolved not to bear it.'

She had gathered her hair by this time in a great shining mass, and knotted it round her head. She felt in disgrace in some way, and savage at injustice.

'Come,' whispered Miss Carden, 'or he'll be so angry. Make haste, Joan!'

'A fig for his anger! Why can't he leave me in peace?' said Joan, reluctantly withdrawing from her room. She was not in the least pretty with those red eyes and tumbled ribbons and untidy hair; but what did it matter?

Arrived at the dining-room door, Miss Carden was almost under the painful necessity of opening it and pushing her cousin in.

'Little goose,' she said, under her breath, 'if she lets such a chance as that go.'

Joan found herself face to face with the man she avowedly hated —her master, her tyrant, her benefactor — leaning on the mantelpiece in the somewhat dim light of the lamps.

Standing there before him—angry, shy, and nervous, all in turn —with one long loose tress of hair that had escaped bondage about her throat, and a mute yearning in her eyes, spite of their fire, she had never looked so beautiful. She meant to say she was sorry if he was still displeased—she desired to be friends with him. Why should they quarrel—why should he always misunderstand her?

'You sent for me, Mr. Challoner,' she said softly, feeling like a culprit, and in unfeigned horror of a *tête-à-tête.*

Perhaps he had found her a suitable situation as a governess— he had before threatened to do so.

Mr. Challoner lifted his head— he beckoned her towards him.

'It was kind of you to please me,' he said, and took the little hand she extended to him.

'Can we not be friends?' said poor Joan huskily, forgetting her part in her fear.

'Why not, Joan?' he said, with an odd smile. 'Am I really hateful to you?'

'No; but you are unkind.' Then naïvely, 'I never quarrelled with any one before.'

'Then I must be a regular ogre, child—a sort of unearthly monster, waging war against all things sweet and fair and true.'

She had never heard him speak before in this strange musing way. There was caressing, beguiling music in the voice; it had none of the harsh, cruel, guttural utterance she had learnt to shrink from; and her face wore a puzzled expression.

Was this Mr. Challoner? He looked decidedly changed—even his dress was altered: he wore a black-velvet artistic suit that gave a rich Rembrandtesque expression to his face, that seemed to her, for the first time, noble, full of fire and tenderness—if it were not for that great red beard.

'Sit down by me, little Joan,' he said, 'for I have been harsh, unkind. I admit it all—and you and I must soon part, Joan.'

Joan turned pale. This was cruelty of a more subtle character than ever; the words cut her like the sting of a lash—for she had been prepared for kindness.

'Leave Ravensdale?' she asked, her large eyes opening wider, even as she shrank.

'Yes, Joan; you see I have resolved to marry, and your temper is so little under control that, even if I offered you the post of companion to my wife, you would both undoubtedly quarrel. You have no meekness, no docility.'

'And when shall I have to go?' asked Joan, the treacherous tears again rising. It was awful—this thought of parting—now that it really had to be faced.

'You like the old place, do you not, Joan?'

'Like it! Like Ravensdale? O, the dear—'

Her voice broke suddenly; she turned on him fiercely as she rose to her feet.

'If this was all you had to say to me, Mr. Challoner, why not have kept it for the morrow?'

He smiled again.

'No, it is not all, Joan. If you will only have patience, I will make my views clear to your small comprehension.'

'You are a cruel man,' she said, flashing a look of scorn on him. 'I shall be glad when I am away; and what makes it so dreadful is the thought of how much I owe you, and,' with a burst of tears, 'I wished to be grateful, as I once was.'

'Joan, will you hear something I have to say?'

'I won't be sent from Ireland,' she sobbed. 'I don't mind Dublin—in fact, I should like it; but London, or anywhere in England —No, no, I would drown myself in the Channel first.'

'Very well, Joan,' he said, amused at her vehemence; 'then listen to the other proposal I have to make. Will you be my wife?'

He was near her again, and had endeavoured to secure both her hands; but she wrenched them away, and though she trembled from head to foot, she had grown calmer, and checked her tears. Her breast heaved, and there came again the old passionate ring in her tones.

'You do me great honour, Mr. Challoner, but I distinctly decline it.'

'Why?' he asked, rising and pacing across the floor. 'You might do worse. I am wealthy, and shall be an indulgent husband; in any case your lot as my wife will be better than either those of a companion or a governess.'

Joan was silent; she thought of her secret and her love; the luxury, the charm of wealth, affected her but little. And she trusted and believed in the truth of the absent with love's supreme faith.

'I do not care for you,' she answered.

'Then you care, may be, for another? Young ladies of your age are not generally fancy-free. Out with it, Joan; let me know who my envied rival is, that I may have the satisfaction of lodging a bullet in his brain.'

'That is my affair,' she said coldly, her cheeks aflame and her little foot beating the ground.

'Well, then, look on me as a friend, Joan, and take me into your confidence. Have I not some little right to inquire who this fellow is, and all about him?'

Joan hesitated, and then shook her head.

'Better not,' she said quietly; 'in any case I shall be true to him. I shall never marry any one else.'

Mr. Challoner reseated himself by Joan's side, and smiled into her sorrowful eyes.

'Was his name Meunier?' he asked slyly.

'Why, how did you know that?' she cried, her heart beating to suffocation; and again he shot a rapid glance at her agitated face.

' O, never mind; a little bird of the air carried the news to me. Did he paint, and teach you to develop skies more after Nature?'

'Yes, he did. It's too bad of cousin to have talked—'

'Did he steal a rose, a bright red rose that you had worn in your hair, and call it "the Rose of Destiny"?'

' Mr. Challoner!' cried Joan, struggling in his embrace, and speaking in the tone of a person driven beyond herself by the flash of a thought.

'Look again, Joan, and tell me if you know me. Off with it, miserable imposture!' and he dragged at the red beard, and completely tore off the grayish-red eyebrows, and the iron-gray wig that covered his black hair.

The girl buried her face on his shoulder, too excited to speak, and over-powered with the first symptoms of faintness she had ever known. He knelt at her feet and carried her hand to his lips.

' Forgive me, Joan, will you not, for the *ruse* I have practised in your pursuit? You must not leave me, dearest—you shall not! I won your love, I have proved its truth.'

Joan found he watched her gently and seriously, and at last some remnants of self-control returned; but she could scarcely speak, and so he kissed her.

'It was too bad, I admit,' he said laughingly, after a volley of reproaches, blended with tears and smiles, had been hurled at him; ' but, Joan, I've been so often deceived by women. Piggott was alone in the plot—he staked his faith on you; and the idea of wooing you in this way first suggested itself to me during an afternoon doze, after our wine and walnuts, on that fatal Sunday of my arrival.'

Joan shivered; she remembered all she had suffered lately.

' But why were you so cruel to me and made me feel so wicked ? I'm not sure that I shall forgive you,' with a demure shake of the head, but speaking in the shy, sweet, broken accents of love.

He took an envelope from his pocket, opened it, and showed her the contents. They were the fragments of a flower.

' Was it not the Rose of Destiny, Joan? But what a little spitfire she is !' he said, turning her round with a playful pat. ' Must I play Petruchio, Joan? You've looked black as thunder lately, and as haughty as any queen; in fact, you want ruling, Joan.'

A modest tap at the door. Mr. Challoner cried 'Come in !' and Miss Carden entered. She was followed by Bridget, bearing a silver tray, on which were lemons, whisky, cakes, and glasses, which collided against each other with dangerous shakiness; for Mr. Challoner had darkened the room till the faintest glimmer was reflected.

'An' shure, miss, it's dark indade,' whispered Bridget nervously.

Miss Carden glanced furtively from Mr. Challoner to Joan, as if dreading to learn the result of the interview. She had lately feared that Mr. Challoner's temper was of the tindery uncertain kind that would make all dealings with him awkward and unpleasant. But he was speaking to Joan in a low voice now, bending his face close to hers, which had a fine colour, and seemed flushed with something that looked like a return of its old happiness. And if they had again quarrelled, and Joan had emphatically refused him, would they be sitting near each other? He rose suddenly, and drawing Joan's arm in his, walked across the room to the corner where Miss Carden stood.

Miss Carden's withered face was indeed a study, with its look of speechless surprise and wonder blended.

'She has learnt the key to the enigma,' he said; while Joan slipped her arm from his and embraced her cousin as she lifted her eyes fondly to his.

'The enigma?' echoed Miss Carden. 'Do you mean that she will be your wife? But now I look at you—you are—'

'Meunier!' he said, laughing tenderly down at Joan. 'She has forgiven me, the dear child, and you must do the same.'

'They say all's fair in love and war,' Miss Carden answered slowly, after listening to his explanations and excuses; 'and if Joan is satisfied—'

'I think she is,' he said, drawing her to him again; 'and I tell her the unforeseen is like a golden empyrean that has all sorts of mysteries and metaphysics of its own, with which it works in Love's service; for who would think that a simple crimson rose, worn in a girl's dark hair, should be Fate's sweet Heaven-sent agent—the Rose of Destiny?'

THE TRYST.

She glided o'er the meadow-grass,
　　And through the green young corn;
Sweet as the summer blooms she was,
　　And fresh as summer morn.
We laughed and loved beside the brook
　　That sang its gay refrain,
And where we met that day, my love,
　　We swore to meet again.

But ere the grass was dry and brown
　　Amid the ripening corn,
Up to the churchyard on the Down
　　A maiden's corpse was borne.
I weep alone beside the brook,
　　All swol'n with autumn rain;
For where we met that day, my love,
　　We shall not meet again.

SUSAN K. PHILLIPS.

SOME REMINISCENCES OF A LADY'S LIFE IN THE FAR EAST.

ALTHOUGH a great deal has been written about China, there is probably no country in the world so little understood by Europeans, and about which so much remains to be told. The following unpretentious little sketches, founded on the writer's personal observations during a six years' residence in China and Formosa, will, it is hoped, form a contribution, however slight, towards a better acquaintance with the manners and customs and peculiar modes of thought which prevail amongst the inhabitants of the Middle Kingdom.

Amongst the most remarkable of Chinese customs are those which are observed at New Year time. Chinese New Year generally falls somewhere about the beginning of our February, and is undoubtedly *the* great festival of the year, the only real holiday enjoyed by the toiling industrious millions scattered over the vast Celestial Empire ; for, although there are in nearly every month certain holidays which are observed by the better classes with more or less ceremony, it is only at New Year that high and low, rich and poor, put aside for the time their ordinary avocations, and give themselves up without restraint to the due celebration and full enjoyment of the festive time. Long before the eventful period arrives, great preparations are in progress, extra bustle is observable in the streets, and extra animation is apparent in every countenance. The shops, especially the provision shops, are filled with tempting wares, the display of slaughtered

pigs hung up at full length in front of the pork-butchers' being particularly remarkable. Lamps are suspended over doors and windows, and attached to the door-posts and window-frames are long slips of red paper, having boldly inscribed upon them mottoes appropriate to the season, ' May the Five Blessings come to this door !'* ' New Year, New Happiness !' &c. Business people are particularly active at this period squaring up their accounts ; for a Chinaman considers it *de rigueur* to pay off all outstanding debts before the old year is out, and thus commence the new year without any arrears and with a clear conscience. Houses are made clean—a rare event in China—and few, indeed, are those who do not supply themselves, or who are not supplied by their husbands, fathers, or other friends, with some new article of dress for the great occasion. Children are in a fever of excitement ; for, besides the new clothes they are likely to have, are there not wonderful toys to be presented to them, or, better still, to be purchased with their own money, during that much-longed-for stroll through the gay streets, which they are to enjoy presently with their father or elder brother as their guide ? Fresh ornaments, flowers, and candles are placed round the little shrine which every house possesses, and every tradesman and shopkeeper decorates his signboard with cloth of flaring red, the Chinese festival colour.

* The Five Blessings are, longevity, honour, wealth, posterity, and a natural death.

At last the happy day dawns. With the first glimmer of light a host of boys, who have been eagerly on the watch for the break of day, commence discharging their stock of fireworks, the fusilade is taken up by the entire row of houses lining the narrow streets, and the New Year is ushered in with a din and uproar which render sleep for the remainder of the morning impossible. The first duty of the day is then performed : children do reverence to their parents, wives to their husbands, servants to their masters, wishing them on bended knee 'a happy New Year.' Early breakfast is quickly disposed of, and then commences the serious business of making calls : old men remain at home in state to receive the congratulations and good wishes of those who have not yet attained the happy and privileged state of old age; but the younger men, clad in their very best raiment, sally forth on their round of visits—in sedan-chairs with an attendant card-bearer, if they are well off; or on foot carrying their own large leather card-case, if they are in less easy circumstances. It is amusing to see the 'get-up' of your old native acquaintances on these occasions. You wonder at first who the swaggering individual can be who comes strutting along the street towards you in all the glory of a Mandarin hat and long silken robe, his left hand placed across his breast, and his right arm, with a sleeve half a foot too long for it, extended at full length, and swaying backwards and forwards in the most approved official fashion. Presently the gorgeous creature stops suddenly before you, joins his sleeve-covered hands in front of him, raises them to his chin, and with a low bow and a grin wishes you in 'pidgin' English a happy New Year. Then for the first time it dawns upon you that you are addressed by your old house-boy, who left you last year to get married and set up in business, and who was reproached by you when last you saw him for wearing such a greasy cap and such a slovenly cotton gown. A-ping tells you in a few hurried words—for he ' wan-chee chin-chin too muchey piecey man'—that he is doing well, and wishing you ' plenty No. 1. good chancey this year,' makes another bow and passes on. Children arrayed in all the colours of the rainbow, and displaying with pardonable pride their recently purchased gew-gaws, are paraded up and down the busy thoroughfares ; friends meeting each other in the street salute in the most formal manner; faces beaming with smiles and contentment are seen on every side. But go where you will, in country or in town, in the richest streets or in the poorest, great and universal though the holiday be, your ears will not be offended by the drunkard's maniacal screech, and rarely if ever will you see the staggering form of an inebriate. For some days the shops are closed and the streets remain *en fête ;* and it is only gradually, and with a certain amount of reluctance, that the ordinary state of affairs is resumed, and things get back to their old groove for one long year more.

It is, I think, a generally received opinion amongst Europeans that Chinese show a great want of humanity in cases where the saving of a fellow-creature's life is concerned, and that it is repugnant to their nature or their religion to risk their own lives merely for the sake of rescuing others. I doubt, however, whether this dishonourable trait can be justly described as a national one, or whether the majority of Chinamen would, either from superstitious or cowardly motives, sit quietly by and see a fellow-creature dying without an effort to save him. An English official in China, to my knowledge, owes his escape from drowning to the spontaneous efforts of a Chinese boatman, who fortunately happened to be at hand; and the incident which I am about to relate, and which came under my own observation, proves that heroism of the noblest kind is to be found amongst the Chinese. At the port of Takow in South Formosa, during the prevalence of the south-west monsoon in the summer months, the bar is occasionally impassable, on account of the tremendous sea which springs up, often suddenly, and without any local disturbance of the atmosphere or other warning. Even the weather-wise fishermen of the place, who generally know so well when it is prudent to venture any distance from the land in their tiny catamarans, are on their return home sometimes caught outside an unexpected and tremendous surf, which they are obliged to pass through at their peril. On the occasion in question two fishermen, a father and son, went out in the early morning to fish. The sky being clear, the sea calm, and the season late—the force of the monsoon being nearly spent—they ventured out a considerable distance from the shore, perfectly sure that no danger threatened them. But a sudden swell having, about noon, set in from the south, they hastened homeward, and found, to their horror, on their return, that the sea was breaking in gigantic crested billows on the bar. There was no room for hesitation, however; the sea was momentarily getting worse, its fury might last for days, and the catamaran, which is only a tiny raft formed of half a dozen stout bamboos lashed together, even if it could live outside, had no accom-

modation for food or sleep. Waiting for what appeared to be a slight lull in the breaking of the waves, the father and son pushed quickly and resolutely on; another minute and they would be once more safe in comparatively smooth water on the shore side of the bar. But it was not to be: a tremendous wave coming behind them like a huge mountain caught up the little raft, and flung it like a feather, men and all, high into the air; the lashings of the bamboos snapped with the violence of the blow, and father and son, with the remnants of their catamaran, were precipitated amongst the seething billows. Fortunately both men managed to get hold of a bamboo, to which they clung with all the tenacity of men struggling for dear life; and as a strong ebb-tide was running out of the harbour at the time, they were carried, almost miraculously as it seemed to the lookers-on, out beyond the breakers once more. The feelings of those who watched the accident without being able to afford any aid can hardly be imagined. Rewards were offered by the Europeans present to any catamaran men who would venture out to the rescue of the poor fishermen; but none were found who would risk their lives in such an attempt. Chinamen, as has been said, are supposed to shrink from the task of saving human life, even when no risk to themselves presents itself; but in this case it did almost seem as if it would be a throwing away of more lives if any dared to venture to the rescue of the floating men. Presently, and whilst the lookers-on were wondering what was to be done, a catamaran, pulled by four strong young fishermen, was seen to shoot, from the opposite side of the lagoon, through the mouth of the harbour, straight out towards the deadly breakers. Can we believe our eyes that these are four *Chinamen*, all poor men, with wives and children to think of, no doubt, going forth like heroes, as they are, in the face of possible, nay probable, destruction, to endeavour to rescue the lives of two others as poor and as humble as themselves? All honour to the brave chivalrous fellows! No hope of reward had they, no stimulus but the conviction that they were doing a noble duty, and, without looking to the right or the left, they drove their little craft nearer and nearer to the breakers, but not to the place where the unfortunate father and son, ignorant of the real force of the waves at the time, had tried to cross the bar. Further north the billows seemed to break with less regularity, and there the brave fellows waited for what seemed a good opportunity, and then with a will they rushed towards the bar; but before they had got too far for retreat they saw an immense wave commencing to rear its awful crest a short distance ahead of them, and, with wonderful dexterity, the catamaran was quickly backed, just in time to escape the breakers, which would probably have dashed the little craft to pieces. Will they succeed in crossing to the rescue? was the query which sprung to the lips of every looker-on. Again they waited patiently for their opportunity, and again they dashed towards the bar; this time with success, and then with all their might they pulled quickly towards the spot where the two men were clinging to the floating bamboo. To the great joy of every one, the two castaways were safely picked up; and their brave rescuers, adopting the same cautious tactics as before, carried their catamaran once again through the breakers, and had the satisfaction of delivering up to their relations the father and son who were

so heroically rescued from a watery grave. As a proof of the disinterested motives which actuated the rescuers, I may mention that on the following day the four brave men were sent for by the European Commissioner of Customs, who offered them a reward, which they politely declined, saying that they had only done their duty, and that the rescued men were their own relatives, or at least belonged to the same clan as themselves; but, at their suggestion, the sum intended for them was devoted to the purchase of a new catamaran, to replace the one lost in the accident by the two poor fishermen.

From the description of an act of heroism in real life to the contemplation of the stage on which scenes equally heroic are oftentimes depicted, is a transition which, it is to be hoped, will not be considered too abrupt. The theatre in China is a venerable and popular institution; like almost everything else in the country, it seems to have made no advance with the lapse of time, and to be to-day what it was hundreds of years ago. What theatricals were in England in Shakespeare's time, such are they in China in the nineteenth century: the stage is generally a roughly put together structure; the acting principally takes place in the open air; the female parts are performed by boys, and the properties and paraphernalia are of the most simple and primitive nature. Immense audiences, however, continue to be attracted by the representations; and it is interesting to observe the intense delight with which the stolid Chinese attend to every action of the performers, and to notice on the uplifted faces of the crowd the varying effect which the alternation of the scenes produces—

'From grave to gay, from lively to severe.'

The plays are generally historical —tragedies with a considerable dash of comedy in them—and abound with sensational and laughter-stirring scenes; but it is questionable whether the popularity of these representations depends much on the literary merits of the pieces that are performed. The greatest commendations of Chinese theatrical critics seem to be bestowed on the gorgeousness of the costumes, and the 'get-up' of the female characters. Another great source of attraction, perhaps the greatest, is the cheapness of the entertainment. The Chinese, as is well known, are our antipodes in all social observances, and in the matter of the stage this national peculiarity is fully exemplified; for whereas theatres at home are at most only tolerated by religionists, and are tabooed by many pious people as the very worst invention of the Evil One, in China religious rites, if of any magnitude, are almost invariably accompanied by theatrical performances, none of which could, I fear, by any stretch of the imagination, be considered religious. On such occasions free admission is almost always accorded to the public; and on the appointed day crowds of people flock from all quarters to stand in front of the stage, and enjoy for hours the dramatic treat provided for them. It is a sight on such a day to see the women hobbling along on their deformed little feet to the rendezvous, dressed up in gala-costume, their cheeks and lips profusely covered with brightest rouge, and their hair heavily gummed and decorated with gaudy artificial flowers. Scores of little children, dressed in all the colours of the rainbow, are carried or led long distances to be present at the entertainment; and in the vicinity of the stage vendors of cakes, fruit,

and sweetmeats drive, literally, a 'roaring' trade.

It is considered a benevolent act, and one highly pleasing to Heaven, to give a public theatrical performance; and wealthy men, who wish to return public thanks for any special piece of good fortune, or who cater for popularity, often expend considerable sums in this way. A rich Chinaman, in whose neighbourhood we once lived, invited us to be present at a performance of this kind. He had been very successful in his commercial speculations, and had recently obtained by purchase the rank of a high-class Mandarin, with the privilege of wearing an opaque blue button on the top of his official hat. At one end of a large open space, near the entertainer's house, a stage had been erected; and at the opposite side, behind the place for the audience, a large temporary box was constructed for the accommodation of the host and his friends. On the appointed day we proceeded to the place, and were received by our Chinese acquaintance with that formal courtesy which the better classes invariably exhibit; and we were shown to chairs from which we could conveniently survey our strange surroundings. In the middle of the box stood a large table or altar, which groaned under the weight of the good things provided as thanksgiving offerings to Heaven. The innumerable varieties of Chinese dishes were here fully represented: roast ducks decorated with gilt paper, sweetmeats of all kinds, cakes plentifully bespangled with raisins and currants, imitation little pigs formed of pork, fruits in great variety, pigs' feet garnished with bruised potatoes, and a quantity of dishes whose composition and names we had no opportunity of discovering, were spread out in promiscuous and rich profusion. Two large pink candles, decorated with gold, silver, and green leaves, stood one on each side of the table, and in the centre a bronze basin containing burning incense was placed. The principal compartment in which we sat was flanked on either side by two small boxes, in front of which were screens, which, while concealing the inmates from the vulgar gaze, permitted from within a view of the stage and the movements thereon; these boxes were reserved for the ladies belonging to the households of our host and his native friends. In the mean time tea was ordered for us; and a servant placed a small table in front of us, on which he arranged Chinese cups, and poured into them some genuine Chinese tea, as consumed by the natives themselves. It is a weak and insipid production, of the colour of pale sherry, and tastes more of hot water than of tea; no milk or sugar is mixed with it; and what with the awkward shape of the cups, with their lids so difficult to manipulate, and the uninviting nature of the beverage, a cup of tea *à la Chinoise* is not a boon much sought after by Europeans. On this occasion we made as few faces over it as we could in presence of our host, and we managed to sip a little without much inconvenience. For some time we sat and watched the actors and listened to their shrill voices; and we could not help reflecting on the immense gap which separated a performance like what we then witnessed from the gorgeous and carefully-planned scenes of a home theatre. The stage had no 'wings' to it; and the only entrances were two doors at the back, through which the actors entered when their turn came round, and retired when they had performed their allotted part; the imaginations of the audience were not assisted by

scenery or stage accessories of any kind; indeed, the entire back of the stage was occupied by the orchestra, and by attendants and hangers-on, who went about their occupations as if nothing else were taking place on the boards. The whole thing appeared childish and stupid to us; but, considering the length of each principal actor's part, set as it was to music—if the hideous din and jargon can be dignified by that name—a vast amount of care and trouble must have been bestowed on the preparation; at all events, judging from the attention and the delight of the audience, this Chinese *opéra bouffe* might be pronounced a success. In a short time, however, we unconsciously became formidable rivals to the actors: the box in which we sat was open in front, and had not the advantage possessed by the side boxes, in which the Chinese ladies sat unobserved; so that, in spite of the gorgeous dresses on the stage, in spite of the vigorous strumming of the orchestra, in spite of the falsetto shrieking of the actors, and the intrinsic merits of the piece itself (if it had any), a large proportion of the audience turned their backs upon the stage, and the 'foreigners' became the attraction on which the concentrated gaze of the multitude was firmly set. Our curiosity having by this time been completely satisfied, we said goodbye to our host, and quietly withdrew, leaving the actors in undisputed possession of their rights as caterers to the amusement of the crowd.

Permanent stages, for the occasional performance of theatricals, are frequently to be seen in China, connected with buildings which, from their construction and the number of idols they possess, with a few priests to look after them, are termed by Europeans ' joss-houses,' or temples. Such buildings, however, are more frequently clubs or halls belonging to one or other of the many guilds which are to be found in all large Chinese cities, and ought not to be confounded with the regular Buddhist monasteries, whose peaceful cloisters are never disturbed by the rude jargon of a Chinese play. Many of these temples are a great source of attraction to the European residents in China; situated, as a rule, in picturesque localities, at convenient distances from the busy haunts of men, and surrounded, as they generally are, by shady groves and secluded walks, it is no wonder that they are so often selected as the rendezvous of pleasant picnics and excursions. Perhaps the most celebrated of the monasteries visited by Europeans is the one situated on Ku-shan, the Drum Mountain, in the neighbourhood of Foochow; and it will not perhaps be out of place here to give an account of an excursion I once made with some friends to that famous temple. Leaving Foochow in a steam-launch, at eight o'clock in the morning, we glided swiftly down the river Min, and in less than an hour we reached the landing-place near the foot of the mountain, where our sedan-chairs awaited us. A short ride, through some paddy-fields and past some comfortable-looking farmhouses, brought us to the beginning of the well-constructed stone road which leads up to the monastery. Abandoning our chairs, we proceeded to walk up the steps; but before we had managed to climb to any great height the unwonted exercise began to tell, and we were delighted to see at a short distance above us a small white house, with the usual Chinese pointed eaves, to which we urged our faltering footsteps; and when we took our seats in the little resting-place we blessed

the foresight of the good monks, who so wisely provided for the comfort of their wearied visitors. Again we plodded up the stone steps, and again, just as our tired limbs began to demand a halt, did a little house, the counterpart of the first one, open its smiling portals and invite us to a most welcome pause in our climbing. Five of those useful little resting-places are met with on the journey up the hill, and they reduce considerably the labour of the ascent. At last we came to a comparatively level road; steps, except at rare intervals, were no longer met with; large trees, which showed signs of much cultivation, began to replace the wild fir-trees which clothe the lower portions of the mountain-side; and the appearance of large Chinese characters deftly cut into the rocks by pious hands, and expressing some holy maxim or the Buddhist invocation, 'O ME TO FU,' became of more frequent occurrence, and we knew we were close to the monastery.

The approach to the monastery lies through an avenue of stately trees, whose wide-spreading branches meet overhead and afford a most delicious shade. The exterior of the building is not very striking; but the large bronze idols in the entrance-hall, the spacious courtyard, and the principal chapel are worth seeing. Like some of 'the monks of old,' the Ku-shan priests have accommodation for visitors who may desire to spend some time in that romantic spot; and in the summer months a few of the guest-rooms are occasionally rented by Europeans, who like the place on account of its comparative coolness and pleasant surroundings. Temporary accommodation for casual visitors, like ourselves, is also gladly given; and a convenient room having been allotted to us, our servants set to work; and with the extraordinary power of adapting themselves to circumstances which Chinese servants show on an emergency, our domestics had, in a wonderfully short time, a complete 'tiffin' laid out for us: nothing seemed to have been forgotten, and everything was in as good order as if we were in our own dining-room.

After tiffin we sallied forth to explore the 'lions' of the place. First of all we visited the belfry, where two old priests, who looked quite happy in their dismal tower, spent all their time in tolling, at intervals of a few minutes, day and night, the solemn monastery bell. The priests take this monotonous duty in turns, and they consider their occupation a most praiseworthy and heroic one. We were told of an old blind priest in a Peking monastery, who believed that every time he tolled the bell he saved a soul! And it is some such pious belief, no doubt, which renders such dreary work endurable. The pond where the sacred fish are kept was next visited; and the attendant priest having supplied us with strings of little round biscuits, we threw a few into the water; and in an instant the surface of the pond near where we stood, which had been unruffled before, became literally alive with thousands of voracious fish with their mouths wide open, ready to swallow any amount of biscuits we chose to throw them. The fish must have been very hungry on that occasion; for when a gentleman of our party, wishing as he said to introduce some variety into their food— rather cruelly, I thought—flung into the midst of the finny multitude the end of his cigar, it was ravenously swallowed; so I fancy at least one fish must have retired in deep disgust with the foreign barbarian.

After a hurried visit to a small temple connected with the monastery, situated in a most romantic mountain-dell, where a bell is constantly tolled by the aid of a waterwheel, we returned to the principal chapel in time to see the priests assemble for their afternoon devotions. About a hundred of these votaries of Buddha came trooping in with their long yellow robes, their hands joined in front of their breasts and clasping their rosaries, and their shaven heads bent reverently forward. The head-priest, a jolly rosy-cheeked individual, who looked as if he occasionally enjoyed something better than mere Buddhist monastery fare, did not join in the service, but stood bowing and smiling by our side; indeed, he had clung to us tenaciously from the moment of our arrival, and was most attentive in supplying all our wants. When we grew tired of the monotonous chanting and turned to leave, the worthy abbot politely escorted us to the gate; and with many a smile he closed his chubby hand over the *douceur*, the prospect of which had all day long filled his pious soul with comfort, and stimulated his amiability and good-nature. Our return journey was soon accomplished, and we reached the foreign settlement of Foochow just as darkness was setting in.

I will conclude this paper with the following little story, which illustrates more forcibly than any mere description could do certain characteristics of the Chinese people. I give it as it was noted by me at the time I heard it from a native who professed to be familiar with the principal actors in the little drama:

In the neighbourhood of Shanghai, some years ago, lived an old farmer named Wang, who by his industry and frugality had, in the course of a somewhat chequered life, managed to accumulate the sum of six hundred dollars. Wang's declining years were not saddened by the reflection, so abhorrent to the Chinese mind, that no male representative would succeed him to burn the votive incense at his grave when he should have passed away. He had two sons; but the satisfaction he naturally felt at this circumstance was considerably diminished by the violent antipathy which his elder son constantly displayed towards the younger one. The cause of this animosity was not far to seek; for it was impossible to look upon the comely appearance of the younger son, and contemplate his erect gait and intelligent bearing, without feeling that there was an object at hand for the envy and ill-will of the elder son, who was as repulsive in appearance, and as vindictive in disposition, as his brother was handsome and amiable. The characters of the brothers might have been estimated, too, by the different manner in which they were regarded by their neighbours ; for the elder was studiously avoided by grown-up people, and the village children hooted at him whenever he appeared in public; whilst the younger one was flattered and caressed by all who knew him. In due time old Wang was gathered to his fathers, leaving the entire management of his little property to his first-born, with the understanding, however, that the younger son was to be as well provided for as the means at hand would allow. When the ceremonies connected with the interment were concluded, the elder brother called the younger one to his presence and thus addressed him :

'For years I have hated you; you have been a thorn in my path, an eyesore in my sight. I have longed for a deliverance from you, and the wished-for time has come at last when I can rid myself once for all of your loathsome presence. Lis-

ten to me. I have unlimited control over the money our father has left behind him. Leave this place at once; swear that you will never again darken my door, and I will give you half of my father's money; three hundred dollars will be yours. But refuse my offer, remain in this neighbourhood, and not a single *cash** will be given to you; no food of mine shall touch your lips; you will be a beggar, and every effort of mine will be directed towards the achievement of your utter ruin.'

The amiable brother having thus delivered himself of his feelings, it occurred to the younger one that separation from such an implacable foe and the posession of three hundred dollars were infinitely preferable to living at home in persecution and beggary; so the bargain was at once agreed to, the dollars were counted out, and next morning the youth was ready for his departure. Secure in the possession of his little fortune, the young man bade an eternal farewell to the only place he had ever known— the scene of his early joys, the spot sanctified with the recollections of his parents, and his boyhood's years. No tears of regret fell as he separated himself from his scowling ill-favoured brother; but his emotion was great when it was necessary to part from the sympathising friends who escorted him a considerable distance on his way. His destination was Soochow, which he had often longed to see, ever since the days of his infancy, when his little eyes used to dilate with amazement at the tales which were then told to him of that wonderful city; of its wealth and splendour, its gorgeous temples, its magnificent yamêns, the rare beauty of its women, and the heroic deeds of its men; and he now hoped, with the

* The small Chinese copper coins are in English called *cash;* about twenty of them equal one penny.

aid of his talents and his money, to win his way in that city of romance to competency, if not to fame. Knowing, however, the absolute need of a good supply of money at the outset of his career in a strange city, he determined to husband his resources during his journey, to walk every inch of the way, and to stop only at the most unpretentious wayside inns for rest and refreshment.

On the first evening after his departure, as he sat in front of a teahouse refreshing himself with a cup of the national beverage, a poor old man came forward with every sign of fatigue and want upon him, and requested assistance. The young man, whose generosity was as remarkable as his other good qualities, immediately felt touched at the poor man's appearance and condition ; and motioning him to a seat at the table beside him, he called one of the attendants, and forthwith ordered a substantial meal for the mendicant. The latter was most profuse in his gratitude, and devoutly prayed that the Five Blessings might descend upon our young adventurer, who, being anxious to avoid notice, picked up his wallet quickly, paid his bill, told the old man to enjoy himself, and proceeded on his journey. Three hours' steady walking brought him to the village where he had decided to spend the night; and having secured a comfortable bed, he retired at an early hour, and was soon buried in the refreshing sleep which is the invariable result of a moderately exhausted frame, a healthy system, and a clear conscience.

His sound sleep was his salvation ; for as he slumbered wellarmed robbers, who would have felt no hesitation in killing him had he awakened, were at work in his room stealthily removing his wallet and his much-prized dollars; and it was almost daybreak when a friendly touch was laid upon his arm, and a voice that had no unkindness in it whispered into his ear that the slightest sound of alarm would be his ruin ; that he was in a den of thieves, who were even then planning the readiest and safest means of murdering him ; and that his only chance of safety lay in noiseless and immediate flight. ' Rely upon me,' said the mysterious visitor: ' I am one of the gang ; but you behaved kindly to me at the teahouse when I was disguised as a beggar, and I never forget a kindness.' ' But my wallet—my dollars! Where are they ?' whispered the alarmed young man. ' Be at ease on that score,' said the robber: ' your wallet has been stolen, but your dollars turn out to be worse than useless; *they are only copper silvered over*, and it is on account of their disappointment and vexation at the trick which my mates believe you have played upon them that they have made up their minds to murder you. Fly, then, before it is too late ; return to your home; here is a little money to help you on your way ; and remember that even a robber can be grateful for an act of kindness.' The young man thanked his preserver and hurried from the scene of danger ; and if he shuddered at the fearful fate which had so nearly befallen him, he was also horrified at the unmanly attempt of his vindictive brother to put him into the iron grasp of the law, and have him thrown into a felon's prison in a strange place, where, without friends or acquaintances, he knew it would be almost impossible to satisfy a stern and pitiless magistrate that the counterfeit coin (the circulation of which in China is a very serious crime) was obtained in ignorance of its real nature.

Little remains to be said, except that the younger brother, released, as he thought, by the elder's treachery from the promise he had made never to return, presented himself soon after at the home he thought he would never see again ; and having accused his brother and threatened to make the disgraceful matter public, the guilty man quailed before the prospect of a just retribution, confessed his crime, threw himself on the mercy of his intended victim, and offered him any portion he chose to accept of the money their father had left them. The young man, not wishing to publish the iniquity of one who, however guilty, was so closely allied to him, took three hundred dollars, making sure this time that they were real ones ; and before any of his friends had heard of his return, or could begin to speculate on the cause thereof, he quietly started once more on his journey, reached Soochow in safety, and, after several adventures, succeeded in winning his way to an honourable position, which he holds to this day with much credit to himself, and with the entire goodwill and respect of the numerous friends he has acquired in his adopted home.

J. G. H.

REQUIESCAT IN PACE.

'She is not dead, but sleepeth ;' so spake He,
The Galilean mild, and they who stood
Beside laughed Him to scorn. But we believe ;
His words to us speak comfort ; and firm faith,
With hopeful eyes beyond the present looks—
Beyond the vale of death. From the sorrows
That darken and perplex this life, from hopes
That find but disappointment here, from all
The ills that turn to shade the light of this
So lovely world, she is at rest. We are
Too poor, too full of grief, enduring but
In silent frenzy the oppressive years,
To pity her who is above our pity.
In her grave verdurous and lily-crowned,
Where vexing dreams come not, she sweetly sleeps,
Till He whose voice the ruler's daughter waked
Shall likewise say to her, ' Arise.' Meanwhile
To us He says, ' Weep not ; she is not dead,
But sleepeth.'

SCEPTRE AND RING.

By B. H. BUXTON,

AUTHOR OF 'JENNIE OF "THE PRINCE'S,"' 'FROM THE WINGS,' ETC.

Part the Second.

CHAPTER I.

A TÊTE-À-TÊTE.

Just as Patty Bray entered the miserable attic in St. Giles's-passage, and beheld her revered mistress ready dressed, and fully prepared to set forth, defying the chill wind and wintry weather, Luke Day was in attendance on the mistress *he* revered at Regency-terrace, S.W. He was assisting Miss Hartley to dismount from her cosy miniature brougham; he disembarrassed her from the furs and rugs in which she had been so carefully wrapped, and, as he closed the front door, eager to keep out the piercing cruel blast, he handed her a telegram.

'Just come, ma'am, this minute,' he said.

She seized the yellow envelope with her wonted impetuosity.

'Surely he will not disappoint me!' she muttered; and then, with her cynical smile, added, 'No, certainly not; I need have no fears on that score, since it is to *his* interest, as well as mine, that we should discuss the business which will no doubt prove more remunerative to him than to me in every sense. He knows he can hold the trumps in our operatic game, and is not likely to miss the chance for want of a confab with his partner.'

After this *sotto-voce* soliloquy, Miss Hartley put an end to further doubts by opening the telegram.

'O, it's Quiz who plays truant!' she says, having studied the hasty message:

'*From Lady Furnival, Bruton-street.*

'John unexpectedly returned from assizes. Cross as bear. Must stay to smooth ruffled soul. You understand, though cannot sympathise with, troubles conjugal.'

Miss Hartley laughed. The contents of the pink paper were eminently characteristic of her sprightly friend, who was as plain as she was witty, and who preferred to save herself trouble by conducting her correspondence entirely per telegram.

'Ah, well, it is all for the best!' thought Diana, tearing the paper into strips, and busily twirling those strips into spills.

When her mind was active the restlessness of her long fingers always betrayed its working.

'Quiz is great fun; but when Campo and I want to talk business—to be serious and to rehearse—her presence is apt to be tiresome; a third person is sure to be a bore where a couple have serious work to do. On the whole, I am rather thankful that the bear requires smoothing to-night.'

'Lady Furnival is not coming,' she added aloud, turning to her major-domo, to whom she handed her heavy sable-trimmed mantle. 'Pile up the logs, Luke, it is bitterly cold; draw the curtains close, shut out every suspicion of the night air, and let us have some of the red seal Burgundy with our dinner. Signor Maestro is always chilly; he will be absolutely shivering to-night, poor dear, I know.'

She laughed as she said the last words; and old Luke rejoiced to see her in such good spirits.

'See that everything is ready by the time I have changed my dress. Send Mrs. Day to my room now; I will be with her directly.'

The servant descended, the mistress entered her dining-room, which, for actual comfort, surpassed all others in the house. Her quick eye noted the disposition of the luxuriously-appointed table; her clever fingers swiftly rearranged the hyacinths and violets in the graceful vases that held them.

She turned the pink-shaded lamps down to subdue the light to a more becoming tone. She knew so well how to adjust all her surroundings with a due regard to their best effect on her personal appearance. She lighted the candles upon the high mantelshelf, and glanced into the Venetian mirror, that stood upon a bracket, with very evident interest. The inspection was decidedly satisfactory.

Yes; she was looking bright, almost radiant. The chill air without had tinged her smooth cheeks with a healthy glow, and the rough wind had curled the soft hair on her forehead with almost artistic skill.

'I must find favour in my Maestro's eyes to-night,' she said, gazing impressively at the bright face that encountered her gaze. 'If he is not wheedled to the top of his bent now, pleasantly coaxed or rigorously forced into the most angelic of tempers, I shall not have him ready with his share of the work in time for the Great Event;

and that would be a disappointment I never could get over.'

The reader has some idea by this time of the vigour of Diana's mode of expression, and also knows that her *never* was not quite as serious as it sounded.

The Great Event, at the prospect of which Miss Hartley looked grave, was the speedy production of a light operetta, joint work of her own and Campo Maestro. The performance was arranged to take place at the house of a certain enterprising lady, who reckoned on Royal patronage for the occasion in question. The object of the fashionable gathering invited to witness the dramatic entertainment—entirely supported by amateurs—was a deserving charity. The only professionals engaged were 'beauties' of that ilk. Miss Hartley had generously taken the burden of the musical arrangements upon herself. She knew she could always reckon on the hearty coöperation of Signor Maestro as long as she contrived to give him a direct personal interest in the matter under consideration. And she had certainly succeeded in doing so on this occasion. She had also arranged a most *recherché* little dinner for him this evening, hoping to impress certain details upon him which seemed of vital importance to her. She was *now* animated by a strong desire to persuade him into undertaking an impromptu rehearsal once the good Burgundy had warmed his fingers and roused the spirit of *musical* enterprise within him.

Campo Maestro was an old friend; one of the few who had remained her steadfast ally during, and since, the gay reckless old Paris days. He was an accomplished musician, and he had been her master for a year before he was made director of one of the lesser opera-houses in the French capital. It was just after she had felt herself so cruelly deceived by the younger and more attractive Lorenzo Martelli (whose desertion she declared she *never* could get over) that the sedate Maestro undertook her musical instruction. He had been the sincere admirer of La Signora Diana, of her gracious self, and her undoubted talents always; but her lover never. Perhaps this accounted for the length, strength, and endurance of the bond so pleasantly uniting master and pupil.

Campo Maestro, whose success in Paris fifteen years ago had given him a secure footing in the musical world, subsequently entered a promising berth awaiting him in London, where, as enterprising *Impresario*, he started afresh on his own account. But though the man had much experience and undoubted ability, he entirely lacked capital: that *sine quâ non* of success, that indispensable backbone for all commercial undertakings. Before he had spent two seasons in London he realised (poor little man!) that the onus and the glory of musical enterprise on an extended scale were not to be his individual delight. He could work for or with others admirably; but he was soon compelled to admit to himself, as a melancholy secret, his lack of capacity for the starting of musical enterprise on a large scale, owing entirely to that absence of capital which has caused so many ambitions to be nipped in the bud, so many glorious schemes to end in miserable failure. He was a wiry dapper little man: brown as a nut, active as a squirrel, gesticulating wildly on all occasions, and speaking with marvellous volubility an execrable language, which he called Eengliss, but which, to the astounded ears of natives, sounded more like an unknown tongue than the speech of civilisation. As his French was as much *Neapolitanised* as his English, Diana soon desisted from her original effort to treat him as a foreigner, and speak a foreign language with him. Indeed, he evidently preferred to be considered one of 'sis Eengliss,' and was himself thoroughly satisfied as to the manner in which he bore himself—a native among Britons.

'You will find me a veritable Shon Boull,' he was wont to declare; and Miss Hartley humoured him on this point as readily as on all others.

The result of her long personal experience was to consider it her primary duty towards men to set them thoroughly at their ease with regard to themselves, as well as in their relations to her; and having first coaxed them into this self-satisfied condition, she mostly found she could deal with them according to her pleasure afterwards.

Il Signor, with his quick black eyes, ever watchful, ever on the alert, soon took in the eminently comfortable state of affairs in his hostess's cosy dining-room. He passed his stumpy fingers, with their abnormally long pointed nails, hastily through his abundant curly gray hair.

'Ah, but it is goot—tru-el-ly goot,' he said, approaching the glorious fire of heaped-up sputtering logs, and, as he spoke, he glanced with overt approval at the elegant figure of lissom Diana as she stood in a graceful pose before him. Few painstaking actresses better knew the value of a good pose than Diana Hartley, who studied and calculated hers with amazing perseverance before that extra-long cheval-glass in her dressing-room. She had now extended one hand; the tips of her fingers rested lightly upon the high mantelshelf; she thus contrived to show to full advantage the pretty outline of her supple figure. Her other hand was laid in approved Vandyke fashion upon her bosom, while the tips of the long taper fingers busied themselves with a crimson rose at her throat.

'I have been to see Lady Buzze to-day,' she said, 'and we have now settled all the stagey pre-liminaries: scenery, accessories, prompter, electric light, the new act-drop—all these details are satisfactorily arranged. The or-chestra and chorus require extra supervision from you, Signor; their fate—and mine—I hand over hope-fully to your tender mercies.'

'And for the sin-kerrs?' he asked, making the *g* into a decided *k*, and rolling out the *r* at the end of the word like a premonitory thunderclap. A dark cloud low-ered upon his brow as he spoke, and Diana knew this meant mis-chief.

'I really think our first choice has proved eminently satisfactory,' she said. 'Of course you were disappointed at the introductory meeting; but I am sure you will be more content by the time we manage a regular rehearsal; for I have been preparing some of the principals by assiduous private practice with each one of them here.'

'And have you found your *in-génue*, your first juvenile? my So-prano with the voice of a night-gall, and the look of a *bambina, hein?* Have you so found one? Tell it to me!'

He shook that stumpy forefinger of his rapidly to and fro before Diana's troubled eyes. It seemed to her as though the acute angle of the nail was intended to lacerate her optic nerve. For the first time during the interview she not only felt herself at a loss, but be-trayed her discomfiture. This was

no moment for crying surrender, however; and with her wonted impetuosity she rose gallantly to the occasion.

'I have firm faith in my never-failing luck,' she cried. 'You may take my word for it that something—somebody—will turn up in our favour even now, at this last mo-ment. I admit that we have come face to face with a great difficulty; but that I love to confront diffi-culties you know, and then it rouses all my ambition to conquer them. That I—that we—shall effect a glorious triumph I am sure. Take it from me; *parole d'honneur!*'

Her eyes flashed as she spoke; she raised her hand on high; her attitude was that of one inspired.

'*Imperatrix, morituri te salutant!*' he cried, bowing lowly before her and pressing the hem of her gar-ment to his lips. She felt that her energy, the strong spirit of vitality within her, had impressed him; the cloud had disappeared from his forehead, and she smiled with satisfaction.

'I have been on the rampage all day,' she said; 'I have sought high and low for the treasure we desire. I have interviewed pro-fessional beauties and ambitious amateurs *ad nauseam*. I have spared neither time nor trouble, and indeed my diligent search has extended over the whole of the past week. Quite as much on your account, dear Campo, as on my own, that you know well. I have even been among schoolgirls, seeking some modest maiden whom I might carry off and launch upon the broad ocean of fame. It looks so inviting to novices; and yet we, who know, are so thoroughly aware of its treachery. But even the anticipation of glorious distinc-tion in appearing at an entertain-ment under "immediate Royal patronage" failed to *inspire* any one of the many young ladies to whom I addressed myself. Those who had innocent attractive faces knew nothing of music ; had never sung anything more ambitious than a Claribel ballad. Those who had voices might have taken the pert soubrette's part and acted it to the life, but were as ill-suited to my rare pale Margaret as I should be to hold your bâton for the orchestra.'

'Ah, but you vould ; and you vould well do, *cara mia !*' said the Maestro, with his most elaborate bow in the style complimentary. And then he remembered the disappointing subject under discussion ; and, as he looked into Diana's face again, he puckered his forehead and drew down the corners of his mobile lips ominously. 'To laugh it is no use,' he said, in a very dismal tone, 'nor more to cry, *in verità ;* but it is bad, bad, all bad ; for *senza* a Margherita *convenable* we must make one *fiasco grandioso.* Not it is tr-rue, *hein ?*'

'Let us sit down to our dinner now, and discuss that before we enter upon any further lamentations, *amico mio.*'

Diana looks into the brown wizen face with so brilliant a smile on hers, as she lays her hand on his arm and draws him towards the table, that he cannot resist smiling in return, but his expression is as rueful as hers is gay.

'I repeat that I have firm faith in my luck—I have proved it so often, remember ; and, in common courtesy, you are bound to believe a lady, you know.'

Old Campo shook his grizzled head, elevated his eyebrows and his shoulders ; then he closed his restless black eyes, nodded his head, and smacked his lips.

'For ze dinnar, yes,' said he ; 'for that I conjugate the verb to belief from Alpha to Omega ; but for dis goot luck, no, no, *cara signora mia.*'

'We have still a month before us,' she replied, in smiling good-humour—'four whole weeks. And before ten days are over I shall have secured our paragon : an ideal Margherita will come to me, as you shall see.'

'From the heaven ?' asked Campo impatiently.

He was getting hungry, poor man, and the savoury soup was inviting him to put an end to the discussion.

'No, nor from spiritland, I hope,' said Miss Hartley. 'We want something tangible, however ethereal in appearance. I believe she is on her road already. I have been haunted by an undoubted presentiment all day.'

'Let us now be hunted, or to hunt our dinner, please you ?'

'By all means,' she answered ; and took her chair at the head of the table, and began to ladle out the soup that smelt so savoury, and which Luke had just brought into the room.

Campo was evidently disposed to dismiss all troublesome subjects for the present, and to devote his undivided attention to the good things which Diana knew he loved well. The great enterprise which filled the mind of each was secretly causing them considerable anxiety at this time, owing to their failure in adequately filling the most important *rôle* in their joint operetta, the leading soprano.

Both author and composer had done their utmost, ever since the first meeting of such amateurs as were deemed most promising *dramatis personæ*, to select a heroine who would not only look the part of a modern Gretchen, but who would also be able to interpret the music of so difficult a composer as Campo Maestro.

There was, certes, no lack of ambitious claimants for the interesting attractive title - *rôle;* ladies who had fortunes, and those who hunted them—old, young, married, single; those who could act, and thought they could sing; and some who had attempted both, but succeeded in neither accomplishment. Of these variously gifted, or totally unendowed, aspirants for future distinction, scores presented themselves, and eagerly offered their services to that 'clever, charming, discriminating' Miss Hartley as soon as Lady Buzze made the details of her forthcoming entertainment known to her select circle.

But Diana proved deaf to the fulsome flattery lavished upon her in her onerous *rôle* of manageress. Indeed, she was far too discriminating, and anything but charming, in her manner towards those who clamoured for a part which she considered them unfitted to undertake. Their abuse when they were driven to retreat from The Presence at the Cottage non-suited was, of course, as shrill and vindictive as their praises had previously been loud and exaggerated. None of this turmoil affected Diana in the least. She, who had hitherto proved so capricious in all her enterprises, appeared very steady, very resolute, in this new operatic scheme. The first idea of the libretto had come upon her so suddenly that she spoke of it mysteriously as an inspiration! And those who heard the avowal whispered with bated breath, and who saw the light shining in the eloquent eyes of the fascinating authoress, were tempted to believe as fully in her genius as she undoubtedly believed herself.

The sober facts of this romantic inspiration were these :

One evening Diana was sitting thinking, or rather dreaming, her eyes fixed on the sparkling logs in the fire, her fancy fully occu-

pied in the erection of visionary castles in Spain, or rather in India. It was just after her visit of exploration to the purlieus of Westminster; and she had felt sick and very sorry ever since. Mind and body were equally nervous, equally out of tune. How could she best distract her thoughts from o'ermuch brooding on her present bitter fate and loneliness ? How should she manage to find some engrossing occupation which would distract her thoughts ? How best fill up her weary, weary days and sleepless nights until such time as the Indian mail brought her a long satisfactory epistle from the man she adored, or—better still—until she should receive the glad intelligence that he was homeward bound ?

This glorious news might come to her at any moment. She did not believe in his prolonged banishment; his starting had been matter of 'a word and a blow;' it was altogether unpremeditated, and had startled every one concerned, from the Lord Greatacre in command down to the youngest subaltern. The return of the expedition might, and probably would, be quite as sudden. O, how she wished for some such speedy turn of the wheel of Fate ! If only the hours did not hang like lead now ! if only her aching heart and anxious thoughts might lend wings to the tarrying minutes !

Ah, she would write ! She would take up the pen of authorship again; but this time she would write poetry. Her mood was melancholy, poetical, lyrical. Commonplace prose at this emotional juncture would utterly fail to express her loving longing thoughts. A ballad ? Sonnets—romances ? No, no. Something soft, flowing, melancholy, tender—something so vividly imbued with pathos that she, the writer, would weep as she wrote, and that those who read her touching lamentations would weep more copiously still.

A love-story ?

Yes ; of course.

The story of a broken heart, of a cruel parting, of injured innocence, of maddening jealousy. A new rendering of that old, old story which seemed ever new, and which most certainly was ever true. Such a story as Goethe pathetically told of a primitive rural Gretchen—such a story would Diana now tell of a modern metropolitan heroine. That was Miss Hartley's inspiration, and it bore psssable fruit in the pretty rhymed scenes she subsequently submitted to Il Maestro for approval.

But O, for a suitable Margaret ! How to find so rare, pale, and precious a pearl among society girls as was required for the adequate representation of the arduous title-*rôle?* Was there one among the many incapable aspirants who would prove able to acquit herself to the satisfaction of the exacting pair who now sat down to an excellent dinner, and who, for the time being, had tacitly resolved to banish all cares for the future ? 'It is the voice, the pure soprano, that I must insist upon,' was Campo's mental resolution, as he hungrily attacked a salmon cutlet *à l'Indienne*, and coughed when he found it so peppery.

'If I find a girl who *looks* the part, I can teach her to act it, and shall not make a *sine quà non* of a wonderful voice,' thought Miss Hartley, as she held up a Venetian goblet filled with sparkling Burgundy ; and she smiled sweetly at her guest, as she uttered a quaint Italian phrase, half welcome, half blessing, which was intended to prove her great satisfaction in his presence at her table.

CHAPTER II.

TREASURE-TROVE.

THAT Campo Maestro thoroughly enjoyed his dinner, and approved of the fashion in which it was served to him, was very evident. Diana had forgotten none of his favourite dishes. The macaroni *à la Néapolitaine* had followed the 'r-roost beef of ze Eengliss,' which he—in all the ardour of his adopted nationality—loved *aussi saignant* as possible. And these heavier delights had been superseded by hot *soufflés* and *méringues glacés*, until the hostess, realising her guest's inexhaustible powers of assimilation, began to fear her hospitality had been excessive, and that she had frustrated her hopes of a serious rehearsal to follow by a too zealous ministering to the prodigious appetite of the Maestro. He was in jubilant spirits certainly ; his laughter was boisterous, his speech more startlingly unintelligible than ever ; for to-day it was profusely larded with phrases of shrill Neapolitan *patois*, such as the natives speak among themselves, but which never fails to puzzle the foreigner, even if he be a proficient in pure Italian.

It is a quiet night, the wind has gone down ; there is at all times very little traffic along the winding road known as Regency-terrace, which, as the reader has been told, was a primitive country lane some twenty years ago.

'That is our gate swinging to,' says Miss Hartley, as the sharp click of the latch in the lock falls upon her ear. 'Who can be coming ? It is not late enough for the last post.'

'*O cielo !* say not it is one visitor for to destroy our peace, our pleasantness, *cara signora !*' cries Campo, lifting his hand in mock entreaty.

'Luke will admit no one now,'

answers Diana, smiling. 'I mean to take you up-stairs presently; the lamps are lighted in the drawing-room; and we must have a serious rehearsal together.'

Then she bends her pretty head in a listening attitude.

'No one has run up the steps,' she says; 'and there has been no knocking at the front door.'

'The gate was open by one who did lost his route,' says Campo, evidently relieved. And with a smile and a bow he selects a cigarette from the dainty case she offers him, and lights it at once.

'And you,' he says—'will you not also?'

'I shall wait for the coffee,' she replies, putting the case he returns to her upon the table at her side. 'Luke will bring it directly; and I will not run away from you if you will promise to come up-stairs with me in half an hour from this, and let us go through the score carefully together once more. I have so much coaching to do in your absence just now; and the responsibility is so great, that I am desirous to acquaint myself thoroughly with your reading of the parts.'

'*Ecco!*' he cries, with a gesture of surprise. 'So please you, hear, hear to this!'

'I am listening,' whispers Diana, and bends her head towards the window, the curtains of which are so closely drawn.

'But it is a voice, the clear voice soprano!' exclaims Campo, rising in his excitement, as the first gentle notes of Olga's song, 'When the elves at noon do pass,' smite pleasantly upon his sensitive ear.

'What a pretty voice, and what marvellous execution!' whispers Diana below her breath. She is listening intently; her expressive face and eager attitude denote rapt attention.

'Alas, it is over; who can the singer be!' she exclaims presently, rising and going eagerly towards the bell; 'she must certainly not escape us. Is it possible that she is a beggar-girl, with such a voice, singing like that?'

'Stir not, you please!' cries Campo, bringing his fist down upon the table impatiently. 'Do notting, notting, *cara mia*, until she have singed one other. If she vant de money, she vill no go, belief dat.'

'But if the poor creature *is* begging, it is only right to let her know that she has not appealed to us in vain.'

'Silence vid your appeal; I vill more song; no talk.'

Campo's enthusiasm covers a multitude of sins in his hostess's indulgent eyes; and as he certainly does not intentionally fail in politeness, she can smile at his rudeness with complacency.

'Ah, vat I tell you? you listen,' he cries, moving towards the window, and throwing the curtains apart, hoping thus to hear better. But the shutters are closed, as we know, and she who stands without is unaware of the attention she has aroused.

Indeed it is at this very moment that Olga—cut to the quick by the manifest indifference of those to whom she has sung her best, and from whose generosity she had hoped much—commences the pathetic plaint of Gretchen.

Both Campo and Diana stand listening with closest attention until the faint echo of the last note has died away.

'It is the song of Marguerite herself—it is my paragon. Now do you believe in the truth of my presentiment, *maestro mio?*'

He stands speechless, amazed. The feverish exhilaration caused by his dinner has predisposed him to exaggerate the excellence of the singer's voice and delivery; but listening intently has already sober-ed him. He is a wondrously kind-hearted man, as well as a true musician, and he feels instinctively that those pathetic strains are ut-tered by one who is terribly weary, whose heart is well-nigh broken.

'We must see her directly—mi-nute!' he cries. He speaks loudly; but his voice has become husky; he coughs, and uses his handker-chief with considerable vigour. 'Shall I go call her in?' he adds pleadingly.

'You might alarm her; she may be timid. I can hear she is gentle by her voice,' says Diana quietly. She also has tears in her eyes, and the compassionate expression of her face at this moment makes her positively beautiful. When Diana thinks only of others, and thinks kindly, she is lovely as well as lovable.

'Here is Luke,' she says, as the servant enters, bearing the coffee-tray; and she at once bids him tell the singer in the garden to come in, because a lady wishes to speak with her.

'With proper training, that voice may become the voice of a *prima donna assoluta*,' Campo declares, in an eager whisper. He speaks Italian now, because that flows more glibly from his lips, and he is moved to amazing enthusiasm. How poor Olga, the incipient *prima donna*, fared when, faint and shivering, she entered that warm scented room, has been told in a previous chapter. Miss Hartley, excited and eager, used all restora-tives to revive the unconscious girl, whom she tenderly supported, kneeling upon the floor beside her, and gazing into the pure white face with unutterable compassion.

'Leave us for a while, *caro maes-tro*,' she says, thankful to see the long-fringed eyelids of the patient quiver. 'Go up-stairs, and wait for me, dear friend; she will not like

to see a man here when she re-covers. By and by you will come down again, and we will talk quietly to her, and find out all about her singing. Poor girl! poor girl!'

As she speaks, Diana takes the white lifeless hand resting upon the floor in her own, and as she eagerly rubs it, her fingers come in contact with a wedding-ring.

'Married!' she whispers, glanc-ing up at Campo, who stands gaz-ing upon the fragile prostrate form with infinite compassion in his wrinkled face.

'She does look dead, poor child! Poor white *bambina!*' he says. Then, in obedience to the command in his hostess's eyes, he suddenly leaves the room.

After a while, Olga recovers con-sciousness, and the first glance of her opening eyes is eagerly di-rected to the mantelshelf. But she is lying with her back towards it now, and her wandering gaze rests with satisfaction upon the face of the lady, who is tenderly support-ing her still.

'How good you are to me,' she says; 'and I fear I have given you so much trouble.'

After that she manages to raise herself a little, and Diana, coming to her assistance, soon settles her in the comfortable armchair by the fire.

'You must drink some coffee; it is here ready,' she says, preparing a cup for the invalid.

While Miss Hartley is leaning over the tray, adding cream and sugar for her strange guest, Olga has managed to turn her head so that she can catch sight of that bonnie-faced boy again, who is cheerfully smiling down upon her from out of the broad gold frame. She longs to ask whose portrait that is, for it most assuredly resembles her baby May; its moving was a delusion of course, and the conse-quence of her giddiness and failing sight. But the likeness is an undoubted fact, as her eager investigation now assures her. Much as she desires information, however, her gentle instincts keep her silent. She remembers that she is in that lovely room on sufferance only, by no means as a guest. Questions from her to her hostess would be sadly wanting in good taste. Having gratefully accepted the coffee and some bread and meat, she declares herself sufficiently strong to set forth again.

'I am most anxious to get home,' she says eagerly; 'my baby will be crying for me, and—and—some one else will be so anxious too.'

'Your husband, my dear?' asks Diana promptly; and as she speaks she mentally concludes that the husband must be an ill-conditioned brute to have allowed that fragile creature to wander forth and beg her bread (or his, most likely) on such a bitter night as this.

'No, not my husband,' says the stranger, covering her wan face with the thin hand on which the massive wedding-ring gleams, as though bearing testimony. '*He* is dead, or I should not be here—like this.'

Diana rapidly crosses the room, and laying her arms gently around the sufferer's shoulders,

'I beg your pardon, my dear,' she says; 'I was very thoughtless, very. You poor child! why, you only look like a child yourself. And you have a baby?'

Diana's tact taught her that this was the safest channel into which to divert the girl's sorrowful thoughts; and in five minutes she had the satisfaction of hearing her patient speak of the young baby and poor faithful Patty, hungry, alone in St. Giles's-passage, with considerable animation.

'And you are really very poor?' asks Miss Hartley, having listened attentively to the stranger's frank lively account of herself and her belongings. 'You with your voice are actually driven to sing in the streets for bread? O my dear child, my poor dear child!' she adds, in tones of profound sympathy, as Olga bows her pretty head in sign of sorrowful acquiescence. 'But all that will be changed now, and at once,' she resumes, with a meaning smile. 'You possess a treasure, a mine of wealth, in that glorious voice, and I intend to teach you how to use your talent to the best advantage. I can put you in the way of earning as many pounds in one week as you have got pence in the streets.'

Olga looks up smiling, but incredulous.

'Ah, you can scarcely believe me,' says Miss Hartley, 'but I can prove the truth of what I have said to you. The gentleman who was in the room when you came in, and who had listened to your songs, is a clever master and an excellent musician. He has experience as well as knowledge; he recognised the wonderful quality of your voice as soon as he heard it, and he told me without hesitation that with careful teaching you might become a *prima donna.*'

'Ah, that is it, careful teaching!' says Olga, relapsing into her erst dejected attitude.

'You must not despond, you must have courage and hope, dear girl,' says Miss Hartley, with more tenderness in her voice and expression than some of those who know her best would deem her capable of. 'Your treasure is planted within your own breast, no one can rob you of that; your future success rests with you entirely; try to understand, try to believe what I tell you; for it is truth—and consolation both. Facts are stubborn things: your voice is a great reliable fact, you may pin your faith to that.'

'But how am I to get the teaching—to pay for it—and how about my poor fatherless babe?' asks Olga, putting her hands to her fevered head, speaking and looking troubled—bewildered almost.

'Do you still feel ill—faint?' inquires Miss Hartley, anxiously noticing the perplexed expression on the stranger's white wan face.

'O no, I am well—quite well; quite able to go home, believe me,' she cries, in nervous haste, and starts to her feet as she speaks.

'Do you mind telling me your exact address, where your baby and Patty are to be found?' asks Miss Hartley, looking searchingly into Olga's frankly uplifted face.

'I don't mind in the least,' she says, with a faint apologetic smile. 'It is No. 1A St. Giles's-passage, a very miserable neighbourhood, and a most wretched lodging; but then we could afford no better, Patty and I. Will you please let me go now? I long to be back with them, and must not stay here any longer, although it is so cosy, so pleasant; and outside—' She shudders at the vivid recollection of the bitter cold she has endured.

Her ingenuous smile might have convinced a more sceptical person than impulsive Diana; but she has lived too long in the world, and has been too thoroughly inured in its ways, to retain much of the trustful simplicity supposed to characterise maidens in general. She has been too often deceived, her charitable inclinations have been too frequently abused, to admit of her placing implicit faith in a stranger. And what a suspicious case is this! A girl looking and speaking as a lady looks and speaks, yet clothed in rags and singing for halfpence, with a voice which Maestro declares may develop into that of a *prima donna!* But— As she ponders on all these things Diana is silent, and takes a little time to reflect as to

her most politic course under such doubtful circumstances. She is always prompt to act as soon as she has arrived at a decision.

'I mean to send my maid, a trustworthy excellent person, to take wine, money, and food to your faithful Patty at once,' she resumes, as soon as she has finally resolved on the best mode of action. 'Then you will not be in a hurry to run away from me, I hope. I am most anxious to have a chat with you about your future prospects, and that teaching we spoke about just now. Will you stay with me for an hour or two when your mind is set at rest about the anxious folks at home? Believe me, I am deeply, truly sorry for you, my poor girl; I know you are a lady, and it makes my heart ache to think of what and how you must have suffered singing in the streets. Will you grant me this favour? Will you stay with me for a while, and hear what that great musical authority, who is waiting on purpose to see you, will have to say as to your prospects from his point of view?'

Olga glances wistfully at her ragged gown, at the great hole in the toe of her boot, and then she looks up into the face of the compassionate lady again.

'Please do not ask me to stay now—like this,' she says, in a tone of entreaty.

Diana, whose enterprising temperament ever leads her into extremes, is at this moment entirely fascinated by the winsome stranger. *Never,* she declares to herself, has she beheld any one so lovely, so interesting before; never have eyes looked into hers with such pathetic appeal in them as those turned upon her now. This is the Margherita—the ideal maiden she had longed for, prayed for, dreamt of —seen in visions. It was the coming of this ethereal being that had filled her mind with strange presentiments of late. Diana had often heard the great question of spiritualism, visions, *séances*, and clairvoyant inspiration discussed. In her quasi-Bohemian circle these were topics of lively interest, and among her friends the dubious cause had some stanch supporters. Hitherto Diana had smiled at the superstitious creed, and at those who held it; but to-night it seemed to her as though benevolent spirits had been at work on her account; for what mortal could have directed this visionary being to wend her way to the door of the Cottage just at the critical hour of Diana's extreme need? Was it her genius or that much-talked-of inspiration which had compelled this startling sequence of events?

'You shall come up into my room, my darling,' she says, flinging a strong supporting arm about the stranger's fragile form; 'there I will change your dress, and put your poor cold feet into a pair of cosy slippers. But I fear my shoes will be miles too long for your wee Cinderella feet.'

'It seems as if I were indeed Cinderella, and you my most gracious fairy godmother,' says Olga, when Miss Hartley has effected the needful change of raiment, and, taking the blushing girl by the shoulders, confronts her with a surprisingly pretty picture of herself in the long cheval-glass. There is a tap at the door of the dressing-room.

Olga starts guiltily, and seems inclined to hide herself behind the long window-curtains; but Miss Hartley promptly reassures her.

'It is only Mrs. Day, my maid,' she says. 'What a timid little Cinderella it is!' she adds, smiling.

'If you please, ma'am, I don't know what name I am to ask for when I gets to the house,' says Luke's discreet wife, waiting on the other side of the door. She knows her mistress well, and is per-fectly aware how completely she will be engrossed by the new fancy which has taken possession of her, and how much averse to any interruption; therefore she does not enter the room. Diana turns to the stranger.

'You have forgotten to tell me your name,' she says eagerly, and most sincerely hopes that it may prove to be a romantic one.

Ever since old Michael Layton turned his unfortunate daughter out of doors, Olga had adopted her mother's maiden name. There could be no shame to any one in that, was her proud conclusion at the time; and when in reply to her patroness's inquiry she answers, 'Laura Bellairs,' no thought of deceiving any one occurs to her. She had never been called Mrs. Strange except by him who gave her that name, and sometimes joked her about it. But when her baby was born the familiar sound of the name of that baby's dead father had become too painful for utterance or hearing. Now, without any hesitation,

'Laura Bellairs,' said she.

Miss Hartley prefixed the name to the address already given to Mrs. Day.

'You will take a hansom, of course,' said the mistress. 'And—I wish you to call at Dover-street on your way. Present my compliments to Sir Gilbert, and beg him to step round for ten minutes this evening, if possible. Ask to see him yourself, and tell him that I particularly desire to consult him.' Miss Hartley had given these orders hurriedly in a low tone; Olga has not heard a word of them. She is busy gathering the waving masses of her hair into coils. As she has been made to look like a princess in that lovely cashmere gown, she thinks it incumbent upon her to bring what order she can into her dishevelled appearance.

CHAPTER III.

MARGHERITA.

'Now, my pretty princess, are you ready?' asks Miss Hartley, as soon as Mrs. Day has received her final directions, and been repeatedly reminded to assure Patty of her mistress's well-being.

'Ready to follow my gracious fairy godmother wherever she bids me go,' answers Olga, smiling; and she lays her hand readily into that of her handsome protectress.

'If you call me godmother, I shall assume the godmother's privilege, and give you a new name, my dear,' says Miss Hartley, as they commence to descend the stairs hand in hand.

'What name will you give me?' asks Olga. 'Cinderella would be the most suitable in every sense, I think.'

'No; the grub period is over for you, I sincerely trust, my dear. You shall have the chance of spreading your delicate wings now, and, as far as I am able, I will do my utmost to assist your flight. I shall hope to see you soar upwards and upwards, until you rest on the laurel crown which befits a *prima donna assoluta.*'

'O,' says Olga, and crosses her hands eagerly upon her breast. 'What lovely words you use, what poetical delightful things you say to me!'

'My darling, my rare pale Margaret!' whispers Diana, clasping her newly-discovered friend in her arms, as they pause side by side on the lower landing.

'Ah, and so at ze last you come!' exclaims Maestro, throwing open the door of the drawing-room as soon as he hears the rustle of the ladies' skirts without. He has been pacing to and fro in a fever of impatience and excitement. If this beggar-maid has a fair share of intelligence—if she is not hampered by the sordid cares of earning bread for herself and other paupers—if she chooses to devote herself to the study of singing, and, with that purpose clearly defined in her mind, will put herself under his guidance professionally, then has she indeed a grand future before her; a future over which he, as leading genius, longs to preside.

When she enters the room, her rags exchanged for the flowing pale-blue cashmere robe, the tangled masses of her fair hair smoothly coiled about her shapely head, Campo screws up his bright eyes as though dazzled by the fair vision before him, and half in jest, but still seriously, he cries,

'*Madonna mia*, but this is work of sorcery! this is the most wonderfullest transform! I do part, and leave wiz you *La Cenerentola*,* and you return to me wiz *La Regina*. Biondina, Bella, Bella!'

Diana, who is still in the first flush of a new romantic excitement, echoes all Maestro's enthusiastic admiration with cordiality. Her best and least selfish feelings have been appealed to by the stranger's gentle helplessness and beauty. And unless some new and unforeseen event happens to distract the capricious lady's attention, the chances are that she will devote time, trouble, and money to the furthering of her new *protégée's* advancement, social and musical. For this night, at all events, she chooses to regard the street-singer as a paragon of womanly excellence, and, what is still more satisfactory, she feels assured that a fitting heroine for the operetta has thus mysteriously been sent to relieve her from the growing anxiety which had threatened to blight all her long-cherished hopes of success on the occasion of that much-talked-of 'Great Event.' His first burst of admiration over, Campo

* Cinderella.

settles himself to a musical cross-examination. Olga, who has grown up among professionals and often been present at interviews between her parents and enterprising managers, is by no means at a loss as to the answers Maestro requires of her. Her mother was a professional singer, she says, and made a great success in St. Petersburg, Berlin, and other cities.

' Her name ?' inquires the curious signor.

' I have adopted it,' says Olga ; ' Laura Bellairs.' And she devoutly hopes that she may escape further questioning on that head. Miss Hartley, who, when interested, is keenly observant, notes the trouble in her *protégée's* face as questions relating to her private history are eagerly pressed upon her by the too inquisitive Italian.

' We do not want to trouble her about her former name or any other bygones,' she says hastily ; and gives Campo a warning look as she adds, ' To me and to you also I think she must always be Margherita in future. As for her parentage, her history, and experiences, she will tell me just what she thinks fit on some future occasion.'

Olga smiles her grateful thanks for this welcome reprieve.

' And you did think of her for our soprano *rôle ?*' exclaims Maestro, on whom the idea, which flashed upon Diana as another inspiration, is only now commencing to dawn.

' Of course I did,' she replies, laughing. ' Did I not tell you that my prayer would be answered— that the heavens would open, or some beneficent spirits would come to my aid just in the nick of time? As all our singers are amateurs, professional experience and *savoir-faire* will not be expected in my heroine.'

' And ze svells ?' whispers Campo,

with a depreciating glance at the ' beggar-maid.'

' I am King Cophetua on this occasion,' answers Diana, also in a low tone. ' I mean to *make* this girl. I shall take her by the hand and lead her on to fame, if she will trust herself to me.'

' But, *cara mia*, she is a singing-girl from the street, a true beggar,' answers Maestro doubtfully. He has known Diana for many years, and has often witnessed the frantic commencement of her passionate caprices ; but has just as frequently noted the tragic disappointment of their sudden endings, and of Diana's victims. Therefore he shakes his head very gravely.

' But she has a voice, the voice that with proper training may lead her to a proud position in the end. You yourself said so, Maestro ; and you are *not* impulsive.'

Diana says this with slow deprecation ; for she gauges the thoughts in her old friend's mind pretty accurately.

' Ah, if I were to have zat training, and if she will place herself, all her strength, all her time, ail her intelligence, all her good-will at my disposal, then there are possibilities. . . .' Campo has uttered the last sentences in Italian, and spoken with rising animation.

' I shall make myself responsible for *all*. This girl training, musical and social, will lend new zest to my dreary monotonous home-life. I mean to take her to live in my house. You shall see. You doubt me now ; but you will find how thoroughly determined I am, and that I mean to keep to my resolve this time.'

Diana also speaks rapidly, and in Italian. Indeed it would be difficult not to believe her, once she is fairly carried away by an idea, as now. She is earnest, eager, eloquent, strangely imbued with the importance of the task she is undertaking, and quite determined to impress all those about her with the happy conviction of prosperous results that leads her so hopefully onward.

'I shall teach Margherita her part in the operetta,' she says, speaking aloud and in English again, as she leaves Campo's side and resumes her former place near Olga.

'Can you once more sing for me ze Margherita of Schubert?' asks the musician, turning to the 'beggar-maid.' He seats himself at the piano, and plays the spinning-wheel prelude.

Olga rises without a word, without a second's hesitation. Her duty is plain to her now. Hundreds of times has she stood thus by her father's side : earnest, intent on the task he has set her, anxious to sing her best always, and hoping for some word of praise or encouragement from him, which (unless he was stimulated by drink) seldom fell from his lips.

She clasps her hands now as she has been taught to do, and stands straight, steady, her chin uplifted, her chest well forward. There is not the slightest affectation about her at any time ; and when she sings, her pose, like her delivery, is equally natural, simple. Campo notes all these details with a master's observant eye. She takes breath with closed lips : good that, and very unusual in amateurs. Therefore he concludes that her professional mother has given the girl a valuable legacy in the way of conscientious preliminary training.

Miss Hartley, seated on the sofa in the small inner room, has watched her Margherita as she stood by Maestro's side ; and has listened with the experienced ear of a connoisseur to each mellow tuneful note that issues from those pretty sensitive lips.

Before the song is over, the handle of the door has been turned noiselessly, and in another moment Sir Gilbert Clive creeps into the boudoir on tip-toe.

Miss Hartley puts her left hand to her lips, and extends the right in eager though silent welcome, just before the song is concluded.

'So you have found your *prima donna* after all? Allow me to congratulate you most sincerely,' he whispers, leaning towards his hostess. 'What a treasure ! Who is she ? Where did you discover her ? What a marvellous woman you are, Diana ! what a head for organisation !' and then—the song being over—Sir Gilbert applauds enthusiastically.

Campo is thankful to see that Miss Hartley is completely engrossed by her visitor, who is asking her question on question in low hurried tones.

'Now,' thinks Maestro, 'it is my turn to talk to my future pupil without interruption.' He speedily resumes the attitude of mentor, and puts the novice through her facings with a promptness and decision that would reflect credit on a drill-sergeant to the manner born. His fierce gesticulation and extraordinary speech alarm poor Olga at first ; but the interest the odd little man takes in her statements is so very evident, and the gleam of his restless black eyes is so benevolent when they do meet hers, that she soon gains confidence in herself and in him. By the time Sir Gilbert is introduced to her as 'Madame Margherita,' Maestro has very clearly explained to her that it rests with herself entirely to take rank among the foremost of the soprano singers of the day. 'But it must be all study, all true vork, and vera, vera littell play. You are young and you are pretty. Can you dis thing ?'

'Madame Margherita' thought she could safely promise to work with all her might and main, if the chance for self-improvement were vouchsafed to her. 'But to be taught costs money, and practice wants all one's time,' she remarked naïvely; and Campo, smiling, answered,

' *Che sarà sarà;*' and then he nodded his head, and closed his eyes in emulation of some favourite oracle perhaps.

'Madame Margherita,' calls Miss Hartley from the inner room, 'my kind old friend, Sir Gilbert Clive, is as enthusiastic about your voice as we others are, and has just had a long talk with me about you and your future. Come into this room, child, it is smaller and more cosy. Let us all sit close to the fire and have a grand consultation. We want you, Maestro, of course. The circle of friends in council would not be complete unless you were in our midst. My proposition is this,' recommenced Diana, after taking a deep breath.

She plunged *in medias res*, as her enterprising custom was, and addressing herself directly to Olga: 'You are to come and live in my house here with me, for one month certain,' she said. 'As I shall require your undivided attention, and a great part of your time, I shall undertake to find a suitable lodging for the faithful Patty and your little one in this neighbourhood. This month will be one of probation. Let us consider it experimental only, if you like. At the end of four weeks I shall offer you the first chance of distinguishing yourself in public. It is to enable you to be successful in that venture, which concerns me personally, that I am ready and anxious to take all possible care of you, if you will allow me to do so. Do not imagine that I am conferring a favour upon you; but believe that I am asking one, and that you can grant it by placing yourself unreservedly in my hands—for one

month. Say yes, or no, and——I do hope it may be yes !' As Diana finished her earnest appeal she rose and took Olga's hand in hers. 'You believe that you can trust yourself to me, do you not, child ? I will promise to be very, very good to you.'

The two men who sat listening were moved with wonder, almost with amazement. Each in his own way admired fascinating Diana exceedingly; but one did more than admire—he loved her. Sir Gilbert had thrice offered his hand and heart to this winsome incomprehensible woman, who, for the last ten years, had held the reins of his destiny firm and close in her clever hands. She would neither be persuaded to say yea or nay; but she would look into his troubled face with her arch smile, and bid him wait or leave her, as he pleased. He pleased neither; but leave her he could not, and so waiting was his safest, indeed his only course.

As he watched her beaming face to-night, and heard her pleading so prettily, so temptingly with this strange girl whom she had called in from the street—a beggar singing for bread or pence—his heart misgave him. What faith could be placed in a woman who took such unaccountable fancies; who was so self-willed; who refused to listen to reason; who persisted in doing things which, to his more prosaic mind, savoured of something stranger than eccentricity ? He had argued with Diana, putting certain risks and possibilities very frankly before her; for he was a man who made a point of calling a spade a spade, and disdained the affectation which would convert it into a ladle. But his warnings and arguments made not the slightest impression upon this headstrong clever woman.

'I know my own mind,' she said; which assertion the reader

will probably doubt, if Sir Gilbert did not. 'And more than that, I can read character at a glance. This sweet woman, whom you disdainfully speak of as a beggar-maid, is a lady, as thoroughly well-behaved, properly brought-up a lady as—I am; or—rather more so, for she is neither aggressive nor self-conceited. She is modest and gentle as an ideal Gretchen, and at the same time she has the true refinement of one who is born and bred a gentle among gentles.'

'Do you mean Gentiles?' ventured Sir Gilbert, trying to laugh off her extreme seriousness.

'I mean a gentlewoman in the true sense of the word, Sir Gilbert!' Diana answered severely; and her old admirer, as usual, collapsed before the sharp reproof on her lips and the angry glance in her dark eyes.

Campo Maestro, though essentially a Bohemian by nature and habit, had lived too long in the world not to consider Miss Diana's decision exceedingly venturesome, and even risky. But he enjoyed his favourite old pupil's eccentricities, and knew her obstinacy too well to attempt any sort of opposition once he saw she had made up her mind to a scheme. And he was less likely than ever to dissuade her in this matter of her new *protégée*, because he himself was favourably impressed by the girl in question, and—because she had a glorious promising voice.

'Of course I will do as you bid me, my gracious fairy godmother,' said Olga, when she had taken some time for reflection. 'And if it be possible for me to render you any sort of service, as you seem to think I can, then I shall be very happy indeed. May I say

good-night to you now?' she added, rising; and, inclining her head to the gentlemen, she left the room.

Miss Hartley followed her, wrapped her in a fur-lined mantle, bade Luke put her into a cab, and promised to come to St. Giles's-passage herself next morning to fetch all the family away.

Olga would gladly have implored her kind patroness not to visit her in her miserable lodging; but, deeming this shrinking a sign of false pride and therefore despicable, she said no word of remonstrance, and, still bewildered by the many novel experiences of this extraordinary evening, she leant back in the cab and felt herself carried home with much shaking and rattling. But her heart was glad within her, and external annoyance troubled her not at all now.

'O Patty, we are saved! Help has come to us; work for me; a home for you and my blessed, blessed baby. I never thought to feel happy or light-hearted again; and now I am, O, so glad, O, so thankful!'

Clasping her baby to her beating heart, laughing and crying by turns, poor Olga tried to tell the wondrous story of the night's adventures to her eagerly listening faithful friend. But about the picture—the picture that looked so like baby May—Olga said never a word.

'Let us put the old life quite behind us, dear Patty,' were her last words that night. 'Promise me faithfully never to mention my father or *him* to living soul. My new friends receive me and think of me as Laura Bellairs; and, as you love me, help me to forget that I ever bore any other name than that of my loving, innocent, saintly mother.'

[To be continued.]

A HEALTH RESORT ON THE KENTISH COAST, IN AND OUT OF SEASON.

By AN OLD BOHEMIAN.

———◆———

'I TELL you what it is, old boy,' said my friend O'Rourke to me a twelvemonth ago, 'you look precious white about the gills. This little village does not seem quite the thing for you just now. You had better take a run down to the sea for change of air.'

'What! in this blessed month of February? How absurd!' I cried. 'Why, people would think me mad as a March hare.'

'Never you mind how absurd, or what people may think,' retorted O'Rourke stoutly. 'You do as I tell you, and I'll warrant you will soon have reason to thank me for my advice, which is solely prompted by my warm interest in you. You must surely see that I cannot possibly have a selfish motive in this.'

Now I must say this of my friend O'Rourke: there breathes not a more unselfish man—except, indeed, in money matters, or where his personal feelings or interests are, however remotely, concerned. And what, indeed, could it matter to him whether I stayed in London or went to the seaside?

So, as I have reason to consider O'Rourke rather an authority on questions of health, and as the advice proffered by him seemed certainly disinterested, I began to look upon the suggestion as not quite so outrageously absurd as it had struck me at the first blush.

'But where would you advise me to go to?' I asked thereupon, somewhat more deferentially.

'To Birchington, man, to Birch-ington!' exclaimed O'Rourke enthusiastically.

'Birchington?' I queried, in some perplexity. 'Where is that to be found on the map?' For I am ashamed to confess I could not just then call to mind ever having seen or heard the name of the place before.

'Not know Birchington!' cried O'Rourke. 'You surprise me.

"A village called Birchington, famed for its rolls,
As the fishing bank just in its front is for soles."

Why, you must have passed it over and over again on your way to Margate!'

'O, is the small shebeen village you mean next on the line from Herne Bay?' I queried somewhat contemptuously, as a faint recollection dawned upon me that I had seen some such name written up somewhere on the road to Margate.

'Shebeen village indeed!' cried O'Rourke indignantly. 'Birchington-on-Sea, as it is properly called, is a town, sir, a town which, but for the lack of a harbour, might have been one of the Cinque Ports, just as much as any of the other five. And as a sanatorium second to none, let me tell you, sir.'

'But,' I ventured to ask diffidently and dubiously, 'will this sanatorium suit my constitution—at this inclement season of the year?'

'Will it suit your constitution—at this inclement season of the year?' mimicked O'Rourke. 'Of course it will. It is the very place for you, man, with your gout and rheumatism, your asthma, your dyspeptic fits, your inveterate hippishness, your eternal colds, and your everlasting bronchitis—and the inroads of old age.' This was merely a nasty ill-natured sneer of O'Rourke's; for, with all the inveterate hippishness imputed to me, I never yet laid claim to anything like half these complaints; and as for old age, why, I might have retorted upon O'Rourke, who is fifty if he is a day, and I am fifty too, only that I look a leetle older —just a leetle. 'Birchington,' O'Rourke continued magisterially, 'with its chalk cliffs, and its dry soil, and its genial breezes, and the splendid facilities for bathing on its sandy shore, and its charming rural simplicity, and its enchanting primitive ways, and its calm repose, will make a new man of you in no time, and give you a fresh lease of life, starting you with a solid capital of health more than sufficient to last you for ten years to come; so you just shut-up and go! And, look you here, old fellow, by a most extraordinary coincidence, I am going to send Mrs. O'Rourke and the chits to this identical town of Birchington; and as I have to go to Liverpool on business, you may as well run down along with them, looking a little after the luggage and things in general, you know. You will infinitely oblige Mrs. O'Rourke. What say you?'

What could I say? I felt that I was in for it, and could not well get out of it, there being a lady in the case; though I must say I saw peep out a little too much of the disinterested O'Rourke's actuating motive to make it quite pleasant.

So, two days after, down I went to Birchington with Mrs. O'Rourke and family of three charming cherubs and a servant.

I am a confirmed old bachelor; and it had never been my fate before then to travel with a family. It is but a two hours and a half run by rail from Victoria to Birchington; but I had quite enough of it. There were twenty-two separate parcels of luggage to be seen to—to get labelled at Victoria, looked after at Faversham, and finally collected on the Birchington platform; for railway porters are apt to be careless if not largely tipped. In short, no slave of the ring or of the lamp in Aladdin's wondrous tale was ever made such a wretched serf as I was to that cursed luggage.

And when at last it was all done, apparently, and our luggage had been safely housed in our new rural residence, it turned out that there were only twenty-one parcels, and that the most important—a large hamper containing the family's provender for a week to come, with no end of table-cloths, napkins, towels, &c.—was not one of them. So I was despatched there and then to the station, to bully the unlucky master, and peremptorily insist upon the *immediate* production of *that* hamper. As the poor man had not got it, I made him telegraph at once in every direction for it.

From that time forward for four days after I was made wretched by that blessed hamper. I was truly hampered by it, or rather by its persistent non-appearance, in all my intended movements in search of health, and in every other way. Every train that happened to stop at Birchington brought me to the little toy station, with the stereotyped inquiry, 'Has the hamper come?'

And as day after day passed without news of the missing parcel, Mrs. O'Rourke grew more and more wroth, goading me, the very mildest-tempered man alive, into unseemly vituperation of the L. C. & D. Company and everybody connected with it, especially the unhappy station-master, who, in the end, dreaded the very sight of me, and had a run for it the instant he saw me turn up the station-road. The three cherubs and the female slavy were also despatched some five or six times a day to make the life of that plagued official a torment unto him. He was forced to telegraph to Victoria and to Faversham and to Dover and to Calais and to Paris and to Ostend and to Brussels—nay, even to Cologne—all in vain. So he told us at last, in desperation, to make our claim upon the company for the value of the missing parcel. And I, upon the strength of some hazy recollection of having once seen a hamper somewhere, and upon the confident asseveration of one of the cherubs that she had seen the hamper taken out of the van at Faversham, was ready to make a solemn declaration that I had seen the missing hamper duly labelled at Victoria and turned out of the luggage-van at Faversham, and—Heaven forgive me !—to swear to the value of the contents, which I had never even cast eyes on. But —*ce que femme veut.*

Well, we were just about sending in our claim for compensation, made out by Mrs. O'Rourke in a fashion testifying equally to a splendidly retentive—perhaps slightly inventive—memory, and to a truly surprising faculty of valuation, and duly supported by me in every item—when lo ! on the fifth evening after our arrival at Birchington, the unlucky hamper came down upon us like an avalanche, sent on by O'Rourke, who had found it snugly reposing on the landing in his own house upon his return from Liverpool. I must say I felt

a happy relief. A load was lifted off my mind. The dread of laying the guilt of little short of deliberate perjury on my soul had happily vanished now into the comfortable domain of things that simply might have been. Of course, I do not claim the gift of looking into other people's souls and consciences, but I have a shrewd suspicion that the unexpected arrival of the hamper did not please Mrs. O'Rourke quite so much as it rejoiced me. Poor lady ! Her great mnemonic feat and her brilliant power of computing values by double-chalk entry went positively for nothing now. She might surely be pardoned, then, for looking upon herself as a woman most cruelly used. No wonder her disappointment was visited upon my devoted head. I caught it hot and sharp and strong. ' If a gentleman undertook to look after a lady's luggage, he surely ought to do it properly. There could be no excuse for laxity or negligence in such a case,' I was told rather bluntly, and I found it no easy task to deprecate the lady's wrath.

And there was another *mauvais quart d'heure* to pass. For had not the opportunity come now for the martyred station-master to bear down heavily upon his unconscionable tormentor ? So I went in fear and trembling to make the *amende honorable* to that most illused official. Luckily the man turned out to be a true Christian. He simply looked at me reprovingly, and, pointing the outstretched index of his right hand at me, said slowly and impressively, ' And you were prepared to swear that you had seen this hamper labelled at Victoria and taken out of the luggage-van at Faversham ! What do you think of yourself now—hey ?' And, without waiting to listen to my apologetic self-depreciation, he turned on his heels and slowly walked away, gravely shaking his head.

I was a free man, then, at last, free from that hampering incubus; and I was permitted by gracious Mrs. O'Rourke to go and look around and about me beyond the quarter of a mile distance separating our urbano-rural residence from the railway-station, to which my explorative movements had up to this been mainly limited.

Now, when one goes to the sea, even in winter, it is but natural that one would like to see the sea. So, on the sixth morning after our arrival at Birchington, I set out for the 'sands;' for I had been told that the coast at Birchington was aranaceous, just the same as at Margate—said sands are about half a mile from the 'town,' as the Birchingtonians will, with true Kentish sturdiness, persist in dubbing their little village. Some of the more ardent natives even call it a seaport, which certainly it might be, only it is not, albeit in most other respects a most excellent place, as I found in due course of time; and as a marine health resort second to none, as O'Rourke had veraciously told me.

On this and on many succeeding days I perambulated the Birchington shore from the bay sea-wall to New Westgate, a stretch of above two miles of smooth sandy expanse, intersected here and there, close to the coast, by patches of chalk, stones, and pebbly shingle, yet altogether an 'illigant sthrand for ladies to bathe in summer.'

Only in February and March the sea is at its very coldest, and much more apt to give you shivering fits merely to look at it, than to invite a plunge. Besides, Birchington most fully shares in that glorious eastern blast for which the Kentish coast would seem to have secured a special patent of its own. O'Rourke had boasted of 'genial

breezes' among the most charming attractions of Birchington. Well, my personal experience of the place soon proved this to be a most deplorable abuse of language. My dear departed friend Jacobsen, known in Bohemia Londinensis as the witty Dane of Westminster, used to call the 'genial climb' the ascent of one hundred and seventeen steps leading to our lofty roost when we were in Paris together in 1867. Upon something like the same principle, the fierce blowers on the Kentish coast might be qualified as 'genial breezes.' I can conscientiously aver that for the last year or so I have hardly ever known two days in succession to pass without some gale or other— eastern or western, generally spiced with a stiff northern blast—blowing gaily through the greater part of the day; occasionally for a long spell of several days and nights running. But I must add, in homage to truth, that, whether owing to the dryness of the soil, or to whatever more occult sanitary influence, the very fiercest gale at Birchington has never yet in any way injuriously affected me. At Brighton I have always suffered from distressing attacks of dyspnœa, and my bronchitis has affectionately stuck to me in all weathers. Here I can breathe freely in the fiercest gale, and cough only just sufficient to give me an occasional gentle reminder that I have chronic bronchitis. In London, a wetting, or a walk through the mud, would always be safe to land me in rheumatic rackings or in gouty fits. At Birchington, neither the very heaviest walk over the wet sands, nor the most thorough soaking, ever seems to have the power to hurt me, or, for the matter of that, any of the many invalids coming in search of health to this truly glorious sanatorium. In my inmost heart I feel grateful to O'Rourke for counselling me to take this trip.

When I had to go back to London last April, I felt as a new-born man; but, alas, certain causes, over which I could exercise but a very limited control, speedily laid me on a most painful sick-bed, with a fierce attack of gastrorrhœa, the most distressful malady I have ever yet experienced in the course of a long life. When I was within the very gates of death, a dear medical friend of mine, a distin-guished West-end practitioner, saved me by advising my instant removal to my old Birchington quarters. I had a hard and pro-tracted struggle for it indeed; but the beneficent, health-giving, tone-restoring *genius loci* of this blessed little place pulled me safely through, leaving me to live the brief re-mainder of my days with compara-tive soundness of body, albeit with just too little stomach, and a great deal too much liver—and sadly shrunken limbs.

This seems to me the proper place to crave permission to ex-press my most heartfelt gratitude to gracious Mrs. O'R. for the un-varying gentleness and untiring patience with which she nursed me through the very worst phases of my fearful malady, bearing with truly angelic sweetness the most wretched outbreaks of temper in-to which my sufferings would but too often goad me. Not alone this; but in the indispensable, pro-saic, and matter-of-fact business relations between us, she showed how lamentably deficient she was in her calculating power, for which I had been disposed to give her such high credit in the affair of the missing hamper. *She* compute with double-chalk entries! Why, her arithmetic was truly deplorable. She made out that a pound ster-ling added to another pound ster-ling came exactly to nine shillings,

and, with woman's proverbial ob-stinacy, she would carry her point. The blessings of an old man rest on her head !

After this somewhat unconscion-able digression, return we to the Birchington sands, where I went for a plunge as soon as I could fairly manage to walk. The sea by this time was genially warm, and I found quite a number of bathers picturesquely dispersed in small knots along the bank, from the Birchington Bay sea-wall to the 'Cliff of the Bungalows.'

The Birchington sands present indeed splendid facilities for bath-ing. It must be conceded also that the ways of the little place are enchantingly primitive. There are certain decayed ports on the Kentish coast where the number of bathing-machines reaches actually up to three, and even four, which, however, are only rarely in simul-taneous use at the very height of the season, when as many as an entire half-dozen families may happen to be down at a time. Now, Birchington, with an influx now and then of some forty or fifty families at a time—many of them belonging to the world of fashion, with a pretty large sprink-ling of carriage people among them —sports not a solitary bathing-box! Nature has generously provided more comfortable and more econo-mical tiring-rooms, in the shape of a number of caves in the cliffs lining the shore. Some of these caves are pretty deep, others are more shallow. By tacit agreement the latter are left to the gentlemen bathers, while the deeper caves are reserved for the exclusive use of the ladies. Sheets or blankets, or a number of newspapers artistically pinned together, secure the privacy of these improvised apartments, whose temporary tenants have no rent to pay.

I may here incidentally remark

that the Birchington ways are perhaps less enchantingly primitive in some other respects, into which it might certainly seem desirable to impart a little modern civilisation. Thus, for instance, the sanitary arrangements are mostly upon the venerable old cesspool principle, which may be a very good thing in its way for the requirements of rural economy, but seems rather objectionable in other important points of view. As for the water supply, almost every house has a well seventy or eighty feet deep sunk in the yard, from which the water has to be laboriously hauled up in buckets, very few of the wells having proper pumps attached to them. There is one comfort, however, in these wells : they do not freeze in winter, and there is no bursting of pipes, as in the late delightful hibernal season in London.

I have mentioned the 'Cliff of the Bungalows.' These bungalows are quite a special feature of Birchington. Properly speaking, taking the term to mean a single-floor house, built of light material, and covered with a thatched roof, only three out of the dozen or so of the buildings on the West Cliff, which are dubbed bungalows by the natives, can show anything like a good title to the name ; the remainder are built of brick and mortar, and several of them are two stories high. Not one of the dozen has a thatched roof; but they are mostly covered with wood, some of them with felt-packing between, to insure coolness in summer, warmth in winter. They are all of them tolerably spacious, with dining, drawing, and reception rooms, from six to a dozen bedrooms, besides kitchen and other offices, stables and coach-houses, conservatories, verandahs, &c. Each stands in its own grounds, surrounded by lawns, flower and kitchen gardens, &c. Most of them face the sea, and have underground passages cut through the cliff, which open straight on the beach—a most comfortable bathing arrangement for the inmates.

These bungalows remain mostly unoccupied for the greater part of the year: their owners will occasionally inhabit them for a few months. In the season—say for two or three months—they are generally let to visitors, at the moderate rent of from seven to fifteen guineas a week, furnished, which it appears visitors to Birchington with large families will cheerfully pay.

In the matter of rent, I may incidentally remark here, Birchington goes slightly wild in summer with a kind of high-season fever. Four to five guineas a week for a moderately-sized, by no means over-abundantly furnished, house, is held by the natives to be nothing out of the way. Yet they will gladly let you have the same place for the year round at the reasonable rent of forty to forty-five pounds. Some of the poorer householders, with pretty large families, will let nearly every nook and corner of their holdings, whilst they themselves will crowd ten together in a small room. Nay, last season I had reason to suspect some of my neighbours of surreptitious nocturnal migrations to the sea-caves, whenever the tide served; at all events I can aver that I have met several of them, rather late at night, stealing their way toward the sea-wall with suspicious-looking bundles on their heads.

Several of the bungalows bear mythological, literary, or fancy names. Thus one is called *Haun;* the next to it, which has a most charming flower-garden and a fine conservatory, *Thor.* Both these are the property of one of the leading notables of Birchington. The next bungalow to *Thor* is called *Woden*—written *Wooden* on the gate-post, the painter's knowledge of Saxon mythology being evidently slightly hazy. This *wooden* structure, which is built of solid brick and mortar, is occupied by an eccentric wealthy lady, who lives here in the sweet company of no fewer than fifty-six pug-dogs, an old mastiff, a ferocious-looking but rather gentle-tempered bloodhound, two ill-mannered goats, some cats, a birdie or two, and a couple of retainers belonging to the human species; also a frequent visitor from London, a remarkably good-natured, albeit rather dirty, dog-fancier, who has a ropewalk somewhere in the Borough, where he carries on a most lucrative business, it would appear. It may seem rather an ill-natured remark to make, but I was told that dogs and dirt formed the bond of union between the well-born lady and the humble roper and fancier.

Then we have Ingoldsby, Corbye Tower, Dilkoosha; the Ingoldsby, named no doubt after the author of the 'Legends.'

One, called the Châlet, is built of wood throughout, and painted black with dark-red cross stripes. This erection looks like nothing else conceivable under heaven, and is a caution both to saint and sinner to behold.

I may here remark, *en passant*, that there are some other rather curious structures to be seen about Birchington, such as, for instance, a small row of villas, specially designed, I was informed by the architect, to stand as lasting monuments to his genius. I had occasion to look at and over them, outside and inside, and I must say they are fearfully and wonderfully built; indeed they must be seen to be 'realised.'

One of the bungalows, planned and built by a Mr. Taylor, is truly a model residence in every respect, admirably appointed and suitably furnished, and provided with every conceivable requisite to make it a snug dwelling in all seasons of the year.

Another, planned and built by the same gentleman years ago, was only finished last year. It is now the West Cliff Hotel, and may be conscientiously recommended to visitors.

These bungalows, with a number of houses, villas, cottages, &c., sprinkled here and there about the railway-station and the cliffs and along the several roads leading to Margate, Ramsgate, Canterbury, &c., also two fine coastguard stations—one near the bay, the other close to Westgate—constitute what may be termed the outlying section of the 'ancient township' of Birchington.

A few short years ago, Westgate, the next station on the road to Margate, had no existence. It was simply a broad expanse of gentle hill and dale along the shore. A large contractor, Mr. W. Corbett, was so struck with the natural beauties of the site, and the facilities which it afforded for building, that he planned what is now rapidly rising into the very respectable township of Westgate-on-Sea, and fast growing into one of the most fashionable health resorts on the Kentish coast.

Now Birchington offers even superior facilities for building purposes. Land may be bought in some parts very cheaply indeed. Near the bungalows it is considerably dearer, it must be admitted, there being actually some illusionists who want a thousand or twelve hundred pounds an acre—only they are not very likely to get it. There is an abundance of chalk and of flint-stones, and two extensive brick-fields, both yielding immense quantities of a very superior article. There is a fine expanse of ground along the shore—

the Birchington Bay Estate it is called—which is even now being laid out with magnificent roads, &c., and awaiting only the advent of a few enterprising enlightened capitalists to burst suddenly upon the world as a splendid new township. And along the coast up to Westgate there are hundreds upon hundreds of acres now offered for sale, which might be turned to most excellent and profitable account in the same way.

The 'ancient town' of Birchington proper consists mainly of a single elbow-shaped street, with a few stunted offshoots, and a square in the joint—at least it is called the square ; but it might with equal propriety have the name of almost any other geometrical figure affixed to it.

To the right of the square stands the ancient church of All Saints, an unpretending building, with an old inside and a new outside (renovated some sixteen years back), and a moderately tall tower, tapering to a shingled spire. It contains a high chancel and an ancient chapel, with a number of monuments, erected to the memory of members of the Quex and Crispe families, who were for many generations the owners of Queker Park and lords of the manor of Birchington.

The inside of All Saints is rather roomy and well appointed, and can conveniently accommodate the entire church congregation of the parish. The respected vicar—as he is universally called here—the Rev. J. P. Alcock, would seem to be a little high—rather gamey, as an old Birchingtonian expressed it to me—much given to chanting and intoning, floral decoration, lighted candles, and 'localisation' of the Deity in the East—just a man after Walker, Tooth, and Mackonochie's own heart. He reads prayers twice every day of the

week, and holds two full choral services on Sunday. He sports a choir of young and old boys—some of the latter very old boys indeed, with more than slightly cracked voices. He has set his heart, it would appear, upon the acquisition and becoming ornamentation of a reredos, for which he is always soliciting the contributions of the faithful in a separate box—with but indifferent success, however.

The Birchingtonian Churchmen clearly must be a simple-minded most accommodating flock, willing to pass without complaint or murmuring from high to low, from low to high, if all I have heard about them is true. The Rev. J. P. Alcock's predecessor, who also was universally called the respected vicar, held no service whatever in the week, and preached only once on Sunday morning, did not trouble much about the choir, held in abomination reredos, floral decorations, and lighted tapers, and stuck manfully to the old Low Church ritual. Yet he gave universal satisfaction. The present 'respected vicar,' who is represented as the very opposite to him, seems equally to give satisfaction to his good-natured and sweet-tempered parishioners. No Westerton here, no Saunders. It may be a moot point whether the parishioners of All Saints, Birchington, are not after all wiser in their generation than the cavillers of St. Paul and Barnabas, Knightsbridge, and St. James's, Hatcham, though the principle for which these latter were and are contending is no doubt in the abstract quite unimpeachable.

The Nonconformist element is strongly represented in Birchington. There is a Wesleyan chapel, built in 1830, with a four-face dial, a most useful ornament, of which the 'Establishment' place of worship is destitute ; a Primitive

Methodist chapel, and a Baptist chapel.

Beer and the Bible, as a somewhat cynical and irreverent friend of mine is in the habit of observing, have a strong tendency to run together. Here, at all events, the 'Establishment' church is flanked on one side by the Powell Arms, on the other by the Queen's Head, and faces the New Inn in a diagonal direction. The West Cliff Hotel is near the railway-station; the Sea-View Hotel is the first house of the village (or town, if you like) coming from the station. A sixth 'pub' is called the Acorn, which makes six 'pubs' to four places of divine worship. However, as the taps of the several inns, hotels, or taverns are mostly unadulterated, no great harm is done. Beer, wine, and spirits are very reasonable in price and of rather superior quality in Birchington. At the Sea-View Hotel, for instance, they sell you a bottle of really good St. Julien at 2*s.*, Niersteiner, 2*s.* 6*d.*; Carlowitz, the same; excellent white and red Catalan, 1*s.* 4*d.* to 1*s.* 8*d.*; superior Old Jamaica rum, 3*s.*; Martell's brandy, 3*d.* under London prices; aerated water, 2*d.* a bottle, with patent stopper; and everything else in the liquid line in proportion.

Altogether living is rather cheap in Birchington. Good bread is sold at 7½*d.* the quartern loaf. Meat is about a penny a pound cheaper than in London; fish, as a rule, low-priced. I have bought as many as a dozen fresh herrings for 4*d.* or 5*d.*, and 120 large sprats at the same low figure. Eggs (new-laid) may be got at 1*s.* a dozen in proper seasons; good butter at 1*s.* 6*d.* a pound; pure milk, 4*d.* a quart; potatoes, 6*d.* to 10*d.* a gallon. Last March I bought five nice cauliflowers for 3*d.* A couple of plump fowls may be got at 4*s.* to 5*s.* Lettuces were 1*d.* to

1½*d.* a head; frame cucumbers, 4*d.* to 8*d.*; and so on in proportion.

Fruit, as a rule, is plentiful and cheap; but last year there was unhappily a destructive blight on the orchards. Yet the prices of strawberries, raspberries, currants, gooseberries, cherries, &c., kept moderate.

There are several extensive nursery-grounds and large well-stocked orchards here, notably the Goodbourn nursery-grounds and orchard, where almost any and every thing can be got cheap that the central avenue of Covent Garden can boast of.

The grocery and other stores need not dread comparison with London establishments. There are notably Pemble's and Hinckley's grocery shops, where everything in the line is to be got, of excellent quality and cheap.

Birchington boasts a local Whiteley (a Mr. Stone) in the drapery and hosiery line. There is also a most unpretending ironmongery, glass, and china warehouse, kept by the parish clerk and registrar, which, under the comprehensive designation of 'sundries,' would really seem to supply all things and any and every thing, from a Seidlitz powder and a peppermint draught or a box of patent pills or *ointment* up to a sheet-anchor, shoes, boots, pans, kettles, coals, and paraffin included. The Birchingtonians altogether are simple-minded, honest, and confiding.

I remember, when many years ago (ahem!) I was in the military service of France, that whenever we happened to import our glorious civilisation into, up to then, yet unexplored regions in Algeria, the very first mark and sign of said glorious civilisation which we set about establishing was the venerable old institution of the *lock-up.* Will it be believed that the ways, manners, and customs of this benighted Birchington are so barbarously simple and primitive that there is positively no lock-up to be found here! and only one policeman, who is hardly ever to be seen, except from Saturday night to Monday morning, when another constable is sent down from Margate to join him on 'special duty, Saturday and Sunday being the two chief drinking days of the lower strata of the Birchington social formation. But even among these, drunkenness is rather rare, and, except with the brick-fielders occasionally on a Saturday night, seldom of the rowing and fighting kind, the votaries of John Barleycorn being preferentially given here to musical manifestations, in which harmless propensity the sober part of the community share to the fullest extent. There is notably a society of bell-ringers, who 'practise' a merry peal on Saturday night in Queker Park. As I find that distance lends enchantment to the sound, I always make it a point to take a walk to Margate on these occasions.

Birchington boasts also an 'Institute,' which is situate in the square. It is a most unpretending and unobtrusive place, as, for the matter of that, all else may be said to be in this sturdy old Kentish village-town, yet it fully answers its intended purpose. It serves to keep boys and youths away from the taproom, and to train them to purer pleasure and higher aspirations. Visitors are freely admitted to the reading-room, &c., on payment of the very moderate charge of one penny a day. Connected with the Institute is a cricket club, which practises in Queker Park, where Captain Cotton, the present owner of the estate, has kindly placed a large plot of ground at the service of the cricketers. I have had occasion to see this team at work, and I must say they play a very fair game indeed, and need not fear matching themselves against more pretentious cricket clubs. They welcome visitors with open arms, and treat them with truly rural urbanity—if the seeming paradox may be permitted to pass.

An admirable feature in the character of the people in general is the almost universal honesty and probity found in even the humblest class of society here. Fencing-in fields would seem the rare exception, not the rule. Cabbages, potatoes, turnips, and crops are left well-nigh unprotected. Workmen's tools are left lying about freely overnight with perfect impunity; so are lots of wood, and occasionally even more valuable portable property. People will take trips to Margate or Herne Bay without securing the doors and windows of their dwellings, yet they expect to find their property intact on their return—and this expectation is never disappointed, they say. Beggars are rather exotics in Birchington, and even that most formidable plague of country places, the tramp, rages here only in an endemic and much mitigated form. Birchington may justly boast of a most fruitful soil. It produces magnificent crops of wheat and all other cereals, also abundance of clover, lucerne, sainfoin, and other fodder-plants. I saw the same field of clover cut four times in the course of last year. Potatoes, turnips, and mangel-wurzel are plentiful. Indeed, altogether the Birchington farmer has but little cause to indulge in extravagant grumblings, nor, to tell the honest truth, is he much inclined to do so.

There would seem to be a strange superstition among Londoners that with the advent of August or September, at the latest, ends the proper bathing season on the Kentish coast. People will flock to Brighton in October, which is comparatively very expensive, and certainly not suited to every constitution.

Now the sea at Birchington happens to be the same as at Brighton and other places on the British coast, just as warm and fit for bathing in October as it is in July, and fine, warm, sunny days all through autumn are rather the rule here than the exception. Even in dreary winter Birchington is comparatively a healthy place to live in.

The 'high-rent' fever passes away by the end of August at the latest, and living is incomparably cheaper in every way here than at Brighton, or any other marine health resort on the British coast. I may honestly and sincerely advise all invalids suffering from asthma, affection of the lungs, skin diseases, gout and rheumatism, dyspepsia, and the manifold disturbances of the hepatic function, to give Birchington a fair trial—both in and out of season.

A SONG OF UNDINE.

I HAVE been where the brooklet flowing
    Rushes onward, untrammelled and free ;
And I would that I too could be going
    With my brooklet down to the sea.
I love not the flowers in the meadow,
    They are silent the summer-day long :
I love better to lie in the shadow,
    And list to my brooklet's song.

My brooklet sings softly and clearly
    Unto me, and the moss and the fern ;
And the swallows come too, and love dearly
    Its waves when the noon-rays burn.
The willow stoops downward, and listens
    To its murmur of yearning unrest,
And a diamond coronet glistens
    On the rose that my brooklet loves best.

When the rose stoopeth down in her splendour
    To mirror her face in its light,
Its song is more pleading and tender
    Than the nightingale's hymn to the night.
And the rose-petals hear it and shiver,
    Like the leaves round the nightingale's nest ;
And they faint and they fall, and for ever
    Float away on the brook's heaving breast.

PEGGY.

A Pastoral.

By EDWARD A. MORTON.

A GOOD many years ago I was invited by my uncle Peter to spend a month or so at his place in Steepletown. I had never seen my uncle in my life to my recollection; and from what I had heard my mother, who was his own sister, say of him on different occasions, I was not at all anxious to make his acquaintance. He had always been represented as an eccentric old bachelor, who had imprisoned himself for life in a large house in a little country town, and was never seen nor heard of by any of his relations. The letter which conveyed the invitation to me, however, brought back many pleasant memories of my uncle Peter to my mother's mind. But I could not help thinking that these were only revived for my benefit, especially as my mother now avoided any disagreeable reference to her brother; and the mark of my uncle's favour did not give me such pleasure as it did my parents, who did nothing else but talk of the grand prospects before me from the time the invitation arrived till the day the visit was paid. The prospects seemed to me anything but cheerful.

Uncle Peter was not the man I expected to find him. When the servant carried my name up to him on my arrival at his house, I became quite frightened as I sat in the drawing-room waiting for him to make his appearance. If he had suddenly sprung through the floor or dropped from the ceiling, I should not have been more surprised than I was when he opened the door and walked into the room; for, instead of the wicked old monster I had expected to meet, I found myself face to face with a man who was everything a man should be—except a husband.

My uncle was a bachelor, and a bachelor by conviction. That is to say, he might have married long enough ago if he had so minded, without having turned single blessedness into married misery, for he was quite rich enough to keep a wife; so rich was he, indeed, that there were few girls who would have had the heart—inasmuch as the heart enters into the contract—to have refused him even when he was old and gray, as he was at the time my story begins. He told me as much himself before we had been many hours together. But the songs of the syren, he gave me to understand, had no charm for him; he had no ear for that kind of music. He told me confidentially that he had only loved one woman, except his mother—and he hoped I loved my mother; and I suppose he took it for granted that I did, for he did not give me time to say so, but went on to observe that he had never loved but one woman in the whole of his life.

When I asked him sympathetically why he had not married her, he laughed outright in my face.

'For the simplest reason in the world, my boy,' he said, clapping his hands heavily on my shoulders. 'Because—'

'Because she refused you,' I

suggested gravely. I certainly did not see anything to laugh at in that, but my uncle took it as a very fine joke.

He explained to me that the lady in question was his niece; and, as I did not know what to say to that, I inquired meekly whether she was still alive.

'She's your cousin Tabitha, boy,' cried my uncle.

'Cousin Tabitha—of course!' I replied. I thought my uncle expected me to answer him, and I did not know what else to say.

'Nicest little woman in the world; dearest little woman in existence; sweetest little woman in creation,' continued my uncle.

'Is she—'

I was going to say 'pretty,' for I felt an increasing interest in my charming cousin; but I hesitated, for fear my uncle had not mentioned beauty with her other attractions for some reason of his own.

'Is she what?' said my uncle sharply, in a tone which implied that he was ready to give me any information I required.

'Is she really?' I returned innocently.

My uncle then gave me a second edition of her praises, with additions, and observed that I should soon be able to judge for myself. Cousin Tabitha, I concluded, was also staying with my uncle.

'And speaking of women,' says he, 'I suppose we shall have to get you a wife presently.'

I remarked that I should no doubt be able to get one for myself. It struck me then that my uncle intended me to marry my cousin Tabitha. I turned that idea over in my mind as I dressed for dinner. I meet my cousin for the first time under my uncle's roof; my uncle represents her to me in glowing colours; she is all his fancy paints her; I fall in love with her, marry her, inherit my uncle's fortune: this is the train of thought which runs through my head as I stand before my looking-glass. I am very careful in the selection of a tie, and unusually long over my hair. I was prepared to fall in love with my cousin at first sight, and, with my heart beating like a *reveille* drum, I went downstairs to meet my destiny.

When I entered the dining-room I found myself alone. I walked to the end of the room, and stood for some time at the window, looking at a dead wall opposite, and listening eagerly for the sound of footsteps on the stairs. I was left alone in a state of dreadful agitation for about twenty minutes; and at the very moment when I least expected it, the door suddenly opened. I was posing in front of the looking-glass, arranging my tie, which was unable to keep stiff any longer, and rehearsing the pretty speech and the polite bow with which I was to receive my cousin. I turned from the looking-glass as the door opened, and confronted my uncle Peter. If cousin Tabitha had been with him I could not have said a word.

'Tabitha not here?' said uncle Peter, as he entered.

'No, sir,' I answered unconcernedly.

'Ring the bell; we'll have dinner up.'

The tread of heavy feet in the passage followed hard on the ring of the bell. I did not wish to betray my emotion to the servant; so I removed my eyes from the door-handle, which I had been watching intently, and fixed them on the table-cloth. As I did so my cousin Tabitha—for it was she who had tramped along the passage—marched into the room.

She marched into the room like a soldier. She saluted my uncle with a kiss; and before I could get a glimpse of her feet—for I was curious to know whether she wore top-boots—she came behind my back and kissed me too; then she took a seat at the table, and I looked up at her for the first time.

She was not the Tabitha I intended her to be. She disappointed me in every way. She was much less than I had thought in every respect, with one exception; for her age was very much more than I had expected. Cousin Tabitha was a woman of forty-five at least, and by no means a pleasant person to look at. A Hindoo might have taken her for an idol, and worshipped her; but my love for my cousin Tabitha flew out at the window as she came in at the door.

Cousin Tabitha was tall, of a stern disposition, and military in her appearance and her habits. She affected high collars and short-braided jackets, and always wore a belt. She was captain of my uncle's household, and had been so many years; and the strict discipline she maintained, together with the loud voice and peremptory manner in which she issued her orders to the servants, often struck me as being very like a way they have in the army. She seemed to be thoroughly contented with a spinster's lot; and, although my uncle spoke to her as to a child, she was not ashamed of her forty-five years, but confessed her age as frankly as an old campaigner. Her love for my uncle Peter was the one gentle trait in her character; to him she was so tender, so kind, so true, that it was not surprising that he, in his unchanging love for her, still saw in her the little niece who had loved him alway.

To me Tabitha was not unkind, but I could not think of making a companion of her; and my uncle, with a delicate consideration which I well understood, avoided me

every morning after breakfast, except when the day was wet; and then he would invite me to his library, saying if I cared to spend an hour with him he should be pleased to see me, but if I had rather postpone our interview till the evening, by all means to do so. He exerted himself much to promote my happiness, devising a hundred little schemes for my amusement; but the idea that an old man was an uncongenial companion to a young one kept him from seeking ever to share my pleasures with me. And so I was left to myself, to row, to ride, and to sketch the country round about.

I had made a number of sketches, all of which my dear old uncle and my military cousin admired and praised beyond their merits; I had taken views of the town, the church, the castle, the lea, the hills, the railway-arch, and the farm, as seen from the north, south, east, and west; and was going to put my sketch-book aside for a while, when my uncle, one evening, suggested that I should take a sketch of the park, between Steepletown and Crumble.

Thither I repaired the very next morning, and, having chosen a spot from which I had the best view of the surrounding scenery, I sat down to work. I had finished my sketch, and was very well pleased with it, and was debating with myself whether I should make an old man coming up the path from Steepletown or an old woman descending the slope from Crumble, when Nature put a model in my way. At first I caught sight of a large straw hat; as it approached, a rosy face appeared beneath it; and presently I saw a young woman, with a basket on her arm, hurrying along towards Crumble. She drew a watch from her bosom, and as she put it back she doubled her pace. She passed me before

I could say 'Good-evening,' but not before I could see that she had a very comely face and a very pretty figure.

She was not many yards beyond me, when I found that she had dropped her purse. I called after her, and she turned her head and walked on. By this time she was already out of hearing, so I started after her, calling to her as I ran ; and once more she looked over her shoulder, and, seeing me pursuing her, she took to her heels. I held the purse aloft, and shouted at the top of my voice; but the more I signalled to her to stop the faster she went, so I put the purse in my pocket and my sketch-book under my arm, and turned towards home.

My uncle was delighted with my sketch. Cousin Tabitha startled me by asking whether I had not forgotten to put a figure in the path. I looked at her suspiciously, and answered that I certainly ought to have done so. I said that I would make a better sketch of the place the next day, as that had been done very hurriedly ; and I should not fail to take advantage of my cousin's excellent suggestion. My uncle, under the impression that I was putting myself to trouble solely to please him—and I was mean enough to encourage him to think so—declared himself thoroughly satisfied with the sketch as it was. The fact was that the figure had passed out of my mind for the moment; but it had since returned, to take a permanent place there.

There was no harm surely in fostering an intention to return the purse, as I had determined to do, even if I should have to sit in the park day after day till I left Steepletown, waiting for the owner to pass by. Thinking that the contents of the purse might help me to carry out my virtuous purpose, I opened it. It contained a little money, a thimble, an elastic band, an advertisement cut from a newspaper, and a half-sheet of note-paper covered with bad writing, which I took the liberty of trying to read, and which, as well as I could make out, referred to certain transactions in eggs and butter with E. Higgles, of 11 Lucifer-lane, Steepletown. There was nothing to be done but to return to the scene of my sketch.

My second sketch was a decided failure; for whereas I had forgotten the figure yesterday, to-day it was the only thing I could think of. My trees toppled over, as if they had taken to drink since I saw them last, and the path deviated from the course of rectitude which it had hitherto pursued. I was vexed at heart because I had not had the opportunity to restore the purse to its owner, and I returned home later than usual, for I had delayed with the hope of seeing her, and presented my shameful sketch to my uncle. He took it, and thanked me cordially for it; but I could see that he preferred my first one, although he would not for all the world and everything in it have hurt my feelings by saying as much. I explained to him that somehow I had not been in the humour for sketching, but as I had promised him a second sketch that day I did not care to disappoint him altogether, however much my sketch itself must do so; I had made up my mind, however, to do justice to the beautiful spot he had pointed out to me, and I hoped to bring back something better another day.

The next day I went to Lucifer-lane, not to sketch, but to interview E. Higgles. E. Higgles was an irascible old woman, and as I was not inclined to tarry long with her, I went straight to the point, and asked whether she could tell me the name of the young lady who had called, I believe, the day before yesterday, to make purchases of eggs and butter. When I had finished, I paused for Mrs. Higgles to reply.

'Well, young man,' she mumbled, 'what do you want? Speak up!' and she literally lent me her ear.

I saw at once that she was deaf, and had not heard a word of what I had said; in fact, she did not seem to know even that I had been speaking.

'If you please, Mrs. Higgles,' I commenced.

'Well, well,' she said impatiently.

'Can you tell—'

'Not well, young man; not at all well,' she murmured.

'Can you tell me—' I screamed.

'What?'

'Can you tell me—*that?*' and I took the bill from the purse and placed it on the counter before her.

She picked it up, and glancing at it, she told me there were no new-laid eggs to-day.

I requested Mrs. Higgles to read the paper.

After reading it over six or seven times, and carrying on a long conversation in whispers with herself, she informed me she did not understand figures, and that her boy John would be there by and by, and that he would explain the mistake to the young lady when she called for the things this afternoon.

Having obtained the information I wanted, I walked out of the shop, leaving Mrs. Higgles mumbling such vengeance against her boy John as she did not seem to me to have the strength to execute.

I went later on to the park to wait for my young lady. After a while I thought I saw her coming up from Crumble, and I rushed forward to meet her. As I advanced, it struck me that I had made a mistake, and my doubts increased as the distance between us diminished; and when they were confirmed, as they were within a hundred yards, I turned back. When the lady upon whom I had wasted so much energy passed me, I was lying on my back, pulling up the grass impatiently, and scattering it to the wind. From the apprehensive manner in which she looked at me as she went by, I believe she must have thought me mad. She stared at me as if I had been pulling my hair out by the roots instead of the grass, and when she caught my eye she made a curve towards the hither side of the path. It amused me highly to think how strange my behaviour altogether must have appeared to such a demure old lady as she was. This idea so tickled my fancy that I fairly roared with laughter; and my roaring, which must have seemed to her as maniacal as my run, so horrified the old lady that she scampered out of the park as if a wild bull had been at her heels.

I should have gone forward to meet my young lady, but there were two roads to Crumble, and I was afraid that she might walk out of the village at one side as I walked in the other way; so I contented myself, as well as I could, with the survey of both roads from the middle of the park. I waited and watched restlessly for her coming. Every bonnet I espied I thought was hers; and the poor specimens of millinery, and the poorer specimens of humanity, which imposed upon my credulity were so numerous that when at length I saw her tripping along, I could scarcely believe my eyes. But there she was, and no mistake about it, basket and all; and if the distance did not deceive my sight, there was somebody with her, and—as I lived—it was a man!

As they approached, he left her side, and walked on in front, and by the time he had reached the park he was so far ahead of her that my peace of mind was restored. He had passed me long before she came up to the spot where I stood leaning against a tree, smiling upon her as she advanced.

To my utter astonishment, she did not seem to recognise me as she went by—did not seem to see me, although I could have sworn that she looked hard at the tree. I coughed slightly, to attract her attention, and as she did not hear it, I walked after her, and touched her gently on the shoulder. She gave me such an indignant look that I was almost afraid to speak.

'Excuse me, miss,' I said politely.

She tossed her head, and told me pertly that she did not know me, and, although she did not say so, evidently did not wish to. I tried to speak to her of her purse, but she refused to hear me. She would not excuse me; she would not allow me to explain; she would not permit me to tell her anything; so dropping all ceremonial phrases, I took the purse from my pocket, and said, as bluntly as if I had that moment picked it up,

'Is this your purse, miss?'

Before we came to the end of the park I had found out that she lived with her uncle, who was a bootmaker by trade; that she had never been to London, but her uncle had; that she came over to Steepletown three times a week, and did not come more frequently because she did not care to; that her age was twenty, and her name was Peggy Giles; that she would not be long in the town, and I might wait for her, if I liked, under a tree she pointed out to me. I had found out, too, by this time,

that I was desperately in love with her.

She soon came back. I expected she would have had some difficulty in finding me among the trees; but she remembered where I was at once, almost as if she had been familiar with our trysting-place. Then I took charge of the basket, and we walked on slowly towards Crumble. In another respect we made rapid progress; for our friendship had grown quite ripe before we reached the end of the park, where we parted; not, you may be sure, before we had arranged to meet the next day.

I watched her out of sight, and then turned homewards, building castles in the air as I went. In thinking of Peggy, however, I had forgotten all about dinner; and when I reached home, I was ashamed to look the clock in the face, it was so late. I entered the dining-room, quietly took my seat at table, and sat in silence, waiting for my uncle, who considered punctuality a point of honour, to call my attention to the time. But he did not say a word, which only made me more uneasy. Cousin Tabitha soon noticed my distress, and, misinterpreting it, asked kindly what was the matter with me. I pleaded a slight headache.

'I suppose you are beginning to find Steepletown dull?' said my uncle.

'On the contrary,' I replied, with no particular meaning.

'What have you been doing today?'

'I've—well, I've been to the park,' I returned, as composedly as possible. 'But I haven't finished your sketch, uncle.'

I had not yet commenced it.

'To the park again!' cried cousin Tabitha. I turned quite pale. 'Do you know what?' she continued, looking me full in the face.

'What, cousin Tabitha?'

'I've found you out, that's what.' The colour of my face changed from white to red in an instant. '*You've been smoking.*'

The next day I went to the park, and as I arrived there an hour before the time appointed for our meeting, I commenced to sketch. I became so absorbed in my work that I did not think of Peggy till I saw her standing beside me.

'Well ?' she said.

'Well, Peggy,' I replied, 'what?'

'What do you want to tell me ?'

'Tell you ? What do you mean, dear ?'

'Don't you remember what you said yesterday when you left me yonder ?'

'Of course I do, Peggy;' and I laughed to think of her innocence. 'And can't you guess what it is ?'

She shook her head.

'Sit down here, then, and I'll tell you. Look at me, Peggy; don't look at that'—she was admiring my sketch—'look straight in my face. Do you know that you are a very pretty girl, Peggy ?'

She told me playfully to 'Go along !'

I declared my love for her there and then in an eloquent speech, ending with an offer of my hand in marriage. I asked her earnestly what she had to say to my proposal. She said 'Go along !' again. I explained to her that I was speaking seriously, for she seemed to think otherwise; and I arranged to meet her again the next day to receive her answer. Then we strolled about the park; and when we separated I flattered myself that I had made some impression upon her heart. I told her at parting to consider well what I had said to her, but not to mention it on any account to her uncle.

Day after day I met Peggy, and wooed her in the park. Sometimes I went over to Crumble

and waited for her at the corner of Whipple-street, where she lived. One day, when she was later than usual, I walked boldly into her uncle's shop. As soon as I opened the door, an ugly little man in his shirt-sleeves popped up from behind a counter, and invited me to come in. He was delighted to see me, and inquired very amiably what he could do for me. It appeared that he thought I had come to buy boots; and when he asked me a second time what I wanted to-day, I had not the courage to tell him what I really did want, so I said shoe-laces.

After opening all the drawers in the shop, and pulling very nearly every box from the shelves, he stepped up a ladder leading to a cupboard, which, when he opened it, seemed to contain nothing but a flight of steps. Putting his head inside the cupboard, he called out,

'Where's them laces got to ?'

'Don't know, uncle,' answered a voice, which I knew at once.

'Jest come down and look for 'em, then.'

'Sha'n't,' returned the voice from above.

'Sha'n't yer? Come down d'rectly, Miss Imperence, will yer? There's a young gentleman, I tell yer, waitin' to be served.'

I fancy I heard Peggy—for of course it was she—say, 'O, bother them laces !' as she appeared at the top of the ladder.

When she saw me she was not the least disconcerted. She stood there, and addressed me with all the simplicity in the world, although I beckoned to her not to recognise me. 'I didn't know it was you,' she said; and her uncle standing by heard every word. 'I shall be ready in a minute. I just want to put a stitch or two into my hat ;' and she vanished.

From that day forth I was a frequent visitor at the bootmaker's shop. On two or three occasions I met my uncle Peter there; but he never referred to our meetings, and actually pretended, as it appeared, to think that my boots really wanted as much attending to as I made out. Peggy's uncle, who became more familiar with me than I liked, seemed to understand how matters stood, although I had never broached the subject to him. In fact, it was presently as well known in the village that I intended to marry Peggy Giles as if I had published the banns at Crumble Church.

Three weeks passed, and I was more in love with Peggy than ever. I had made up my mind to marry her; but I had no idea precisely when, and I was therefore very much surprised when she asked me one day whether my father was aware of my intention. I replied that I had not yet told him anything about it; and I was sorely worried to think how I should ever be able to do so. And from that moment my love for Peggy commenced to be a trouble to me as well as a pleasure.

I was sketching, and Peggy was sitting beside me, when the conversation just alluded to took place. I had arranged to meet her in the park that day, having heard my uncle say at breakfast that he intended to drive over to Crumble to see Giles the boot-maker, and not wishing to excite his suspicions by meeting him there again, if I had hitherto been fortunate enough not to have done so. Peggy was very late, so I set to work again at the sketch which had been left so long unfinished. I did not expect to see her that day, it was so late; but at length she came. She told me that she could not stay long with me, and bade me go on with my work. I promised to give her the sketch if she would wait till I had finished

it. After the conversation I have recorded, however, I continued it, as I had commenced it, with the intention of presenting it to my uncle. At any rate, Peggy did not wait, for she rose to go in less than twenty minutes. I accompanied her only to the end of the park. I wished her good-bye, and was going to kiss her, when she said that there was somebody coming; and with that she snatched her hand out of mine, and was gone. I looked down the road and saw a lady, tall and erect, walking briskly up the hill. She carried her umbrella like a soldier carries his gun; and, as she advanced, I recognised my military cousin.

I returned to my sketch, and was busily at work when cousin Tabitha entered the park. She halted in front of me.

'It's you,' she said, 'is it?'

I could not make out what she meant; but I turned very red as I answered,

'Yes, cousin Tabitha. I'm just finishing—'

'Haven't you finished that sketch yet? Well, little man, you're sitting near a very unlucky spot, let me tell you. Your uncle Peter lost a diamond ring there,' and she pointed with her umbrella to our trysting-tree. 'I say,' she continued, after a pause, 'you've been up to your tricks again, I see.'

'What tricks, cousin Tabitha?'

'You know,' she replied; and she shouldered her umbrella and marched away, leaving me to brood over my doubts and fears.

As soon as I reached home cousin Tabitha told me that uncle Peter wished to speak to me, and was waiting for me in the library. I guessed at once what he had to say, and, pale and trembling, I sought his presence. When I entered the library my uncle was writing.

'I daresay you know what I have

to speak to you about?' he said, after a few minutes.

'I think so, uncle Peter,' I replied, looking down at my boots.

'Of course you have found Steepletown dull,' he resumed, 'very dull—eh?'

I made no answer.

'Don't say you haven't,' he continued, 'because I know you have.'

I thought this was intended for satire, so I said nothing.

'Perhaps you have managed to amuse yourself pretty well—pretty well.'

I thought we were coming to it then; but here, to my astonishment, he turned off in another direction altogether.

'But a week or two in Paris would perhaps induce you to think better of Steepletown when you return to London. Now what do you say to a fortnight in Paris?'

I said 'yes,' with all my heart; and we arranged forthwith that I should drive over to Dover on the following day, and go by the night-packet to Calais.

The next morning I went over to Crumble to take leave of Peggy, and once more I met my uncle at the bootmaker's shop. As I walked into the shop he took up his hat and walked out, and I found myself alone with Peggy. I told her that it pained me much to part from her, but I was obliged to go that very night to Paris. I begged her not to grieve at my absence, and she promised me that she would not.

I returned to England at the end of a fortnight, and from Dover I drove straightway to Crumble. I passed through Steepletown, but I did not call upon my uncle, as the picture I had in my mind of Peggy waiting for my return hurried me on to the bootmaker's shop in Whipple-street. But no welcome was waiting for me there. When I pulled up at the bootmaker's shop I found it closed, and Peggy and her uncle were gone, no one could tell me where.

I consoled myself with the reflection that it was really the best thing that could have happened. By the time I reached Steepletown I felt very pleased to be released from my engagement, and I wished never, never to see Peggy again; and so, with a clear conscience, I went to pay my duties to my uncle. I found him in his library, and his wife was sitting at his side—for my uncle had actually become a husband since I saw him last.

He had married Peggy Giles!

STRAWBERRY LEAVES.

By RICHARD DOWLING,
AUTHOR OF 'THE MYSTERY OF KILLARD,' 'THE WEIRD SISTERS,' 'UNDER ST. PAUL'S,' ETC.

Part the First.
THE DUKE OF LONGACRE.

CHAPTER VIII.
ON BOARD THE YACHT SEABIRD.

THE bodily and mental conditions of the Marquis of Southwold, which forbade him living ashore any length of time, were many, and almost insurmountable. The greatest doctors had of course been consulted, but without being able to afford any relief. They had called his lordship's symptoms by a number of very learned names, seldom heard in the medical profession. They could go no farther than that. They had tried every resource of their art, and had failed. Men at the top of the profession can afford to confess failure much better than their brethren of a less degree. When the greatest doctors declare a patient must die soon, the sooner that patient dies the better for conventional decency.

The doctors had not said that Lord Southwold must die soon, but they had declared him incurable, and advised him to try the sea. He tried the sea, and the remedy was most successful. On shore his eyes were tender and dim, his limbs were dull and nerveless, his appetite failed, and his spirits sank almost to melancholia. But no sooner did he go on board a ship than all these symptoms began to abate. His eyes grew stronger, his sight improved, the lassitude abated, he could eat with relish, and his spirits gradually returned.

The Marquis of Southwold was now a man of thirty-eight years of age, tall, lank, long-cheeked, and without the hereditary bow-legs. His features were vague and expressionless. He had a remarkably large mouth, and dull faded gray eyes. There was upon his face always the look of pain past rather than pain present. His face was that of one who was fading out, rather than of one who suffered any violent assault. He was more languid and subdued than his father, but, like him too, he was very taciturn.

His health was good while on board the yacht, although she only lay at anchor in Silver Bay, beneath the ducal castle. Thus, for a good portion of the year, his grace's schooner-yacht, the Seabird, lay at anchor in Silver Bay. The bay was excellently suited to the requirements of the ailing nobleman; for it was protected from the wind by high lands on three sides, and from the rolling sea of the German Ocean by a barrier of rocks, extending more than halfway across the bay from the northern side. The best anchorage was just under the shelter of this jagged barrier of rocks. Here, even in the most severe gales from the east, the water was always smooth. The holding ground also was excellent; and the rocks, as they rose twenty, thirty, forty feet high, protected the hull of the schooner from the force of the wind.

The entrance to this bay was safe and easy. It was about a quarter of a mile wide, and quite free from rocks. The largest vessel afloat would have water enough in any part of that opening, from a point twenty fathoms from the end of the bar to a point twenty fathoms from the opposite shore of the bay. The only great danger was if, in tacking in or out in heavy weather, anything should give way; for it was necessary to reach in or out on the one tack, there being no room for tacking in the passage itself in a strong wind and high sea.

Of course, if Lord Southwold wished for a steam-yacht, he might have the finest that could be designed. But he could not endure a steamer. It was almost worse for him than being on shore. The air is never brisk aboard a steamboat, and then the vibration jarred upon him horribly.

He was not an adventurous sailor, and did not court adventure. He did not love the sea for its perils, or for the chance it affords of enjoying the sense of struggling successfully against an enemy. He looked on dwelling afloat as a birthright, or birthwrong, against which there was no good in growling. His father allowed him twenty thousand a year pocket-money. He would have given up his twenty thousand a year and his right of succession to the title and vast estates, if he might have a thousand a year and the constitution of a navvy. It is not utterly impossible that a navvy may become a duke, but it is utterly impossible that a man with such a constitution as his could enjoy the health of a navvy.

He found it impossible to spend his pocket-money, and he hated the notion of it accumulating at his banker's. When he had a large balance, it always seemed as if it were placed there as the wages of his bodily infirmities. He hated money as honourable men hate debt. When he found a balance of ten or twelve thousand at his banker's, he could, he knew, draw it out and drop it over the side of the yacht. But that would be wilful waste. He might have given it in charity; but he had so little contact with the world that he had hardly any sense of the necessity for charity, except through reading, which is a cold and formal way of kindling one's sympathy. He might have gambled; but he had hardly ever attended a race or coursing match. They very rarely had a guest at the Castle or on board the yacht; and he did not care for cards, even if guests were more numerous. He led an isolated and dreary life; but he had experience of hardly any other. He could not, with comfort, live more than a few days ashore, or, with safety, more than a couple of weeks.

He was now no longer what might be called a young man, and he intended not to marry. His feeling was, that when such as he was the only representative of his race, his race ought to die out. On this point his father had expostulated with him in vain. He never would marry. The vital power of his race was dying in him: let it die. When his father died he should be Duke of Shropshire, with three to four hundred thousand a year. What better off should he be then than he now was? No better. He should, in fact, be worse, for he would have lost the only friend and companion he had, his father. He should have to draw more cheques, to see more people, to transact more business. But he should eat nor drink nor lie no better, nor should his health be improved. His capacity for enjoyment would be in no way increased, and there would be a great addition to his labours. His father was hale and hardy, and might live twenty-five years yet ; and the heir hoped with all his heart he might die before his father.

He marry ! Why should he marry ? What woman would care to share the stupid life he was compelled to lead ? No woman would be likely to love him for himself; for he knew he was an uninteresting invalid. Thousands of women would marry him because he was Marquis of Southwold and heir to the great dukedom of Shropshire. That went without saying. But no woman would willingly share his life ; and why should he marry a woman who would unwillingly abide by him, or insist upon keeping up fitting state in London and the country while he was a frail despised rover of the sea? No ; let the race go, and let the lawyers pocket the spoil—the spoil would be enough to found fifty families — and let the title die. What good would the title be to him ? Could he soothe the winds with it, or stop a leak with it, or claw off a lee-shore with it?

Neither the Duke nor the Marquis was an intellectual man. But when one is everlastingly on shipboard he must do something. Common sailors who cannot read cultivate superstition, a knowledge of the weather, and the use of abnormal quantities of tobacco. A sailor carries away, from a book he has read, a more accurate notion of what is in it than any other class of man of similar intellectual lights and acquirements. As the sailor who has studied his chart by day can see, when approaching an invisible shore through the trackless darkness of water and night, in his mind's eye the shore and the bea- cons of the shore that still lie hidden below the horizon, so the sailor who has read a book can see that book by aid of the chart he has made of it when the book has been closed up for ever.

As neither father nor son played the fiddle, or carved ivory, or cared much for shooting at bottles in the water, or hunting the great sea- serpent to earth, if the phrase may be allowed, or discovering the North Pole, or exploring cannibal islands, or going in search of novelty in foreign parts, a great deal of their time was spent in reading and fishing. Fishing at sea is not a very high or exciting art. Indeed, it is an art that is almost independ- ent of the artist. And it is almost necessary to have some other oc- cupation at the same time, so that reading goes hand-in-hand with fishing.

Thus it happened that both the Duke and his son read enormous piles of newspapers and books. The Duke read newspapers chiefly, and political books, and articles in the quarterlies. When a young man he had been active in politics, but now he took only a reflected interest in them. He hated Radi- cals with a complete and abiding hatred. He would root them out of the country at any cost. They disturbed his cities and boroughs. They were a low lot, and never washed their hands.

The Marquis of Southwold, on the contrary, took little or no in- terest in politics. As far as he had any political feeling, it was against his order and in favour of the Radicals. This feeling he kept to himself, not because he was afraid to put forward anything opposed to his father's views, but because he did not care to speak on a subject he knew so little about. Personally he had a poor opinion of dukes, but they might in reality be better than Radicals for all he knew to the contrary, for he had met two dukes besides his father, but never a Radical. He knew there was a wide gulf between dukes and Radicals. He had an idea a Radical was a kind of political poet. He didn't think much of poets; he knew little of Radicals; and he was perfectly sure dukes were useless. He had a vague general conviction that politicians who were not dukes were fools or rogues, but he was quite sure dukes were supernumeraries without parts in the play of life.

But if he did not care anything about poetry and politics, he was much interested in fiction. One of the few ways open to him, by which he could now and then reduce by a few pounds the balance at his banker's, was by ordering all the new novels which appeared, and ordering them, not at a library, but from the publisher, through his bookseller. Thus, while this arrangement existed, every author who got out a novel was sure of finding at least one buyer.

It so happened that in the same month of June Edward Graham set up his easel to paint that landscape under Anerly Bridge, a novel was published called the *Duke of Fenwick*, a romance, by Charles Augustus Cheyne. According to the ordinary rule, the novel had been published in three volumes before it had fully run out through the paper in which it appeared from week to week.

The same week the book was published it found its way down to Silverview Castle, and from the Castle to the yacht Seabird, into the hands of George Temple Cheyne, by courtesy called Marquis of Southwold.

The title naturally attracted the nobleman, who had no faith in dukes. He opened the book and found, by a curious coincidence, that the book had been written by a namesake.

'A book by a namesake,' thought he; 'but by no relative! There never yet was a Cheyne who could write anything more worthy of public notice than 'Trespassers will be prosecuted. Dogs found in these preserves will be shot.'

But a book by a namesake dealing with a duke was of much more than ordinary interest; so he immediately found the easiest of couches, and lay down under the awning on deck to hear what his namesake had to say about a duke.

Certainly he had never met a duke like his Grace of Fenwick; but then he had met only his own father and two more. The two strange dukes he had met were like the farmers who came to pay his father rent. But then his father was very like a groom or jockey, and yet was not particularly fond of riding or of horses; so that it was, perhaps, not the nature of dukes to look like what they were. His namesake had no thought of drawing any member of the Shropshire family, for his duke was represented as being tall, well-made, and handsome. None of the Shropshire family had been tall, well-made, and handsome. They had all been short and bandy-legged until he had come. He was tall, it was true, and not bandy-legged; but then he was not handsome or well-made.

Stop, there had been his uncle, Lord George Temple Cheyne, who had been tall, well-made, and handsome; but he had died upwards of thirty years ago. What a strange thing that the two last representatives of the race should have escaped the hereditary bowlegs! What a pity his uncle had not lived! He would have married, no doubt, and then his sons would have come into the title, and the property and the old name might have been carried down generations by men of wholesome make.

'What a ridiculous way that story ended! A violoncello-player turned out to be the real Duke of Fenwick. I wish to goodness he could turn me from being Marquis of Southwold into a man who had only warts on his fingers from the strings of the big fiddle. He wouldn't catch me going back again to the Marquis or Duke of Anything or Anywhere. Not I. I'd very soon pay off that land-lord. But stop! How could I pay him off if I had no money? If I was the poor violoncello-player, I shouldn't have any money. But I am always wanting not to have any money; and if I had none when he came, I'd tell him I couldn't pay him then, but that I would the moment I got my next quarter's allowance from the duke— But I should be the Duke of Fenwick then, and there would be, as far as I should be concerned, no Duke of Shropshire. Who really should I be then? It is the most puzzling thing I ever thought of. What's the good of writing a story that twists a man's head round and round like that, until he doesn't know which is front or which is back—I mean, which is his face or which is his poll? Before I had got rid of tutors they had so twist-ed my head round and round that, although I have been trying ever since, I have not been able to twist it back again.

'I know why this fellow wrote this book. I know it all now. Cheyne is an assumed name. He knows our name is Cheyne, and that the race dies with me. He knows I am an invalid. He knows —some one told him—I get all the novels which are published; and he has written this one to spite me,

and offend my father. Low cad! But I will take good care my father does not see the filthy rubbish. Boy, bring me a marline-spike and a piece of spun-yarn.'

The Marquis of Southwold bound up the three volumes of Charles Augustus Cheyne's *Duke of Fenwick*, and having looped to them the marline-spike by way of a sinker, dropped them slowly over the side of the Seabird into the still blue waters of Silver Bay, under the Duke of Shropshire's stately castle.

CHAPTER IX.

THE MARQUIS OF SOUTHWOLD'S LETTER.

'O, WHAT a way it is up! My wind isn't now what it used to be, when first I met you warm and young, Cheyne, is it? Such con-founded stairs!' said Mr. John Wilkinson, a very stout *puffy-look-ing* man for thirty-six years of age, and editor and staff of the *Coal-Vase Reporter*, one of the most prosperous of the minor trade pa-pers in London.

'My wind is as sound as ever,' said the Duke of Longacre, *rising;* for Wilkinson was not alone.

'Going up and down these breakneck flights once a day would keep a man in training. Cheyne, allow me to introduce my *friend* Freemantle. He has a great taste for poetry, writes very beautiful poetry indeed, and is most anxious to make your acquaintance. He has just read your book, *the Duke of Fenwick*, and is delight-ed with it. I haven't had time to read it yet; but I shall read it this week, and review it in next week's *Reporter*.

Cheyne shook hands with Free-mantle, set a chair for him, and pushed his new acquaintance down on it in his jovial freehanded manner.

'And how are you, Freemantle?' asked Cheyne, as though they had known one another for many years. Turning to Wilkinson, he said, 'Look up a chair for yourself.'

'I'm quite well, thank you, Mr. Cheyne.'

'For Heaven's sake don't Mister me. I am never Mistered by any one but duns.'

'I beg your Grace's pardon,' said Wilkinson. 'May I have the honour of presenting to your Grace Mr. Harry Freemantle? Mr. Harry Freemantle, his Grace the Duke of Longacre.'

The two men rose and bowed profoundly to one another. Then Cheyne, again bowing profoundly and causing his head to describe a semicircle parallel to the horizon, said,

'The interesting preliminaries of introduction having been disposed of, his Grace left the room to draw the beer out of his four-and-a-half-gallon cask, kept on the landing outside his Grace's bedroom.'

He returned in a few minutes with a jug and three glasses. When the three men had settled themselves and lighted their pipes, Wilkinson said,

'I hope we are not disturbing you now, Cheyne? You are not busy?'

'No, not a bit. I have just written a reply to a letter I had this morning from the Earl of Sark. He is an old chum of mine, and has read my book. He wants me to go and stay with him for a while. But I can't—not just now, anyway.'

'Well, you see,' said Wilkinson, 'Freemantle here is very anxious to do something in the way of verse—publishing it, I mean. He has several poems ready for publication. Poetry isn't in my way,

Cheyne, so I thought I'd bring him to you.'

'May I ask if you expect it to pay?'

'Well, no,' said Freemantle, with a candid smile.

'You are independent of it?'

'In a certain sense I am. I am an attorney, and am employed in the office of Baker & Tranter, Bedford-street.'

'O, that is all right! Is your purpose to publish a volume?'

'No, I do not aim so high as that.'

'I am glad to hear it. There aren't more than six men whose volumes pay the mere expenses of printing and publication. Poetry is the most beggarly of all arts now. Living poets of fame and exquisite merit do not make as much by their trade as the humblest Italian artisan employed in casting plaster-of-Paris in Leather-lane. Writing and publishing poetry is an expensive luxury, and the readers of poetry are now a lost tribe.'

'I thought of a much more modest attempt than a book. I thought I might be able to get a few little bits of verse into a magazine or two. I have brought a few little bits with me; and I should feel very much obliged to you if you will look at them, and tell me what you think of them, and if there is any chance of their getting in anywhere; and if there is, when?'

'O, I'll be glad to do more than that, if they are all right. I'll give you an introduction to an editor or two, whom I think likely to take them. In fact, if they are all right, I think there can be no question of our planting them somewhere.'

'I am sure I am very much obliged to you. You were speaking a moment ago of having had a letter from a nobleman who has read your novel.'

'Yes, my old friend, my kind old chum, the Earl of Sark.'

'Well, if both of you will promise me to keep a secret anything I may say about another nobleman who has read your book, I can tell you something which will interest you a good deal.'

The promise asked was given.

'I know I may depend on you both.'

'Entirely.'

Wilkinson answered for the two.

'Now, you know of the Duke of Shropshire and his son, the Marquis of Southwold? And you know they happen to bear the same name as you, Cheyne?'

'Yes,' said the Duke of Longacre guardedly. If Freemantle had not thus early mentioned the identity of names between the two, no doubt Cheyne would have claimed acquaintance with both; but here was the wretched name springing up again. Should he never get rid of this odious name?

'Well, Baker & Tranter have had a letter from the Marquis of Southwold, saying he has read your novel (Baker & Tranter are the Duke of Shropshire's lawyer's), and that he thinks it a most impudent and barefaced outrage upon his father and his house—'

'What!' exclaimed the Duke of Longacre, in the profoundest astonishment.

'It is a fact. He says the book is all about a dukedom which is on the point of becoming extinct, as in the case of the dukedom of Shropshire. That you have no claim or title to the name of Cheyne—'

'He lies!' cried Cheyne, all the more vehemently because he was not certain.

'And he wants to know if criminal proceedings cannot be taken against you for slander, malicious injury, and assuming a great name, with a view to annoy or—'

'Go on.'

'Or possibly extract money.'

'Great Heavens! What next?'

'Of course, Cheyne, you do not confound me with any of the opinions expressed in this letter. Indeed, I now think it would have been better I had not mentioned it at all. And, indeed, for more reasons than one, I should not have done so, only that, of course, the whole thing is utterly absurd. Baker & Tranter have written back that, having had the book and the case placed before counsel, counsel and they agree no action of a criminal or civil nature can be taken in the matter. You will, of course, make no use of anything I have told you?'

'What, sir! Do you, too, doubt my word, question my honour?'

He struck the leaf of the table a mighty blow of his right fist. The leaf of the table flew to the ground, torn from the table; the table tilted up; and all the glasses, pipes, books, and papers went flying in wild confusion around the room. He sprang to his feet with an oath, and stood, pale as death, except his eyes, which were blazing. He looked like a wild-beast ready to spring.

The other two men were also standing now.

'No, no, no, old man!' said Wilkinson, in a soothing voice. 'Nothing is farther from the thoughts of any one here. Why, we *know* you—old man!'

Wilkinson did not like to call the furious man either your Grace or Cheyne now. Mortal offence might be in either.

'For if any man asperses my mother's name or impugns my honour, I shall take him by the hips, and pitch him head downward through that window.'

He meant what he said; and they both felt sure he could do it.

'Do be quiet, old man!' said

Wilkinson. 'I am sure either Freemantle or myself would be one of the very first to defend your mother's name or your honour, if any one here had dared to call either in question. But no one here has dreamed of any such absurdity.'

'Then where is this leprous Marquis, who has dared to do both? By ——, I'll choke him with the tongue that said these things, as sure as my name is—' His whole frame was convulsed, the muscles of his throat and his face flushed, deepened into purple. He could not speak. The conflict was too terrible. At last he got breath. 'O God, is it not horrible that a wretch whom Thou hast marked with the sign of Thine own displeasure should try to sully spotless names, and spit its unclean venom on wholesome men with wholesome honours? As sure as the same Great Power made you and me, you shall answer to me for this, foot to foot, eye to eye, life to life!'

Without saying another word, he took up his hat, crushed it down on his head, and dashed out of the room, leaving the two men mute, incapable of speech.

Freemantle was the first to recover.

'Don't you think we ought to follow him? He'll do mischief to himself or somebody else, I'm afraid. He's a raving maniac at this moment.'

'I don't think he will do any mischief.'

'I never saw a man look so like as if he meant what he said.'

'No doubt. But I have known Cheyne many years, and you have met him for the first time to-day. All the time I have known him he has been the most peaceful of men.'

'Yes; but these peaceful men when they break out are always the worst. How infernally un-lucky I was to say anything about that letter!'

'But no one could have foreseen the consequences. Ninety-nine out of a hundred would have laughed at the whole thing. But you did not know Cheyne is sensitive about his name being the same as that of the Duke of Shropshire.'

'I hadn't the slightest idea of anything of the kind.'

'Of course not, or you would not have spoken. Cheyne is the very soul of honour, and a very excellent fellow, although he tells lies about knowing peers and big pots of all kinds. He said to you he had just had a letter from the Earl of Sark. Now I'll lay you a level shilling that there is—'

'No such title.'

'O no! Cheyne isn't such a fool as that. But I'll lay you a level shilling that if you look in a morning paper you'll find the Earl of Sark has been doing or saying something. He has either spoken in the House, or written a letter to the secretary of a club, or laid the foundation-stone of a church, or bought a racer of some note, or done something else that has for the moment lifted him out of the ruck of the peers.'

'Then you don't attach any importance to what he said?'

'I think he is very angry now, but that before he has got half a mile he will cool down. How far is it from here to where this Marquis lives?'

'O, a long way! A couple of hundred miles or more: two-fifty.'

'It would be sheer nonsense to suppose his anger could last half the way. And I believe this Marquis spends most of his life at sea?'

'A good deal of it. He was so knocked up by reading this book that he put out to sea almost at once, he and the Duke.'

'Then we may dismiss the matter altogether from our minds. I'll lay you another level shilling he draws no blood over this affair. What a horrible mess he has made of the place ! He has spilt all the beer and tobacco. There's no cure for spilt beer, but there is for spilt baccy. Let us pick up a fill each and have another pipe before we go.'

CHAPTER X.

ROUSING THE LION.

But, notwithstanding John Wilkinson's opinion to the contrary, there was not a man in all London so sure of the endurance of his rage as Charles Augustus Cheyne. That letter of the Marquis of Southwold had hit him on two of his sore points, namely, his doubtful parentage and personal honour. It used to be his boast that he never lost his temper, never once in all his life; and even still he might say the same thing. He had not lost his temper, his reason had fled him. He was not in a legal sense insane, but morally he could scarcely be held responsible for his acts.

Ever since he had been old enough to be capable of appreciating feelings of the kind, his most anxious thoughts had been devoted to reducing as much as possible all inquiry respecting his parentage. And here now was the wretched, drivelling, imbecile Marquis not only directing attention to his early history, but putting forth in as many words the horrible suspicion that he, Charles Cheyne, had no right or title to the name he bore ! The one great fear of his life had been realised. He had been called an impostor of the most shameful class, and in addition to this, his own honour had been impugned. He had in effect been called a knave, a liar, a cheat, a low-minded bully, who wanted to levy blackmail on unoffending people. It was intolerable, monstrous, unendurable.

Nothing but a personal encounter with the man who had dared to say or insinuate such things would appease him.

He would go to this wretched Marquis of Southwold; he would give the man his name ; he would confess his authorship of the book, and then—

Suppose, when he had done all this, the Marquis said nothing: what further should he do? For had he not promised the man who told him that he would not speak of the nature of that letter? What should he do? How could he bring that wretched man to book? Yet the thing must be done somehow, anyhow.

Then he suffered a revulsion. All his life he had been boasting of his acquaintance with lords, and yet he had never, to his knowledge, spoken to one. Now he was quite resolved to meet and to speak with one, no matter what the risk, no matter what the consequences. He would never allude to the aristocracy in the old way again. He was conscious that there was a kind of poetic justice in the fact that a fatal stab to the reputation of his mother and his own honour had been dealt by one of the class with which he claimed intercourse. Henceforth and for ever let that class be to him accursed. Henceforth and for ever he would be a Radical, a Socialist.

But how should he manage to keep his word with Freemantle, and yet be able to taunt Southwold with his calumnies? He could think of only one way. He would go to the Marquis, declare who he was, state he was the author of the *Duke of Fenwick*, and await the course events might then take. It was more than likely that the Marquis would say something offensive to him. He would then challenge the heir; and if the latter would not fight him with pistol or sword, if the Marquis declined such a combat, Cheyne would, after warning him, attack him with such weapons as Nature had given him —his hands and his vast strength. He would take the neck of that man in his hands, and strangle him with his thumbs; then they might hang him upon the nearest tree.

He knew the Marquis was a man of delicate health, of poor physique. He, Cheyne, would first offer him an equal combat, that the matter might be settled with pistols. If the heir refused, Cheyne would then offer him swords, in which skill would compensate for strength. If swords were refused, then he should tell the Marquis to defend himself as best he could, as he, Cheyne, meant to kill him as they stood.

No doubt in a stand-up, man-to-man fight for life without artificial weapons, the Marquis would have no chance. Still, was it in essence an unequal fight? Who had struck the first blow? Who had given the affront? This man had slandered his mother and himself. Suppose what had been published to the few had been published to the many; suppose, instead of writing to his lawyers, he had written to the newspapers, and he, Cheyne, had taken an action against him, and recovered, say a thousand, say ten thousand pounds damages, what injury would that be to the heir to one of the richest dukedoms in England? But the stain could never be washed out of his own or his mother's character. Give a dog a bad name, and hang him. Give the lie twenty-four hours' start of the truth, and the truth will never overtake the lie. In any conflict whatever, a rich nobleman must have enormous advantages over a poor commoner except in one. There is no law or rule for giving the rich noble as fine a physique as the poor commoner. When, therefore, the rich noble has a physique inferior to the poor commoner, all the noble's other advantages must be put into the scale with him before the two are weighed for a physical encounter. Therefore he, Cheyne, would be perfectly justified in using every resource of his muscles, and, by Heaven, he would; and he would strangle that libellous ruffian as he would strangle a venomous snake.

Cheyne found himself in Hyde Park before he had any consciousness of surrounding objects. In every man, it is a common saying, there is a chained down madman. We are all capable of being driven mad by something or other—we may not know what. Men have gone mad for joy, for sorrow, for success, for reverse, for love, for hate, for faith, for unfaith, for gold, for lack of gold. All Cheyne's life he had been devoted to the nobility and the concealment of his own early history. This blow therefore fell with a double weight. It was dealt by a member of the nobility at his early history. So that his own mind, never very well rooted in firm ground, was torn up and scattered, and he could not now recognise any of the old landmarks, or see anything in the old way. All mental objects were obscured by one—the figure of the man who, he believed, had done him irreparable wrong. He did not wait to see whether the Marquis had merely made a random guess, or had spoken from ascertained facts. To Cheyne it was as bad as bad could be even to hint at the chance of his having no right to the name he bore, or the title of an honourable man. If he had known anything, no matter how small, of his parents, his birth, his early history, he should not have minded it so much. But here was his titled namesake, the head of all the Cheynes in the empire, plainly suggesting that he, Charles Augustus Cheyne, had no right or title to the name.

Then, out of the depths of his own mind, depths which he did not dare to explore, came the question : Was the Marquis's shot a chance one, or did he, the Marquis, absolutely *know* that he, Cheyne, had no right to carry the name?

Horrible! Horrible question! Most horrible question because it was unanswerable—because he had no more clue to it than he had to the mysteries that would be solved by man a thousand years hence. The Marquis and he were of the one name. Could it be the Marquis knew his history? Could it be the Marquis knew the history of Charles Cheyne; and into that book, at no particular leaf, at no single paragraph, should he ever be permitted to look, save with the sanction of the Shropshire family?

After thinking over this for a while he dismissed the supposition with a contemptuous gesture. The thought was worthy of no consideration. The idea of the great Shropshire house knowing anything of his humble history was absurd. The Marquis had merely shot a random shaft, which hit an old sore and rankled. But the very fact that it had been shot at random made the offence the more grievous. Why should a titled scoundrel be privileged to blast the name of a woman whom he had never seen, never heard of— that of a man of whose existence he had not heard until the publication of that novel?

It never occurred to Cheyne for a moment to think that, when the Marquis spoke of his possibly having no title to the name, the writer might have meant that the name Cheyne had merely been assumed for literary purposes, and that the man's real name was Brown, or Jones, or Robinson, or Smith, and that the Marquis did not intend the slightest imputation on the character of any woman who ever lived. Long brooding on the subject of his birth and parentage had made Cheyne's mind morbidly sensitive to any allusion of the kind; and one might as well try to talk down a storm, or to obtain practical results by expostulation with an earthquake, as to make him see the matter in any other than its very worst and most offensive light. Hence his wild homicidal fury.

When he became conscious, he was in Hyde Park. He never noticed the warm sweet sunshine, the bright-green well-kept grass, the wholesome-looking well-dressed people, the fair slight blue-eyed children, the brilliant equipages and stately footmen and coachmen, the trees in the pride of their full primal leafiness. He took no heed of all these; and yet they all contributed in an obscure way, in a way he could not trace, to bring his mind suddenly back to the one object which constituted the shining brightness of his own life. He thought of his bright and sprightly May.

Under the circumstances, the vision of her was anything but quieting. It was all very well for him who had no relative in the world to talk of killing this man, and being himself hanged on the nearest tree; but if he had no relatives in the world, he had one with whom he purposed forming the closest of all human ties. To the world it would not matter a fig whether he were hanged or died quietly in his bed. He was no cynic. There was not a flaw of cynicism in his large generous nature. Yes, he knew the boys would be sorry if he died in his bed, or were hanged. But then, May? How would it be with his little May—his bright, gay, winsome little sweetheart, who was to be his wife?

It was easy to ask that question, and easy to answer it. May would be heart-broken. What heart he ever had to give woman, he had given her. He knew that what heart she had to give man, she had given him. On neither heart had there been a previous mortgage. Each heart was perfectly unencumbered. Yes, it would break May's heart, as the saying went. That is, it would take all the brightness and hope out of her life. It would crush her for ever. She would never again be the same gay, animated, cheering darling she was now.

Then for a long time he walked about the Park, with eyes cast down, brooding over the image and the memories of May.

The question arose in his mind, whether he owed more to the name of his dead mother than to the happiness of his affianced wife? To him there could not be a moment's pause in answering this question. A man, whether married or single, engaged or free, was bound, if occasion demanded, to die in defence of his country, of his home, of the honour of his name. The last part of the code was growing a little obsolete now. But the man who could sit still while they blackened the memory of a dead mother must be that worst of all reptiles—a cowardly cad.

No. He had resolved not to go near May. Seeing her might jeopardise his revenge; and revenge his mother he would at any peril. How could a man who was not ready and able to defend his mother's name be considered capable of defending a sweetheart or a wife? It would be a poor rascally world for us, if men learned to sit still while evil tongues wagged over the fame of their womenkind, mothers or sisters or wives.

So he set his back towards Knightsbridge and walked in the direction of Longacre. When he arrived at his own place, he gathered up the papers which had been scattered on the floor, kicked the broken glasses into one corner, and then, taking some notepaper, wrote three notes, two of these being to editors, and one to Marion Durrant. The last was as follows:

'My darling May,—News which I heard quite by accident this morning obliges me to leave town very suddenly. I am unable to say good-bye. In fact, I haven't time to write even a reasonable long letter; for the train I go by to the east leaves very soon, and I have to pack a portmanteau and get to the station in a very short time. I am not sure how long I shall be away; a few days, anyway. I hope my darling girl will take great care of herself until I get back, for her own ever fond
'CHARLIE.'

A whole week passed, and she heard no more of him than of the dead. What had happened to him —to her darling, darling Charlie? She knew him too well to think he could write and would not. She knew him too well to think he had deserted her for some other woman. What had happened to her darling Charlie? When, hour after hour, she heard the postman knock in the street, and yet no tidings came to her of him, she began to think the postman must have been bribed to suppress his letters.

Only two men suspected whither Cheyne had gone, and they waited in fear and trembling of some terrible catastrophe; and at last news was at hand, filling the whole country with his name.

From the day Charles Augustus Cheyne set out for the east coast of England his name never appeared to another story or on the title-page of another book.

CHAPTER XI.

AT BANKLEIGH.

WHEN Cheyne had packed his portmanteau he took it and a hatbox down the steep staircase, carrying at the same time his letters in his teeth. He wore a low-crowned soft hat, instead of his ordinary silk one. He jumped into the street, and having thrust his letters into a pillar-box, hailed the first empty hansom and drove away to the railway-station.

Either his watch must have been slow or he must have looked at a wrong line of figures in the time-table, for when he got to the station they told him the train was on the point of starting, instead of his having, as he had calculated, a good ten minutes to spare.

He took a first-class single ticket to Bankleigh, the nearest railway station to Silver Bay. Then, with his portmanteau in one hand and his hatbox in the other, he dashes along the way leading to the platform from which the train for Bankleigh starts. The door was shut against him. The train had not yet started, but the time was up. The next train was not till evening, which meant getting into a small unknown town long past midnight, a thing no one cares to do, particularly when he does not know even the name of a hotel or the hotel in it.

The gate was closed against him. The man refused to open the gate. The gate was five feet high, and Cheyne about six. Cheyne raised his hatbox and portmanteau over the barrier and let them fall. The man inside thought the traveller merely wished to get rid of the trouble of carrying his luggage any longer. Instantly Cheyne stepped on the lowest cross-rail of the gate, bent his chest over the top-rail of the gate, seized the ticket-taker by the leather waist-belt, and lifted him slowly over the gate. When he had deposited the ticket-taker safely on the ground he thrust half a crown into the man's hand, vaulted the gate, and taking up his portmanteau and hatbox, ran for the train, and succeeded in scrambling into a carriage just as the train was in motion, and before the astonished but grateful ticket-taker could climb over the gate and regain the platform. Two or three of the porters had seen the feat, but it was not their duty to interfere. One of the guards saw it also; but having been, when younger, something of an athlete, and admiring the way in which the thing had been done, affected not to have seen it, and absolutely held the carriage-door open for Cheyne when he was getting in.

At the first station the train stopped at, the guard who had seen Cheyne lift the man over the gate, thrust his head into Cheyne's compartment, there being no one else in it, and said,

'That was a very neat trick, sir, very. It isn't often we see a thing like that nowadays, sir.'

'Confound it!' thought Cheyne, 'this fellow must have his tip too.' He put his hand into his waistcoat-pocket and drew out a coin.

The guard saw what the passenger was doing, drew back and said, 'No, sir. Nothing for me, sir, thank you. It's not often nowadays we see a trick like that done, and I'd give a trifle myself to see it done again. But 'tisn't every one, or half every one, could do it.'

And he moved along the platform shaking his head to himself with the intelligent approval of one who knows a good deal of the difficulties in the performance of the feat which he applauded.

The train took eight hours to get to Bankleigh, but at last it drew up at that station, and Cheyne got out. It was then dusk, and the traveller having learned there was only one place in the town or village which accommodated strangers, and that it was only a few hundred yards away, gave his portmanteau to a porter, and bade the man lead him to the Shropshire Arms.

Now on the local London lines of railway, where there was a chance of meeting a friend or acquaintance, Cheyne always travelled first class, the difference in the fares of first and third being only a few pence. But when he went further out into the open country, where there was practically no chance of meeting any one who would know him, and where the difference came to many shillings, he always travelled third class. This was the most important journey of his life. He, a gentleman, was about to call upon another gentleman and demand satisfaction, and it would not do to travel in any way that did not befit the station of men of their class.

All the way down in the train the deadliness of his design had not been lessened. He would meet this man, he would tell this man who he was, and then he would challenge him. There should be no seconds and no doctor. If the Marquis declined pistols and swords, then Cheyne would try to kill him with his hands, his fists,

his thumbs dug into his throat. It was not every man, it was not one in ten thousand, could have lifted that burly ticket-collector over that gate with the neat precision he had shown. He could have thrown that man headforemost twenty feet, and broken his neck against a wall.

Cheyne engaged the best room at the Shropshire Arms, and ordered supper. It was only meet that a man come upon such a mission should be housed and fed as became a man of blood.

It would have been quite impossible for Cheyne to indulge in the luxuries of first-class travelling and first-class hotel accommodation, only he was a man who always lived within his means, and had by him, when starting from London, all the money he had got for the right of republication in three volumes of his novel, the *Duke of Fenwick*. The money would not last for ever, but it would keep him going comfortably for a month or six weeks.

Cheyne was not in the least superstitious; but he did look on it as an extraordinary coincidence that the money he had got for the book which had exasperated Lord Southwold now enabled him to come down from London, and seek satisfaction for the affront which had been put upon his mother and himself.

He asked the waiter who served the supper if his Grace the Duke was at home.

'No, sir, I think not. His Grace the Duke and Lord Southwold, that is, you know, sir, his lordship's only son and heir—'

'Yes, yes, I know.'

'Well, sir, the two of them are gone to sea in his Grace's yacht, the Seabird, a couple, ay, or maybe three, days ago.'

'And where have they sailed for?'

'Nowhere, sir.'

'Why, what do you mean?'

'They never sails for nowhere, sir, great folks like them; and they never go nowhere, just as a man might walk out into the middle of a grass - field and come back whistling no tune, nor bringing no daisy nor buttercup, nor as much as cutting a switch for himself in the hedge. I have never been to sea, sir, never. Where's the good of going to sea? But I've seen my share of salt water in my time, and all I ever saw of it was as like as two peas, ay, liker; for some of the green peas is yellow, and some of the yellow peas is green. But all the sea-water I ever saw was the same in colour and smell and beastliness of taste and disposition, only fit for sharks and alligators and sorts like them. And not a single useful fish would be in the sea but would be poisoned by the beastly sea-water, only for the sweet waters of the rivers running into the sea and cheering up the fishes, poor souls, like a pint of cold bitter after a long walk of a hot day.'

'And when do you think the yacht will come back?'

'There's no telling that, not unless you was a prophet. Even the sporting prophets knows nothing about it; for his Grace has no dealing with dogs or horses, no more than the miller's wife that's been dead this five year.'

'Are they often long away—months?'

'No, sir, not often months. But they are often away a tidy bit. It's like hanging a leg of mutton Christmas time; it mostly depends on the weather, whether the leg will ripen by Christmas-day, or will ripen too soon or won't be ripe enough.'

'And is it the bad or the good weather that brings them home?'

'Well, sir, seeing that this house is built on the Duke's property and called after the Duke, and that the landlord, sir, holds it by lease under the Duke, it wouldn't be becoming in me or any one else of us to call it bad weather that brings the Duke back to us; but I'm free to say it isn't the kind of weather that everybody would order if he was going on a desolate island and wanted to enjoy himself on the sly away from the old woman. We call it the Duke's wind here; for if he's afloat it brings him home, and that's the only good it ever brings, but the doctors and the coffin-makers and the gravediggers. Most people call it the nor'-east wind. You see his Grace is over sixty now, and has got all his joints pretty well blocked up with rheumatism; and the minute the nor'-east sets in it screws him up, and they have to run for home. His lordship stops aboard the Seabird in the shelter of the bay, and his Grace goes up to the Castle, and never goes out of his warm rooms at the back of the Castle, farthest away from the nor'-east, until the wind changes.'

'And how far is the Castle from here?'

'About four mile, or, may be, a trifle less. We like to think we're a trifle nearer to it than four miles. Anyway, we're sure of one thing—we're the nearest public-house or inn by a mile.'

'There is no railway, I suppose, from here to Silverview?'

'Railway! Railway! Why, it's my belief, his Grace would rather have a row of public-houses opposite the Castle gate, and the courtyard made into a bowling-green with green wooden boxes all round for refreshments, rather than see the snout of a railway-engine within a mile of his place.'

'Then I shall walk over to the place and have a look at it to-morrow morning,' thought Cheyne, as he strolled out into the porch to smoke a couple of cigars before going to bed.

But he did not smoke even half one of his cigars there. The air had grown suddenly chilly, nay, down-right cold. So he left the porch and went into the cosy little bar, where there was a fire for boiling water for those who liked a drop of something hot.

Here were half a dozen men smoking and chatting and drinking. As he entered, all were silent.

'Turned quite cold, sir,' said the host, who was sitting at a table with the rest.

'Yes, indeed,' said Cheyne, taking a chair. 'I thought I would smoke in the porch, but it's too cold to sit there.'

'Ah,' said the landlord, 'I think we're in for a stinging nor'-easter—the Duke's weather, as we call it hereabouts, sir.'

'Do you think so?' said Cheyne.

'Ay, no doubt of it.'

'Then,' thought Cheyne, 'I shall not have long to wait.'

[To be continued.]

A RUSTIC LOVE.

———

I MET my love where the crystal brook
    Blushed rosy red in the sun's last glow,
And I parted a tangle of flowers to look
    At the happy faces that laughed below.
Ah, bright was the picture reflected there,
All blushes, dimples, and waving hair!

Pure love's first dawning and maiden fear
    Played 'hide and seek' in her radiant eyes;
While the flower-kissed zephyr that murmured near
    Hushed its fairy voice, for her virgin sighs
Filled the blissful silence with music sweet,
And bade my heart with wild rapture beat.

'My love,' I whispered, 'no wealth have I—
    These hands must toil for our daily bread.'
'Brave hands!' she laughed, with a joyful cry,
    And clasped them close to her lips so red.
With love to brighten our toil and care,
Ah, we shall be wealthy beyond compare!

' When spent and weary, my loving words
    Shall greet thee, dear, at our cottage-door,
And the soft " Tweet, tweet," of the happy birds
    Soothe thy world-worn spirit when toil is o'er ;
And love's dear knowledge will teach me how
To soothe the clouds from thy troubled brow.'

I fondly lifted the blushing face
    That nestled close to my throbbing breast—
' True heart,' I answered, ' the lowliest place
    Thy love enriching must aye be blest :
With the gold in thy locks, and thy eyes' blue sheen,
I am rich beyond measure, my love, my queen !'

I kissed her hands as they lay in mine—
    I kissed her cheeks and her gleaming hair ;
How her dear eyes danced as she watched me twine
    A daisy crown for her temples fair,
Where the bright locks rippled and waved and curled—
The brightest, the dearest, in all the world !

I placed a rose in her kerchief white—
    A wild-rose, dewy and fresh and sweet—
But its soft leaves trembled with shy delight,
    Then fluttered down to her dainty feet,
Where the leaves flashed crimson and gold and brown
Mid the graceful folds of her rustic gown.

O'er hill and valley the gloaming fell—
    The lovely gloaming, so weird and dim !—
While my darling's voice, like a silver bell,
    Mingled its tones with the vesper hymn.
Then we said ' Good-night' mid the slumbering flowers,
And we deemed there was never such love as ours.

FANNY FORRESTER.

———————————

SORDID VENGEANCE.

By BYRON WEBBER,

AUTHOR OF 'IN LUCK'S WAY,' ETC.

I.

'As I was saying—do leave off snivellin', Bertha; if any one on these premises ought to snivel or snarl, it is your father—as I was remarking, when you interrupted me, it is a pretty sum already; and at the rate the items accumulate, it will be a much prettier sum before six months are over!'

'Six m-m-months, pa?'

'Yes, six m-m-months, Bertha. Expostulation is thrown away on you, Bertha; so go to bed.'

'Willingly, pa, if I cu-cu-could sleep.'

'Exactly. Theodore has murdered sleep, and all the rest of it. *Macbeth* adapted for the occasion. Now, Bertha, listen to me; and let us have no more nonsense.'

'I'll try, pa.'

'Very well. What is your age?'

'You know—I have arrived at my majority. I—'

'Yes, Bertha, you have. You accomplished that feat two years ago. Now at three-and-twenty a well-favoured female cannot be said to be on the shelf. In other words, she does not belong to that class of matrimonial goods ticketed for immediate sale at an alarming sacrifice; she—'

'Papa, I wish you would not speak of me as though I were a—'

'Box of last year's raisins. Well, Bertha, I will not. However, let us confer together on the subject of your engagement.'

'It is no longer an engagement, papa, as you know. The subject is obnoxious to me, and what good

can come of a conference which I have told you must not end in your suing Theodore?'

'A great deal, Bertha—a great deal. I know your rooted objection to going into a witness-box, and I must say that I sympathise with it. We should get swingeing damages, I am sure; and Mr. Theodore Hobbs would unquestionably suffer in the estimation of a newspaper-reading public, through his letters to you; but, Bertha, my dear, I must consider you in the matter. And the business. You are quite determined to give him up?'

'Papa, you are too bad. You know the faithless wretch has saved me the trouble.'

'Yes, yes, yes. That is not quite what I mean. He has taken flight; but he might be lured back again.'

'Never!'

'Very good. You are resolved?'

'Obdurate.'

'Excellent. And so am I. Hand me that letter-case.'

The scene of the conversation was a little room behind the shop of Simeon Scarth, grocer, tobacconist, wine-merchant, and Italian warehouseman, Stainsby; and the conversers were the aforesaid Simeon (who was a widower), and his only child Bertha. Mr. Scarth's position in the borough of Stainsby was one 'of credit and renown.' He was an alderman and a member of the Board of Guardians, and in relation to properties of various steadfast descriptions he was reputed 'warm.' The business, which he conducted in a slow solid manner, was the best of the kind in the county. Bertha Scarth was comely and fat. Twenty-three years of age, she, the particular friends of her very early youth averred, 'looked her age to an hour.' In fact, the fair Bertha's appearance leant more to the side of the womanly, not to say to the matronly, than it did to the girlish; and yet, to the surprise of her appreciative married friends, who were never weary of saying to each other, 'How is it Bertha Scarth does not get off?' she not only remained single, but unengaged. It was Theodore Etty Hobbs, artist, and temporary resident at Lahore Lodge, Stainsby, the abode of his uncle, Major Chutney, who first set her mind running on Love's young dream. He was nineteen, tall, and broad for his age, with manners that had received a metropolitan polish, and the invincible courage of an experienced flirt. He saw her, and loved her. It was a long vacation—she was an awfully jolly girl—and old Scarth's wine and cigars were unexceptionable. Sketching by the side of a purling stream or in the recesses of a bosky dell, accompanied by an awfully jolly girl, was—well, awfully jolly. This was the view Theodore took of it. Bertha's view was different. Taxed by her very particular friends on the subject, she had admitted, with great reluctance, and under considerable cross-examining pressure, that 'it was not a regular engagement. Theodore's friends were *so* particular—he would not on any account tell his uncle, Major Chutney, yet; and as for his aunt—that would be too dreadful!' Simeon Scarth's view was Bertha's. At any rate, he gave expression to no other. There was no harm in the young fellow, that he could see; and he (Simeon Scarth) was

Major Chutney's equal any day in the year. In his youth he had belonged to the Yeomanry cavalry, and he was about to be elected Mayor of Stainsby. Major Chutney's view, and that of his military wife, were not public property. It had been all along suspected by the special friends of Bertha that the Major knew of his nephew's proceedings; but—it is high time we returned to Mr. Simeon Scarth and his daughter.

'Ah, here it is! As you are aware, Bertha, my love, Major Chutney is a good customer. He recognises a good glass of wine when it passes between his experienced lips; and he has told me more than once that my cellar is a credit to the county. His cellar, my dear, was once mine. And Mrs. Chutney has what I may call a generous idea of a breakfast. I daresay her notions of dinner are equally noble, but I do not supply much of that meal. Here we are: caviare, hams — York and Westphalia, Bologna sausages, truffled liver, Schabzieger cheeses, Bath chaps, Strasbourg pies, devilled ham, tongue, ptarmigan, salmon, bloater-paste—whew! After that, Bertha, and there is as much again, I do not feel that I can comfortably enter the Major's cellar. Well, as I have twice observed, it is a pretty tidy amount as it stands; and it is one of those little bills which grow. Bertha, I must trouble you for that letter.'

'Theodore's, pa?'

'Yes; and also the enclosure which was never intended to meet your gaze or mine.'

'O papa, spare me! Consider how recent it is.'

'I spare no one, not even myself. He says here that his family have discovered all (*his family!*), and that, although it will break his heart to say adieu, you must separate! His uncle, the Major, has placed him upon one of the horns of a dilemma. (Only one, eh?) He is entirely dependent upon his uncle for means to pursue his studies, and—well, he must either give up the Major or the grocer's daughter.'

'Do Theodore justice, papa; he does not put it that way.'

'He does not; but his uncle the Major does. Mr. Hobbs was evidently in a state of bewilderment when he despatched this letter to you, Bertha; for it was by accident this note of the Major's became an enclosure. Just by way of a mental tonic—a moral pick-me-up—I will read what *he* says:

"Theodore, you are the talk of this scandalous little town—you and the grocer's daughter. Were she in the same social sphere as yourself, your taste would astonish me; but as she is so far beneath you, I will refrain from discussing a disparity of age—*and size*—which has provoked more derisive comments than you would care to hear. Understand me. I will have no common retailer of figs in my family. The man Scarth is, I daresay, decent tradesman enough—as such creatures go—but none of his brood put their feet under my mahogany. Choose! The grocer's daughter or your uncle!"'

'That is a scandalous, infamous letter, papa.'

'My dear, do not forget that it was written with an object, which it secured. The nephew is worthy of the uncle.'

'I am afraid he is.'

'I am sure of it. He is gone, is he not?'

'He left this morning by the first train for London. He is going to travel.'

'O, you know his intentions?'

'I knew them long ago, papa.'

'How long does he—or did he —propose to remain away?'

'About six months.'

'Um !—six months. That will do. Now, Bertha, take possession of these letters, and when you feel yourself softening towards Mr. Theodore Etty Hobbs, read them; especially read the Major's. Recollect you are the fat daughter of a common retailer of figs, and that you were only prevented by the interposition of my friend the Major from luring a distinguished artist into the perpetration of a *mésalliance*.'

'The wretch !'

'Which ? Theodore or his uncle ?'

'Both. Of course you will have something to say to Major Chutney.'

'Not yet, my dear. For the present, and for some time to come, we are the best of friends. Good-night, Bertha, my love. I must look out for a husband for you in our own sphere.'

———

II.

IT is six months since Theodore Etty Hobbs went on his travels, and to-day has been appointed for his return to Stainsby. This is the day also of the annual ball at the Stainsby Assembly-rooms, under the patronage of Lord and Lady Dewlap, whose seat is five miles distant, of the county members and their wives, and of the Mayor of Stainsby. Mr. Simeon Scarth is the Mayor, and of course Bertha is the Mayoress. Major and Mrs. Chutney are present, and it is no small satisfaction to the grocer and his daughter to have to open the ball with the noble patroness and patron of the assembly. The Major and his lowly friend the wine-merchant and fig-dealer are no longer on speaking terms. Mr. Scarth, after allowing the uncle of the perfidious Theodore to make considerable additions to that little bill of his, pressed for the amount, and met with, what he had anticipated, a polite rebuff—'It was not convenient.' According the Major enough time to make it convenient, Mr. Scarth renewed his application for a settlement, and was again repulsed, whereupon he placed the matter in the hands of his solicitor with instructions to proceed to extremities. If he, Simeon Scarth, Esq., Mayor of Stainsby, is not out in his calculations, the final blow has been struck that day.

With an appreciation of dramatic effect remarkable in a family grocer and Italian warehouseman, the father of Bertha has arranged a scene for Mr. Theodore E. Hobbs, who, apprised of the ball, is now on his way from London with a view to reaching the Assembly-rooms in time for supper. He will, of course, have to call at Lahore Lodge to dress. If Mr. Scarth has timed his effect with accuracy, Mr. Hobbs's going without his supper is amongst the contingencies of the festive occasion.

Having himself performed the dance which was expected of him as Mayor, and ascertained that Bertha was provided with quite a list of distinguished partners, Mr. Scarth proceeded to hover between the cardroom and the entrance to the principal hall. Ah, Mr. Hobbs had arrived! In brief space the young gentleman had paid his respects to his uncle and aunt, and was engaged in a quadrille, in the same set as that which included his former sweetheart Bertha. 'Washing his hands with invisible soap in imperceptible water,' Mr. Mayor waited for the sequel. This arrived in the shape of a breathless servant in livery, who inquired eagerly for Mr. Hobbs.

'There he is, dancing,' said Mr. Scarth; 'but will not Major Chutney or Mrs. Chutney do as well? They are in the cardroom.'

'No, sir. It is Mr. Hobbs, and he must come at once.'

Mr. Hobbs was informed that he was wanted imperatively—something that would not wait—and the fiendish chief magistrate of Stainsby, satisfied that his diabolical plot was working, saw the artist and the excited man-servant depart, and proceeded to enjoy the ball with a mind full of tranquil rapture.

'Now then, what is it?'

'Somethin' too orful to tell the Major, sir, or Mrs. Chutney ontil you can prepare them for it. Somethin' I daresn't mention to none of the other servants except Mrs. Hustler, the 'ousekeeper, sir. *There's a man in possession.*'

'A *what?*'

'A bailiff, sir; a man in possession. It's 'orroble. I offered him all I could raise, including my watch, to get him out ontil the mornin', when Mrs. Chutney would see 'im paid; but I might just as well have talked to the town-pump for any impression I made.'

'You are a good fellow, Oakham, and my uncle and aunt will thank you, I am sure, for your discretion in the matter. You are sure that only Mrs. Hustler knows?'

'Not a soul else, except me, sir. I told them it was a party as wished to see you very particular.'

'Yes, that was prudent. Well, here we are. He did not tell you who was proceeding?'

'No. I asked him, but he said it was no business of mine. He'll tell you, sir.'

'Where is he?'

'In the smoking-room, sir.'

Theodore proceeded straightway to the retreat in question, and there was confronted with the disagreeable emissary of the law.

'Now then?'

'Mr. Hobbs, I believe, sir?'

'Yes. Who is it—how much?'

'Mr. Simeon Scarth, Mayor of

this borough—a 'undred and seventy-three pounds and my expenses.'

'O !'

'Look here, sir. I am on the job, and I must do my dooty ; but you'll not find me orkard. *I* can tumble to anythink in reason. Call me a friend of the fammerly, a cousin of the kernel's from Horstraliar, or Mrs. Chutney's long-lorst uncle. If I'd had the orfice sooner and knew that you did not want me to be orkard, I could ha' come in as the butler's son, or the 'ousekeeper's brother ; as it is, I can't see no help for it. I am one of the fammerly.'

'Not yet, Mr.—'

'Chivers.'

'Mr. Chivers. Oakham, my traps have arrived from the station, have they not ?'

'Yes, sir.'

'Very good. No, Mr. Chivers ; I do not think it is absolutely requisite that you should figure as a kinsman of Major Chutney's, or of my aunt's, or of mine. Mr. Chivers.'

'Sir to you !'

'Did you ever have your portrait painted ?'

'Once, but it did not come out proper.'

'Ah, the operator did not understand the peculiarities of your head. Oakham, and Mr. Chivers, listen to me. You have followed me from London because, when I saw you in London, I told you it would be impossible for me to finish my great picture without your assistance. You would have to sit.'

'Yes, sir.'

'And being an artist's model in continual request—full of engagements—you came down here solely to oblige me, because—'

'Becos I'm fond of you. Well,

I don't mind all that. But I want to just say a word about the picture. I once had a pal who was indooced to have his portrait painted. The painter told him he was to come just as he was, not to trouble to shave or dress or do up his hair, of which he had a heap. Well, if you believe me, he never could get a look at what the painter was a doin' of, but, determined not to be had, he went to the exhibition ; and what do you think he see ? W'y, that he'd bin a-settin' for the head of Goliath when it was orf ! If you believe me, he was known as Goliath ever after ! I don't mind settin' as long as you like, but no larks ! I am a married man, and it would not soot me to be Goliath'd.'

'I promise you, Mr. Chivers, a strictly family portrait.'

Mr. Chivers proved to be an excellent model. And he enjoyed his novel occupation so much— with its accompaniments of 'rests' and copious refreshment—it was several times on the tip of his tongue to express a wish that Major Chutney would *not* put himself out of the way to get that money. When Major and Mrs. Chutney returned from the ball (Theodore had taken care to apprise them beforehand of what occurred and was in operation) they found the billiard-room converted into a studio, and their nephew hard at work on a study of slumbering Mr. Chivers. It was not convenient for many days for the Major to pay out the man in possession. Meantime Mr. Hobbs had finished two careful studies of the head of Mr. C. One of these he presented to that gentleman, and the other he sent with his best wishes to Mrs. Gibson (*née* Scarth) as the beginning of a gallery of portraits of *historical interest*.

STOLEN KISSES.

Two lines of a lingering song
    For ever fall soft on my ear,
And echo, the whole day long,
    In tones that are tenderly clear.
Wherever my wandering feet
    May stray, still rings the refrain:
'Stolen kisses are always sweet,
    And love is never in vain!'

In silence and hush of a dream,
    With never a sound to be heard,
But a touch of lips in the gleam
    Of the fire, and never a word;
The echo will ever repeat,
    Breaking the silence in twain,
'Stolen kisses are always sweet,
    And love is never in vain!'

For a kiss would a maiden wake
    From the charm of a dreamful sleep,
And a touch of true love would break
    The peace that the blue eyes keep.
For ever the echo shall greet,
    Like song of a ripening rain,
'Stolen kisses are always sweet,
    And love is never in vain!'

When hearts and lips have grown cold,
    And love lives but for an hour;
When life's romance has been told,
    And kisses have lost their power,
Then shall soft memory fleet,
    No more a dream to enchain;
Yet stolen kisses *are* always sweet,
    And love is *never* in vain!

G. C. BINGHAM.

TINSLEYS' MAGAZINE.

April 1881.

SCEPTRE AND RING.

By B. H. BUXTON,

AUTHOR OF 'JENNIE OF "THE PRINCE'S,"' 'FROM THE WINGS,' ETC.

Part the Second.

CHAPTER IV.

TRANSMIGRATION.

PROUD Miss Hartley had been somewhat taken aback, not to say shocked, when, true to her rash promise, she found herself early the following morning at the entrance of that miserable slum known as St. Giles's-passage.

She had driven over in a cab, intending to bring the whole party away with her; but she felt almost ashamed to let the cabman see the house to which she was going, and congratulated herself on the prudent foresight which had prompted her to leave her own brougham and coachman at home, and her people in ignorance of her destination.

Mr. and Mrs. Day knew her eccentricities too well to heed or wonder at anything she might choose to do; but Johns, the coachman, was jobbed from the livery-stable with the carriage and horse; and Miss Hartley never forgot that a stranger would be likely to view her proceedings less leniently than her own trusty servitors. Theoretically Miss Hartley gloried in defying the whole world,

and yet she shrank from being misjudged or ridiculed by her groom.

When she had wearily toiled to the top of the steep grimy staircase, she paused for breath on the landing outside the door of the attic, to which she had been directed; and, for the first time, her heart was filled with misgivings anent her hitherto tempting enterprise.

What manner of girl was this who seemed so gentle and fair, and yet contented herself with so poverty-stricken, so mean a habitation? What could have happened to a gentlewoman to bring her to this miserable pass? Had she no decent friends? Were there no relatives of her late husband who could have procured her more suitable shelter, some fitter lodging, than this?

Mrs. Day's report on the attic in which she found Patty crooning to the baby by the spluttering light of a 'farthing dip' had not sounded encouraging; but Miss Hartley (making due allowance for the fastidiousness of her 'pampered maid') had paid scant attention to the depreciating account she gave of her inquisitorial visit.

Now, as Diana stood irresolute before the closed door, she positively shrank from opening it; poverty in its unromantic aspect was loathsome, revolting, to this highly-imaginative, sensitive woman. The mere sight of Margherita's patched gown and worn boots had filled her with disgust yesterday; but then the pauper attire had chiefly struck her as incongruous amid the luxurious surroundings of her own wealthy home. The contrast, startling as it was, had thrown a glamour of romance over those rags which was heightened by the beauty and refinement of their wearer.

Now, however, matters were very different. On the other side of that door there would be no fictitious glimmer of unreality to throw sad poverty into attractive relief. All would be squalid, mean, revolting. How could decent people live in such hovels?

What could have prompted her (Miss Hartley) to the quixotic enterprise of hunting out this pauper family, of volunteering to carry the strange trio away to a fashionable district?

She had actually undertaken to find board and lodging for the Irish slavy and the squalling child in her immediate vicinity. And this was the most astounding reflection of all at this prosaic moment—she had positively been so far carried beyond the bounds of prudence as to offer the street-singer the shelter of her own refined home. So intense was the revulsion of Diana's overwrought feeling, as she realised the extent of what now seemed folly, that poor Olga's future hung trembling indeed in the balance of her would-be patroness's indecision.

She, poor girl, was fortunately as unconscious of the lingering footstep outside her door as she was of the battle against her own rash impulse that raged in Miss Hartley's mind, and stayed her hand even as she lifted it intending to turn the handle.

'"Meine Ruh! ist hin—meine Herz ist schwer." No, O no, baby mine, baby mine! Our trouble is over, darling; mother will work; mother will sing to the world—sing aloud, gay bright songs. That will please people, and make them pay; pay money to buy pretty, pretty clothes for baby mine, baby mine!'

Margherita's melodious voice smites on Miss Hartley's ear reassuringly, tempting her to enter at once, and not waste any more time in unworthy vacillation.

'Lor, ma'am, I am sure I humbly axes your ladyship's pardon,' cried Patty, suddenly opening the attic-door, and beholding the handsomely-dressed lady who was waiting on the threshold.

Her irresolution was over. The sudden hardness that possessed her had melted under the subtle influence of Margherita's *recitative* to her baby, as a thin crust of ice dissolves beneath the warming rays of bright spring sunshine.

Miss Hartley, with a gracious inclination of her proud head, entered the attic, and was agreeably surprised by what she saw there; poverty was evident, but cleanliness more so. A large bed, a deal table, a wooden chair, and three-legged washhand-stand completed the furniture. There were neither carpet, curtains, nor tablecloth; but the window was bright, sunbeams danced on the wall, table and floor were scrubbed by one who evidently was an adept in the art of scrubbing.

Margherita, her baby on her arm, rose to meet her guest with that first duty of hospitality—an eager smiling welcome.

'How glad I am to see you! how thankful you have come!' she said.

She wore the thin patched gown again; but a fresh linen collar around her throat, and snowy cuffs at her wrists, lent it quite a dainty finish.

'I have come to carry you all away with me at once,' said Miss Hartley, her demonstrative admiration of the baby (enacted solely for the mother's benefit) over. She had neither interest nor tenderness for babies of any kind; and in the case of her new *protégée* could not fail to consider the young child a decided nuisance. But this stumbling-block, like all other difficulties, had to be accepted and made the best of; and Miss Hartley was not easily daunted once she had resolved upon a course that suited her inclination.

Within an hour the grimy old landlady (a perfect ogre, Miss Hartley called her, shuddering) had been interviewed. Madame Margherita's affairs were summarily taken out of her own hands, and their future conduct assumed in a very businesslike spirit by her patroness. The rent was paid in full, and the sticks of furniture carefully counted over by their miserly possessor, who watched her mysterious tenants depart under the guidance of a fine lady, in a manner even more mysterious than the way in which they had existed beneath her squalid roof.

The past lay behind Olga—far, far behind. As the cab bore her away from St. Giles's-passage to the luxurious south-western suburb, she mentally resolved to ignore all that had gone before as far as possible. She could not forget, but she could certainly contrive to bury the remembrance of, those eventful bygone days; and this she was more than ever determined to

do. 'Let us put the old life quite behind us, dear Patty,' had been her last words on the previous night. 'Promise me faithfully never to mention my father or *him* to living soul.' Patty had understood her, and was as willing as her mistress to 'let the dead past bury its dead.'

Miss Hartley, who took up a new caprice, a tempting suggestion, or an attractive friend with all the amazing energy of her exuberant temperament, now took up her Heaven-sent heroine with even greater impetus than her steadfast old friends were accustomed to see her exhibit. There was a delightful mystery about this Margherita that appealed directly to Diana's fertile imagination. The young girl-widow's charming face, her pretty modest manner, her lovely voice—all these were potent attractions, and each one contributed its fascinating share to the romantic whole which exercised such magnetic power upon the impressionable mind of the authoress. Women as a rule possessed scant attractions for Miss Hartley, and of girls—the girls of the period—she always spoke with impatient scorn. She never could put up with people or things who neither amused nor attracted her in special fashion; and her emancipated views on social subjects carried her far beyond the possibilities of any girl, even of such as took advanced rank among the strong-minded votaries of society.

But now she felt that she had discovered a *rara avis* for herself. An ideal young woman, simple yet accomplished, beautiful but modest, deserving all kinds of friendship, sympathy, and encouragement, and left desolate by adverse fate. Therefore Diana's heart warmed to her *protégée* with most uncommon ardour. Here was a friendless orphan, a gentle ladylike creature, without guiding hand to direct, or experienced friend to protect, her. She had drifted out alone into the cold cruel world, poverty-stricken, helpless, desolate. She had been providentially led to Diana's very door; she had asked for charity in a voice that made one think of the angels. She had met her hostess with a grace and dignity that betrayed gentle birth and gentle breeding. She had the sweet innocent face of a young girl, and yet she had passed through the keenest ordeal of loving womanhood. She had been a wife: she was a mother and a widow. The halo of romance about *her* Margherita no doubt served to strengthen Diana's affection and interest at first; but as her *protégée's* charming disposition, musical aptitude, and general intelligence became known to her, her attachment grew with every passing day. She soon came to regard the interesting girl-widow with as much interest as she had formerly bestowed upon her novels and plays. She devoted hours to the study of the new character brought under her notice, which greatly *intrigued* her.

A living ideal with a mysterious history, possessed of undeniable beauty and considerable culture, was certainly far more amusing than the pen-and-ink creations of one's own brain. Here was a heroine, who moved, thought, and spoke of her own accord; whose ideas were startlingly unconventional, and yet revealed more power of thought than pages upon pages of the society stories that had just come into literary vogue. The fact of this heroine's absolute dependence on Miss Hartley's pleasure or whim added another attraction to those already set forth. The career of no girl, whose story it had pleased the authoress to indite, could be more entirely left to her tender direction than

was the fate of the stranger now living within her gates, who knew so little, and cared still less, for the doings of what Miss Hartley called 'the world in general.'

Margherita was quite frank in the recital of the many happy years spent, with a mother she had adored, in foreign travel. She told of St. Petersburg, Moscow, Berlin, and Vienna with the knowledge of one who has lived in those cities for some length of time, and can therefore speak with authority. She told of her mother's professional life, and of what she herself had learnt during those pleasant schooldays in Germany by which she had profited so much.

She would dilate with truly maternal delight on the marvellous strength and increasing beauty of her baby May. She was, indeed, ready to meet Miss Hartley half-way on any given subject of conversation, save one—the husband she had loved and lost. Of him she never spoke, and being somewhat persistently questioned on this tender point of reserve, she became suddenly and absolutely silent. Miss Hartley, who was deeply interested, and eager to be answered (as she asked) minutely on all subjects, was greatly perplexed, and thought herself injured by this repelling silence.

'When I venture to speak of the child's father,' she told Campo confidentially, 'the poor girl turns pale and trembles. The change in her on such occasions positively frightens me, and I cannot induce her to give me any information. She creeps into the shell of reserve like a snail, until her silence makes me almost nervous.'

'How much more well it will be to leave this subject, so *pénible!*' replied Campo, in his blunt wisdom. 'It may be that the brute husband was cru-ell to the poor gentle night-gall. She has poesy in her nature; and she, being a woman who know to love, will not bring her to confess that him she love make her to suffer. Thank the heaven he have not rob her of her voice; and for the rest, verefore shall it matter to ve vat he have done or he have not done? You once have tell me not to ask questions to make the poor girl sorry; I shall now say to you keep a great silence on all *tempi passati*; for it is evident that in them our Margherita has had to suffer much.'

Diana, who hated all interference with her modes and methods, resented Maestro's kindly-meant hint; but she acted upon it nevertheless, and thus the mysterious stranger escaped from any further questioning as to that past which, according to Campo's wise inference, had truly been *pénible*.

A clean comfortable apartment, in the immediate vicinity of Regency-terrace, was secured for precious, thriving, baby May, and Patty, her faithful attendant.

Olga—or, as she was now called by all about her, Madame Margherita—went across the Brompton-road twice a day to spend the happiest half-hours of the forty-eight in that neat little sitting-room with her darling. She sang to the child, nursed and fondled it. She dressed and undressed the little one, keenly enjoying the pleasure of handling the pretty wax-like body, and its dainty new clothes. As far as the baby was concerned, all was easy and delightful. But Patty, hitherto the most tractable of mortals, now began to prove refractory, and the painful task of reasoning with her repeatedly devolved upon her mistress. She had to talk Patty into acquiescence with her changed circumstances. Patty resented her curtailed liberty. She did not care to be made comfortable when nothing was expected of her in return for such pro-

vision. She fully appreciated Miss Hartley's generous kindness to her beloved mistress, and considered it a fitting tribute to her sweet lady's 'iligant' qualities; but she could not be brought to understand the necessity for separate establishments for mother and child. Surely she, Patty, might be allowed to pursue her former scrubbing avocations; the baby might go to its mamma's new home, and there be efficiently tended by that comfortable-looking body, Mrs. Day, of whom Patty had thought very kindly ever since she came to St. Giles's-passage with welcome tidings of the wanderer, and good food for them all.

Olga, gentle and submissive, as she had always shown herself to those she loved, had her share of pride also; and there were times when she nervously shrank from the load of obligation her generous patroness was hourly heaping upon her. It was only Miss Hartley's oft-repeated emphatic assurance that Madame Margherita could render her estimable service, which reconciled the poor girl to her novel position. If she should succeed in doing justice to Miss Hartley's heroine, and in singing Maestro's music to his satisfaction, then she would be wholly reconciled, quite content in her changed condition. If she could please her patroness, and prove herself worthy of the great musician's teaching, she would really be making some return for the lavish favours bestowed upon her; and then she might indeed rejoice.

But if she should fail? Alas! then there could be nothing left for her but to run right away, to hide her diminished head, perhaps to drown herself, and so be rid of the burden of sorrow and trouble for ever.

But there was baby May to be considered. Whatever happened,

she, a mother, must fight the battle of life bravely for the sake of her child. The winsome little creature grew merrier, prettier, day by day, and more and more like that portrait in Miss Hartley's dining-room.

'Whose picture is that?' Olga once ventured to ask of her hostess.

'The son of Sir Gilbert Clive,' said Miss Hartley, and a curious change came over her face as she pronounced the name.

'Is he dead?' asked Olga wistfully.

'Dead! Good God, no! What can have induced you to suggest anything so terrible?' The very colour left Miss Hartley's cheeks and lips, and her voice sounded changed and harsh, as she added, 'He is far away now, and in constant peril, fighting for his Queen and country.'

After this remark no further information was vouchsafed to Margherita, and she of course felt herself constrained to ask no further questions on the subject, which haunted her with increasing interest, but which she now felt to be tabooed for ever.

The only evidence of strong emotion which Miss Hartley had ever betrayed, the only sign she had outwardly given of some deep well of feeling within her breast, was her manifest trouble as she mentioned the son of Sir Gilbert Clive, who was 'far away, and in constant peril.'

Olga would have been thankful for the opportunity of some glimpse into the hidden nature of her kind protectress, who showed so easy and smiling a front throughout their pleasant daily intercourse.

Margherita had suffered so much and so keenly that her heart longed to sympathise with the troubles of those about her. She was shrewd and observant; and she felt that she had unwittingly detected the clue to the secret sorrow which she was sure Miss Diana was hiding under her pleasant smiles; but she also knew that she must abandon all further inquiries as to the bonny-faced boy in the picture, who was now a brave soldier fighting for his Queen and his country. Sir Gilbert Clive, that soldier's father, was a constant visitor at the Cottage, and already began to regard capricious Diana's *protégée* with very favourable eyes; for her presence in the house certainly added to the cheerfulness of its mistress. But though she liked the baronet, Olga was in no little awe of him; and he was the last person in the world of whom she would ever have asked a question regarding the portrait that haunted her with its smiling resemblance to her own child.

CHAPTER V.

PROBATION.

THANKS to the exacting watchfulness of her enthusiastic benefactress and the professional anxiety of her painstaking singing-master, Madame Margherita's time was so completely filled up that she very soon found she had scarcely an hour left which she might fairly call her own. Her brief glimpses of unalloyed happiness—the furtive visits to her baby—became more and more hurried every day, as Miss Hartley seemed to require her *protégée's* presence at the Cottage incessantly for study or rehearsal.

Like most individuals given to rash impulse, but strong in their determination to carry out the sudden prompting of their capricious will, Diana was both exacting and autocratic. Having taken the poor singer out of the cheerless streets into her cosy home, bestowing clothes, food, and shelter upon her with a generosity that amounted to lavishness, Miss Hartley considered the girl's identity as submerged completely in her sovereign will and pleasure. Every thought in her *protégée's* mind, every hour of her time, was claimed by her hostess as her due ; indeed, she made no secret of her intention to exact the girl's complete self-abnegation. Olga, unselfish by nature, yielding by dint of private reflection as to her duty, and in consequence of the bitter experience of her troublous past, now contrived to submit unconditionally to the sometimes tyrannical exaction of her patroness. The only part of Miss Hartley's dominion which was always painful, and soon became almost intolerable, to the girl-widow, was that lady's growing unmistakable jealousy of her *protégée's* love for her fatherless babe. For a time Olga, who was both observant and keenly sensitive, simply wondered at Miss Hartley's frowns and sharp speeches whenever mention of baby May was made ; but she very soon learnt to interpret these signs of displeasure correctly, and was the more distressed by them when she understood their origin. After a while she actually began to feel guilty when she contrived to escape from her hostess's presence to put on her hat and cloak and run away to see her child. At last Miss Hartley's evident displeasure became so intolerable to poor Olga that her visits to the farther side of the Brompton-road were made in fear and trembling, and finally became matters of clandestine manœuvring. It was only when Diana happened to drive out alone, Madame Margherita felt at liberty to speed to the nest that held her darling, to be with whom was the mother's sole glimpse of unalloyed happiness.

Miss Hartley's painful unnatural jealousy was the one bitter drop in her guest's cup of peace and prosperity ; and there were times when she felt tempted to throw up her pleasant prospects and the promise of all good things in the future, as well as her immediate comfort, for the sake of that liberty of action of which she was now deprived, and which is so dear to every independent human being. If she escaped entirely from the Cottage and her exacting patroness, she would at least be free to live with her child again, and to have some sort of home of her own, which poor Patty would so thankfully share with her.

One day, about a fortnight after the migration from St. Giles's to South Kensington, when Olga's trials became so irritating that she could no longer bear the worry of them alone, she confided all her vexatious thoughts to her trusty old servant.

'I am ashamed of myself for complaining,' she said. 'I feel I am ungrateful—ay, almost wicked —to say a single word about that kind Miss Hartley that is not in her praise. But, O Patty, to be made to feel that it is a crime to wish to see my darling baby is more than I can bear without rebelling.'

It was now Patty's turn to reason with her mistress, and she rose to the occasion with astonishing foresight and skill. Indeed, Olga herself was amazed at the ability so unexpectedly displayed by this illiterate advocate. Patty certainly managed to prove to her mistress how bad it would be for the darlint child's sake to throw up the chance of the pleasant home and future comfort with which Miss Hartley evidently intended to provide them all.

For herself, Patty would a thousand times rather have trudged away to do the day's charing which had comfortably supported her in the old days in Sidney-street; but for her gentle mistress and the young child certain luxurious comforts were absolutely indispensable, and on no account would Patty allow them to be rashly abandoned.

'It's only to be a month on trial, mistreth darlint,' pleaded Patty persuasively. 'You told me so, and so did Miss Hartley, when first she spoke of our coming. We would try the experiment just for four weeks, she said; by that time we should all of us be settled in the new kind of life she meant to offer us. And at the end of that time we could, any one of us, make any change, if so be as we wanted to try some other experiment.'

Olga smiled at Patty's *naïve* arguments; but the smile expired in a sigh, as she said,

'Yes; that is so, and at the end of the month, if I do not sing as well as they expect me to do, and if I do not succeed in satisfying Miss Hartley and my master in the part they are teaching me, I shall be turned out of doors summarily, and there will be no choice in the matter. But that would not break my heart, for I should be free and my own mistress again; and however poor our circumstances might be, I should certainly have my baby to do as I like with.'

'O Miss Olga, to hear you speakin' of *your master* is more than I can stand ! Who ever dared to say that they had the right to order you about ?'

Patty spoke with great vehemence in rising wrath, and 'Miss Olga' laughingly explained her mistake, and the relative positions of herself and Signor Maestro. As she mentioned that name, she suddenly remembered that he would be at the Cottage awaiting her in ten minutes' time; so she hugged

her baby, cried 'God bless you both !' and sped hastily back to what, in her present ungrateful mood, she termed her prison.

Miss Hartley was still out; but Maestro came punctually, as was his wont.

'It is now a half month, two entire week, since we have begin to sing togedder day after day,' he said, taking his pupil's hands in his and pressing them cordially. 'You give to me a great satisfaction, my dear child. You have improve already; and so much ! You are good, and you have patience, the one great secret of success eventual.'

'Do you really think I shall sing the part you have given me tolerably ?' asked the pupil anxiously.

'I no sink, I be *sicuro, cara mia*. For dis one occasion you vill all that can be require; but then you will be with the amateurs, de know-noddings—ze fools !—it is a *divertissement*, a recreation, a experiment, and—it will be well, it will be well, for it will give pleasure of the greatest to our gracious Signora Diana. For ze rest—ah !'

Maestro, with both hands uplifted, and his eyes fixed on his pupil's face, made so long a pause that she thought he had forgotten to finish his sentence; but suddenly he brought the hands down upon the keyboard of the piano with a crashing sound. 'For ze rest,' he repeated, 'I have much ambition for myself, and big hope for you, my child; you shall take your place, not among amateurs, not among the stoopid svells and peoples of pretension, but in ze great world of ze art—of true music—of big artist of talent, of genius. There you shall have the chance to shine, to make a great name for your pretty self, perhaps to make a littel extra fame also for your humble, but much-hoping, old Maestro !'

'I will try—indeed I will try—with all my heart and strength!' cried the grateful pupil, fired by a noble ambition, and profoundly touched by the great musician's flattering appeal. He; saw that he had struck the right chord in her sensitive nature, and he went on discoursing about her promising future in a torrent of words, so rapid and strong as to appear eloquent and convincing, in spite of mispronunciation. He pointed out to the attentive girl the immense obligation under which she undoubtedly was to her generous benefactress ; and he insisted that, for the time being, no consideration whatever should be allowed to outweigh her first duty, the duty to Signora Diana.

'But my child!' cried the troubled young mother, breathless with sudden apprehension. Something in her master's tone and manner was arousing the suspicion already lurking within her. 'You will not deny that my baby should be the first thought always, and that her claims upon me are paramount.'

'Zis, I do deny,' said the Italian promptly ; 'for a veritable artist it is ze art, and ze art alone. Ze heart it must never be listen to, it must not be allowed to give us trouble, or the voice and the attention most securely go—exit—so!'

He then went on to point out to his painfully-excited pupil the imperative necessity to abjure all lesser interests for the sake of her musical training. If she had honestly determined to achieve the position her glorious voice entitled her to hope for, she could thus best secure the future well-being of the child she loved. A leading singer could command her own terms. Money meant power and independence both. With money of her own earning at her command, she would be free to devote

herself entirely to the care of her child, if she thought fit to do so, then. But for the present her best, indeed her only, chance of ultimate success lay in abstracting herself completely from all outside interests. Even her share in the Great Event, the singing of the part of the modern Gretchen, was a distraction from the steady onward path of musical training, and therefore to be regretted as likely to prove detrimental to one who was entering on a serious career.

'But it will not distract me, it will only make me the more attentive—this I promise you faithfully,' cried Olga impetuously ; 'and if I am successful—O, if I really should be so happy as to satisfy you and Miss Hartley !—think how hopefully I should then work on in the future.'

Her passing rebellion was quelled already. To sing, to be a successful artist, to hold a sceptre among *prime donne*, had been the latent ambition, the dream of her life. Until to-day her master had not cheered her by any such auspicious praise as he now poured into her delighted ears. With the vision of the glories to come so temptingly rising before her, all other misgivings fled, and she listened to Campo Maestro's further propositions in perfect patience, without any outward sign of demurring. But her heart bled inwardly at the notion of the sacrifice he now demanded of her. He asked her to allow her child to be taken away into the country, and to live in a farmhouse with Patty.

'Until you give your undivide attention, all your thought, to your study, you can never have no entire success,' insisted Maestro, with very determined emphasis ; and his pupil, thoroughly reasonable as she was, acknowledged that, from his point of view, he was right, and told him that she had

resolved to do just as Miss Hartley pleased in this matter also.

'You will remember what I tell
you; you are a good, a no-bel
woman. You have a great purpose
before you; you deserve success
and you will obtain him; all ze
help it is mine to give shall be for
you; and in ze good time, in two,
tree, five year, you shall make one
big triumph. You will have money,
too much for your vant; and that
vill be good, veritable good, for
ze loving moder, and for ze lovee-
ly *bambina* also; *hein ?*'

Campo Maestro had received
elaborate instructions from his 'admirable Signora Diana' as to the
conduct of this difficult interview
with his pupil, and he felt that he
had acquitted himself exceedingly
well.

'You are quite sure that if I
follow your advice and do all you
suggest, that that will be the quick-
est way to make money of my own;
to be able to pay for my lessons,
and to obtain a home for my child
and myself?' asked Madame Margherita, with intense eagerness.

'Diss it will be, I svear it to
you,' replied Maestro, trying to
hide the smile which her *naïve*
earnestness brought to his cynical
lips. How very evident was her secret desire to escape from patronage
of any kind! How childlike her
efforts to restrain her natural love
of liberty and to assume a contentment she was far from feeling in
her present condition of absolute
dependence on the will and pleasure of others!

When Miss Hartley returned
from her drive, Maestro, smiling
the while, told her how gloriously
he had won her battle, and how
soon he had brought his pupil to
elect the better part. He had reasoned with her to such excellent
effect that he had succeeded in
bringing her to a most important
decision. She had resolved to give
up the care and companionship of
her child for the sake of the art
which is the most exacting mistress of any, and to it she was now
prepared to devote herself wholly.
Diana also smiled as she listened,
not cynically, but in triumph. Now
at last Margherita would be really
hers. Her time, her attention, her
thoughts, all would be at the disposition of her benefactress. Even
that troublesome baby would cease
to be a stumbling-block in the
paths of pleasantness and peace.

Baby May, whose name and existence had become as thorns in the
flesh to autocratic Diana, would interfere with her comfort no longer,
and would make no further claim
either on the time or the active
attendance of her mother, whose
soothing presence had become a
comfort and a necessity to jealous
exacting Miss Hartley.

But though Diana was so egotistical in regard to her home relations with her *protégée*, she was by
no means inclined to withhold the
praises of her new-found treasure
from her social circle. She paid
visits by the score for the sake of
rousing the curiosity of her friends
and acquaintances anent the mysterious Madame Margherita, of
whom she positively raved in
every available drawing-room—her
beauty, her grace, her intelligence,
her refinement, above all her marvellous voice. When Campo Maestro chanced to hear these promiscuous laudations, he was sorely
displeased, and remonstrated with
the enthusiastic signora almost angrily. But his attempt to stem the
torrent of Miss Hartley's vocifer-
ous zeal was vain indeed. Useless to assure her that this injudi-
cious heralding would do their
pupil more harm than good, by
over-exciting the anticipations of
those who were coming to hear a
novice, and might after all be disappointed at the young singer's

first attempt at so difficult a *rôle* as that which had been given her.

'Zime alone can prove if ve have right on our side,' was Campo's very just remark. 'Vy for spoil ze chance of ze child's first triumph by over-estimating her possibilities in advance?'

He might have known (well-meaning but evidently still inexperienced man) that Miss Hartley was never to be checked once she was possessed by any fresh impulse. Sir Gilbert, who had profited far more by his experience of Miss Hartley's leading characteristics, did not attempt to check her exuberance in any way. Indeed he could find no fault with her; it seemed to him that Diana was perfection incarnate; she was the one woman in the world to the infatuated old man—'his *rêve* and his rave,' as little Lady Furnival was wont to say, with her sarcastic laugh.

He smiled on Madame Margherita now with ever-increasing benevolence, solely on account of the evident pleasure her society afforded to the indifferent mistress of his 'evergreen heart.'

CHAPTER VI.

PREPARATION.

THE month's probation, the ceaseless studying of pose and part, the secret but growing anxiety of Miss Hartley and Campo Maestro as to the ultimate result of their lessons—all these occult but potent influences were brought to bear on Madame Margherita, who probably suffered under, but certainly in no way resented, them. She lent herself to the perpetual experiments of author and composer with a gentle graceful obedience that fairly secured the hold she originally took on their goodwill. Singing lessons, prolonged and arduous practices of *fioriture*, *tours de force*, and the *pesante* style of recitative, none of these wearisome ordeals came amiss to her. She anxiously desired to perfect herself as far as in her power lay, and certainly rendered the tribute of unflagging attention to those who were good enough to instruct her.

She had thought long and anxiously over her present position, and had come to the conclusion that her first, her most earnest endeavour must be to do her utmost to further the success of that Great Event on which her generous benefactress had so evidently set her heart.

Campo Maestro—far blunter of speech (by reason of his imperfect English) than he himself was at all aware of—had given his sensitive pupil a clearer view of her absolute dependence and of her present position than she ever had before. His vigorous insistence of speech and gesture forced the forlorn girl to realise the debt of gratitude she owed her generous benefactress, until the weight of it seemed almost to crush her. Perhaps the suddenness of the change in her circumstances, or the strength of impulse with which Miss Diana was wont to overwhelm all those who came in contact with her autocratic will, had some share in bewildering Olga's usually correct judgment. She certainly had not as yet had time to diagnose her position, and the responsibilities it carried with it; but no sooner had the loquacious Italian demonstrated these to her than she fell into his practical views. She was too innocent of the ways of the world, and far too unsuspicious by nature, to imagine for a moment that Maestro was but acting as Miss Hartley's mouthpiece on this occasion. The guileless girl gave the anxious foreigner credit for his astuteness, and wondered at her own stupid want of appreciation as regarded the great bounty of one on whom she certainly had no claim of any sort.

To submit herself absolutely to Miss Hartley's sovereign will and pleasure was evidently her first duty now, and must at all hazards be conscientiously fulfilled.

As an instant proof of her reformed intention, the lonely girl resolved upon the sacrifice suggested to her by Miss Hartley's clever agent, to part at once and entirely from her child, her darling and delight — that bonny baby May, whom her patroness had always regarded with such scant favour.

Once this tremendous sacrifice was made on the altar of gratitude, all else would surely be easy. The child was bound up in her widowed mother's heartstrings, and once those loving ties were cruelly severed, no other task could present any difficulties.

Patty and the baby were sent away to a farmhouse in Surrey. The former grew plump on the home-made bread and the enforced leisure she so little appreciated, and the child certainly throve on the fresh air and new milk she so heartily enjoyed.

Patty had endeavoured to rebel, when first the fiat of banishment had gone forth; but her 'darlint misthress' had smiled so sweetly, and told her with such comfortable assurance that it was all for the best, that Patty yielded, of course. It was in her nature to obey implicitly where she loved, and her devotion to 'purty Miss Olga' was surely a pure and unselfish affection.

As soon as her *protégée's* child was temporarily disposed of, Miss Hartley felt that the chief stumbling-block to her peace and comfort was removed. Her autocratic nature craved unlimited sway over all whom she honoured with her affection, and she was pleased to find Madame Margherita willing to resign the child she adored, for the sake of the benefactress who exacted her undivided allegiance.

It was evident to both Campo and Diana that their promising pupil progressed more rapidly as soon as her attention was perforce concentrated on what went on within the four walls of the Cottage; indeed each day added to their hopeful anticipation of the girl's ultimate triumph in her difficult part. Determined not to overtax her industrious *protégée*, Miss Hartley took her out driving every day. This exercise, and the consequent change of air and scene, provided both ladies with the rest and recreation they required as a relief from concentrated study and attention. The weather was uncommonly mild and spring-like. An open victoria had been substituted for the close brougham; and Miss Hartley, who preferred to be kind and considerate when things went smoothly, took pains to ascertain her companion's preference, and, having done so, gave her coachman orders to avoid the London parks, and to drive out into the country lanes beyond Ealing and Hanwell, or through the unfrequented roads traversing Kew or Richmond and its glorious park. The Row, the Ladies' Mile, the Horticultural and Botanical Gardens, had evidently very little interest for unsophisticated Margherita; but the lanes leading to Harrow, full of sweet promise of the coming spring, seemed to delight her. She revelled in the rich fragrance of the newly-upturned earth; she listened to the chirping tones of mating birds with a happy smile on her innocent face;

and after such rural outings she always returned home in radiant spirits, prepared and eager to devote herself to her all-absorbing studies. She took very kindly to her interesting *rôle*, as heroine and *prima donna*, in the new operetta. And Miss Hartley, in great glee, was soon able to assure her that she possessed a 'very precious gift in her 'strong dramatic instinct.' This was a pet phrase with the ambitious authoress; and as its utterance evidently afforded her great satisfaction, both Campo and his anxious pupil heard it thankfully.

The time was very close at hand now for the public display of the result of Miss Hartley's untiring private tuition. And although the preparatory month of probation was so nearly at an end, fickle Diana's sudden adoration for her *protégée* had as yet shown no sign of diminishing. Both her stanch old friends were considerably surprised by the unwonted endurance of the capricious lady's latest infatuation; but both sincerely rejoiced in this novel sign of steadfastness: it seemed to their ancient but ever-youthful hearts a hopeful augury for that future to which each, in his own way, still looked forward with intense individual interest—the one as an admirer of ever-developing talent, the other as a constant devoted lover.

Although Miss Hartley absolutely refused to give her friends the chance of hearing her *protégée* sing, she frequently took her into the houses where she herself felt most at home; but the jealous way in which she guarded Madame Margherita caused those friends a considerable amount of amusement, and gave rise to much uncharitable discussion anent Diana's odd selfish ways. The fact was that the romantic authoress still looked upon her chance discovery of the mendicant singer with the glorious voice as something so mysterious and wonderful that it removed them both from the vulgar comments and criticisms of ordinary mortals. She cherished her treasure, hugged herself in the sole possession of it; while she continued to guard it with jealous secrecy as far as untoward circumstances permitted. At full rehearsals Margherita was naturally heard and seen by the rest of the *dramatis personæ;* but even Lady Buzze's urgent entreaties had never as yet prevailed upon Diana to permit the presence of an alien auditor at these preparatory trials. It was only after they had entered on the last week of preparation that Miss Hartley so far condescended to gratify the rising and impatient curiosity of Lady Buzze as to consent to her ladyship's presence at a private rehearsal, and there to hear the much-talked-of Margherita sing.

Her ladyship was charmed, 'most charmed, indeed,' she said, with a fine smile on her large face; but the smile soon faded, and pleasantness was changed to considerable irritation, by Miss Hartley's subsequent refusal to have the rehearsal repeated before an extended circle of her ladyship's intimates.

'That conceited Diana is so crotchety, so provoking, just as full of fads and fancies as an egg is of meat:' this was Lady Buzze's indignant verdict on the authoress's persistent refusal. But all this hubbub and discussion, the secrecy on the one part and futile chatter on the other, added fuel to the flames of excitement rising and growing in intensity as the day of the eventful *début* and Great Event was just at hand.

Sir Gilbert Clive rejoiced at the bright change Margherita's advent had wrought in the home of the woman he had so persistently (though secretly) adored for many years; and he actually covered three sheets of thin blue paper with an elaborate account of Diana's present devotion to a new-found *protégée* whom she considered a treasure, and perfect; and this minute description the communicative old gentleman sent across the seas to the son he dearly loved, and whom he had so sternly driven into exile.

' Shall I find dear old Di installed as my gentle stepmamma whenever I do get back to old England?' thought young Cyril, smiling as he conned his father's lengthy epistle; and then with an impatient sigh he resolved to put the pleasant thoughts of his father, of ' dear old Di,' and of all else he had left behind him, out of his mind. Those recollections were fraught with so much that was sad and bitter, that they always gave rise to feelings of rebellion in the young man's breast; and when these became too poignant he was wont to escape from them by rushing headlong into whatever excitement or dissipation presented itself at the moment.

Now he dispelled the thoughts of Diana, whom he had ever regarded with an almost filial affection, and of another woman whom he had held dearer than all the rest of the world, by getting into his dress-clothes. He sallied forth with a jaunty air, determined to take an active part in the great ball given by the lady of his chief that night. Cyril danced *con amore.* He had already won the reputation of a flirt for himself, and he recklessly strove to keep up this distinction. He flirted with all the prettiest young women, and allowed himself to be made love to indiscriminately by frisky matrons, officers' wives, or those numerous grass-widows whose husbands were either shooting in the hills or running the risk of being shot themselves in those dangerous

plains still persistently inundated by irrepressible warriors.

It was not a year since Cyril had been so suddenly sent away from home, and yet he was already a changed man. He himself felt and sometimes wondered at the transformation; but it seemed to him the natural result of a very bitter sorrow, and for the most part he endeavoured not to think about himself, or that scarce realised trial, at all.

Diana, who so eagerly read his few letters, and imagined so much more between the lines than the writer himself put into words, very soon marked the signs of the growing change in her ' darling boy's' nature. She marvelled a little and sorrowed much over it. The spirit of his letters now always filled her mind with a vague uneasiness. The old Cyril was either dying— or dead. The youth with his surplus of sentiment, who was clever, imaginative, but pure withal and truly good, had vanished. The Cyril who now wrote to her appeared as a cold man of the world already. He had an undue idea of his own importance, and sneered at the women who ran after him in no measured terms. The strange bitterness with which the boy habitually spoke of women now seemed to his chivalrous old father almost blasphemous.

Miss Hartley, who possessed a sense of humour most unusual in the fair sex, was considerably entertained by the bright caustic descriptions Cyril gave her of the women he had met, and with whom he had entered into violent flirtations. But the tone of these confidential disclosures shocked old Sir Gilbert exceedingly. He, who rejoiced in the wholesome but now antiquated notion that ladies should never be ' talked about,' was really horrified by his son's flippant allusions to the weakness of the sex which showed itself prodigal of favours to the handsome new-comer. Indeed the *preux chevalier* of the old school was quite disgusted by some of the remarks in his son's last letter to Diana, which arrived the very day after that voluminous blue-paper epistle had departed. Sir Gilbert was vexed with himself now for attempting to keep that 'frivolous boy' so thoroughly *au courant* with all the interesting details of the simple happy home-life of those two gentle ladies at the Cottage.

'It is all the fault of that wicked, designing, evil-minded Olga Layton,' thought Miss Hartley, with ever-increasing bitterness, as she listened to the baronet's indignant comments on his son's flippant disclosures. And then Miss Hartley discreetly resolved to withhold Cyril's confidences from his father in future. Why should the old man be grieved, and be made to sorrow over the change in his boy, which to him was quite incomprehensible? Diana, who flattered herself on her marvellous powers of penetration and her wide sympathies, could understand it all so well; and with that hasty generosity always characteristic of a jealously-prejudiced woman, she lavished the entire blame for the change in Cyril upon her own hated though unknown rival.

'It was that woman, that vile, unscrupulous, designing woman, who perverted my noble boy's heart. She began by estranging him from his home and from me; and now I see, alas, that she had managed to rob him of that beautiful faith in all women which was at once his safety and his happiest creed.'

There were times when the capricious lady most earnestly desired that Cyril might see and know lovely lovable Madame Margherita; and at others she was profoundly thankful that there was no immediate chance of his meeting that exceptional and fascinating woman.

To Margherita herself Miss Hartley now spoke often and at length of Sir Gilbert's valiant soldier-son. The young widow was evidently attracted and interested by the theme on which the elder lady loved to dilate. She made a mental picture of Miss Diana's hero to herself, and she invariably thought of him as of a man of middle age. Miss Hartley had probably determined to bring this inference about; for she was keenly sensitive, and, delighted by her listener's interest, could not have endured a suspicion of ridicule as to her own infatuation, which she by no means strove to hide. She was as communicative by nature as Margherita was reserved; and it would have been impossible for her to live long under one roof with a sympathetic friend without revealing some of the thoughts that constantly preoccupied her. But, youthful and ardent as her own feelings still were, Diana was quite aware that the direct confession of her hero's age would startle, and perhaps shock, the sympathetic widow, who considered Miss Hartley's affection for Sir Gilbert's middle-aged son natural and interesting; but who would certainly have recoiled had she learnt that the man Miss Hartley spoke of with such touching sentiment was the lady's junior by full fifteen years.

Sir Gilbert's personal attachment to Diana was considered by many on-lookers (who do not always see most of the game) as purely platonic, or indeed paternal. Diana herself was not likely to fall into this error; but she strove to keep the veteran himself as ignorant of her suspicions as that guileless companion, who regarded Miss Hartley's very old friend in the light of her grandfather, if not as a father-in-law.

To descant at great length on the courage and other estimable qualities of that dear son of Sir Gilbert's had been Miss Hartley's latest caprice; and during most of those extensive country drives which she so thoroughly enjoyed with her companion, this interesting theme formed the chief subject of their conversation.

'We are going to drive over to Richmond this afternoon,' said Miss Hartley one morning, as Campo Maestro took leave of her and his pupil, with whose singing he had declared himself 'verry most content.'

'You will still make that our *prima donna* have so a cold she cannot sing not at all ven de great day come,' he answered, with lowering brow. He had all a southerner's horror of our variable climate, and considered Miss Hartley's excursions in the open carriage as 'veritable mania.'

'And verefore it is you go all dis miles to Richmond?' he growled, buttoning his fur-lined cloak close up to his throat.

'Lady Furnival is there just now, staying with the old dowager, her mamma; they give a great musical reception this afternoon, and Lady Buzze has asked me as a special favour to drive over with our heroine. I was undecided about accepting the invitation, although it was couched in the most flattering terms.' (Here Diana smiled her most cynical smile.) 'But as the child has sung so admirably this morning, and you seem so delighted with her progress, I am tempted to make this fashionable at home into a sort of preliminary *début*, as it certainly will be a crucial test for the powers and the nerve of our *prima donna*.'

'*Ma, cielo, cielo!* and you vill dat she sing in so a crowd, and vid

not her master to her help!' shouted Campo, clenching his fists and looking unutterable things. He was fairly staggered by this sudden and more than usually amazing change in La Signora's intentions; but he might have known, as well as all others who came in contact with her, that Diana truly was but another name for caprice.

'I have resolved to acclimatise the child by degrees, and I mean to begin the experiment at once,' answered Miss Hartley, with prompt decision. 'You might have known by this time, Maestro, that I was leading up to a surprise of this kind when first I began to take Margherita into society with me. I feel that we have been making too much of a recluse of her already, and I am afraid she will be too frightened to do herself or us justice this day week, if I keep her persistently shut up until then. To breathe a social atmosphere requires a certain amount of experimental preparation. You seem to me, *caro* Maestro, to have lost sight of the fact that the Great Event is now so close at hand.'

Campo Maestro was completely taken aback, and very much inclined to indignant protest; but after a few minutes' silent reflection, during which La Signora had not forgotten to fix the full power of her compelling eyes upon him, he yielded. Every one was wont to yield, sooner or later, if once Diana took it into her head to insist; but poor Margherita herself shrank painfully from the proposed ordeal, at the discussion of which she had been present. She had looked forward to one of the long pleasant country drives in which she delighted, and this startling intelligence of a grand reception at which her presence was desired filled her with dismay. But to demur where Miss Hartley ruled was out of the question, and with a very heavy heart the poor girl took her accustomed place in the carriage by the side of her exacting friend.

———

CHAPTER VII.

REBELLION.

IT was Saturday afternoon; heavy rain had fallen all the morning, but the sun was shining pleasantly now, and the streets were thronged. As the victoria turned rapidly into Kensington High-street, the ladies became aware of a gathering crowd in front of them.

'Music hath charms, you see,' said Miss Hartley, laughing as she perceived the cause of the commotion in the crowded thoroughfare. 'All that mass of people attracted by a common fiddler. He is no expert either, to judge by those feeble melancholy strains.'

'He is drunk, mum,' vouchsafed Miss Hartley's coachman, turning upon his box and touching his hat deferentially as he delivered this private information with a wide grin.

An active policeman was clearing the road in front. Miss Hartley, who always rejoiced in everything savouring of excitement, stood up in her carriage and looked across the heads of the people. Margherita sat silent, preoccupied. She hated crowds as much as Diana loved them, and the mere tone of a violin brought thronging reproachful thoughts of her father into her mind.

'Move on!' cried the energetic policeman, addressing the coachman; 'you are causing a block.'

Miss Hartley sank back into her seat. The horse, animated by a flick from the impatient coachman's whip, bounded into his collar.

At this moment the fiddler, who had been fighting his way out of

VOL. XXVIII.

the rough jeering crowd, stumbled forwards and fell, almost under the horse's feet.

'O, help! O, help! It is—it is my—' cried Miss Hartley's companion distractedly.

She would have flung herself out of the carriage had not Diana, ever prompt as she was vigorous, forcibly held her back. The drunken fiddler had already been propped up by those nearest to him. He had heard that startling cry of terror, and now he turned his bleared bewildered eyes on the occupants of the carriage.

'My girl, my precious Ol— !' he cried, in a whining tone; and he stretched forth his trembling hands, making the rags of his coat-sleeves painfully apparent.

'Drive on !' cried Miss Hartley, in her most imperious tone; and the coachman, startled into instant obedience, overcame his growing desire to see some more of the rough-and-tumble fun. He revenged himself on his good horse, which instantly answered to the undeserved reprimand of the whip by breaking away in a hurried amble, but soon trotted steadily onward again, followed by a volley of hiccupping anathemas from the tipsy and now furious fiddler. The brave horse trotted fast, but not so fast as to save the ladies from hearing the torrent of frantic abuse showered after them by the irate drunkard. They glanced at one another in alarmed questioning silence. Both were greatly shocked, and each at this moment felt afraid of the other. What possible connection could there be between this low tipsy ruffian and her gentle *protégée*? thought Miss Hartley. What had she said? How far had she betrayed the bitter, the most humiliating truth? These were the anxious questions uppermost in Olga's mind. But her selfish fears were soon crowded out by a most

AA

acute twinge of conscience. What had she done? How kept the sacred vow made to her sweet mother? Was not she herself responsible fot this degradation of her father? Was not she to blame for his having sunk so low?

For many years she had devoted herself to him entirely. She had made him her first, indeed her only, consideration. From lodging to lodging she had moved at his bidding; she had argued with hard-hearted landlords on his behalf, and pacified irate landladies time out of number. She had used such part of his salary as he 'could afford' to bring home to the utmost advantage. She had patched his clothes, washed his linen, darned his gloves, brushed his hat, waited on him hand and foot; indeed, she had faithfully rendered him all those countless services which a loving woman alone understands. This devotion on her part had certainly brought her the only reward she craved. It was for her sake her father came home at night. It was her presence that compelled him to pay over some of his earnings for their joint lodging; and it was she who made that lodging— such as it was—into home. She knew well in those old hard days that, if she left her father, and thus broke the last link of the frail chain that bound him to outward respectability, he would infallibly sink lower and lower, until he reached the depths of the drunkard's degradation.

And it was to this she had driven him. Alas and alas! She had been selfish, neglectful of her poor weak old father, thinking only of the strong masterful lover whom she adored, and who had lovingly insisted on taking his wife unto himself. He meant well—he had surely meant to make all of them happy; he had intended to give her poor dear father a safe com-

fortable home, and to do everything that was best for them all. But that did not excuse her. Her slumbering conscience was startled into sudden alarmed wakefulness by the terrible sight of her father's present miserable plight, by the hideous sound of his drunken curses. What should she do? How help, how save him? To whom should she turn for advice and assistance in this the fatal hour of retribution?

A sob escaped her as her anxious remorseful thoughts came to a climax.

'Will you deign to explain these mysterious alarming occurrences, or give me some idea of the subject so strangely preoccupying *you?*' asks Miss Hartley, glancing quickly at her companion, whose sigh was decidedly an audible one.

She makes her inquiry in so startlingly harsh a tone that Margherita recoils as if struck.

'O Miss Hartley, do not be angry with me! I am too utterly wretched as it is,' cries the poor girl; and she buries her face in her hands, sobs wildly, and rocks herself to and fro, utterly regardless of the fact that they are driving in an open carriage, and have reached the Hammersmith Broadway, *en route* to the Suspension Bridge.

Her grief is real; her remorse as keen as it is profound. In those ten minutes of silence, during which Miss Hartley has been surreptitiously watching her, the penitent girl has reviewed the past, and has found herself utterly blameworthy. The reaction is painful in the extreme, and renders her for the time quite oblivious of the present and her surroundings. Her first impulse, on recognising her forlorn parent, was to fling herself out of the carriage, to seize him in her arms, to cling to him with all the old love and tenderness, with all the old sense of protecting the weak, of raising him who had sunk

so low. In this quixotic inclination Miss Hartley had vigorously
checked her; and she had been
waiting ever since in silent but
growing displeasure for some explanation of her *protégée's* amazing
conduct. She knew Madame Margherita's quiet reserve well by this
time, and had long since given up
futile questions or allusions to that
mysterious past from which the
forlorn girl evidently shrank.

But now some interference on
her part had become absolutely
necessary. She had not heard the
actual words Madame Margherita
uttered, nor had she been able to
attach any definite meaning to the
blasphemous shouts of that fearful
old drunkard. But that he had at
some time played an important
part in the life of her *protégée* was
plainly apparent.

The girl's blanched face and
lips, her scream of terror, her desire
to save the stumbling beggar, her
subsequent alarm, and the hysterical sobs which were now beginning
to attract the coachman—all these
proved her profound interest in
that vulgar fiddler, beyond the possibility of doubt. Miss Hartley
was first amazed, then indignant;
and, by this time, her scant patience had come to an end. Vague
suspicion was changing to disagreeable conviction. She now recalled
the ambiguous facts of Margherita
singing in the street like a common beggar; she remembered that
horrid lodging in St. Giles's-passage,
and a strong sense of dissatisfaction,
doubt, and distrust grew upon her.

What manner of woman was this
she had sheltered in the sanctity of
her bijou home? She had fed this
unqualified stranger at her table;
she had clothed her in purple and
fine linen (in as much of each, at
least, as she felt inclined to discard
from her own luxurious wardrobe),
and now she found her, who had
never, by word or sign, alluded to
her past life or afforded any information about it, sobbing wildly,
the victim of overwhelming excitement; and all this frenzy occasioned by an old beggar rolling
about the street with his fiddle.

'Have the decency to consider
the gross impropriety of your conduct, even if you do not choose to
consider me in the slightest degree,'
cried Miss Hartley, when her furious indignation reached a sudden
climax. 'I shall soon be compelled to introduce you to a fashionable circle, and I do not intend
to be laughed at because you seem
inclined to make your *début* a fiasco.'

She spoke with concentrated intense bitterness, which put her
companion's melancholy regrets to
sudden flight, and brought her
back to the stern reality of her
present dependence as effectually
as a physical blow would have
done. A moment ago she was in
a condition of abject misery, self-
condemnation, and meekness. But
Miss Hartley's insulting tone roused
and revived the pride within her.
What right had this ill-tempered
woman to address her in a tone of
vulgar reproof, looking contemptuous, and speaking scathingly?

Madame Margherita's spirit rose
to the occasion.

'I am your grateful dependent,
your willing pupil, Miss Hartley,'
she said, and her tone was as in-
cisive as that of her patroness;
'but I am not your slave. There
is a limit to my endurance, and I
can no longer consent to submit to
your caprice and exaction as a
child might do. I do not choose
to expose you to the humiliation
of being laughed at on my account; nor will I be introduced
to your fashionable circle at a moment when I am utterly unfit to
meet strangers. I shall, therefore,
request you to allow me to get out
and walk back at once. If—after
this unseemly scene—you would

prefer my leaving your house at once, I will do so. I feel I have grievously offended you, and that you have a right to command my instant departure.'

She spoke in a low tone, but there was no mistaking the steadfast resolution which prompted her.

The carriage rolled on; the coachman whipped his horse, and pricked up his own red ears, anxious to ascertain the sequel of those audible sobs which had attracted his attention. But the ladies behind him were silent; the horse trotted on over the jolting pavement at Mortlake; and still Miss Hartley had not sufficiently recovered from her amazement to find any vent for it in words.

Had this sweet-faced, sweet-voiced angel suddenly changed into a strong-willed demon?

'Do you mean that you refuse to accompany me to Lady Furnival's "at home"?' she asked at last, and her voice sounded strange to them both.

'I mean that I am too much upset to go into society of any sort,' said Madame Margherita. 'I intend to return home on foot; the walk will quiet me. I have but one question to ask you, Miss Hartley: will it not be better for me to leave your house at once?'

'You are off to that blessed baby of yours, I suppose?' asked Diana promptly, and by no means pleasantly; her irritation was getting the better of her amazement.

'I gave up my child out of consideration for your wishes,' answered the girl, proudly and steadily. 'I felt that the concession was due to your great kindness and generosity; but I shall not give up

my liberty of thought and action to any one. If you exact these we had better part.'

'I exact nothing. I do not dream of asking you to do anything you do not like, my poor darling!' cried Diana, with a sudden rebound, an outburst of feeling as characteristic of her impulsive nature as it was incomprehensible to her reserved consistent companion.

'Stop a moment, if you please, Johns,' cried Margherita, addressing the coachman; and she hastily descended from the carriage.

Miss Hartley seized her hands.

'Promise, swear to me, that you will not bear malice, child, and that I shall find you quietly at home when I return.'

'I need not swear,' said the girl, with a sorrowful smile. 'I deeply regret my hasty words already, and will do all in my power to atone for them by my future conduct.'

And then she stepped on to the curb, and was soon walking briskly townwards. In less than an hour she found herself back in the most crowded part of Kensington High-street, and was eagerly asking questions about the drunken fiddler who had so narrowly escaped being run over.

Miss Hartley leant back in her carriage, and her mind was filled with misgivings. How could she depend on her *protégée* in future? What sort of fiasco might happen on the night of the Great Event, if a drunken fiddler who cursed, or the squalling baby she adored, chanced to cross the smooth path and trouble the hidden sensibilities of that reserved, incomprehensible Madame Margherita!

[To be continued.]

BOAT-RACE QUERIES.

ARE you going this year
   To the race on the Thames?
When the peasant and peer
   In a heaving crowd hems
The banks of the river, to witness
   A struggle the doctor condemns.

Do your sympathies lie
   With the dark or the light?
Does the boat from the I-
   sis or Cam, in your sight,
Appear as the one that should carry
   Your hopes in the forthcoming fight?

And what bet have you made
   On the coming event?
Have you 'taken' or 'laid'?
   O, you know what is meant
By *taking* or *laying*, for ladies
   Now gamble to such an extent!

Have you taken a place?
   But no doubt you'll drive down
Just in time for the race,
   In the brougham, from town;
That saves all the crush at the station,
   And many a fret and a frown.

And you'll mount the box-seat
   A good view to command?
But it's no easy feat
   There unaided to stand;
So *I* will be by to assist you,
   And offer a steadying hand.

Will you take it, Miss Flo?
   For you must be aware
That 'twas yours long ago
   With my heart. If you care
To own it, then eights we can laugh at,
   And journey through life as *a pair*.

SOMERVILLE GIBNEY.

THE UNTRAVELLED TRAVELLER.

By WILLIAM GEORGE BLACK.

A few months ago I stood on the platform of the Kronborg at Helsingör, which commands the sound lying between the Danish and the Swedish coasts. Opposite, the houses stood out with startling vividness in the clear air, and white sails glittered in the mid sea path. There were cannon to the right, and to the left a sentry noting the colours of each vessel that passed. Above us rose the tower, from which an even finer view is obtained, and the tramp of soldiers resounded on the pavement of the court. The scene was one to repay even a long journey, so full was it of combined vivacity and harmony, of cool tones and the bustle of life. We had sailed from Copenhagen, and this is without doubt the best way of approaching Elsinore; for although the railway route is shorter, and passes through the prettiest scenery in Zealand, it is a mistake to miss the voyage in the blue Baltic waters when early light is tinting alike shore and sea. The town of Helsingör is itself a simple shipping port of small size, and requires no long visit. To cross the meadow, where soldiers in the dingy Danish uniform were awkwardly going through their drill, was our course when we had found the direct line to the castle; and in a few minutes after leaving the steamboat-pier the stranger passes up a dusty road, and, entering under a dark archway, finds himself in the castle of the Kronborg.

It would be well if, when mentioned in literature, this castle were always called by its Danish name. It should be remembered that the present building was built in the end of the sixteenth century, and there can therefore be no reason even in romance for claiming it as the castle of the ghost and the tragedy. It is, speaking historically, a modern building. Saxo-Grammaticus, the chronicler to whom we owe the historic Hamlet, was himself laid to rest in Roeskilde three hundred and fifty years before this Renaissance building was begun. But there is a source of disappointment to the student of Shakespeare in the absolute difference between the scenery which Shakespeare describes, and the scenery of this point of Zealand. Here is no

> 'dreadful summit of the cliff,
> That beetles o'er his base into the sea.'

Had Kent been speaking to the blind Lear, he might have said,

> ' The very place puts toys of desperation,
> Without more motive, into every brain
> That looks so many fathoms to the sea,
> And hears it roar beneath.'

But that Hamlet, born, as Shakespeare would have it, in Zealand, should not know the rippling on the shore, the absence of cliffs and dreadful summits and precipices, is inconceivable.

To criticise Hamlet and Hamlet's Elsinore is not the intention with which this paper has been written: it is rather with the hope of withdrawing the attention of students from the gamesome chases of fancy which have made of their master what lay in their own hearts, to the qualities which, though he were all his life no more than stay-at-home and playwright, must have been there, that I have ventured to touch upon a subject which has often been handled before—I mean, the supposed travels of Shakespeare.

It has been a fertile subject of discussion to what trade, profession, or calling Shakespeare may have been put, and fertile too often of weeds. Lawyers have proved he knew of law, printers that he knew of printing, when both lawyers and printers should have remembered that there are very few lawyers or printers of intelligence who have not made themselves familiar with other things than text-books and types; and that, like the novelist and the physician, the dramatist and poet must mix with many ranks and classes, whose talk is so eminently of their trade or of the shop, that it is impossible to associate with them and not learn the phrases and the cant-words of their business, and not infrequently to have rational intercourse with them, unless the outsider is already so familiar with their daily interests, that his talk can be appreciated and intelligible to them, and theirs in turn be profitable to him. Any counsel with practice at the Bar, in the course of a few years, becomes conversant, or at least professionally and intellectually conversant, with a hundred ways of life, of custom and social usage; and Ministers with a Budget are not without the glib use of trade terms and trade devices; yet no one, except the student who is himself shut out from the highways and byways of life, would say that the barrister must have spent a weary apprenticeship to a dozen masters, or that the minister had been boy in a brewery.

I hope that I shall not be thought inconsistent when I say that a totally different degree of interest and of importance seems to me to attach to the question whether Shakespeare was indebted for the general knowledge to travelling by sea or land, professionally or otherwise, or whether, by an acquisitiveness almost as superhuman as his dramatic genius, he had, from sources known and unknown to us, steeped himself in the very essence of foreign knowledge.

The late Mr. Bruce, in a paper contributed to the first volume of the *Transactions* of the former Shakespeare Society, asks the question, 'Who was Will, my lord of Leycester's jesting player?' When Leicester went to the Netherlands as Governor-General of the United Provinces, he was accompanied by a large and magnificent retinue, and with the five hundred tenantry and retainers went the means of making them merry. Funds, however, ran short, and Sydney wrote remonstrating to his father-in-law, Wolsingham. The last paragraph refers to a letter sent already to Wolsingham by the hands of 'Will, my lord of Leycester's jesting player.' Who was this jesting player? That it was Shakespeare was for some time supported by Mr. Thoms; but it has been settled that in this instance, at least, there is no proof of Shakespeare's travels, for 'Will' was William Kempe.

That English players frequently visited the Continent at this time we are well aware, thanks mainly to the labours of Mr. Cohn; and Professor Elze, in his essay on this subject, the supposed travels of Shakespeare, says, 'Holland, Denmark, and particularly Germany, swarmed with English actors, musicians, dancers, and other performers; and it cannot be doubted that even members of the circle in which Shakespeare moved, travelled and performed for some time on the

Continent.' This is all very well, and it is easy and allowable to go further, and to say, as Professor Elze says, that we may take it for granted that Shakespeare, like all young men, had a desire to see foreign lands. It is a different thing whether we can find any internal evidence that he ever gratified the desire of a young man, and saw foreign lands. I will not do more than suggest that his duties in London, if we consider his abilities were early recognised, would probably soon become such as could not well be done by deputy; that we are justified in conceiving that he had a definite object in life; that he wished, while yet strength and health were his, to provide for the serene retirement of old age; and that he was not free from social and family burdens not lightly to be thrown aside. This is not the question which we consider here. If it can be proved that some means were found of getting free for a time of all his responsibilities, all that is asked is that evidence should be brought forward of Shakespeare's having done so. It is only reasonable to conclude that some trace of those travels should be found in the plays and poems which make so many goodly volumes.

We have seen how Mr. Bruce and Mr. Thoms associated Shakespeare with soldiers; let us now see how others have made him a sailor. There is almost more to be said for the former idea. It is not difficult to find passages descriptive of wars and weapons, but the references to sea are less frequent. Lord Mulgrave has referred to the opening scene of the *Tempest* as proving extraordinary knowledge. A correspondent, in the third volume of the first series of *Notes and Queries*, calls attention to the line in *Hamlet*,

'The wind sits in the *shoulder* of your sail.'

Professor Elze refers to such passages in the same play as,

'And yet but yaw neither, in respect of his quick sail;'

and,

'My sea-gown scarfed about me;'

and says of the following passage in *Cymbeline*, to which Malone's note drew his attention, 'It looks very much like personal experience:'

'Sluttery, to such neat excellence opposed,
Should make desire vomit emptiness,
Not so allured to feed.'

Malone says of this: 'No one who has ever been sick at sea can be at a loss to understand what is meant by vomiting emptiness;' and so on. All these passages, and others, refer obviously to the sea; but it surely does not follow, as a matter of course, that Shakespeare was a sailor, or even that he made a long voyage. It is uncommon for those who have been on board ship to narrate experiences, in which the disagreeable is always absent; and, so far as evidence has already been led, it cannot be admitted, as a matter not disputing of question, that Shakespeare's nautical knowledge was derived from personal experience, and that he did not draw from the sailors of the roving age many a yarn of shipwreck, storm, and calm. That 'our poet was not wanting in sympathy with, and in the knowledge of, life at sea,' is not in question. Shakespeare's universal sympathies have made his fame what it is. If he wrote, to cite the trite adage, not for an age, but for all time, he wrote also not for one class, but for all. The audiences in Elizabethan days were not more cultured than are ours. When Rosalind, in *As You Like It*, spoke of Troilus, who 'had his brains dashed out with a Grecian club;' of Leander and Hero, and Sestos, there must have been many to whom these were but names, as they are still. There were sailors as there were soldiers, there were travellers as there were shopkeepers and shopkeepers' boys, in the audience ; and no one play was written either for one class or another. Why then, because he speaks of the shoulder of a sail and sea-sickness, should Shakespeare be sent a-voyaging ?

Now, dismissing those subtle questions whether Shakespeare went abroad as a soldier, player, or sailor, let us ask if he ever went abroad at all. I feel sure that, although troops of English actors may have visited Germany and Denmark, Shakespeare was not at Elsinore, for the reasons indicated at the beginning of this paper. It is inconceivable that he who described so well the scenery he knew—Windsor, and the woodland scenery of his own home country—should have wilfully perverted Elsinore. I do not doubt he had heard often of the beauty of Elsinore, of its commanding position, of the far view to sea and inwards ; the rest he made for himself. His estimate of the Danish character is substantially the same as that of Baron Riesbeck, who travelled in Denmark a century and a half later, and seems to have fed on tradition ; I mean as regards heavy and boorish living. When Hamlet jestingly asks Horatio, in the first act,

'But what is your affair in Elsinore?'

he adds,

'We'll teach you to drink deep ere you depart.'

But two scenes further on, when he speaks of the King's draught of Rhenish to the bray of kettledrum and trumpet, he says :

'This heavy-headed revel east and west
Makes us traduced and taxed of other nations ;
They clepe us drunkards, and with swinish phrase
Soil our addition ; and, indeed, it takes
From our achievements, though performed at height,
The pith and marrow of our attribute.'

Such was the Elizabethan repute of Denmark, and so too in the reign of the Georges ; the Danes, says the Würtemberg traveller whom I have cited above (as given in Pinkerton), 'are the most melancholy, most untractable, and most clownish people I have hitherto seen. Their debauchery, bigotry, and brutality distinguish them so much from the greater part of the Germans, that it is only necessary to be among them to be convinced of the inefficacy of religion alone, when other favourable circumstances do not concur.' It is pleasant to think that neither the judgment of Hamlet nor of Baron Riesbeck is applicable to the Denmark of to-day ; and for the historic credit of a beautiful and brave nation we may hope that, as the Baron may have been misled by prejudice, Shakespeare may have been misled by the boasting roisterers who had shared the hospitality of a Danish sailor. The allusions to 'German clocks' and 'German hunting in waterwork,' and suchlike, are not founded upon by those critics who have referred to Shakespeare's travels ; and it has been well said that there are no indications anywhere in his works of familiarity with Germany and its inhabitants, or with the German language and manners.

One question remains, if we dismiss from consideration the query if Shakespeare was ever in Scotland, Was Shakespeare in Italy ? It must be owned that there is more evidence of knowledge of Italy and Italian habits than can be lightly disregarded. Mr. C. A. Brown has worked out an Italian journey, about 1597, with great ingenuity ; and other writers, among them Lady Morgan, have incidentally adduced proofs of, at the very least, Shakespeare's most anxious realisation of Venice, Genoa, and Florence. Professor Elze seems in clined to support Mr. Brown, and quotes with approval his remark that although it is true Shakespeare might have learned in London each single fact of those he enumerates, yet their totality borders upon the miraculous. But the German critic has anticipated the objection that Schiller could describe Switzerland, and Jean Paul the Borromean Islands, when neither had seen the place he professes to describe. His introduction of a reference to Elsinore rather detracts from the merit of the admission, and makes one wonder if he has himself been there; but, on the whole, the pros and cons have been argued with so much fairness and impartiality, that to his learned pages those may turn who care to pursue the green lanes of literature. For my own part, I cannot admit the completeness of the proof of an Italian journey, startling though it sometimes is; but I must enter my protest against any such phrases as 'I will scarce think you have swam in a gondola,' being regarded as a bit of powerful testimony. Of gondolas every traveller would tell.

In conclusion, in the present state of our knowledge and of our criticism, I am fain to hold that Shakespeare was what Dean Stanley has well called 'an untravelled traveller.' With an appreciation of strange lands and men, of adventure and merry-making in which no man in England could excel him, he was tied by destiny to the desk of the playwright. To him there was to be no gadding abroad, and his entertainment must be taken in London and his rest in Stratford. That members of the circle in which he moved had travelled and performed over the Continent is of itself explanatory of much of his knowledge. It should also be remembered that those who went far afield in Elizabethan days had, as a rule, some diplomatic mission or talent for amusement. Of Shakespeare's employment as even a nominal diplomatist of the humblest kind, we have no tittle of proof, and that he was an actor of eminence we may doubt. A man of strong sympathies and great powers of assimilation, he went about from coterie to coterie, from actor to author, from patron to playboy, everywhere gathering new thoughts and garnering fresh conceits; from one and all getting the ready welcome and the cordial appreciation which was the due of the great spirit that knew no earthly pilgrimage beyond his England.

THE DIAMOND RING.

By E. M. ALFORD,
AUTHOR OF 'HONOR,' ETC.

CHAPTER I.

A PERFECT September morning, the blue sky softened by fleecy white clouds; late reaping going on in the upland fields, while in some places the waving golden corn and yellow barley still stand; freshly-mown meadows enlivened by grazing cows and sheep; hedges rich in blackberry blossoms, and decked here and there with autumn-tinted leaves—yellow, red, and brown. And through this land of delight, threading its uncanny way like some creature of a wild imagination, slides the black line of the train, headed by that wonderful monster of the nineteenth century, the panting puffing engine, the signs of its gigantic power lingering behind it in the blue atmosphere, in those soft curling wreaths of white cloud. Truly the simple every-day occurrence of a railway journey is a marvellous thing. One might write an essay on the subject which, could it have been published a century ago, would have been regarded by men of sense as too fanciful a fairy tale.

The train is full to-day, especially the first and second classes; and as it pulls up at a quiet station, a gentleman, who had been looking in vain for a place in the more select carriages, springs hastily into a third, replying to the apologies of the station-master, 'O, never mind, Adams; I shall like it for a change: it will be a new phase of life to study.' And then the train whistles, and they are off again.

The gentleman settles himself comfortably into his corner by the window, and begins glancing with the eye of an accustomed traveller at his fellow-passengers. This is not one of the new and luxuriously-padded third-class carriages, but one of the old kind, open all through, and with bare boards for seats. But all the more amusing, says our passenger to himself, who is evidently in a happy state of mind, easily to be pleased, and interested in whatever may happen.

'What a change there is in third-class travelling!' he says presently to his opposite neighbour. 'Before I went abroad, ten years ago, none of the better sort of people thought of going third; and now I am told that the clergy patronise it largely, and the professional class generally. Indeed it seems to me, on looking around us, that it is quite as select as the second-class is now, and much more amusing.'

This remark was made as he was busily adjusting his railway-rug comfortably around his legs, and without looking up. The person to whom it was addressed was a young lady—yes, certainly a lady, though her dress was of the plainest—who was gazing in such rapt attention out of the window, that she hardly seemed to take in her companion's words. The rug being arranged to his satisfaction, he looked up for the expected rejoinder, and was met by a pair of thoughtful gray eyes and the calm confession,

'I beg your pardon, I was thinking; did you ask me some question?'

'O no; I only made a remark. It was of no consequence. Excuse my having interrupted your train of thought,' replied the gentleman, a little huffed maybe at his good-natured effort at sociability being so quietly ignored.

The girl relapsed into her former attitude of entire absorption in the sweet country through which they were passing. It was as though she were alone there. Talking went on in the other divisions. A hearty Yorkshire farmer began descanting on the crops in his north-country dialect; a Somersetshire yeoman took up the cudgels for the south; the talk grew eager and racy; others joined in it; there was a hearty hail-fellow-well-met tone amongst them all, which interested and amused our young gentleman vastly. A cleric in the farther corner raised his head from the note-book on which he was dotting down notes for his Sunday's sermon, to give his kindly word, and point out the merits of the rival modes of farming. A lady, travelling apparently with her maid, joined in the discussion, in accents that contrasted strangely in their purity with the provincial tones of the farmers. Our friend of the rug added his quota, and the friendly talk became general; but still the gray-eyed girl remained preoccupied.

Another whistle, another stoppage, more passengers crowding in; amongst them a poor pale lad, evidently leaving home to get work; for a motherly woman is seeing him off, and bidding him take care of his health and not over-do it, as the train starts again. The girl in the corner brings her eyes back from their abstraction then, and turns them on the lad with a tender pitiful glance. Presently she draws out a little bottle of wine from her travelling-bag, and, offering it to him, begs him to take some. The poor lad starts, and a passing flush comes over his white face, as he says, with a pleased smile,

'Thank you kindly, miss, but mother gave me some before I started.'

'Are you going far?' asks the girl, her face lighting up with interest.

'Only to B—, miss. I've heard of a clerkship there; and I'm main glad to have a chance of earning my own living.'

There was a touch of bitterness in his tone, as he made the concluding remark, which evidently struck a chord of sympathy in the girl's heart. A beautiful smile stole into the gray eyes, as she said gently,

'But you must not go beyond your strength; your mother values your health far above your earnings.'

'How do you know that, miss?' he asked, almost sharply. 'And yet it is true. Mother, she does; but father, he don't like "useless lumber." I'm bound to strive, come what may. If I'd only my health, like the rest of them, I wouldn't care. But I won't be a coward, and cave in for a little, anyhow.'

'Those also serve who only stand and wait,' said the girl softly, as if to herself; and the gentleman of the rug, as he glanced up from his paper, thought he saw tears in the steadfast gray eyes.

The lad said no more till they reached the next station, where he had to change for B—, and then, just as he was preparing to leave the train, he turned to his new friend, and said,

'Thank you kindly, miss, for that thought; maybe I shall need it to cheer me before I've done. I wish you good-day, miss.'

And the pale lanky lad tried to make a sort of bow as he passed. But the girl held out a little white hand, on which a diamond ring glittered, and said good-bye with a tremble in her voice, which was not lost either upon the poor lad or the luxurious gentleman opposite.

Several passengers turned out here, and our two friends were left alone in their division of the carriage. The girl's face had relaxed some of the intentness of its expression; it would seem that she had gained a clue at last to the puzzle that had been engrossing her, and a look of quiet pleasure stole over her face, as she gazed on the smiling landscape.

But her eyes were still fixed on the outer world, and her thoughts were evidently abstracted too. Our friend of the rug felt somewhat nettled at this continued ignoring of his existence. He was not accustomed to be thus overlooked. This very morning he had left his aunt's country residence, followed by the tender regrets of charming young ladies, cousins and otherwise. Ever since his return from India in the spring, he had been fêted and petted by all his friends. Was he not a very eligible young man, in receipt of an income of 1000*l.* a year from the Indian civil service? And had he not come home to old England now, with the expressed intention of taking a wife back with him? No wonder the mammas made him welcome; no wonder the young ladies were ready enough to respond to his overtures of friendship. And here was this quiet gray-eyed girl ignoring him altogether, not troubling herself even to collect her thoughts to respond to his remarks, and yet going out of her way to speak kindly to a poor lad who had made no claim on her attention ! Mr. Clive Fenton folded up his newspaper, un-

fastened his rug, and strolled across to the opposite window. The people in the next compartment were napping; the farthest division was occupied chiefly by children. ' A dull set of passengers,' he murmured to himself; 'I have half a mind to change my carriage at the next station.' But just as the train slackened speed, the gray-eyed girl said,

'Do we change here for London, if you please ?'

' O no,' replied her companion, forgetting his intention at once, and coming back to his former corner. ' We don't change till we get to ——, and then we shall have an hour to wait.'

' An hour to wait? O, how delightful ! Then I shall have time to go and see the cathedral. Is it far from the station, I wonder? But I *must* go; I have never seen a cathedral in my life.'

What a pleasant voice she had, and how naturally and easily she spoke, now that once the ice was broken ! Clive Fenton made a rapid decision in his own mind that he too would visit the cathedral at ——. Why not? He had been away ten years; it was his duty to see all he could.

' Not very far,' he answered; ' there will be plenty of time. I intend paying it a visit myself. I have not seen an English cathedral since my return from abroad, and I shall like to recall old impressions.'

The gray eyes were turned fully on him now, and with such a depth of earnestness in them, that he was fairly startled, as the girl said,

' Have you been abroad? O, then perhaps you can tell me what I want so much to know ! Would it cost a *great deal* to go to the South—to Nice, or Mentone, or anywhere on the Mediterranean— for the winter? I want *so much* to know the cheapest way of getting there, and of living when there.'

So pathetically earnest was the gaze of inquiry fixed upon him, that it cost Clive an effort to answer, as he felt bound to do,

'Well, I fear it is an expensive place to live in, from the fact of so many invalids being ordered there by our London doctors. But I am hardly an authority on the subject, as I have but recently returned from India, and know very little of the Continent. I should fancy you might probably find some smaller place on the Riviera, where lodgings at least would be cheaper. May I ask how many your party would consist of?'

'Only of Donald and myself, that is if I can get him to go. But I'm afraid I sha'n't. He can't bear being made a fuss over, and you see we are all so poor. And then Donald was never strong; he says it must have come sooner or later, and that it is useless pinching others to try and add a few years to his life. But the clever doctor he has seen says it is his only chance, and I shall break my heart if he dies for lack of trying it.'

There was no hysterical emotion about the girl as she spoke. Her trouble was far too deep for sobs or sighs. Her companion wondered no longer at the intentness of abstracted gaze that had nettled him before. The poor child was living through a phase of life's tragedy as she sat so calmly in her corner. His kind heart was deeply touched. She looked so young and fragile to be bearing such a burden of care. Had she no parents, no brothers or sisters to share it with her? Why did she appeal to him, a perfect stranger, in her private perplexities? He had the chivalrous feeling towards women that we often take note of in men who have been in other lands. An English girl in

all her innocence and freshness had a sort of sacredness in his eyes. It hardly seemed right that she should be allowed to travel unprotected, especially in a third-class carriage. Would she be met in London, he wondered? He must find out all he could about her, and then give her what help he might. His own business was not pressing; even if it were, he would not begrudge some little sacrifice to help this poor sorrowful child.

'I must think if I can help you in any way,' he began. 'Let me see. I have a friend at Nice; I could write to him for information, if you would allow me. Will you be staying with Mr. Donald, your—'

'My brother? Yes, I shall stay and nurse him while he needs it; and when he is better, I shall try and persuade him to go away somewhere with me.'

'Will he be well enough to meet you at the station this evening?'

'O no, he is far too ill; and besides, he does not know I am coming. I daresay he will be vexed at first,' the girl went on, responding to the stranger's friendliness by telling her sad little tale with confiding simplicity; 'but I couldn't help going to him when I knew how ill he was. You see, Donald is everything to me. Mamma is very good to us, but she has the little ones; and though we are all very fond of each other, of course they belong mostly to her. Our own mother died when we were very young—Donald and I; and our father died five years ago in India of cholera, after only three days' illness, just a year before he would have retired with a large pension. So then Donald and I had to leave school: I to come home and help mamma with the little ones, and Donald to go into a London bank. I think it was splendid of him; for it was all his own doing. He was at the top of the school, and so clever; and he was to have gone to Cambridge very soon; but he gave it all up for the sake of the little ones, and has been drudging ever since at bank-work. And now this morning we had a letter to say that he could not come home for his holiday, for his cough had been worse, and in fact he had been spitting blood; and so he had been to a clever London doctor, who had ordered him to lie by till his cough was better, and then to go to the south of France, or somewhere, for the winter, as his only chance. Mamma was very unhappy, and couldn't tell what to do; so when I begged her to let me go to him, she said I might, though she did not see how that would help. But I have been thinking hard about it all the way, and I have a plan now,' concluded the girl, a glad light coming into her eyes as she looked at her companion with a childlike confidence.

' Have you? I am so glad,' he said, answering her look with one of like friendliness. ' I suppose I must not ask what it is?'

She seemed doubtful for a moment, and then said,

' I think I had rather keep it a secret, if you don't mind.'

' Certainly; in truth I had no right to ask,' he answered, feeling wonderfully interested and amused by her *naïve* simplicity. Evidently here at least was a girl unspoiled by society and conventionality. He fell to musing on the sort of domestic life she had probably led among those little half-brothers and sisters, and that apparently weak stepmother. And the whole story seemed to him most touching: the father's premature death—of how many such had he himself known! —the clever brother's early life of

self-denial and failing health, the sister's unselfish devotion.

' Here we are at —— !' he exclaimed presently, as the train drew up. ' Shall I look after your luggage for you while you go and have some lunch? I will join you in the refreshment-room, and show you the way to the cathedral, if I may.'

The girl looked puzzled for a moment; evidently, unsophisticated as she was, this plan did not quite commend itself to her judgment.

' Thank you very much,' she said; ' but I like puzzling out ways by myself. I shall have to be clever at that if we go abroad, you know.'

And so, with a little bow, which was very pretty in its attempt at dignity, and yet its simplicity, she left her companion, and engaged the services of a porter to look after her luggage.

Clive Fenton watched her as she walked along the platform talking to the porter; and as he noted the faultless neatness of her gray dress and hat, of her neatly-coiled glossy brown hair, and the simple dignity of perfect unconsciousness with which she moved and spoke, he said to himself that here at last he had found his ideal of an English maiden, in her fearless frankness, her gracious courtesy, and her quiet self-respect.

———

CHAPTER II.

ALL the bustle and stir of a refreshment-room at a busy railway-station at midday. Little family groups of father, mother, and children at one table, of elderly father and attendant daughter at another, young bride and bridegroom at a third, enjoying their honeymoon. With what fresh interest and bright intelligence those gray eyes scanned the various faces, and how entertaining it all was to the stay-at-home girl! How she would enjoy talking it over with Donald to-night, if he were only well enough for a chat! Her young spirits rose with the change of scene and life around her. She ate her own modest lunch of egg and roll with keen relish, and took advantage of the opportunity of passing the salt to a pleasant-looking lady, who stood next her at the counter, to enter into a little chat. The lady was nothing loth, and it ended in their starting off together presently to walk to the cathedral.

A certain gentleman, who was eating his lunch at the farther end of the room, and keeping his eye meantime on the figure in gray, started up as he saw the pair disappear, and hastily paying his reckoning, followed in their rear. He had a settled purpose in his mind; it was to keep respectful watch and guard over his young travelling companion. So young, so inexperienced, what snares might not beset her! Probably he had an exaggerated sense of the need of protection by the weaker sex; he had hardly been long enough in England to realise the independent line taken nowadays by so many of his young countrywomen. At any rate, all the chivalrous part of his nature was called forth towards this artless unprotected child, as he called her to himself; and no one would have guessed at the wild dreams of knightly service that were seething in the brain of the faultlessly-dressed gentleman who sauntered so leisurely that bright afternoon through the streets of ——.

He purposely kept in the background, even when he joined the party of strangers in the cathedral, whom the verger was about to take round. But not a word did he lose of the eager questions or excla-

mations of pleasure which sprang forth irrepressibly from the girl in gray. And often he was surprised at the culture and quickness of perception which these same remarks showed. Once or twice, indeed, he left his retirement to answer questions which went beyond the routine knowledge of their guide, and was rewarded by a bright glance and a quiet 'thank you' for his pains. The lady to whom his *protégée* had attached herself was evidently a wise selection on her part, so that he felt his watchfulness was so far superfluous. But it was not superfluous to warn them of the lapse of time, and to offer to fetch a cab when the danger of their not catching the train was found to be imminent. The girl hesitated, but her companion promptly accepted his offer.

'Yes, thank you. I must not lose this train on any account,' she said. 'I have an appointment in London which I must keep.'

So the cab was hailed, and they all three jumped into it, and were speedily set down at the station again. The girl had her purse in her hand, and earnestly begged to be told her debt; but Clive Fenton laughed at her, and said,

'It was my cab, and you ladies only honoured me by your company.'

'A pretty speech; and we are indeed indebted to you, for here comes our train,' said the elder lady. 'Shall we not keep together still, and get into the same carriage, if we can? O, but I travel second, and doubtless you are going first class?' she added, glancing at Clive's well-appointed person.

'On the contrary, I am travelling third to-day,' he answered, smiling, 'otherwise I should have been most happy.'

'And you, my young friend?'

asked the lady, turning to the girl in gray.

'I am travelling third class too; but I wish I could go on with you. The third is very comfortable; won't you try it?'

But the lady laughingly shook her head as she answered,

'No, I dare not. Picture the dismay of my cousin, on meeting me in London, to find me a third-class passenger! It is all prejudice; but one must consider one's friends.'

And with a friendly nod the good-natured lady stepped into the train, just as a porter came up with the girl's wraps, and calling out, 'This way, miss,' put her into a most comfortable third-class carriage. He was about to close the door, when some one stopped him and sprang in just as the train was about to move.

'I was nearly too late,' he said; 'I had lost sight of you, and was looking for you in the forward carriages.'

'Looking for me?' said the girl, and the gray eyes were turned on him in startled surprise.

He saw he had made a mistake. Of course she could not know anything of his secret vows of knightly service and brotherly watchfulness over her. He hastened to add,

'Yes; I thought you might be glad to feel that you had an acquaintance, if but a railway one, with you for the remainder of your journey; and that perhaps I might be of some help to you when we reach the busy metropolis, as you do not expect Mr. Donald to meet you. I have cousins, if not sisters, of my own,' he added kindly; 'and I should not like one of them to have to look after herself all alone at the big London station.'

'You are very kind,' answered the girl, quite reassured, as much by the frank friendly manner as by his words. 'Indeed,' she added,

'I think everybody is very kind. Do you know, I have been wondering over it as I came along—over all the happiness and brightness and kindness there seem to be in the world. I liked watching the people at the station; I did not see one sad face among them nor in the train as we came on, except that poor lad's;' and at the thought of him the smile died out of her face again.

'And he was cheered by your sympathy,' said her companion. 'It must be a great consolation in suffering to feel how the hearts of the good and gentle are drawn out towards the sufferer.'

Perhaps he was thinking of his own mortification at being overlooked for the poor lad, and wishing that he could get up any claim of trouble upon this sympathetic girl's feelings. But, indeed, things had gone very smoothly with Mr. Clive Fenton. No doubt he had been diligent and steady, and in so far had earned his success; but then he had had good health and good brains to start with, two gifts of inestimable value. Moreover, although an only son and an orphan, he was rich in relations who had always made much of him. No, he could not make out a case to enlist the sympathy of those gray eyes; he must content himself with doing their owner service, and with earning a glance of gratitude as his reward. So he produced a book which he had purchased at the bookstall at —— for this very purpose, and offered it to his companion.

'I think you will like it,' he said; '*The Autocrat at the Breakfast-Table*, by Wendell Holmes. Just the book for travelling, very suggestive and original; so that you can get an idea and then lay the volume down and ponder over it at your leisure.'

'Thank you; yes, that is the

only reading I could do in the train. I almost begrudge taking my eyes for a minute off this peaceful country,' she said, receiving the book with a pleased smile.

She began reading with evident interest; but after a while the book was laid on her lap, and her eyes were gazing out of the window again.

'You do not care for it, I fear?' asked her companion.

'O yes, I like it extremely. But, do look at that dear little homestead yonder among the trees! See! they are putting up the last of the corn on the rick; and look at those two little toddling children riding away in the empty wagon. Ah! you are too late; we have passed.'

'I see you are reading the book of Nature, and find that more interesting than the printed article,' said Clive.

'I can have printed books any day, but not such a series of living pictures as these you see,' she said simply.

'I expect you are not a great traveller? It is quite refreshing to come across any one genuinely enjoying a railway journey, instead of looking upon it merely as a necessary nuisance between getting from one place to another.'

'Is that how you look upon it?' asked the girl, in evident astonishment.

'Not to-day; but sometimes, I must confess,' said Clive.

'Well, to-day is exceptionally lovely, no doubt,' she answered, entirely overlooking the implied compliment. 'Perhaps on a *very* wet day it *might* be dull.'

Clive laughed at the grudging admission, and answered gaily,

'I don't suppose *you* would find even that dull; you evidently carry about so much pocket sunshine with you that you must be nearly independent of cloudy skies. But

we are not all so happily endowed.'

'Ah, no! I am not always bright, I assure you. Ask mamma. I am dreadfully discontented sometimes, when the little ones are dull and won't learn, and when there are heaps of clothes to be mended on sunshiny days. But to tell the truth—I daresay you will be surprised—this is the first railway journey I have taken since I was quite a tiny thing, and it is all so new and so delightful to me.'

'You are indeed a *rara avis,*' said Clive. 'I congratulate you on the vast amount of pleasure in store for you, with your keen appreciation of Nature. Think of all the lovely places there are to be visited, and with what a freshness you will view them all.'

'Yes, if I ever do view them,' she said, with a merry laugh. And then more gravely, 'I hardly like to think of what it would be to go abroad with Donald. I think we should both lose our heads at the sight of the blue Mediterranean.'

Always Donald. He was evidently first and foremost in her heart. Clive fell into a study. He was thinking how delightful it would be to watch the unfolding of this girl's sweet nature, to see her face glow with pleasure, soften with sympathy, kindle with new thought, as the treasures of Nature and art were unrolled before her. And then he went on to think that he could afford himself this pleasure, that he had come home with the avowed intention of finding a wife, and how far all other girls he had ever met fell short of the charm of her refined simplicity and sensibility.

But how was he to cultivate her friendship—a mere stray fellow-passenger, without any sort of introduction between them? It seemed almost hopeless, except for the promise to inquire particulars of his friend at Nice. He must make the very most of this opening, and request the brother's address before they parted company.

There had been a long silence. The carriage had got fuller as they neared London. In another half hour the journey would be at an end. Clive was quite taken aback at the despair which came over him at the mere thought of the parting with his quiet *vis-à-vis.* He must make an effort to gain some clue by which he might meet with her again. So, folding up his newspaper with a rustle, he remarked on their nearness to their journey's end, adding,

'And about my friend at Nice: I will write to him by to-night's post to make all inquiries, if you will kindly give me your brother's address, so that I may communicate to him, or to you, what particulars I may learn.'

'O, thank you very much,' replied the girl quietly. 'But I have been thinking it over, and I don't fancy Donald would like my giving so much trouble to a—a stranger. Though indeed it is most kind of you to offer to help us,' she added quickly, as if afraid the first part of her remark might have sounded ungracious.

'Then is there nothing I can do for you?' he asked, in a tone so despondent that the girl thought it must be assumed in joke, and glanced up with a merry answer on her lips, till, seeing how grave he looked, she changed her mind and said,

'Yes, since you are so really anxious to be kind, you can tell me the most respectable jeweller I could go to, on a little matter of business.'

He mentioned the name and address of one of the best West-end firms.

'Thank you,' she said, taking out her purse and writing the name

on the tablets therein. As she did so, his attention was again attracted to the glittering diamond ring. It was evidently one of great value, and the gold in which it was set was curiously chased.

'I would advise you to keep your glove on whilst going through the streets,' he said, in a low tone, and glancing at her ring. 'You will forgive the suggestion, but that ring is too evidently of value to be exposed recklessly.'

'Thank you for the hint,' she answered, drawing on her glove. And then she added, with what struck him afterwards as assumed carelessness, 'I wonder what its money's worth really is; have you any idea? It was my mother's engaged ring. My father bought the diamond, and had it set in India, I have been told.'

'Indeed, that must make its value priceless to you; but I should think its market value could hardly be less than fifty pounds,' answered Clive.

'Really? O, I am so glad!' exclaimed the girl, her eyes glistening with pleasure.

Clive felt annoyed, he hardly knew why, at her evident appreciation of £ *s. d.* And yet after all was it not natural, a girl who had known the gall of poverty, no doubt?

But there was no time for reasoning on the matter, for here they were, arrived at the great city, and all was stir and commotion.

'Would you be so very kind as to help me find my luggage?' asked the girl, as Clive handed her out.

Of course he would, and secure her a cab too. The sagacious young man thought that thus at least he would be safe to find out the brother's address. So he put her into the four-wheeler with all her goods, and then asked eagerly,

'What address shall I tell him to drive to?'

'O, to the jeweller's, please,' replied the girl, repeating the name of the shop he had suggested.

The driver caught the well-known name in a moment as he leaned down for his orders, and before Clive had had time to repeat it, he had whipped up his horse and the cab was off.

As Clive Fenton stood staring after the disappearing vehicle in blank despair, some one touched his arm, and looking round he saw the lady who had shared his cab at ——.

'Will you befriend me once more?' she said. 'My luggage has been stupidly left behind at ——, and I can't get hold of the proper official to telegraph for it. It is a shame to trouble you; but my cousin and I have no gentleman to help us, and I have already proved your willingness to aid.'

Of course Clive had no alternative but to go back with the good lady and the cousin who had come to meet her, and see to the telegram being sent. But I am afraid he felt very savage at the delay, and forgot his wonted chivalry in his impatience at the folly of women going about travelling alone, who could not look after themselves.

Full ten minutes had elapsed since his other travelling companion had set forth for the jeweller's, and his first impulse to follow her in another cab would now be utterly futile. What could he do? He racked his brains in vain, as he was whirled along in a hansom, to the boarding-house he had patronised earlier in the summer. It was a sign of how much his heart was in the matter that he actually forgot his dinner, and had no sooner deposited bag and baggage in his old quarters than he was off again on his hopeless search. Presently he found himself staring into the jeweller's shop aforesaid, and in a minute more he had entered it,

without any definite intention, but urged on by a restless despair.

As he strolled up to the counter, thinking what trifling article he should ask after, his eye was suddenly caught and dazzled by a glittering diamond ring that lay upon it. Surely he knew that curious setting? Yes, there was no mistaking it—it was the same ring concerning which he had warned his young travelling companion so short a time ago, when her eyes had kindled with pleasure at the high price he had valued it at. In a moment his resolution was taken. He would purchase the ring, cost what it might—it was his only remaining clue. The price was a heavy one; but Clive was pleased rather than otherwise at this, for he knew that the sum realised by its owner must have been good in proportion, the jeweller being an honest man. And as he walked off with the precious bauble on his finger, his spirits were so much lighter, that he remembered how hungry he was, and, turning into a restaurant, enjoyed a hearty dinner.

CHAPTER III.

ALTHOUGH Mr. Clive Fenton felt considerably relieved by his possession of the precious ring, it was difficult to see how that fact alone brought him any nearer the object of his search. The private business which had taken him to London kept him somewhat busy during the next two or three days; but in all the intervals of business those gray eyes haunted him, and the vision of the demurely-clad maiden, with her bright look of intelligence and her quiet self-possession, was never long absent from his mental vision. As time went on, and the chances of ever meeting her again seemed to grow less, he tried to argue himself out of his infatuation, as he called it; but in vain. He was obliged to confess himself hopelessly in love, and to marvel at this utterly new experience in his hitherto prosperous career.

For Clive Fenton was not one of those men who have been always in the habit of falling in and out of love from their childhood upwards. He was a very sensible practical sort of person in general, and his life heretofore had been too wholesomely occupied with work to leave him the temptation of idleness to fall into folly. It was in keeping with this practical side of his character that he had come home now on two years' leave of absence with the clear intention of taking a wife back with him, to preside over his Indian home. But it was not in accordance with this side of his character that he should have fallen head over ears in love with a little unknown maiden in a third-class railway carriage, who had neither beauty nor wealth to attract him—nothing, in fact, beyond the pleasant comeliness of a fresh English girl in her simplicity, a pair of steadfast gray eyes, and evidently a heart equally steadfast and true. Perhaps for the man who had never known the nearer ties of mother or sister—his mother had died at his birth—the sisterly devotion he had discovered in this *incognita* possessed an especial charm. At all events he had been unwittingly taken captive, and soon ceased to try to disentangle himself from these new chains.

As soon as the pressure of his business was over, and he was at leisure not only to think but to act, he suddenly resolved to pay another visit to the jeweller, on the mere chance of finding a clue to the former owner of the ring. He guessed now what 'the happy thought' had been which had occurred to the girl in the train, and which she had preferred to keep a secret. Evidently it was the selling of her dead mother's ring, to enable her to try the last chance, humanly speaking, for her living brother's life.

Doubtless they were already on their way to the sunny South, two poor inexperienced children as they seemed to this man of thirty, little guessing how soon their small fortune would be swallowed up in the expenses of English life abroad. It was foolish of her surely, and over-prudish, not to accept his offered help. And yet he liked her all the better for the intuitive self-respect which her courteous refusal showed.

Thus thinking, he strolled preoccupied into the shop, and was not a little surprised when its owner hastened towards him, exclaiming,

'I am so glad to see you again, sir. I have been hoping much that something might bring you this way.'

'Indeed; and why?' asked Clive.

'You will remember the diamond ring, sir, I sold you a few evenings ago?'

'Perfectly,' answered Clive, touching the ring on his finger. 'Here it is, you see.'

'Well, sir, I should like to repurchase it from you, if you have no objection. But I must tell you its story, in order to excuse what may seem a cool request. I had purchased it of a young lady about an hour before you came into my shop, giving her its full value; for I confess I was touched by her story of a brother's illness, and of her adopting this means of raising money to take him abroad. Her simple confidence in me led me to give her perhaps even a better price for it than prudence might have dictated, with the probability of its lying long on hand.

You may imagine, therefore, that your speedy purchase of it was no little relief to my mind. Next morning, however, the young lady visited me again to re-purchase the ring, at her brother's urgent desire, he having been much distressed at her having parted with it, as it had belonged to their mother. She was dismayed to find it gone, and asked if I could not prevail on its purchaser to allow her to buy it back. I told her how unlikely it was I should ever see you again, but promised, if you should revisit me shortly, to lay the case before you.'

'Return her the ring, by all means,' said Clive, slipping the costly bauble from his finger and laying it on the counter.

'Thank you heartily, sir,' said the shopkeeper, beginning to count out the money to return to his customer.

'Nay,' said Clive, with a short laugh, 'I do not sell jewelry; I am not going to compete with you in your own trade. The young lady must take it as a gift, or not at all.'

The jeweller stared in open-eyed astonishment at this very extraordinary young gentleman, who seemed to value fifty pounds at so easy a rate.

'Your generosity is too great, sir; and, pardon me, I do not think the young lady's pride would allow her to accept it. There was a quiet dignity in her manner, young and simple as she was, that would not make it easy even to offer such a gift to her from a stranger.'

'But what if I am not such an utter stranger to her as you think?' replied Clive. 'Stay,' he added hastily, taking a note-book from his pocket and writing a few lines on a slip of paper which he tore out from it. 'Stay. Enclose this with the ring when you return it— that will surely do away with any scruples.'

The lines were as follows:

'Your fellow-traveller in the train trusts you will allow him the privilege of returning you the ring, concerning the care of which he cautioned you, and which it has been his privilege to secure from other hands. C. F.'

Nothing more. No clue to his whereabouts, no possibility permitted of returning him the money.

The jeweller glanced at the lines dubiously, as Clive added,

'I happened to travel up from the country with the owner of the ring, and, like yourself, was interested by her simple dignity and evident trouble. And as I can well afford to indulge myself in my whim,' he added, with a laugh, 'I do not see who is to hinder me. Now I will wish you good-day.'

So saying he turned and left the shop, ere its master had time for further expostulation.

It was wonderful how light-hearted he felt after this little episode. It led to nothing further, as far as he could see, in his chance of meeting again the girl in gray; but it seemed to have set up a subtle link of sympathy and comradeship with her, which was all the more delightful, perhaps, for its very intangibility.

Clive Fenton went about his business as usual, visited old friends, and attended to all his social duties with even more than his customary genial pleasant manner; for deep down in his heart lay the thought of his unknown ideal, the surety that sometimes at least he would be remembered with gratitude by that artless maiden, and perchance be a topic of conversation between her and her sick brother.

Sometimes a dread would come over him that the brother might be worse, and that she might be passing alone through a season of suffering and sorrow. At such times a great longing would seize him to try and find her out, to go again to the jeweller, his only clue, and make him his confidant. But his feeling for her was too sacred to be breathed to any indifferent person, much less to a mere stranger; and he had purposely kept away from the jeweller's neighbourhood lest, on any casual meeting, his money should be again urged upon him.

So the weeks slipped by; and the time came when Clive Fenton, according to a previous arrangement, was to accompany his aunt and cousins in a trip to the Continent. Clive himself determined their route, including visits to Nice and Mentone, and other resorts along the Mediterranean on their way, with motives half hidden from himself.

A merry party they were, the young cousins taking their first glimpse at foreign climes, and being proportionately enthusiastic at the first sight of the blue Mediterranean, and at the varied beauties of the Riviera. But although merry kind-hearted girls, Sibyl and Flora were, after all, little better than frivolous butterflies at this stage of their existence, flitting from flower to flower with careless joyousness, and with little real appreciation of what their pretty eyes rested on, and their pretty lips admired. Clive looked on with the half-indulgent half-critical air of an elder brother, and was often rallied by his fair cousins for his grave looks and absent thoughtfulness. Was it a pair of gray eyes that haunted him with their bright intelligence? Was it the remembrance of what he had said to their owner of the delights in store for her, as he had watched her enjoyment of their quiet English scenery in the train, that set his thoughts wandering? At all events, he grew graver and more absent as time went on, and

Nice and Mentone had both been explored and passed. The girls wondered why their cousin was so eager in perusing the lists of visitors at these places, and rallied him on his lonely explorations of the less fashionable parts of these towns. Clive bore their raillery good-naturedly, but his spirits were unusually—and as he declared to himself unreasonably—depressed as the party turned their backs on beautiful Mentone, *en route* for Bordighera and its palms.

CHAPTER IV.

CLIVE had established his aunt and cousins in the comfortable Hôtel d'Angleterre as soon as Bordighera was reached, and then sallied forth to explore the old town, and to revel in the beauty of the surrounding palm-trees.

He had mounted to the town, and, taking a path to the left round it, had reached an arched passage which formed the entrance to a steep street, when his eye was arrested by the beauty of the scene.* He was gazing towards the west, over some rough old battlements in front, with graceful palms below them, and a solitary cypress in striking contrast to the feathery palm-fronds. Below him lay the level olive-groves, and white against the deep-green sea the picturesque Hôtel d'Angleterre, where he had left his friends; while beyond again, his eyes rested on the Fort of Ventimiglia, and the promontory of Monaco, and the still farther stretching coast.

It was late in the afternoon of an October day, and the setting sun was flooding sea and sky and land with a glory of light. Clive's

* For a description of this scene, see Dean Alford's *The Riviera*, p. 72, from which it is taken.

depression passed away, like a cloud lifted, in the presence of all this beauty. Involuntarily he took off his hat, as though in a church Suddenly, as he stood there bareheaded, a voice broke the stillness which set his heart beating with unwonted eagerness.

'Donald,' said a clear young voice, 'we had better go in now. The sun will be down in another half hour, and then it will grow chilly all at once.'

'As you will, little one. I feel as if I had taken in as much beauty as I could digest for one day,' answered a voice equally clear, but less firm and strong.

'Yes, indeed, it is almost too perfect. I feel sometimes as if I could hardly bear it,' answered the first speaker, in awed tones. 'O Donald, think of this, and then think of your London attic!'

As the last words were uttered two figures arose from a sheltered nook hard by, and suddenly faced Clive as he stood spellbound, hat in hand.

The girl started, and blushed brilliantly at this unexpected apparition. Donald felt the arm on which he rested tremble, and turning kindly to his sister, said,

'What ails you, Dorothy?'

Before she had time to answer, Clive had recovered his self-possession, and coming forward, with a flush mantling in his dark cheek, said,

'I have had the great privilege of meeting your sister before, when travelling in England awhile since, Mr. Donald. May I introduce myself as Clive Fenton of the Bombay Civil Service, staying just now with my aunt and cousins at the Hôtel d'Angleterre below there?'

Donald held out his hand—a thin and wasted one, alas!—as he said,

'I am indeed glad to have met you, sir, and to have an opportunity of thanking you for your

unheard-of generosity to strangers like ourselves. And also—you will pardon me, but it must be so—of returning you the ring which you could not bring yourself to resell to us. Dorothy, give it to the gentleman.'

Dorothy's glove was off in a moment, and she slipped the diamond ring from her finger, and moved shyly to place it in Clive's hand. She feared it seemed an ungracious thing to do; but she and Donald had often discussed the matter together, and Donald was very emphatic in his decision, that they could not be under so great an obligation to a stranger as the receiving the ring back for nothing would place them; and that, as he had declined the money, their only alternative was to keep the ring in charge for him until, through the jeweller or otherwise, they should succeed in hearing of him again. Meantime Dorothy always wore the ring, with perhaps an added interest from the little romance connected with it. Nevertheless she agreed with Donald as to what would be their duty in the matter, and held it out now in her little brown hand for Clive's acceptance, saying, as she did so,

'You must not think that we do not value your generous kindness, but indeed we cannot keep the ring.'

The words were said so gently, and there was such a kindly deprecating look in the gray eyes, that Clive could not be offended. He took it quietly from her, saying as he did so,

'It is a great disappointment to me to have to receive it. I had hoped that little affair had been happily arranged; and I have no use whatever for the ring, which must be so valuable to you. However, I will submit to taking charge of it on one condition,' he added more lightly, 'namely, that you and your brother will allow me the privilege of your friendship, and of introducing you to-morrow to my aunt and cousins.'

To this proposal both brother and sister acceded gratefully, and, as Clive walked back with them to their modest lodging over a baker's shop, at the top of a steep street, and commanding a lovely view of palm-trees, blue sea, and distant rosy hills, Dorothy expatiated on the wonderful kindness they had experienced on all hands since they had come abroad.

'It is your old story of that day in the train,' said Clive, with a kindling face as he bid them good-bye; 'but I think now, as then, that it is your own pocket-sunshine that makes the world seem so bright to you.'

And lifting his hat deferentially, the young man walked away.

At the *table d'hôte* that evening his cousins were delighted with his altered manner; he was the very life of the party, and described in such lively colours the beauty of the views from the old town, that they and his aunt were all eager-ness to visit it on the morrow.

'And, by the way,' he added with assumed carelessness, 'some recent acquaintances of mine are lodging up there, a brother and sister, travelling for the brother's health. I should be glad, aunt, if you would call on them when we are up there, and ask them to join us in any excursions we may make.'

'Certainly, my dear Clive. What is the name did you say?' inquired the lady innocently.

Poor Clive, what an awkward position for him! His aunt and cousins all raised their eyes expect-antly, and, to their extreme sur-prise, observed an unmistakable blush on their self-contained rela-tive's face.

'Upon my word, I haven't a no-tion!' exclaimed Clive at last,

laughing in spite of his self-con-sciousness. 'To tell the truth, I met the young lady travelling in Eng-land, and we had a little conversa-tion together, and cemented our acquaintance when we met just now in that region of palm-trees. Her brother is in a decline, I fear, a gentlemanly talented young fellow; and their father is dead, and their stepmother has children of her own, so these two are everything to each other—quite a pattern bro-ther and sister,' he ended, with a forced attempt at lightness.

'You seem to know a great deal about them, for a mere casual ac-quaintance,' said pert Miss Sibyl, looking mischievously into her cousin's perturbed face.

'Considering I don't even know their surname, I can't be said to have made much progress as yet,' replied Clive quietly; 'but I hope our friendship will ripen speedily now.'

And with that he left the ladies, and retired to enjoy his daydreams under the star-lit skies, with the aid of a cigarette.

Mrs. Fenton was not at all sure that she cared to cultivate the ac-quaintance of this unknown bro-ther and sister, but she never thwarted Clive; and accordingly, on the very next morning, a pil-grimage was made to the baker's shop in the old town, and Clive introduced his relatives to his un-known friends.

Dorothy's happy ease and charm of manner came to his rescue at the awkward moment of introduc-tion.

'How very, very kind of you to come and seek us out!' she said, as Mrs. Fenton made rather a stately bow in response to Clive's introduction of, 'This is my aunt, Mrs. Fenton. Allow me to in-troduce her to you, Miss—' 'My name is Dorothy Durnford,' the girl went on, setting chairs by the pretty window for her visitors, 'and my brother Donald will be here directly, and will be cheered by fresh English faces.'

Donald entered just then, looking very refined and very fragile, with sharpened delicate features and lustrous dark eyes. The lady's interest in him was aroused at once. She had lost her only son at nearly the same age, and she could hardly keep the tears out of her eyes as she hastened towards the invalid, and took his wasted hand in her own.

From that moment the thing was done. The two families were daily together; and not only was the stay at Bordighera prolonged in order that it might be so, but Mrs. Fenton persuaded Dorothy to join their party in travelling still further south, pointing out the advantage to her brother of constant change and easy travelling, which would be better secured to him as one of their party.

Dorothy could not but accept, with tears of gratitude, when, in answer to her protest of lack of means, Mrs. Fenton begged them to be her guests for the time, urging as her plea the interest she felt in Donald as recalling her own lost son.

And so a time of enjoyment beyond the very wildest of her daydreams came to pass for quiet happy Dorothy. They went as far south as Florence, then up to Venice, and thence to the Italian lakes, where they lingered till the time for the Fentons' return to England drew near.

Nothing was wanting to Dorothy's content. Donald daily improved, and his spirits as well as his health revived among such kind and congenial friends; for he was petted and made much of on all hands, and he began to talk of returning to his work with quite a new hope for the future. Then

the joyous light-heartedness of Sibyl and Flora was very catching; and Dorothy felt a child once more, as, throwing off all her cares, she joined in their merry fun. Mrs. Fenton's presence, too, gave a feeling of propriety to it all, which was an important item to demure little Dorothy's satisfaction. But, above all, ever at hand to point out fresh beauties, to describe and explain works of art, to suggest historical associations, to throw, in short, the charm of a cultivated intellect and of a refined taste over everything, was Clive himself. He said not a word of love to scare Dorothy at the outset. He was more than content to see all her faculties waken up in her new surroundings, to meet the glad look of welcome in her eyes whenever he entered the room, to watch her ready response to the thoughts he treasured up for her. Day by day his only endeavour was to please and interest her; and, almost unconsciously, happy ideas seemed to flow into his mind, and pour themselves forth to her. He gave her of his best, and there was a great deal of value stored up in his cultivated intellect and thoughtful mind. And in return she not only drew him out, as he had never been drawn out before,—till not only his aunt and cousins, but he himself also, was surprised at this revelation of his unsuspected powers,—but her fresh keen interest threw a new charm into everything, till Clive was often carried beyond himself, and could hardly maintain his usual calm demeanour. It was a happy idyllic sort of time, a bright spot, for ever radiant in the memory of two at least of the party.

But the most delightful times must have an end. And the day drew near at last when Mrs. Fenton must return to England. A friendly consultation was held between her and her guests, and it was decided, in spite of Donald's arguments to the contrary, that it would undo all the good he had gained, were he to return to England for the winter. Mrs. Fenton had written to a friend of hers at Nice, and had secured remunerative employment for Dorothy as a teacher of English, and thither the brother and sister were to return shortly; whilst their kind friends were to pursue their homeward journey over the Simplon Pass, so as to give the girls a passing glimpse of Switzerland.

It was the last day of their sojourn together on the banks of Como, and Clive had planned a row on the lake for the afternoon. But the wind blew a little fresh, and Donald feared to venture. Mrs. Fenton declared she could not leave her invalid on this last day, and Flora and Sibyl decided to remain with her.

'Won't you have pity on me, Miss Dorothy?' asked Clive, looking very wobegone.

'Shall I go?' asked the girl, turning to Mrs. Fenton with an eager face.

'By all means, my dear. Clive must not be cheated of his row because the girls are lazy, and I cannot tear myself away from our dear invalid,' replied Mrs. Fenton, glancing at Donald with almost a motherly smile of affection.

So Dorothy went off with a light heart to don her hat and jacket, too happy in the present to be sad about the parting on the morrow. Clive, however, was unusually grave and preoccupied as he rowed the light boat out into the rippled lake. At last he lay on his oars, and they drifted quietly along, still in silence, for his gravity rather awed Dorothy; and though she longed to break the stillness, she hardly knew how. The remark she made at last was not *apropos* of anything in particular, unless glancing at her own hand, which she was trailing in the sparkling water, suggested it.

'You never wear your ring?' she said, looking up at him suddenly.

'No, I am keeping it for my wife,' he answered laconically, and there was silence again.

'For his wife!' Somehow the idea jarred upon Dorothy. Of course he would marry; but who would be good enough for him? Not Flora or Sibyl, kind and bright as they were. It must be somebody very different, very clever and beautiful and good, and above all very devoted to him, who could be worthy of such high honour.

So thought the demure little maiden, as she lay quietly back in the boat, giving no sign of the feeling stirred within her. Clive, glancing at her, thought to himself, 'She cannot care for me; she did not even start or blush when I spoke of my wife; it is nothing to her whom I marry.'

Perhaps the impending gloom of the parting on the morrow had depressed him unduly; at all events, it was in a very dolorous voice that he spoke again.

'But it is nonsense to speak of my wife; I am never likely to marry. I have lived a lonely life heretofore, no doubt I can live it again; and it will come to an end some day, as far as this world is concerned.'

Dorothy looked up now, with an expression of startled wonder in the gray eyes.

'Something has vexed you?' she said, in a tone of most gentle sympathy. 'Cannot I help you? There is nothing I should like so well.'

Clive's countenance brightened at once.

'Yes,' he said, 'you can, if you will—you, and you only. You can help me to a wife.'

'I! Can I do that?' asked the girl, in most unfeigned surprise. 'But I know no one good enough for you; you ought to have some one so wise and beautiful and good, I cannot tell where to find her for you.'

There was something very sweet in the earnestness of her simplicity. Clive could contain himself no longer; he must risk his all on the venture now, come what might.

'O Dorothy,' he said, leaning forward, and looking eagerly for his answer into her truth-telling eyes, 'do you not know that it is *you* that I want, your own sweet self, and nobody else; and that if you say me nay, I shall remain a lonely bachelor to the end of my days, with only the bright memory of the past few weeks to cheer my solitude!'

The colour mounted into Dorothy's cheeks now in a brilliant fashion, and her eyes fell before his gaze, as she said, in a voice so low that he had to lean nearer to catch the precious words,

'I am not worthy of you, but I cannot say you nay.'

And then, before she could look up, her left hand was lifted out of the water, where it had been lying all the time, and the diamond ring was slipped on the fourth finger, and Dorothy's fate was sealed.

We will not intrude further on their happiness, as they drifted about on the glittering lake till the sun sank in the west. But when at last Dorothy set foot on *terra firma* again, she felt as if she had passed through a whole lifetime of bliss, as if the bright beams of the setting sun had thrown a glory over her path in life which would lighten it to the end.

The parting had not to be gone through on the morrow, after all. Instead, the whole party travelled back to Nice together, and there, in due course, a quiet wedding took place.

And when at last Mrs. Fenton and her girls returned home, it was without their escort. But Mrs. Fenton's motherly heart was comforted by the knowledge that she had left Donald now in the best of hands, and that, with Clive as well as Dorothy to attend to him, he would want for nothing that was good.

LITERARY AMATEURS.

By J. A. B. OLIVER.

IT is a reflection full of consolation for those despondent ones whose productions uniformly meet with a polite repulse from hard-hearted and unappreciative editors, that all writers, great as well as small, must have begun sometime, and that, as a rule, their first efforts underwent the same heart-breaking process of repeated postings and receptions, accompanied by the laconic 'Declined, with thanks.' Thackeray had many of his earlier compositions returned to him. Mrs. Henry Wood, it is said, collected a drawerful of rejected tales before *East Lynne* made her name. Carlyle was rejected as a contributor to the *Edinburgh Review*. Not articles merely, but works destined to live in the page of history have suffered the same fate. Defoe sent *Robinson Crusoe* round the English publishers before he found one willing to print it. The travels of *Jane Eyre* in search of a purchaser are well known. Carlyle's *French Revolution* was rejected. Likewise Motley's *Dutch Republic*. Did not Milton, too, sell his immortal *Paradise Lost* for five pounds? Let beginners, then, be not cast down, for the same hard apprenticeship must be served by all. First attempts, even although they may bear the strong imprint of genius, are invariably crude in expression. They have immaturity or 'greenness' written in every line. Either the beaten tracks are too closely followed, insipidity and namby-pambiness being the result, or all rules are boldly defied, and an original style adopted which the public will not tolerate except in men like Carlyle and Ruskin. To hit the happy mean between ordinary and extraordinary writing is the study of all who wish to catch the public ear ; and it is not wonderful that beginners fail when practised writers are not always successful.

Amateurs are very apt to look upon editors as their most implacable foes. The cool persistence with which they decline to avail themselves of contributions which the contributor is convinced would make the fortunes of the journals, if they only knew it—such blindness to self-interest—rouses pity in the breast of the worldly-wise amateur. He indites a letter of remonstrance to the misguided editor, and is promptly crushed. In some a less tender emotion than pity is aroused by such conduct. Rage very often agitates the bosom of the rejected poet. Smarting under a sense of gross ill-usage, he pours out the vials of his wrath upon that incarnation of fraud, injustice, and wickedness, the editor. Why should *his* poems be rejected when so much trash is inserted? Why is no reason for rejection vouchsafed to him? He hysterically demands satisfaction. The amount of this sort of correspondence that goes on is surprising and distressing. It is distressing because it shows such a lamentable want of tact on the part of the contributors. No editor can reasonably be expected to reconsider his decision. If he were to do so, every rejected article would be sent in half a dozen times, each time with a slight alteration here and an addition there; and it would be necessary to have six editors instead of one to examine the contributions in their successive stages of development. How such an economical system would work, we leave the reader to imagine. Naturally this badgering of editors never leads to 'business.' If an editor declines a proffered contribution because it is unsuitable for his magazine, it is not likely that he will be bullied into taking it; and any attempt to do so will be resented and remembered. The bad taste as well as bad policy of amateurs who adopt such a course of action cannot be too strongly censured. If they really believe that their article, or poem, or whatever it may be, is worth publishing, let them send it the round of the periodical press from the *Nineteenth Century* downwards; and if it fail to find a haven of rest from its wanderings somewhere, its proper place is in the fire. It ought to be borne in mind that, although the reading public devours an immense amount of rubbish, and pays for it too, it will not swallow the literary garbage produced by all who choose to scribble on paper with a pen. There is a vast difference between well-written nonsense and the clumsily-hashed encyclopædia or over-strained sentiment of beginners.

There has recently been published for the guidance of embryo Salas, Taylors, and Yateses, who do not know how to begin, a little book entitled *Journals and Journalism: with a Guide for Literary Beginners*, by John Oldcastle (London: Field & Tuer, 1880). That such a book was needed, or at all events wanted, is testified by its sale. Beginning is undoubtedly the most difficult step in a literary career, and aspirants owe a debt of gratitude to Mr. 'Oldcastle' for his kindly aid. He is convinced that there are thousands eager to follow in the footsteps of our great writers, nearly all of whom, whether journalists or not, began by contributing timorously and obscurely to the newspaper and periodical press; and in the hope of lending a helping hand to the Macaulays and the George Eliots of the future, he has drawn up this little book, which will enable them to proceed to work in a business-like manner. It is to be expected that, having such an excellent manual of procedure in their hands, amateurs will renounce those many little eccentricities of conduct—gushing notes on crested note-paper, lofty disclaimers of any wish for remuneration, pathetic narrations of personal grievances and woes, and frantic appeals for the reason of rejection—that have hitherto constituted them a peculiar and very objectionable people in the eyes of editors; but it is also to be feared that the encouragement afforded by the knowledge that Mr. Tennyson, until lately, received from one firm 4000*l.* annually for his copyrights, that Sir Walter Scott got 2000 guineas for the *Lady of the Lake*, and that Lord Byron made 24,000*l.* by poetry, will cause fountains to spring up all over the country, from which ceaseless streams of inspiration will flow into the editorial waste-baskets. Such never-drying wells of sentiment are plentiful enough already.

Mr. 'Oldcastle' does not believe in the efficacy of introductions to editors. He says: 'There is an impression universally prevalent among beginners that to be introduced personally or by letter to an editor is one of the essentials of a literary *début*, albeit the only introduction which really avails is good and marketable work. It is difficult to convince them of the fact that recommendation will not do a great deal for them, or that they can possibly receive justice without it. "A good word from a trustworthy source will induce the editors to read my things," says the amateur invariably; "as it is, I am certain they do not read them." The unpalatable fact is, however, that when a MS. is not read, the reason in eight cases out of ten is, that the editorial eye, which is as practised in gauging at a glance the quality of literary work as is the eye of an art collector in determining instantly the approximate value of a picture, has summarily given a decision adverse to the offered contribution. Good things are too well worth having to be carelessly foregone.'

In accordance with these views, Mr. 'Oldcastle' advocates the practice of sending manuscripts from editor to editor until a satisfactory destination is found. 'This is a common way of getting a footing in periodical literature, and one which we have heard, perhaps, the most experienced editor in London recommend to young men who came to him for counsel.' A recent writer in *Belgravia*, who complacently pointed to 14,000*l.* as the gross earnings of his pen, took quite a different view of the matter, and regarded this method as hopeless, because he did not believe that such fugitive contributions are ever read by editors. In thus giving the lie to the editor of the *Contemporary Review*, who returns proffered articles with the comforting assurance that ' it is too able an article not to have been read with interest,' he has probably a measure of truth on his side; for to suppose that every editor conscientiously reads every paper that any casual contributor thinks fit to send him is to give him credit for a capacity for doing work far beyond what Nature has endowed any other members of the human family with. Of course it is purely optional whether editors read the unsolicited contributions of outsiders or not. Nearly all magazines and journals have an adequate staff of their own. Hence the productions of amateurs can only be accepted if they are of exceptional merit, or if the subject dealt with happens to be particularly suited to the times. This the editorial eye can discover at a glance; and so beginners may be satisfied that rejected MSS. are really unsuitable, or they would not be sent back. But our having arrived at that conclusion does not afford much consolation to the amateur, who wants to know how to get his articles accepted—how, in fact, to make a start in the career of letters. If he follow Mr. 'Oldcastle's' advice he will write articles and despatch them to suitable periodicals; he will keep them constantly circulating round the periodical press; he will frequently augment this floating literary capital by fresh additions of 'copy;' he will not be discouraged although the manuscript ring thus formed shows signs of circulating for ever without a break being made in it by the abstraction of an article; and he will do all this in the sublime consciousness that 'persistence is the secret of success.' We hope Mr. Oldcastle bore in mind the circumstance that editors are mortal. They are more patient and long-suffering than the generality of mortals, we admit; but it seems doubtful if they would consent to expend their valuable labour and time upon the examination of an interminable series of worthless articles sent in by an individual who has adopted for a motto ' Persistence,' and who hopes to attain success by acting up to it. We need not quote the saying about a bad name adhering to an animal of the canine species. Our persistent amateur would soon become well known in the editorial offices. The character of his productions being already known, they would be returned to him without being looked at. They might improve and become really readable articles; but the improvement would not be noticed, and unless he could enter a new field where more impartial treatment would be accorded him, his progress might long be impeded by the effects of his youthful ardour. There is another reason why this ever-circulating plan is not likely to meet with success. Nearly all magazines, or at least all those of the better class, have individual characteristics both of scope and style. The flavour of *Chambers's Journal* is unmistakable. *Cornhill* is æsthetic. *Good Words* gives a prominent place to travel. *Cassell's Family Magazine*, as its name implies, is essentially domestic. If, then, an article be written with a view to insertion in, say, *Chambers's Journal*, unless the author means to insure rejection, he will endeavour to catch the general tone of that magazine, and follow it as closely as he can. Should his article be refused in that quarter, is it likely that it will find acceptance in another? It may happen to deal with a very general subject in such a very general way as to render it suitable for almost any periodical; but, as a rule, if refused by the editor for whom it was specially prepared, it will run a poor chance of being accepted by any other one unless it be carefully remodelled and rewritten before being submitted in a second quarter. The absurdity of sending a paper intended for *Cassell's Magazine* to *Cornhill*, or a light article designed for *London*

Society to the *Nineteenth Century*, is sufficiently apparent. Although we do not recommend the adoption of Mr. 'Oldcastle's' plan, which is obviously calculated to try alike the patience of editor and contributor, we are far from wishing the beginners to consign all rejected MSS. to the flames. When an article has the misfortune to be declined on its first candidature, let the writer fix upon another journal or magazine within whose scope the topic dealt with falls, and rewrite his paper in a style suited to it. Nothing can be lost by doing this, and a great deal may be gained. In the first place, the article itself will be improved. Second thoughts are generally the best. We are told that Macaulay and Cardinal Newman penned many of their pages twice, thrice, and oftener; that George Henry Lewes re-wrote everything before submitting it to a magazine; and that Mr. Albany Fonblanque frequently wrote an article ten times over before it contented him. With such examples before him, surely the amateur need not feel himself degraded by revising his work. And secondly, the process will prove the most useful exercise the beginner could possibly have. After all, the principal difference between the regular journalist and the tyro is one of practice; and the more practice the beginner gets the sooner will he develop into a full-blown journalist. The amateur will doubtless think this a very slow way of beginning. It is so; but it is sure. The man who goes to work in the way that we have suggested will not, perhaps, turn out so many articles as he who dashes off anything that comes uppermost in his mind, and sends it hither and thither in search of an asylum; but he will have fewer returned to him, and he will be first in the field as an efficient writer.

A MASTERPIECE OF CRIME.

By JOHN AUGUSTUS O'SHEA.

I.

SOME mortals are born under an unlucky star. Jonathan Smith was of them. There was his vulgar name to handicap him in life's race, at the outset. Then, he was poor and had no brains to speak of, and—unkindest of all—he considered himself a man of genius.

His first anxiety on reaching the age of puberty—which for him did not mean the age of discretion—was to adopt a pseudonym; his second, to adopt another; and so on for ten years, until he had exhausted all the *sobriquets* within his fantastic reach in the effort to throw the curiosity—the fancied curiosity rather—of his contemporaries off the trail of his identity.

No matter what name he took—noble, middle-class or basely mechanical, foreign or home-made, romantic or prosaic—Cavendish, Thompson or Sikes, Giovanni Romano or John Bull, Guy Chastelar or Tom Merry—he remained in the depths of obscurity. The least known of workers at the pen, the most unrecognised of novices, the poorest of the horde of Grub-street, glory would have none of him.

' E pur, si muove !' he used to exclaim, as he tapped the bony casket of his skull with his index finger. ' I have something here.' He believed his skull was profound because it sounded hollow.

'Were not Sheridan and Disraeli failures in their parliamentary beginnings? and yet see to what greatness they arrived ! And I, Jonathan Smith, shall I despair? No. Perish the thought !'

The aberrations to which literary vanity can push those who are afflicted with it are inconceivable. There are men of genuine ability whom it has made ridiculous, if not worse. It has sometimes induced them to give way to shameful or odious follies. What may not its effect be, therefore, when it racks an unfortunate wretch of notorious incompetency? Worn-out patience, wounded pride, the growing sense of impotence, a career wasted in futile attempts to succeed renewed again and again at the stimulus of ambition—these accumulated trials are surely enough to drive a weak man to thoughts of suicide or crime.

Jonathan Smith shrank from the idea of death. He was not physically brave enough to throw down the gauntlet to the King of Terrors. Besides, his pretensions to intellectual superiority might find gratification in doing something bad and base, not to himself, but to his fellows. He reasoned that his genius had so far gone astray in following the dreams of art, and that destiny marked him out for the violences of action. On the other hand, crime might bring him a fortune, and, at last, riches might conduct into the full blaze of noonlight this transcendental mind which was withering in the chill of poverty. From the artistic and moral point of view, the unappreciated Jonathan convinced himself that it was absolutely necessary that he should commit a crime.

He did commit one. And, as if Fate wished to justify his reason-

CC

ing, for the first time in his life, he accomplished a masterpiece.

II.

ABOUT two years before the day when Jonathan Smith sold himself to the Devil, he had lived in the fourth story of a tenement house in Stockfish-court, in the parish of St. Giles. Lost in the crowd of squalid lodgers, known only under one of his numerous pseudonyms, he had there cultivated the acquaintance of a buxom and youthful, but garrulous, serving-wench, who made him the recipient of all her small confidential gossip. She waited on an aged widow, very eccentric and excessively rich, who occupied a floor in a house in Great Coram-street. When this female had finished her day's work she returned to Stockfish-court. Jonathan Smith had resided in the place for about a month.

One evening, as he was quitting the Strand Hospital, where he had been to visit a friend, a resident pupil, he recognised his former acquaintance of Stockfish-court in a dying state in one of the wards through which he was passing. She beckoned him over, and told him she had left the widow's service but three weeks before, that she had been replaced by a woman from a Home, that her mistress was too infirm to come and see her, and that she felt quite miserable.

'I can understand that,' said Jonathan. 'Naturally, you would like to have an interview with her.'

'No, no, not that at all,' muttered the moribund female; 'but I'm afraid, if I die here, that she will read all the letters I left at her place, and despise me after my death.'

'And why should she despise you?'

'Bend over me, and I will make a clean breast of it. I want to make my wickedness known to somebody, and to whom rather than to you? I may confess now that I always had a hankering after you; but you were above me in station. You are a scholard, and I was only in service. But there was another man in the 'ouse at Great Coram-street, a mechanic, a cabinet-maker, by the name of Wiggins. If the missus only knew that horrid fellow's carryings-on with me, 'twould be my ruin. He was all for money, he was—the wretch; but I was a fool to listen to him. He is the father of my child. That was his hold upon me. He always kept promising that he would acknowledge the baby, and marry me. Now, I know it was all make-believe on his part; but never mind. I have enough money to leave after me to keep my little one above want, and my missus, who is a good soul at bottom, will look after her; for I have a letter written to her, telling her all about my misfortune.

'The letter is under my pillow, and I want her to get it when I am dead, but only if my papers are burned beforehand. If that is not done, I would eat the letter first. I don't want the missus to suspect how bad a girl I have been. She would have no pity for my child if she knew it to be the daughter of an unmarried woman and a thief.'

'Don't take on so, my poor friend,' said Jonathan brusquely; 'but explain to me exactly how the land lies. You are talking too fast, and mixing things higgledy-piggledy. If I am to do you any service, I must know the truth, the whole truth, and nothing but the truth. I'll do all I can for you, but I must know everything first.'

At that moment Jonathan Smith had no notion of crime. He was simply yielding to his literary curiosity; for he scented the plot of a tale, and prepared himself to hear the materials of sensational 'copy.'

'Hold up my head, and I'll try and tell you my story. That's better. I fell down in the street with an attack of apoplexy, and they brought me here. The missus left me here, for the doctors said I was too ill to be removed. I wrote to her, and she answered me. The woman who is in my place came to see me on her behalf. But neither to her nor to missus could I speak of what is on my mind. I have a bundle of letters from the cabinet-maker—from the father, you know. They are full of villany, of encouragement to commit thefts, and of thanks when I had committed them; for I robbed, yes, I robbed my missus, and all on his account. The cussed letters! I should have burned them. But they were sweetened with flatteries and words of love, promises of marriage, and vows that he would acknowledge our child. I kept them. One day the scoundrel threatened that he would take them and expose me. I refused him money, and he gave me to understand that, once he had the letters, he would do what he liked with me. I was weak enough to believe him; for I was in an 'orrible state of fright. All the same, I did not like to destroy the letters. To get them out of the way, I asked the missus to let me put some family documents, of value to me, into a bureau, where she kept her own.

'Missus gave me a drawer for myself, and a key. I know I have only to let her have a message that I want the papers, and she would send them immediately. But I have no confidence in the woman that's with her, and she's the very one that would be sent with them. From some words she let drop, I can guess that *she is the cabinet-maker's friend now!* He is paying her attentions, and she has let herself be taken in by them; for he is a handsome soft-spoken bla'-guard. But if he is wheedling her, 'tis only to get those letters. Now, you understand my trouble. O, if you would only do me a kindness! I have no claim on you, 'tis true; but it would be a real mercy if you would render me this service.'

'What service?'

'To bring me my letters.'

'But how am I to get at them?'

'It is easy as possible. Every evening before bedtime missus takes chloral, and at ten she is as sound asleep as a 'umming-top. At that hour there is nobody in the place but herself; the serving-woman always leaves at seven in the evening. She does not know that missus takes chloral, for missus kept that very quiet always, through fear of robbery. She only told it to me—to me, because she trusted me so much, the poor old lady! Well, you can enter her rooms at ten—she will never hear you going in or coming out—and you can fetch me my letters. There is no danger of nobody noticing you; besides, even if they do, you can pretend that you are going into the cabinet-maker's shop.'

'You're silly, woman. How could I open the bureau? and the widow's set of rooms, how could I get into them?'

'I have a duplicate key to the bureau. To my shame I had it made to help me rob the missus. Here it is; the little one opens my drawer. One of these others is a latchkey for the hall-door, and the other opens the missus's rooms Do me this kindness, I entreat you. I don't know why, but I have faith in you. I am sure you will act a friend, and aid me to die in peace.'

Jonathan Smith took the bunch of keys. His eyes were set. A sudden paleness overspread his face. Nervous contractions twisted his thin lips. The possibility of a crime had flashed across his mind. This woman, by whose couch he was leaning, once out of the way, the thing was easy of execution.

'My poor girl,' said he, 'I would go far to do you a kindness; but tell me, may not the cabinet-maker be on the premises and guess what I am after?'

'No, no; he is never there at night; he only works in the shop on the ground-floor.'

'And how am I to get into it, if anybody interrupts?'

'I have a key for that, too; it was there we used to meet. There it is.'

Jonathan took the key—he had now five—and chuckled to himself that he was almost as well-furnished as a locksmith.

The conversation had been carried on in an undertone; but now a short sharp gurgling cry came from the bed.

'O, I'm choking, I'm choking!' gasped the patient, who was exhausted by her long narrative. 'Water, water! something to drink!'

The ward was in semi-obscurity, faintly illuminated by a nightlight. There was no attendant near. The occupants of the neighbouring beds were in profound repose. Jonathan lifted the head of the sick woman, drew back the pillow, and, clapping it to her mouth, pressed upon it with all his strength and weight. He had the awful determination to preserve that position for ten whole minutes.

When he raised the pillow and looked upon the woman's face, all was over. She was suffocated. She had been unable to make a single movement, or utter a single moan. She had the appearance of having succumbed to cerebral congestion. He replaced the pillow under her head, and drew the coverlet under her chin. The corpse had the tranquil aspect, to those who might pass carelessly by, of a wearied sufferer in a deep sleep.

The murderer walked quietly out of the hospital, passed the porter with a nod, and an instant afterwards was in the mad whirl of the busy tumultuous Strand, with its streams of rattling cabs and carriages, its crowds of hurrying pedestrians, its lively shops, its cheerful noises, and its blaze of glaring gas.

It was twenty minutes past nine o'clock.

Jonathan Swift walked as far as Drury-lane, entered a tavern there, and drained a pint of ale; then, hastening across Holborn, he made his way to the house in Great Coram-street, which he reached at five minutes to ten.

On the road he had matured his plan.

He opened the hall-door and coolly passed in. There was none to perceive him. Seizing his opportunity, he unlocked and pushed ajar the door of the cabinet-maker's shop, and groped his way to where a working-suit lay roughly thrown across a bench. By the dim rays cast into the shop from the fanlight, he perceived a coarse cotton-mixture necktie. He tore a strip from one end of it, and then, stealthily shutting the door, stepped boldly but cautiously up the stairs till he reached the entrance to the widow's set of apartments. He turned the key, and walked on tiptoe into her bedroom. She was sleeping, as he had been told and expected, 'sound as a humming-top.' He grasped her firmly by the throat and held her in his vice-like clutch for a full quarter of an hour, until the eyeballs, released from the lids, projected in glassy bulbous stare, and the tongue, tinged with froth-specks, protruded some inches. She would never wake again.

Jonathan then opened the bureau, and found in the large middle drawer a medley of railway bonds, leases, assurance papers, and parochial and other receipts. These he pushed aside with a gesture of disgust. In the drawers to the right and left he was more fortunate. In one there were piles of tempting yellow sovereigns; in the other, bundles of crisp bank-notes—five thousand four hundred pounds sterling in all. He had the demoniac self-possession to count them.

He next searched for the letters the woman he had smothered in the Strand Hospital charged him to find. He burned them in the chimney, taking care to leave intact the fragments most compromising for the serving-wench and the cabinet-maker. A few, well chosen, were sufficient to reconstitute the story of the baby, of the provocations to theft, and the thefts committed: He arranged them so as to give rise to the suspicion that they had been set fire to in a hurry, and that the murderer fled before they were completely destroyed. He put the shred of the necktie in the rigid right hand of the dead lady. He slipped out then—again unperceived—and rushed to Holborn, where he subsided into the easy gait of an honest citizen immersed in thoughts of business.

Decidedly Jonathan had genius—genius for crime; and he had worked his evil deed with the hand of an artist.

III.

No crime is a true masterpiece unless its author gets off scot-free, unstained even by the breath of suspicion. On the other hand, impunity cannot be perfect unless 'justice' condemns an innocent man.

Jonathan Smith enjoyed this perfect impunity.

There was no hesitation in laying hands upon the assassin. Evidently it was the cabinet-maker, Wiggins. The remains of the burnt letters were infallible clues to his guilt. Who but he, the accepted lover of the servant, could know so well the favourable moment for the atrocity? Who else could have got the keys into his possession? Did he not commence by robbing the widow in concert with his paramour? From robbery to murder is but a step. Besides, did not the accusing shred of that torn necktie speak trumpet-tongued? To crown his misfortunes, the cabinet-maker had bad antecedents. He was the associate of burglars. Finally, he was unable to give any satisfactory account of how his time had been employed at the fatal hour. Thus the last frail plank of safety fell from under his feet. It was useless for him to make denial, or protest his innocence. Everything went against him. There was not a single valid plea in his favour.

He was tried at the Old Bailey, condemned to death, and strung up by the neck in the raw of a winter's morning within the precincts of Newgate. Judge, jury, the bar, the press—all were unanimous that for once Scotland-yard had shown vigilance and vigour, that the law had been vindicated and a foul assassin made a condign example of, as warning to the tribe of ill-doers. The public conscience was tranquil on this head. There was but one obscure point in the whole business. What had become of the widow's money? It was obvious that the scoundrel, Wiggins, had hidden it in some well-chosen spot. That the money had been taken by him was unquestionable, for was not robbery the motive of his crime?

It was universally admitted that never, in the annals of turpitude, had a murder been brought more providentially home to the Cain who had imbrued his hand in the blood of an unoffending fellow-creature.

IV.

THE consciousness of a good action, they say, brings balm and peace to the soul; but few thinkers have the hardihood to maintain that impunity for a bad action can also carry happiness in its train. Nevertheless, it is true. Jonathan Smith was happy. He had the full enjoyment of his double murder, and tasted of the fruits of his criminality in the most undisturbed ease. He felt neither remorse nor terror. The only sentiment which chafed him, and which swelled by degrees, was an overpowering pride. An artistic pride, above all. The very perfection of his work, and the sense that he was inaccessible to attack, caused him to forget every moral consideration. In that reflection alone, his thirst for the sentiment of superiority found wherewith to slake itself—even to drunkenness. But, apart from that, he was as before—a weak, mediocre, justly unknown man. In vain he tried to force the gates of fame with his stolen money-bags. Literature would recognise himself, but not his writings. He contributed generously to the Newspaper Press Fund, the Royal Dramatic Fund, the Newsvendors' Benevolent Fund; he gave suppers and drinks to the hangers-on of third-class journals; he wrote a drama, which was produced at the East-end and damned; he started a magazine, which died after the first number of a plethora of his own prose; he feasted Grub-street: but the British public would not hearken to him but to laugh at him. His articles, tales, rhymes, and plays were uniformly stamped with the trade-mark of incapacity. Under the pseudonym of Horatio Primrose he was known to men in the world of letters as an amateur who had more bullion than brains. But that stern unbribable public made a mockery of his money, and refused to give him credit for an ounce of talent. He stood convicted of mental imbecility.

'Notwithstanding,' he often said to himself, with a flash in his eyes, 'notwithstanding, if I only wished! If I were to recount my masterpiece—for masterpiece it was! There can be no doubt about that. Horatio Primrose is an ass—be it so; but Jonathan Smith is a man of genius. All the same, it is bitterly mortifying to think that an act so admirably conceived, so powerfully carried out, so neat and successful in all its details, should be condemned to everlasting oblivion. Ah! that day I had the true inspiration; that day my breast heaved under the *divinus afflatus* of brightest malice. I have done but one great thing in my life. Why did I perform instead of writing it? If I had written it, I should be celebrated. I should have but one tale to point to; but everybody would read it, for it would be unique of its kind. I have accomplished a masterpiece of crime.'

In the long run, this idea assumed the force of an hallucination. For two years he fought against it. He was devoured, first, by the regret not to have conceived a fiction instead of having done an action, and, next, by the desire to recount the action as if it were a fiction.

It was not the demon of perversity which pushes criminals to avow their crimes, as in Edgar

Poe's tales, which haunted him; it was purely a passion for literary renown, a craving for reputation, a sort of prurigo of glory.

Like to a subtle counsellor who demolishes objection after objection, and brings captious arguments into play, his fixed idea pursued him with a thousand questionings:

'Why should you not write the truth? What do you fear? Horatio Primrose is sheltered from the law. The crime is stale. Everybody has forgotten it. The author of it is buried in quicklime under an unchiselled flagstone. You will be thought merely to have woven an artistic narrative out of a few columns of police intelligence. You can put in it all your dimly-shadowed thoughts, all the grudges that drove you to murder, all the shrewdness and address you brought into exercise to compass it, all the circumstances that were furnished like gifts by that most marvellous of inventors whom fools nickname Chance. You alone are in the secret, and none can guess that you sought out your plot in the actual. They will only discover in your story the opulence of a rare imagination. And then you will be the man you wish to be, the great writer who reveals himself late, but by a stroke of undeniable genius. You will enjoy your crime as malefactor never enjoyed his. You will reap from it not only gold, but laurels. And who knows? After this first victory, when you shall have a name, you will cause them to read your other works, and compel them to reverse the unjust opinions they have passed upon you. On the highway of fame, it is only the first stage which is planted with thorns. Have pluck, man! Summon to your aid but a tithe of that marvellous temerity you had one day in your existence. Recollect how it succeeded. It must command success

again. Take opportunity by the topknot. The ball is at your foot again: kick it! You cannot conceal from yourself that the job was splendidly done. Chronicle it as it happened, without fear or equivocation, proudly, in its majestic horror. And if you have any faith in me, you will do the big brave thing —sign the narrative, not with a pseudonym that looks like your name, but with your real name, which they are sure to take for a pseudonym. It is not Cavendish or Chastelar or Tom Merry, not even Horatio Primrose, or any of that crowd, you must link to immortality, but yourself alone, Jonathan Smith.'

Accordingly, one fine evening, Jonathan Smith sat down to his desk, a block of virgin paper before him, his head on fire and his hand in a fever, and, like some true poet in the throes of a great composition, at a single sitting he dashed off the vivid history of his crime.

He told of the miserable commencements of Jonathan Smith, his Bohemian existence, his multiplied failures, his proven mediocrity, his fierce rancours against society and fate, the hot wayward impulses towards suicide and sin which held epileptic revel in his brain, the revolt of a heart deceived by the chimerical, and yearning to avenge itself on the real—in short a penetrating psychological romance, a remorseless scalpel scrutiny of the inner man. In a style of studied soberness and with a harrowing precision, he described the scene in the Strand Hospital, the scene in Great Coram-street, the scene in Newgate gaol, and the triumph of the actual assassin. Then with a satanic incisiveness he analysed the causes which had induced the writer to publish his crime, and finished by the apotheosis of Jonathan Smith—who placed his signature at the bottom of the confession.

V.

A Masterpiece of Crime was brought out in the orthodox three-volume form, and had an immediate and an enormous sale. It took the town by storm. Within six weeks, it ran into nineteen editions. Some faint estimate of the sensation it created, may be gathered from the following excerpts from the notices which appeared at the time in exponents of public opinion—that is, opinions of professed critics —in organs of various and varying altitudes of importance :

'It is the secret of Polichinelle that, under the *nom de plume* of Jonathan Smith, is to be recognised the facile pen of Mr. Horatio Primrose, a gentleman who takes a particular delight in this harmless species of literary masquerade. After having too long wasted his abilities in minor fields of culture, less grateful to the peculiar mode of mental husbandry he affects, he at last has hit on a golden vein, and has gratified us with the revelation of unexpected power. His *Masterpiece of Crime* is, indeed, a masterpiece of inventiveness, of lucid disentanglement of a ravelled skein of intrigue, and of strenuous character-painting. It would be uncharitable to the subscribers to our libraries to divulge the plot ; but we may broadly state that the moral of the narrative—for there is a deeplying moral—'&c.—*The Times.*

' This is a book of depraved and debasing tendency, utterly vicious in intent and execution, and the more dangerous that it bears evidence of having been written by a man of unrivalled art in his profession. We pray—and we ask our readers to join with us in the prayer—that he may be brought to see the error of his ways.'—*The Christian Gnomon.*

' Not since as a gentle child, with a gigantic appetite, I sat at my father's knee and made faces at my elder sister, have I read a tome so entrancing. It is almost as wholesome as, and far more interesting than, the trial of Palmer. Only Gubbins could have been its hero ; only the Gineral could have written it ; only Yonder could read a stolen copy of it with true appreciation.'—*The Sporting Times.*

' Thomas de Quincey (good master printer, prithee, do not capitalise that *d* !) once wrote a paper on murder considered as one of the fine arts ; and Barbey d'Aurevilly has left on record, in his admirable *Diaboliques*, a novelette in opuscular form entitled *Le Bonheur dans le Crime.* Both were right according to their lights, although wrong, peradventure, taking their productions as far as their moral influences are concerned. Murder may be elevated to the dignity of a

learned profession ; the criminal may rise to the height of mental serenity. But this merely *en passant*. Horatio Primrose, a promising young writer, whom I am proud to welcome to our Republic, has just given us a work, *A Masterpiece of Crime*, which lies before me on my escritoire as I sit down to collocate my weekly Echoes this present Wednesday—a work which I am fain to own has yielded me much, albeit not unmixed, pleasure. The author is of the school of Grimod de la Reynière and Restif de la Bretonne. In his truly remarkable performance, the quaint elbows the *bizarre*, the passionately tragic runs in double harness with the broadly droll, the poetically impossible is cheek by jowl with the improbable. It is as if the late Mr. Calcraft were to dance a saraband with the spirit of Duns Scotus, the ghost of the dead Garrick with the living J. L. Toole. I have known but one other man in the course of a tolerably chequered and extended career—*ay di me !* our hairs *will* whiten and the crowsfeet spread in expansive splaydom—who could indite such a volume. It was at Metz I met him in the very hot autumn of 1870—at Metz, whither we were both blown by a simoom from Fleet-street. A small man, but of heroic stomach and venturesomeness astounding, was O'Goggerdean of the *Avalanche.* He had been, they said, a colonel of American Federal cavalry, a Confederate bushwhacker, a Mexican guerillero, a Spanish contrabandista, a Garibaldino, one of the Milia di Marsala of course, a Fenian centre, and a Pontifical Zouave. He had the *Newgate Calendar* by rote, had travelled hundreds of miles to witness a revival of *Jack Sheppard*, held Robert Macaire in adoration, was ready to maintain at the sword's point that *Dick Turpin's ride to York* was the finest spectacle in the world; and yet he paid his poor's rates. Of kidney with him is Mr. Primrose, and I trust he too pays his poor's rates. His book I can recommend, provided only he be, like my irascible friend O'Goggerdean, "sound on the goose."

Mem.: Can any of my many correspondents tell me where I can find a complete set of Restif de la Bretonne's tractates ? I have sought for them in vain at the British Museum.

Item: What is the exact meaning of *caboulot ?* I fancy it is loaned from the Franche-Comtois dialect. Mr. Primrose uses it nine times in his volume.'—G. A. S. in the *Illustrated London News.*

' You have doubtless heard of the new novel, the success of the season, *A Masterpiece of Crime.* It is admitted on every side to be one of the most magnificent productions which has emanated from the press since Tom Moore electrified the universe with his Melodies, and set human nature in accord with the music of the spheres. Need I tell you it is the offspring of an Irish mind ? The author is a distinguished member of the Home Rule party, who is hoping shortly to have the privilege of going to prison for the good of his country.'—London Correspondent of the *Dublin Freeman's Journal.*

'Consummately utter, utterly consummate—in brief, clever, quite too awfully clever, this enchiridion.'—*The Æsthete.*

'A deucedly amusing study of murder, this of Primrose's (no relative of my Lord of Dalmeny), but blotted by the ugly blemishes of conceit, cynicism, Crichtonism, and the like. The man knows nothing of the ramifications of Scotland-yard. Now when I was at Washington (D. C.) I met,' &c.— T. T. in *Truth.*

M. Hans van Braun, the celebrated commentator on Beaumarchais, delivered a critical and exegetical conference on *A Masterpiece of Crime,* at John-street, Adelphi, at which members of most of the great literary clubs, such as the Savage and the Junior Garrick, were in attendance. The learned gentleman established analogies between Primrose and Hoffmann, elucidated the predisposing organic incentives to wrong-doing, made a few happy digressions into the Pelasgian attributes of the earlier rhapsodical drama, and finally arrived at the deduction that Primrose was almost clever.

To sum up, the book was a hit. It was praised by the judicious, it was damned with faint praise by the envious and those anxious to be smart, but it was read by all.

The publisher rubbed his hands in secret, and smiled as if he had good conscience and appetite.

Nevertheless, in all those criticisms, even the most flattering, two things inevitably turned up to worry Jonathan Smith.

The first was that the writers obstinately persisted in taking his true name for a pseudonym, and in calling him Horatio Primrose.

The second was that there was too much said of his rich imagination, and that the wonderful realism of his narrative was not brought into sufficiently strong relief.

The absence of these two desiderata irritated him to such a degree that, in pondering over them, he forgot all the happiness of his

dawning renown. Some sensitive *littérateurs* are thus constituted; even when the critics spread under them a bed of roses they are querulous if there be the slightest rumple in one of the leaves.

As an instance of how he felt, it is well to give an anecdote of this stage of his experiences. Walking down Oxford-street one afternoon, an acquaintance congratulated him on his book; there was the ring of the genuine metal in the work; when would he give them something again like *A Masterpiece of Crime?*

'My good sir,' said the coming great man, 'your congratulations would take another turn if you only knew the word of the enigma. My story is founded, not on fiction, but on fact. The crime *was* committed, literally as I have written it down, and I am the assassin. My real name is Jonathan Smith!'

He said this coldly, with an air of profound earnestness, choosing his phrases deliberately, after the fashion of a speaker who wishes to impress his auditor that he is speaking the simple truth.

'Capital, by Jove! capital, Mr. Primrose!' exclaimed his acquaintance, with a grin. 'The joke is worthy of Theodore Hook, ha, ha! Of Theodore Hook, did I say? Of Ned Sothern, rather.'

The anecdote was printed in the gossipping columns of all the society papers the same week. The mystification by which Horatio Primrose sought to pass himself off as an assassin was regarded as delicious in its humour. The rising author was, palpably, an original of the first water. And then upon Primrose, as a peg, were hung a set of funny anecdotes of the McArdle, whose lurking foible it was to be taken for a circus clown; of Vere de Vere, who had cards printed, 'Mr. Marwood, P.E., Horncastle, Lincolnshire,' which he loved to distribute among casual companions; and of little Lord Sheepshanks, who always represented himself in his cups as a bandmaster in the Japanese Imperial Guard.

Jonathan Smith was infuriated by these allusions. In making his awful confession he had acted without exact sense of what he was doing. Now, he felt an overpowering need to be believed by somebody.

He renewed his confession to every man he met about town. The first day, this was spoken of as an excellent piece of drollery. The second, the farce was called monotonous. The third, Primrose was voted a bore. By the end of the week, he was declared an infernal nuisance, with his played-out 'chaff' and his self-conceited whimsicality. His unexpected success had turned his head. It was plain that the man had a bee in his bonnet; and his circle of good-natured friends bantered him to their hearts' content.

'Ah! this is too much of a good thing,' he cried to a knot of incredulous auditors in a corner of the Gaiety bar. 'Not one of you fellows is willing to credit me when I am telling you the candid truth. You won't admit that I have not only described, but executed, "a masterpiece of crime." All right. I shall soon put it beyond yea or nay. By this time to-morrow all London will know who is Jonathan Smith!'

VI.

THE following day he presented himself at Bow-street, before the magistrate who had committed the man, Wiggins, for trial.

'Your worship,' he said, 'I have come to give myself up. I am Jonathan Smith.'

'It is unnecessary to prolong the joke,' said the magistrate amiably. 'I am a subscriber to Mudie's. I have read your story with a great deal of interest and pleasure; and I am glad to have the privilege of complimenting you upon it. I am also not unaware of the pleasantry you have been playing off on your friends for the past week or so. Another in my place would be annoyed at your attempt to turn a police-court into a theatre for practical joking; but I have dabbled in literature myself in my time, and I can pardon the sally, since it affords me the pleasure of making your acquaintance.'

'But I tell your worship,' cried Jonathan, impatient at this long-drawn-out urbanity from the bench, —'I tell you emphatically that this is no practical joke! I swear to you on my most solemn oath that I am Jonathan Smith; that I did commit the murder in Great Coram-street; and, more than that, I can prove it to you.'

'Very good, sir,' said the magistrate: 'as we are not mightily busy to-day, and as I have got through the morning charges, I don't mind humouring the pleasantry. I tell you, beforehand, that I shall look upon it as a treat to hear how a subtle intellect like yours will set about demonstrating the absurd.'

'The absurd! But I have written nothing but the absolute truth. The cabinet-maker was innocent. It was I who made away with—'

'My dear sir, I am under the impression I told you I had read your story. If it pleases you to relate it to me *vivâ voce*, it will give me infinite gratification; but that will demonstrate nothing except what is familiar to me already— that you have a singularly rich and weird imagination.'

'I needed no imagination to commit my crime.'

'Not to commit it, but to describe it, my dear sir, to describe it. With your permission, since we are on the subject, I'll let you have a bit of my mind frankly. As for the style of the book, there, of course, you are the better judge. To my thinking, you gave just a little too free a rein to your imagination; you passed the legitimate bounds of fancy; you invented certain circumstances which outrage all probability.'

'But, again, I tell you—'

'Allow me, allow me! You will admit, at all events, that I have some competence respecting crime. I can assure you candidly that yours was not what I should call combined naturally. That meeting with the nurse in the Strand Hospital, for example, savours too much of the *deus ex machinâ*. The chloral is difficult to swallow.' (Here there was laughter in the court.) 'There are many other small details which trip in the same way. As a piece of literary handicraft, your story is charming, original, most skilfully worked up—in fact, what you gentlemen would call thrilling. As a writer, I admit that you are perfectly justified in travestying the reality, but your famous crime of itself is impossible. My dear Mr. Primrose, I am sorry to say anything to hurt you; but, whilst I admire you as a man of letters, I must say you would make a very indifferent criminal.'

'I'll soon show you whether I would or not!' yelled Jonathan Smith, springing towards the magistrate.

His mouth foamed, his eyes were bloodshot, his whole frame shook with passion. He would have strangled his worship if an usher, a warder, a police-constable, and a reporter had not rushed to the rescue.

After considerable scuffling, the madman was mastered, his hands were handcuffed behind his back, he was seized by four stout con-stables, turned face to earth, and treated to a 'frog's march' to the cells at the other side of the street.

Five days afterwards he was immured in Bethlehem Hospital.

'Genius, like beauty, is a parlous gift,' said Atlas, in the *World*, the following Wednesday. 'Poor Primrose—by chance, the censorious may hint—one morning woke to find himself famous. He achieved a solitary *chef-d'œuvre;* and so possessed with it did he become, that in the end he believed in the substantiality of his dream. It is the old fable of Pygmalion growing amorous of his statue.'

VII.

THE most terrible feature in the case was that Jonathan Smith was not mad. He was in perfect hold of his faculties, which but added to the tortures of his disappointed mind.

'Gracious goodness!' he said to himself, in the solitude of his cell, 'I am the most unhappy of men. What have I done that I should be thus crushed under the weight of misfortune? They will neither believe in my name nor in my crime. When I am dead I shall pass for simple Horatio Primrose, a newspaper hack, who had the luck to imagine one clever story, and only one; and they will take for a creature of fiction this Jonathan Smith—my very self, the man of coolness, of decision, of action—the hero of ferocity, the living negation of remorse. O, let them hang me, if they choose—I ask for it—but at least let the truth be known! If it were only for a minute before putting my neck in the halter; if it were only for a second, while the white cap was being pulled over my head; if it were only during the space of a lightning flash — I wish to have the certainty of my glory, the vision of my immortality.'

But the doctors only looked upon him as madder than ever. They took his complaints for hysterical ravings, and treated his paroxysms with shower-baths.

At length, as the inevitable effect of living in this fixed idea and of keeping the company of lunatics, he became a complete and confirmed lunatic himself.

And then, precisely then, O irony of Fate! the doctors pronounced him sane, and discharged him with a certificate that he was cured.

Jonathan Smith ended by imagining that he was really Horatio Primrose, and that he had never been an assassin.

He died in the conviction that he had *dreamed* his *Masterpiece of Crime* instead of having *committed* it.

FISHERMAN'S SONG.

O, THE fisherman's life is a dangerous life,
   As he rides o'er the wave's high crest,
From the sunrise flush to the midnight hush
   On the ocean's unquiet breast!
     And brave and undaunted
      His heart should be
     Who daily dares death
      On the treacherous sea.

And the fisherman's life is a lonely life;
   Full slowly the hours pass by;
No whisper, no sound breaks the silence around;
   No trusty companion is nigh.
     O, loving and tender
      His bride should be
     Who dares for her sake
      The restless sea!

Yet the fisherman's life is a noble life,
   For he calls no man his lord;
And little he recks on his foam-swept decks
   Of the gold that the landsmen hoard.
     For fearless and brave,
      Untrammelled and free,
     Is the life that is passed
      On the bounding sea.

STRAWBERRY LEAVES.

By RICHARD DOWLING,

AUTHOR OF 'THE MYSTERY OF KILLARD,' 'THE WEIRD SISTERS,' 'UNDER ST. PAUL'S,' ETC.

Part the First.

THE DUKE OF LONGACRE.

CHAPTER XII.

THE DUKE'S WEATHER.

THAT night Cheyne slept heavily. The journey and the change of air had helped to deepen his slumbers. Then there had been the exhausting excitement of the day he had just passed. It was near nine o'clock when he opened his eyes. For a while he lay awake, unable to recall the events which had brought him to this strange place.

'The sea,' he thought—'is that the rolling of the sea? Have I gone to Brighton or to Margate in my sleep?'

He jumped out of bed, and approached the window. Before he had crossed the floor, he remembered all. This was Bankleigh, whither he had come for the purpose of settling affairs with the Marquis of Southwold, and this roaring sound abroad was not the beating of the sea upon the shore, but the headlong flight of the wind across the land.

How did the wind blow?

He pulled up the blind, and looked out. The wind beat at an acute angle against his window, but as he did not know how the house faced, he could not tell from what quarter the wind blew. He rang the bell.

When the waiter entered, he asked abruptly,

'How's the wind?'

'Regular Duke's weather, sir. Your boots and the hot water, sir. It has been blowing a gale all night, sir. A gale, sir, it would take soda-water bottles to hold. You couldn't bottle a gale like that in any of your flimsy fifteenpenny claret bottles. Schwepps himself might be proud of a gale like that. Some of the early customers that came in this morning says that the sea is awful, and that many's the tree there's down here and there along the road. Duke's weather all out.'

'And you think there is a likelihood the Duke's yacht will be in soon?'

'She will, sir, as sure as country eggs are eggs, which they mostly are, sir. But town eggs, sir, especially them at thirteen for a shilling, are very often not eggs at all, but young chickens which hadn't the heart to face life. Talking about eggs, sir, reminds me to ask what you would like for breakfast. I never could make out, sir, why we should eat eggs more in the morning than any other time of the day, unless it may be that we are vexed with the whole breed and generation of fowl by being woke up at first light by cocks crowing, and then, when we see an egg, we revenge ourselves.'

Cheyne gave the necessary order for breakfast, and dismissed the talkative waiter.

The wind had not fallen. It was blowing a full gale from the north-east. The landscape, which yesterday had been flushed with the mellow green of early summer, now looked cold and bleak and dispiriting. The trees bent in the blast, and showed the dry faded green of their underleaf to the ashen sky. The grass and corn lay flat and quivering like a muddy green lake. The clouds were low and long, stretching in great jagged strips up into the wind, down into the lee. Birds were silent, and rarely left shelter. Everything was parched and gritty. All the life had gone out of the scene, all Nature looked barren, forlorn.

Cheyne dressed himself with deliberation and care. The yacht might come in to-day, and she might not. It was well to be prepared. When she did come in, he would lose no time in going aboard. He should go aboard, ask for the Marquis of Southwold, tell the Marquis he had something of importance to say which should be said to him alone. When they were alone, he should lock the door, and say what he had to say—do what he had to do. He should not be very long in coming to the point, once he found himself face to face with this cowardly nobleman. Nothing should move him from his resolution of wiping out, in blood, the deadly insult of that letter. When the good name of a man's mother was called in question, and when, at the same time, a man's own honour had been assailed, no one but a mean dastard could for a moment hesitate as to the course one ought to pursue.

No doubt Lord Southwold would refuse to fight. In all likelihood he would refuse pistols or swords. Then he should tell this arrogant liar that they should fight as they stood, armed with only manhood against manhood. If,

again, this lying miscreant refused, he should strike him, with his open hand, across the face. If this son of seven dukes did not respond to this, he would tell him, in plain words, what he was going to do. Then he should seize him and crush the vile breath out of his body, as sure as that they both owed their breath and their bodies and their manhood to the one great Maker.

They would call this murder. But was murder of the body of living man worse than, anything nearly so bad as, murder of a dead woman's fair fame? Eternal curses attend this reprobate wretch!

He ate his breakfast, but what it consisted of he did not know. The talkative waiter kept up a running fire of words; but what they meant, or what his answers conveyed, he did not know.

He had made up his mind to walk over to Silver Bay, and, as soon as breakfast was over, he asked the way and set off.

The gale had not moderated; and although Cheyne was one of the strongest men in England, he could not make rapid headway against it. In ordinary weather he would have backed himself to walk the four miles in less than three-quarters of an hour. This day, at the end of three-quarters of an hour, he had got little more than half-way.

He was in no hurry, and he liked the wind. He liked to feel it beat against his face and tug at his clothes. He exulted in the conflict, for at every pace he was conquering the enemy. He was in an excited angry humour—in a rage, the first rage he had ever known in all his life—and he exulted in having some kind of foe in front of him.

Then again, if what that loquacious waiter had told him was true, the wind against which he fought here was fighting for him out at sea, was driving that yacht with its accursed passenger towards him. When this thought crossed his mind, he reached out his arms to embrace the wind. It was no longer a foe, but a loyal friend, doing his work with all its might.

He wondered, Would the yacht come in to-day? Almost certainly not. She had, according to the man at the Shropshire Arms, gone to sea two or three days ago. This gale had been blowing only twelve hours, and it was not likely she had been last night within twenty-four hours' sail of this bay. But then one should remember that twenty-four hours of such a gale would do more than three days of light winds. That was so if the light winds had been fair winds, and the gale was a fair wind. But if the light winds had been fair, and this was foul, how would that be? To answer this question, one should know particulars as to the course the yacht had sailed, and where she was when the gale had struck her first. He knew none of these particulars, and therefore he had no choice but to give up trying to solve the problem.

Thanks to this wind, his victim would soon be in his hands. Unless—what an intolerable disappointment that would be!—unless the waves swallowed his victim up, that victim would soon be in his hands. It would be too bad if the sea robbed him of his revenge. Vengeance for an insult to a mother was the inalienable right of a son, and it would be monstrous to take it from him.

He pressed onward through the wind and blinding dust.

What should he do if this man refused to see him? Suppose, when he tried to get aboard that yacht, they would not let him, what should he do? He had never thought of that before. In case they refused to let him go on board, he should have to go on board by force. He should have the strength of ten. Ay, but he should have more than ten against. He could not hope to fight his way on board, across the deck, down the companion, and into the cabin, against such odds as would be opposed to him.

What should he do? What could he do?

Ah, that was a good thought! He should send in the name of Baker & Tranter, and make no other use of the name of the firm or of the information he had got through Freemantle. What an excellent thought that was! With the proceeds of the book, the *Duke of Fenwick*, he had been able to undertake this journey, and face any reasonable delay. With the name of the firm to which this man had written the libel on himself and his mother, he should gain admittance to the loathsome detractor. Here was a complete circle of poetic justice!

When asked for his name, he should say,

'A gentleman on business. Kindly mention the name of Messrs. Baker & Tranter. I do not happen to have a card of the firm by me.'

When he found himself in the presence of the Marquis, he should announce his own name, and say that he had written that book.

But suppose, when all this had happened, the Marquis said nothing, made no accusations, no admissions, what then?

O, confound it, Southwold would say something. Surely the Marquis would betray his opinions in some way or another, and then—

'Ah, is this the bay? Silver Bay? And here is the Castle—Silverview Castle.'

The gale struck him with its full force; for he now stood on the top of the high land by which the bay was surrounded. On his right rose the favourite home of the great Duke of Shropshire. He was in the ducal grounds, opposite the vast castellated pile of buildings, where the Duke lived when on shore ; and before him lay the unquiet gray waters of the bay, bounded on the seaward side by the reef of gray rocks and the narrow opening through which the heavy waters wallowed in huge uncouth billows towards the shore at his feet ; while all along the reef, and high above the summit of its rock, rose and fell at regular intervals a slow - moving irregular wall of dingy white spray. Beyond the reef lay the German Ocean, heaving and tumbling beneath the impetuous blast.

On the left or northern shore of the bay the water was comparatively smooth, and here a few fishing-boats lay moored. Somewhat south-west of the fishing-boat rose and fell the buoy at which the yacht Seabird swung when in port. At the northern corner of the bay lay the only strip of level ground on the shores of the bay, and here stood a few fishermen's cottages ; and from this rose a long private road of gradual ascent to the level of the Castle, reaching the upper land a little to the north-east of the Castle.

Except at that one strip of land at the north-east corner of the bay, at the right angle formed where the reef joined the mainland, the water of the bay was unapproachable by cart or carriage. There were three precipitous paths leading, at different points, from the top of the cliffs to three small sandy coves below. The road and the cottages had been the work of the present Duke. He had made the road, that he might have easy access to the water ; and he had built the few cottages, that

he might have at hand a few seafaring young men, from whom he might fill up vacancies in the yacht's crew, for neither he nor his son liked strangers. While the wild north-east wind swept over the sea and the downs, the cottages lay in secure shelter under the shadow of the high cliff and gaunt rocks, while the huge Castle stood up white against the withering blast.

The road to the little jetty was visible the whole way from the Castle to the water. That cluster of cottages was the only one within three miles of the Castle.

For a while Cheyne stood leaning forward against the wind, contemplating the scene. He looked out under the low clouds streaming up towards him, and could see no craft of any kind. He looked into the bay, and saw a few fishing-boats rolling slowly in the comparatively smooth water between him and the reef. He looked at the reef itself and the cataracts of white foam and waving haloes of dun spray. He heard the thunder of the ocean billows on the reef and swash of lesser waves upon the shore.

'What a storm !' he thought. 'And that yacht is out there—out there where the long waves, each with the weight of thousands of tons, press onward ceaselessly to the shore. It is wonderful to think man can build anything which can withstand the onslaught of such mighty waves, the fury of such relentless wind. It is almost incredible that any structure of wood could live afloat under conditions such as these.'

He pressed his hand firmly over his eyes, drew his coat tightly round him, and, leaning still more forward into the wind, pushed resolutely down the road leading to the jetty.

CHAPTER XIII.

A NOR'-EASTER AT SEA.

WHEN this north-east wind began to blow, the yacht Seabird was well away to the southward and eastward of Silver Bay. The reckoning was that she was from the bay a hundred and thirty miles as a crow flies. The gale had not come on the schooner suddenly. The Duke, the Marquis, and the captain were standing together when the south-west wind on which they had been sailing began to die, and finally shook out of the sails.

It was a beautiful moonless starlight night. When the wind fell, and the sails flapped idly against the masts, the Duke turned to Captain Drew and said,

'Well, captain, what do you think of it now?'

'I don't think much of it, your Grace. I think we're going to have a stifner. I don't like the look of it at all.'

'Where do you expect it from now?'

'Not out of the south'ard and west'ard again. No such luck. It would not surprise me a bit if it went all the way round to north, or even the east'ard of north. The glass is falling, it's been unnaturally hot for days, and I think we'll have a change.'

'So do I. I think the thermometer must have fallen also. Has it, captain?'

'Yes, your Grace, it has dropped from sixty-seven to sixty, and it is going down still.'

'I'm sure it isn't sixty now. I think you're right, Drew. I think it will be out of the north. I feel it in my shoulder. I feel the north-east is coming. What do you think, George?'

'I think so too. I am almost sure we shall have to put about before morning. It is growing colder and colder every moment.'

For a while there was silence on deck.

A tall raw-boned man with hollow cadaverous cheeks was at the wheel. He was a man of forty-five years of age, and one of the best seamen in the crew. It was the second mate's watch, and the next man who spoke aloud was the man at the wheel. He cried out, in as low a voice as would reach the officer in charge,

'Mr. Mate!'

'Ay, ay!' answered the mate from the waist, as he turned and walked aft to Pritchard, the gaunt cadaverous man at the wheel.

There was a loud flapping of sails at this time. For a while Pritchard and Starclay, the second mate, whispered. Starclay took the wheel for a moment, put it three spokes to starboard, put it three spokes to port, and then asked of Pritchard,

'When did you notice it?'

'Not until after the way went off her. I was playing with the wheel, and I felt something wrong.'

'Ay, something wrong, no doubt. I don't know what. We must see to it at once. I think we're going to have a bit of a twister. Awkward to have anything wrong there if we get into heavy weather. The captain is talking to the Duke, and I don't like going to him just now. Mr. Yarmould is lying down. I'll ask him to turn up.'

Yarmould was the first mate.

In a few minutes Yarmould, the first mate, came aft with the second mate, and taking the wheel in his hand, turned it three spokes to starboard, and then three spokes to port of 'steady,' shook his head, and then asked,

'How much was it free before from steady, Pritchard?'

'One spoke, sir, or maybe two. Did you notice, sir, that when you put it over three spokes and were putting it back six, between the second and third spoke you felt something?'

'Yes. It didn't come back smooth. I felt a check at about steady. That's queer, isn't it, Mr. Starclay?'

Mr. Yarmould was stout and low of stature.

'Yes, sir. I can't make it out. It goes over freely three spokes, and yet when it's coming back, it grates between two and three.'

The chief mate spun the wheel backward and forward once more, and then looked up quickly. It was impossible to see the expression of his face; but evidently he had made up his mind as to what was wrong with the steering apparatus of the yacht Seabird.

He said,

'The carpenter is in your watch, Mr. Starclay?'

'Yes, sir.'

'Ask him to step aft.'

When the carpenter had come, the first mate said,

'Carpenter, yesterday two spokes or three spokes of the wheel picked up the slack of the rudder-chain when the wheel was at steady in smooth water, now it takes six hands to pick up the slack. Try the wheel, and tell us what you think of it.'

The carpenter caught the spokes, and put them over, and put them back again.

'At half-way back I feel something,' said the carpenter. 'That is bad. It's not the chains, it's not the wheel, it's not the tackles—'

He paused a while, and all the men looked gravely into one another's face, but no one spoke.

The boom, with the great mainsail, lay over at the starboard side of the schooner. The Duke, the Marquis, and the captain were standing by the starboard main shrouds. The two noblemen were leaning up against the bulwark, and the captain was standing five or six planks to windwards, amidship from the bulwark, and in a line with a line drawn from a point about half-way between the mainmast and the companion. Thus he could not see anything of what was going on at the wheel, and the flapping of the sails prevented his hearing any of the words spoken further aft, beyond the cry of 'Mr. Mate!' to which he had attached no importance.

The lower portion of the bodies of the four men now at the wheel had been all along visible to the Marquis of Southwold. Such a gathering of the crew on the quarter-deck was, under the circumstances, exceedingly unusual, and it attracted the heir's attention. At last he spoke:

'I say, Captain Drew, what can all these men want aft in a calm at this time of night?'

The captain turned quickly round, stooped so as to be able to see under the boom, recognised by the bulk and stature of the four men who they were, and guessing from the fact that the first mate, whose watch it was below, was on deck, and in consultation with Pritchard, who he knew was at the wheel, the second mate, and the carpenter, said, 'I'll go see, my lord,' and dived under the boom and disappeared, all but the lower part of his body.

'What is it, Mr. Mate?' asked the captain.

'Well, sir, it looks bad enough.'

'The weather? I know it does. We're going to have it, and I think, Mr. Mate, a good deal, too, of it, out of the north. But we are able for all we can get. Eh?' The final interrogative was spoken, evidently, not with a view to an answer to the question it put, but with the intention of encouraging the mate to speak out and explain why a council should be held on the quarter-deck without him, at such an hour, and in a calm.

There was a perceptible pause.

' We think,' said Yarmould, in a whisper, ' that there's going to be a gale—'

' Well,' cried the captain impatiently, ' we're not feathers or chaff that we need be afraid of our being blown away, my sons.' He spoke with the impatient irritation of a man who knew he was being fenced with, and knew the men who were fencing with him would not be so unstraight, only that they wished to break to him some unpleasant fact.

' What is it?' the captain asked, seeing them all hesitate.

' We think, sir, there is something wrong with the steering-gear.'

' With the steering-gear ! With what part of the steering-gear? The chain?'

' No.'

' The tackles ?'

' No.'

' The wheel?'

' No.'

' The helm?'

' No, sir.'

' Then, in the devil's name, what is it?'

' We think the cap-irons of the rudder have worked loose.'

' *What!*'

For a few seconds no one spoke.

' Are you sure?' asked the captain.

' Take the wheel, sir, and see what you think of it.'

The captain spun the wheel first one way and then another. He thrust his cap back off his forehead, thrust his hands into his trousers-pockets, and remained motionless for a few moments.

Over the rudder-head was an ornamental seat.

' Carpenter,' said the captain, ' bring your tools and a lantern.

Knock away this seat, and let us see how things are.'

As the captain gave these orders the sails ceased to flap. Slowly the boom went over to what had, a little while before, been the weather-side ; the sails filled, and the schooner began to forge slowly ahead.

' Drew !' cried the Duke.

' Yes, your Grace.'

' Put her about and run for the bay. Good-night.'

' Ay, ay, your Grace. Good-night.'

' Anything wrong, Drew ?' called out the Marquis.

' I hope not, your lordship. We are going to try ; and when we know I will go below and tell you.'

' All right. Good-night, Drew ; good-night, men.'

' Good-night, your lordship.'

The carpenter brought the tools and a lantern. In a few minutes he had knocked away the ornamental seat, and revealed the rudder-cap to view.

There, unmistakably, was the explanation of the irregularity which Pritchard had noticed. The rudder-head was rotten ; and the cap-irons of the rudder had worked loose upon the wood, so that the helm, to which the cap-irons were fixed, played a little free to starboard and port before it gripped the rudder-head.

' What do you think, carpenter?' asked the captain, when the four men had recovered their upright position, after bending low to examine the rudder-head by the light of the lantern.

The carpenter shook his head gravely.

' It doesn't look wholesome, does it, captain? You're going to put the ship about, sir ?'

' Yes.'

' All right, sir. Put her about, and then we'll see what we can do.'

The sails were now full with the

north-east breeze, which was yet light. The yacht was put about. Her head was set for Silver Bay, and she lay over slightly, steered half a point to the northward of north-west, on the wind with the wind abeam.

When the yacht was tidy once more, the four men came aft again to where the man stood at the wheel.

'What do you propose to do, carpenter?' asked the master.

'Well, sir, you see there is no time to be lost. It was a bad bit of timber to start with, and now it's dozed. It's the first rudder she ever had?'

'It is the first rudder she ever had.'

'And it's five years since she has been on the hard or in a dry dock?'

'Five years since she got a good overhauling.'

'It is my opinion, sir, that any one would pass that rudder by sight until it began to give, which can't be longer ago than a few days.'

'What do you propose doing?'

'Well, sir, I'd say the best thing would be to wedge it taut inside the cap-iron. What do you think, sir?'

'You couldn't fish it?'

'No, sir, in no way. There's no room.'

'I think you're right, Mr. Carpenter. There is no other way but to wedge it. Do you think it will hold?'

'Yes, sir, I think it will. We'll lash it with half-inch as far as we can below the iron, and then we'll wedge it inside the iron. That'll hold it,' said the carpenter confidently.

'Ay,' said the captain. 'I don't think you can do anything better.'

The carpenter set to work at once. The man at the helm kept the wheel steady, and coil after coil was slowly wound round the rotten rudder-head. The carpenter wound the rope round and round as far down as the space between the rudder-head and the rudder-case would allow. Then he improved on his original plan, and wound the line over the coil already formed, thus doubling the thickness of the serving. When this had been done, the carpenter brought some pieces of oak, and cut them into long wedges. These he drove down with a caulker's mallet inside the cap-iron all round the rudder-head.

While the carpenter was lashing the rudder-head and driving in the wedges, the captain and first mate were walking up and down the quarter-deck together. As the carpenter had driven in wedge after wedge, he had noticed with satisfaction that each succeeding one required more driving. Hence it was obvious the wedges were telling. It was also plainly revealed, by the light of the lantern, that the play of the rudder-head within the irons of the rudder-cap had been reduced to almost nothing. This was exceedingly satisfactory. Now and then the captain had stopped in his walk to see how the carpenter progressed.

When the carpenter had driven in ten wedges he paused a moment, asked the captain to look, and said:

'What do you think of it now, captain?'

'What do you say, Mr. Carpenter?'

'Well, sir, I think 'twill hold now. See.' He caught the rudder and shook it forcibly.

'It works a little yet.'

'It does, sir. Do you think, sir, I might put in another wedge or two?'

'You see, Mr. Carpenter, it works a little free now; we're going to have a gale; if it works a little now, it will work a great deal more by and by, and I don't like the notion of that iron working freer and freer with a lee-shore under my bow. I don't like that notion at all. Do you think you could make it taut with a couple more wedges?'

'Yes, captain, I think I could, if—'

'If what?'

'If the iron will hold.'

'Ah!' said the captain, and the three men looked down gravely at the face of the carpenter, who was kneeling on the deck, and whose tar-stained caulker's mallet was partly illumined by the light of the lantern. The lantern was tilted up by a spike nail, so that most of the light was thrown on the rudder-cap and down the rudder-case.

'And what do you think of the iron, Mr. Carpenter?'

The man did not reply immediately. He took up an iron hammer and struck the iron sharply with it. The paint cracked and fell down the rudder-case into the black invisible water below. When most of the yellow paint had fallen off, the rusty wasted iron became visible.

'It looks all right, captain,' said the carpenter, raising his head.

'Well, knock in two more wedges. I don't like the notion of that thing working loose while we are in a gale with a lee-shore under our bow. I promised the Duke I'd tell him about this as soon as it had been put straight. I suppose I may count it straight now, Mr. Carpenter?'

'Yes, sir, I think you may. With the lashing and the wedges I don't expect anything will stir, and I have no fear of the iron.'

The captain walked forward and disappeared down the companion.

————

CHAPTER XIV.

TWO DISCOVERIES.

THE captain knocked at the cabin-door, and, having received permission, entered.

'Well, Drew, what is the matter?' asked the Duke, from a couch.

'The rudder-head is dozed, your Grace.'

'Dozed, Drew! And you found that out only now!'

There was a tone of alarm and reproach in the old man's voice.

'You see, your Grace, it is some time since she was overhauled.'

'Yes; but the rudder-head, Drew, the rudder-head! That is not a thing to trifle with.'

'Your Grace will remember I could not get at it, owing to the seat.'

'Well, talking won't undo the evil now. What do you propose doing?'

'We've cured it so far, your Grace. We've served the rudder-head with the half-inch, and driven wedges inside the iron all round.

'And you think it is safe now?'

'Quite safe for the run.'

'And you do not think it necessary or advisable to put in anywhere?'

'That's what I came to speak to your Grace about.'

'There's Izlemouth a couple of hours nearer than Silver Bay. How is the wind for Izlemouth?'

'Fair, your Grace. We'd carry it over the quarter.'

'And how is it for home?'

'Abeam.'

'She'd make a couple of knots more an hour with the wind on the quarter.'

'Yes, your Grace, and less leeway.'

'I am half inclined to run in there. And yet, if you are satisfied that the rudder-head will hold until we can reach Silver Bay, I'd much rather go home.'

'The rudder-head will hold, your Grace. I answer for that. Would your Grace like to come and see it?'

'No, no, Drew. I'll take your word for it. You know all about it. It's a wonder you never thought of running a knife into that rudder.'

'Well, your Grace, you see, it wasn't easy to get at. You see, there was the seat.'

'Ay, ay! So there was—so there was, Drew! I forgot that— I forgot that. You are not to blame. We must lay the Seabird up when we get in. We can hire or buy another yacht while this one is under repairs. What do you think we ought to do, Drew, sell her or repair her? What do you think?'

'You have had her a good many years now, your Grace.'

'Yes, yes. You think I ought to sell her. I think you are right. What course are you steering now, Drew?'

'Nor'-west, your Grace; for home.'

'Well, then, keep her on that tack—keep her on that tack. If you answer for the rudder, we'll go home. What do you think she'd fetch as she swims?'

'Fittings and all?'

He looked round at the superbly-fitted and furnished cabin.

'Yes. Just as she swims. We'd take our personal baggage ashore, and sell all the rest.'

'She's worth thirty pounds a ton builder's measurement, although, if she was a merchant ship, she would now be off the letter. Thirty pounds a ton, if she's worth a sovereign.'

'Then I tell you, Drew, we three have been shipmates many years now, and you shall have the old Seabird as she stands; and if you don't want to better yourself— you are too young a man to retire— you shall get us a new and a better boat, and be our captain still.'

'Your Grace, I shall be glad to command your new yacht. I am very proud to think you have still confidence in me, notwithstanding my oversight of the rudder—'

'The fullest confidence, Drew. As you say, there was that seat in the way.'

'But, your Grace, I would scarcely bring myself to take a present of the Seabird—'

'But you shall take a present of it. Neither I nor my son want her any more.'

'Well, if your Grace insists, I have no choice.'

'You have no choice. She's beginning to heel over already. She is beginning to feel this nor'-easter already, and so am I. My pains grow bad. I feel it in my shoulder now. You may go now, Drew, and lie down, or take a watch on deck, as you consider best. Anyway, have just another look at that rudder-head before you turn in, and come then and tell me what you think. We will then finally decide as to our course.'

When the captain regained the deck, he found the wind had freshened. There was as much wind now as she could bear with all fore-and-aft canvas set. It was not yet necessary to think of taking in sail, but it would be if the breeze got any stronger. She was now quite comfortable, with flying jib and gaff-topsails. The covering boards on the port-side were under. But Captain Drew would rather keep her going than insure a dry deck. The dead-lights were all closed, and everything snug except the rudder-head. It was worrying to think he should not have found out about that rudder-head until he was a hundred and fifty miles from Silver Bay, and upwards of a hundred and thirty from any port. But the wedging was sure to hold. In fact it couldn't help holding unless the wood was ten times worse than it looked.

Captain Drew went aft. The carpenter and first and second mates were still at the rudder-head. The broken-up seat had been carried away. Pritchard was still at the wheel.

'Well, Mr. Mate, what do you think of the cap now ?'

'Taut as a drum now, sir.'

'How does she behave ? How does she feel, Pritchard ?'

'Answers as good as new, sir. Look !'

He put the wheel a little to port, and then a little to starboard ; at each side, before he got the wheel two spokes over, there was a check, and plainly the jump of the rudder.

The captain rubbed his hands. He really thought now she would fetch forty pounds a ton, and to-morrow she would be his.

'Have you looked at the cap-iron, Mr. Carpenter ?'

'Yes, sir ; most careful.'

'How is that ?'

'Sound as a bell.'

The captain rubbed his hands again. What a fortunate thing for him, after all, was this fault in the rudder-head ! Only for it the Duke might not think, for goodness knew how long, of parting with the Seabird ; and, of course, until he did think of parting with her, he could not think of making her a present to him, Captain Drew. Wonderful how things fall out !

As far as the rudder went, all now being in a satisfactory condition, and the watch sufficiently strong to deal with the duty of taking in sail, the captain told the first mate to turn in and the carpenter to go forward to his own duties, having ordered him to leave the lantern behind him. To the second mate he said,

'I'll take charge, Mr. Starclay. You can turn in, if you like.'

'Thank you, sir,' said the second mate ; and he, too, went forward. The captain and Pritchard were now the only men on the quarter-deck. The latter went below, told the Duke, and came back to the deck.

Captain Drew was too full of thought for sleep. His pay was very good, more than very good. He was perfectly content to remain as he was. The Duke and the Marquis had always treated him well. He had nothing to complain of, and he had never complained. When he was afloat he lived like a prince. When he was ashore he had a comfortable home, and a wife and children, who were dearer to him than all the rest of the world. But, notwithstanding the liberal pay of the Duke, and that he had been many years in his Grace's employment, he had, owing to no extravagance on his part, but to the way in which he had kept his home and brought up his family, been able to lay nothing aside for a rainy day. Now he was between forty and fifty ; all his children were still upon his hands, and his pay was no more than kept them and his wife comfortably. He had of late felt some anxiety as to what he should do with his boys and girls. He knew that if anything happened to himself, the Duke would pension his widow. But the children were now old enough to have their careers indicated at least, and he lacked the means of starting them.

Now all had been changed. This yacht would become his property the moment they reached Silver Bay, and she would fetch from five to six thousand pounds !

What a blessing! She was as good as his own already. They all thought the rudder-head would hold. For anything else he cared nothing. She was a good sea-boat. She was stiff. He knew her from stem to stern. If the rudder-cap held, he feared nothing wind or wave could do. This gift had made his fortune, and from the Seabird's deck he would not go until she had dropped anchor safe inside the reef-protected Silver Bay.

He told the steward to bring him a cup of coffee, and having put on his pea-jacket, and lighted a pipe, he shook himself, and began pacing the quarter-deck at the windward side.

As his feet fell upon the plank, he thought, ' My own ! My own ! The craft I've sailed these many years, the best years of my life, now is all mine, to do with as I please ! And what shall I do with her ? Sell her ! Sell her, and put my little ones fair before the wind ?'

' How does she answer now, Pritchard ?' he asked the man at the wheel.

' Fast as a racer, sir,' replied the man.

' That's right ! That's right !' said the captain, rubbing his hands, and drawing his pipe heartily.

It was the rule of the yacht that the officer in charge, be he captain or mate, should not smoke. This was the captain's first infringement of the rule, but there were excuses for him. There was no likelihood that either the Duke or the Marquis would come on deck again that night ; he was taking charge of a watch which did not belong to him, and in less than four-and-twenty hours the craft he commanded would be his own. He was now in the zenith of his fortune. All his worldly future was fairly provided for, and he was mapping it out with a loving hand.

He paused in his walk, and caught the bulwark, tried to shake it, that he might enjoy the consciousness of the vessel's — his vessel's—strength. He laid his hand on the main boom, as one pats the head of a favourite child. He looked down the skylight. and saw the satin-wood panels, the silver fittings, the rich velvet curtains and upholstery.

Then he took up the lantern and directed the light from the bull's-eye on the unshapely ragged rudder-head. The carpenter had not been able to drive all the wedges fully home, nor had he cut them off level with the rudder-cap. The clean newly-cut wedges, standing up in the rude oval formed by the line inside the cap-iron, looked like a double set of irregular teeth laid flat and open or dislocated. The upper surface of the rudder appeared lozenge-shaped, but only the outline of the iron was lozenge-shaped. The wood and the inner side formed an octagon, the sides of which were arcs of large circles, the plain being longer by one-third than broad. The irons, when they reached what may be termed the base or after-line of the octagon, increased greatly in thickness, and at the line of the base were pierced by an iron bolt which was riveted over a pair of washers, and this bolt formed the base line of the iron-work aft. The iron sides of the octagon were continued aft, and brought together at a gentle angle, until they met the iron helm, to which they were firmly welded ; the strength of this joint being enormously increased by a stout exterior ring clasping all three together, and welded to all three ; following the helm-iron forward, between those two side bands over the bolt, through the rudder-head, it was finally riveted over a washer in the foremost iron side of the band.

The workmanship was excellent,

and the whole looked as firm as human hands could make it.

The interior of the iron was an irregular octagon, the exterior was rounded and lozenge-shaped. The captain now, for the first time, noticed two things: namely, That the lozenge-shape, which looked so well, had been obtained at the expense of strength; and, That the helm-iron must be broken off short at the point where it entered the rudder-head. The exterior oval had been produced by thinning away the iron at points exterior to the interior angles. Unless the the helm-iron had been broken, the cap-iron could not have worked so freely a while ago.

These two discoveries filled him with uneasiness. He knelt down on the deck and turned the full glare of the bull's-eye on the jagged rudder-head and the symmetrical mass of iron-work.

This closer examination somewhat allayed his fears. If, as he knelt, he could have seen what was slowly, surely, creeping upwards towards him in the darkness, he would have sprung to his feet in despair.

CHAPTER XV.

AN INVISIBLE FOE.

THE wind increased. It now became obvious that the captain's predictions would be verified, and that it would blow a whole gale before morning. It was midnight, and gradually Captain Drew had been taking off canvas. The sea had begun to rise. The yacht was now close-reefed, but it had not been necessary to turn up the whole crew. The wind had come on so gradually that the watch had been able to make the necessary reductions. Captain Drew was a considerate man, and never gave any unnecessary hardship to his men.

In the dim light of a moonless June night the sea looked dreary and forlorn. Although the wind was high, and round the rigging and the spars it seemed secret and furtive, it appeared to cling closely to the water, to leave the hollows between the waves stealthily, and to leave them only when goaded forward by something behind. Then it leaped the crests of the waves swiftly, and flung itself in the hollows once more.

The water looked cold and pallid. From the heavy swash at the bows to the almost human murmur of the back-water under the counter, there ran all along the side a gamut of depressing sounds, into which every now and then ran the swirl of spray, mounting from the bow and falling with a groan on the deck, to run aft in whispered hisses, until it found its way to a scupper-hole, whence it fell with a weary drone into the sea to leeward.

Captain Drew was not, for a sailor, a very superstitious man. But in the atmosphere of this night there was something which daunted him. The mere fact that a flaw should have been found in a vital part of the yacht, and that this flaw had never been discovered until it was, under existing circumstances, past effectual cure, was depressing. But then again there was the sustaining fact that this yacht, which he had sailed for years, was now practically his own property. He was now in effect five to six thousand pounds a richer man than when that day had broken.

How was he to regard that rudder-head? As a friend or an enemy? If it had not been for the defect in the rudder, the Duke would, in all probability, not have thought of getting rid of the Seabird; and if he had not thought of getting rid of her, it would never have occurred to him to give her to his captain. If the rudder-head held until they got back to Silver Bay, it would undoubtedly be the best friend, after the Duke, he had ever had in all his life. But if the rudder-head gave, what then? No one could tell. They might be driven ashore and all lost, or they might be able to live through the gale, and be picked up by some steamer or sailing-vessel, which would stand by them until a tug or some other kind of succour could reach them. Of course, if the rudder gave, they could do something with a few spars towed behind them, but not much. It was better to keep on hoping the rudder-head would hold.

It was now more than four hours since the Duke and the Marquis had gone below, and these four hours had settled one thing. There was no longer any chance of their putting in anywhere. Silver Bay was now the nearest harbour. The watch had been changed, and a second new hand was now at the wheel.

'Does she answer well, Jefferson?' asked the captain.

'As well as ever, sir,' answered the man at the wheel.

By this time, every man aboard knew what had happened, and the means which had been taken to meet the emergency.

The captain had slung the lamp on a belaying-pin on the weather-side, abreast the companion. He unslung the lantern, and once more went aft and turned the bull's-eye full in the rudder-head.

He could notice no change. The iron looked taut, the wedges looked unchanged, the helmsman found the wheel worked as well as ever. And yet all this time there was creeping up, at an infinitesimal rate, from the inner side of the rudder iron, that which would be sufficient to dash all Captain Drew's hopes to the ground.

As he gazed at the rudder he thought:

'If the Duke does give her to me when we get into the bay, I'll let her swing there at anchor until I get a new rudder into her. She shall have the best rudder they can make for her at Izlemouth. It will cost fifteen—ay, maybe twenty—pounds. It ought not to cost more than twenty pounds. But cost what it may, she shall have the best. Whatever the ship carpenter asks, he shall have. I will not cheapen him a penny. If he says five-and-twenty pounds, he shall have five-and-twenty pounds. You must not look a gift-horse in the mouth, and I won't haggle over a few pounds to make the craft I sailed so long, and that now is going to bring me a fortune, ship-shape and seaworthy. She doesn't want anything else. We never knew anything she wanted that she didn't get. Not likely, with such an owner as the Duke, God bless him!

'Ay, it's a fortune, and a large fortune, too, for a man like me. The most I ever had any reason to hope for was a few hundred in the will of the Duke; and here now it has come to thousands all at once, and with the Duke alive and friendly to me yet, and promising me a new ship, and giving me the old one.'

He bent forward, and felt round the rudder-head carefully, tenderly, as though it had feeling. Then he rose, hung up the lantern on the belaying-pin, and resumed his walk. His thoughts went on:

'I will run no risk with her. Any plank or beam or stanchion may get dozed any time. It is likely everything else in the Seabird is as sound as a bell. But this matter of the rudder-head is a warning. I'll never take her to sea again at my own risk. I'll sell her in the bay, and will take good care I have the money in my pocket before she goes to sea again. How do I know but that the mainmast may be gone, or the stern post? No, no. It won't do to throw away a chance like this. Not twice in a lifetime does a man in my position meet with a chance like this. It will not do to throw away a chance like this.'

He filled and lit another pipe, and continued his walk.

It was now gray dawn, and the wind continued still to increase. Captain Drew was in no way uneasy about the wind or the sea. She was equal to it all, and much more, if the rudder-head only held. Although the wind had now double the force it had when he ordered in the flying-jib and ordered down the gaff topsails, so skilfully had sail been reduced, and so free from anything like squall had been the gale, that she had never been more than a plank or two under to leeward. Water was now coming over the weather-side in bucketsful; and now and then the schooner plunged her nose under a big sea, and washed her decks fore and aft.

It was a dismal daybreak. The sky was all overcast with low-flying gray clouds, the sea a tangled maze of irregular billows. As day advanced there was no encouraging element in the scene. No land, no vessel, was in sight. All looked void and purposeless. The water and the air were given up to the tempest, and the schooner seemed an impertinence, the presence of which air and water resented with deadly hatred.

Still dreary as the dawn, Captain Drew preferred it to the night. He kept the deck. He was resolved to carry out his determination of not going below until the Seabird was safely at anchor in Silver Bay. It was now between two and three, and, if all went well, and all had been going well, he might, in reason, hope to be in smooth water in less than a dozen hours.

Every half hour, as morning grew into day, he paused and examined that rudder-head. It held admirably to all appearances. He could discover no sign of any weakness, of any working, of any giving out. He rubbed his hands once more in satisfaction. He now felt assured the rudder would last until they had reached security. Of course there was no great strain on the steering-gear. It was not as if they had been tacking up a narrow river, where they had to come about every few minutes. A couple of spokes to port now, a couple of spokes to starboard at another moment, sufficed to keep her in her course. He should not have to put any strain on the tiller until they ported to enter the bay; that was, of course, provided they did not encounter very much worse weather or the danger of a collision. As soon as he saw anything he would be able to tell better how they were, but he calculated that they would fetch Silver Bay on this reach without changing the course a point; and he ought to know if any one did, for it was not the first nor the fiftieth north-east wind he had run away on in this same yacht, Seabird.

When he was getting that new rudder made, there was one thing he would be certain not to have like the old one: there should be no sacrifice of strength to appearance. If there were to be interior angles, there should be exterior angles also.

All this while the silent invisible foe was slowly, but surely, working its way upwards.

At eight o'clock the Marquis came on deck, and was informed of the way in which the night had gone over, and that Captain Drew hoped to let go anchor in Silver Bay at about two o'clock that afternoon, if the wind kept steadily as it now was, and the sea did not get very much worse. The Duke did not come on deck. He feared to face the bitter air.

As day grew the wind and sea rose considerably, until the gale became a storm, and the Seabird had not a single dry inch of deck. The rudder held bravely, although it now had to contend against hardships which the captain had not foreseen for it a couple of hours ago.

At noon they made out land under the port-bow; and by what Captain Drew could see he knew he was right in his calculation, and that the yacht would, on her present course, sail almost into the bay.

For miles and miles there was no other place of refuge but that bay. In such a storm it was a serious thing to have such a lee-shore, for at this part of the coast the land tends north-west, making a lee-shore for a north-east wind. Captain Drew would have felt no anxiety if no accident had happened; but in the face of a damaged rudder in a lee-shore such as this, and in such a storm, he felt very uneasy. If anything went at the rudder there would be no hope for the yacht, and little or none for any man aboard her.

The schooner was now able to show only a storm-jib and a close-reefed scandalised mainsail to the storm.

At half-past one the foe, which had been so long invisible, came into sight, the Seabird being then about three miles to the south-west of the entrance to Silver Bay.

At a quarter to two the carpenter, who had been ordered to watch the rudder-head, saw the foe, which had so long been working in darkness, and reported to the captain. The carpenter said to the captain,

'In the starboard side of the rudder cap-iron—'

'Yes.'

'There's a crack.'

'Good God! a crack! If that goes, we are all lost.'

'I think it's going fast, sir.'

While the carpenter was telling this terrible news to the captain, on shore Cheyne was standing among a knot of fishermen watching the approaching yacht.

[To be continued.]

FIFTEEN MONTHS WITH THE JESUITS.

THE carrying-out of the French decrees against unauthorised Religious Orders has naturally excited in this country an interest which, purely speculative though it is, has its grades of intensity both for and against: the sympathy that weakness claims, they had; and that fictitious conscience which reaction instils into the breasts of a people moved many Protestant onlookers to compunction, even when they, in the main, indorsed the decrees as ending an anachronism.

With us, it may be hoped, religious feud is a bygone. Never to be aroused in the name of Christ, Wolsey's intemperate zeal, Cranmer's stern retaliations, brought within the domains of ordinary human criticism only through having passed the ordeal of fire; the insolence of Puritan, the wrongs of Covenanter, all sleep in one grave, now that we, whose fluent public opinion finds its level without corroding or breaking bounds, are at one upon the merits of religious toleration.

It would be hard to evoke a spirit, in our time, such as animated the Lord George Gordon rioters upon the 8th of June, and days succeeding, of 1780. Catholic Emancipation passed and became law, being but a paragraph in that great unwritten deposit of justice resident in the bosoms of our race from the beginning of time, that prescribes liberty to all men; a deposit which may be obscured by passion or covered up in time of great emergency, but whose natural bias is upward to the light, and laterally to the furthest limits of the empire.

While rancour is of the past, suspicion is not yet laid, nor does its cloud rest more heavily upon any social institution than it rests upon the monastic system. But recently, a bench of magistrates memorialised Government, drawing attention to 'the existence of institutions in which persons are immured for life, and prevented from holding free communication with the outer world,' and, backed by an English peer, would have chivalrously brought freedom of mind and person to the Fulham nuns by *tour de force*.

The Fulham nuns were found, upon investigation, to be in exercise of all the freedom a lady should desire; nor was the search after lunatics, it appears, very successful; yet the people of this Protestant country feel persuaded, on grounds which are both historical and conjectural, of the possibility of abuse attacking monastic systems together with everything that is human. Such views rest not merely upon the yelping corroborations of Voltaire, the sardonic humour of Rabelais, for the St. Bernards of the Church equally deplore a transient phase of declension from pristine morality obtaining at no very distant epoch. If, however, the monastic spirit be generally deemed, irrespective of denomination, obsolete as a power, excrescent upon modern society, and peculiarly counter to British instincts, most admit the obligations we are under to the monks of the early past in science, art, and letters, and are willing to concede that they were, upon the whole, exemplars of morality. Our feelings towards the monk, outside the boundaries of romantic and dramatic literature, are like those we should lavish upon some crustacean of the fossil age, whose cumbrous scaly body might be caught dragging its painful way along our clean macadam ; pity mingling with respect, and both steeped in the sense that the monster had no business to mingle his unwieldly frolics with our young vitalities. One order is, it is true, customarily exempted from commiseration and amnesty—nobody pleads for the Jesuits; but the order that produced heroic Southwell, mild Xavier of Navarre, simple James Laynez of Almazan, and chivalrous Loyola, meets with nearly universal obloquy.

This may be just, since intrigue and subtlety are difficult to drag into daylight ; and with this I have nothing to do directly, mine being but the record of a Protestant's impressions, who lived with them for a considerable period. I had been some years in Canada, one of those 'rolling stones' which 'gather no moss,' when Fortune threw me into the companionship of a member of the Roman communion, whom I shall always be honoured in terming 'friend.' His bread was earned by skilled hand-labour ; mine, as circumstances, born of varying conditions, might dictate. I had just finished an engagement as teacher of languages in the high and public schools of the town of Guelph, in the Province of Ontario, and, being offered a like post in the college for boys belonging to the Society of Jesus, closed with it.

That it was unusual for a Protestant to fill such a place in a Roman Catholic seminary is probable; but, negotiations being frank and aboveboard on both sides, I trust there is nothing upon which to reflect, yet much for which to be grateful, I having been treated with the greatest kindness and consideration

during my stay. For the train of incidents leading up to my engagement, I myself was responsible. A Jesuit father may not seem a very promising subject for the professional interviewer, and, indeed, my first operations were not directed towards the result attained, which came about quite naturally. Having casually dropped in at the church to hear one of a series of missionary sermons that drew many Protestants to listen, I arrayed my objections in phalanx upon paper, and posted my letter to the talented preacher. Upon the next occasion, my vanity was excited by a sermon specially designed to meet my points advanced ; and thinking it courteous to reveal my personality to one whom I respected both for his learning and for his attention to small matters, I called at the college for that purpose. Some weeks then passed before I became installed in my quiet cell; a mark of favour which, whatever the mutations of opinion, I shall always prize, knowing it to be one of great rarity.

As for proselytism, so much dreaded, and a calamity to which my position left me peculiarly exposed, there was none of it, although I of my own free will went through a good deal of theological literature, especially that portion which bore upon the nature and evidence of miracle, a department of inquiry nearly enough allied to my favourite 'Ghost-Lore' to be of interest. Free to hold any heresy I pleased, the propounding of false doctrine met with courteous and rational, if sometimes severe, treatment from the kind fathers, who, I am inclined to think, viewed their stray Protestant 'child' rather as a psychical oddity, fashioned for some inscrutable purpose by a wise Creator, than as a walking menace to the Holy See. And so they allowed me to shake up the bottle of blessed water from the Grotto at Lourdes against the light, mildly pitying the want of faith which debarred me from its use. Meanwhile, Canadian pilgrims kept returning from the scene of miracle with sound bodies, peaceful minds, and quart-bottles : evidences that ought, I fear, to have convinced me; leaving, indeed, upon my mind the assurance of sincere belief on behalf of the votaries, with the wish, on my part, to imbibe a like faith in mysteries, which is, after all, more conducive to tranquillity than the blank scepticism that often passes for strength of intellect.

Discussions bearing upon vexed points of doctrine were, of course, frequent, I being champion of the Reformed Church for the time being; yet nothing could discompose or annoy these meek men : intolerance was as far from their minds as from those of the most liberal of Protestants. Hints of rack or thumbscrew in the cellars beneath were good-humouredly laughed at, while one well-conditioned father invited my search after the horns which, said he, were supposed to adorn the heads of Loyola's lambs. The expression is my own, however. Remarking that my closest scrutiny failed to detect either horns or cloven foot, evoked some mirth and a cigar. While my first impressions of the renowned Order of Jesus were thus genial, it can profit nothing either to ignore facts or avoid seeing things to their logical issues; and a strong English popular sentiment in this order's disfavour must be owned, just as the probabilities of its extension in England, with or without molestation, offer subjects for interesting surmise.

It seems that the Catholic Emancipation Act gave no unrestricted liberties to monastic orders : ' Jesuits and members of other religious orders, communities, or societies of the Church of Rome, bound by monastic or religious vows;' pronouncing, on the contrary, that ' it is expedient to provide for their gradual suppression and prohibition.' Members entering the realm unlicensed are liable to life-banishment, and, in case of return, transportation, replaced, now, by penal servitude, a penalty whose severity might easily defeat itself in failing to secure enforcement. Most likely, indeed, the greater number of recently-exiled French monks, Jesuits included, are in England now; yet the ship of State has not taken to ' heeling' through displacement of ballast, and it may prove that the Order of Jesus is no present menace to it or to the Establishment.

It may be a question, moreover, how far a partial legislation, which was calculated, like intermittent suspensions of the Habeas Corpus Act, and recently effected measures of coercion in Ireland, to meet cases of emergency, could take approved effect just now, in the face of that apotheosis of individual freedom which makes the Protestant ideal of to-day.

' Why should not monasticism exist ?' might become the easily-raised query, for sentiments are not to be crushed at will ; and, remembering that Christian monasticism, itself a parasite, dates from the year A.D. 305, when monks Anthony and Paul retired to the deserts of Thebais, British reverence for vested rights should prove stronger than a prejudice.

Yet a historian eminent in his day, and writing in the beginning of the present century, predicts : ' If we may hazard a conjecture, there will be scarcely any monastery found remaining in any country of the Roman Catholic communion at the end of the present century.' Current events appear to make good the prophecy ; yet who shall say that Gallic and Teutonic dicta are to be final, or that, a smoky wrack scudding over the sky towards the horizon, the whole set of modern crude opinions be not shifted to bring old aspects of faith and ethics again into view?

That the 'close orders' are not wanted more, is possible: seclusion no longer insures safety, for men can view a nun without impertinence; just as ladies can, by virtue of cultivated self-denial, spare a Jesuit to the cloister with easy grace. But that among the throng of people of either sex whose lives are devoted to doing good, as we would gladly think, and this throng of no special persuasion, they alone are to be excised from the 'fruitful tree' because of being under 're-ligious vows,' should be strange in-deed.

The Jesuits are no 'close order,' but live in the world as much as out of it; and, except by sending obnoxious members to the tread-mill, it is hard to see how to quell the corporation, unless laws be en-forced only to be unconditionally repealed.

The College of St. Ignatius is an imposing building that, with a con-vent (devoted to teaching and open to the closest scrutiny) upon its left-hand side and the Church of our Lady between, crowns the summit of a hill, which is the first object to strike the eye upon near-ing the town of Guelph. Irrever-ent people call the college 'the barracks;' yet it is the rendezvous of a body of able and genial men, who, with single-hearted purpose, serve the Master according to their lights: faithful ever, flinching never; equally at home in pulpit and parlour, yet most characteristic in the cells which the glorious tra-ditions of many ages have invested with a charm certainly not owing to 'ormolu' or 'rosewood.'

Equally inaccessible to the hu-man exaltation that comes of pro-sperity, as impervious to all assaults of adversity, they wear a uniformly cheerful look, which is engaging because real, yet is apt to arouse in the stranger a feeling of personal neglect, the Jesuit's cheerfulness being usually unattached to any mundane object. This cheerful air, which is the normal condition of a Jesuit, does not, however, ade-quately convey my complete im-pressions upon the subject, for I have noticed a distinctly triune character in my clever friends: first, the cheerful habitual tone; second, a very stern air levelled against enemies to Mother Church; and third, a peculiarly angelic side, whose facial expression marks a point in the ethics of phy-siognomy.

Cheerfulness is infectious; and, in defiance of principles, a voice sometimes whispered of a religion greater than creeds, within whose ample pale Jesuit and Protestant might agree; where, turning from the gloomy abyss, which is often all that departmental philosophies offer the groping human soul, one might seize upon the firm flesh and substance of the idea underlying the motto of the order in question, '*Ad majorem Dei gloriam.*'

No blinds beautified our win-dows, but a stern sameness ruled, so that no wonder the college was reputed, by schismatic urchins, to be haunted. Occasionally the moon and stars might be seen, by one standing in front, through the windows in the rear of the edifice, but a face was seldom shown, even in day-time, the priests disliking manifestations of curiosity. Rarely were the rooms all lighted up; yet my room was an oasis in the waste, curtains, and a flower-garden on the window-sill, forming, I fear, an eyesore to my ghostly hosts. It has been suggested to me that no account of a residence among the Jesuits would be complete without a description of my cell. Now, to begin with, mine was no cell, but a room; still, the inventory of my furniture is so simple that I can well trust my recollection for its enumeration. Seeing that I was 'of the earth, earthy,' my 'uncanny' hosts had considerately painted and varnished my floor brown, the nearest approach to a carpet permitted in that 'eerie' establishment, all but the bishop's room, an apartment devoted to the reception of dignitaries of the Church on tramp. Severity so naturally slides into Scotch and Calvinistic vocabularies, that I offer no excuse; but the fathers were mostly French or French-Canadian, with a sprinkling of Germany and Ireland. Well, my bed, protected by a screen, adjoined the window, from whose top I had suspended a cow's horn, which I found in one of my rambles, and filled with flax-seed, that speedily formed a cascade of drooping verdure and blue blossoms. Thus, quite innocently, my 'horn was exalted' among the dread order that I had been taught to fear; and there all attempts at adornment ended, for a stove burning wood, a table, and two chairs made my entire furnishings, barring my two boxes and a small bracket I put up myself. What little 'midnight oil' I burnt was of the prosy paraffin brand. We retired early, as a rule. A library of good and valuable books was placed at my service, but most were beyond my depth, being unable to read Latin fluently as the Jesuits. Everybody in the house had his own number upon the bell, mine being eight strokes, not as being the most important member in the household, but as the last-comer only. Once I felt much disconcerted when a brother, whose duty it was to summon us all to meals, rang a second peal of eight upon the 'gong' before I had finished

my toilet, and just began another course of exercise as I was halfway down-stairs, where I passed a bishop in purple, only to run against an archbishop in the passage. The papal legate was expected about that time; and the hasty fear swept over my nerves that I might perhaps look papal in my embarrassment; and how should I bless the archbishop and bishop, if required?

Large grounds were attached to the college, together with a farm at some distance. In the front of our building was a garden, well kept, but with an eye to purposes of utility rather than of ornament, potatoes and a wilderness of Indian corn supplying our table abundantly. Amongst fruits, we had apples, plums, strawberries, cherries, and one pear-tree, while grape-vines festooned the trelliswork bordering the walk; so that the saucy Canadian robin—a large bird—and the wicked crow, showed a marked predilection for the Jesuits' larder.

This adjunct of our house was, by the way, equally sound within as without, vegetables being brought to a point of perfection that might have put half the farmers to the blush, and all without noise or interruption of daily duties, severe enough at times. Our pig was the model of a priest's pig, portly and affable; while our poultry seemed in perpetual jubilee of chanticleer, whether feast or fast day.

Be it not supposed that the priests themselves tilled the soil, as is the case with the Trappists, most stern of orders.

To begin with, they have no time for such things, nor is it necessary where there are so many able farmers at hand in the brothers of the society. These, who never attain the dignity of orders, do the menial work of the houses, and this in as deft a manner as if they had been housemaids born; while they have only to don white surplices to be ready for their duties at the altar. Each must know or learn some trade, so that the order has, among other craftsmen, skilled carpenters, smiths, farmers, tailors, and especially noble cooks. The culinary art is, I was told, self-taught; and, indeed, these otherwise modest brothers are disposed to advance a tentative claim to cook upon inspiration, which, since they are certainly poets in the art, may safely be conceded. Ours was a French-Canadian cook, whose *menu* was, upon occasion, worthy of a Soyer, yet so meek was the good brother, that he claimed no merit whatever: it was his duty, and he did it well, employing odd moments reciting his rosary; both vocations, the solemn and the sordid, being equally *ad majorem Dei gloriam*. Many of the brothers are of superior education and birth, taking upon themselves those lowly duties as a voluntary burden. One had originally been trained for the priesthood, but felt the honour too overpoweringly great for his modest nature, and thus bound up his sheaf of learning with a wisp of wormwood, and laid it at the feet of his superior: a true martyr for conscience' sake. We had a Belgian brother whose talents were of an inventive kind, and so he exhibited his improved stove at several provincial exhibitions with success. He was our gardener also, tilling our garden upon the economical system of his country, and waging destructive warfare upon the 'potato-bugs,' as the Colorado beetle is termed locally.

It is often the case that a man's talents divert attention from himself; but brother B—— was a marvel in his own right, his iron frame and constitution having

been the subjects of a long series of terrible accidents, from which the Blessed Virgin rescued him in the nick of time without his turning a hair.

The principle of Jesuit *cuisine*, arrived at by a process of inductive reasoning, is, enough of all things, as good as reasonable care can make them, but neither waste of time nor superfluity. We were not always feasting. Lent came in its season, when Catholics take but one meal a day, and that of the meagrest; as for the fathers, they always fast before offering mass on Sundays, and, in turn, during the week. When visiting the sick and bearing the Sacrament, they invariably set out on empty stomachs; a great hardship where the distance is, as often happens, far, or during the bitterly cold winter weather.

Speaking is against rules at such times; and I shall long remember the stoical *sang froid* of a worthy old priest of the order in such an instance. I was, as frequently occurred, his companion and driver, when, the road being in bad condition and full of ruts, I nearly spilled my venerable friend in the mire. He neither winced nor looked round—never spoke one word. To my great relief, I pulled through, landing my priestly charge in safety, although to have added one to the already glorious roll of Jesuit martyrs would not have troubled the order half as much as it must have discomposed me. Our rambles were both interesting and instructive; everywhere we met with the greatest respect, children and live-stock being carefully marshalled under the eyes of the Jesuit and his acolyte, as though our joint prayers were understood to be secured in advance.

Severe as was the exterior of the college, it was comfortable enough inside, although, in truth, not lavishly furnished. The Society of Jesus is known to be rich; yet the individual may own nothing, everything being held in common. Speaking of Communism one day, a member of the order said, 'We are a true Communism, and manage to live 'in harmony, but the world can never do this.'

It is true; for the world is not quickened by the one spirit of goodwill, nor, while animal feelings interlace so closely as they must with nobler passions, can social Communism do more than provoke loathing. The Communisms of the Church are epicene. Life is, and is meant to be, complementary and strong-typed. We lop some branches from a tree to give strength to the rest, a measure of exigence that may justify the cenobite; but paradisaical growths should develop volume and stature without application of the pruner's hook.

Reviewing the history of the renowned Society of Jesus, those who see the hand of Providence at the helm of human affairs will recognise the fatality, romance, and import of that story. Born in 1491, among the hills of Guipuzcoa in Spanish Biscay, and of illustrious race, Ignatius Loyola was contemporary with Luther; 'the antidote to the poison,' as Catholics hold, but, according to good last-century Protestants, more properly Hell's last firebrand cast at the Gospel. We are wiser now, and may pay tribute to the memory of a gallant and chivalrous soldier, who, at the siege of Pampeluña, being indignant at the cowardice of the garrison, rushed like a lion into the van of combat and got his wounds. The bone of his shattered leg having been badly set, he insisted upon the projecting portion being cut off, submitting to the operation

with fortitude. Lying upon his litter in the hospital with only the *Flos Sanctorum* to beguile the weary time, his headstrong, yet at heart reverent, nature underwent a change, so that he only exchanged the lazar-house of Manresa for a cavern and penance. Then, resolved, to use the current language of the time, to devote to the Queen of Heaven the remains of the powers with which he had served his king, he, having hung his arms upon the walls, spends a night in solitary prayer in the Church of Montserrat, taking vows of romantic knighthood. In this church the abbot caused an inscription to be written, setting forth how 'Ignatius à Loyola, multa prece fletûque, Deo se Virginique devovit.'

About this time occurred an incident that distinguishes in a striking manner the age of Ignatius Loyola from ours. Riding towards Valencia, our knight overtakes a Moor on horseback, and, notwithstanding a protracted discussion in a friendly manner, debates as to whether he shall kill the Moor or not, finally leaving the delicate point of etiquette to God and the two horses, deciding to wish the Moor 'good-night' if, upon meeting a certain crossroad, the animals diverged into different paths, but otherwise, to slay him. Bismillah! Would not the Moor have stirred up his beast, had he known of what was passing in the mind of 'El Caballero de Nuestra Santissima Virgen'? But the infidel brute must have had a presentiment; for, taking the bit between his teeth, he bolted along the proper path, saving the scarcely convalescent knight a little trouble.

Next, the knight founds his order at the hospital of St. Jacques at Paris or upon Montmartre Hill, just as one chooses to prefer, the infant society being of both places. Some five comrades formed its nucleus—Xavier, Laynez, Salmeron, Rodriguez, Bobadilla. Then came pilgrimages and arrests, the tour to Venice being performed on foot amid many strange adventures, and Jerusalem was also visited.

We know with what opposition the Jesuit Order was met; how the Pope himself at first condemned it, relenting only when the vows of the order, engaging to uphold the Holy See, were shown him; and we know the rapid progress made by it—how a Jesuit was thrown forward to meet each heresy as it arose, and those were troublous times. Jesuit missionary work advanced, so that Japan was brought under Western influence; but the work was not to last, scores of zealous priests being cruelly tortured and put to death. The *Lettres édifiantes et curieuses*, sent to head-quarters annually by the outlying missionaries, are, apart from their scientific interest, full of pathos, telling of sufferings undergone and success attained. We read, too, in the *Histoire de la glorieuse Mort de neuf Chrestiens Japonois, martirisés pour la Foy Catholique*, of the noble deaths of good men; how Father Constanzo was burnt at Nagasaki, while thirteen Dutch and English ships were in port, his majestic stature towering above the flames as, quite calm and unmoved, he uttered the word 'Sanctus' five times before dying. Then again, in 1622, thirty-one Japanese Christians were led up to Maritzi's Mountain to be roasted over slow fires. Father Spinola went first, followed close by Father Kimura and seven novices, singing 'Laudate, pueri, Dominum;' and Father Spinola, as became the leader, was 'insensible to pain.' The list of martyrs in Japan is long and painful, yet ended by a note of triumph such as a Jesuit alone can produce from what ordinary people take for a wail of

anguish: 'Dieu soit éternellement loué'—runs the concluding paragraph of the book—'qui communique une si grande force et constance à ses fidèles serviteurs.' Simultaneously with the Japanese successes, for such the far-sighted Jesuits deem them, missionary enterprise was being pushed in South America. The fierce zeal of the chaplains accompanying the armies of Cortes and Pizarro flashed from the rapier's tip, to deaden rather than convince; but Paraguay became, under Jesuit dispensation, the ideal of a Christian commonwealth, the shepherd's crook sweeping mildly into the fold of Christ hordes of man-eating savages— swept them in and taught them wisdom and the arts, until this Acadia was, proudly by some, enviously by more, admitted to be the one state under the sun wherein the law of the land and the moral law were coincident. This was not the work of ambition either, but undertaken at request of the Dominican, Francisco Victoria. It was too good to last.

Spanish viceroys undid what Jesuits had done; clinging to their children to the last, teachers and taught shared the same ruin. Ousted from one spot, the fervent apostles turned to others; and in 1634 Father Peter d'Espinosa died, massacred by a cruel tribe that, however, accepted conversion a little later on. Time is too brief to dwell upon details; dates must serve to bring the order upon a level with our age.

Jansenism, supported by the Fronde, agitated France in 1648, to the distraction of the Roman Church and the especial loathing of Mazarin; but, in spite of the witty attacks of Pascal, who, for a time, held all Paris in his cause by the brilliance of his *Lettres Provinciales*, the Jesuit fathers manfully met, and finally quelled, the trouble. The Pope would have conferred honours upon them; they refused, for their work was all *ad majorem Dei gloriam*, and not for the sake of human applause. If I failed to notice the Titus Oates' conspiracy of 1679 I might be charged with partiality, even in so slight a sketch as this; but it was with this plot as it had been with the 'Gunpowder Plot' before it : nothing was proved against the Jesuits. In the former case, a priest replied in the confessional very broadly to a very broad question, nor, except for his own admission, would this much have been known; torture failed to elicit more. Why Father Thomas Jenison was thrown into prison at Newgate is, I confess, not clear to me. The whole plot was a farce from beginning to end, and most unlikely to commend itself to a Jesuit. However, guilty or not, the expression of Father Jenison, when slowly dying, is not that of a criminal : ' O, how sweet it is to suffer for Christ !'

That English feeling was adverse to the order is true, as we see by the subsequent ' Lord George Gordon riots,' already spoken of, an outbreak that had a Scotch savour about it, if the truth were told, in more than the leader's name.

Speaking of the dislike manifested by the Jesuits, both priests and lay-brothers, to accept Church honours or private gifts, brings to mind several rebuffs I encountered in so simple a matter as the proffer of a pipe. Nothing of the least value will be accepted; and the only article I could prevail upon a worthy friend of mine in the college to take was a small vial half-filled with mucilage, the gum of which I myself picked from our cherry-tree in the garden, and which was certainly more the property of the Jesuit than it was

mine. Delicacy forbids my describing the interiors of the rooms, which, as an inmate of the house, I was privileged to view : yet I may say that the very simple furniture was occasionally supplemented, with creditable ingenuity, by small extras, as when one of the fathers, who was fond of birds, finding a cage desirable, made one out of a sieve. Our sitting-room, not used much except by visitors, was, however, more elegantly arranged, the comfort of the fastidious outside world being in question ; the reception-room, also, was neat, and, considering the sternness of Jesuit criticism, comfortable. Our dining - room was spacious, hung round with portraits of famous members of the order, and with a big crucifix at the head of the table.

The little chapel attached to the building received, of course, the loving care which considerations of personal comfort could not evoke ; but, fearing to break the beautiful privacy which is there, like the hush after some sweet melody, the Jesuits' chapel shall not be described, except I say that there is a very fine, though small, painting over the altar.

The famous society of which I am speaking has given to the world men of science, as it has given to heaven saints and martyrs ; and I may, I trust, without offence, publish the fondness which the members betray for living things, whether finned, scaled, or feathered, together with the devices I learnt to contrive in the pursuit of natural science, under their direction. Being presented, by a father with a bent for ' crustacea,' with three or four sturdy little crayfish, I put them into a basin half-filled with water, and ornamented with stones and moss. For some time all went well ; but one morning I awoke to find my pets missing. I never discovered them; but in my sleep for several nights an uncomfortable feeling oppressed me of slimy crayfish crawling down my back.

Father W—— was a bird-fancier, and his room an aviary. In the summer weather, his casement being thrown wide, the birds were suffered to fly in and out at will, sure to return at their master's whistle. He would be walking in the garden, open Breviary in hand, and a robin on his head, while an unhallowed screeching from the bushes seemed making light of the good priest's orisons; the birds were but asking for worms. My pet robin, a legacy from this worthy father at his departure for another station, regaled me for a time with his antics, only to commit suicide in my washing-jug.

What with daily morning services, both in the church adjacent and at St. Joseph's Hospital at some distance; marriages, christenings, burials, private devotions and visits, to say nothing of feast and fast days, there remained but scant time for private study. Yet some of these men will probably be heard of in science or literature: one was already an accomplished musician, another a learned author; but they came and went at a moment's notice, and without warning, just as the fiat might be sent forth. Having lived for years in one place, they were liable to be called away suddenly, perhaps to meet the latest doctrinal error upon the altar-step of an English or French cathedral; but, as likely, to go forth, alone and unprepared, save with fortitude and faith, to battle for the faith among savages. Fame is no bait for them; undue celebrity is roughly checked: they are seldom allowed to bear ecclesiastical honours, reputation being suffered only as it may chance to benefit the Church. Implicit obedience to authority,

the reins; humility, the curb: see here the harness in which a Jesuit would live and die.

Whether his bones be inurned within the Basilica at Rome, or left to bleach clasping a rude crucifix in the wilds of the vast untrodden territories of North or South America; whether sliced up in Formosa, or impaled in Malaya; if met in the line of duty, the end is the same—*ad majorem Dei gloriam.*

This unquestioning obedience to superior authority has, it is true, been charged against the Jesuit; but is not this submission universally desired by rulers? Even the cry of *imperium in imperio* loses its force, remembering that the Jesuit recognises all *de facto* conditions as permitted by God. He may be pictured as a gloomy ascetic; far from it, he is most genial of men, and cheerful as the English squire of the olden school. Smoking and the use of spirituous liquors are against the rigid rules of the order, yet many exceptions hold with regard to the former habit, some being ordered to smoke by their medical advisers. Wine is not brought under the heading of spirituous liquors; and that certain fathers can both smoke and toss off a bumper, I can vouch for. One of the most pleasant scenes upon which my eyes rested during my stay at the college was that of a portly German father, at the end of a long pipe, in the garden-walk, labouring over some ponderous theological knot, and grunting with Teutonic phlegm. Such judicious relaxations of rigour as this must widen the recruiting-grounds of the society; for what son of Vaterland would cap the martyrdom of a life involved in taking the Jesuit vows by an abjuration of tobacco?

Affable to me, and wearing the air of polished men of the world, once in the pulpit, and all was changed. Feared, as well as loved, by their flocks, these men spoke their minds with a force and dignity peculiar to them; feeble or infirm, the man became merged in the apostle, indecision falling away before the conscious sense of authority, until there spoke the spirit of prophet or judge, rather than of priest, from the frame which had struck one, a few minutes ago, as being that of a broken-down man.

The respect excited by the Jesuits is genuine, yet they are seldom approached in the same tone of cordial intimacy claimed by the parish-priest of the secular clergy. Why this is so, I cannot undertake to say. For my part, I found them liberal in polemics, and genial as companions, more so, indeed, than ordinary priests; but there can be no question that they are invested in the eyes of the masses with a superstitious halo, as though gifted with supernatural powers. While the parish-priest may be often seen by the fireside of a parishioner, dandling the baby or sipping tea, no one would think of inviting a Jesuit to the family circle. Possibly it is known that they have no time for such human unbendings, so they get credit for an austerity which they really have not at heart.
- It is charged against the Jesuits that they can be 'all things to all men;' yet the power of adaptation to circumstances and the condition of people is nothing so enormous after all. Another imputation under which they labour is that of 'making the end justify the means;' but there are only two methods of proving the charge—either from the internal evidence of their rules, or by circumstantial evidence from outside points. Upon the first question, I can only say that I have spoken to them plainly face to face, and they deny the existence of such a principle among the laws of their order, declaring

it to be opposed to all the facts of their corporate history, subversive of morals and society. Good certainly often comes out of apparent evil, for *omnia cooperantur ad majorem Dei gloriam ;* but, believing, in common with all Christians, that all things work together for good, they do not teach the responsibilities of individuals to be abrogated on that account. 'Sin must come, but woe unto him by whom it comes.' The idea of flexibility which is underlying these vague accusations can never resolve itself into more than a question of degree, and who is judge? Any sensible pastor seeks to adapt himself to the capacities and, sometimes, humours of his audience, for undue rigidity bars approach and encourages the meanest of all vices, hypocrisy. The Jesuits in turn, not so much from what I have been told as from what I infer, think the Protestant section of the Church superficial in judgment at times, and prone to panic ebullitions of unnecessary antagonism, while, of course, most doctrinal or disciplinary points may be warped to suit a turn. Perhaps one of the most marked instances of this crooked vision is, when hastily disposing of a Jesuit, and probably Roman Catholic, dogma, which places an apostasy below a murder in point of blackness. 'What!' cries one, ' do they palliate the taking of human life ; making the capital offence of an idea that cannot attain an act effectually at all?' The answer is, Church dogmas are both practical and speculative. Murder is in the thought, and not in the act. Society would be equally justified in punishing for the malicious intent as for its diastrous consequence, were society omniscient. Apostasy, of the theological type, aims at the dignity, rights, all but the life, which it cannot touch, of the Godhead, and merits divine punishment and secular reprobation. Since God is superior to man, the crime of apostasy exceeds murder. Apostasy includes blasphemy, which must be deliberate and genuine; it includes separation, both in theory and practice, from every point of divine law, the privilege of taking human life being reserved, indeed, among the other breaches of the Decalogue. Thus apostasy, which designs the nullification of all the commandments, is blacker than the offence levelled at one only; the sum includes the parts. But the Inquisition, the *auto da fé*, the usurpation of conscience? These phases, say the Jesuits, were less frequent and cruel than represented; further, the Church was ever the bulwark of the people against oppression; granted a few burnings, the body social was fenced against communisms, heresies, loose-thinkings; and, after all, the souls were, in most cases, 'saved alive.' Candidly, the Jesuits strike one as being not such bad fellows, and we are driven to search for the distrust in which they are held, not only in Protestant but Catholic countries, in two directions. First comes the inflexibility which they evince in holding their ground on important issues; secondly, political intrigue, more or less justified by theoretical advantage to the State, whose interests the Jesuits can never view separately from those of the Church. Running counter—as these are apt to run—to the social interests of communities, and carried generally to their full logical issues, discords arise more frank than edifying to professing Christians. Personally, as has been intimated elsewhere, I found the Jesuits liberal in argument, and, moreover, quite devoid of the abject superstition which chokes the higher functions of thought.

Having once asked their views upon 'Spiritualism,' as the disjointed mass of hallucinations paraded for money is called, they replied by asking me whether 'the shadow did not always imply the substance.' Of course they do not lightly receive narrations of the supernatural, yet give credit implicitly to the possibility of miracle, but explain the phenomenon intelligibly, so as to widen the human reason by leading it safely up to the point at which its penetration fails; 'faith' being taught to be a higher effort of mind rather than a childish credulity.

In doctrinal matters they set limits, yet do not cramp, owning frankly that a Protestant may be as good a Christian as a Catholic, if he act in good faith. My impressions may have been crude; but methought that, discarding popular prejudice from either camp, Jesuit and Churchman might be left to poise in tranquillity the meagre weight of the doctrinal atoms which sever them.

Persecution is what English people dread; but being common to all, this blot should be eliminated from all creeds before delivering sober judgment. Public opinion must in future rule the world, whether cowl or cassock dispense morality.

I was treated well; but the Jesuits are too conversant with human nature to expect that I should be grateful on that account, and if I should abuse them in place of doing justice they would not be surprised; on the contrary, it might give them pleasure. This pleasure I did not propose to do them, however, when I took pen in hand; but my object was to give my private impressions of life among the members of the order. Our schoolrooms were models of neatness, and although there were pictures of the Holy Family against the walls, as well as a crucifix above the chief desk, I could only see the scholars' decorum and the Jesuits' devotion to them ; nobody worshipped the paintings, nor did they harm me. Left free to attend my own English church if I pleased, my greater privilege was to study the manners of my hosts and their flocks in theirs. We had many excellent preachers visiting us from both England and the United States, and the services, I find, were the very same as are performed in the London Catholic cathedrals. For my part the burial services pleased me most, and these I often attended, finding the solemn music soothing rather than depressing. Occasionally a young novice took her vows, surrounded by her white-veiled attendant maidens ; or some strange ancient ceremony of blessing salt carried me, in mind, back to the early centuries. But when the father who had been officiating left the church, looking cheerful as ever, and followed by a knot of people demanding to be 'confessed,' I felt myself no fossil after all, but went to my dinner with good appetite and wholesome mind.

There were not, to my knowledge, any fixed confessional-boxes in our church ; but ingeniously-contrived screens separated the sinner who confessed from the one who heard his confession. It chanced once, before my residence at the college, that, drawn by the eloquence of a missionary priest, I made one of the congregation, being obliged to remain standing at the entrance of the church, so great was the press of people. Now, upon occasions like this, good Catholics, of the mature softer sex chiefly, improve the occasion by unburdening their minds of their iniquities ; and I was close to the confessional, from which I could not stir. Judge, then, of my embarrassment when an

elderly lady, kneeling down, began to open upon the delicate matter of her misdeeds in no abashed style. A church-attendant nudged me, whispering ' Not here ;' the congregation near me seemed viewing me with reprobation, seeing, no doubt, that I was a heretic ; and just then, the penitent, stone-deaf apparently, after several fruitless endeavours to hear, raised her head, and, looking right over the screen at the sacred functionary behind, prepared to speak ; but some one plucked at her skirt, and turning round to glance at me she heaved a sigh only.

Fortunately, my efforts to escape were successful, and before I had mastered the nature of the sin that weighed on the good dame's mind ; of which I was glad, fearing lest I might be placed in the predicament of the grandson of whom a story speaks. He, resorting to church to confess, as the result of contrition after a scolding, found his relative there before him, who, losing temper at not hearing her confessor, lifting her head, said, beneath shaded mouth : ' Twice, father ; did I not just tell yez so ?' The young man is said to have gone home unshriven that day.

The essence of religion is not held by the Jesuits to be a thing of forms and ceremonies, any more than it should depend on their absence ; conformity with the will of God is their brief thesis, only it happens that folk differ much in their readings.

The Jesuit Order has a fine college at Montreal, the church, although small, being reputed one of the prettiest in the world ; but the head - quarters upon the North American continent are at New York, and known as Fordham College.

Roman Catholicism is making great strides in America, not amongst savages alone ; so that it is interesting to reflect how there was once a time when native Americans were declared by the Synod of Lima unfit for reception of the Eucharist, as wanting the reasoning faculties. This uncharitable decision was reversed by Pope Paul III. in 1537, and Lima has given a saint to the Church since then —the Rose of Lima.

There had been standing for many years, on the grounds at the back of our Church of St. Bartholomew—since rechristened Our Lady —a ring of ruins, forming the foundations of a most ambitiously-conceived building, but commonly termed 'Father——'s folly.' Partly from these ruins, partly from private quarries leased by the building committee of the congregation, a beautiful edifice has been erected, though only half finished, and stated to be exceptionally correct in design. It was dedicated with great ceremony by the late Bishop Conroy, Papal Legate at the time. We had triumphal arches, and my floral talent was enlisted in the work of beautifying our somewhat severe-looking front garden; so that when the Pope's vicegerent bestowed a blessing upon the crowd assembled to do him honour, my feeling was that I merited my share. In 1827 the town of Guelph was first prospected by Mr. John Galt and others, representing the Canada Company; but where forest-glades then existed are brisk and well-built streets now, noted for the excellence of their public buildings. Fancy a wolf coming sniffing up to our church-door! Not a bit of it; none of these animals are to be found within thirty miles of the city; and as for forest, the one difficulty is to find a retired walk at all.

Although this Jesuit college is found perched upon the most commanding hill in the neighbourhood,

Ontario is strongly Protestant, and agitated by warm feelings of sect and party, so that the fathers have their enemies as well as their friends. Indeed, the Orangemen, an energetic, perhaps conscientious, yet noisy army of young men, parade the streets at intervals under the very noses of the Jesuits. Once upon a time, many years ago, I was told, these zealous Protestants fairly besieged the Catholic church on the hill, talking of burning down that 'nest of Popery.' But priests and brothers, poking the muzzles of their guns, spiritual and material, through the crannies of their then primitive church, defied the powers of the world to the onset; so the Orangemen, playing 'We'll kick the Pope before us,' marched away down the hill to dinner. Taking all in all, the feeling subsisting between denominations is good enough at present; but Canadian society bears much the relation to ours that a shallow pool does to an ocean, the one to be set in uproar by any wanton breath, the other not to be lifted but by a tempest.

Our sober college was occasionally given up to levity of an instructive kind, as when, to swell the building fund, our schoolboys and the young men of the congregation donned sock and buskin in the religious drama. At these times, the indefinable charm brought by the fair sex wherever they come, illumined our three flights of stairs. Ladies of all persuasions, and, for the greater part, pretty and inquisitive, took summary possession of Loyola's domain. Our efforts drew approbation, and were repeated. Scenes were painted on the premises by my associate in tuition, a clever Frenchman, some literary work falling to my share. To see those talented Jesuits superintending the erection of staging, slides for the scenes, footlights, and other matters, one would have deemed them playwrights ' to the manner born.' Whatever the Jesuits do is well done. From the hot air of the theatre to the cool glades of our garden is a natural step, and so I will there end my narrative of experiences in a Jesuit college.

The open air is God's temple after all, but our Jesuits' church came next; and sometimes, indeed, the one seemed to explain the other, as upon May-day, dedicated to the Blessed Virgin and her *protégées*, the young. Then, the flowers sending up their fragrance from the garden, butterflies and birds holding jubilee of colour and sound, one turned in to the cool aisles of the Church of Our Lady, only to see new colours and a higher music, as scores of young voices warbled gentle melodies in unquestioning faith and native innocence. In the garden, too, it was my pleasure to walk, upon ordinary occasions, after the day's work was over, beneath the bending trees, and between purple clusters of grapes, red tomatoes, pink apples; through patches of towering maize and creeping melons: a land of plenty, offering shelter from the dying but yet fierce sun, and immunity from the driving dust of the streets.

Sweet voices and strains of music were wont to rise in tremors on the evening air, from the convent close by, as some grand hymn might be sung by the pupils; or the deep-toned bell rang out for a special vesper service, or the organ pealed forth its sonorous tones beneath the skilful touch of Father F——. Mystic and solemn and melodious, such accessories could only deprecate credal feud, arousing sympathy with religion's self, which is equally remote from arbitrary designations of Protestant or Papist. Even the Christian sentiment of exclusiveness was apt to become merged in a wider feeling, wherein all flesh is the care of a beneficent God. And, reader, here let us part, leaving old sores unprobed and problems unsolved; leaving the Jesuit fathers to their load of obloquy and life of self-immolation.

Perhaps we may be wiser and better as communions; we rarely are either the one or the other as individuals, unless appearances are snares; fifteen months' experience, all wrong; and the human book of feature and expression, a lie. My wish has been to deal fairly. I have only to say that I am personally responsible for my inferences, and trust to have made few incorrect statements.   H. U. S.

WINIFRED'S CONSERVATORY.

BY JEAN MIDDLEMASS.

———◆———

'THERE's only one thing wanting now, Arnold dear, to make our little house perfect,' said Winifred Moreton, as she clung coaxingly to her young husband's arm; 'and that is a conservatory—a wee conservatory to keep us in flowers all the winter long. Look here, in this corner now, there are really three sides of it ready built; we should only want a front and a roof, and that old door we took from between the lower rooms, and the shelves inside.'

'*And* the apparatus to warm it, *and* the plants to stock it,' added Arnold, with a smile.

'O, as for those, my friend, Mrs. Wodehouse, has promised to send me most of hers; she is going abroad shortly, and doesn't care about them, she says; and she appears anxious that I should have them.'

'So—so you are jealous of your dear friend's conservatory, is that it? You forget, little woman, that the Wodehouses are rich folk, while you have been foolish enough to marry a poor young fellow in a Government office. However, *ce que femme veut;* have your conservatory, my Winnie, only don't be extravagant about it.'

A month later the conservatory is finished, and Winnie is superintending the arrangement of a cargo of fine plants just sent by Mrs. Wodehouse. All have, as usual, a label affixed to a little peg at the side of the pot, on which the botanical name of the flower is written; but she suddenly observes that this, in the case of the finest plant, is not a label merely, but a carefully-folded and sealed note directed to herself.

She opens it, and her blue eyes grow first round with astonishment, then moist with pity as she reads. Finally she sits down among the flower-pots, and looks at them as they stand just where the men have left them, and there is a sort of superstitious awe depicted on her face, as if she fears lest the arrival of these pots of flowers is also the arrival of a great misery in her home. All her pleasure, her almost infantine delight over the new conservatory, is gone; it seems to have passed away as rapidly as the short exclamation of joy with which she had hailed the advent of these floral treasures. In her hand she still holds the note containing the cloud which, wreathing itself about her mind, is already beginning to dim the clear horizon of Winifred Moreton's bright young life. She is reading it once again with much intentness, when she hears her husband open the outer door with a latchkey. She thrusts it into her pocket with hurried eagerness, and then strives, but rather vainly, to compose her face into an appearance of creditable tranquillity. The first secret has sprung up between her and Arnold, and the keeping it then and in the future will prove a heavy tax on Winifred's candid nature.

He cannot avoid noticing that something is amiss, and exclaims,

'Why, little wife, how grave you look over your new toy! You have got your conservatory ; you have some lovely flowers to put in it—very kind of Mrs. Wodehouse to send them—and still you look as if you had some heavy care on your mind. What *is* the matter, my dear Winnie?'

' Please, Arnold, let me send for old Roffey the carpenter to put up some shutters and a bar across here, and a couple of bolts to the door.'

' Foolish Winnie, do you think your plants so very precious that all the burglars in town will be after them ? However, have your way. Send for that old carpenter with a face like a battered half-penny, and make your floral treasures quite secure. Meanwhile, perhaps you will treat me to a smile and a kiss.'

Days passed into weeks, and the conservatory was never out of Winifred's thoughts, reminding one forcibly of La Fontaine's fable of ' Le Savetier et le Financier :'

'Tout le jour, il avait l'œil au guet ; et la
          nuit,
Si quelque chat faisait du bruit,
Le chat prenait l'argent.'

Alas, poor Winnie ! her plaything had become her *bête noire,* nor could all the care and solicitude of her husband, whom she loved to adoration, lay the ghost which seemed to be wandering about her heart.

The London season was over ; she accompanied Arnold abroad for his holiday, but the preoccupation and listlessness of his little wife became a serious source of anxiety to him. Nothing seemed to amuse her ; nothing seemed to have any place in her thoughts save the one overwhelming desire to get home. Arriving at last in the first week in October in the bijou house in South Kensington, she rushed instantly into the conservatory, looked carefully at all her plants, and counted them to see that the number was correct. Arnold had some thoughts of sending for a physician, as he positively was beginning to fear that Winifred had some mental disease, which was developing itself into a phase which he was pleased to call ' plantomania ;' and not a little delighted was he to receive a telegram from his brother-in-law, who had been for some time past with his regiment in India, saying that ' he is coming home as fast as ship and railway can bring him, and that he may be expected in London any day.'

' He will perhaps be able to throw some light,' he thinks, ' on this extraordinary infatuation of Winnie's, not only for watching and tending her plants, but for locking them up and thinking about them ceaselessly.'

But Captain Verschoyle is not more able to account for his sister's peculiar mania than is her perplexed husband ; and after many conversations between them on the subject, and much confabulation, they agree to consult the family doctor. Dr. Jones, however, laughs at their surmises, and pooh-poohs their fears.

' He has known Winnie ever since she was a baby ; he'll guarantee his reputation that there is nothing mad about her.'

So he says ; but when he comes to see her, at her husband's suggestion, the pained anxious expression of her face, once so bright and smiling, the restraint of her manner, once so lively and gay, staggers even the belief of the faithful old Hippocrates. What can it possibly mean?

' Look here, Mrs. Winifred'—he had always called her Mrs. Winifred since she married — ' look here, Mrs. Winifred, I believe the odour of these flowers is making you look thin and wan. I shall tell your husband to have them all carried away, and that little ugly conservatory pulled down.'

'No, Dr. Jones, no. I wish to Heaven that it had never been built; but to take it down would be worse than death to me.'

'I do not understand,' said he, watching her keenly as he spoke.

'No, perhaps not; but plants are such a worry: they always die when you want them to flower. I am very sorry I asked for them. I was so much happier before I had them.'

The doctor was nonplussed, and began to think, with her husband and brother, that the worry these flowers occasioned her must be the result of a weak mind.

To his repeated suggestion, however, that if they were troublesome to her, the wiser course would be to get rid of them, she persistently offered the most determined opposition.

Altogether, Winifred's conservatory was a puzzle to these three men's heads, the like of which they had never previously been called on to solve. She was perfectly sane, perfectly coherent, perfectly wise on every subject, except about these carefully-tended plants. What course, then, remained to those who were interested in her, save to imagine she was afflicted with monomania?

The winter passed; spring, with bright days and sharp winds, came at last, and brought once more a series of countless invitations for Winifred and Arnold Moreton; for they were in good society, though their means were somewhat limited; and Winifred, moreover, was a beauty. Nothing, however, had the effect of distracting her from what appeared to be the one sole amusement of her life—tending the flowers in her conservatory.

In the first week in May there was a splendid ball given by Lady Olive Farnham. The Moretons

were there; and Winifred, in a pale-pink *crêpe*, which Arnold had insisted on ordering from Paris for the occasion, was surrounded by admirers; in fact, she was on the straight path for becoming a fashionable beauty—a state of affairs to which Arnold would especially have objected, had he not been in a frame of mind to hail with joy any event which would make Winnie forget to devote herself to that hateful conservatory. She seemed to be enjoying herself to the very utmost; and Arnold felt quite happy.

While she was standing talking to a distinguished French diplomat, the colour suddenly forsook her cheeks, and she looked as if she were going to faint. Arnold, who had been watching her at a little distance, was at her side in a moment.

'My dearest Winnie, what is the matter?' he exclaimed.

'O Arnold, the Wodehouses—how dreadful!'

He looked round, but he saw no one, heard nothing that could give him any clue to her meaning.

'Would you like to go home?' he asked.

'Yes, please.'

He took her down-stairs, and called for the carriage. It was not till they were seated in it that she told him that while she was talking to M. de Merinan, she overheard, from a conversation that was going on behind her, that Mr. Wodehouse was locked up in a French prison for some bubble-share transactions in which he had been concerned in connection with a South American railway, and that Mrs. Wodehouse was dead.

Arnold Moreton was not an unfeeling man, and he was truly sorry for this heavy affliction which had fallen on the family of his old friends. Still he could not be brought to understand why Winifred should be so desperately upset by it; for no sooner had she been released from her finery by her maid than she threw herself on her sofa, sobbing convulsively, and by turns rejoicing and lamenting over what had happened. Arnold grew angry for the first time in his life, really angry with his little wife.

Dr. Jones had more than once recommended a certain amount of discreet wrath; for the first time, to-night he felt inclined to follow his advice.

He represented to Winifred that she was by no means fulfilling the mission that either love or duty imposed, wounding her sensitiveness, too, not a little by telling her that, while he did everything he could to give her pleasure, she seemed to take a tacit delight in receiving all his advances with indifference—nay, almost with contempt.

His words went like a sharp dagger into poor Winnie's heart; but still she offered no word of explanation: only after a while she raised her tear-stained face from the sofa-cushion on which she had hidden it, and looked at Arnold with her large swollen eyes.

'One more favour, dearest Hubby. I know I do not deserve it; but you will grant me one more, will you not?'

'What is it, my love? You know I shall be delighted to give you anything in reason that will make you happy.'

'Send for Blanche Wodehouse, and let her come and stay with us.'

Arnold's brow contracted into a frown. It was not that he objected to Blanche Wodehouse coming to stay with them, but that he was totally at a loss to conjecture what the affinity was that existed between his young wife and these people, even to the extent of rendering her unfit for all her home duties. She saw his hesitation, almost amounting to displeasure, and threw herself into his arms with a sudden outburst of affection.

'Arnold dear, grant me this request—do, there's a darling Arnold, —if you don't, I shall be compelled to go off to the Continent myself, in search of Blanche!'

'You, Winifred! You must be quite mad!'

'O no. I am not in the least mad, only I have a terrible secret to keep, and the keeping it nearly sends me mad, Arnold dear. O, how I wish I could tell you all about it!'

'A secret in connection with the Wodehouses?'

'Yes; and you will let Blanche come, will you not?'

'I do not object to your having Blanche Wodehouse to stay for a little while, if her coming is at all likely to remove the incubus which has lain over you of late.'

'It will, indeed it will, at least I hope so. O you dear darling old pet, you are much kinder to your little wife than she deserves, though she is not such a bad little woman as I know you have been thinking her of late.'

'Now let us to bed,' he said, 'or you will look so jaded to-morrow, you will no longer merit the name of my pretty Winnie.'

To bed for Arnold Moreton was not to sleep. He was perplexed beyond everything to imagine what this extraordinary secret could be which had so changed Winnie. That the flowers in that conservatory had something to do with it he felt sure; but turn the matter in his mind how he might, he could make nothing of it; and after thinking it over in all its varied phases for hours, he decided that it was perhaps as well he had given permission for an invitation to be sent to Blanche Wodehouse, since her presence in the house might throw some light on the matter.

At last Mr. Moreton fell asleep, to awake after a while with the sort of nightmarish conviction that some one had arrived, and that this some one was Miss Blanche Wodehouse. It was eight o'clock, and the sun was streaming gladly into the room. He was not dreaming then, and it was actually the voice of the butler outside the door, informing him that a young lady in deep mourning had arrived from abroad, and wanted to see Mrs. Moreton immediately. Of course it was Blanche Wodehouse, and of course Winnie, in her dressing-gown, rushed off without farther delay to receive her; and 'most extraordinary,' muttered Arnold, as he peeped over the staircase to see them meet, 'they have actually gone into the conservatory and locked the door.' He went into his dressing-room to perform his morning toilette, with a sort of desperate resolution to give up all attempt at guessing the very difficult conundrum that had been presented to him. He did not hurry himself in the least; having resolved to give the matter up, he wrapped himself in a sort of gloomy resignation.

Quite an hour later, when he came out of his room, thinking that if possible he would get a little breakfast and go straight to his office out of the way, he met Winnie at the door. She had dressed very quickly, and appeared in the freshest and prettiest of morning dresses, a glad smile on her lovely face, an open letter in her hand.

'O you great, dear, naughty Arnold, you look as grave as if you had the weight of the whole world on your shoulders!'

The cloud partly passed from his brow when he saw the changed look on her face, and he held out his hand for the letter.

It was the same that had been attached to the largest of Mrs. Wodehouse's flower-pots. With no small astonishment Arnold read as follows:

'Forgive me, my dearest friend, for the subterfuge to which I am compelled to have recourse; for the trust and responsibility with which, without even daring previously to ask permission, I am about to burden you. Sooner or later you must know the sad secret of my life: my husband is a confirmed and desperate gambler. This fatal passion has gradually made our whole life one miserable acted lie. It was necessary to keep up appearances in order to avoid suspicion and retain his business credit. The more deeply we sank in debt the more wildly he sought to retrieve his fortunes at the gaming-table. Heaven only knows how soon and desperately this may end. My own little fortune, which by the culpable carelessness of my guardian was left in his power, has been dissipated. The only thing left for me and my poor daughter when the crash comes, as come it must, is the handsome *parure* of diamonds I inherited from my mother. These are indeed, by every right, my own; but already my infatuated husband has his eye on them, and I dread lest any moment they may be gambled away. For my child's sake I entreat you, help me to save them. They may some day realise a sum which to her will be invaluable. Deep down in the mould of the flower-pots you will find them buried. There, for the present, let them remain; keep them till a day comes when I or my daughter may reclaim them. Do not betray my secret even to your husband. I trust entirely to your goodness and your loyalty.—Your unhappy friend, 'MARIAN WODEHOUSE.'

'So,' exclaimed Arnold, putting

his arm round his wife, 'this is the terrible secret, little woman, which has been wearing your life away. I do not feel obliged to Mrs. Wodehouse for not letting you confide in me.'

'O Arnold dear, poor Mrs. Wodehouse, she is dead.'

He shrugged his shoulders and followed Winnie down-stairs into the conservatory, where they found Blanche, a rather sad-looking tearful beauty of seventeen, whom Winnie's brother, Captain Verschoyle, was not altogether quite unsuccessfully seeking to console as they stood together taking the plants out of the flower-pots and shaking the diamonds from their roots.

Arnold looked at Winnie and smiled as he saw the picture; perhaps he had a sort of vision of a matrimonial pendant. A few minutes later they all four went down to breakfast together, Blanche's *dot* lying before them in lustrous beauty on the white cloth.

Mr. Moreton being a busy man, Captain Verschoyle undertook the sale of the jewels; but though he was always on the point of clinching a good offer, somehow or other he never quite achieved it, and already Blanche Wodehouse had been nearly a month under the Moretons' hospitable roof, when she rushed into Winnie's conservatory one morning—now, since the finding of the diamonds, become once more the young wife's plaything—and threw herself into her arms.

'O Winifred, he has asked me to marry him, and says I am not to sell the diamonds after all, as he has quite enough money for us both.'

'My dear Blanche, I am so very glad. You will make the sweetest, dearest little sister-in-law. Only fancy a marriage arising out of my building a conservatory, and then having, as Dr. Jones says, "diamonds on the brain"!'

SPRING IN THE SOUTH.

By Mrs. ADOLPHE SMITH.

EVERY one talks about the splendour of winter in the South, about the warmth and brilliancy of December on the Riviera, when one can run up the hills at the back of the sunlit towns and pick a handful of wild honeysuckle for Christmas morning—about the vivid colouring of the winter sunsets, the profusion of winter roses; but little has been said about the splendour of the early southern spring—the spring that comes at the beginning of February, when every growth throughout this blest corner of the world is budding and bursting into leaf and blossom. The hills are covered with anemones of every shade, from the palest lavender to the deepest purple; the plains are yellow with jonquils growing wild by thousands; the hedges are brilliant with wild roses, with honeysuckle, with iris and asphodel; the maidenhair fern grows abundantly in every damp and shady corner; the Oriental lenticus shows its crimson berries and glossy foliage on every southern slope; and the orange and olive, the myrtle and the almond, the cypress and the lemon-trees are on every side, on every ledge of every hill; and above all is the deep-blue sky that is beyond the imagination of those who have never travelled southwards. Even in January a few rays of sunshine will suffice to set these towns of the Riviera aglow. The rain will come down in a genuine deluge at night, and the sun will rise in the morning as complacently as if nothing had happened, and will dry up all the roadways and pathways, will strengthen and encourage the almond-buds that are ready to burst into odorous masses of brilliant bloom, will fortify the millions of roses that blossom in the fields, and will send the exposed thermometer up to ninety-five degrees Fahrenheit!

The *hivernants*, as all the foreigners who come to pass the winter and spring in the South are called, are able to bask in the sun in February, and sometimes in January! They can sit at the open windows, their rooms needing no warming element but the sunlight. They can watch the lawn-tennis, they can linger about the flower-kiosks, they can read their English journals at the English reading-room windows, which overlook either luxuriant plains of palms and cypresses and yuccas and orange-trees, with glimpses of umbrella pines beyond, or ample expanses of the 'sapphire sea' of the Mediterranean. They can take their newspaper to the Promenade where the band plays, or to the terrace by the water's edge; in fact, they can behave on the Riviera, as a rule, in the early spring months as they would behave at the English seaside in July and August.

These observations apply to all the Riviera towns, but perhaps more especially to Hyères, the 'Garden of Provence,' as it is often called, which is the most sheltered corner of the vast coast-line, and which has as yet been one of the quietest of the health-resorts. People who have come here have meant business : they have come to linger in the sunlight and to go indoors at sunset ; they have been through the six months' season without getting a glimpse of the light of a street gas-lamp ; they have insisted upon being visited by one of the doctors every day ; they have been drawn up the hills in bath-chairs ; and some of them have even required to be accommodated with a seat when they have entered upon a campaign at the dark little post-office, where sits the official whose tousled head of hair looks as if he were perpetually rubbing his hands through it in despair at the multiplicity of the demands upon his time.

The foreign element at Hyères is mainly English, for the moment ; but a considerable change will doubtless be effected when fashion steps in, and the various improvements contemplated—the instalment of the Casino, the erection of the kiosk or pavilion for the municipal band, the arrangement of the gardens below the kiosk, the contemplated tramway from the English quarter (known among the natives as the Quartier des Moustiques and the Quartier du Mistral, for both of which cheerful accompaniments to a southern resort the west of the town, where the English do congregate, is remarkable) to the *orient* district—put Hyères more on a level with Nice and Cannes as regards civilisation.

To some of us, however, it is not the lesser or greater development of civilisation that charms us in these southern towns ; it is the boundless beauty of Nature, the splendour of the scenes that surround us. We forget to note the existence or non-existence of a Casino, as we stand on the olive- and pine-clad hills and look away towards the blue Mediterranean ; we do not sigh for a tramway as we follow the windings of the narrow white roads where there is only just room for the passing of the *diligence ;* on the contrary, we worshippers of that Nature that ' never did betray the heart that loved her' are prone to conceive that each step taken towards what are called commonly improvements will rob us of some treasured corner, some picturesque group of trees, some well-loved glimpse of field and forest.

The spring that begins in February lasts till May, each day bringing forth fresh charms, fresh beauties. The warmth of the air, the clearness of the sky, the indescribable brilliancy of everything, makes one feel sometimes that the privilege of life is a blessed one after all. We sit on our broad stone terrace shaded by the vine, and look around us : the orange-trees are in full vigour at the foot of the terrace, the aloes and the prickly pears and the palms and the almond-trees are within a stone's throw, and the unbroken expanse of deep-blue sky is crossed in the distance by the line of purple hills. As we glance around us, and sip our coffee with a touch perhaps of southern indolence, it is hard to remember that we are at the very beginning of March. The *hivernants* are indulging in all the outdoor amusements connected with July in England. They are picnicking in the woods, they are hunting butterflies up the hills, they are gathering wild-flowers in the fields, they are collecting ferns in the shady lanes, they are sauntering along the Rue d'Antibes at Cannes, or the Promenade des Anglais at Nice, or the steep streets of Mentone and San Remo, or the varied Boulevard National at Hyères, in broad-brimmed hats and light clothing, carrying big white umbrellas lined with blue or green, and very often wearing blue spectacles in order to protect their eyes from the glare of the sunlight. The natives of Provence contribute largely to the picturesque aspect of the various places. The people of this land of troubadours and roses are not classically handsome; but when they are young there is a fire about their eyes, there is a brilliancy in their smiles, that remind the ethnologist of their Moorish ancestors. The men in their blue working clothes, with their broad red sashes and wide-brimmed gray or black felt hats; the women in their red skirts, black bodices, and enormous flat white straw-hats, make effective pictures in their youth. In old age they are, both men and women, hideously ugly.

The Provençals have no sense of art, as a rule; they utterly fail to appreciate the beauty of their own country; they spend their lives in their native villages, utterly destitute of the spirit of adventure that should induce them to explore even their own province. There were people in Hyères who, at five-and-twenty and thirty years of age, had never left the town, except to spend three days at Toulon at the time of their marriage! Marseilles seemed at as great a distance to them as New York to the Englishman. They are amazed at the English love of travel, and they are often amazed also at the English people's admiration of their country. They cannot understand that one should pay attention to the blue sky, and the palms, and the alleys of Oriental plane-trees; and they cannot realise that in London these things are unknown, that our streets are not lined with palm- and eucalyptus-trees, that Ludgate-hill is not a sea of anemones, and Lincoln's-inn-fields yellow with jonquils.

Spring has a startling advantage over winter in the South, in the matter of mosquitoes. If the winter be mild, these abominable insects linger on through November, December, and even into January; but then they die out, and are never to be feared in February, or March, or April. They appear in March or April, but they are too young to do any harm. Only those who have suffered from mosquitoes will appreciate the full force of this argument.

TINSLEYS' MAGAZINE.

May 1881.

SCEPTRE AND RING.

By B. H. BUXTON,

AUTHOR OF 'JENNIE OF "THE PRINCE'S,"' 'FROM THE WINGS,' ETC.

Part the Second.

CHAPTER VIII.

THE GREAT EVENT.

THERE can be no doubt that a reception of more than ordinary importance is destined to take place at the magnificent residence of hospitable Lady Buzze this evening. The verandah running round three sides of the substantial red-brick mansion in Kensington Gore has often been ridiculed as quite out of harmony and date with the rest of the quaint-looking house; but its real usefulness has now been proved and demonstrated; for by the aid of enterprising upholsterers it has been converted into additional reception-rooms, the walls (?) of which consist of red-striped canvas, all decked with flags, ribbons, and garlands of bright-hued flowers. Quaint Chinese lanterns throw a dimly suggestive light over everything, and make the dazzling brilliance of the thousand wax-candles within the farther spacious 'state' apartments the more apparent. Great masses of verdure, ferns, palms, and other exotics seem to have sprung up out of gorgeous-hued carpets, as though by magic; sweet-scented sprays of perfumed waters fall in rippling showers over the fern-grown rock-work heaped in the dimly-lighted corners; and these form a picturesque background for the living figures of elegantly-dressed women, who seek quiet and fresh air in these secluded nooks, and feel that here at least they may safely reply to the whispers of the black-coated men, who escort them, and who also rejoice at having escaped for a moment from the noisy restless crowd in the ballrooms. Lady Buzze is a clever woman, as well as a generous and hospitable one; she is quite aware that there will be many of her guests who will prefer the opportunity of a quiet *tête-à-tête* in the cool verandah-rooms, which she has improvised, to being perpetually *en évidence* before the throng assembled to do homage to Royalty, and, as soon as Royalty shall have made them happy by appearing, to look on and applaud the *tableaux* and the operetta so carefully prepared and rehearsed for their benefit during the last six weeks.

Lady Buzze, who some years ago took an active and a very prominent part in all the very best theatricals organised by amateurs, and always acted with great success, has of late been reluctantly compelled to yield her *rôle* of leading lady to more youthful, if less competent, rivals; but she has borne this compulsory change fairly well; and as her husband's sudden inheritance of an immense fortune proved an immediate consolation at a critical moment, so the farther favour of knighthood (bestowed upon him by a gracious sovereign in return for some civic hospitality over which Sir Thomas Buzze had successfully presided) served to lift Lady Buzze's drooping wings. And she had arisen again after this temporary discomfiture, animated by her husband's promotion; refreshed, vigorous, and quite prepared for far more ambitious flights than ever plain Mrs. Thomas Buzze would have ventured to contemplate.

Over the stone-pillared gate at the outer entrance to Lady Buzze's hospitable mansion, a great marquee is arranged to-night; carpets cover the gravel-path of the garden and the pavement outside; and it is on this latter spot that another eager crowd has assembled expectant already, and watching the arrivals, in the quickly succeeding carriages, with craning necks, critical eyes, and growing interest. Sometimes a fair youthful head of exceptional beauty is greeted with the expressive 'Ah!' of admiration; and then the advent of some portly dowager, whose attraction consists in her wondrous size and in that of her flashing diamonds, provokes a general ' O!' which sounds as much like disapproval as surprise.

'Move on, move on, *if you please!*' is the occasional reminder of a passing policeman, who evidently suits his polite address to the exigencies of the occasion, impressed by which, he, who is but mortal, thinks he also would like to stand and look on at the goodly show of arriving guests; but innate respect for the force, of which he is proud to be a member, checks his first impulse to stand with the crowd looking on. He strongly resembles its component parts, and he feels that he shares the inquisitive proclivities of those lingering expectant men and women; but to betray this weakness would be derogatory, so he discreetly crosses the road. He walks with measured official steps; but he has a clearly-defined purpose, and presently takes up a favourable position in the shelter of the dark trees overhanging the railings at Kensington Gardens. From this coign of vantage he also can look on at the fast-arriving guests, and he indulges in frequent though unspoken comments on the appearance of such as he can see tolerably well. Suddenly, however, he leaves his comfortable post of observation, and hurriedly crosses the road again; for there is a surging movement in the crowd opposite, and a cheer rises into the still clear air of the spring night, as a neat dark brougham, on C springs, draws up at the curb, and a face, dear and familiar to all Londoners, is recognised by the crowd, who feel that now their patience is well rewarded. They have gazed upon Royalty face to face, and the hem of the skirt of an august personage has swept the ground within an inch of their weary feet.

Lady Buzze sails down the broad stone steps in a fine flutter of excitement. The great event of her life has come to her. This triumphant moment crowns her socially, and rewards her for countless hours of mental and physical anxiety and fatigue. All her tedious manœuvring is rewarded; the diplomatic talent brought to bear upon the organisation of this exceptionally brilliant *fête* has led to unqualified success; and to-morrow morning the chronicles of fashion will teem with elaborate accounts of Lady Buzze's grand reception, of the beauty and talent present thereat, and, better than all else, those who run will be able to read that her ladyship's charitable enterprise was graced by the presence of her august patronesses.

The news of this eagerly expected arrival passed swiftly from lip to lip in the crowded rooms above, and is repeated with ever-increasing excitement.

A professional beauty of considerable renown, who is preparing to pose in a preliminary *tableau vivant*, hastens to the glass and adds an additional *soupçon* of rouge to the cheeks, which have suddenly blanched at the stirring news of the latest arrival.

Miss Hartley, who is as active and preoccupied behind the scenes as any 'acting and responsible manager' on a 'first night,' requires no rouge. Feverish excitement has flushed her face in a most becoming manner; and her eyes sparkle with a brilliant vivacity that makes her appear more youthful than ever. So far everything appears auspicious indeed. No irritating telegrams have arrived at the last critical moment to vex the souls of author and composer. No apologies have been tendered for the 'unavoidable absence' of some person or persons whose presence is absolutely necessary for the unblemished success of the evening's entertainment.

Campo Maestro, quicksilvery in his movements, directing, gesticulating with ever-increasing violence, shouts out would-be English phrases, interspersed with passionate Italian oaths, to the bewildered and somewhat helpless crowd of amateurs about him, who, as is their wont, appear utterly at a loss the moment their services are put to a professional test.

'The Beauties'' only anxiety concerns their personal appearance, and each one of them is secretly animated by the flattering hope that, on this auspicious occasion, she will be able to assert herself triumphantly as far lovelier than her *soi-disant* rivals. The would-be actresses—those who sing and intend to take an active share in the performances—are naturally more nervous and excited by their responsibilities than those who only require to look their best in the dumbshow of *tableaux*. But all these more or less ambitious amateurs belong to a certain social sphere; they form a select class, of which each member is in some degree known to the others; they have tastes, opinions, and friends in common; but Madame Margherita finds herself isolated among these fashionable ladies, an alien among strangers—quite alone in the busy, chattering, familiar crowd.

Both Miss Hartley and Campo Maestro are too thoroughly engrossed by their respective duties, and the exigencies of the situation, to have thought or word to spare for the *débutante*, their *protégée*. And so she has retired to the farthest corner of ' the greenroom,' which, in this case, is a red chamber; for it is the breakfast-room of the mansion which has been thus utilised by the enterprising stage-manageress, who has assumed the right to turn Lady Buzze's house topsy-turvy on this momentous occasion. And Lady Buzze, though she nominally retains the proud position of commander-in-chief of the ceremonies, is sufficiently shrewd to appreciate the cleverness of an active general, and, as far as the stage is concerned, willingly hands the managerial *bâton* over to experienced autocratic Miss Hartley, who certainly seems born to hold dominion over those about her.

As Margherita sits alone and unnoticed in her corner, she is thinking over the events of the past sorrowful weeks; and her heart, which has been very heavy within her ever since she beheld the abject condition of her very wretched parent, is still aching with the prolonged pain of regret and repentance, under which her sensitive nature suffers acutely. She had inquired about the fiddler from door to door in Kensington High-street as she made her way back through that crowded thoroughfare; and, after these countless fruitless inquiries, she was finally directed to the police-station.

'If he was a beggar, a vagrant that is, you'd be sure to hear of him there, miss,' said a good-natured red-faced butcher, to whom the anxious girl had applied for information. 'I wonder what her game is?' remarked he of the blue blouse, turning inquisitively towards the buxom partner of his joys and jokes, who was comfortably ensconced in an office that resembled a glass-case.

'No good, you may be sure, my dear,' said she, with truly feminine charity, and then she went on with the customers' account-books.

Margherita made her way to the police-station, which she entered in fear and trembling. To her surprise she was most courteously received by the inspector in the office, who seemed quite prepared to give her any information in his power. He—worthy man—had been considerably taken aback by the manifest trouble and earnestness of the beautiful girl, whose presence in his gloomy official apartment brought a radiance with it that fairly dazzled the veteran. Why should this pretty lady in fashionable attire trouble her head about an old beggar, who, according to her own reluctant statement, was certainly intoxicated; for he had stumbled in front of her carriage because he was unable to hold himself up? Her reason for requiring such information was her own business, however; and the inspector (who might, with advantage, have set an example of reticence to many of his superiors in the fashionable world) forebore to inquire into matters which did not concern him, and contented himself by promising to seek out the fiddler, and to make his whereabouts known to the lady, unless he had wandered on through Hammersmith into Surrey, which was most likely, since beggars on this road mostly found their way out of the county to Richmond or Kingston.

'If the old man had been hurt by your horse, miss, we should have heard of it sure-*ly*,' continued the civil inspector, going forward to open the door for his gracious visitor, who was fain to content herself with his assurance that she should be informed of the fact if the fiddler should be heard of in those parts again. She left her name, 'Madame Margherita,' and Miss Hartley's address; and then she continued her way towards Regency-terrace. She was ashamed to own to herself that she felt relieved by the knowledge that, for the present at least, there seemed to be no chance of ascertaining her degraded parent's whereabouts. The inspector had hinted to her that, if her business with the beggar were of real importance, he might be traced, and would surely be discovered, time and money being allowed for the research. Then she had declined to make any further stir in the matter at present, and had left it to chance whether or not she should receive any farther communication on the subject, which, from the inspector's point of view, was evidently one likely to compromise 'a lady.' But no sooner had she left the police-station than her tender conscience reproached her. She was afraid and ashamed of her father. She had refused to take any active steps in the matter of finding him, because she had no urgent desire to do so; and when she remembered her mother, and the promise made by that beloved parent's deathbed, the troubled girl was filled with sudden consternation as she realised her own wicked ingratitude.

It was in this mood that she arrived at the Cottage; and there, to her surprise, she found Campo Maestro. He could not rest in peace, he said, knowing of the folly Miss Hartley was about to commit by anticipating Madame Margherita's *début* without his sanctioning presence; and so he had come back again, half hoping they had never started at all; and, in any case, fully prepared to await their return.

Mrs. Day was already busy cooking some cutlets for him, which the old Bohemian, thoroughly accustomed to cater for himself, had purchased at a butcher's shop as he came along. One glance at his pupil's pale troubled face showed him that matters had gone wrong with her; and as, where his professional interest was at stake, he was not a man to be deterred from his purpose by any notion of etiquette, or what he would have called 'a false delicacy,' he so persistently questioned and cross-questioned the shrinking girl that she finally had to confess the cause of her trouble to some extent. Campo, with true Southern impulsiveness and redundant phrases of conversation, vowed absolute secrecy as to anything she

might confide to him; and this promise induced her to tell him that the man who had frightened her, and who was playing the fiddle for money in the streets, was a near relation of hers, whose present poverty was the result of his intemperance.

This reluctant confession was welcomed with secret delight by Campo, for he at once saw in it an urgent motive-power which he might bring to bear on Diana to influence her judgment and gain her consent to a fondly-cherished scheme of his own, to which he had hitherto been unable to induce her to lend a willing ear. To Margherita herself the shrewd old man gave no hint of his secret intentions, plans, and aspirations; but he comforted her as best he could, and, having promised to give her an extra hour's lesson if she would consent to sit down and dine with him first, he had the satisfaction of seeing her face brighten a little, as a faint flush of colour came back to her cheeks.

'Noting can more make pleasure to *la signora* than to find you perfeck in that last *aria, cara mia,*' he said, as he rose from table and prepared to accompany his willing pupil to the drawing-room. 'I can see that our goot Diana has troubeled yourself and herself, and that you have fear of her; but that shall pass—it shall all pass, *foi de gentilhomme*—if but you meet vid her quite as on an ordinary, and say no littel vord for vat has gone before.'

Miss Hartley remained at Richmond, and dined there with her friends. It was past ten o'clock when she returned to the Cottage; and she was almost afraid to enter lest she should hear that offended Margherita had fled. But when the sound of that mellow soprano greeted her anxious ears as she drove up the gravel road, she felt immensely relieved, and, though somewhat surprised at Maestro's unexpected presence, betrayed her satisfaction in the cordiality of her greeting; and she very soon put her alarmed *protégée* quite at her ease by a smile of encouragement, and a request for that very *aria* at which the girl had just had an extra practice with her devoted painstaking master. And neither by word nor look did Miss Hartley allude to that terrible scene in Kensington High-street again; but she reassured the timid *débutante* by every means in her power, urging her on to perfect herself for the fast-approaching 'great event,' at which Margherita was now present, fully prepared to do her best for the sake of her much-interested friends, and fervently hoping that her success on this occasion might prove a stepping-stone to her proposed professional career.

As the girl sits alone in the green-room she is thinking over all these things; and she has so completely forgotten her present position and her novel surroundings that she fairly starts when Campo Maestro suddenly taps her on the shoulder, and says,

'It is ze hour; ze time it has come, and now it is for you to appear. Be brave, my child; have a great courage, a good heart, and all must be very well. Belief dis.'

Though startled for a moment, she is not long at a loss, and is surely the most tranquil and self-possessed of all the ladies, who are trembling with mingled apprehension and delight at the blissful prospect of appearing before Royalty and its attendant crowd. They who thus tremble are wrapped up in exciting ideas of themselves, their appearance, their reception by the guests, and anxiety as to the effect they are likely to produce on others.

Margherita is thinking only of the part she is so eager to do justice to, and of those kind hopeful friends who, as she knows, are in some measure reckoning on her for the success of their joint enterprise. The crowd—and the possible or probable opinion of those who compose it—affects her not at all; she longs to sing and to act well; but it is the thought of the art to which she aspires, and the friends to whom she is grateful, that preoccupies her, rather than the approval of outsiders, as she steps upon the stage with quiet dignity.

It is her appearance which provokes a burst of applause; for this greets her before she has uttered a note. She is clad in a simple gown of creamy cashmere, which looks pure white behind the footlights. A Marguerite satchel of brown leather depends from her waist; her hair is gathered in two great plaits, and its waves are pushed off her forehead behind the delicate shell-like ears. She wears no ornament of any kind. The perfect simplicity is a welcome relief after the tinselly appearance of all the velvet-clad kings and queens of romantic history, and the heroes and heroines of historical romance, who have been posing in a succession of dazzling *tableaux vivants* during the past two hours.

Miss Hartley—who has a natural talent for stage management—has accurately calculated the kind of appearance which will cause the best impression after the meretricious pictures in which painted beauties have so generously exhibited their charms. She has allowed Margherita to follow the bent of her own inclination, and, saving the touch of rouge upon her fair young face, she has insisted upon no further 'professional' preparation.

Margherita's eyes shine with their own clear light; her lips are unstained; she has escaped the hare's-foot, the black pencil, the white wash, and stands before the crowd of upturned faces a very incarnation of purity.

'Lovely!' 'Exquisite!' are the words that greet her; but she has no ears for the audience at present. Her thoughts are concentrated upon her part; and in another moment she responds vocally to the silent command of Campo Maestro's *báton* by commencing her first recitative.

The scene is laid in a modern drawing-room, and the lady who follows Margherita on to the stage is a handsome bold-looking girl, clad in a crimson-brocade dinner-dress. She is evidently bent on displaying as much of her figure as the costume of the day permits. She is a sparkling brunette, and has by no means disdained the use of colour and cosmetic in her desire to heighten her attractions. In Miss Hartley's modern drawing-room version of the familiar Faust and Gretchen story, the part of designing Mephisto is given to a handsome unscrupulous woman; and no one could have been found to interpret this difficult *rôle* better than Miss Aurelia Armstrong, who is required to present the incarnation of evil in the guise of a tempting insidious Delilah.

Miss Armstrong is a practised coquette. She has proved herself a proficient in every variety of the art of flirtation during the last five seasons. Her mother had played the part of an aspiring adventuress in polite society with such signal success that she had secured the wealthy Sir Jacob Armstrong as a partner for life. And Miss Aurelia was so thoroughly imbued with the teaching and tactics of her diplomatic mamma that she was doing her best to emulate that brilliant and successful example.

No more startling contrast could have been presented to an attentive, eager, and interested audience than that which now appeared before the surprised eyes of Lady Buzze's guests.

Pure pale Margaret, with her lowly-bent fair head and modestly-downcast eyes, clad in softest folds of white drapery, and brazen Beatrix, her proud dark head lifted defiantly, her bold eyes seeking the eager glances of the spectators, her gorgeous crimson gown, as startling in its splendour and eccentricity as Margaret's was simple. The outward appearance of these two women differed as widely as did their characters, both in the play and in real life.

Yes; Miss Hartley had certainly been very successful with her dramatic scheme this time, and, with her usual good fortune—or shall we say discrimination?—she had happened on the very women best fitted to do justice to her libretto, and to carry out the parts of the heroines most satisfactorily.

Miss Armstrong (Beatrix) has a contralto voice, and she knows how to use it as effectively as she uses her eyes. She has enjoyed the advantage of regular study, under a painstaking master, for many years, and her proficiency as a singer is very soon apparent. She has long ago won renown for herself in drawing-room entertainments, and is considered preëminent as a contralto among amateurs.

The soprano (Madame Margherita) is richly endowed by nature, her first song proves the fact; but, from an artistic point of view, the contralto decidedly has the advantage.

There is a 'la-di-dah' tenor of average drawing-room capabilities and more than average affectation; but as he has simply to languish in strains of adoration for arrogant Beatrix, his lack of special vocal and dramatic power makes little difference to the *tout ensemble.* Miss Hartley, like so many lady-authors, has not succeeded in endowing her heroes with life-like vigour. She has concentrated her attention upon the women of her play; and she has certainly given them very effective parts. She flattered herself that she had acted upon the *inspiration* which prompted her libretto in the first instance; and she believed that the tenor's *rôle* was a faithful representation of her own adored hero, Cyril Clive. That gallant young soldier would certes have been no little amazed had he been told that lisping Mr. Ladidah was intended to represent him (Cyril) from his dear old friend Di's point of view.

Besides the soprano, tenor, and contralto, a basso-profundo is, of course, required for the completion of the cast and the proper distribution of the score. He who interprets the *rôle* of Margaret's father is a Signor Demetrio, an Italian by birth, and a familiar friend of Maestro's. Demetrio is not a professional singer, or his appearance in this exclusive circle of amateurs would have been prohibited; but, though hardly qualified to take part in regular concerts, he has not the least objection to accept the fee, which is invariably tendered to him, *sub rosa,* by professional *entrepreneurs* on such private occasions as the present.

CHAPTER IX.

THE PROGRESS OF THE PLAY.

MADAME MARGHERITA'S cosmopolitan education, the various phases of life she had passed through when travelling abroad with her parents, and her constant contact with professional people in the old days, all tended to give her confidence as an actress now. She was quite able to represent the heroine of Miss Hartley's play with becoming dignity; and those old experiences endowed her with an admirable self-possession. Modest and unassuming as she appeared, she was still possessed of that easy tranquillity which inspires confidence in all beholders. She had talked often and earnestly with her patroness concerning the character she had undertaken to portray; she thoroughly realised its motive-power; and she had so thoroughly identified herself with the 'rare pale Margaret' of Miss Hartley's creation that she felt assured she could do justice to the part, more especially as it was one eminently sympathetic to her. The undercurrent of passion which animated Diana's heroine was so strongly imbued with a powerful reality that Madame Margherita's honest nature responded to it readily. Diana had betrayed the secret passion smouldering within her own breast in the words which she put into the mouth of her troubled heroine. And the girl-widow who now played the part had known the terrors and the delights of a clandestine, but all-engrossing, love only too well. Now that she was called upon to interpret such suffering, such hopes and joys, she felt herself in a congenial element.

If there be spiritual influences at large which obey the bidding of *soi-disant clairvoyants*, and busy themselves with the affairs of ordinary mortals, then surely these visionary beings had interfered to some purpose with Miss Diana when she was 'inspired' to create that innocent wronged Margaret of modern society, who eventually was portrayed with touching fidelity by the natural prototype of the fictitious character, around which the authoress had skilfully grouped all the subordinate actors in her realistic libretto.

Miss Armstrong (Lady Beatrix), perfectly aware, and decidedly rejoicing in the fact, that she had the advantage over that mysterious *protégée* of Miss Hartley as far as vocal culture went, was too experienced in theatrical performances of all kinds to deceive herself for a moment as to the impression created on the audience by that innocent pale-faced rival of hers.

The Margaret of the piece, and the Madame Margherita who played the part, had won the sympathy of those who beheld and listened to her from the moment she made her entry. Lady Beatrix might gain their admiration by the effrontery of her glances and bearing, and by the undeniable attractions of that brunette beauty which was so well adapted to the Mephistophelian *rôle* she was playing; but though she might hope to please their eyes and win their attention, she realised, with a sudden pang of jealous envy, that she could neither touch the hearts of the men, nor bring tears to the eyes of the women.

For Madame Margherita these tributary evidences of subtle power were evoked before the end of the first act. This was a trying but most effective scene: Lady Beatrix, roused to a passion of jealousy, bids the poor girl, who is her dependent, go forth into the world to practise her allurements elsewhere. Her ladyship, who pretends to be envious of attentions which her affianced husband has *not* paid to her humble companion, amazes the latter by a torrent of reproach and recrimination. Here Mr. Ladidah, animated in spite of himself by the passion of the ladies on the stage and the enthusiasm of the audience, suddenly rises to the urgency of the situation. He certainly sings his great

air admirably. He is carried beyond himself by the impetus of his companions; their powerful emotion moves even his sluggish nature; and as he is really possessed of a fine voice, which Campo Maestro has taught him to use to the utmost advantage, he now manages to deliver himself of his crowning scena with undeniable *éclat*.

Campo Maestro, in a white heat of excitement, wipes the beaded drops of mortal anxiety from his troubled brow. Musically speaking, this elaborate end of the first act is *the* climax of the opera, and Mr. Ladidah—heroically supported by the ladies—had helped to achieve a decided triumph for all concerned. His solo had led on into a trio fraught with passion, in which the tenor still kept a most melodious lead; and both Margaret and Lady Beatrix had followed his mellow effective voice with truly artistic skill.

Royalty had been moved to an outward and visible sign of approval. A pleased smile parts the lips of the face so familiar to, and eagerly welcomed by, Londoners always; this gives the final impetus to the wildly-echoing bursts of applause that greet the singers on their reappearance before the curtain.

It is said that too select an audience fails to encourage actors by a signal want of enthusiasm; but surely no combination of gallery and pit in a popular theatre could have been more demonstrative in clamorous approbation than the *élite* of the fashionable world, gathered together by enterprising Lady Buzze, here showed themselves.

Miss Armstrong was a familiar figure to all present. They were well acquainted with her vocal powers, her coquetry, and her histrionic talent; but Madame Margherita had as yet been an interesting *incognita* only ; and stormy discussions as to her birth, antecedents, and present social position followed immediately on her second recall, and led to quite a tumult of asseveration and denial. Every one had some fresh version of her romantic story to offer; contradiction was rampant. One imaginative lady suggested that she was a foreign princess; on which another immediately said, ' Russian ;' a second, ' Prussian ;' and a third capped these statements by declaring that eccentricity had prompted this aristocratic personage to make her *début* in the London world under the auspices of that other eccentric, Diana Hartley.

One of the authoress's former Parisian acquaintances flatly contradicted all other accounts by coolly asserting that they were entirely mistaken ; and then this better-informed person vouchsafed a new and startling hypothesis.

' Madame Margherita is a foreign adventuress,' said the unimpeachable authority. ' Her antecedents would make it impossible for her to hold her own in our fashionable world. But good-natured Miss Hartley, animated by one of her sudden caprices, has taken the girl up *con amore.* She has determined to launch her *protégée* on the ocean of fashion, and leaves her future fate to chance. To judge by the sensation she has made to-night, the launch appears a propitious one ; and who can tell to what golden shore this pretty singer may be wafted by the flattering breeze of social adulation ?'

An hypothesis so plausibly put could not fail to meet with some approval. But the notion of Madame Margherita being a foreigner was soon and eagerly disputed again by those who chose to judge for themselves, and who, listening

attentively, had noted her pure pronunciation. These observant people emphatically declared her to be English by birth and breeding. And all those present who were not biassed by some personal feeling of spite or envy, with one accord declared the interesting stranger to be a lady herself, no matter how or whence she came.

There was present among the audience one Sir Conway Joy—a widower, young, wealthy, handsome. Most of Miss Armstrong's brilliant glances were directed towards the corner in which Sir Conway had taken up his position. He was the man whom the dark beauty preferred to all others ; and she had set her heart on becoming Lady Joy before the season—barely begun as yet—should have come to an end. That Sir Conway had in no way responded to her overt and flattering regard discomposed ambitious Aurelia not at all. He had not long been a widower; he was inexperienced and shy. He led the life of a recluse, and appeared wholly devoted to the infant daughter his lovely young wife had confided to him on her deathbed. Aurelia, who had known the lady well, was acquainted with all these interesting domestic details, and occasionally presumed on the fact of her previous intimacy with the poor wife. Indeed she now treated the widower with a certain familiarity, which his reticent attitude neither warranted nor encouraged. Miss Armstrong, who never undervalued herself, was fully aware of the extent of her undeniable attractions as the Lady Beatrix of the play; she therefore looked forward with much eagerness to this opportunity of fascinating the ungrateful man who had hitherto rewarded her unceasing efforts to please by most exasperating indifference.

Sir Conway was an intimate

friend of Miss Hartley, and between the acts he made his way into the greenroom. Miss Armstrong espied him instantly, and swiftly crossed the room to where he stood patiently waiting until Miss Hartley (to whom he had just turned for some information) should be at liberty to answer his inquiries.

'And how do you like the performance and—*us?* asks Miss Armstrong, bent on attracting Sir Conway's eyes and attention.

'Delightful; most interesting indeed!' answers he promptly.

There is new brightness in his eyes and a smile of unwonted animation upon his face, which cause Aurelia's susceptible heart to beat with sudden hopeful excitement. She has moved him at last. She has not seen him look bright and cheerful like this since that poor Amy died—more than a year ago. But, though young, Conway looks eager; his thoughts are certainly preoccupied still; she has failed to distract them from their object; for, without entering into the conversation so eagerly commenced by her, he seizes the first opportunity of securing Miss Hartley's attention. As soon as he sees her alone he hurries across the room again, and is evidently impatient for some information, which he thinks she can give him.

Miss Armstrong, discomfited, but not discouraged, loses no time in following him in her turn; and the crowd which divides them covers her advance. A minute after he has escaped from her she has taken up her position within earshot of him again. She distinctly hears the word 'Margaret,' then 'Madame Margherita;' and, to cap these suggestive nouns, the adjectives 'charming,' 'exquisite,' 'lovely.' He makes no mention whatever of Miss Armstrong—Lady Beatrix; indeed he is so

engrossed by the whispered information Miss Hartley affords him, that he has evidently forgotten all else at the moment.

'Madame Margherita,' says Miss Hartley, laying her hand on the arm of her *protégée*, as she leads her forth out of the corner into which the girl had retired, as soon as (in obedience to imperative orders) she had hastily exchanged her Marguerite dress for a gray gown suggestive of Cinderella, 'Sir Conway Joy asks me to introduce him to the most charming actress it has ever been his good fortune to see on any stage. Was not that the pretty speech you asked me to deliver for you?' adds Diana, turning towards the young man with a smile, which ends in a laugh as she sees his blushing discomfiture.

'You are very kind,' says Madame Margherita, bending her pretty head in modest acknowledgment of the interpreted compliment. 'I wish I could feel as well satisfied with myself as the indulgent audience appears.'

'I shall leave you two to fight out the measure of praise my heroine deserves by yourselves,' says Miss Hartley hastily.

She has no time to lose in idle parley. The fifteen minutes allowed between the acts are almost over.

Signor Maestro is at his post again, waiting—expectant. There is a scene between tenor and bass before the ladies are wanted. Madame Margherita, having obeyed instructions, is ready; but Miss Armstrong, whose attention was otherwise engaged, has deferred the changing of her dress to the last moment. Miss Hartley, with a frown of displeasure creditable to a manageress, now hurries the dilatory one into her dressing-room, and she goes off, leaving Sir Conway talking to her unconscious rival, a flush of anger on her face,

sickening jealousy in her heart.
The widower has taken his place
close by the side of the *débutante*,
and is talking to her with an
amount of *empressement* most unlike his customary reserve.

'But I shall bring him to his
senses *now*,' Miss Armstrong assures herself, as she confronts her
wondrous likeness in the cheval
glass. She is clad in a most elaborate maize ball-dress. The golden
glory of her apparel suits her admirably, and her secret determination to triumph over every one
seems warranted.

The second act is more trying
and less effective than the first.

Margaret, at the lowest ebb of
her fortunes, is tempted by the
lover whom Lady Beatrix, with a
wicked woman's wily skill, has
herself led on to play the traitor.
Her ladyship's noble ambition is
to compromise the girl whom she
affects to consider as a rival. This
course will enable her to banish
the dependent, upon whose ruin
she is resolved. The obedient
lover behaves as an irresponsible
agent in the matter. He is as unconscious of her ladyship's wickedness as Faust, in the first instance,
was of the danger of Mephisto's
companionship. Moved beyond
herself by the vindictive feeling
aroused by her innocent rival—off
the stage—Miss Armstrong enters
into the spirit of the second act
with fresh enthusiasm. Such life,
such vigour, is in her impersona-
tion now, that even those who
have long considered her an accomplished actress frankly acknowledge that she is surpassing
all her previous efforts to-night;
and her success is the more apparent because Madame Margherita
displays far less power than she
did in the opening scenes. She
has to render a phase of the heroine's character now with which she
does not sympathise. To be made

love to by Mr. Ladidah has always
tried her temper and patience during the rehearsals, and the task of
enduring these unwelcome attentions becomes more embarrassing
in the presence of an audience.

In spite of Miss Hartley's hopeful verdict it is very evident now
that Madame Margherita has not
sufficient 'dramatic instinct' to enable her to pretend to feelings
which conflict with her sympathies.

Miss Armstrong could bring herself to act the part of an unselfish
ingénue, and would acquit herself
cleverly, however uncongenial the
rôle. But Madame Margherita is
as little able to act the part of a
designing traitress on the stage, as
she is incapable of treachery in private life.

And so the second act does
not move the audience to as
much enthusiasm as the first has
done. Both authoress and composer are dissatisfied. But though
Madame Margherita has gone back
several degrees in their estimation,
she has made a wondrously pleasing impression on the heart of that
shy young widower. The *débutante*
herself is fortunately not aware of
the latent displeasure of those who
have hitherto led her on with fulsome praises and lavish promises
of undoubted success. She has
thoroughly studied her part, and
identified herself with it; and she
acts and sings from first to last with
unvarying steadfastness, fully resolved to do all that in her power
lies for the ultimate success of the
much-discussed operetta. Sir Conway Joy watches her every movement, and listens to the sweet tones
of her voice with rapt attention.
He is as unconscious as she is herself that this part of her performance is less satisfactory than what
has preceded it. To him the sad-
faced interesting heroine of the pathetic dramatic story appears perfect
from first to last.

CHAPTER X.

AN UNEXPECTED CONQUEST.

ALTHOUGH twenty-four years of age now, Sir Conway is still almost a boy in feeling and manners. He has, to a great extent, recovered from the painful effects of the one sudden and terrible sorrow, which frightened him and sobered his youthful spirits; but he has lived the greater part of his life in the country, and his worldly experience resolves itself practically into *nil*.

He had married almost as soon as he attained his majority. The match was of his father's making; and the old baronet (since deceased) probably cared more for the legal annexation of two contiguous estates than he did for the happiness of the young people concerned in the compact. He had always desired that the day might come when his son should marry the orphan who was his ward, and an heiress in her own right. Young Conway, who had regarded his neighbour, gentle little Amy Ray, as a favourite playfellow for many years, was not unwilling to convert the ties of child friendship into the more binding chains of matrimony, when he ascertained that this was the ruling desire of his indulgent old father. He—poor man—did not live long after the realisation of his pet scheme. He was thrown on his head while hunting, and killed on the spot. Then young Conway reigned at the Abbey in his stead. And very soon he was left quite alone in his glory; for Amy, while still a child in years, became a mother, and left her heart-broken young husband a widower with an infant daughter.

Such was Sir Conway Joy's position when he went up to town to try and divert himself by a glimpse of the gay life of social London, which was still almost *terra incognita*

for him; for his only experience of it had been when, as a schoolboy at Eton, he came up for occasional holidays, which he spent with Miss Hartley, who had for many years been a stanch friend of his father. It was to the Cottage young Conway's sense of duty and gratitude called him as soon as he had established himself in his new quarters in St. James's-street. Miss 'Di' had been a very kind and indulgent friend to him in those old schoolboy days—not so very long ago, after all—and he longed to shake her hand again, look into the bright kindly-smiling face which illumined the recollection of those holidays spent in town with quite a special radiance, apart from those ever-welcome surreptitious golden gifts invariably bestowed upon him at his leave-taking.

At the time Sir Conway unexpectedly called to pay his first visit to Miss Hartley, she was entirely preoccupied by the preliminary rehearsals and arrangements for that 'great event' which left her so few moments' leisure during the weeks of its preparation. The much desired—and almost despaired of—heroine had but just been discovered, and the first private rehearsal was taking place in the drawing-room above, when the visitor was hurriedly ushered into the dining-room, and asked 'to take a seat and wait awhile,' until Miss Hartley should be disengaged.

During a pause above, the hostess hurried down, welcomed her quondam schoolboy cordially, but in unmistakable haste and preoccupation, which he was too modest to misconstrue or resent.

'You are busy, and I am interrupting you,' he said simply; 'please let me go away without detaining you now, and give me leave to come again another day.'

'You are quite right, and most considerate. I will be as frank as you are,' answered the lady, pleased with his honest face and perfect straightforwardness. 'But stay,' she added, suddenly remembering, 'you must not run away until I give another old friend of yours the chance of meeting you again. Miss Armstrong heard your name mentioned (she is at the rehearsal up-stairs), and begged to be allowed to see you before you left the house.'

'Miss Armstrong?' he repeated, puzzled.

'Yes, yes; Aurelia Armstrong. She was at school with your poor dear little Amy—don't you remember?'

Sir Conway had some vague recollection of a tall dark-eyed girl who spent the summer holidays in Torshire at the Rays', and who insisted on being rowed on the river by him, when he would much rather have practised in the Eleven, who intended to disport on the Abbey cricket-ground in some pending village festivities. He remembered that Aurelia gave herself airs of *grande dame* because she was grown up and a parlour-boarder at the school where his little Amy, the youngest boarder, was petted and treated as a baby by her seniors.

He had no particular desire to revive any of these dead associations with a past that had now become fraught with sadness to him; but he had neither choice nor alternative.

Miss Diana, moved beyond even her usual impetuosity by the exigency of the situation, and her desire to be back at her post, grasped her visitor's hand suddenly, wrung it warmly, said, 'Good-bye—or rather *au revoir*. Don't run away. Aurelia will be with you in a moment;' and fled precipitately, leaving the bewildered young man to wonder at the offhand fashions of town people, and vainly striving to recollect some-

thing more definite concerning the lady who claimed to be 'an old friend' of his. He had had no desire to interview any one but comfortable 'understanding' Miss Di, and had therefore called at an unusually early hour; but now he had no chance of escape left him, for even as he rose, desperate and hoping to get out of the house undiscovered, he was confronted by Miss Aurelia Armstrong.

She extended both hands in the eagerness of her welcome, and considerably amazed the young man by informing him that she was indeed overjoyed to recognise one of her earliest, best, dearest friends in him.

'Loving my sweet May blossom as I always did,' she said, with a catching of her breath that sounded very like a sob, 'it is only natural that I am filled with joy—with joy and pain—at the sight of him who was *my* friend even before he became Amy's husband.'

Sir Conway was taken aback; but he could not resist feeling flattered by the profound interest with which he so evidently inspired 'poor Amy's friend.' Their interview lasted close on an hour, and the time fled swiftly and pleasantly. Aurelia dwelt with touching pathos on every detail of those happy old schooldays, in which, as now appeared, she and that 'sweet Amy of yours' were inseparable and most devoted companions. By degrees the conversation, under Miss Armstrong's skilful guidance, was led from sentimental to mundane topics of interest. The pleasing task of introducing her darling Amy's husband to all the people worth knowing—to all the sights worth seeing in town—would devolve upon Aurelia, of course. Perhaps Sir Conway had reckoned on Miss Hartley; but Miss Hartley—poor dear!—was far too much engrossed by her latest theatrical scheme to spare an hour to any outsider; and therefore Miss Armstrong insisted, with pretty imperiousness, she should take upon herself to look after the stranger in every way.

Had he chosen and found rooms to his liking? St. James's-street would do very well. He must give afternoon tea soon, and invite all the ladies with whom he had any acquaintance. By and by, with Miss Hartley's assistance, a dinner or a supper might be arranged. That was what all the best bachelors did now, and just the sort of entertainment the ladies enjoyed above all others.

Miss Armstrong kept her rashly-made promises very well. When Sir Conway had paid his first ceremonious call at her mother's house, the young lady considered all the proprieties were duly observed, and very soon began that career of general introduction to the people and sights worthy of recognition to which she had alluded at the first interview with her much-favoured friend. His youth and inexperience enabled her to assume a dictatorial manner with him, which one less modest and unsophisticated would probably have resisted.

Young Conway thought and spoke of her as 'very kind,' and was really grateful for the unbounded measure of trouble she took on his behalf. She selected the operas she wished to hear, and he had the privilege of conducting her; sometimes other friends accompanied them, more often they went alone.

'I look upon him as a child—a mere schoolboy. Poor lonely fellow, his wife was my dearest friend; we were all children together.' This was Aurelia's overt explanation of the intimacy existing between the handsome young widower and herself.

People shrugged their shoulders and talked, as people always will talk of such attractive and enterprising young ladies as Aurelia Armstrong. But those who knew her best were quite satisfied that she was but playing a waiting game, and that ere the season was over she would triumphantly disclose a band full of trumps. When asked if she were engaged to the widower, she would reply by an ambiguous but uncompromising smile; and she continued to take him about with her to routs, balls, and kettle-drums *ad lib*. By and by she told him they would join river picnics; then there would be Ascot, Goodwood, and—Henley Regatta. She had the list of forthcoming pleasures ready cut and dried, even beyond the season; and meanwhile she was putting the novice through a trying preliminary canter in the midst of the social throng.

Miss Hartley, who, at the time of young Conway's advent in town, was engrossed by far more serious matters than the entertainment of one whom she really regarded as a schoolboy still, was delighted to be relieved from all responsibility by the readily-tendered services of Miss Armstrong. And so matters went on to the perfect satisfaction of the ladies, although the object of their solicitude was perhaps less pleased by the impartial distribution of their favours than they were themselves.

From the first hour of her meeting with the interesting widower, Aurelia conceived the notion of supplying the place at the head of the Abbey so suddenly and sadly left vacant by the death of poor little Amy; and from that hour she steadily set herself to the accomplishment of her ambitious scheme. Her first move was unbounded eulogy of the dead; her next, enthusiastic offers of present service and lasting friendship for the living.

So touching was the eager warmth of her many protestations, that Conway bitterly reproached himself with ingratitude, since he was really quite unable to respond with proportionate eagerness to her generous declarations of friendship and interest. He was shy by nature, reserved from habit; but Aurelia was ready to make the tenderest allowances for his lack of enthusiasm; and as long as he did not rebel against the arrangements she made for the disposal of his time, she was quite satisfied to provide him with a never-ceasing round of amusements. Thus time went on pleasantly, if not profitably, for the young man; and Aurelia, as well as her friend, had no doubt that she would soon gain the prize for which she had so assiduously angled. Young Conway was so docile by nature that a child might have guided him in the leading-strings of affection; and clever Miss Armstrong did pretty much as she chose with him. Indeed, he would probably have allowed her to carry her point without much opposition on his side, had it not happened that on the very night to which Aurelia looked forward as certain to complete her triumph, the man she admired and coveted saw, and fell desperately in love with, Madame Margherita at first sight.

Perhaps it was the startling contrast of her reserve and modesty with the effrontery of his late constant companion which in the first instance fascinated young Conway. His quite provincial life had left him with 'antiquated' notions about women which would have delighted Sir Gilbert Clive, but would have moved the greater number of the young man's new town acquaintance to unbounded ridicule and mirth.

As he stands on this eventful evening intently watching and lis-

tening to the progress of the play, it certainly seems to him as though Madame Margherita is the incarnation of all that is lovely, pure, and most attractive in woman. Had his poor little innocent bride lived long enough, she might eventually have blossomed into as nobly perfect a creature as that fair-haired singer with the dark pathetic eyes, whose voice and appearance are filling him with keenest admiration as he looks and listens now. Until this night, Sir Conway had not even seen Miss Hartley's *protégée*. He had been taken to Lady Furnival's 'at home' in Richmond by Miss Armstrong; but the 'mysterious soprano,' about whom Diana's intimate friends were beginning to twit her, had not made her *début* on that occasion, owing to circumstances with which the reader is already acquainted. As Conway Joy concentrated his attention upon the fair singer, whose simple pathos appealed so directly to her audience, Aurelia's bold glances and apparent effrontery filled him with a sudden sense of keen dismay that was akin to disgust. He was amazed at himself. How could he so long have condescended to follow the bidding of that wicked-looking brazen beauty! He had submitted himself to her will. She had, to a great extent, ruled his actions: he had come or gone as she bade him; he had accompanied her whenever and wherever she had chosen to demand his presence; he had obediently awaited her advent at the various houses to which she procured invitations for him, and he had done all these things without reflection, but certainly without hesitation.

To-night the veil is ruthlessly torn from his eyes; he sees the woman who has exacted his homage by the side of one to whom he would have rendered it with glad spontaneity, and a sudden tremendous revulsion of feeling oppresses him.

Perhaps it is Aurelia's crowning achievement as a triumphant actress that suddenly breaks the spell she had hitherto exercised over her callous though constant companion. Certain it is that, with the fall of the curtain, Sir Conway fiercely determines to escape from the galling leading-strings of his feminine Mentor.

Like Telemachus of old, the young man suddenly longed to be free, and, with the instinct of a hero, decided to act with alacrity and vigour.

'Is Madame Margherita staying at the Cottage with you, Miss Hartley?' he asked, as soon as he could obtain speech with the successful authoress, who was beset by a crowd of eagerly thronging congratulators; and when the lady replied in the affirmative, added:

'May I come and see you to-morrow evening, and tell your *protégée* how thoroughly she has charmed—me—all who have heard her? Every one is saying things of that sort to-night, I know; but to-morrow they will seem to have more meaning, and I am also most anxious to talk to you about your delightful libretto.'

The young man's handsome face looked very attractive in Miss Hartley's observant eyes. 'I have neglected this poor boy shamefully,' was the thought in her mind, and aloud she said,

'You must make up for lost time now, my dear Conway. Why, I have seen nothing of you; but I am free to some extent again at last, and very much at the disposal of my *intimate* friends. By all means, come and see us to-morrow evening. We dine at eight, quite *sans cérémonie*, you know; that is the best way to make people acquainted.'

'Delighted! Many, *many* thanks!'

whispered Sir Conway, with much earnestness. Any little private grievance he may have smarted under hitherto, consequent on Miss Hartley's seeming neglect, vanished before her bright smile and cordially repeated invitation.

'Do not forget that we are going to Mrs. De la Vere's "at home" to-morrow, Con dear,' said Miss Armstrong, as she laid her hand on Sir Conway's arm to attract his attention. She had made her way to his side through the pushing crowd with some difficulty, and as her voice fell on his ear, he started. How much of his conversation with Miss Hartley had she overheard?

'As it is to be an early affair, and I am down in the programme among the first singers, you had better come and dine with us at seven, and then we will go on together. Mamma does not want the carriage to-morrow; so I can have it. Shall we say seven o'clock?'

By this time Aurelia was close by her friend's side, and instantly aware of the troubled indecision in his frank young face.

'I am so sorry, dear Miss Armstrong,' he said, and his contrition was evident; 'but I had completely forgotten the engagement for to-morrow; indeed, I hardly think you had mentioned it to me; in any case I am forced to decline the pleasure of accompanying you, as I have promised to dine and spend the evening with a friend.'

Miss Armstrong's face was not pleasant to look upon. It was disfigured by a sudden sullen cloud of anger.

'You are treating me shamefully, Con,' she whispered; and her words sounded like hissing.

'I can only express my sincere regret,' he answered, with perfect composure. 'I have had so few engagements of my own hitherto that you naturally took my being at your disposal to-morrow for granted. I think, on reflection, you will find that, though you once mentioned Mrs. De la Vere's party to me, neither date nor hour was fixed, nor was my acquiescence required.'

The red sullen flush of anger dies out of Miss Armstrong's face, and leaves it very pale.

'With whom have you promised to dine to-morrow evening?' she asks, after a prolonged awkward pause.

'With our mutual friend, Miss Hartley,' he answers.

'And there you will meet Madame Margherita?' she says.

'I sincerely hope so,' is his reply; and as he utters it he sees a threat leap into his companion's dangerous dark eyes that reminds him painfully of the furious glances bestowed by wicked Lady Beatrix upon her inoffensive rival in the operetta.

'I am going now, at once,' says Miss Armstrong. 'May I trouble you to see me to the carriage?'

He offers his arm instantly; but though the movement is prompt it is without alacrity. He had hoped to escape in time to see Miss Hartley to her carriage, perhaps—who knows?—to assist Madame Margherita also.

'Good-night, Conway,' says Miss Armstrong, as he stands bareheaded at the door of her brougham. 'Can I give you a lift?'

'No, thanks; I am going in the opposite direction,' he says hurriedly. He is longing to escape from the persistent reproach in her accusing eyes. 'The opposite direction' would be the high-road to Bath. It does not seem probable that he intends to journey countrywards in the small hours of the night. But Miss Armstrong refrains from farther question. She knows the mesmeric power of her glances, and thinks her eyes have troubled him sufficiently for the moment.

'But he shall *not* escape me,' she mutters, as she flings herself back in the carriage. 'I will not be beaten by that little quiet palefaced nobody. If he dines at The Cottage to-morrow, I will dine there too; quite unexpectedly, of course.'

[To be continued.]

THE FAMILY GAMP.

By SOMERVILLE GIBNEY.

———◆———

NEVER mind about my early days. If at one time I certainly was nothing but *a stick*, that is my business, and mine alone. The fact remains. I am a descendant (or would not *a parachute* be the more correct term?) of an honourable family; a family whose birthplace, I believe, was in China, many, many years ago, and among whose members we are proud to number *royalty*. For what person has not heard of 'the royal umbrella of such and such a monarch'? But, as I said before, my early days have no interest to any one save myself, and we will therefore pass quickly over the time when I had little or no covering to my ribs, and when I did not possess that slim, elegant, and upright figure which I afterwards obtained; and we will go on in one stride to the time when I made my *début* as a highly finished *paraplui* in the window of Mr. Grain's shop in the High-street of Barkstown.

From my position I had every opportunity of seeing the world; and my leisure I employed in endeavouring to guess what kind of a person would eventually choose me as his companion and friend. For I have always been accustomed to look upon the members of our race as the friends rather than the servants of men. In England this is more especially so; summer or winter, it matters not; where the Anglo-Saxon prevails, there will be found umbrellas. We guard him from the rain, we shade him from the sun, we support his weary frame; we occasionally fight his battles for him; when flourished, we act as signals to the passing omnibuses; and, in short, we do everything in our power to add to his comfort and convenience, only asking in return that we may be tightly rolled, carefully brushed, and kept free from mud-stains; for among our higher grades vanity is our great failing.

But to return to myself. I had been in the window some three weeks without finding any one as a companion; not that I had lain there the whole time unnoticed—not a bit of it. I am vain enough to say that my personal appearance forbade that. Several gentlemen had been struck with my good looks, and had entered the shop to make inquiries about me; but I liked none of them; there was not one whom I felt I could look upon as a friend, and I therefore made myself as awkward as possible to them. I puffed out my hitherto tightly-wrapped folds, I loosened my handle, and I made myself as heavy as I could; and with the desired result, for they one and all left without me.

At length, one evening, just as it was growing dusk, I awoke from a nap I had been indulging in to find a pair of laughing, merry, blue eyes gazing on me through the shop-window. I was wide awake in a moment. I felt I could believe in the owner of those eyes; there was an honest, downright, straightforward look about them that took my fancy at once, and my heart thumped loudly against my ribs with pleasure when I heard the owner of the eyes enter Mr. Grain's shop, and ask to look at me. I was taken out of the window, opened, held up, examined; and eventually Mr. Gilbert Joyce purch—no, I don't like that expression—agreed to make me his companion and friend, and we left Mr. Grain's shop together. I liked him better and better the more I saw of him, and he was proud of me. He always took me with him wherever he went. While he was busy in the bank during the day, I used to wait for him, and keep guard over his greatcoat and hat in the clerks' room. And many and curious were the acquaintances I there formed. I soon came to know a good deal of the ways of the world from distant connections of mine. You see we had plenty of time for conversation during the day. Our duties did not really commence until the close of business. I had not long been the friend of Bertie when he gave me my name. It was not an aristocratic one, nor one that I should have chosen myself; but after the first few days I grew accustomed to, and began to like, it. I looked on it more as a term of endearment than anything else; for I was always addressed by it in a friendly hearty way. It was '*Toby.*'

I soon discovered that Bertie was *spoony*—a curious word used by mortals to express the state of their feelings towards one of the opposite sex. The object of Bertie's affections was a pretty little motherless girl, of some nineteen years of age, the only child of the principal solicitor in Barkstown. The price of Jessie's birth had been her mother's life. Her father, Mr. Ralph Sorrell, had become a changed man on the death of the wife he loved so dearly. All his kindly feelings seemed to have been buried in her grave. He grew taciturn and morose, living only

for his business. At first the baby was hateful to him, and it was months before he would consent even to see it. He looked upon it as his wife's murderer. Time flew on, and Jessie grew up without the knowledge of a father's love. She was tolerated; but that was all.

In her sad condition, the wife of the Rector of Barkstown took pity on her, and proposed to her father that he should allow Jessie to share the advantages of the Rector's governess, and the companionship of his girls. To this suggestion Mr. Sorrell offered no objection; nor did he take any further notice of the matter beyond sending his quarterly cheque regularly, with a polite note of thanks. The friendship commenced in childhood continued after Jessie left the schoolroom, and she grew to look upon the Rectory more as her home than her father's house. She was constantly there; for alas, poor girl, the Rector's family were her only friends. I learnt the foregoing facts later on, but I state them here that you, my readers, may the better understand what follows.

Bertie Joyce was the Rector's nephew. He had been educated at Winchester and Oxford, and was reading for the Bar when his father died suddenly, and instead of leaving behind him a substantial fortune as everybody expected, Bertie found himself a beggar, his only stock-in-trade a good education. It was absolutely necessary that he should give up all thoughts of the Bar, for it would be years before he could hope to make enough to live upon, and in the mean time he must contrive to exist on that hope, or starve. In his difficulty his uncle came to his aid, and through his influence with the bank manager procured him a clerkship there at the salary of eighty pounds a year to start with. This Bertie always looked upon merely as a stop-gap, until he could find something better. With his uncle he was a great favourite, for the Rector was quick to recognise the good points in his character. He was delighted with the grateful way in which his nephew fell in with his views, and the cheerful manner in which he gave up the course of life he had chosen, for one which never could offer any fascination to him. It was more of a trial to Bertie than people were aware of; for he dearly loved the law, and his great ambition was to become a shining light in Westminster Hall. In the path of life now opened before him he would have to mix with men his inferiors both in birth, education, and feeling, with whom he could have little or nothing in common. Yet he made a virtue of necessity, and cheerfully followed his uncle's advice. The good Rector's wife found him rooms suited to his limited income, and did all in her power to make his new life tolerable to him. He had a standing invitation to dine and spend his evenings at the Rectory, and it was here that he made the acquaintance of Jessie Sorrell. Was it to be wondered at, that Bertie should feel pity for the pretty little motherless girl in whose companionship he was so much thrown? But pity, they say, is akin to love, and so it proved in this case; for it was not long before he fell, or rather glided swiftly but surely, over head and ears in love with her; and that Jessie should reciprocate the feeling can cause no surprise. Bertie was the first young fellow with whom she had been acquainted, if we set aside the red-eyed sandy-haired curate, Mr. Jacobson. They had known each other some six months, without a word of love having passed between them; and yet they were each aware of the other's secret, as well as if it had

been spoken. But human nature is weak; and one evening, as Bertie was seeing her home, the old, old story was told, and answered in such a manner as to satisfy both the young people. It was raining hard at the time; and spreading myself out to my fullest extent above them, to shield them from the wet, my ribs rattled with satisfaction as I heard what was taking place under my protection; for I had often, on former occasions, thought the matter over, and had come to the conclusion that a better-suited pair never existed. Jessie was a simple child-like girl, who knew nothing whatever of the world, was totally unable, by herself, to fight the battle of life; to her Bertie's protecting care would be everything. Bertie, on the other hand, was rash and impulsive, and required ballast, and this I was convinced he would find in Jessie's love; but however rosy and bright the future might appear to my young charges just then, I, with my superior wisdom, for I had thought a good deal in my leisure time, foresaw trouble. There was the consent of Jessie's father to be obtained; and from the little I knew of him, I judged that would be no easy matter.

Bertie was too honourable a young fellow to wish for any concealment, and the next day he had a quiet interview with his uncle and aunt in the Rectory study, and laid the whole matter openly before them. From the confidential conversations which took place with Jessie afterwards, while seeing her home, in which I was always a silent participator, I learnt that he had written a letter to Mr. Sorrell, stating the plain facts of the case in an unvarnished manner. The reply this drew was curious, and yet at the same time characteristic of the writer. As well as I can remember—for he read it to Jessie one evening under a street lamp— it ran as follows :

'Dear Sir,—Yours of the 6th to hand. Its contents, I need hardly say, surprised me; for up to the moment of my reading it I was unaware of your existence. You say you love my daughter; I am not in a position to deny the fact, but can you provide such comfort for her as she has hitherto been accustomed to? From the amount of your present income, apparently not. When you can come to me and show me that you are possessed of 800*l.* per annum, it will be time enough to talk the matter over; in the mean time I cannot sanction any engagement. I presume my daughter is attached to you, though she has never honoured me with her confidence on the subject ; and as I do not wish to cause her any unnecessary unhappiness, I shall not forbid the present intercourse which appears to exist between you. I leave the rest to your gentlemanly feeling, and trust I may not be disappointed.—Yours faithfully,
'RALPH SORRELL.

'G. Joyce, Esq.'

And so the father dismissed the subject as one in which he had very little concern.

Under these circumstances, the Rector and his wife saw no reason for their interference, and so the lovers were allowed undisturbed enjoyment of each other's society ; and many a happy stroll I participated in after banking hours, and again when Jessie was returning home at night. Of course I heard all the soft nothings they said to each other, conversations which are intensely interesting to the parties engaged in them, yet simply idiotic to the general public. But my family is, and ever has been, a strictly honourable one; and I stoutly refuse to divulge a single word that might be considered confidential. As the courtship was carried on under his roof, the Rector felt bound in duty to stipulate for one thing, and that was, that Bertie should promise not to have anything to do with a runaway match ; and so matters went on, the young couple contriving to exist on love and the hope of brighter days in store for them.

One dark evening in November Bertie was seeing Jessie home about ten o'clock. They had chosen the longest way round, by the river-walk. There were no lamps there, and for some reason or other they always seemed to prefer it. The banks were high and steep, and the water could just be seen hurrying along to do the old mill-wheel *a good turn* a little lower down.

'And so, Jessie,' Bertie was saying, 'I really don't know what to do. I sometimes think it is not right of me to hold you to your engagement, when my prospects are so indefinite. If I continue in the bank I see no chance of ever earning 800*l.* a year, and I have no capital to embark in business. I am afraid we shall have to wait a long, long time yet.'

'Well, dear, if you can wait I'm sure I can ; and please don't talk about releasing me : you know I should never wish for such a thing. Hark ! did you hear anything?'

'Yes. By Jove, it's a fight or something,' as the sounds of a struggle were distinctly audible a little distance ahead in the darkness. 'It's a nasty place for a row. Let's go on. There ! Some one's calling for help. Stay here, darling, if you're frightened; I'll be back in a second or two;' and I and Bertie hurried on to the rescue.

We were soon at the scene of action, and discovered two burly navvies attacking a gentleman with sticks. He was doing all in his power to defend himself, but it was evident he could not sustain the unequal struggle much longer.

'All right, sir!' shouted Bertie, as we joined in the fray. 'You tackle that beggar, while I attend to this one;' at the same time making a dash at the bigger. It was well that I was there to look after my friend, for I only just succeeded in stopping a tremendous blow the blackguard levelled at his head. It landed full on my ribs. O, how it made them tingle! But it raised my blood to boiling-point, and I thirsted for revenge. I did my best, I can tell you. I lunged out and hammered away without doing much harm until I saw an opportunity, and then I came down with all my weight and the strength of Bertie's arm on the rascal's head. The shock nearly stunned me, for his skull was very hard; but I can remember, even now, the glorious feeling of satisfaction I experienced as I heard him give one groan and fall senseless in the mud. During this time the other two combatants had been going it tooth and nail; but the gentleman appeared to be getting the worst of it. They had dropped their sticks, and were struggling together very near the edge of the bank. As soon as the villain saw his comrade fall, he knew the game was up, and made a tremendous effort to free himself, so as to be ready for our joint attack. By a dexterous twist he made his adversary loose his hold, and with a push sent him backwards into the river; but he was not as quick as I was, and I again had the satisfaction of dropping my man. That second blow hurt me even more than the first, and I felt that three of my ribs were gone.

'Where are you, sir?' gasped Bertie, out of breath.

'Here! Some way off from the bank, and drifting to the mill-wheel. I can't hold up against the current,

it's too strong. Unless you can get to me, I'm lost! Tell them to stop the wheel! Get a boat, a rope, anything! Good Heavens! Do something, or I shall be drowned like a rat!'

But Bertie returned no answer; for we had run back to where Jessie had been left. She was there.

'Run, darling,' exclaimed Bertie, 'and tell them to stop the wheel! There's a fellow in the river, and unless we can get at him he'll be done for. I'm going to try and catch him from the beam just above the mill-race. Come along, dear!' And off we all three set; for Jessie's way was ours, until she came to the road leading from the banks to the front of the mill. Here she parted from us, and we groped about in the darkness for the beam. All the time Bertie kept shouting to encourage the swimmer.

'Where are you now?'

'Here, right in the middle of the stream. I can't keep up much longer. Why don't they stop the mill?'

'I've sent to tell them; it's all right. Hold on a little bit longer, and keep shouting, so that I may know where you are.'

By this time we had clambered along to the middle of the beam; and then Bertie found, to his horror, he could not reach the water; it was too far beneath him. He lay down all his length; but it was no use, his hand was even then three feet from the water.

To make matters worse, Jessie came rushing back, saying the door was locked, and the noise of the stones was so great she could not make the men inside hear.

'Go back, Jessie, and try again; remember a man's life depends on it; for I can't reach him, after all.'

'Haven't you got your umbrella with you?'

'By Jove, so I have! What a fool I was—I forgot all about it!

But go back, there's a good girl; we shall want help to get him out, even if I do manage to reach him.'

Off set Jessie once more, as we heard the drowning man's voice close at hand.

'For God's sake, save me! I'm not fit to die!'

'All right; where are you?'

'Coming straight towards you. I can just see you.'

'Well, clutch hold of my umbrella as you come under the beam. There! Have you got it? Don't struggle, man, or I sha'n't be able to hold you.'

And I felt myself convulsively seized. O, what a wrench it was! I was aching all over before, and with three ribs broken; but then to have them crushed and squeezed was fearful. I could only just keep myself from crying out.

'Don't struggle, I tell you!' shouted Bertie angrily. 'Can't you keep quiet? I'll let you go if you don't!' For as it was he had hard work to hold the swimmer against the current, and at the same time keep his own balance; and it would have been impossible to do so if the exertion were added to.

'Now then, hold tight!' he continued. 'I'm going to crawl back till we come to one of the piles which support the beam, and then you can get up it. Look out!'

Very slowly we worked our way back, my agony every moment becoming more intense, until the friendly pile was reached and the strain was in a great measure taken off.

'Hold on to that for a minute or two, and get your wind, before you try to climb it,' were Bertie's directions; and very faithfully they were carried out. Just then we heard the *thud, thud, thud* of the wheel growing slower; and, as the current slackened, we knew Jessie had been successful, and that help would soon be at hand. We had

not long to wait. Down rushed the miller, with a rope in one hand and a lantern in the other; three or four of his helpers, with Jessie, were close behind; and very soon the man was landed safely. But the exertion had been too much for him, and he fell fainting on the grass. Jessie knelt down beside him to fan him, and as she caught sight of his face, exclaimed, in a frightened whisper,

'Bertie, it's papa!'

'What! Are you sure, dear? Here, lend me the lantern a moment. So it is, true enough. Well, I'm very glad for your sake, Jessie. He'll be all right in a few minutes. Let him have plenty of air.'

Very soon, under Jessie's treatment, Mr. Sorrell opened his eyes, and it was not long before he was sufficiently recovered to sit up. Seeing Bertie he held out his hand, saying,

'I don't know who you are, sir; but you have saved my life, and I can never repay you; at present I can only thank you.'

'No, sir, you must thank a higher One than me, and afterwards my umbrella; without the latter I could never have reached you.'

A thrill of joy ran over my shattered frame as I heard those words, and knew that my friend recognised the little I had been able to do.

'O papa, don't you know who it is?'

'Jessie! You here? I don't understand.'

'Never mind about it now, sir,' said Bertie; 'wait till we have got you comfortably at home, and then you shall hear the whole story. Jessie, you go with your father. Some of the men will help you, and two of the others had better come with me. I must go and look after our friends on the bank; they will be thinking it's time to get up by now. Bring the rope along with you. I'll come round and see how you are, sir, as soon as I've seen them safely lodged.'

To make a long story short, the navvies were caught, and duly suffered for their crime. Mr. Sorrell, it appears, was returning home from settling a large purchase at a neighbouring town; he had a considerable sum of money about him, and by some means the fellows had found this out, and had waylaid him as he was taking the short cut from the station to his house, with the result already known. From the name with which I have headed this narrative, the upshot of the adventure may be gathered. Suffice it to say, Mr. Sorrell was a changed man from that evening. Bertie left the bank, and entered his office as an articled clerk, with a view to an ultimate partnership.

The following summer there was a marriage in Barkstown, at which all the chief personages of my story, except myself, were present. I, however, accompanied the happy pair on the honeymoon.

I am an old umbrella now, and long past service, except as a plaything or hobbyhorse for Mr. Sorrell's grandchildren.

IN THE GLOAMING.

LIKE the wan beckon of a lifeless hand,
    The fading daylight trembles at the door,
    And ghostly footsteps seem to press the floor;
Dim shadows fill the room, and round me stand;
I feel alone in a deserted land,
    No sweet humanity to reach me more.
    How swift the darkness rises life before,
And withers its warm bloom with death's cold brand!
My thoughts, transfixed, on strange sadness gaze,
    Letting their shuttles fall; dreams, drear or fair,
Fade mistily away in pallid haze;
    Until the moon smiles slowly, and the air
Grows merry as it ripples through her rays,
    That, trooping hither, far night's phantoms scare.

ELLYS ERLE.

POETRY OR PROSE?

BY ANNABEL GRAY.

'Tu rougis quand je te regarde.'

LADY CLARISSA LAWLESS is the only daughter of a peer. She is fairly wealthy, and young; but she is not beautiful—not poetically, unprofessionally, æsthetically beautiful. This want of perfection in feature, this absence of faultless curve and outline, is her one great, always unassuaged, agony. It has even, at times, affected her usually sound nervous system and vigorous young appetite, making her keep in bed for a week and exist on soup, salmis, aspic jelly, and champagne; but these foolish freaks of temper occurred in her 'salad' days. She has since learnt wisdom and found consolation. It seems to her one of the most monstrous injustices of life that third-rate women—mere glazed earthenware—searching in vain for ancestors, and at one time scouring London for invitations—should reign supreme in society by right divine of loveliness and audacity. Lady Clarissa's proudest smiles and calmest disdain affect these gentle creatures nothing. They come and see and conquer, with *Après moi, le déluge* for their crest and oriflamme; they have their partisans and puppets, their 'Adams' furniture, Oriental tiles, and rare old blue, their columns in fashionable journals and lovers in the Row. They know how to *aborder* men and women with the most charming insolence and 'chic' in the world, and Lady Clarissa and her noble sisterhood can do nothing to stem the fulsome tide of popular adulation steadily setting in their direction. She,

alas, is baffled individually for want of a profile. It is the only one thing lacking in her otherwise perfect rose-coloured life; it defies her absolute enjoyment of costume, it curbs her *luxe effréné* in a thousand sinister ways; it mocks her at balls, operas, garden-parties, *fêtes*, and races. She is *almost* ugly in nautical costume, her little blunt nose being scarcely piquant when the strong sea-breeze blows the fluffy little curls off her forehead. She has one of those clever irregular faces, the despair of *modistes* and milliners.

All her position and power seem wasted to a great extent; she hears no murmurs from an impassioned chorus of æsthetic admirers; she has never been compared to a nocturne or admired by Court painters in *tableaux vivants;* she has, indeed, been frequently overlooked at 'crushes.'

To a vain woman and a dainty aristocrat, nothing blunts the benevolent faculty, sharpens the wit, and 'improves occasions' like the vinegar sauce of neglect.

'Why was I born in such an age,' she cries, 'when beauty is indispensable to enjoyment and success?'

She tries to make up for her cruel loss of personal charms by flirting; and she flirts hard and well. Her suppressed bitterness makes her *espiègle*, sometimes (when the wind is in the east) quite *farouche*. Men like her awfully; there is so much 'go' in her; her animal spirits are splendid, so also is her health.

Il y a compensation pour tout. She adopt mechanical contrivances to reduce her pretty plump waist to eighteen inches? She get into a pair of stays like a strait-waistcoat, for the sake of a figure looking like a slim willow-wand at Ascot or Goodwood? Never! Strait-waistcoats, either physical or moral, are not much in her line, and she is tall enough to be independent of purgatory on three-inch heels. Knowing she can never be a beauty, she cares for no false standards of art or absurd pretences: paint and powder will do a good deal, but they will not add half an inch to an audacious perky little nose, or give a finer slope to a voluptuous kissable chin.

Hence, declining to be a fashionable martyr, Lady Clarissa can walk and drive and ride with the ease and freedom of a man. She has no aches and pains, no spinal curvatures or malformations of any kind; she escapes all immolation at Fashion's shrine.

When poor Beauty has headaches, and is reminded of the vulgar necessities of stomach and liver; when Beauty's friends look grave, and her devoted husband finds, in more senses than one, *la situation est tendue, diablement tendue*—wishing he could take her from her surfeit of social gaieties—Lady Clarissa laughs in her jolly, frank, characteristic way, as she scampers down the Row on her lively chestnut, with the Hon. Jack Pytchley of the 10th, or Sir Lancelot Howarth, Captain of the Hotspur Guards, by her side.

At the present moment Lady Clarissa is sitting on a low couch, in a rose-wreathed boudoir, at the Malmaison's mansion in Queen's Gate. Subdued lights exert a soothing effect on the senses. Strains of music are faintly distinguishable, to say nothing of the fragrant odours of the most delicate scents Rimmel can furnish.

'Is not this our dance?' a voice murmurs in her ear. There is the least dash of irritation in the tone.

Lady Clarissa does not answer: she clearly intends to apparently snub her *preux chevalier*, the handsome Guardsman, Sir Lancelot Howarth. She is surrounded by her three lovers, and she is eating an ice.

Scented blossoms are fastened with a diamond butterfly to her very *décolletée* ball-dress. It is composed of the richest and darkest ruby velvet, trimmed with gold-tinted lace; the skirt of the palest rose-leaf-coloured satin, embroidered with gold flowers. Her shoes are worked with roses and seed-pearls; her pretty back and shoulders (they really are superb, and worthy of a Falconnet) are carelessly reclining against a blue-satin cushion; one dainty foot peeps beneath her satin flounces—she is too clever to reveal both at once; and her dimpled hands are perfectly charming.

'Our dance?' again suggests Sir Lancelot.

She has a motive for her indifference. The lover she intends to marry is no other than his Grace the Duke of Tremayne, a grave thoughtful-looking man of fifty years, with a rent-roll of thirty thousand a year. He is lover number two, and he adores her jauntiness and *bonhomie;* but Lady Clarissa prefers Sir Lancelot Howarth, who is nearer her own age, to any man living—he is more than capital fun. As much as her heart will permit she loves him. He will be her fate, she knows, in some way or other. He is lover number one. He can make her blush when he likes, which is saying a good deal. Besides, a *grande passion* for a handsome Guardsman has a comfortable warmth about it, and she is tired of being left out in the cold.

Her third lover is the Honourable Jack Pytchley, a man who never committed a *bêtise* in his life, a dandy of the first brilliance, rich enough to occasionally drop four 'thou' on the Derby, and ditto at gambling clubs, without feeling it. His sensations will, however, be agreeably aroused on the day when Judea walks into his inheritance, while he is walked off in an opposite direction. All this Lady Clarissa considers, and looks upon Jack as a 'detrimental.'

'I shall not remind you of our dance again,' Sir Lancelot whispers a little angrily, as Jack seizes Lady Clarissa's ice-plate, and then refreshes himself with a brandy-and-seltzer ere turning into the second ballroom.

She rises instantly and takes her Captain's arm. The Duke does not see her amatory glance at Sir Lancelot: only the toss of her well-shaped head, the curve of her adorable arms, the slow unfurling of a large fan, are visible to him. She fans away some of the crimson-hearted blossoms from her breast, and, with all the *abandon* of gesture and grace of a Mdlle. Lange, she half swoons on her partner's manly shoulder towards the close of a maddening waltz.

'Your dancing is too charming,' he whispers, as they retire into a boudoir conveniently free of humanity, and now Sir Lancelot begins to talk plain English.

'You don't mean to say you care for that fellow?' the Captain says, referring to the Duke, and scowling at a harmless old gentleman, who has raised the velvet *portière*, and contemplates cooling himself in the boudoir. Sir Lancelot's deep dark eyes have unutterable longings, but are wrathful and flashing. A fine colour darts to her cheek.

'I prefer Jack,' she says artlessly, with that mischievous smile of hers which works so much riot in masculine senses, and makes the languor of conscious supremacy and the cold pale eyes of Beauty nowhere, ' or' — hesitating — 'better than Jack, you.'

'You're an awfully jolly little pet,' says Sir Lancelot, forgiving her, and averse to making her cry, since she really looks almost pretty to-night, indeed quite kissable. He thinks of a Latin sentence he learnt at Eton, beginning with 'Amantium iræ,' as he speaks with all the familiarity of a favoured lover. 'But, Clary, you'll not throw me over for Jack or Tremayne, will you? Because I'm ridiculously fond of you; as much in love as a fellow can be, don't you know; completely knocked off my appetite, wretched, *désœuvré*—'

She half believes him, and then recollects she is not beautiful. She vainly struggles against the fascination of his mild melancholy.

'I daresay,' answers Lady Clarissa, palpitating, but sceptical. 'How many games of billiards and cards have you played? How many cigars have you smoked? How much cham have you floated in? How many pretty girls have you—'

'Eh, what?' cries Sir Lancelot, as her voice, trembling with something like passion, grows thick from jealousy.

'Kissed?' ends Lady Clarissa, lowering her long eyelashes.

'It's Jack goes in for that class of cattle,' he says, trifling with her gold bangle; 'he's regularly tacked on to the skirts of the Delamere.' (Lady Clarissa shudders at the name of this professional beauty.) 'But, Clary darling, you must know how I love you;' and his dark moustache hovers about that rebellious fluffy little fringe. 'I'd give up Hurlingham and the Vauxhall, if you wished, and forget there was ever such a bird as a grouse.'

'Don't let's miss this enchanting waltz by silly spooning,' she says, starting up, and remembering the Duke and her numbered hours, her large velvety eyes now liquid and passionate with pleasure. He reflects what a fiery volcano may be often concealed under an apparently calm exterior.

Lady Clarissa ascertains that the Duke, whom she means to marry, is in the card-room, hence she waltzes with a vengeance. One thinks of Watteau's pictures, Arcadia, and 'The Loves of the Angels,' all in a breath, as fair women, leaving their waists longer than necessary in their partners' arms, glide, with half-closed eyes, through the mazes of the giddy dance.

After the waltz, Lady Clarissa and her partner seek refreshments, and then they secure a very quiet corner in a deserted conservatory, beautifully sheltered from worldly eyes by some enormous bigonias and indiarubber plants. Here they retire and talk delicious nonsense, the delight of low replies, &c., with only azaleas, roses, and camellias for listeners.

'My diamond pin!' suddenly cries Lady Clarissa, after a somewhat lengthened embrace has crushed her scented blossoms all to pieces. 'It's tumbled out of my dress!'

Sir Lancelot dives after the article in question, and at last discovers it under the leaves of the friendly indiarubber. Is he losing his equilibrium, or is it a lurking consciousness that she means to throw him over after all, and that this is his last chance?

'You are too lovely in evening-dress,' he says quietly, endeavouring, but vainly, to make that butterfly look like flying among the scattered petals. He is in a half-vindictive, but yet admiring, mood; his dark closely-cropped head descends lower; he prefers contemplating the diamonds encircling the milk-white throat, to the lips, which, if not those of a Venus, are still bewitchingly human. It is but an instant's work to crush the scented blossoms still more, to read the meaning of that passionate wistfulness in the stormy gray eyes. He will be sacrificed to the tyranny and exigencies of society, and while she is kindest and sweetest, she means to deal him his *coup de grâce*.

His voice is unusually soft and gentle; he has abandoned himself to the delights of dreamland, and dreams, as they ever will do, steal away his common sense. He feels convinced that his chronic impecuniosity, even when allied with a faultless profile and indisputable 'form,' will prove fatal to his hopes; but the sentimentalism generally ascribed to the raw schoolboy characterises his mood to-night. He bends forward and kisses her once —a furtive, foolish, violent embrace —on the lips.

'You wicked, abominable, dare-darling wretch!' cries Lady Clarissa, a shade paler after that sudden osculatory seizure. 'You positively deserve hanging!'

'With a silken rope made of these tresses,' says the Captain, tenderly indicating her beautiful nut-brown coils.

She pauses, looks pensive, then recollects her duties to society, and coldly points with her Marie Antoinette fan to the distant ballroom. The poetry of her existence is centred in her handsome lover, the solid sober prose of her future is bound up in the Duke. Dreams and poetry, reality and prose; and, alas, she knows so well the separate value and meaning of each; for the dark days of approaching age and *ennui* will romantic love suffice?

'I am tired, Sir Lancelot,' she says wearily, but rather too much in the tone of a stage queen. ' Be good enough to find me a seat.'

She has seen the Duke in the doorway. Her woman's Jesuitism saves her ; she is well on guard.

'Is not this our dance, Lady Clarissa?' asks his unconscious Grace ; and she takes the arm of the man she means to marry.

Six months have passed away, and Lady Clarissa is Duchess of Tremayne. *Ce que femme veut*, &c. There are moments when she is resigned to the loss of the brilliant Guardsman ; but there are also times when she is in a rage with herself and every one else. Moments when his Grace discovers there is a 'hidden want' in the woman he loves. During these feminine frenzies she will slash away at her satin couches with penknives, or hurl paper-weights through plate-glass windows. She flatters herself she is almost handsome in a passion. When mild reason resumes its sway, Lady Clarissa acknowledges the wisdom of her choice. Could *she* ever have hoped to be immortalised on meerschaum, or have added to her reputation by photography? She is fairly clever and witty, but Sir Lancelot—that fastidious and very *blasé* emotional epicure— would have surely tired of her in the long-run, seeing that she is not beautiful. Things are just as well as they are; they would be better, perhaps, if Sir Lancelot were here. Her personal fascinations having secured her a duke for a husband, she is inclined to think that beauty does not invariably have the best of it.

'I can always write to Lancelot,' the Duchess is saying, sipping orange Pekoe out of her Sèvres china cups; her eyes wandering over the home-park, where deer are browsing, and no sound in the room beyond the ticking of a French clock. ' I do wonder he's never made an attempt to see me ; he was rather cool, I thought, at Cowes; he flirted with horrid women. Of course I threw him over for the Duke; but we can be friends all the same, and my money would never have held out for both our extravagances.'

Here the sighs of the robust coquette swell a perfumed tender breast, and a few drops of diurnal *pleurnicheries* fall into the orange Pekoe. Sir Lancelot, however, arrives at the castle in a somewhat hurried and unexpected manner; certainly in a way he neither desired nor anticipated.

The Duchess is now at Abbeyholme, the Duke's seat in the North; she has crammed her mansion with visitors. The Honourable Jack Pytchley, his mother and sisters, two or three foreign noblemen, Count and Countess Valmey, both remarkable for general slanginess, fastness, and 'horsey' tastes; some rich old bachelors, inclined to make matrimonial *fiascos ;* a fair sprinkle of pretty girls, musical signors of infinite affectation and melancholy, and a brace of mild poets of the Burne-Jones school, are among her guests.

She looks gloriously happy tonight sitting at her dinner-table, wearing a splendid diamond and emerald necklace, and a rich black velvet, trimmed with cobwebby filmy lace; her antique point is worth a queen's ransom. The Duke's gaze follows her with the sombre intensity of all graybeards who rejoice in the possession of a youthful spouse; but he is universally pitied as a man infatuated enough to be in love with his wife, instead of somebody else's. He is admiring in a sleepy appreciative way that ugliness *du diable*, that roundness of contour, those silvery bursts of laughter which first won his heart, when a meek little man, with a pale scared expression, suddenly appears in the midst of the festive throng, and the Duke recognises his old friend the Rev. Anthony Gilchrist, rector of St. Mary's.

One of the German visitors, who has been mentally blessing the roe of the sturgeon, presented in the form of caviare, through the aid of which the gastric-juice has proved satisfactory, cries, 'Ach, mein Gott!' at the unexpected apparition. The leaner of the two disciples of the Burne-Jones school has lost a super-subtle thread of thought, and looks pleadingly at his hostess.

'What is wrong, Gilchrist?' asks the Duke, fearing his new model cottages must be on fire, or that his favourite shorthorns have wandered into the river.

'A frightful railway accident has happened,' the Rector explains, 'but a few hundred yards from your park; an express has dashed into some trucks laden with petroleum—over fifty people are injured, and many killed. Knowing your Grace's goodness of heart, I venture to implore immediate aid.'

Something like the panic in the last act of *Lucrezia Borgia* now occurs. The Duke's one thought is to relieve the sufferers. He gives orders to his servants to prepare certain rooms of the castle, which will be converted into a temporary hospital for the reception of the injured, and, accompanied by several friends, starts off for the scene of the accident.

The ladies, left to themselves, yawn and retire to the drawing-rooms, where they loll on ottomans and sofas, and foresee a slow evening.

'How very dreadful this accident is! But only fancy every one rushing out of the house in this way!' Countess Valmey is saying, in the tone with which she has just discussed the frocks at the Hunt ball.

'Wilford is so good-natured,' answers the Duchess, sighing, her eyes resting on the fine frescoes of the ceiling; 'but the idea of any one taking upon himself the duty of seeing to hundreds of wounded people!'

Her dinner-party is disturbed; her husband has not consulted her wishes, or listened to her suggestions; her temper is roused—that ready temper which makes 'lightning of her eyes,' and a fit of hysterics imminent.

The ladies withdraw to their boudoirs. The Duchess is slowly ascending her staircase, when she hears a well-known voice humming a favourite air:

> 'Lisette, ma Lisette,
> Tu m'as trompé toujours.
> Mais vive la grisette!
>   Je veux, Lisette,
> Boire à nos amours.'

It is Jack. He smiles at his hostess, but feels too hungry just then to appreciate a flirtation.

'Is every one mad?' he asks. 'I've just come through the terrace-gardens, and seen people rushing wildly over the park with lanterns. What does it mean?'

She explains, in her pretty practical way; and soon after, grave, almost to sadness, she leaves him somewhat abruptly. She feels irritable, restless. She hates the society of her lady-friends. She is listening to a hurried tramp of feet below; and after it has passed, and all is still again, she descends into the hall with a beating heart.

There, in a corner, she sees an apparently lifeless figure lying on a mattress, blood flowing from a wound on his temple. What does this strange likeness mean between her old lover and this man? Sir Lancelot! Can it be he, brought here lifeless under her very roof? Awe-stricken and overwhelmed she approaches the sufferer, and, kneeling by his side, she begins to tremble. The dark hair, matted with blood, the perfect outline of the smooth chiselled features, all that splendour of manhood she had once adored, are his, her knight's, Sir Lancelot's. She bows her proud head; remorse assails her. She has grown hardened and chilled by training and temperament to most things; she has fancied herself proof against all emotion; but at this crisis she is natural, for she is pained. Her lips tremble, her eyes are dim; she bends over Sir Lancelot, and, moving with a caressing hand the hair from his brow, whispers,

'Lancelot, do you not know me? Can you not speak?'

The words are uttered with a tremulous cry; her whole attitude expresses an all-absorbing grief; he has evidently not been thrown off without a pang. It is a comforting reflection to Sir Lancelot to think she *may* die of a broken heart, after all.

She has forgotten for a moment the golden fetter on the third finger of her left hand, and with it her social successes, her extravagance and luxuries. Why should an old memory evoke such weakness and regret? Her words have been overheard by the Duke, and that touching attitude of a modern Niobe has revealed the secret of her life.

Sir Lancelot does not seem much the worse for his accident after a few days; for, beyond an ugly scar on his manly brow, he appears to all intents and purposes himself again. As time passes on, however, the Duchess never understands why his friendship (cracked as it has lately been, but now cemented by her repentant tears) should grow small by degrees and threaten to vanish altogether, or why she is hurried off suddenly to the East.

Many things puzzle her. Sometimes she half suspects the truth; for the Duke changes his tactics, makes her respect and fear him, reminding her, with a curious smile, that he has not been engaged in diplomacy all his life for nothing. He has passed from the fine frenzy and rose-decked imagery of the lover to the more sober and practical stage of the spouse; hence, what in the former case would have been exciting and added ardour to the chase, in the latter disposes a man to severity of action.

Taken thus in hand by a sensible and strong-minded husband, society has nothing to complain of in the conduct of the Duchess. Her virtues are all her own, her faults such as her education and training have fostered and increased. She is saved from herself, and she is fairly happy. The Duke is a man of endless resources, a shrewd judge of human nature, and with a rooted horror of all the sophistries and fallacies concealed under the brilliant form of platonic pyrotechnics, which he considers only harmless when let off at a safe distance, with nothing inflammable at hand.

WILLIAM HOGARTH.

By H. P. PALMER.

IT has often been observed that every experience of life, every emotion of the soul, every thought, wish, and hope, exercise a lasting influence on the human mind. Their effects may for a time, perhaps, be lost to view. Still it is certain that at some future day impressions long since forgotten, in the unceasing whirl of business or pleasure, may determine the mind at a most anxious crisis, or even display their presence when the agent is unconscious of the power which has shaped his will. Momently we are weaving the intricate chain, the subtle web-work, the delicate fibres, forming the complex and majestic structure of the mind. The gladness or passion envisaged in the faces we see, the splendour of the summer sunset, the sigh of the rising wind, the songs of birds, the melody of voices, all the ever-varying sensations— sweeping, as though by harpist's touch, across the soul, and with wondrous magic stirring it to its depths—fleeting and evanescent as they seem, have yet a vitality in them which, while this life endures, remains, and perhaps shall last for ever.

It is the privilege of man that he is able consciously to mould and fashion this changeful experience, and to colour, with the glorious light of thought and imagination, this apparent chaos of discordant elements. It is, I think, in childhood that the bent of the mind is most easily discerned. We can trace the mould in which the outside world is cast in the language,

not yet become conventional, of the child who can make himself understood. The joys he so vividly realises, the objects he sees, the faces that bend over him, present to his imagination a strange and mysterious meaning. And though the fanciful or grotesque garb in which they appeal to him may seem flung, like a husk, away, as he grows older, yet the time must come when he will feel that his childish visions and dreams have tinged his whole after-life.

It is easy to trace the influence of his youthful surroundings on the mind and spirit of William Hogarth. Buried, as it seemed, during the weary years of his apprenticeship, it broke forth at last, when he exhibited himself to an astonished world as one of the keenest observers of human character and life, as well as one of the most brilliant humorists who have enriched the stores of literature and art. It is of his life and character —of the purpose, method, and history of those wondrous works which have made his name immortal—that I wish briefly to speak.

Born in 1697, the future painter did not find a silver spoon in his mouth. His grandfather had been a north-country yeoman in affluent circumstances. Unfortunately for himself, he espoused the cause of Charles I.; and when that monarch's fortunes were ruined, the enemies of the vanquished party seized the estates of numerous loyalists. The unhappy yeoman was partially dispossessed, and brought to the brink of ruin. When Charles II., at his accession, inaugurated brighter days for the loyalists, Hogarth regained his property, but found he had sustained losses from which he should never recover. By dint, however, of the greatest thrift and industry he was enabled to rear a large family. His third son, Richard Hogarth, studied at St. Bees; and, being unwilling to take holy orders, went to London, and henceforth spent his time in teaching and flogging the youth of his generation, after the approved fashion set by Dr. Busby. His finances were never in a flourishing condition; and those of his sister, the dressmaker, were not sufficient to allow her to afford him any assistance. Like his father, however, he worked hard, spoke the truth, and brought up his family in a wholesome fear of God, the law, and himself.

William Hogarth, his son, spent his youthful days in an ineffectual attempt to learn to spell, and in a subtle and minute study of life and customs. In order to understand his works and trace their history, we must take a cursory view of London as it was when Hogarth, released from the eye of his watchful parent, roamed therein at large, and came to know nearly every brick of Wren's churches, and all the statesmen, divines, ballad-singers, muffin-men, thieves, rogues, vagabonds, who were in the habit of spending their time in the metropolis, to dupe others or be duped themselves. If the Cockney of the present day could suddenly be transported to the London of King George II., he would scarcely recognise his birthplace and his home. St. Paul's, Westminster Abbey, Lambeth Palace, would still be as prominent features in the place as they are now. But he would hardly know, except for these great landmarks, that he was not in an unknown city. Fleetstreet would astonish him by the strangeness of its house architecture, the presence of signs, the meaning of which he would be at a loss to conjecture; the whirl of vehicles, carrying him, in imagination, to some unknown land. If, on a Sunday, he could visit the church of St. Clement Danes, he would recall the hideous pulpits and the galleries, and the pew wherein Dr. Johnson sat; but the parson with his monstrous wig, the congregation fast asleep, the beadle caning the idle young scoundrel in the churchyard, would make him fancy that he was watching the ceremonial of religious inmates of Bedlam. He would hardly call the miserable edifices, lighted with flaring lamps, making night hideous, by the well-known term of theatre. The boats and hoys plying on the Thames would strike him with amazement at their size and inconvenience; the language of the boatmen would almost make him faint with horror. Appalling as the London street-cries now are, they would be as the sweetest music compared with the ceaseless din which Hogarth has described in the picture of 'The Enraged Musician.' At night he would hear an uproar, which, unless he were of a highly phlegmatic temperament, would almost unhinge his mind. He would see Mohocks, the crutch-and-toothpick young men of the period, prowling about with huge clubs, half murdering men and insulting women. He would incur the risk of being run over by a drunken drayman or the impetuous horses of the Right Honourable the Prime Minister. If he ventured on the pavement, he would have to call at Mr. Filby's on the morrow for a new suit of clothes and a new wig. At Vauxhall he would witness scenes of immorality such as, in these days, could not be detected in the lowest quarters of the town. In the streets and alleys of the city he would see more destitution, cruelty, and vice than would equal the heaped-up misery of many of our largest towns taken together. He would see murders and suicides committed almost under his eye; children run over in the darkness; women, intoxicated with gin, devoting their own offspring to death; men fighting, and almost killing one another.

Leaving these squalid and miserable scenes, our Cockney might pay a visit to a tavern. There, perhaps, he would see Parson Ford mixing punch for an uproarious company of clerics and laymen; through the clouds of tobacco-smoke and the dust of snuff he would hear the grossest ribaldry, and be a spectator of such scenes as the rending of a man's coat or the burning of his periwig. In another tavern he might witness the scene delineated in ' A Midnight's Modern Conversation.' Drunken roystering gamblers would be now trying to swindle one another, while a sober sharper robs all of their money. Having threaded his way, with frequent stumbles, to an inn near Covent Garden, he would be unable to sleep. The cries of the watchmen would rouse him more effectually than the best American alarm-clock. The drunken crews turning out of the taverns would break the short slumber which, perchance, he might hope to seize in the early morning. Covent Garden would then remind him of its existence, as the trucks and wagons containing vegetables, such as would now be considered refuse, rattled along the streets. If he looked out of window, he would behold a noisier and dirtier set of men than could now be found in Irish districts most impregnated with the spirit of Home Rule. He would probably get up, swallow some beer and bacon, and, after a preliminary thrill of horror at the

grisly heads impaled on Temple Bar, would proceed to Tyburn. While wending his way thither, he would observe his Majesty's Guards, clad in uniform at which Smike might laugh. The melancholy *cortège* would at length rise to his view. The culprit, borne to his doom on a cart, with his coffin behind him, and maddened by the exhortations of a self-constituted divine, would occupy a prominent position. He is guarded on all sides by mounted officials of the law, while the predecessor of Mr. Calcraft waits, like Dennis in *Barnaby Rudge*, to 'work him off.' Turning at the spot, our visitor from the present to the past would see a huge crowd standing on a rough platform, smoking, drinking, ogling, and eagerly awaiting the cheapest popular entertainment of the day. His ears would be assailed by deafening cries. Among these, the hoarse notes of the wretch who is reading the criminal's dying speech and confession, just fresh from a Grub-street hack, would startle him by their hideous congruity with the rest of the performance. Such are a few of the sights which would arrest the attention of an individual freed for a few days from the ordinary conditions of time. Upon returning to his former existence, he would probably be unwilling to reëmbark on a similar undertaking; and if a pessimist before, would never in the future allow that England was better or healthier or wiser then than now.

Such, too, were some of the sights most attractive to the taste of the future painter. Many of them, doubtless, will be recognised as collected from those wonderful materials which he, like Swift, Addison, Steele, Fielding, and Smollett, has given us for forming a true estimate of London as it was in the earlier part of the eighteenth century. It is essential that his merits as a historian should be rightly understood and appreciated. Equally necessary is it, in judging of his works, that we should recall the history of his mind in recalling the environment by which it came to be what it was. I shall have to say something more on this subject. Meanwhile I will briefly conclude the biographical part of this paper.

When about fifteen years of age, Hogarth was apprenticed to Mr. Gamble, at the Golden Angel, in Cranbourne-street. Mr. Gamble was an engraver on silver; so Hogarth's genius was for some years cramped in a bondage to a morbid taste for heraldic ornaments. He did not, however, as Mr. Herbert Spencer puts it, 'adapt himself to his environment,' but was weary at the deprivation, caused by hard work and protracted hours of business, of his accustomed leisure. He could no longer go to Southwark Fair or Tyburn, though he might occasionally be enraptured and cheered by the Lord Mayor's Show. He seems to have left Gamble in 1720, and to have spent the four following years in illustrating squibs and drawing cartoons. In 1726 he illustrated Butler's *Hudibras;* the pictures are coarse and rude, but show signs of the 'prentice work of a master-hand. At any rate, they brought him into relation with Sir James Thornhill, an eminent painter, with whose daughter he subsequently eloped. He then took a house at South Lambeth; the ' Harlot's Progress' soon appeared, and from that time to his death he was continually producing fresh pictures. As a man, he seems to have been shrewd, jovial, and fond of company and amusement. His acquirements, of an artificial order, were small. His immodesty was excessive. From his point of view, the great painters of the sixteenth

century were incompetent dunces. Frenchmen were particularly odious to him, as they were to Dr. Johnson; and he regarded them with that peculiar abhorrence which yet lingers in the vulgar English mind. A well-spread table, loaded with a coarse plenty of food, and foaming tankards of the strongest beer, formed the painter's Utopia of felicity and enjoyment. There is extant a long poem written by one of the party, recording a tour taken by Hogarth and four friends in the neighbourhood of Sheerness. It seems that they spent much of the time in drinking, smoking, and eating shrimps. The bill of fare at one inn visited by them consisted of viands which might well astonish the present century. It is thus described in the flowing, but hardly elegant, metre of Tothall:

' In our first course a dish there was
Of soles and flounders, with crab-sauce;
A stuffed and roast calf's head besides,
With 'purtnance mixed, and liver fried;
And for a second course they put on
Green peas and roasted leg of mutton.
The cook was much commended for 't:
Fresh was the beer, and sound the port.'

It is pleasant to turn from the outer empirical life of Hogarth to his works and teaching. These details are only interesting as showing the kind of experiences through which he went. I have spoken of him as a historian, and, in that capacity, his works are really invaluable. They describe, with the fullest accuracy, a past century and a past society. The morality of that era, its politics, its customs and amusements, are traced by the hand of a child of genius. Art, we are told, must copy Nature. And Hogarth studied Nature, not in the symmetry of leaves and the colours of flowers, nor even in the sweet loveliness of human beauty, but in the surroundings of a busy London and English life, with all its jollity, coarseness, and brutality. He is a brilliant artist, and, because a brilliant artist, a true historian. No department of English life escaped his keen-sighted vision; nothing was too vulgar, nothing too commonplace to be passed unnoticed. We have now to consider him as a moralist. The moral teaching of Hogarth is sufficiently simple to be appreciated by the weakest understanding. He warns men that idleness leads to dissolute habits; dissolute habits to law-breaking; law-breaking to transportation and the gallows. The lesson is indeed easy, but there are many who never learn it. It is most eloquently taught in the set of pictures known as 'Industry and Idleness.' These, it may be interesting to remark, were drawn from the study of two actual lives—those of John West, a youth who rose to be Lord Mayor of London, and Thomas Randal, a rogue, who was executed at Tyburn in March 1696. Every one knows the story. West works industriously at the loom with the 'prentice's guide before him; while Idle neglects his work, drinks copiously of beer, and spells out ribald pamphlets, recounting the doings of Moll Flanders. West lends his master's daughter his hymn-book, and worships devoutly in the gallery; while Idle plays hustlecap in the churchyard, surrounded by the worst of London roughs. He then commits felony, and is sent to New Guinea. West rises daily in his master's confidence and favour, and at length marries the beautiful Miss West, and becomes Lord Mayor of London. Idle returns from New Guinea, commits murder, and is hanged. The moral is similar in all Hogarth's works. Occasionally, indeed, we meet with a more philosophic analysis of conduct. In 'The Four Stages of Cruelty' the gradual genesis of evil habits is illustrated in a style which might per-

haps have satisfied Aristotle. The cruel boy develops into the yet more savage man; the disposition becomes more and more hardened, less and less amenable to softer influences; until Herod out-Herods Herod, and the completed hero works the sad deed of havoc and ruin which brings him to a merited fate. Hogarth, then, is a great moral teacher, expounding and illustrating truths as old as the hills, but continually lost or obscured by the shortsightedness and ignorance of men. He taught these lessons by a forcible appeal which could strike home to the hearts of the most depraved, and influence the reason of the most infatuated follower of vicious habits. There is no possibility of deception. Facts of every-day life are brought vividly before the mind; it would be perilous, nay suicidal, to neglect them.

The question naturally suggests itself, Has art any business to moralise, and what should be its scope and aim? Modern critics tell us that art is meant, and only meant, to give pleasure, to intensify moments of exalted spirituality, to lend a charm to the passing moment, and to crystallise in richest form the æsthetic sighs of humanity for the beautiful. Whoever takes this view will find little in Hogarth for ardent admiration. He may indeed praise his works as true to Nature and true to life. But he will find no exquisite tints to delight him, no divine beauty in the faces of the women whom Hogarth paints; no loveliness, delicacy, or comeliness wherewith to enthral his soul. Hogarth painted designedly to teach a lesson, to preach an old gospel, to revive a proverbial morality. Those who deny his right as an artist to set up for a preacher will lose much of the inner meaning penetrating his works. Art, like all else, should be subservient to the true interests of man. It is right, as Plato says, that a man should be surrounded by its choicest productions, imitative of all that is noble, excellent, and good. Thus the soul becomes filled with an inward longing for the beautiful, and an abhorrence of the abnormal and mean. Stamped with the impress of the Divine nature, it cleaves to the excellent creations of art and imagination akin to it, and turns with loathing from all that is incongruous and depraved. This is indeed an admirable view of art for those whose happiness it is to be able to develop and perfect that innate love for the beautiful and right which, though frequently crushed and stamped under foot, is imminent in man. But the highest service art can render to men whose education and lives render them incapable of these higher emotions is surely to direct their course towards habits of industry, temperance, and self-control. Hogarth speaks primarily to those who have never tasted the higher satisfactions, or experienced the loftier aspirations of which our nature is capable; and he warns all who are drifting into vice with an earnestness which demands attention.

Hogarth is not merely a moralist, he is a moral satirist. The frivolity of the nobility, the miserable parade of Court assemblies, the idleness of the clergy, are described by him with inimitable skill. He tears away the veil covering the inward corruption of society, and shows that the whited sepulchres are full of dead men's bones. He does not lash society with the unsparing hand of a Juvenal, nor with the cruel, almost demoniacal, spirit of a Swift, but he delineates living and unquestioned facts. I have often thought that town life in 1720 affords a more fruitful field for a satirist than any in modern times. Everything in it, when tested and examined, seems to display signs of a deep-seated canker and corruption. The system of parliamentary corruption inaugurated by Sir Robert Walpole, its effects in the provinces as illustrated in the scenes of an 'Election Contest,' had poisoned the fountain of political purity. The trading system of matrimony, depicted in the plates 'Marriage à la mode,' had exercised an equally destructive influence on the happiness of social and domestic life. The subjection of the political life of the country to a narrow and ambitious Whig oligarchy, with few aims beyond its own aggrandisement, made the Government more oppressive than that of a Periander or a Tiberius. The poor man, whose labour rendered luxury possible, was regarded with an ignorant and cynical contempt. He was absolutely without vote or influence, and considered as little better than a living tool. Such was the state of society which Hogarth successfully strove to depict, and, in depicting, to amend.

Before I close this part of my subject, I should like to mention a belief which strikes me with renewed conviction every time I read a great literary or study a great artistic performance. We are told now that vice and virtue merely represent obedience to, or rebellion against, the dictates of society; and that they have, the one no intrinsic value, the other no intrinsic defect. The distinction between vice and virtue is, in short, merely conventional. Literature and art point indisputably to a far different belief, implanted in the depths of the consciousness of the man who is worthy of the name he bears. They show, indeed, that the 'strait gate' does lead to happiness; and the broad indefinite area of vice to misery and ruin. But beyond this there is a feeling finding its way into all masterpieces of art, not only that the virtuous life means a conformity with law dictated by reason, but that man is free, and, because free, a responsible being. Those who admire Hogarth as a moralist and moral satirist may, perhaps, say that he undoes with one hand what he does with the other; that his pictures are low and vulgar, pandering to the diseased taste of prurient minds. That Hogarth is occasionally coarse cannot be denied, nor can this coarseness be sufficiently explained by the kind of life he describes. Certain of his pictures, indeed, seem to be useless in aim, and worthless as artistic productions. Their publication can in no way be excused. They subserve no good end. They tend to gratify the lowest elements in the nature of the uncultured, unregenerated man. At the same time, it is but fair to mention that Hogarth shared this vice with the majority of the great humorists of his time. Swift took an insane pleasure in bringing all that culture and civilisation lead men to conceal into the light of open day. Pure-souled as was Joseph Addison, there are passages in some of his papers in the *Spectator* which would shock a modern reader of the *World, Vanity Fair,* or *Truth.* These facts but further elucidate what has already been stated, that the society of the eighteenth century was saturated with vice, and no author or artist could escape its malignant influence. As a humorist, Hogarth is unrivalled in the field of art; and a minute consideration of this point is unnecessary. A few remarks on his method must conclude this discursive paper. Hogarth's faces were all drawn from life, and well-known Londoners were frequently astonished to find themselves in conspicuous, though hardly complimentary, positions in his pictures. Whenever Hogarth

saw a striking countenance, he immediately drew a sketch of it, sometimes on scraps of paper, and even occasionally on his finger-nail. This habit easily accounts for the absence of extravagance and absurdity in all his portraits.

In the introductory part of this paper I drew attention to the influences by which Hogarth's mind was shaped and moulded. He could never transcend these influences. His pictures of sacred subjects are lamentable failures. His landscapes are entirely wrong in perspective, and have but few touches of the beautiful. In order to paint sacred subjects, the painter must be brought under the soul-stirring power of mediæval religion. His mind must come to be strangely affected by the sight of priests in long procession, or the perfume of choicest incense, or the measured tone of the curfew-bell. The mind, when thus touched, becomes keenly alive to the more sentimental side of human life and beauty; and it was after this fashion that the souls of the painters of pensive Madonnas and saints were moulded. The rough London painter heard no strange or heaven-sent music in the sound of St. Paul's bells; beheld no transcendental vision in the sight of his ministers of religion. He looked at everything from a plain practical point of view. This attitude, also, he was compelled to adopt by the circumstances of his life. But still, if on earth there be inspired God-directed efforts of genius to teach, instruct, and warn, surely in that great category Hogarth's works may claim a place. He taught men, not indeed to be sentimental dreamers and gloomy ascetics, but to lead active and useful lives, to purge from their lives all falseness and baseness, and to leave therein the ennobling virtues of sincerity and truth. He preached, indeed, to a generation hard and selfish, but his preaching and his life were not in vain.

Art can have no nobler object than the rectification of errors and the reform of abuses. Systems of philosophy and theology, revered by one generation, are often rent asunder or neglected by the next. Art and its votaries share these vicissitudes. The popular will is ever changing; a permanent and absolute belief is, in the nature of things, impossible. Yet, amid the many signs of hope and consolation, we may note with gladness that the genuine efforts of gifted men to benefit their kind have never lacked their merited tribute of gratitude and love. The less talented are ever eager to profit by the teaching of those who come forward with the will and the power to benefit their kind. They are ready to have breathed into their souls the breath of a higher and purer life, and to catch at loftier feelings manifested in the works of those so far above themselves. Among those who have impressed on mankind a nobler spirit, who have struck with unsparing hand at the vices which mar the fair beauty of the world, Hogarth may claim a conspicuous place.

LIFE.

MOSTLY in acquiescence, helpless, dumb,
　Sometimes arising to divine content,
　We mortals take our mortal punishment:
The blows that through our sunniest hours come,
Blighting the upward path, the happy home;
　The blows that seem in pitiless random sent.
　Yet, so Faith whispers, mid their smart is blent
Mercy and lesson, blessed with balm for some.
Pray not for succour, O despairing heart!
　Pray not for strength to thrust the doom away:
In every drama the foredestined part
　Each actor, till the curtain falls, must play.
Ask for the power to trust, to kiss the rod,
Accepting so His will, our Saviour God.

SUSAN K. PHILLIPS.

UNDER THE MIDNIGHT LAMP.

𝔉𝔬𝔲𝔫𝔡𝔢𝔡 𝔬𝔫 𝔉𝔞𝔠𝔱.

I AM a doctor, a busy professional man, whose time is money; whenever therefore I can save it, I do. Many and many a night have I passed in the train, counting the hours thus gained as a miser does his gold. Upon this point, unfortunately, my little wife and I do not agree; and it is, I think, the only point upon which we do not. Eight hours in a comfortless railway compartment, rolled up in your plaid like a snake in its blanket, instead of in your comfortable sheets, stretched over a comfortable spring-mattress—no, she cannot be made to see the propriety of the exchange, nor will she believe that I sleep quite as well, if not disturbed, in the plaid as in the sheets.

The train was just off as I sprang in, and the shock of the start landed me in my seat. Being of a slow placid nature, I was in no hurry to recover from the shock; and we were fairly off, speeding away as only an English express can speed, before I looked round. I had not the carriage to myself, as I had at first supposed: a lady occupied the farther end; and at the first glance, spite of the dim light and the fact of her veil being down, I saw that her eyes, unnaturally large and intense in their expression, were fixed upon me. I at all times prefer a carriage to myself, and, if companion I must have, let it be a gentleman, not a lady; but there was no help for it; the lady was there, and, moreover, she was looking at me. 'So she may,' I said to myself; 'that shall not prevent my making myself as comfortable as circumstances will allow.' Slowly and deliberately, therefore, I removed my hat, substituting for it a cloth cap, which I drew well down over my ears; then I folded my arms, and composed myself to sleep. But in vain: the eyes of my fellow-passenger haunted me; I saw them as distinctly as if my own were open. Was she watching me still? Involuntarily I looked up and round, and my look met hers, full, burning, intense, with far more of meaning in it than I could at all fathom. It was getting decidedly unpleasant, and I was growing decidedly uncomfortable; try as I might, I could not keep my eyes closed: hers were on me, and meet them I must.

In her attitude, too, as well as in her look, there was something strange and mysterious. Huddled up in the corner, she seemed to be holding something close pressed to her, beneath the long loose mourning cape, bending low over it in a crouching posture. Once or twice, her eyes still fixed upon mine, I saw her shiver; but for that slight convulsive movement she sat perfectly still and motionless.

Was she cold? I offered her my plaid, glad of an opportunity to break the ominous silence. If she would but speak, make some commonplace remark, the spell might be broken.

'I am not cold.'

A commonplace remark enough; but the spell was not broken. The mystery that lay in her eyes lay also in her voice.

What should I try next? I looked at my watch — 11.30; our train speeding on at a furious rate, no chance of a stoppage for some time to come, and the full wide-open gaze of my motionless companion not for one moment removed from my face. It was unpleasant certainly. If I changed my position, faced the window instead of her, she must remove her eyes from my face at last. But there was a sort of fascination about her and her look, which I preferred meeting to shirking, knowing it was on me all the time.

There was nothing for it, then, but to give up all hope of sleep, and make the best of my position and companion, whom I now observed more closely. That she was a lady there could be little doubt; there was that in her dress and appearance that was unmistakable. That she was pretty, there could be little doubt either; those great dark, intensely dark eyes, the thick coils of warm burnished hair, the small pale features, seen dimly beneath the veil; yes, she was young, pretty, a lady, and in trouble. So far I got, but no farther. How came she to be travelling alone at that time of night, and with that look on her face? What could it be that she was holding pressed so closely to her, and yet so carefully kept out of sight? From the size and uncertain outline, I should have guessed it to be a child; but, then, there was not the faintest motion, nor could she have held even a sleeping infant long in that position. I think that something of curiosity must have been betrayed in my look, for her own darkened and deepened into a perfect agony of doubt and fear.

Ashamed, I withdrew my gaze at once, and drawing out my note-book, was about to make a memorandum, when, with a sudden forward movement, she fell at my feet, arresting my hand by the agonised grasp of her own, its burning contact sending through me a painful thrill.

'Don't betray me! Don't give me up to him! O don't! I am so frightened!'

It was but a whisper, breathed out rather than spoken, yet it shuddered through me like a cry.

'I cannot always hide it! I cannot always bear it about with me; it breaks my heart, and — I am so tired.'

And letting the hand which still held, pressed closely to her, the mysterious burden that had so raised my curiosity drop heavily to her side, there lay at her feet and mine a little dead baby, a tiny creature evidently not many weeks old.

Then the woman threw up her veil, and, withdrawing her eyes for the first time from mine, clasped her hands before her, her figure thrown slightly back, and looked down upon it. A pretty picture: the poor young mother, with her pale child's face and deep mourning - dress; the wee baby, gleaming so white in its death and baby-robe against the heavy crape skirt on which it lay — a pretty picture certainly for a railway-carriage, and lighted by its dim midnight lamp.

'Dead!' was my involuntary exclamation.

She stretched her clasped hands downwards towards it with a despairing gesture, speaking with low, wild, rapid utterance.

'It was not his look that killed it, but my love. He hated it, my baby, my firstborn; for all the love I gave him, he hated it; and that his look might not kill it, I held it in my arms, so close, so close, till it was dead. O my baby, my baby!'

The outstretched hands had

reached it now, and raised it from the floor to the seat, folding it around until the enclosing arms and the down-bent face hid it once more out of sight.

Was ever luckless traveller more awkwardly placed ? — the dead child; the prostrate woman; the scene, a public railway-carriage; the hour, midnight. Would not my little wife have triumphed could she but have known how infinitely I should have preferred the spring-mattress and snowy sheets to my present position !

I am of a blunt nature. Mrs. Merton often scolds me for my blunt straightforward speeches; but then she has such a pretty way of beating about the bush, which it would be as absurd for me to imitate as it was for the ass to mimic the tricks of his master's lapdog. I must go straight to the point as soon as ever I see it. I did so now.

'How come you to be travelling alone, and with a dead child ? Are you going home ?'

The question seemed to rouse her once more to a perfect frenzy of fear. She turned to me as before, clinging to my hand with small hot fingers, and the old heart-broken cry,

'Don't betray me; don't give me up to him ! His look would have killed my baby; it would kill me if I had to meet it. She is safe, for I killed her, and she is dead; and he hates me, and I have no home—no home !'

I was in a perfect maze of doubt. Could the pretty soft young creature at my feet be indeed a murderess ? and could it be her husband of whom she seemed in such abject terror ? My blood boiled; I felt ready to defend her against a dozen husbands : but how ?

It was midnight now; we could not be far from London; the guard might be popping his head in at any moment. I jumped to a sudden conclusion.

'Were you going to any friend in London ?'

'I know nobody in London.'

'The poor little thing is either mad or her husband is a brute,' was my mental exclamation.

'Then you must come home with me to my wife; she will see after you.'

An upward glance of wild agonised supplication :

'She won't betray me, or—take baby from me ?' And once more the wee dead thing was lifted up into the arms that seemed almost too frail to hold it, and hidden away beneath the long mourning-cape.

I took her home. Mary received her with a broad look of amaze that made me smile, but that found no expression in words. When, taking her aside, I told her all I knew, she wrung her hands in sheer sympathising pity.

'Murdered her own baby—her firstborn ! O, how sad, how dreadful !' And involuntarily she glanced towards the door that hid from us our own little ones, safely cradled and asleep. Then she went back to our strange guest, who sat huddled up in my own big easy-chair, the dead baby still at her bosom.

'I must get her to bed,' said Mary, with a quick determined nod; and she really did contrive to do so by soft, tender, cooing words, and solemn assurances of safety for herself and baby, whom she kissed and cried over, and considered as she might some living object of solicitude, much to the little mother's comfort.

'And you won't betray me; and he won't come and take her from me, or hurt us with his angry look ! O dear, how nice it is to lie down ! I am so tired, and baby is so cold; but I think I can sleep now a little and—forget.'

She was half asleep already; the heavy lids had dropped together, the small pale face had drooped downwards upon the little downy head that lay against her bosom.

'Her husband must be sent for,' I said resolutely, when we found ourselves once more alone ; and I glanced at an envelope I had taken from the stranger's pocket :

MRS. TREMAYNE,
Grantley Lodge,
Grantley.

Mary stared at me aghast.

'Her husband, who hates her, and would have killed her baby ! O John, you would not be so cruel ! She seems so frightened of him, poor little thing ! You may be sure he is some horrid wicked tyrant. And if she really killed her baby —O dear, how sad it is ! Whatever will become of her !'

'But, my dear, if she has a husband or friends we must restore her to them. Why, she is little more than a child ! It's very strange, very, and sad ; but the mystery must be cleared, and the baby buried.'

Mary still pronounced me cruel and unfeeling beyond anything she could have conceived.

'Of course her husband is a madman, who will murder her as soon as he gets her into his hands. You know, John, that husbands are always murdering their wives.'

'Middle - aged wives, dear, or elderly, whose lives are heavily insured. I shall telegraph at once.'

'Then her death will be at your door, sir—mind that !' and too indignant to waste upon me more words, away went Mary to take a last peep at our own sleeping babes, at the dead baby about which there was so much mystery, and the poor young mother whom she had doomed to a violent death.

She was still bending over her, and had called me up to the bedside to notice the extraordinary length of the lashes, and the beauty of the face in repose, when we were startled by a knock at the front door.

'It's the husband ! I know it is. O John, don't betray her, don't give her up ; you wouldn't be so cruel.'

'Nonsense, child ; watch by her till I return. If she awakes say nothing about—'

'Her husband. *As if I should !*'

Our household having long since retired, long indeed before my return, I myself opened the door.

The street lamp lighted dimly two figures ; one tall, stout, and muffled.

'Mr. Merton ?'

I answered in the affirmative.

'You have kindly given shelter to a lady ?'

'Just so.'

The speaker nodded to his companion, who touched his hat and vanished.

The other stranger had now entered the hall, and grasped my hand.

'Mr. Tremayne ?' I asked hesitatingly.

'Captain Tremayne. How is she ?'

'Asleep, under my wife's care ; sleeping as peacefully as a child.'

'Thank God ! So young—at such an hour—in such a state—'

I saw a long shudder run through the tall powerful frame.

'And the child ?' he added, after a pause, in a horror-stricken whisper.

'She had it with her ?'

I hardly knew what to answer ; but he had thrown off his heavy ulster and travelling cap, and now stood before me as handsome and pleasant and honest-looking a young fellow as I ever saw, and my heart warmed to him. He was no assassin, or ruffian, or cowardly bully, whatever Mary might say. The shadow of a great horror that lay in the blue mellow eyes had been laid there by terror, not crime.

'The child is dead,' I said softly.

'It died two days ago, died suddenly in convulsions in her arms, and the shock turned her brain. She was doing so well, poor little thing; but afterwards she grew delirious, and in her ravings she accused herself and me. I could do nothing; she would not have me near her, but beat me off with her hands, as she couldn't bear the sight of me. And I was so fond of her and she of me!' Here the man broke down. He walked to the window, then turned and asked abruptly, 'May I go to her?'

I thought of Mary, and hesitated.

'She is sleeping so peacefully just now; and if she awoke suddenly and saw you—'

'She shall not see me,' he broke in eagerly. 'I will be so quiet; but I must see her. I nursed her through a long illness a year ago, and she would have no one near her but me; and now—'

Under the heavy military moustache I saw his lip quiver; he paused, then added: 'I must go to her!' not in command, but yearning appeal, both in voice and eyes.

'Will you wait here a minute? I will see whether she still sleeps.'

She still slept, the heavy peaceful sleep of a tired child, Mary keeping a stern watch and guard over her. I beckoned her out of the room.

'Well?' with fretful impatient eagerness. 'You have seen him? What is he like? Is he horrid?'

'Judge for yourself; he is in the dining-room. He says he must see her—he must come in.'

'That he sha'n't, the cruel wretch; or it shall be over my prostrate body!' tragically.

'Well, go and tell him so.'

'I will!' And away, nothing daunted, went Mary.

I smiled. 'She will no more resist the pleading of those blue handsome eyes than did her husband. He will win her over with a look.' I was right; she soon returned, and not alone.

'He will be very quiet, and she need not see him. I thought it would be better;' all this apologetically.

He crossed the room as noiselessly as a woman, stooped over the bed in silence, then sat down beside it. Mary shaded the lamp, so that the room was in twilight, and so we all three sat down to wait.

For more than an hour we waited, then Mary stole out. Captain Tremayne looked up as the door opened and closed; then, with a quick sigh, laid the brown curly head down upon the pillow as close as possible to that of the poor young wife without touching it, and his hand moved up towards hers where it lay on the coverlet, but without touching that either, for fear of awaking or disturbing her.

It was not until the first gray streaks of daylight were struggling in through the window, beside which I sat, that there was a slight stir; she was awaking at last.

'Hugh!' she breathed—dreamily at first, then urgently—'Hugh!'

'Yes, dear.'

She turned her face towards his where it lay beside her. She was only partially awake as yet, her eyes were still closed; but the hand on the coverlet crept up softly towards him, fluttered over his face, rested one moment caressingly on the brown curls, then, with a long contented sigh, her arm stole round his neck.

'Husband, kiss me!'

'His presence has saved her,' was my mental comment; 'there is nothing now to fear;' and, unnoticed, I left the room.

Chilled and cramped with the

long sitting after the night's journey, I was not sorry to find the sitting-room bright with lamp and firelight, the kettle singing on the hob, breakfast as comfortably laid out for two as if the hour had been nine instead of six, and Mrs. Merton as neat and fresh and trim as if that midnight tragedy had been all a dream. Let cavilists sneer as they may, there is nothing for a man like a wife, if she be a good one. I myself *may* have had my doubts on the subject—wives are but women after all, and must therefore be trying at times, even the best of them. But I certainly had no doubts whatever as I stretched out my feet to the blaze, and resigned myself cheerfully to being petted and waited on.

'Well?' questioned Mrs. Merton, when my creature comforts had all been duly attended to, and not before. I told her how matters stood: she was delighted.

'And so they are fond of each other, after all; and his being unkind to her and her poor little baby was only a delusion. How dreadful! How delightful, I mean! Poor fellow—so young and handsome and nice! I felt so sorry for him.'

'He must have travelled down in the same train as she did.'

'O no; he told me all about it. He had been summoned up to town on business, and left home yesterday morning. In the evening the nurse left her, as she thought, asleep, to fetch something from the kitchen.'

'Have a gossip there, you mean.'

'John,' solemnly, 'you don't like nurses, especially monthly nurses; you know you don't!'

'My dear, I am a married man, and moreover an M.D. A well-balanced mind must hate somebody or some class of bodies; and,

as a rule, medical men hate nurses, especially monthly nurses.'

'Nonsense, John! Well, Mrs. Tremayne got away while the nurse was down-stairs, and, being traced to the station, where she had taken a ticket to London, Captain Tremayne was telegraphed to, and was stopped as he got into the train on his way home. Some one must have seen you leave the station.'

'As he came to look for her here, somebody must have brought him; two came to the door.'

'It will be all right now that he has found her, and is fond of her; she will get quite well, and he will only have to comfort her for the loss of her poor little baby.'

I wipe my pen, blot the MSS., and rise. My story is done, and, as it is the first, so will it probably be the last of which I shall be guilty.

Mrs. Merton looks up from the glove she is mending. '*The story done!* Why, all you have written is only the beginning of the end! You could not surely have the heart to break off in that unsatisfactory manner. Not a word about Captain Tremayne's gratitude, or the hamper they sent us at Christmas, or the birth of their little son last year, and the pretty way in which she coaxed you to be godfather, though her uncle, the duke, was only waiting to be asked; or how she insisted upon our bringing baby and Johnny and Freddy, and how baby—'

But I have seized my hat and gloves. Mary is, as I have said, the best of wives, if just a little trying at times, and her baby the most wonderful of all *created* babies—but I have an appointment at twelve!

HOTELS.

By G. DE M. SOARES,
AUTHOR OF 'TAHITI,' 'A HELL IN PANAMA,' ETC.

CAN anything new be said or written on the subject of hotels? Possibly not, if one were obliged to limit one's observations to the beaten tracks of the ordinary tourist; but my lines have fallen in out-of-the-way places, beyond even the range of Messrs. Cook, where, if hotels exist at all, they possess such strange characteristics as to be worth describing. Besides which, if Carlyle has demonstrated the possibility of establishing a philosophy of clothes, why should not the Darwinian theory be applicable to hotels?

For fifteen years I have lived mostly in hotels—*tant pis pour moi*. I have partaken of, and paid dearly enough for, the hospitalities of the best, and have deplored the discomfort, while I paid equally dear for it, of the worst. Familiarity with them in all the 'six quarters' of the world, geographically speaking, has bred in me contempt for their extortions; and I am fain to denounce them as unsatisfactory, but necessary, evils.

My memory leaps into the Pacific, and alights on the island of Tahiti, where I was staying a few years ago, on a cotton plantation. Queen Pomare (since dead) gave a ball at Papeete, thirty miles distant, and thither I repaired with a young Hussar officer, to pay our devoirs and see the fun. We should not have consigned ourselves to the tender mercies of the Hôtel Impériale—for we had many and serious misgivings as to the nature of the entertainment afforded—had we not been obliged to do so in consequence of the influx of visitors precluding all hope of our throwing ourselves successfully on the hospitality of any of our European friends.

As it was, however, every house being stretched to its utmost limits of accommodation, we went to the hotel, and demanded of the proprietor, one Mons. Alphonse Lacroix, if he could provide us with rooms.

'Mais parfaitement, messieurs.' And he committed us to the care of a waiter, who had the appearance of doing duty generally in a straw-yard, with directions to take us to Numéro —.

Following our guide across a capacious yard, ornamented with an immense manure-heap, round which were basking many pigs and much poultry, we arrived at a door, indicated by the *garçon* as the entrance to our bedchamber. Undoing a piece of cord which served instead of a latch, he pushed open the door, and we beheld before us the interior of a rude barn, with a pent-roof, so poorly thatched with plantain-leaves as to render a window not only unnecessary, but positively unadvisable.

Our entry had the effect of startling a large family of small birds, which flew out through the spaces in the roof, chirping disputatiously, as though they considered their ejectment as a matter of hardship and injustice; and with their sudden clatter they awakened a large hog that was gracefully reclining in the centre of the apartment, with one of his legs attached by a string to the corresponding member of a skeleton four-post bed. In this attitude he put me in mind of a gouty old gentleman, more especially as he grunted most querulously upon being disturbed, as did also a barn-door fowl that was roosting on the curtain-rod over his head, so far as his crowing propensities would permit. Although their continued residence was dispensed with, the visible and odoriferous indications of their tenancy filled us with horror at the thought of putting up in this extraordinary domicile.

There was, however, no help for it; so, submitting with the best grace we could assume, we deposited our effects on the floor, there being no other furniture apparent, excepting a few rusty nails stuck in a beam by way of wardrobe, which had been lately used by the departed birds as temporary perches; and we petitioned the servant for a basin and a stool, with which we were supplied with cheerful alacrity. We then sat ourselves to scouring the basin, which had evidently served as a platter for the pig, being encrusted with potato - parings and other kitchen refuse of a similar character.

In this place we dressed for the ball, entertaining each other with conjectures as to what Mr. Poole, or any other London tailor, would have said had he witnessed the donning of his works of art under such circumstances.

As we divested ourselves of our travelling garments we were compelled to pack them up in our portmanteau, in order to keep them from the birds and vermin, with which the place was infested; and we formed the resolution to remain as late as possible at the ball, in order to dispense with the necessity for using the bed. As to any attempt to *sleep* upon it, we decided at once that that would be utterly futile and unavailing.

I omit any mention of the other departments of the hotel, as they were more or less comfortable after the manner of country cabarets throughout France, with which, doubtless, the reader is already acquainted. I must, however, testify to the superiority of the cuisine and *salle à manger*, to which the proprietor, being a Frenchman, had especially devoted himself.

The island of Carnicobar, in the Indian Ocean, where I remained a week at the beginning of 1869, being peopled by savages, did not boast even of such accommodation as I found in Tahiti, so I was lodged, like Mahomet's coffin, between heaven and earth. No, not in a balloon, but in a sort of exaggerated pigeon-house, supported on a colonnade of palm-tree piles. The floor was simply a large sieve, made of split bamboos, through the interstices of which the dust went down, while the air came up, thus rendering the habitation both cool and clean. Besides this, it possessed a certain springiness highly conducive to comfortable rest. At all events, in the company of my host, an island chief, and sixteen of his relations, I therein enjoyed my limited sojourn exceedingly.

Levantine hotels are, as a rule, detestable, more especially those of Roumania. I except, of course, some in the large towns—Misserie's, at Constantinople, and such establishments, being far from uncomfortable; but, generally speaking, Levantine hotels are detestable. For the most part, they are as morally disreputable as they are socially disgraceful. Their proprietors not only allow, but encourage vice, as an inducement to visitors. From beginning to end, they are foul in the extreme.

For curiosity's sake, let us enter one : the chief hotel in the town of Braila will afford a good specimen of the class to which I allude. It is kept by a Polish Jew, of evil appearance and worse reputation. The staircase is narrow and dark, and the passages correspond. There is a prevailing odour of paraffin-oil proceeding from the dirty lamps which here and there are hung against the walls, backed by tarnished reflectors : underneath each is a wet stain on the floor, caused by the dripping from the oil above. In the centre of the passage are a bell and a sort of clock-face, furnished with a single hand and the numbers of the different rooms in the corridor, so that when any visitor requires attendance he is forced to leave his room, traverse the passage, set the indicator, and ring the bell : and even then the chances are greatly against the arrival of a servant.

Push open a door—you *can*, for the fastenings are seldom in order —and enter a bedroom. There is no carpet ; the floor is dirty, so are the windows ; so, in fact, is everything in the room. The bedstead is of stained wood, and, like the rest of the furniture, is of the poorest manufacture of Vienna or Pesth. The mattress is of the commonest description, and feels as though it were stuffed with walnut-shells and toothpicks ; it is covered with a sheet that is very rarely changed, and surmounted with a quilt, on which is buttoned another sheet that is never changed at all. Let me forget the vermin, which have occasionally been sufficiently rampant to oblige me to remove to the table in search of sleep. Look at the chairs, table, washstand—all of the same brown-stained wood, all dirty and repulsive.

The feeding department is on a par. Bad oil pervades everything. It floats on your soup, in your gravy, in your tea or coffee—everything appears to be cooked in it. Roasting is unknown : all the meat is baked, and tastes sodden in consequence.

The plates, glasses, knives, &c., are also greasy. The servants are all squalid, frowsy, cringing Jews, from Austria or Hungary. Pay them, and there is no degrading service that they will not render you in their abjectly crawling reptile-like servility. Pah ! the very recollection of them makes me shudder.

And yet there is no necessity for such a revolting state of things. It is possible to live as comfortably, as regards cleanliness, in the Levant as elsewhere. When I had my own house, in the very town of which I have been speaking, I got good servants, and lived as properly as I could desire. This, however, is not general, even in private houses ; the fact being that the Levantines, be they English or what not, by long residence, become careless, and grow accustomed to the disgusting habits of the East.

Hungarian hotels, save at Pesth, are but a shade better.

Hotels in India are worth noticing. The first with which I made acquaintance was at Vizagapatam, kept by one Baboo Krishna Ghosal Bhat. It was a very fair sample of native hotels in India.

Something like a Pompeian house, composed of pillars, half-roofs, peristyles, atrium, &c., furnished with punkahs and kus-kus tatties (*i.e.* mats made of fragrant fibre, hung against open windows and doors : in the hot winds they are wetted, and the draught blows through them cool and refreshing). There was no furniture to speak of, save two lame tables, three bottomless chairs, and plenty of dirty whitewash and cobwebs, relieved by some coloured German prints, such as are purchasable at the Nuremburg fairs for a few kreutzers apiece. 'Pegs,' *i.e.* brandy and soda-water, were procurable and drinkable; but eating was out of the question, everything was so abominably filthy.

I was rescued from starvation by a friend who lived some three miles distant—at Waltair—or I should have had to perish from hunger or nausea. In travelling up country in India, people always take their servant to cook for them, unless they can depend upon the hospitality of a friend. They also take bedding with them, which is arranged on a sort of horizontal harp, supported by four legs, called a 'charpoy.'

This last precaution is very necessary, as a charpoy *au naturel*, as used by the natives, would not be considered comfortable by Europeans, who prefer mattresses to knotted cords, which, to say the least, are calculated to impress a pattern on the flesh of whoever reposes thereon.

In the large towns in India there are, of course, hotels kept by Europeans, or, at all events, of a superior order to that described above; and they are so similar that, in describing one, I cannot fail to give an idea of all. I shall, therefore, select the Great Eastern Hotel of Calcutta, in which I was resident for many months.

The Great Eastern Hotel, then, is a large three-storied building, capable of 'making-up' more than a hundred beds. It contains many marble-paved corridors, where, at any hour of the day or night, you may see dozens of servants stretched asleep, and drowsy punkah-wallahs lazily pulling their ropes, sometimes with their toes, sometimes with their hands, according as it best suits their squatting attitude. The servants in the hotels are, in fact, the feature that principally attracts a European's attention when he first goes to India. They *swarm.*

Besides the hotel servants, and their name is legion (say one to each visitor at least), each guest has always one, generally two, and often three, private servants. When the hotel has been comparatively empty, they swarm; and when it is full, I suppose there must be over two hundred and fifty of these disagreeable necessities sleeping, chattering, smoking, and wandering about the house.

Out of the season I have seen as many as thirty-five servants in a room where half a score of diners were protesting, with perfect reason, that it was impossible to get waited upon, the service was so inefficient. The chief occupation of these kitmudgars (table servants) always appeared to me to consist in pushing one another about, squabbling amongst themselves, clattering plates and cutlery, or else standing a little on one side behind their masters, and watching intently every mouthful as it sped from plate to mouth. At first, the sight of all these servants, clothed in white, amused me—it was so droll to see them, their black faces surmounted by immense turbans, rushing hither and thither aimlessly, or to watch them standing statue-like, while their eyes rolled as if by machinery; but at last I only viewed them with a disgust for which I can find no expression.

One advantage that Indian hotels possess over European houses is that of baths. Every bedroom has a bathroom attached, and in that they are superior to our sleeping chambers at home; but only in that, for otherwise sleeping chambers are comfortless in the extreme: simply whitewashed, containing a round table, a brass bedstead hung with mosquito-curtains, a rickety washstand, and two arm-chairs (all chairs have arms in India); everything is covered with dust during the hot weather, or mould during the rain. There is a matting on the floor full of holes and ants; and there is a musty smell pervading all, which is caused by the damp-heat that is eternal.

The reading-room is worse; it is like the bedroom, but minus the bed and washstand; it is without sofas or lounges, so that unless one be either dining or playing billiards there is no comfort out of bed, and even then it is of a very limited description.

The worst feature of Indian hotels, however, is that of the inner-man administration.

It is impossible to give an idea of the monotony of the bills of fare. Every dish, whether boiled fish or roast joint, omelette or curry, chop or vegetable, tasted of, and was impregnated with, *ghee*, which is about the most disagreeable de-scription of grease with which I am acquainted. It is worse than the bad oil in Wallachia. It would be vain for me to attempt to de-scribe the distaste with which I ap-proached the table, or the disgust with which I left it.

The whole of the ground-floor of the hotel is devoted to a store, where anything from bacon to a bicycle can be purchased, at double the European price. In every way the hotel is a failure—pecuniarily and otherwise—probably because it is under the management of a board of directors and clerks and stewards and secretaries without end.

The visitors, however, are inter-esting and amusing. They are most varied in class, occupation, and character; but, as a rule, they are in good spirits. This arises from the fact that they have come to Calcutta, either because they are going home, to which they look forward with immense delight, or because they have come *from* home, and are full of hope and anticipa-tions, which, alas, are but rarely realised! It is curious in the ex-treme to mark the different aspect of these birds of passage, when a P. and O. or Messagerie steam-boat is leaving, or when one has just arrived. The new-comers are fresh, anxious, sanguine, and healthy, glad to get ashore, and sceptical as to the horrible pro-phecies which are dinned into their ears. In three or four days they disappear, either up country or into lodgings, or somewhere or other; and they make room for bilious, 'livered,' jaded, faded, Mofussilites, who, notwithstanding all their past miseries, are cheerful in the thought of the new era open-ing upon them, in their escape from bondage, and the prospect of reviving health that is before them.

One word more about hotels in India before I take wing to Ame-rica. In the large towns there are hotels of decent, but deceptive, appearance; they are nearly all uncomfortable. Throughout the whole of my Indian experiences, I only found one hotel—Harrison's at Lucknow—really comfortable. In all the capitals there are, of course, a quantity of Jack-ashore lodging-houses, the refuge for the disreputable, and frequented by the class of loafers who infest all sea-ports.

And now for America, where hotels are most unequal.

Those which are the pride of Yankees, on account of their size, their publicity, and their grandeur, I found to be objectionable in the highest degree. On the other hand, those which are unpretend-ing and quiet and private are far from uncomfortable, due allowance being made for their existing in the United States. In point of fact, the great question of comfort or discomfort consists in the style of servants employed. It rests mainly with the servants whether you feel at home, or whether you find yourself miserably abroad.

Now I believe it is impossible to get good servants in the Northern States. Fenianism is their predominant characteristic; and although they are taken from the lowest and most ignorant classes of Ireland, yet they vaunt themselves, not as your equals, but as your superiors; and their rowdyism and insolence are observable to a far greater degree in the 'big' houses than in their less pretentious neighbours. I may cite as an example that I heard a gentleman, who complained that he had ordered some salad, which was not forthcoming, told by a ruffian, 'You are a liar!' and when the gentleman felled him to the ground, he took up a knife, and endeavoured to stab the man he had so unprovokedly insulted. Such things arise from the necessity, in these 'big' houses, of engaging a great number of servants, of which there is an inadequate supply.

The above occurred at the Fifth Avenue Hotel at New York, which, perhaps, takes the lead, and is a type, of the hotels I dislike so much. They need but little description.

We have all read of the bars down-stairs, which are little else than public thoroughfares — frequented by chewers, spitters, readers, smokers, drinkers, and loungers; where drinks of the most delicious descriptions and most disagreeable nomenclatures are mixed, with a sublime science, from sunrise to midnight; where the prices of cotton and the operations of Wall-street are discussed equally with political views or election squabbles; where lank-jawed men sit facing the window, supporting their legs, on a

level with their hats, upon rests provided for the purpose, chewing and ruminating by the hour, while they lethargically contemplate the kaleidoscopic aspect of the humanity that passes in review before them; where youths strut and ape their elders; and where you are surrounded by barbers' shops, and tailors' shops, and hat-makers' shops, and every other kind of shop imaginable.

We are also familiar with the oppressive magnificence and chilling grandeur of the ladies' saloon upstairs—rich in great mirrors, and superb sofas, and curtains, and carpets, and filled with majestic furniture, but not with people. I used to feel awe-stricken when I entered, and could no more have summoned up courage to have traversed its length—the cynosure of all the observant eyes belonging to some dozen very strong-minded ladies therein — than I should dare to walk Regent-street at midday in the garb of a Carnicobarean.

Then the meals, which never finish and never begin, and are never fresh; or the bedrooms, which are small, ill-ventilated, and showy—all these things made me rejoice to change to such houses as the Brevoort or the Clarendon, where, barring the servants (a great improvement on those I mentioned above), one might almost fancy oneself in England, so homely and comfortable are they. By this I do not mean to say that I think English hotels bear off the palm of all hotels. By no means. English hotels are passable; so are the Australian, which resemble them closely. So are also French hotels, or Austrian, or those of most of the European capitals; but the hotels in which I found the greatest excellence were at the German watering-places, or rather at the gambling baths in the Rhine region.

Perhaps their *tables d'hôte* are not so famous as those of Bruxelles or Paris; but the society that frequents them is infinitely more agreeable. If their rooms are not so stately as at Vienna, they are at all events better provided with comfortable appliances; and the kind attention, the quantity of water, the cheerful and ready service, the excellence and freshness of everything to eat, is beyond all comparison.

The best servants are undoubtedly to be found in hotels in Germany. They are well educated, understand their position, appreciate kindness, and thoroughly know their business—it being a fact that many of the German waiters are the sons of hotel proprietors, serving their time and learning their trade.

Italian hotels are not famous, though there are some nice houses —at Florence, for instance, the 'Pension de Milan,' where, for eight francs a day, you eat, drink, and sleep as comfortably as may be; but as a rule they are dirty, smell close, and are economical with the water-supply.

Of a totally different nature are those queer old inns in Switzerland, the Tyrol, and Transylvania, which one views so gratefully in out-of-the-way districts. They are homely, but cheerful; simple, but comfortable. I enjoy the dining and supping all together in the great kitchen, where the rafters overhead are hung with future feasts; where the bedchambers are perfumed with the sweet herbs on which the snow-white linen is dried; where the torrent hard by provides a delicious bath, and the lowing herds and belled and bleating flocks wake one with a promise of lactean draughts; and where, if one chooses to be sociable, he is cordially received and entertained, more as a friendly guest than as a profitable visitor.

I would willingly dwell longer on this theme; but my space is filled; and although my say is but half said, I must perforce close my reminiscences on the subject of hotels.

FAITHFUL FIDO.

By JAMES HUTTON.

I.

COMMITTED for trial! A simple formula, but full of terrible significance. It means that a grave, sober-minded, experienced, and impartial magistrate, learned in the law and exceptionally conversant with *primâ-facie* evidence as regards criminal cases, entertains very serious doubts of the innocence of the unfortunate being then standing in his presence, and charged with the perpetration of an offence too heinous to be dealt with summarily. To a certain extent it is a sentence of condemnation. An individual who has so conducted himself as to incur the suspicion of guilt not only on the part of reputable witnesses, but also on that of the presiding magistrate, must at least have been strangely off his guard, and must altogether be a man in whose discretion one would be unwise to place over-much confidence. There is only one exception to be made, and that is in a case of mistaken identity. Even then, perhaps, a stigma will attach itself for ever to the victim of adverse appearances. The stain will never be quite effaced. The world will still eye him askance; and few of his previous acquaintances will care to be seen in his company in places of public resort. A respectable and innocent man, against whom a grand jury has found a true bill, is of course in a still worse plight, for he is, socially, condemned for life. He may escape imprisonment; he may be told by the judge who has tried him that he leaves the court with unsullied reputation; his friends and relatives may crowd around and shake him heartily by the hand as he steps out of the dock; but never again will he hold up his head among his neighbours —never again will he be welcomed to their hearth and table as in the days that went before his calamity. He cannot get over the fact that he has been accused of a gross violation of the laws of the land; that he has been deemed capable of committing that particular crime; that he has been, possibly, denied the privilege of bail, and has been locked up in a House of Detention as though he were, in very truth, a malefactor. That frightful burr will stick to him to his dying day. The memory of it will follow him to the grave; and when his neighbours read the newly-engraven inscription on his tombstone they will whisper, one to another, their long-smouldering doubts as to the rightfulness of his acquittal. This prologue would be more appropriate as an epilogue; but thoughts that burn are the readiest to find words that breathe, and whoso reads the story of the little episode in my life which, with trembling hand, I am about to describe, will, perchance, not wonder at the emotion evoked by a reminiscence that haunts me by night and day, though, in truth, I have neither been imprisoned nor actually committed for trial.

My name is William Hamilton. On attaining my twenty-first birthday I succeeded to a small inheritance bequeathed to me by my father, of sufficient amount to deprive me of the best motive for exertion, though not large enough to excuse absolute idleness in one whose tastes were somewhat fastidious and expensive. Dabbling mildly in light literature, combined with desultory raids into journalism, I was enabled to ride my few harmless hobbies without incurring debt, and while living well within my income. At the time to which I am about to refer, and which is not yet very remote, I was a little over twenty-six years of age, the golden era of manhood when not adulterated with any base alloy. My chief friend and ordinary companion was many years my senior. Indeed, he was not unfrequently taken to be my father; but this was partly due to the kindly gravity of his demeanour, touched with a softening ray of sadness. He was the head of an important department in one of the Government offices, and possessed, in addition to a comfortable salary, private property to a considerable extent. His father, the late Admiral Sir John Boyle, had seen a good deal of service at one time and another, and had contrived to save more money than usually falls to the lot of naval officers, not generally the most provident of mankind. Him I never saw, nor yet his only daughter, who, as I afterwards learned, died in giving birth to her first-born child, a bouncing boy, with quite a crop of hair. On the death of her husband, a few years later, my friend had taken charge of the little urchin, and brought him up as his own son. He was, I believe, tenderly attached to the youngster, who turned out altogether unworthy of his kindness, and repaid his constant good offices with shocking ingratitude and treachery. Shortly before I became acquainted with John Boyle, his nephew, Stephen Jervis—at that time about twenty-two, which

was also my own age—was caught by him, in the middle of the night, in the act of forcing open a *sécrétaire*, in which he had locked up a considerable sum of money while talking to Stephen; for naturally he could not suspect the young man of having descended to such a depth of infamy as to be capable of robbing his benefactor. The guilty wretch was incontinently shipped off to the colonies at his uncle's expense, who likewise arranged with a bank at Melbourne to pay him two guineas a week until such time as he should show himself worthy of being again taken into favour. In the mean while it was understood that no allusion of any kind was to be made to the absent scapegrace; and, for my part, as he was a perfect stranger to myself, I never felt the slightest desire to break through this tacit understanding.

Boyle and myself lived in the expansive region known as Westbournia, in different streets, but within a few minutes' walk of each other. We were, both of us, bachelors, and apparently—at all events, so far as he was concerned—without any intention or desire to add to our respective responsibilities. Of the two, I was thought the more likely to take the leap in the dark, because I had no living pets of any kind, and in a querulous, impatient, blundering sort of way, tried to manage my own small household whereas my friend indulged in a housekeeper and in a little dog. Fido was a black-and-tan terrier, with a strain of the Italian greyhound, which imparted a singular grace and airiness to all his movements, and he was seldom at rest except when coiled round and fast asleep on my knees. Next to his master, whom he certainly preferred to all other human beings, he loved me more than any of the frequenters of that hospitable house. I say so not from vanity or conceit, but because everybody knows that it was so, and because subsequent events caused him to transfer his allegiance to myself. At this moment he is watching me from his little round wadded basket, which, when I am writing, is always placed on the table in front of me. In that position he will remain watchful and contented as long as I am engaged in scribbling; but no sooner do I take up the pen-wiper than, with a sharp shrill bark, he springs out of his lair, jumps down on the floor, and capers about in wild delight, for then the time has come for a walk if there be neither rain nor snow, and, in any case, for a game of romps.

It had become an almost invariable custom with John Boyle to give cosy little dinner-parties twice a week, on Wednesday and Saturday. To my dying day I shall see, as clearly as though reflected in a mirror, the minutest incident connected with the last of those social gatherings. On the occasion to which I refer, there were three guests besides myself; for he affected odd numbers, and was fond of repeating the somewhat free French translation of the old Latin phrase, *Deus numero impari guadet* —*Le numéro deux se réjouit d'être impair.* Next to myself sat George Heneage, vaguely described as a rising barrister; and on the other side of the table his brother Henry, a keen clear-headed solicitor with a large practice; and a man whom I never liked, and whom I now detest, named James Barclay, in the same department of the public service as our kindly host. Everything seemed to go wrong that day. The fish was over-boiled, the *entrées* were detestable, the joint half raw, the guinea-fowl scorched and shrivelled, and, finally, the sherry was corked, the claret cold and flat, and the port had been shaken—at all

events, that is what I seem to recollect. Boyle himself was strangely silent and depressed, and, so long as the servant was in the room, scarcely uttered a word. Conversation was consequently constrained and spasmodic—the more so that Barclay appeared to think it incumbent on him to imitate the melancholy mood of him who certainly could not that day be called our entertainer. After the wine had gone twice round, Boyle suddenly rose from his chair and, with a few words of apology, left the room, promising to return in a few minutes, and begging us to excuse his momentary absence.

'The old man seems upset and out of sorts,' remarked the barrister. 'Has anything of a disagreeable nature happened at office?' he asked of Barclay.

'Nothing whatever, to my knowledge,' the latter replied; 'but I observed an air of depression when I went into his room at an early hour. He hardly listened to what I was saying, and answered me at cross-purposes. When I advised him to go home and lie up for the day, he looked at me with a sad expression, and murmured, "Who shall administer to a mind diseased?" Presently he pulled himself together, and said, with a forced smile, "I shall be all right as soon as I have had my lunch. The fact is, I received some very unwelcome news this morning, which spoiled my appetite, and lost me my breakfast."'

'Ah!' exclaimed the solicitor. 'He must have heard from that rascally nephew of his. I hope to goodness the fellow is not coming back to England.'

'What if he has already arrived?' I suggested, for the sake of saying something, and because I hate to be left out in the cold.

At that moment the door opened, and Boyle returned to his seat.

He held in his hand a sheet of paper, on which a few lines were apparently written, and his face was as white as the paper, though it wore a resolute and almost defiant look. Hastily tossing off a glass of wine, he handed the paper to the solicitor, and, in a tone of assumed carelessness, asked if it were all right. Heneage started, and fixed his sharp eyes upon myself; but as I met his gaze without flinching, he gave back the paper, and dryly answered,

'Ye-es. I daresay it is right enough from a legal point of view; but—'

'That is all I want to know,' said Boyle, with an abruptness quite unusual to him, and which made us all uncomfortable; but the next moment he laid his hand softly upon Heneage's arm, and almost whispered, 'Bear with me, old friend. I am not quite myself to-day. I will tell you all about it another time. I am quite myself, however, in one sense. I am sitting here clothed and in my right mind, and perfectly understand the purport and meaning of the few lines I have just written upon this paper, to which I am about to affix my signature, which I shall request Barclay and George Heneage to attest in due form.'

He then asked me to bring him pen and ink from a small fancy devonport, which stood in a corner of the room, and then, calling upon us to charge our glasses in honour of his adopted son and heir, he read aloud the memorandum which had excited our curiosity:

'This is the last will and testament of me, John Boyle, at present residing at No. 9 Cheshire-villas, in the parish of Paddington, Middlesex. I hereby give, devise, and bequeath, all and singular, my property and effects, of what nature or kind soever, of or to which I may be possessed or entitled, unto my dear friend and adopted son, William Hamilton, for his own absolute use and benefit; and I hereby appoint the said William Hamilton sole executor of this my will.—Dated this twentieth day, &c.'

The astonishment with which three of us listened to this extraordinary document may be easily imagined. For myself, I could scarce believe the evidence of my own ears, and sat speechless, and as one half awakened from a dream. What first recalled me to myself was the malignant and diabolical expression that distorted the usually serene countenance of James Barclay. The civilised man had gone under—the savage was once more in the ascendant. I took in at a glance the false position in which I should be placed among Boyle's friends and associates through envy and disappointed expectations. Besides, I was never a covetous man, and, as I have already remarked, my income was quite as large as was good for me. Should I chance to want more, I felt that I could earn it without very much difficulty. Trying in vain to clear my throat and steady my voice, I implored my friend to tear up the paper; and when he, smiling sadly, shook his head, I begged the witnesses not to attest his signature, to compel him to wait until at least he had recovered his ordinary spirits, and to spare me the constraint I must always feel thereafter in the company of one whose friendship I should appear to many to have shamelessly abused. The barrister shrugged his shoulders, and quietly remarked: 'I wish I had half your complaint, old fellow.' Barclay, however, in a sneering sarcastic manner, objected to mock heroics and tinsel sentimentality. 'A man does not necessarily die,' he continued, 'because he has made his will. Sometimes, no doubt, a curious coincidence ensues, but that is not likely to happen in your case. There are such things, too, as codicils. Besides, Boyle may outlive you, or he may change his mind a dozen times. He may take to himself a wife, and surround himself with any number of olive-branches. I will sign my name with pleasure, and hope you will make a good use of the money when you get it.'

Boyle was evidently somewhat pained by the bitterness of Barclay's tone, and by the undisguised ill-feeling he manifested towards myself. The Heneages exchanged significant glances, but said nothing, while I remained silent and stupefied. The strange memorandum was then signed and witnessed, and committed to the safe custody of Henry Heneage, the solicitor. If conversation had flagged during dinner, it died away altogether after the completion of this unexpected interlude. Our host made two or three futile attempts to rally himself, but finding that no one seconded him, he told us good-humouredly that we were the dullest people he had ever met with. We neither drank nor talked, we neither laughed nor made him laugh, and from choice, he thought he would as soon be in bed. Then we all rose, and, shaking him by the hand, hoped he would be all right after a good night's rest. As we went out into the street, I overheard Boyle half whisper to the solicitor, 'Stephen is in London.' 'I feared as much,' replied the other, in a low but clear voice; 'call upon me tomorrow as you go to office—or, still better, come and breakfast with us'—for the brothers lived together. I heard no more, but when the door had closed, I said to Henry, 'I really could not help it, but I overheard what Boyle said to you. For Heaven's sake, persuade him to

cancel that will, and make a natural provision for his nephew.' He made no reply, beyond pressing my hand, and the three went off together in one direction, while I hurried home with my mind in a whirl, and my thoughts in an inextricable tangle.

II.

ONE bright spot, however, did gleam on the horizon. Happy, as I ought to have been, I was not quite contented with my lot. There were times when fancy conjured up, on the other side of my hearth, a certain bright joyous face, with the merriest smile and the whitest teeth in the world. That I could maintain a wife in reasonable comfort, I never doubted; but how about a family? I have always objected to dealing with unknown quantities, and abhor all algebraic symbols from the bottom of my heart. Moreover, I professed, in those days, to be somewhat of a Malthusian—at least in my writings. Neither was I at all confident that the young lady's parents would look benignly upon a suitor whose income, all told, seldom attained to 700*l.* a year, and one-third of that precarious. Great expectations might make all the difference, and Benedick might end by being benedict. These speculations murdered sleep. I tossed and tumbled from side to side. I threw off the counterpane and pulled it up again. I sprang out of bed, walked about the room in light attire, drank several tumblers of water, and at last, in despair, determined to dress and go out for a long walk in the cool air of a summer morning.

My little bedroom timepiece had just struck five as I completed my hasty toilet. There was a sound of hurried footsteps on the pavement, and then, almost immediately, came a fierce scratching at my street-door, accompanied by a most pitiful whining. A sudden chill struck at my heart. Undoing the fastenings with a degree of nervousness of which, even at the moment, I felt half ashamed, I opened the door, and little Fido rushed in and crouched at my feet in abject supplication. He then set up a dismal howl, which went through me like a sharp sword, and, suddenly ceasing, caught my trousers in his teeth, and began to drag me towards the door. Snatching down a hat from the hall-stand, I at once yielded, and, with rapid strides, tried in vain to keep up with the dog, who would every now and then turn back and pull at me, and then gallop on again. At the corner of the street I met a policeman whom I knew by sight, and with whom I occasionally exchanged a few words. Though somewhat afraid that he would laugh at my fears, I stopped to tell him how anxious Fido seemed that I should go to his master's house. While I was speaking, the little dog came running back to us, and tugged now at one, now at the other. 'Blest if there ain't something up there!' the constable exclaimed—a little to my satisfaction, I confess—and went off with me at a round pace towards Cheshire-villas. On the way we had to pass a house, hideous by night by reason of a red light over the door, and, almost instinctively, I pulled at the night-bell. The policeman, instead of grinning, nodded approval, and continued to follow the dog. To my intense relief an upper window was instantly thrown open, and the surgeon made his appearance, dressed for the day.

'For Heaven's sake,' I cried, 'come on as quickly as you can to Mr. Boyle's house, No. 9 Cheshire-

villas! He is either very ill, or something dreadful has happened.'

'Very well,' he answered sharply. 'I am coming as fast as I can; but Mr. Boyle is not the only sick person in the neighbourhood.'

I felt annoyed and angry, but was in no mood to waste time at such a moment. Swallowing my rising choler, I ran on, and overtook the policeman just as Fido darted down a side-road which led to the back of Boyle's house. Surprised, but without hesitation, we went after our guide, who made several futile attempts to spring on to the garden-wall, which was higher on the outer than on the inner side. Accepting his discomfiture, Fido sidled up to me, as though begging me to lift him up. Jones, the policeman, being the taller of the two, took him out of my arms and reached him up to the top of the wall, whither he himself scrambled with my assistance, and then, sitting astride, helped me to attain the same eminence. The puffy little surgeon, who had kept us in view, now arrived, panting, on the scene, and between us we pulled him up also. It was easy enough to drop down into the garden; and poor Fido was impatiently awaiting us at the back-door, which was wide open. Again he led the way, I next to him, and the policeman almost close to my side. On reaching the hall I made a dash at the bedroom-stairs, but Fido whined, and threw himself against the door of Boyle's library and usual sitting-room when alone. There we found him, lying on his face, his skull horribly shattered. The deadly weapon had been flung down carelessly after it had done its accursed work, and was lying across his legs. It was a heavy war-club from one of the South Sea Islands, taken from a rack over the mantel-piece charged with the arms of savage peoples. He was quite dead, and must have been so for several hours. His watch was missing, and the *sécrétaire* was open, the papers within having been much tumbled about.

'Can you give me any clue, sir?' asked the policeman.

'None whatever,' I replied; but as I spoke, my thoughts flew off to Stephen Jervis. 'We must send at once for the Heneages,' I continued. 'But how is it that none of the servants are moving? They must have heard our steps.'

'Likely enough,' answered Jones; 'and we shall find them under their beds.'

I went to the door to call to them, but Walters, the surgeon, intercepted me, and said, with a determined manner,

'No; you don't leave this room. Policeman, take this man into custody! I charge him with the murder of the deceased gentleman.'

For a moment I stood rooted to the spot. Then it struck me that the little man, of whom I knew nothing whatever, had been making a night of it, as the saying is, and was talking at random.

'Stand aside!' I cried somewhat imperiously. 'This is no time for fooling. We must send off one of the servants immediately to the police-station and another to poor Boyle's solicitor; he may be able to put us on the right scent.'

Instead of giving way to me, the little idiot planted his barrel of a carcass in the doorway, and again called upon Jones to do his duty and make me his prisoner. Thus adjured a second time, the policeman asked him if he had any grounds for suspecting me.

'Grounds of suspicion!' he exclaimed. 'I have proofs—proofs that will bring him to the gallows! Listen to me. I had been sitting up all night with a patient, and had just got home and undressed,

when a tremendous pull at my bell made me throw up the window and look out. There, on the pavement staring up at me, stood this fellow, his face swollen with passion, and, now I come to think of it, dressed somewhat differently from what he is at present. He struck me as being rather seedy, and he wore a sailor's wideawake instead of a hat; but I could swear to him among a thousand. "Come down directly!" he shouted, with a husky voice. "There has been foul play at No. 9 Cheshire-villas. I am off for a policeman," and with that he was off like a shot; but I also observed that little dog flying at him furiously, though he seemed to take no notice of the brute, beyond kicking at him sideways whilst speaking to me. The dog followed him when he again started off at a run. Before I could get my clothes on, he was again pulling at my bell; but in the mean time he had changed his dress and put on a hat. For all that I recognised him at a glance. Where did you get those things?' he asked.

I was quite cool and self-possessed, for now I was convinced that the murderer was Stephen and no other. So I answered, with perfect good temper,

'I am Mr. Hamilton. I reside at 17 Devonshire-road, not very far from your house. Fido and I are old friends. I was going out for a walk, and had barely opened the door when he dashed in and made me come here. I was fortunate enough to meet Jones almost directly, and told him how anxious the dog seemed that I should go with him. He at once turned back with me, and we knocked you up, to be provided against the worst. Would a murderer have acted in that way?'

'I really don't know,' he replied. 'This is the first time I have ever had to do with one, and I hope it may be the last. You have effrontery enough for a dozen; but Tom Walters is not easily imposed upon.'

'Well, Mr. Walters,' said I, still good - humouredly, 'I am quite willing to constitute myself a prisoner, and shall give Jones no trouble whatever; but will you call the servants, and especially Mrs. Davis, the housekeeper? Their rooms are on the second floor above this.'

I walked across the room to Jones, who laid hold of my cuff, after the manner of his race; and the doctor began to shout up the staircase loud enough to awaken the dead. But there was no answer.

'This is a rummy go,' said Jones; and I too felt uneasy and sick at heart.

'Go up to them, man,' I cried to Walters. 'Break in the door of their rooms, if they won't open to you.'

'They're afeard of housebreakers,' sententiously remarked Jones. 'That's about where it is.'

'Help! Help!' screamed the little man; and we both rushed up-stairs—the policeman forgetting, in the excitement of the moment, that I was supposed to be in his custody. The fact is, he never believed that I was guilty, and stuck to his belief stoutly. The housekeeper's room was empty, and it was evident that the bed had not been slept in; but in the adjoining chamber an appalling scene awaited us. The cook, who slept in a little bed close to the door, looked—except for the leaden hue of death—as though she still slept. She had been stabbed to the heart, and had died without a struggle. The other girl had been awakened, but too late to defend herself successfully. She had, however, made some sort of resistance,

for there were wounds on her hands and arms, and in her throat, with marks of fingers, as if she had been partially strangled. In her case, also, the *coup de grâce* had been a blow aimed directly at her heart; but, unlike the cook, her eyes were starting from their sockets, and her features were distorted with horror. The murderer had then washed his hands in one of the basins, and wiped them dry upon a towel. For a brief space we were all three too awe-stricken to utter a word. The wretched little doctor was the first to recover his voice. Thrusting his hand into my collar, and half throttling me, he shouted,

'You villain, you shall not escape me! Were you twice as big and strong as you are, I would drag you to the gallows, and hang you with my own hands!'

With a sudden effort, I flung him off.

'You d—d fool,' I cried, 'if you don't keep your hands to yourself, I'll pitch you over the baluster! If you want to be of use, go off to the station, and tell the inspector to come at once, with a couple of his best men. Now, Jones, let us search for Mrs. Davis. She is probably hiding in her own parlour, next to the kitchen.'

Idiot as he was, Walters had sense enough to see that I was right about giving information at the police-station, and started off at a brisk trot, after being enjoined by Jones not to say a word to anybody he might meet on the road, not even to a constable. We then proceeded to look for the housekeeper, after drawing a sheet off poor Boyle's bed, to lay over him. I forgot to mention that we had placed him on the couch, with faithful Fido at his feet, who every now and again uttered a low subdued howl of anguish. Mrs. Davis was neither in the kitchen nor in her own sitting-room, but had been struck down in the dining-room, into which she had apparently fled for her life. She had been stabbed twice in the back, close to the spine, and death may have been accelerated by horror.

Up to this time the excitement had enabled me to bear up, the necessity for action preventing me from realising what had actually happened. But now that all was known, and yet nothing could be done until the inspector arrived, I turned sick, and fell fainting into a chair. With the instinct of a sleuth-hound, Jones darted at the sideboard, upon which stood a decanter of brandy, half empty, and beside it a tumbler that had been recently used. He had too much good feeling to give me anything in that glass; but, taking another from the dinner-wagon, he poured down my throat a dose that nearly choked me, but quickly restored me to myself. The rest he tossed off in two gulps, and smacked his lips.

'As good stuff as I ever tasted in my life,' he remarked; and neither of us said another word until a cab stopped at the door.

'Thank God!' I cried. 'There they are at last!'

'Good!' he grunted. 'That sounds honest; but there's no knowing.'

While thus speaking, we had moved into the hall and opened the front-door. 'There! There he is!' screamed the odious little wretch. 'That's the villain! Seize him—hold him fast!' The inspector said something to Jones, who replied in a low tone. The former then turned to me, and told me civilly enough that, from what Mr. Walters had stated, he must take me into custody, but, if I made no resistance, he would not put the handcuffs on me. I drew back in horror. For the first time

the sense of my position came upon me; but the knowledge of my perfect innocence sustained me, and with the renewed necessity for action I recovered my self-possession. I acknowledged the inspector's forbearance with heartfelt thanks, and expressed my desire to afford him every assistance in my power. At the same time, I reiterated my wish that a messenger should be despatched without further delay to the two Heneages; and the cab was accordingly sent for them, the driver being instructed to bid them come in all haste, as a serious accident had happened to the gentleman at No. 9 Cheshire-villas. They declared to me afterwards that, when they received the cabman's message, they looked at one another, but said never a word until they arrived at Boyle's villa, and found their worst apprehensions more than confirmed.

Of course I was driven off to the police-station, and locked up in a cell by myself. In vain did the Heneages assure the surgeon that they could answer for me as for themselves, that they were certain of my innocence, and had reason to believe that they could name the actual murderer. The inspector mused for a moment or two, and then said, in a somewhat oracular tone,

'If this gentleman is innocent, as you and Jones seem to think, a few hours' detention won't do him much harm, but it will do us much good.'

'How so?' I asked.

'Because it will throw the other off his guard. As soon as he learns that suspicion does not point towards himself, he will do something foolish.'

'All right,' I replied. 'Lock me up, then, by all means.'

III.

LET me not forget poor Fido. As I stepped into the cab at Boyle's door, he sprang in after me, and, standing on my knees with his forepaws on my shoulders, he licked my face, moaning between times. One of the policemen wanted to turn him out; but the little fellow bristled up like a wild-boar, snarled, and showed his teeth. 'Let him be—let him be,' said Jones. 'He is a witness for the defence.' I felt grateful to him for his thoughtfulness, but still more so when he brought a cup of water to my cell. I tried to slip a sovereign into his hands, but he refused to take it. 'Not now, sir. Not now, if you please. When you are back again in your own house I will drink your health with pleasure.' However, he took a half-crown piece to get a cup of coffee for myself and a piece of boiled liver for Fido, and I was not troubled with any small change.

As soon as possible I was driven to the police-court, charged, on the testimony of Mr. Thomas Walters, surgeon, with the murder of my dearest friend, John Boyle, of his housekeeper, and of his two servants. The court was crowded, a rumour having somehow gone abroad that a gentleman had been taken up for murdering a whole family near Westbourne-grove. Jones gave his evidence in an honest straightforward manner, which drew from me an expression of entire acquiescence when the magistrate asked me if I wished to put any questions to the witness. The inspector, of course, had little to say that could throw any light upon the perpetration of the crime; but his prepossession was so clearly in my favour that I could not help bowing to him, and saying, 'Thank you.' Very differ-

ent was the tendency of the statement volunteered by the surgeon. One would have thought that the deceased was his nearest and dearest relative, and that I had done him personally a foul wrong. The magistrate was more than once obliged to desire him to confine himself to facts within his own knowledge, and to avoid comments and, above all, abusive epithets. Neither Henry Heneage nor myself could shake his conviction that I was the individual who, dressed somewhat shabbily, and with a sailor's cap on his head, had given him the first intimation of foul play. And when the police produced a sou'-wester that they had found hanging on my hat-rail, and which, in a weak moment, I had purchased at Ramsgate, he swore positively to its identity. The other clothes had not been found, but the search was still going on for them. My own servants, though quite unwittingly, did me some harm by stating, in reply to the magistrate's inquiries, that I was not usually an early riser, and that they had been surprised, on going down-stairs about seven o'clock, to find my bedroom-door wide open and the street-door unfastened. My case took a still worse turn when Mr. Barclay, whom the Heneages had summoned, under the impression that he would testify to the intimate friendship which existed between the deceased and myself, purposely overshot the mark by relating the incident which occurred after dinner on the previous evening. For the moment the remembrance of Boyle's almost paternal kindness so thoroughly unnerved me that I failed to see the mischievous drift of Barclay's revelation, until I observed the malicious smile on his lip and the evil twinkle in his eye. The two Heneages smothered an indignant exclamation; but the magistrate scrutinised me keenly, and even Jones looked disconcerted. Instinctively aware, perhaps from my emotion, that something had gone wrong, little Fido, who had been suffered to lie in my arms, climbed up against my chest, and began licking my face. The tears stood in my eyes at this demonstration of attachment and fidelity, and involuntarily I pressed him close to my breast. That simple action saved me from much shame; for the magistrate was already talking to his clerk about my committal. Until Barclay appeared upon the scene there was no conceivable explanation of the conduct ascribed to me by Walters; but now a motive had been shown, and, for obvious reasons, the Heneages hesitated as yet to disclose their suspicions of Stephen Jervis. But in drawing Fido away from my face, I had caused him to look over my shoulder, when his keen bright eyes caught sight of a face he knew too well. Suddenly he howled in a tone that thrilled through every one, and, struggling out of my arms, he clambered upon my shoulders and leaped down to the floor. Worming his way through the crowd, he sprang at a man who stood in a corner of the court, but had exhibited an interest in the proceedings that caused some annoyance to the *habitués* of the place, one of whom had already told him that he was 'no gentleman' to make so much fuss about nothing. The intelligent Jones had watched Fido's movements with interest, and no sooner saw him fasten his teeth upon a dissolute-looking scoundrel than he was by his side, and ready to support the four-footed detective. The fellow was so confounded by the unexpectedness of the attack, that he cried out, 'Down, Fido! Down!'

'So you know him?' remarked Jones interrogatively. 'Come forward, my man, and tell the court all about it.'

'What is the meaning of all that noise?' asked the magistrate. 'Officers, clear the court if there is any further interruption. Well, what now? Who is this?' as Jones half-led, half-dragged Fido's captive to the front.

'Seize that man!' shouted the two Heneages, with one breath. 'That's he! That's he! That's the murderer!'

'God bless me!' murmured Walters. 'I have done a great wrong. Sir, sir, I have sworn falsely! That is the man who first came to me this morning. I could swear to him anywhere—to his dress—to his cap—to his wicked bloated face.'

I was so disgusted with him that, on the spur of the moment, I said, 'You will swear to anything. Half an hour ago you swore it was I who came to you, and now you swear it is that drunken wretch.'

What made me so savage was the idea that any man in his senses could have mistaken that broken-down vagabond, with bloodshot eyes and chalky face, for myself. That there was an extraordinary likeness in our features I could not even then avoid recognising; but surely there is a vast difference between an habitual criminal down on his luck and a gentleman so eminently respectable in appearance—although he did write for the papers—that he might have passed for a churchwarden or a director of a City company. The magistrate looked hard at me for a moment, and slightly smiled as he read my thoughts; but his attention was diverted to Jones, who held up in triumph a gold watch he had adroitly extracted from one of the trousers-pockets of the new prisoner. The watch had been presented to Boyle on his last birthday by the Heneages and myself, as was attested by an inscription engraved inside the cover.

Stephen Jervis—for of course it was he—stared at me, as though bewildered and stupefied, and then, by a rapid movement freeing his right arm from the constable who held him on that side, he drew a long sharp-bladed knife from his breast, and drove it into his chest with such force that he could not draw it out again. The wound, however, touched no vital part, and a healthy man would soon have recovered from it. It nevertheless proved fatal in a few days to a man whose constitution had been destroyed by excesses, and who even then was subject to frequent and terrible attacks of *delirium tremens.* In his lucid moments he seemed to find a strange pleasure in dilating upon the minutest details of that fearful night. He stated that on his return to England he had written to his uncle for assistance, and had received a five-pound note, with a prohibition to apply for further aid in that quarter. He determined, therefore, to see him personally and make one more appeal to his old feelings. Unwilling to be seen in that neighbourhood, and perhaps recognised, he had put off his visit until about the time his uncle usually retired for the night. He met the Heneages and Mr. Barclay, but slunk past them without being noticed, as they were seemingly engaged in very earnest conversation. Poor Boyle must have strolled down to the road after we left, for he was standing at the gate of the carriage-sweep in front of his house, gazing abstractedly into space. He started and made for the door, when he first became conscious of his nephew's presence; but stopped, turned round, and spoke to him kindly and pityingly.

'Uncle, my dear uncle!' sobbed the poor wretch. 'Hear me for one minute! Give me one more chance! You will never repent it. I swear to you I will do whatever you wish me to do.'

His uncle hesitated for a moment, and then made a sign to him to follow. Taking him into his library, he went to the top of the kitchen-stairs, and called to one of the servants.

'Tell Mrs. Davis,' he said, 'that nobody need sit up for me. I shall be engaged some time with a gentleman, and wish not to be disturbed.'

The damsels must then have taken themselves off to bed; but, for one reason or another, the housekeeper could not have followed their example. Stephen protested that when he entered the house he had no idea of harming any one. He only wanted his uncle to advance him a little money, and allow him a small sum weekly until he could do something for himself. At first, he said, his uncle was much affected and wept bitterly. He agreed to give him the twenty pounds he asked for, and to make him an allowance of three pounds a week for six months. He then began to question Stephen as to his plans and projects; but when he found that his nephew had formed no designs of any kind beyond 'looking about to see if anything would turn up,' he spoke harshly, and warned him that he would do no more than he had promised, adding that he had made his will and left his property to one who would make a good use of it. This imprudent avowal filled Stephen with rage and despair. When his uncle turned his back to go to the *sécrétaire,* he rose noiselessly from his chair, took down the club which was close at hand, and with two strides came up with his victim, and struck him down at his feet. With two more blows he despatched him, and then flung down the deadly weapon. As he did so, the door opened. Whether

Mrs. Davis had been tempted by curiosity to listen at the keyhole, or whether, in passing, she had been alarmed by the noise of her master's fall, will never be known; but there she stood, dismayed and horrified. Screaming aloud, and dropping her candlestick, she ran wildly into the dining-room, closely followed by Stephen with that formidable knife in his hand. He struck at her two terrible blows, and she never moved again. He then retraced his steps, picked up the candlestick, and lighting the broken candle at the gas-lamp in the library, went back to the dining-room, as he said, to 'finish his job.' He had done his work only too well.

Tormented by thirst, and seeing the key in the cellaret, he helped himself to half a tumbler of raw brandy. His next proceeding was to secure his uncle's watch and purse, and to take from the *sécrétaire* a pocket-book containing half-a-dozen five-pound notes. Some time was spent in examining his uncle's papers, in the hope of finding the will referred to so unfortunately; but all at once he fancied he heard a noise overhead. Stealing softly up-stairs, he came to the servants' bedroom, and, in an evil moment, opened the door. The dawn was already breaking, but the women slept soundly. When he came to this part of his narrative the unhappy man began to rave incoherently, and yet his story was all too plain. 'I could not help it!' he gasped. 'The Brandy Devil—I had not seen him since—well, it don't matter—since a long time ago in Australia—he made me do it—he pointed to the bed and showed me how to do it. Then he woke the other, and I would have run away, but he caught me and held me, and—and—that is all I know about it.'

And what was poor Fido doing all this time? At first the faithful beast was overjoyed at the return of the prodigal, his former master, who had left him in his uncle's kindlier keeping. But as the demonstrativeness of the affectionate animal grew troublesome, Boyle opened the door and ordered him off to bed. Fido wagged his tail and obediently trotted up-stairs to his master's room, and, no doubt, had jumped on to the bed and curled himself up in his usual place at the foot. Anyhow Stephen saw nothing more of him until he came down from his awful butchery on the upper floor. As he passed his uncle's room, Fido ran out after him, and joyously scampered down to the library. There he stopped and stood like a pointer. Crawling up to the prostrate body, he went all round it, sniffing at it and trembling in every limb. Then he gave three piercing yells.

'I could stand anything but that,' raved the dying wretch. 'The Brandy Devil stood jeering at me, and pointing at—at—that thing—and the dog grew bigger and bigger —till I thought he would tear me to pieces and eat me. I fled—down-stairs—to the back-door—into the garden—and over the wall. There was the dog, bigger and bigger. I ran away from him, but he followed till I saw a red eye—all fire—it was the Brandy Devil's! I pulled at a bell for help—a round-faced man said something from a window—and I said something—and the dog flew at me; but I ran away, and he left me.'

Growing quieter after a while, he went on to say that he began to feel weak, and thought he was going to die, when he came upon a coffee-stand and drank two big cups that scalded his throat. The men standing about laughed, but slunk away when he looked at them. After that he got a bed somewhere, and slept for three or four hours, and when he awoke it was as if he had had a bad dream. However, he went down to the coffee-room and tried to eat some breakfast; but he could not swallow anything but brandy, which was brought in from somewhere outside, and the girl who fetched it said that a murder had been committed in a street not far off, and that the murderer was caught by a dog and held till a policeman came up and took him into custody. He was a gentleman, and confessed that he had killed everybody in the house.

'Then I knew,' said Stephen, with a ghastly laugh, 'that the Brandy Devil had saved me, as he told me he would when I was asleep. So I went to the police-court to see what he had done for me, and there I saw myself as I was—ah, it's many years ago—and I wanted to get away, for I thought he' (pointing to me) 'would disap-pear and then they would catch me; but I durst not move: the dog was there, and I knew, if he saw me, he would tear me to pieces.'

In this way he would ramble and rave by the hour together, when the fit was upon him, but on the fourth day he was at rest.

What remains to be told? Barclay has been cut by all our friends. Walters sold his practice and went elsewhere. Jones is no longer a policeman; neither do I reside in Westbournia. The Heneages mostly spend Sunday with us—I mean with Mary and myself; she is their cousin, you must know—in our pretty villa by the river-side. But I have lost my taste for journalism, and taken to grafting rose-trees. Fido is the real master of the establishment, and is somewhat of a tyrant. At all events, he has his own way in most things.

THE PEASANT'S VISIT TO THE CZAR.

I was but an earth-born peasant,
  All my life a trampled slave,
Till there came a joyful message
  Of the gift our father gave :

We were free ! the golden sunrise
  On us, bondsmen of the clod,
Opened in a field of glory,
  We were free !   Then prayed we, ' God,

Bless our sovereign Alexander
  For the good gift of his hand ;
Though too late for us, our children
  Shall be freemen of this land !'

Twenty years had aged and bowed me .
  Since that joy of long ago,
When I saw the blood-red sunset
  Glare upon the field of snow ;

When there came a sound of wailing
  To the village of the plain,
To our holy city Moscow,
  That our lord the Czar was slain.

Then our eyes that ne'er beheld him
  Wept for sorrow, and we said,
' We will travel forth together,
  We will look upon him dead.'

To the city of St. Peter,
  All the long and weary way,
With my mates I journeyed, sleepless,
  All the night and all the day.

When we neared the great cathedral
  Where they watched him as he lay—
Priests in sable robes and silver,
  Warrior chiefs in bright array—

They made way for us, poor peasants,
  And we fell beside his bier ;
Thrice our foreheads struck the pavement
  Wet with many a bitter tear.

Then they swept aside the garlands
  Where his coffin lay beneath;
On the bosom of our father
  Did we place our humble wreath,

On the heart of our deliverer,
  On our martyr! Sore we wept—
From his face the veil was lifted,
  And we saw him as he slept.

Long we gazed, in stone-like wonder,
  As cold fear had stopped our breath:
Thrice we bent the knee in homage,
  And we kissed his hand in death.

Snows had blanched his beard, his temples
  Wreathed about with snow-white flowers;
Cares of Empire pressed upon him
  With a heavier load than ours.

Traces of the crime that slew him
  Seamed his eyelid and his cheek;
But those lips had met destruction
  With a smile so calm, so meek!

He was glad to burst the harness
  That had galled him in the strife;
For the grave and birth hereafter
  To exchange the worn-out life.

They who did that cruel murder
  Might have melted at the sight;
They may call him an oppressor,
  They may talk of human right.

In that day when all the accursèd
  Shall depart from God's right hand,
'Gainst the faults of power and nature
  One blest deed of his shall stand.

Yes, I knew the fire had tried him
  By the look on his dead face;
Twice he bore the curse of Adam
  Thronèd in the highest place.

Yes, these eyes have seen our father;
  Where the holy lamps burn dim,
I, who ne'er beheld him living,
  Looked upon the last of him!

                  EMILIA AYLMER BLAKE.

STRAWBERRY LEAVES.

By RICHARD DOWLING,

AUTHOR OF 'THE MYSTERY OF KILLARD,' 'THE WEIRD SISTERS,
'UNDER ST. PAUL'S,' ETC.

Part the First.

THE DUKE OF LONGACRE.

CHAPTER XVI.

ON THE ROCKS.

GRADUALLY the group on the ledge of land hard by the cottages increased as the yacht drew nearer. A few women joined the men, and the talk about the yacht and its owner became general. Cheyne stood a little apart, within hearing, to leeward. The yacht was still half a league from the shore, heading for the bay.

'She has got as much as she wants now,' said one of the men.

'Ay, and a trifle more.'

'As fine a sea-boat as ever swam!'

'Ay, ay; but this is near as big a gale as ever blew.'

'O! There's her keel from the bow to the foremast!'

'And there it is from the rudder to the main chains!'

'She'll pick up her moorings in a quarter of an hour.'

'And I don't think any one aboard will be sorry when she's in smooth water.'

'Especially the Duke. For my part, I don't like even looking on, and I'd like it still less, only I know she's fit for it, and only plays with it. Fancy how an old collier would behave in a gale like that. It's very well the sea is no worse, or it might poop her.'

'Poop her with that way on! You are a fresh-water sailor, you are!'

'But suppose she made a stern bound?'

'Or flew over the moon?'

'But if she carried away her mainsail she'd pay off, and then she might be pooped.'

'If the sky fell, we'd catch larks. Get along with you, for a mud-pilot!'

'I daresay they're all on deck.'

'Every soul of them. Why, who could stay below in a gale like that? Everything in her is jumping about like dice in a dice-box.'

'They haven't a plate or a cup or a saucer left whole, I'll warrant.'

'What odds about the cups and saucers, so long as the Duke—God bless him!—is safe.'

'And the men.'

'And the men too—and the men too!'

By this time the Seabird was within a few cables' length of the southern or cliff side of the opening to Silver Bay. She was now keeping a little more to windward than she absolutely wanted, and, according to a landsman's eye, it might seem Captain Drew meant to run his ship ashore about the middle of the reef. But when you have your vessel well in hand, and know all about her being a little to windward of where you want to fetch is like having a fine unencumbered estate and a large balance at your banker's, after paying the last penny you can be called upon for.

'Time for him to port now,' said one of the men on shore.

'Nice of a mud-pilot like you to teach Captain Drew how to bring the Seabird into Silver Bay! Why, if you were an admiral you'd teach the ships how to graze on the side of mountains, and the marines how to furl a t'gallant sail, you would!'

'Port!' cried Captain Drew. He was standing by the weather bulwark, abreast of the companion. 'Hard a port!' he added.

'Port!' cried Pritchard, who was again at the wheel, as being the best helmsman aboard. The wheel flew round. 'Hard a port it is!' called out Pritchard mechanically. The wheel had gone round, and it ought to have ported the helm; but he knew very well it had not. It had spun around as though nothing had been attached to it. When the first few spokes had been put down, the wheel had suddenly run away in the direction he had been forcing it. He looked instantly behind him, sprang forward to where the captain stood, and whispered in a choked hoarse voice:

'She won't answer, sir. The cap-iron's gone!'

'All hands aft! Cut away mainsail!' sang out the captain.

Two men sprang into the main rigging, and went up upon the lee side hand-over-hand. Two men sprang on the peak of the gaff, and scrambled up. Three men got out on the boom, and in less than three minutes the mainsail had been cut adrift, and was rolled far away down to leeward.

'Your grace,' said the captain, 'the rudder-head iron is gone, and I have ordered them to cut away the mainsail.'

'Good God!' exclaimed the Duke, who had heard the order, and guessed that something had gone terribly wrong with the rudder-head. 'Then we are all lost!'

'She may pay off enough to fetch in,' said the captain.

'She will not,' said the Duke.

'She will not,' thought the captain; but he held his peace.

By this time the men on shore had become aware something was wrong. They had seen the men spring aft, and cut away the mainsail. They had seen the man at the wheel leave it, and they had not seen him or any other man return to his place. From the fact of cutting away the mainsail, and leaving the wheel untended, they came to the conclusion some accident had befallen the steering gear. For a while there was nothing but startled looks and violent exclamations, which to Cheyne conveyed no clear idea beyond the fact that some kind of danger assailed the schooner.

The first word of definite import which Cheyne caught was spoken by a powerful-looking man of forty. He said,

'She'll never pay off fast enough. She'll be on the rocks in five minutes.'

This announcement was received by a low moan, which told too plainly that there was no gainsaying the words of the speaker.

Upon hearing these words, Cheyne moved up more closely to the group.

'Where will she come ashore?' he asked.

'On the reef, man,' answered a fisherman hotly; for no man who knows of such things likes to talk at such times.

Cheyne moved back to his old position, and fixed his eyes upon the doomed schooner.

The men and women assembled on the ledge of ground, on the northern side of Silver Bay, knew too well there was no lifeboat or rocket apparatus within fifteen miles, yet still there was no good in giving way to despair. The yacht was unmistakably going ashore in a few minutes on those rocks. There was little or no hope she could hold together there for anything like the time it would take to send word from Silverview to Bankleigh by horse, and from Bankleigh to the lifeboat station by telegraph, and then have the boat or apparatus round. Yet no chance, however slight, ought to be neglected; and accordingly, before another minute had elapsed, the swiftest man of the group was on his way at the top of his speed to the Castle, to give the alarm, and order the immediate despatch of the fleetest horse in the Duke's stables to Bankleigh.

Once more Cheyne drew near the group of men and women, and listened.

'What can be done when she strikes?' asked one of the women of one of the men.

'Nothing that we know of.'

'Couldn't a boat go off to her?' asked the woman.

'No boat ever built could live in those breakers, except a life-boat.'

'Could not a line be got to her?'

'How are you to get a line to her? We have no rocket or cannon here. There is no chance for them but to swim.'

'Swim!' cried the woman, in terror. 'How could any one swim in that sea, and where would any one swim to?'

'Hush!' said the man impressively, and for a minute all were mute.

The schooner plunged onward through the foam, for she was already in the white outwash from the shore and threw it madly from her bows. She was now showing nothing to the wind but a storm-jib; and although she was paying off, she was paying off too slowly to give any grounds for hope. She had her anchors still, no doubt; but to let go her anchors under her nose in such a sea and with such a way on would be the wildest act of madness. They would drag her nose under or tear the bows out of her, capsize her the moment she broached to and came athwart the sea. Better the rocks than the anchors.

And those rocks looked terrible: huge spikes and feline teeth, over which mounted and broke the irregular billows, white with the sullen back-wash of former waves. When the wallowing billows flung themselves mercilessly upon the rocks, the white spray toiled slowly upward, like hopeless signals of distress.

The ill-fated yacht was now within a cable's length of destruction. There was nothing to be done but hold on, await the end, and take advantage of everything in favour of one's life.

The men were all clinging to the fore-rigging at the weather side. The two mates, the captain, the Marquis, and the Duke clung to the after-rigging on the same side. Absolutely nothing could be done. If there had been a little more time, they might have tried the effect of a little more head-sail on her.

At length one huge wave seized her, flung her aloft, and threw her, as a giant might cast a mighty javelin, upon the rocks. There was a tremendous shock, a mighty crunching sound, an explosion like a cannon when the deck burst up in the waist, the scream of torn metal, the groan of yielding planks and timbers, the loud plunging swash of the water—all in a conflict of broken torrents hidden under a pall of blinding spray that rose over the wreck like smoke over the victim of a sacrifice.

'Her back is broken,' said one

of the men on shore standing close to where Cheyne was.

When those on shore could see more clearly, they agreed that the vessel was of course a total wreck, but that the hopes of saving those on board were much better than they had had any reason to hope for.

She had, it was true, broken her back; and as she had struck the rock about amidships, and her fore part was firmly wedged in between two rocks, and her after part hung over the ledge of rocks on which she lay, it was most likely the after half would very soon fall off. But it might be fairly counted that the fore part would last some time. The foremast still stood, but the jib had been blown away. No fisherman on the shore thought for a moment the fore part of the Sea-bird could possibly hold out until the arrival of the lifeboat; but five minutes ago the chances were the schooner would be in staves in ten minutes. Now half of her might be reckoned on to last an hour or two, and in an hour or two—well, there was less certainty of all of them being drowned than if she went to pieces in five minutes.

The two mates, the captain, the Marquis, and the Duke had all gone forward and secured themselves to the weather fore-rigging.

Before many minutes had elapsed, the yacht broke in two, the after part settling down in deep water.

CHAPTER XVII.

VOLUNTEER I.

IN some respects the position in which lay all now above water of the Seabird was favourable to those on board. When she struck she had had a heavy list to port. As she had struck, so she settled down with a strong list to port. Thus

her high shoulder was against the weather, and every sea did not sweep her deck. It so happened that the weather side of the fore rigging was in the lee of one of the rocks between which she was jambed. Thus the heavy broadside wash of the water did not reach the men, but only the thick spray of waves which broke on the sea-face of that rock, and the spray of the waves that struck her aft.

There was no chance whatever of landing on these rocks. They were almost perpendicular, tapering so as to yield no hold for the foot or hand, and at their bases was deep water surging tumultuously up and down. Once in water on the outer face of that reef, nothing could save a man in such a gale and sea. His arms, his ribs, his head, would be smashed against those pitiless fangs of gray smooth stone. These teeth-like rocks rested on an irregular bed of flatter rocks; but this bed was visible only at low water, and the tide would now be at its greatest height in an hour, or, taking the wind into consideration, an hour and three quarters.

Three of the crew were natives of the little hamlet, and their wives were spectators of their husbands' danger.

'For God's sake, men, can't you do anything?'

'Anything!' repeated a man sadly, pointing his arm to the sheer inner wall of the reef. 'What could mortal man do there?'

The inner side of the reef differed from the outer one in being much more regular and straight. It was a wall of low spires, with here and there an opening down to the water, through which the foam-mantled sea shot shafts of hissing water. No human hand or foot could rest upon any part of that inner wall now in view. Nothing grew or lived on the shore-ward side of that reef; not weed or barnacle or mussel. There was nothing to rest on, nothing to cling to, nothing but the cold clean side of the pitiless gray stone.

'Can nothing be done? Can nothing be done?' asked the woman, wringing her hands helplessly. 'Are my babies to be made orphans, while you all stand idle there? If you can't do anything to save the men, you might in all decency turn your backs, and not let them see you with your hands in your pockets in front of their own doors, while they are drowning under your very eyes!'

The men drew aside from where the women stood, and held a brief council.

Meanwhile Cheyne hardly moved. He was sheltered from the full violence of the wind, but now and then a gust burst in upon him, striking him full in front. He could see all the figures on the deck, and he had heard the people say that the undersized man, with the fur-cap tied over his ears, was the great Duke, and the tall lank man behind him was the Marquis of Southwold. His thoughts ran:

What an extraordinary thing fate was! Here was he, as it were by a mere accident, awaiting the arrival of that yacht which for years had sought and found safety in this harbour, and, by an extraordinary coincidence, that yacht would never enter this harbour again.

For the first time in all his life, he had formed the design of committing fatal violence upon a fellow human being, and here was that human being withheld from the sphere of his vengeance by an appalling disaster. Was this man to be snatched from his clutches now that he was in sight? Was there no means of rescuing this crew? There was a double source of regret in seeing those men helpless on the vessel, and these men helpless here. It was a pity to see the good and useful lives of the sailors in danger; and it was a pity that, after all, this man was about to escape his natural and most just vengeance.

After a somewhat lengthened council, the knot of fishermen broke up. It was plain they had come to the decision of making some effort on behalf of the unfortunate men in peril. Two men went immediately towards the cottages; each one entered his own. The man who came out first carried a long coil of light line, and when the other man, whose name was Bence, appeared, he had nothing on but his under-clothing.

'Bravo, Bence!' cried the men, with a cheer.

They made the line fast round his waist, and in another moment he had plunged into the sea.

The dangers and difficulties he faced were enormous. Although, to the mind of a sailor, the water inside the reef was smooth water to a landsman it seemed tempested. No open boat could possibly swim in it, for the cross-swells and huge choppings formed by the rush of water through the long narrow slits between the rocks would swamp any ordinary small boat, such as those at the command of the fisherman. Besides, the fierce wind bursting through the clefts would almost blow a small boat out of the water. The anchorage for the yacht and the fishing-boats was not close in under the reef, but some way inland in the bay, where, in case of storms, the sea became regular once more, and any decked vessel might roll lazily too and fro in security through the strongest north-east wind that ever blew.

The swimmer had to contend with a great number of discouraging circumstances. The only thing in his favour was that the water was not very cold. It was his interest to keep as close as possible to the rocks, for ultimately he had to try and force his way through one of the openings between them. How this was to be done, no man there could tell. A man could only try and fail, and be pulled ashore, dead or alive, if he failed.

The first of these narrow openings he met he passed without any disagreeable experience. But just as he got under the second one the creamy foam-mantled water dashed through it, and, striking him, turned him round and round in the water, and drove him a long way out of his course.

He recovered himself quickly, and was soon swimming obliquely for the reef again.

He had not got more than five times his own length when he encountered the spent torrent from another opening. This did not turn him over, but it drove him still further away from the reef.

Another difficulty now was added. Every time a wave burst through one of those openings, the torrent from it caught the line and drew Bence away from his right course. He felt this tug him, pluck him from the straight course, and, although he was not discouraged, he knew the disappointment of men not full of resources when, in moments of anxious endeavour, they meet obstacles they are not prepared for.

However, he set his heart manfully to the work, and still kept on obliquely for the reef. But he gained no ground. He rather lost. Six of these openings had to be passed, and three out of the six had delivered the spent force of their torrents against him.

As he got further and further from the shore, he had a longer line to drag through the water, and a greater quantity of the line became exposed to the disturbing influence of the six currents. So that, when he came opposite the seventh opening, the one through which he should pass with the rope, he was many hundred yards to leeward, and a good deal spent. The original line had been run out long ago, and other lines had been bent on. But now, when he turned about to swim straight for the goal, or rather for the rock at the northern side of the opening he desired to gain, for it was essential he should keep in the slack water, he had an enormous weight of line to drag through the water and against those six adverse currents.

But Bence had a big heart and a good cause, and he knew his mates on shore were watching him with pride as he tried to fight the wind and tide in the interest of humanity. Bence was a hero, not a fool; and although he had, from motives of pure humanity, volunteered to try and carry the line to what remained visible of the Seabird, he did not hide from himself that one of the richest men in England was on board that wreck, and that if he were the means of saving that man's life he might look on his fortune as made.

He swam with all his might, but made little or no progress. Now and then he looked over his shoulder at some mark on the shore, to find he was not making more than a third of what he had counted upon. Into every stroke he put all his skill and all his vigour. He began to wonder whether his strength would last until he reached the reef. Even if he had strength enough to reach the reef and then found himself with no reserve he could do nothing, for the work to be done on the reef itself was almost as arduous as that to be done in the water. The perilous passage through the rock had to be forced before those on board could throw him a rope.

With the dogged determination

to fight out to the last, he swam on. He had arranged before leaving that when he threw up his right hand those on shore were to haul in ; when he did that he had been vanquished.

At length, after a desperate struggle, he reached the reef, and paused here a moment to rest, treading the water in the shelter of a rock where there was a slight backwater. But the backwater acting on his body was not enough to overcome the strain of the water on the line, and he found himself losing ground slowly. This ground had been too dearly won to be lightly lost now. The moment had arrived for the supreme effort. He must force that passage at once, or give up all hope of success.

Having pulled in some of the slack of the rope by a few vigorous strokes, and waited until the water of a wave swept past him, he fronted the opening.

The opening was little more than wide enough to admit a man. He was nearly spent, and owing to the narrowness of the passage, he was obliged to change the ordinary arm-stroke for 'dog-fashion,' and this caused him a loss. But then when he could touch the rocks, and although they were as smooth as polished marble, he was able to get a purchase on them, and force himself forward more successfully than if he had been swimming in the ordinary way in ordinary water.

But when he looked up the cleft through which he had to make his way, his spirit failed him. It was at least fifty feet long, and straight as a gun-barrel. At the exterior mouth it was wider than at the interior. Hence, as the water rushed through, it would gain in force and height. Who could withstand such a rush of water? Who, so spent as he, could hope to stem the fierce fury of that on-rush of water?

These thoughts passed almost instantaneously through his mind. He had made only four strokes after entering the cleft when he heard the next wave burst upon the beach, and saw the hoary head of the bore rushing down upon him.

He prepared to dive. But the fierce waters struck his head and shoulders before he was under water, and threw him upright in the water, turned him over on his back, and shot him head foremost from the cleft into the open water beyond. Then the torrent turned him over and over until he was half stunned, and when, at last, he came to the surface, he had only enough strength and consciousness to hold up his arm, the signal of recall.

The men on shore pulled the line with a will; and in a short time Bence, the best swimmer of the village, was drawn ashore, defeated, insensible.

'Send for a doctor at once,' said Cheyne, in a quiet tone.

The people, to whom by this time had been added many servants from the Castle, stared at the stranger in unpleasant surprise. Who was he that should give orders to them when their own lord and master, their husbands, and their brothers, were in danger?

Cheyne spoke with the easy confidence of one who knew he would be obeyed.

'Groom,' he continued, 'take a dog-cart, and don't spare the horse. Bring back a doctor with you. Mind, not the best, but the nearest! We shall have other cases presently.' And he pointed towards the yacht.

'Not a soul will come ashore alive out of her,' said one of the fishermen.

'How long will it take you to go and come?' asked Cheyne of the groom.

'An hour,' said the groom.

'Don't be any longer. By that time there will be work for him.'

The groom hesitated a moment.

Cheyne nodded a dismissal to him, turned his back upon him, threw down his hat, and began undressing.

The men drew closer, until they made a ring round him.

He spoke in his former tone of easy confidence.

'Let the men take that anchor there up to the knoll, dig a hole for the fluke, and back it up with a grapnel—two claws buried.'

'Why, sir,' said one of the men doubtingly, 'what are you going to do?'

'When the whip comes ashore, make it fast to the ring of that anchor, and make the hawser, when it comes ashore, fast to the same ring. I can see nothing else that will do. We'll manage the rest aboard. When all is fast, you will haul the men ashore one by one in a coal-basket. Now then, look alive! Make that line fast round my waist.'

'But it would be murder to let you go when Bence has failed.'

'By —, if any man tries to let me in this, there will be murder! Do you hear?' he roared, at the top of his voice, as he drew himself up like a lion at bay, and shook himself ominously. It was a startling oath, a startling transition of tone and manner from the tone and manner of a moment before.

'Give me the line,' he cried, 'you palsied idiots! Give me the line and half a pound of sheet-lead!'

The man who held the line handed it to him mechanically.

One of the women whose husbands were in the yacht ran to her cottage and returned, in a few seconds, with a long narrow strip of sheet-lead, such as fishermen use for making net-sinkers.

'How far below the present level of the water is there rock in those open places?' Cheyne asked, as he made the line fast around his waist.

'Two fathom,' answered one of the men.

The men were by this time fairly taken aback and submissive.

Cheyne measured off three fathoms on the line from the place where the line was made fast to his waist, and rapidly rolled on the line a piece of sheet-lead weighing more than half a pound. This he tightened on the line by biting it hard; and, having ascertained that the lead would not slip easily, he walked over to the edge of the little quay, and, having told the men who tended the line to pay-out freely—in fact, never check it —he dived into the turbulent sea.

CHAPTER XVIII.

VOLUNTEER II.

CHEYNE had been a careful and intelligent spectator of Bence's failure, and he had learnt two of the great causes of it.

In the first place he had seen that Bence swam at such a distance from the openings as not to receive the full force of the bore, but at the same time to be very much thrown out of his course by the spent water.

In the second place he had noticed that at least half Bence's difficulty arose from the rope he towed getting into these currents, and dragging him still more out of his course.

In both these cases were precious time and enormous labour thrown away. It occurred to Cheyne that both sources of loss could be easily avoided. If the swimmer kept under the absolute shelter of the rocks, close to them as possible where there was a slight backwater, and waited to swim across the open spaces until all the force of the wave had been spent and the water in front of the opening was still, he would avoid any loss of way owing to the former cause in Bence's case.

If, instead of towing a long slack-line after him, he could manage so as to cause the line to sink almost perpendicularly from his waist to a depth below the influence of the water rushing through these openings, then the line, if allowed to run freely out at the shore end, would lie straight behind the swimmer.

Now that he was in the water he struck out for the reef, keeping as close to the northern shore as possible, in order to avoid any direct influence of the currents from the reef, and in order to get the advantage of the backwater, if there should happen to be any.

When he reached the reef he swam in under the rock, and there awaited the bore. When the water had subsided he made a few vigorous strokes, and crossed the open without losing a foot of ground. Adopting the same plan at the next open, he passed it with equal success.

'He knows how to go about it,' said one of the men on the shore.

'And he's a powerful swimmer.'

'He'll be as fresh as a daisy when he gets to number seven.'

'Ay, but how is he to get through number seven?' asked Bence, who had by this time been restored to consciousness, and comforted with warm dry clothes and brandy.

'Leave it to him. When a man makes a good beginning like that, it isn't for any one to doubt him until he shows that he's weak. That's what I say.'

'And what I say,' retorted Bence, 'is, that no one who has not been in one of the guts does not know what they are.'

'Well, we sha'n't be much longer in doubt; he's at number seven now.'

From the time Cheyne left the shore, he had not, owing to his keeping so close to the rocks, been able to see even the topmast of the Seabird.

He paused under the last rock for a while—not to rest himself, for he felt no fatigue, but to consider what he should do.

He first of all resolved to look into the opening. He waited until the water had rushed through, then swam in front of it, and looked in. He was a much bigger man than Bence, and the first thought which occurred to him was, Could he squeeze himself through? At a mere glance it appeared as if he could not; but upon a closer examination and reflection, he came to the conclusion that the passage was at least four feet wide, and almost of a uniform width. He waited to see the bore coming, and then, with a few vigorous strokes, put himself once more under the shelter of the rock.

Owing to his enormous chest capacity, Cheyne swam very high, and in sea-water he could move about with almost as much ease as on land. In the deep water under the rocks the sinker on the line, even if it hung perpendicular under him, would not touch the bottom, and consequently impeded his swimming only by its weight in water, which was, of course, much less than its weight in air. But there were only two fathoms of water in the cleft; and if he entered the channel towing that loaded line after him, the chance was it would get jambed somewhere, and he should be obliged to turn back, or come back somehow, turning being out of the question on account of the narrowness of the place, in order to free the sinker.

Remembering the free way in which the line had been paid out, and the fact that the sinker was now almost perpendicular under him, he concluded that the whole of the line now run out was far below the influence of the bores. These were not, by the way, real bores, but the term fitted them better than any other in the language.

When the next wave had gone by, Cheyne seized the edge of the passage, and catching the line in his feet and left hand, began drawing it up. At the approach of a second wave he was obliged to desist, but before a third was upon him he had the lead in his left hand, and was tearing it off with his teeth.

He had also another object in drawing the slack of that line. It was more than advisable that he should take with him into that cleft as much of the rope as would reach through; for if he had to overcome the friction between the line and the corner of the passage, his progress would be very much slower than if he could pay out as he went. Therefore, while treading the water in the slack, he made a small coil of about fifty feet of rope. He could swim with his right hand and legs.

Everything was now ready; and having waited his time, he filled his chest, threw back his head, and struck out for the opening.

The place looked forbidding. But its narrowness was greatly in the swimmer's favour. If it had been five feet wider, no man in his senses would have dared to enter it at such a time; but because of its narrowness there was only one point to expect motion from, namely, ahead. When the bore had swept through, the water was calm; there was no room for perturbation; and in so narrow a place, where one could touch both sides with hands and feet, there

was not much chance of being dashed against the sides.

Cheyne had, like Bence, resolved to dive under the bore. But he did not forget what Bence had forgotten—that beneath the surface of the present smooth water the bore would rush with as much fury as in the body of the bore itself. This was not like a wave which moves with only the force of its undulation, and which has no more power than its onward tidal force.

It is not the lateral force of the sea that beats the beams out of ships, and tears away the most enduring walls of man and the adamantine barriers of Nature. It is the shoulder of the wave that gets under the ships and the walls and the cliffs, and pushes them to destruction. At sea we never find the water flying up into the air. Of its own accord the water would not leave the bed it lies in. It is only when it meets with an obstacle and is broken that it leaves its own bed. Then, being broken and weak, it is caught by the wind, and flung over the rocks and cliffs in spray.

But in the case of the passage in which Cheyne now found himself, it was quite different. Into this entered a new body of water, a perpendicular section of a wave which had been torn from the general body of water, and as a projectile blown through this opening by the wind.

Now Bence had not calculated on this; he thought that if he got under the body or lowest level of the bore visible, he would find himself in still water.

Cheyne had also resolved on diving, but for a very different object.

Suppose he remained on the surface, the force of no mortal man could resist that wild rush of water, and the upward thrust which would strike him in the place where such a blow would be most effective, the chest. It would turn him over as a wind would a leaf. It would in all likelihood lift part of his body out of the water, and hurl him backward into the open beyond. The rush of the water must be borne; there was no way of avoiding that, but the uplifting might be avoided.

It was plain that when a torrent, or when in repose, the cleft held just the same quantity of water, from the dead level line down. Not a gallon more water was below the low-level water-line when the bore dashed through the cleft than a second before the incoming of the wave.

Therefore the bore, as it were, ran along the low-level water; and although the water beneath would be pushed violently forward, the horizontal motion would not be quite as much as above, and there would be no upheaval whatever.

But Cheyne knew what Bence did not know—that no man could, by swimming alone, stem the force of even that undercurrent.

'When I dive,' he said to himself, 'and get down there, I shall let go a pretty powerful grapnel. I shall moor myself on all fours with my hands and feet.'

He swam up the cleft, paying out his little coil of rope as he went, until he heard the roller break upon the outer rocks. Then, without waiting another moment, he dived.

When he found the descending force of the dive spent, he thrust out both arms and legs until they reached the sides, then working his legs up and his hands down, until he could get the full measure of his enormous strength to bear laterally upon the rocks, he thrust forward his head and awaited the onset.

When it came it was not quite as bad as he had anticipated; but it was bad enough. He had no difficulty in resisting it; but another man, a man of ordinary strength, would have been taxed to the utmost, and in all likelihood driven from his hold.

Cheyne waited until the rush had passed, and then rose to the surface. He found himself a few feet in advance of where he had dived.

He had not got many more feet when he heard the thunder of the roller on the rocks once more. Again he was under water before the bore entered the cleft. He had resolved to risk nothing, and his curiosity to know what his foe was like could not induce him to wait and see it.

This time the conditions below water were slightly altered. The passage was wider, and the hold, consequently, less secure; but, to compensate for this, the rush of water was less swift.

The fact that the passage widened thus gradually was a matter of surprise and much anxiety to Cheyne. He had a considerable distance to go before he got out of the cleft and within sight of the yacht, which lay to the southward a little of where he was.

If the passage went on widening as it approached the mouth, then there must be a point, and that too not far off, at which it would be impossible for him to reach from side to side, when, in fact, he would have nothing to rely upon but his powers as a swimmer. A baby would be as potent against that bore as he, if he depended on his powers as a swimmer merely.

It was necessary to proceed with the utmost caution. Should one wave overtake him, unprovided with secure holding-ground under water, all that he had hitherto achieved would be undone, and his own life most likely endangered.

He must, so to speak, pick his steps. That is, thenceforth all his progress must be under water.

When the present bore had run its course, he rose for breath. The period of his submersion was never more than ten to fifteen seconds. After a few hasty inspirations he dived again, and, feeling carefully along, crawled forward hand over hand and foot over foot for a few seconds, until it was time to expect the next wave. Then he set himself to resist it as before.

The moment the current slackened, he rose once more, took breath, and dived again.

At last he came to a place beyond which it would have been obviously unwise to advance, if he were to depend on the means hitherto adopted of stemming the torrent.

What was to be done now?

He was still a good distance from the mouth of the cleft. He had heard the men on shore say that if once he were at the mouth of the cleft he should be all right, as he should then be in sight of the yacht, from which a rope could be thrown to him.

He now was cut and bleeding in a dozen different places.

Another thing, too, troubled him greatly. He had, during the few last dives, tried to pull up some of the rope he towed after him, and he began to feel that the few small coils he had left would not be sufficient to reach the end of the passage.

What could one do in such a strait?

Desperate cases require desperate remedies. There were two coils of that rope round his body. If he unwound these he would be able to add considerably to his few remaining coils. He could tie the end of the line to his left wrist, and then he should be no more incapacitated than he had been with the coils.

To effect this, under existing circumstances, was an enormous labour. Wave after wave he dived under; time after time he rose again to his work.

At length the line was ready, and he had only now to face his desperate swim.

He had by this time begun to feel faint. His head was somewhat dizzy and confused from long and frequently holding his breath. He was bleeding now from twenty small wounds, of not one of which he felt the pain. He was too desperate, too battered, too exhausted, to feel paltry pain. He knew he had to swim between wave and wave to the end of that passage, and for the moment he thought of nothing else.

At last the moment came, and he thrust himself forward through that narrow channel with the supreme mental and physical concentration of a man whose whole being is absorbed in the determination to succeed.

At last he reached the opening, and found himself in shallow water. With a dim hazy sense of triumph he staggered to his feet. He was conscious of smiling, then he was conscious of standing before a gray-green barrier of water, and then, for a while, he was conscious of no more.

[To be continued.]

POPULAR PHRASES MISUNDERSTOOD AND MISAPPLIED.

IT is, I believe, generally admitted, by those who have given any thought to the subject, that the most dangerous kind of falsehood —the most likely to deceive—is that which contains a modicum of truth ; and for this reason the practised gossip or slanderer rarely resorts to pure invention ; because, knowing the value of a slight admixture of truth, for the purpose of plausibility, a trivial fact or circumstance is made the nucleus, around which is woven a tissue of lies, or, to use another simile, a fabrication of falsehood is raised on a slight substratum of fact, thus giving an appearance of stability to a superstructure which has little or no foundation to rest upon.   Mere idle gossip may prove very mischievous ; but it is a far more serious matter when the character of an individual is affected, in consequence of words and acts, perfectly innocent in themselves, being coloured and distorted by the ingenuity of a mind intent upon this sort of malevolent amusement.

However, it is not of intentional misrepresentation that I wish to write, but rather concerning a kind of unconscious perversion, that seems prevalent in the public mind, with regard to the meaning of some common phrases, which may truly be said to be 'in everybody's mouth ;' and my reason for the above introduction is that I desire to show how subtle falsehood is, and how very fine the line between it and truth; consequently how easy to accept the false for the true, the counterfeit for the genuine coin. This is particularly the case with reference to one or two familiar sayings, the fallacy of which I hope to prove.

Perhaps no lines have been more widely quoted than the following from Hood's poem :

' Evil is wrought by want of thought,
As well as want of heart.'

The frequency of the quotation is no doubt due partly to the constant occurrence of cases to which the sentiment seems to apply, and partly again to the readiness with which shallow minds adopt sayings, the real meaning of which few pause to consider ; the sound is more attractive than the sense ; a short pithy sentence that pleases the ear is easily remembered, and readily applied, when it happens to suit the capacities and humours, and, I may add, the prejudices, of the people ; thus a currency is obtained for sayings that are regarded as proverbs, yet contain no deep lesson of wisdom, which was the pride of the old philosophers. But even in the case of a sound moral lesson being intended by an author, it is often lost, and the original meaning becomes changed through frequent quotation by various writers and speakers ; thus a false sentiment is substituted, which is all the more mischievous because of the authority with which such aphorisms are usually repeated and accepted. These remarks are particularly applicable to the lines quoted from Hood : it is not probable that the author of them intended to excuse either 'want of thought' or 'want of heart;' but that is the interpretation put upon them by the majority of writers, who make use of the quotation to finish up a description of some 'tragedy,' or some so-called 'accident,' the result of gross carelessness; and in these days of morbid sympathy for offenders against the law, an attempt is too frequently made to save an individual from the rightful penalties of a really culpable act by attributing it to thoughtlessness: now 'want of thought' does *not* excuse the 'evil that is wrought' by a person that has arrived at the 'years of discretion'—the inexperience of childhood is quite another thing. Want of thought, therefore, is blamable because thoughtlessness, although a passive state of mind, is yet a *voluntary* condition of obliviousness to consequences; and by the non-exercise of the controlling power of the will and the judgment, the individual becomes an active agent for mischief. Experience ought to bring wisdom, that is to say *caution*, in connection with the present subject; if it does not have that effect, the heart is wrong; for where there is right feeling there will not be want of thought; at all events, the same mistakes will not be repeated when there is a real desire to avoid them.

'*Honesty is the best policy*' may be mentioned as another saying which is often wrongly interpreted. Of course, really honest people are not likely to put any but the true construction upon that phrase, which means, 'Honesty is *best*, because it is *right*;' but is that the incentive which actuates the classes whose ideas are rather hazy on the subject of '*mine and thine*'? I fear not; for instance, a ragged urchin picks up a purse containing money; he knows that should he discover the owner he will most likely be rewarded, and he also knows that, in the event of his keeping the purse, he would almost certainly be detected and punished; he is aware of the penalty, and prefers not to run the risk; so that the 'best policy,' according to his idea, is not the reward of a good conscience, but the prospect of a bit of silver as a recompense for his self-denial in not keeping what does not belong to him! It would be well if parents and teachers would inculcate the true meaning of this saying, and others of the same kind.

But I had no intention to write a lecture on 'thoughtlessness' and 'dishonesty;' my object being to show, by means of the examples given, that serious mistakes may be made by too readily accepting popular phrases, under the erroneous impression that '*what everybody says must be true*'!

M. A. B.

THE CAREER OF A WIG.

By HAL LOUTHER.

I WAS born in affluent circumstances, and, from my first recollection, inhabited a crystal palace, otherwise known to the common herd as a glass shade. The window wherein I first saw the light was that of a fashionable perruquier in the West-end. The said window was crowded with all kinds of perfumery, set out in the most elegant and artistic manner. We had wigs, scalps, long silken tresses of all colours, and in fact every kind of article necessary for the restoration of faded charms, to say nothing of two revolving wax figures trimmed and dressed in the grandest style.

Yet in the midst of this artificial world, such was the singular beauty —pray pardon the egotism—of my appearance, I could always attract to the window my special crowd of admirers !

My webbing was as light as gossamer, while my hair was of a soft rich brown streaked with golden threads, which glimmered here and there in sunny tints. I was always of a poetical nature, mind, and must express myself accordingly. My parting was as clear and white as a marble pathway, and was embowered on each side with a perfect grove of little curls, so neat and tiny, and clustering together so naturally, that they were regarded by the most critical observer as a wonderful evidence of master's skill.

I was justly proud of my position. I cared not for the gaping wonder of plebeian passers-by ; my chief delight was, when the sun shone on my glass palace, lighting up the golden meshes of my locks, to feel that I merited the compliments showered around my transparent shrine from the lips of my aristocratic admirers.

There was one gentleman I used to notice particularly : he would walk past the establishment wherein I held my daily levées, and then saunter back, stopping, as if by accident, in front of the window. Having nothing better to do, he would of course examine the articles ; but, no matter what object engaged his attention, he always finished his observations by looking fixedly at me; then he would turn and hurry away as though he wished to avoid some temptation.

So often did this occur that I made it my business to watch him. He was a man of that peculiar military bearing which can only be acquired by ardent Row and Piccadilly practice. Not that I wish to infer that he had never been in active service, or that he was only a toy soldier; some said he had never been a soldier at all, but the world is full of envious people. However, there he was, and no one but an enemy, of course, could doubt that martial tread. He was a very martinet in his attire, his boots were polished till they looked like mirrors, and the heels had the appearance of being adorned with invisible spurs. His strapped trousers were of the regulation cut, his coat bore the air of a braided frock, his hat was worn as though it were surmounted with a plume of feathers belonging to a field-marshal at least; in fact his appearance altogether gave the idea that he must undoubtedly have been present at no less than three general inspections.

One day I saw this hero of Mayfair pass through our doorway. My curls quivered and my parting turned a shade paler: was it of me he meant to inquire? I felt that my fate trembled in the balance: was I to be launched upon the world? Was I— But why look back to those harrowing moments of suspense? I was dragged from my crystal palace and consigned to the hands of the military stranger.

Having secured me, he hurriedly entered the cab which had brought him, and I was whirled away to his home. His dwelling was approached by a number of steps in a semicircular form, while the frontage generally gave you the idea of a palatial residence. But I was soon undeceived; for on ascending the broad stairway I was astonished to find doors opening, and heads popping in and out, as if the place were a human rabbit-warren; and I afterwards learned that the building was nothing more or less than a lodging-house on a grand scale, used by impecunious people who wished to appear in the world's eyes as if born to boundless wealth.

When we reached the topmost story of all, we entered a room noticeable at once for its faded grandeur: every article had an unmistakable second-hand air about it. The look-out comprised a full view of the backs of other houses, and a solitary tree so melancholy and depressed that it looked as if it had been stolen from some churchyard, and so refused to put forth bud or leaf in consequence. The walls were brightened with prints and pictures of famous beauties, past and present, which proved that my owner was an ardent admirer of the fair sex, especially ladies of stage notoriety.

The bedroom—which was a sort of enlarged cupboard with a window looking into an untenanted mews—was furnished on the same principle.

I soon found out that my new master was a wealthy wife-hunter of the most determined type. His income was derived from a legacy left him by an admiring relative, which income he managed to expend on outside show.

Well, the morning after I had left my first home I awoke and found my master already at his toilette. The table was laden with cosmetics of all kinds, and he was busy concealing the ravages of Time with an artistic touch which at once proclaimed long experience. When he had finished, he lifted me tenderly from my resting-place and fixed me on his bald head. Running his fingers through my curls, they fell so naturally about his temples that even I was lost in wonder for a moment as to whether I was really a wig or not. The effect upon him was magical. He looked twenty years younger in the instant.

'Dear,' he muttered as he looked at himself, 'very dear, but worth every farthing.'

And for a long time he lingered before the mirror with a pleased smile beaming over his face, till at last, placing his plumeless hat jantily on his head, and seizing his gloves and cane, we left the room. As we descended the stairs the rabbit-heads were again at work. Morning salutations were exchanged, and I noticed, with surprise, the lower we descended the stairs, the higher we rose in the social scale. On the first landing he was addressed as captain; on the second he was a colonel; and so quick was the promotion accorded him, that by the time he reached the hall he was made a general!

Once in the street, I was in

hopes he would pass by my old home, for, like all beginners in life, I had an emotional yearning towards the place of my nativity; but he studiously avoided it. We wandered to the club, found some birds of the same feather as ourselves, were complimented on our improved appearance. We lounged about, chatted over the newest scandal; then did the Row, bowed and smirked at imaginary acquaintance, returned to club again, beguiling the way by ogling the girls. Dined, and having an order for a theatre, we patronised the performance, then supped at our club, toddied ourselves with the proverbial 'night-cap,' and, seeking the skyward portion of our mansion, retired to rest. Such, with an occasional invite to an 'at home,' was our daily life.

It was at one of these parties an event occurred that changed the current of my career. I have already said that my master was on the look-out for a rich wife. Well, we were introduced to a middle-aged lady with the requisite banking account. My master at once laid siege to her heart, and soon found that, through me, his attentions were not displeasing— 'She adored a fine head of hair,' she said—and so he attacked her affections like a redoubtable knight of old.

When matters had sufficiently ripened he found an opportunity, and, after a burst of loving words, he fell upon his knees, propounding the conundrum, 'Will you be mine?' With a spasmodic 'Yes!' she fell upon his neck, and, in so doing, her hand caught me, and in an instant his bald head was bared to her astonished gaze.

That night he left the house a rejected suitor, with despair in his heart and his wig all awry.

Onward we went through the darkness to our home, sad and sullen. Just as we had reached a lonely part of the way, my master was suddenly knocked to the ground. I was seized by a rough hand, as a voice uttered a startled imprecation; then the hand, after a momentary clutch, thrust me into a most capacious pocket, where I swooned away in a state of utter collapse. How long I remained in that condition I know not, but when I recovered my senses I found I was not alone in my prison; there was something moving beside me, and I shivered with dread to find it was a young dog.

Into what hands had I fallen?

I was not long in doubt, for, on being released, I saw that I was in a dingy garret, the atmosphere of which was redolent of gin and tobacco-fumes. My captors were two of the most brutal-visaged ruffians it had ever been my lot to see. From their conversation I soon learned that they were professed garrotters, combining the light and elegant occupation of dog-fanciers.

'By thunder!' said one of them, 'it give me a lift when I seized the swell's hair and found it was a *jasey*.' Then he continued, in a rasping kind of chuckle, as he threw me on a rickety table with a bandaged leg, 'but his ticker is all right, though his puss is light.'

My dreams that night were not pleasant.

When the occupants awoke in the morning, I was picked up and examined with curiosity.

'It don't look a bad un,' said one of the ruffians.

'I wonder if it would fetch anything?' mused the other, looking at me critically.

'Take it round to barber Jack's,' ordered the first speaker—'he knows you—and try him, though I'm afraid it is too swell for his window.'

I was again stuffed in a greasy

pocket, and, without another word, carried away.

I saw no more till I was produced in the barber's shop, where, after a great deal of haggling, I was left. How I shudder as I think of that horrid shop-window, where I was placed on a featureless block, surrounded by frowsy wigs and dishevelled fronts! What a change from my Mayfair home—to be mixed up with cobwebs and curls, unsaleable razors, squares of petrified soap, paper collars, and tarnished shirt-studs. The sear was in my heart, and no amount of admiration could compensate for my degradation.

I was in one of my deepest fits of despondency, on a certain day, when I suddenly became conscious that a gentleman was regarding me with a fixed expression of wonder. My limp manner and languid bearing changed in an instant. There could be no mistake in that admiring look—hope kindled in my heart as I watched that face anxiously—it was a strange face too, clean shaven, severe, and strongly marked, with the muscles under the eyes standing out in bold relief over the white cheeks. His glance was proud and defiant, his lips had a chronic curl of scorn about them, and, as he stood there, with his right hand poised in the breast of his buttoned frock-coat, he looked like a monarch vainly striving to disguise the imperious majesty of his nature.

He entered the shop, and I was taken from my odious pedestal. I was to accompany the stranger, no matter whither. My heart throbbed with joy to leave that hated realm of soapsuds, rough conversation, the snip of scissors, and the rasping of coarse razors.

That night I made my first appearance behind the scenes of a theatre, and a strange atmosphere I found it. My new possessor was an actor—a tragedian whom, fortunately for me, chance had brought into that locality. My first appearance was as Virginius, and a most successful one it was. What a throb of pride went through every curl, as I sat enthroned on my master's heroic brow, listening to peal upon peal of applause!

From that night I became a declaimer of blank verse, varied occasionally with a touch of highflown prose. I was happy in my artificial world. I always played good parts; so from night to night I went on my way, now rescuing from wrong, now being wronged myself, and invariably winning my reward in the tears which lovers of tragedy always indulge in shedding, and the sight of which affords the actor the greatest joy.

One fatal night an event happened which cast a shadow over my life. My master was playing one of his favourite parts to an unusually large house, and using an extra amount of energy. His efforts were received with deafening plaudits. Not content, he thirsted for more, and so received his deathblow; for in denouncing the proverbial 'double-dyed traitor' he burst a blood-vessel, and was carried home. In a few days he breathed his last; and a self-elected jury of his brother-actors gave it as their verdict that he died of an unnatural greed of applause.

So I was again to be cast on the world. There was a sale of my master's effects, and I was purchased by a theatrical wig-maker; and, being operated upon by hot bran, I was again placed in a window for public inspection, amidst companions of my own tribe of all possible shades and colours, to say nothing of endless whiskers, beards, and moustaches, together with heaps of masks frowning or grinning around me.

Before long I was purchased by

a young lady of gaudy appearance who played boys in burlesque, and I was at once conveyed to a scene of glitter and frivolity. So great was the change from Virginius to a boy in burlesque, that I was completely dazed. I was fairly plunged into a perfect whirlpool of gaiety. With the exception of the titled inanities in the wings and green-room, we had but few men in the theatre; but, O, what crowds of the opposite sex, and what dresses too, and so varied the colours that if they had been melted down they might have served for a whole generation of rainbows!

My mistress was the pet of the theatre; no brain was required to please our patrons; only face, figure, and an impudent saucy manner, and these qualities she possessed.

To me the change was startling. In my last home, where the Tragic Muse reigned supreme, both actors and actresses were, as a rule, stately and grand; and as for the theatre, when you passed the stage-door, it was as if you had entered a church by mistake, so solemn and staid was everything around. Figures glided about the wings saluting each other in whispers, while in the greenroom all conversation was carried on in a grave and quiet way, as became the character of a serious theatre. The curtains hung in depressed folds, the furniture looked as if at one time it had mingled with a sinful world, but since then it had happily seen the error of its ways. The walls stared at you severely; jokes were never heard, or else they were told in muttered tones and acknowledged in suppressed laughter; a pious gloom pervaded the air, breathing in your ears demure precepts, while the very clock ticked at you in a sort of moral and improving manner. And from this sober life I was launched into a most frivolous world.

What bickerings and scandal, friendships born to-day and buried to-morrow, rivals meeting each other with kisses on their lips and stings in their hearts, faces that were but as smiling masks, insincere praises, joyless laughter, a rooted desire to outdress and out-jewel each other, with here and there a slighted figure shrinking as much as possible from contact with this brilliant sisterhood; and so the hollow whirligig went its nightly round, dizzy with compliments and champagne! O, how I sighed for my blank-verse home again! Dear old blank verse! No cannonading of champagne-corks deafened our ears! O dear no! in our wildest moments we never rose above whisky-and-water.

But the end of the hateful time came at last. I was one night ordered back to the hairdresser's to be re-dressed. The man who had charge of me, being a thirsty soul, called on his way home at a favourite public-house; though I could not see the place, I knew, by the clamour of egotism around, and the fumes of tobacco, that it was a low-class theatrical tavern. The thirst of the hairdresser's man required so much to quench it that, when he left, his memory was drowned, and I was forgotten. I was carried away by some unscrupulous person, and sold to a provincial light comedian.

What a Bohemian life I then led! He was a gay rollicking fellow, moulded by Fate for his business; it always seemed to be a battle between his purse and spirits as to which should be the lightest. Nothing ever troubled him, so elastic was his nature. He looked upon life as one huge joke, and laughed at it accordingly; with him all was sunshine and no shade. If his manager did not pay him at the end of the week, he would borrow if he could find any one who would trust him; if he failed in that, he would owe those who had already given him credit. When he did receive his salary, he would divide it in this fashion: 'That is for the landlady,' he would say to some invisible confidant; 'that is for the tailor, I promised him faithfully this week; and that is for myself. There is very little for self,' he would add, after a pause; then brightening up he would continue to his invisible confidant, 'Well, I will pay the landlady half, the tailor nothing, and that will leave a better share of loose silver for dear old self;' so that it ended in his paying as little as possible. Yet everybody liked him (at least those who had not lent him money), he was so genial and affable. I remember once, during a farce we were playing, a lady of the company came to him, and, with tears in her eyes, asked if he would follow her recently defunct daughter to the grave; whereupon he instantly replied, with one of his sweetest smiles, 'Certainly, Mrs. D., *with pleasure;*' as if it had been an invite to the poor creature's wedding!

With him I lived a considerable time, flitting hither and thither in a sort of hand-to-mouth existence.

At last we were doomed to part. During the night-time the theatre, wherein we were then engaged, took fire, and was speedily a complete wreck. By a miracle I escaped with life, but was so severely singed that I was crippled for the rest of my existence.

Then commenced the chequered part of my career. No one could have recognised me; the shock had turned me prematurely old. I was a ragged object; the golden sheen of my glossy hair was gone, its lustre was shed for evermore, and my spirit was broken down.

After many vicissitudes, I at length found myself in the hands of a poor utility-man at a minor theatre; and O, the drudgery of such a life for a bare and miserable existence! Your utility-man is the bloodlet of anger for all who are above him; he is a victim to those in office; for when their tongues are tied with regard to the errors of others of the company, poor utility is sure to bear the brunt; in fact, he is the parochial orphan of the theatre, the stock sacrifice always at hand and ready to be offered up on the altar of blame. It may be easily imagined what my life was when it is known that my owner, who had all kinds of parts to play, had only one wig (myself) in his possession. I have begun a performance by being ruffled up to play the Bleeding Sergeant, and afterwards fairly haunted Macbeth all through the play. I have been smoothed down and with a back piece of a different colour have trembled through Lennox. I have turned my side portion to the front, and served as a witch. With the aid of a beard hastily glued on, I have impersonated one of the Murderers. Then I have again transformed myself into a witch, appearing shortly afterwards as the Apparition of an Armed Head, sneezing behind a caldron illuminated with offensive red fire. Sprinkled with powder, I have played the Physician; and finally, with my hind part turned to the front, I have startled poor Macbeth by appearing before him as both the speaking officers in the last act. In the farce, and on the same night, I have played a countryman and a bailiff with the prospect of a doubtful treasury on the Saturday.

I thought in this capacity Fate had for me plumbed the lowest depth, but I have found a lower deep: I am now, with the addition of a couple of greasy side-locks, cracking coster songs in a low concert-room, to the clapping of coal-heaving hands and the melodious clanking of pewter pots.

PERILS OF THE DEEP.

By A LANDLUBBER.

———◆———

'PERILS of the Deep' is a title which seems to wear a forbidding and unpleasant aspect; but a certain class of nautical casualties is occasionally attended with an element of humour. No doubt a similar element could be discovered in many of the accidents which occur on *terra firma*, but it is only a thorough-paced 'old salt' who could do justice to the subject. A 'landlubber' views the deep with eyes of a different hue from those with which he gazes at things of the earth earthy, just as the sailor will often find little to laugh at in the most amusing (to a landsman) sea yarn. It would be found on inquiry that the sailor, when ashore, frequently chuckles over 'Perils of the Street,' which would give a shareholder in an Accident Company a fit of the blues, or in his snug fo'c's'le laughs until the tears stream down his weather-beaten cheeks as he reads the record of a 'Shocking Railway Collision.' Most of us have heard the story of the tar who, while his ship was laying-to in a gale under close-reefed canvas, exclaimed, 'What a dreadful time the poor folks ashore must be having— slates blowing off the houses, chimney-pots tumbling down by the score, umbrellas turned inside out —'tis something awful to think of it!'

Most of the details of maritime misadventures which I shall attempt to give an account of were, in the cases which did not come under my personal observation, related to me, not with a view to evoking merriment, but with the intention of creating in my breast feelings of sympathy, indignation, or horror.

With every shipmaster to the manner born there exists no positive or comparative degree when his craft is the topic of conversation. Her qualities are, in some respect at least, superlative. If she is not the swiftest ship afloat, she is the strongest, or the steadiest, the easiest on her gear or the lightest on her ballast, the tightest or the best-looking, or she keeps the best cabin. In fact a shipmaster will tell you that his ship is the slowest or the leakiest in the world rather than steer clear of superlatives. This is an invariable rule.

It was once my fortune to know a master-mariner, whose ship was 'the fastest of her build afloat.' He was an excitable man about everything, but his excitability knew no bounds when the sailing powers of his vessel were called into question. Upon one occasion he was standing on the pier-head of a certain port, watching his idol moving out of dock, when the master of a neighbouring Yankee clipper addressed him: 'Say, you've been bragging to no end about your sailing. I'm going down Channel this tide. There's a nice whole-sail breeze nearly dead aft. Now I'll give your tar-nation tub a topsail, and lick her into a cocked hat.'

This was too much for my excitable friend. 'Clap on every inch of your canvas, you lubber,' he cried, 'and I'll show you what *sailing* is! By Heavens, I will! If I don't put you hull down before sunset, I'll scuttle my ship! Get ahead now! You'll be out of dock before me; and look out for the Tiger—that's all!'

The Yankee proceeded down the Channel in gallant style, closely followed by the challenged craft. Every available yard of canvas was put into requisition, and never did the crews of racing yachts settle down to their work with greater energy and determination. The master of the Tiger stood on the fore-deck alternately shouting his orders to the sailors, and straining his eyes after the ship ahead. Gradually the Tiger gained upon her rival, until at length she came within easy hailing distance.

'Get out of my road, you cursed Yankee!' roared the excitable skipper. 'Steady your helm!' to the man at the wheel. 'Get out of my road, or by Heavens I'll run right into you!'—and he did. Fortunately no lives were lost, but it took some hundreds of pounds to put the damage to rights.

A man of a totally different temperament was the master of the coasting schooner, Harvester. He was one of the laziest of mortals, and his ship, perhaps through sympathy, was one of the slowest afloat. Over his crew he somehow contrived to exercise autocratic control, and by them he was set down as 'an exceedingly knowledgable skipper.' His chief anxiety was to act up to this estimate of his abilities so long as the effort caused him no extra amount of locomotion or 'wear and tear' of brain-tissue.

One evening, bound for an Irish port, he discovered himself at the mouth of the Bristol Channel, with a dense fog creeping up from the south. Expecting that the fog would clear away before daybreak, and being too lazy to alter the course of his ship, he continued blindly onwards. At daybreak the fog showed no symptoms of decay. It was now too late to turn tail; for it would be just as difficult to find the way backwards as the way forwards; so the ship's head was put to the S.W., in order to keep well out to sea until the atmosphere brightened. For four days the fog enveloped the Harvester like a shroud. The master was in despair, but exhibited no traces of the anxiety which was gnawing at his vitals. At last, on the morning of the fifth day, he was rudely shaken from his bunk (where he usually spent eighteen hours out of the twenty-four), and informed that the weather had cleared. And now he was in a mental fog, which bade fair to outrival the actual one in density; so he determined to avow his troubles to the mate, and accordingly the 'chief officer' was summoned to the state-room for consultation.

'You see, Mr. Mate,' said the skipper, 'I don't, to be candid with you, know where we are, or what we ought to do. We have been keeping rather a random course for the past four or five days, and for all I can tell, we may now be in foreign parts. Perhaps the banks of Newfoundland are under our bows, if we only knew it. No doubt we shall come across some homeward-bound ships before long, and we can ask our latitude and longitude; but I daren't expose my ignorance to the men. Now I want you to rob the harness-cask.'

'Rob the harness-cask? What for?'

'That's *my* business. Stow all the beef and pork here in my state-room without letting the crew be any the wiser, and then I'll go on deck with a light heart.'

That evening the sailors were

summoned aft, and their skipper gravely said,

' I'm sorry, men, to tell you very bad news. The mate informs me that we are running short of provisions; in fact—keep up a brave heart, men—there is only a few days' grub on board altogether; so we must put up a signal of distress at the masthead, and, please God, we'll fall in with some vessel before another twenty-four hours. You know we're now right in the track of homeward-bound ships. We must all go on short allowance for the present.'

Next morning a barque was observed on the horizon, and before noon the Harvester was alongside. The sad tale of short supplies was told to the master of the barque, in the hearing of the Harvester's anxious crew, and a supply of beef and pork in exchange for other commodities was quickly negotiated.

' Where are you bound to ?' inquired the Harvester carelessly.

' Portsmouth, for orders. We ought to sight English land before sundown. Oughtn't we ?'

' How's your reckoning ?'

' Well, we calculate we should be about eighty miles due west of the Land's End now. We are steering east and by south.'

' Ay, ay. That's about my reckoning too, my sonny; but you might put her a point or so more to the south'ard, as the wind is freshening a bit, and the sky looks all southerly.'

' Thank you. Where are you bound ?'

' O, farther north ! It's square yards for me — east, south-east ought to do you nicely—but keep a good look-out. Safe voyage !'

Thus was the all-important information obtained without loss of prestige, and ' Square away !' was the order of the hour on board the Harvester.

' Decent fellow, that stranger !' said the skipper to his crew; ' but it was the mercy of Providence he fell in with a knowledgable man like me. Only that I gave him some instructions about altering his course, he'd find himself ashore somewhere about the Scilly Islands before night.'

Shortness of provisions recalls an anecdote which might afford food for another ' Nancy-Brig' ballad. Captain B—— was a man who claimed to have been in every possible sort of nautical scrape. Ships on fire, sinking ships, collisions at sea, desolate islands, icebergs, waterspouts, and cyclones were all in his way. His experiences would make a drama more sensational than the *World*, and more improbable. I once asked him if he had ever fed upon his fellow-man for want of a more palatable dish. ' Well, not exactly,' he replied; ' but certainly the next thing to it. I'll tell you how it occurred. We were caught in a double-shotted gale in the Western Ocean.' The Western Ocean was usually the scene of his wonderful adventures, and it seemed a vague and terrible expanse of waters when Captain B—— referred to it. ' Our masts had gone by the board, and we were making six inches of water an hour. This was bad enough, in all conscience; but worse was to follow. After knocking about helplessly for several weeks, never once sighting a strange sail or a spot of land—not even a coral reef or an iceberg—we discovered that provisions were exhausted. We managed to get along nicely for a while on the rats which infested the ship, but which, owing to hunger and fright, were now as tame as cockroaches. We had a French cook aboard; and blow me, but we had a gay time of it on those rats ! Even this source of supply was soon cut off; for rats don't last for ever any more than salt junk and lime-juice. We turned next on our boots and the pump-leather, and then we fell back on all the parchment documents on board. By the way, that's how I lost my certificate of competency—made soup of it, sir! At last we were almost at our wits' ends, and determined to cast lots amongst ourselves. I had my eye on the bo'sun, a fine able-bodied fellow, who would be safe to keep us in condition for another spell. By a curious coincidence the fatal lot fell upon this very bo'sun, but damme if the scoundrel didn't rebel! He produced his clasp-knife, and swore he would die hard, at any rate. You may guess I felt more enraged than I can tell at such mutinous conduct; but rather than create any unnecessary unpleasantness and bloodshed, I advised a friendly consultation, and called the officers of the ship into the cabin. After some deliberation we decided that perhaps it was best to let the boy, a young lad about seventeen, be sacrificed first. He had no wife or family depending upon him, and, moreover, he could be easily knocked on the head from behind. Just as I came on deck to make an end of the youngster, we sighted a sail. It was just as well we did, for it would fret me all my life to have taken an unfair advantage of any lad. As soon as we were safely landed at Falmouth I lodged a complaint with the collector of customs against that bo'sun, but they would not allow me to stop a stiver from the rascal's wages. What do you think of *that?*'

I have already attempted to show in what an ugly predicament a fog can place a seafaring man; and the following yarn will prove that, helpless and persecuted as Londoners consider themselves during the dull days of November, they know little of the terrors which King Fog can exercise in his maritime domain.

Late in December the good ship Sarah Jane, bound for Glasgow, tripped her anchor in the Tyne. The wind was in her favour, and she proceeded northwards rapidly. On the evening of the second day she passed Long Hope lighthouse, in the Orkneys. Already the skipper was congratulating himself upon a quick and profitable voyage; but he was a stranger to the coast of Scotland, and he little knew the affectionate manner with which the Scotch mist clings to the northern shores in the winter season. Before daybreak of the third day the Sarah Jane was surrounded by a fog, the density of which was only equalled by the mental condition of my friend of the Harvester when he decided upon robbing the harness-cask. By the way, is a 'harness-cask' so called because it contains 'salt horse'? This would be an interesting inquiry for nautical philologists. But to return to the Sarah Jane, which was now floundering about the northern seas, uncertain what course to pursue. The skipper would have decided upon laying-to with the ship's head to the north, so that he might give the land a wide berth, but, unfortunately, he was not quite certain in what direction the north lay—an awkward state of affairs for a mariner in a fog. Too late he remembered that his solitary compass was not all that a respectable compass ought to be. He had intended getting it adjusted at Newcastle-on-Tyne, but, owing to some fatal forgetfulness, the adjustment had not been performed. The compass might, of course, be all right, but he dare not rely blindly upon it in his present predicament. There was no alternative but to take all sail off the ship and trust in Providence. It is a remarkable fact that the most impious son of Neptune will invariably declare his intention of 'trusting in Providence' when he finds himself in a fix.

As the shades of night descended, the fog showed no signs of disappearance; and the crew of the Sarah Jane, to a man, were in a state of abject terror. Suddenly, towards the small hours of the morning, the lowing of cattle broke the stillness, for during the night the wind had almost died away, and little could be heard save the lazy surging of the waters.

'All hands on deck!' was the alarmed cry.

Every ear was strained, and again the voice of the 'lowing herd winds slowly o'er the *lee*'-ward.

'Heave the lead—we are all lost!' sobbed the skipper.

'Can't make this out, sir,' said the mate, as he held the lead-line over the side. 'There's practically no bottom here, and yet we must be close in shore to hear the cattle.'

'There is one chance left,' said the skipper. 'The wind must be right off the land to carry the sound aboard so clearly. Let's give her the topsail, and run before the little breeze that's left.'

The topsail was loosed, and the Sarah Jane soon forged slowly ahead.

'Clap on more canvas!' cried the skipper, as the lowing of the cattle grew fainter every moment. 'Give her all the square sail you can spread. 'Tis our only chance of escape.'

In about half an hour the cattle could be heard no longer, and the crew of the Sarah Jane were beginning to indulge in hope when another and more pronounced 'boo-o-o' electrified them.

'Merciful Heavens!' said the master. 'I see how it is. We're in a land-locked bay. Out with

the boat, men. Quick, lads! The land is right atop of us!' he shouted, as a black mass could be distinguished rising, like an Ethiopian Venus, from the waters.

The boat was swung into the davits, when the black mass drifted alongside, and a voice exclaimed,

'Hey, mon, but you be making a pretty course of it! Where be you bound to?'

'Damn your eyes, you lubber! Why, don't you carry a light? You've frightened our wits out.'

'A light! Dang it, who wants a light in our wee craft? We be only bringing a handfu' o' coos fra the Orkneys. 'Tis nigh daybreak, too, and the mist's clearing awa.'

Although, strictly speaking, 'mud-pilots' are not creatures of the deep, still their connection with seafaring life is so intimate that a tale of the perils of mud-pilotage may not be out of place here. Perhaps some little explanation is necessary concerning 'pilots and pilots,' for there *are* distinct gradations in the scale —the coasting, the licensed river, and the mud pilot. It is a matter for grave doubt if the licensed river conductor would allow his coasting brother to take precedence of him, but certainly both regard the mud-pilot as a creature of immeasurably inferior rank, socially, intellectually, and professionally. The son of a coasting or river pilot would not dream of contracting a *mésalliance* with the daughter of a mud-pilot; nor would the son of a mud-pilot be presumptuous enough, even in his cups, to aspire to the hand of the daughter of a coasting or river pilot. Again, if you are a seafaring man, or connected in any way with seafaring life, a mud-pilot will fearlessly ask you for the price of a drink, whereas the most delicate and subtle tact has to be employed in forcing a liquor upon him of the coasting or licensed river ilk.

The coasting-pilot takes charge of ships at sea (usually ships which sport three masts and double top-gallant yards); the licensed river-pilot confines his peregrinations to the quarter-decks of crafts in pilotage waters; and the mud-pilot exercises his profession in places where pilotage waters exist no longer. It may be stated *en passant* that 'pilots of the purple twilight' have no connection with the sea, or the perils thereof.

The duty of the mud-pilot, whose acquaintance I once had the honour of making, was to conduct ships up a river to a place about a dozen miles distant from a seaport town. He was not the monarch of all he surveyed, as he could boast of at least two rival practitioners; and of course it was his interest to do all in his power to damage the reputations, moral and professional, of his rivals, and secure for himself, by fair means or foul, all the vessels he possibly could. On the average, three or four ships a week proceeded up the river in charge of the mud-pilots; but occasionally the vagaries of the weather would cause a number of crafts to be overdue; and when a favourable change of wind took place it was not unusual to see almost a dozen little vessels riding at anchor, awaiting the assistance of one of the rival conductors before proceeding to their final place of discharge. As a general rule, the ships intrusted to my friend, who knew every square inch of the river, reached their destination safely in a tide or two; but when this extra pressure of work arose, a rather curious phenomenon might have been observed, namely, the occurrence of a series of accidents. Two or three of the ill-fated argosies would be certain to find a temporary home about half way up the river, in the mud or on a sand-bank. My curiosity was aroused, and I determined to discover the cause of the phenomenon. I knew it was due to design rather than to accident, but I was unable to imagine the why and the wherefore. I consulted my pilot-friend, and in a moment of confidence, inspired by judicious applications of whisky, he disclosed the awful secret.

'You see,' he said, 'times are so bad that a man must study things carefully in order to make both ends meet. There are a lot of ships, let us say, waiting for pilots; and of course, if I can get done with my ship sooner than the other two fellows—a bad lot they are too, I may tell you—I can come back and take charge of a second ship before the other scoundrels are half over their journeys; so I manage to put one or two of the little vessels in a soft handy spot up the river. O, I have a conscience, I can assure you, and wouldn't let hurt or harm come to anything in my charge for the world. They lay there, nice and comfortable, for a few days—just as safe as if they were in a dry-dock—until the spring-tide floats them off. I take charge of them for the remainder of the journey then, when work is slack with me. I can earn as much as the other two fellows put together, just by studying matters in this way. It goes to my heart though if the tides are cutting, and leave the poor ships in the mud a week or so; but then we manage to dig 'em out somehow; and there isn't a great deal of time lost after all. 'Twill be all the same in a hundred years, anyhow. Here's your health.'

Another 'long-shore yarn' will illustrate the saying, that there is a special Providence which protects a drunken man; and it will also exhibit the utter recklessness and devil-may-care-ism which is frequently to be found in those who brave the dangers of the seas.

I was standing one evening on the deck of a brig, which had just discharged a cargo, and was being prepared to receive another freight. A tipsy sailor was lounging about the ship, and in an evil moment he approached the open hatchway. He suddenly staggered, and fell backwards into the empty hold. In a few minutes he was hoisted on deck; and, in common with the others on board, I expected to find he had been killed. The depth of the hold was over fourteen feet, and the unfortunate man had fallen right across the iron-bound keelson—the dorsal ridge, if one may call it so, of the ship. All were agreeably surprised to see that, though stunned, he was beginning to recover consciousness. I sent at once for a doctor and a pint of brandy. The brandy arrived first, and the injured man swallowed most of it before the doctor appeared. Then he eased his mind by giving vent to a string of very robust oaths. The doctor ordered a stretcher to be procured, and the sailor was conveyed to the hospital. I heard every day that he was progressing most favourably; but I was more than surprised, in a little over a week, to see him on board the brig again, looking not much the worse for his accident, and smelling strongly of rum.

'You had a miraculous escape,' I said. 'I hope you will take a little more care of yourself for the future.'

'That's all right, governor,' he replied. 'I'm hard up now, and I'm game for another back tumble if you'll stand another nip of brandy.'

The most irritable seafaring man on record was the commander of the Nautilus, a clipper schooner of about two hundred tons. When first I met him, warm and young, he would relate the most highly-spiced yarns concerning the speed of his ship, and it was actually dangerous to assume an incredulous air, or hint in the most delicate manner that he was an unmitigated liar. Later on in life he was obliged to take command of a very dull craft called the Troubadour; and having been always accustomed to a ship that could do her ten or twelve knots an hour in moderate weather, the transfer to a ship whose top speed in a hurricane was six or seven knots completely soured his already dangerous temper, and rendered him the most saturnine, the gloomiest, and most misanthropical navigator that ever sailed the wintry main. On his first voyage in the dull vessel he was beating up the English Channel, the wind dead in his teeth. It was bright, cheery, wholesome weather, but sunshine had no charms for the irascible skipper, who paced his narrow quarter-deck with the strut of a freshly-caged tiger. He had not been long beating about, when he observed another vessel creeping up towards him. Both ships were making short tacks in and out, but it was easy to see that the strange sail would soon overhaul the Troubadour, and, irony of Fate, the stranger was none other than the lively little Nautilus! Slowly, but surely, the Nautilus lessened the distance between herself and the Troubadour until she was almost in a line with her. The Troubadour then reached in shore with the wind a point or two in her favour, and the Nautilus reached out, close hauled on the wind. When meeting it is the duty of the ship having the wind slightly in her favour to give way to the close-hauled ship; and it is almost unnecessary to say that the rule of the road was never adhered to with fewer manifestations of good-will and politeness than on this occasion. On the next tack the Nautilus met the Troubadour again, and gave way in turn.

'Well, yours *is* a slow craft!' shouted the master of the Nautilus. 'I'm just playing with my vessel. I see I could sail round you without straining a rope-yarn. I'll just ease her a bit, and meet you on the next tack. 'Tis such a pleasure to see a man give way good-humouredly like you do.'

'Better keep clear of me!' roared the commander of the Troubadour, now lashed into fury. 'If you come near my bows again, I'll run you down as sure as there is a sky above us!'

The Nautilus, however, took no heed of the warning, and on the following tack gaily approached the Troubadour, expecting, of course, to have another little joke with the 'stern commander' as he passed.

'Give way, give way!' bellowed the Nautilus, as all on board saw they were getting rather too close to the other ship. 'Give way, man! Give way!' was the cry, an alarmed cry this time.

'Damned if I do!' roared the skipper of the Troubadour, as he took the helm into his own hands; and before the Nautilus could alter her course she found a strange cutwater imbedded three deck-planks deep in the vicinity of her fore-rigging.

A tedious law-suit ensued; but there was such a plethora of 'cross-swearing' that the master of the Troubadour came out of the ordeal without a stain upon his character. However, he was destined to bid a long farewell to his lazy craft before another twelvemonth had elapsed. He was sailing out of a harbour in company with a vessel belonging to a rival owner. As the breeze freshened he could see he was doomed to be distanced; and as he reflected that in his former ship he could 'walk away' from this very Mary Jane which

was now about to 'walk away' from him, a flood of thought came o'er him which filled his eyes with tears. He could bear this state of affairs no longer. 'Better perish,' he muttered, 'than be perpetually beaten and scoffed at.'

'Look here, men,' he said to the crew, 'I'll give this cursed Troubadour one more chance! When we get round the next bend in the river we'll have to make a tack. If I can't cross that beggar's bows' (pointing contemptuously towards the hated Mary Jane), 'and take the wind out of her sails, I'm blowed but he may run me down! Do you think I could ever hold up my head again if that fellow licked me? Get the boat over the side before we tack! If we don't weather him, damme if I don't go ashore and follow a plough!'

The crew, who could not make up their minds whether their skipper was mad or drunk, humoured him by getting the boat into the water; but when they saw him deliberately take the helm and seek a collision, they thought it was nigh time to mutiny. But the resolution came too late.

'Take to the boat, my lads!' cried the worthy skipper. 'We'll never weather her! The Mary Jane wouldn't give way an inch to save my life; and he's on the right tack now—steady, men, we'll do it yet!' as the two ships swiftly approached each other. 'Never! She's into us!' he yelled. 'Over the side with you, men—quick!'

The Troubadour continued on her career, her stern just shaving the jibboom of the Mary Jane; but no crew, no captain, stood on her sturdy decks. From the ship's boat they watched the deserted vessel sail blindly onwards, and seek an asylum on a friendly reef of rocks. She was afterwards towed off and repaired, the injuries sustained being, strange to say, very slight; but never again did her *quondam* commander make an entry in her official log-book.

The history of the strange and mournful death at sea of Commander Augustus Winter may appropriately bring to a close this paper on the perils of the deep, and, in addition, may serve as a warning to those who, in time of illness or pain, think professional advice and professional aid may be carefully ignored. Augustus Winter was a mortal possessed, from time immemorial, with an enormous belief in himself, and not wholly without cause. If he were to tell you the wind would come out from the nor'head and east'ard before midnight with heavy squalls, or that it would chop round to the sou'-west before daybreak, you might, with security, 'make a book' on either of these events. So correct was he in his weather forecasts that, in his old age, he began to believe he was endowed with full prophetic powers. Now all this has very little to do with the death of Augustus or the manner of his death, but it will afford an insight into the character of the man. Augustus suffered much from tooth-ache, but he had always treated himself successfully for the ailment. His recipe was, ' Take of thin marline six or seven yards ; secure one end of the marline firmly round the mainmast of your ship, and make the other end fast to the erring-tooth; walk gently backwards until the line is nearly taut; then close your eyes and suddenly fall backwards, always taking care that the deck behind you is swept clear for action.'

Augustus always followed out his own recipe to the letter, and with most satisfactory results ; for at the age of sixty-three his lower jaw was quite unencumbered with teeth, and his upper jaw could boast of but a solitary stump. Feeling a slight face-ache one dark night at sea, he determined to do away with this solitary stump, and accordingly he proceeded to follow out the rules and regulations laid down in his own recipe. Unfortunately he omitted to attend to the final clause, and, in his backward career, his head came in contact with an old block which lay unheeded on the deck.

He was buried at sea with honours.

IN MEMORIAM B. H. BUXTON.

'IT is but a step from the known to the unknown.' On Wednesday evening, March the 30th, Mrs. B. H. Buxton, whose name is well known to our readers as the authoress of *Nell—on and off the Stage*, &c., returned home from a pleasant evening spent with friends in her neighbourhood, looking unusually well and speaking with her wonted cheeriness, to sink down with a quiet sigh on to her sofa, and pass painlessly into the land of shadows. Heart-disease, unknown and unsuspected, was the secret and insidious complaint that thus abruptly cut short the brave bright life—a life that, for several years past, had battled courageously with troubles which would have prostrated most women, and that had but recently won for itself some return of peace and happiness.

Mrs. Buxton was born on the 26th of July 1844, and when only a girl of eleven years amused herself by writing stories for her schoolfellows at Queen's College, Tufnell Park. Her taste for acting was as strong as her taste for writing; and, whilst a mere baby, she posed in *tableaux vivants*. Both her parents were German—her mother being Madame Therese Leupold, well known in musical circles —and with them she travelled in America, Germany, and Holland during her fourteenth and fifteenth years. Her careless girlish days, however, did not last very long. At sixteen she married Mr. Buxton, but still pursued her literary work as an amusement, translating a German operetta into English, and writing a modest one-volumed

novel, which was published at her husband's expense, and appeared under the title of *Percy's Wife*, obtaining some capital notices.

In 1875, nearly fifteen years after her marriage, the page of her life was abruptly reversed. Domestic troubles arose, and from a rich woman, surrounded with every comfort and luxury, she suddenly found herself poverty-stricken and entirely dependent on her own exertions. Then it was she turned to writing for her living. She took her youngest child with her, and settling in a modest cottage close to town, devoted all her energies and abilities to the production of a good stage novel. She was one of those conscientious workers who would only write about what she had thoroughly studied and mastered; and to carry out her determination she persuaded a manager at Exeter to let her go on the stage as a walking-lady. Telling him exactly what she wanted, he allowed her every facility for studying life 'behind the scenes.' In the green-room she was known and respected as ' the little lady.'

Having gathered together the materials she needed, Mrs. Buxton returned to her London cottage, and in 1876 her labours were rewarded by the great success of her novel, *Jennie of 'the Prince's,'* which at once made her name; best of all, it brought her what she most needed—plenty of other work. Mr. Edmund Yates asked her to write a serial for the *World*, which she accomplished during the following year; bringing out, during the same year, a story for children entitled *Rosabella,* and published under the name of 'Auntie Bee.' The following Christmas another child's book was published, entitled *More Dolls,* illustrated by Mr. D. T. White, and dedicated, by special permission, to the Princess of Wales, who said, in a letter which she caused Miss Knollys to write, that she had herself read every word of it to her own children.

Mrs. Buxton was now getting on admirably, and earning more than enough for herself and child. Peace and content reigned in the little London cottage, when once again the wheel of Fortune struck the brave worker to the ground. In 1877 an accident while out riding caused a terrible illness, which paralysed her energies, and reduced her to that physical and mental state when work seems to be an impossibility. Broken in spirit, needing rest and refreshment, she found instead that she must begin her fight with Fortune all over again, under greater disadvantages even than before. But she would not be beaten; and making a desperate effort, managed to complete *Great Grenfell Gardens,* which bore traces, however, of the effort it had cost the author.

As soon as she had recovered a little health and strength, she resolved to try once more the style which had proved so successful in *Jennie of 'the Prince's ;'* and with this view, obtained introductions to Mr. and Mrs. Bancroft, Miss Ellen Terry, and Mr. Irving, who all showed her great kindness and courtesy, giving her every opportunity to familiarise herself with London stage-life. The result of this was the serial, *Nell—on and off the Stage,* which appeared in these pages, followed by *From the Wings.*

Mrs. Buxton was a most careful painstaking writer, and spared no trouble of re-writing and revision, however urgent the work she had in hand might be, or however great the need for the payment she was to receive ; for she supported herself and her boy, refusing all help, except a little occasionally from her mother, who has been her best friend through all her trials, giving her frequent and bright encouragement, though compelled by delicate health to live abroad. The pen has dropped from her hand in the prime of life, in the full tide of successful work ; and many will regret the loss of a warm and sympathetic friend and a pure true-hearted woman.

TINSLEYS' MAGAZINE.

June 1881.

MERELY PLAYERS.

By ERNEST WILDING,

AUTHOR OF 'SONGS OF PASSION AND PAIN.'

'All the world's a stage,
And all the men and women merely players.'

CHAPTER I.

LADY ARIADNE AT HOME.

IT was Thursday afternoon, and Lady Ariadne was 'at home' from five to seven o'clock. Human vitality is said to be at its lowest at these hours; and probably tea served by negro pages in cups that had once been Louis Quatorze did much towards reviving life's languid flow in Lady Ariadne and her guests. Lady Ariadne's soul was intense; the form it inhabited frail, but most beautiful. She was mated to a man whose body was immense, and who, if he had a soul at all, had never given the slightest indications of possessing one.

But she never sighed in vain for a community of kindred spirits. She was ever the fair centre of a group—not, indeed, of graces; but geniuses, gentle, and mostly long-haired: men and women endowed, as she said, 'with divine gifts, whose efforts were directed to idealising and rendering beautiful lives whose lots were cast by perverse Fate in a commonplace and vulgar age.' She had, wonderful to relate, never written a line for the public; all language, she was heard to murmur in her dulcet tones, failed to express the high form of her conceptions. Lamartine reflected his soul on smeared manuscripts and printers' proofs, and sold its sacred and treasured memories to an enterprising publisher. Byron annually broke his heart, and described the process in so many cantos for general perusal; but she hid secret conceptions in her virgin soul, and only a stray sentence, a half-uttered expression, a mere glance from her sweet sorrow-fraught eyes, gave indication of the rich mine that lay within.

' 'Tis the world's loss,' said Adrien Messieurs the poet, in talking the subject over with his patroness; 'but the world's well lost.' And he sighed gently, looking at his reflection the while in an opposite mirror, wreathed with long-stemmed silver lilies.

How the gods had ever permitted the union of a being like Lady Ariadne with a creature like Sir George Beldon—whose highest interests lay in agricultural pursuits; whose greatest ambition was the gaining of cattle-show prizes; whose chiefest pleasure was in producing wondrous mangel - wurzel; who wore short, coarse, tweed coats, thick-soled boots, let his beard grow in a tangled mass of tawny-coloured hair, and had rough red-looking hands—was ever a marvel to the heaven-gifted group of young poets, painters, and musicians who followed in her train.

It was one of these subtle mysteries which Fate loves to weave in the lives and destinies of the best and brightest, they said. But had Lady Ariadne, the tenth daughter of an impoverished Scotch earl, deemed it wise to inform them why she listened to the suit of the wealthy baronet who eventually became her lord and master, doubtless she could have thrown a new light on the subject. Sir George Beldon's name was little known in society. He hated town life, and lived principally on his Scotch estates; a thorough country gentleman, an exemplary landlord. The world knew his wife as Lady Ariadne—that is, the world in which she lived. An heir to the Beldon estates had presented himself, much to his mother's inconvenience; a baby with great dark eyes, and a charming dimple in his chin. It was pretty, Lady Ariadne thought, pretty as babies went; but its crying fatigued her, and it was consequently consigned to the charge of nurses and hidden away in the wilderness of a nursery.

On this Thursday afternoon the talent of the present and future crowded her rooms. Wonderful rooms they were, all the world admitted. Sweet Eastern perfumes filled the air and stole upon the senses with subtle sensuous pleasure; the walls of the larger room were hung with sage-green velvet, wrought with passion-flowers, white lilies, and tendrils of many plants; the light was subdued as it fell through windows on which a life-sized copy of the sad-eyed Beatrice

Cenci, and the sinuous sweet form of Venus of Milo were painted; the tiny figure of a maimed Bacchante found in Pompeii rested on an ebon pedestal; white-flowering fragrant plants were ranged against the walls at irregular intervals; an unfinished sketch by Antonio Allegri Correggio lay on an easel, and a piano designed by Alma Tadema and painted by Mr. Burne-Jones stood in the centre of the room.

But the smaller drawing-room was Lady Ariadne's sanctum sanctorum. Here she sat in a low-seated antique chair of dark oak, on which many griffins and weird animals were carved. She wore a robe of creamy hue, gathered full beneath her breast, and lying in many graceful curves and folds at her feet. On her wrists were coils of scorpions wrought in dead gold, and jewel-eyed; around her white throat a single snake in silver, a lily in her fair tangled hair. The walls of this inner room were covered with tapestry; music so soft as to be heard only in the hush of conversation played perpetually; and in the shadow of a far corner stood a life-sized statue of a white-limbed, vine-crowned Apollo, before which a crimson lamp gleamed shrine-like.

Mr. Hal Vector was sitting at the piano playing one of his latest inspirations—a Symphony in Sorrow, a composition in many wondrous intricate keys, with deep-sounding bass chords. It was written evidently for the purpose of making its hearers as uncomfortable as possible.

When it was almost finished Charlotte Weston and her mother entered the room. Though their tastes in common with Lady Ariadne were few, they kept up a friendship which, if not deep, was continuous. Charlotte Weston was beautiful; all men, and, indeed, most women, though the latter somewhat reluctantly, acknowledged that. It was one of

Lady Ariadne's first principles to fill her rooms and surround herself with all that was beautiful in Nature and Art. 'It is a duty one owes to oneself, to make life beautiful as a dream of heaven,' said Cyprian de Ruch the artist, laying down the canons of his belief; and then he laid his dark head, handsome as a Greek god's, against a white-velvet pillow, and waved a Portia fan to and fro, as if beating time to the measure of some haunting rhythm.

'Who is that pretty girl?' queried Mrs. Frumage of her friend and neighbour, Lady Everfair.

'O, Miss Weston. Positively charming, is she not? Though she makes the most of her beauty, dear girl.'

'Ah, of course; I remember now. Her portrait was hung in the Academy last year—granddaughter of old Lord Broton. Yes, very charming indeed.'

'That is her mother. Clever woman—designing, it is said;' and Lady Everfair carelessly played with her gold-rimmed eyeglasses.

'It's said, my dear, Miss Weston is engaged to Mr. Grayford. He has great expectations. Speak of an angel—not that he is one, if gossips be relied on—and you see his wings. Why, here he comes!'

'He is a handsome man!'

'All handsome men are bad,' said Mrs. Frumage, who was twice a widow, and had much experience of the opposite sex. She sighed and thought of the late Mr. Frumage; he was no saint. 'Here is Mr. de Ruch. Ah, Mr. de Ruch, I have not met you for some time! You devote all your time to art, I suppose?'

The artist thrust his hand within the recesses of his velvet coat.

'Yes,' he said, with a sad smile on his pale face, 'I am about to give the world the result of a fresh conception.'

Mrs. Frumage started for a second.

The artist paused and looked wearily away.

'May I come and see it?' said Lady Everfair.

'I shall be very pleased if you will favour my studio with a visit,' he answered. 'At present the conception is but in embryo; time and study can alone render it supremely complete.'

'I'm sure it will be beautiful,' said Lady Everfair.

'Sublime,' suggested Mrs. Frumage.

The artist again smiled faintly, as if all praise was to him mere senseless sound.

'The appreciation of friends alone compensates the true artist for his highest endeavours; it more than rewards for the indifference of an outer world.' He bowed and moved slowly away.

'Senseless young man!' said Lady Everfair. 'What did he say about the other world?'

She was rather deaf, and frequently misinterpreted words.

'It was the outer world he said; but surely he might pay the *friseur* occasionally, and look more rational.'

'Long hair means high culture nowadays.'

'What strange music that young man has been playing! Strange and unpleasantly weird.'

'That is Mr. Hal Vector, one of the musicians of the future; and the dear Dean has just come in,' Lady Everfair said, as a High Church dignitary entered the room.

He had a pale handsome face and long black hair that curled on his shoulders; he wore the ecclesiastical apron, his thin legs were covered with black-silk stockings, and his shoes, pointed at the toes, like those of a stage Mephistopheles, were adorned with great silver buckles.

'We have just had such delightful music, Dean,' said Lady Ariadne; 'a Symphony in Sorrow. You should really ask Mr. Hal Vector to play it as a voluntary at one of your services.'

'I should be delighted if he did,' said the Dean, brushing back his hair with his slender white hand. 'True music, I think, is ever sad in its undertones. It speaks to the soul; and in what place could it more fittingly do so than in church?'

The Dean's services were noted for good music.

'True,' said Lady Ariadne; 'we must render religion beautiful before it attracts. Mr. Vector plays divinely; he is all soul.'

At that moment Miss Fletson, an art-student of the Slade school, in a Greek dress, came up, and the Dean tripped lightly across the room on his toes to speak to Lady Everfair and her friend.

'Have you seen the sketches Mr. de Ruch has made of water-nymphs for Lady Ariadne?' asked Cecil Grayford of Miss Weston. 'No? Will you come and see them?'

'His latest is Undine rising from the sea,' said Lady Ariadne, overhearing his question. 'It is full of divine vigour; it is a dream idealised—you should see it!'

They rose, and went to an adjoining room entirely hung with sketches and water-colour pictures: it was called the studio, and contained plaster casts, some quaint furniture, lay figures, and easels. It was like, indeed, a toy studio, where no one ever did or could work.

There was no one in the room when they entered, and Cecil Grayford said at once,

'I did not ask you to come and really see this rubbish; I asked you because I wanted the chance of speaking a few words to you.'

Charlotte Weston did not move.

'You have scarcely selected a fitting opportunity,' she said slowly.

'Charlotte,' he said, with some determination in his voice, 'let me ask you one question?'

'Not now; I hear some one coming.'

She raised her eyes to his once; there was a look in them she had not seen before. The colour mounted to her cheeks.

Mr. Fruitwell, the Royal Academician, and some friends, came in just then to see the sketches, and Cecil Grayford and Miss Weston moved away.

'I shall call on you to-morrow morning,' he said, in an undertone that left little doubt of the purpose of his visit.

Pink blushes came upon her cheeks. She lowered her eyes.

'Let us go back to the drawing-room,' she said.

On returning they found another child of genius had taken his place at the piano, and was playing a 'Nocturne in Death.' A great actress had arrived too, and was smiling and chatting in the midst of a group of dramatic critics and *literati*; a pleasant murmur of voices fell upon the ear, a gentle movement flowed to and fro. Lady Ariadne was in the larger drawing-room talking to Adrien Messieurs; she suddenly waved her fan, and a silence fell upon all. Mr. Messieurs stood up to recite his last poem, 'Passion's Death.' His voice was soft and low; he sighed once, and then commenced:

'Here, in the garden quaint and gray.
    And sombre in the yellow light
Of sundown, whilst the summer day
    Sinks restful in the arms of night,
        Let us live o'er once more
        Our love-life as of yore.
Let me kiss close your cheek and mouth,
    Right rare your mouth and hot and red;
Your fleet breath rich as winds from south.
    Ah, bliss was in those dear days dead—
        Mad bliss, and deadly sweet,
        Like passion dreams and fleet.
Rose-scented is the darkening air,
    Full fragrant from the sweets of night—
The night all hushed and passing fair—
    Pale lilies stand as spectres white
        Against the garden-wall
        With lichen covered all.

I kiss you on the lips full sweet—
  Ah, tremulous your wild heart throbs
When lip and lip in rapture meet.
  Wild in your soul are passion sobs,
    I feel your quivering breast
    Sweet close against mine prest.

The purple shadows fall apace,
  The gold streaks in the far clouds die,
Too quick the young night veils your face,
  Your tired head on my breast let lie—
    Alas, for light love dead,
    And sear and sad and fled !

Ah, days in the early dawn dead!
  Ah, sweet nights we may know no more!
Our pleasure dreams full fleet have fled,
  Leaving us sad on life's gray shore.
    Let me drink, sweet, your breath ;
    Good-bye, kiss true as death.'

There was a pause for a moment as he finished the last lines slowly. Lady Everfair looked at Mrs. Frumage, and that lady in turn looked away and waved her fan vigorously.

'It is more beautiful than Byron,' said Miss Fletson, 'though, like some of his best poems, it throbs with the sorrow of a great passion.'

The Dean turned to examine the unfinished copy of the great Italian.

'It is like sweet slow music, glad to the senses,' said Mr. Vector. 'I think I could sit down now and play it over.'

The great actress came up and touched the poet's hand.

'Thank you so much,' she said, 'though thank you is not what I meant to say; but I think I can read between the lines, and they are very lovely.'

She smiled with her old winning grace.

'It is entirely supremely beautiful,' said Lady Ariadne slowly— her eyes were fixed on vacancy. If only her lord and master could write like that, wear velvet and long hair, shave his chin, and think no more of cattle and tenants and mangel-wurzel ! It was a vain wish, alas ! She smiled as Adrien's eyes met hers, the very ghost of a smile it seemed, and toyed with her marriage-ring.

It was seven o'clock, and several people were departing.

'Allow me to see you to your carriage,' said Cecil Grayford to Mrs. Weston. Charlotte followed with the Dean. 'I shall do myself the pleasure of calling to-morrow,' he said to her, in a low voice, just as she drove away.

Mrs. Weston overheard him, and smiled.

CHAPTER II.

BEATRICE BARRINGTON.

AN old man and his daughter sat by the fire in a small room of a house in Gray's-inn-road. He had just come in, laid down a violin-case, and taken off a great old-fashioned chocolate-coloured coat, such as Dr. Johnson might have worn in his palmy days. He played second fiddle in an orchestra at one of the Strand theatres. To him music was not only the solace, but the support of life.

'Supper will soon be ready, dear,' said Beatrice Barrington, his daughter.

She was about four-and-twenty years, and what most men would call a very lovely woman. There was almost a southern tint in her clear olive complexion, her eyes were large and gray, her hair rich brown, with an underlying tone of gold.

'And after supper, if you have patience to wait, dear, I have some news for you,' she continued.

The old man looked at her with a nervous startled expression.

'Tell me now, Beatrice.'

Her face had been bright when she spoke; but at her father's question a shadow of care and sorrow crossed it, as if some sudden thought had risen in her mind : the smile faded from her lips.

'News,' she hastened to say, 'only from my old manager, Mr. Ainsworth.'

'Ah,' said the old man, sighing as if relieved.

'He writes to say he has taken a theatre at Rockstrands, and is trying to collect as many members of his old company as he can.'

'I felt sure he would soon make another effort at management.'

'He opens with *Henry Dunbar*, and asks me to play Margaret Wentworth at the same salary as before.'

'He's a good-hearted generous man. God bless him !'

'But that is not all, father.'

She went over to his side, and, kneeling by his low chair, placed one arm round his neck, and laid her head upon his shoulder. 'He knows how hard it would be for us to part, and he wants you to play first fiddle, and conduct the orchestra.' She kissed him fondly as she finished.

The fire grew bright just then; one flame leaping up showed the tears glistening in the old man's eyes.

'Are you not glad, father?'

'Yes, dear, if you are. Don't let any consideration of me influence your going back to the provinces. I am very happy now —indeed, indeed I am;' and he laid his hand gently on her head, and stroked it as if she were a child once more.

Almost unconsciously she cast one swift glance round the room, seeming mentally to note its threadbare comfortless aspect.

'I must go back to the provinces, it is impossible for me to get a town engagement. I am sick of those agents and their promises; and then I am personally unknown to managers, and have little chance of succeeding with them, there are so many others more attractive and better dressed than I, waiting for vacancies,' she said, speaking like a true woman.

She waited a moment, and then continued, 'I have thought it all over whilst waiting here alone for you.'

'Well, my dear?'

'Well, father, we shall accept Mr. Ainsworth's offer !'

Then she was silent again ; her great gray eyes were fixed on the fire, as if she sought to read her future from the grim pictures and shapes the ruddy embers presented. She looked very handsome then, as the flickering firelight played upon her pale face and touched to brighter hues the rich masses of her hair.

'Have you faith in presentiments?' she asked suddenly, looking up. 'Do you believe that in our inner lives there is a voice heard only in the silence of deep thought?'

'I think I do.'

'Well, to-night I have listened to its whispering of a happier life ; to-night for the first time.'

'God grant it, Beatrice !' he said, with solemn and wistful earnestness.

'Since our return to town, when I had nothing to do but stitch or read all day, life was wearisome. I continually went over my past life ; lived it all over again ; its first days so peaceful, bright, and innocent—days that seem centuries away ; then its dream of feverish happiness and its cruel cold awakening.' She shuddered as she spoke, then continued, 'I often wonder you can forgive me, father, and take me to your heart again as you do.'

'My darling, my only hope and comfort,' he said, putting his arm around her fondly, 'don't say that. Why did you never tell me you were so dull and lonely?'

'Have I not given you trouble enough, dear?'

'We will leave all our cares behind us in town,' he said cheerfully.

'Yes, I want excitement in my life again. There is something more than mere woman's vanity in knowing that hundreds of eyes watch you, that hundreds of ears listen greedily for the words falling from your mouth; to see night after night strange faces turned to you; to feel intuitively you have touched the crowd by a phrase uttered in a certain tone; by a gesture, an expression, by some subtle power which is only half comprehended by an actor, and yet which only he can realise.'

A new light came into her eyes, a colour just tinted the olive of her skin, she stood up to her full height, tall and graceful.

'When does Ainsworth open this theatre?'

'Monday next; we can start on Sunday, I shall be quite ready.'

Then they sat down and had supper. When it was over, and the old man resumed his place by the fireside, Beatrice took the violin from its case and handed it to him.

'Play me something, father; anything you please; I feel as if I must have music to-night.'

His face brightened; he stretched out his hands and took the instrument as tenderly as if it were a child. Music was not mere professional drudgery to him. He drew the bow across the strings and commenced a symphony sweet and low, yet wild with plaintive tenderness in its minor chords. Sitting in her low chair, Beatrice laid her elbows on her knees, and covered her face with her hands. Some music touches us indescribably, bringing back thoughts we have tried and tried in vain to bury in the past, voices we can hear, and faces we can see never more, times and places we would fain forget.

When the old man ceased, she stood up; her face was pale.

'Good-night, dear father,' she said.

There were tears in her eyes.

CHAPTER III.

AT ROCKSTRANDS.

MEANWHILE Mr. Ainsworth made Rockstrands his head-quarters. The place was remarkable for nothing in particular. It boasted of some long streets, straggling up the side of a hill, with shops of all sizes, whose solemn peace was never disturbed by the intrusion of customers save on market-days. It seemed at the manager's first view to lie dosing in the glare of a August sun, soothed to peaceful rest by the murmuring sea rippling lazily on the broad strand at its feet.

The inhabitants were numerous and tolerably innocent of the crime of poverty; a race who believed in their own superiority with unflinching faith; whose lives, pleasures, prejudices, and morals were bounded and influenced by stern unflinching rules of provincial propriety.

The manager was a corpulent man, clad in velveteen that had seen better days; rings glittered on his stout fingers, and his breast was ornamented by a massive chain and several appendages in the way of lockets, seals, and miniature designs of household furniture. In the absence of the partner of his joys, and their stock of numerous children, he stayed at the Crow's Head, the principal hotel the place boasted of. He found the town rather dull, for no one seemed anxious to make friends with him. A stranger in Rockstrands was usually looked on with suspicious eyes. If he were rich, how could they tell—good souls—that he was not a diabolical bank director, forger, or midnight assassin, living on his ill-gotten gains, who might any conveniently dark night murder them in their innocent sleep? whilst if poor he was certainly a vagabond, for poverty and vagabondism ever go hand in hand.

One night he strayed into the little billiard-room attached to the inn, where a solitary muscular-looking young man was knocking the balls about in a listless manner.

'Do you play, sir?' he asked of Mr. Ainsworth, who, with arms folded across his chest, was looking at him from the end of the room.

'No, sir; though I take an interest, I may add a vast interest, in all modern games.'

'Rather a pleasant pastime, and almost the only one the town boasts.'

'Indeed! a very healthy and delightful place it seems,' he remarked conciliatingly.

'Certainly, if dulness means delight.'

'My dear sir,' said Mr. Ainsworth, pleasantly familiar with his new acquaintance, 'the air is invigorating, the quietness soothing, after leaving the tumultuous concourse one everlastingly encounters in great cities.'

He waved his hand with a graceful gesture towards the window, as if the cities he referred to lay just outside.

'Then you live in—'

'London. I have the honour of being one of the four million inhabitants popularly supposed to live in that mighty and magnificent metropolis. "One in a populous city pent," as Milton expresses himself,' he ended, bowing as if his words were addressed, not so much to his hearer, as to an invisible crowd situated somewhere at the end of the room.

'We are much quieter here in winter,' said the billiard-player; 'you have just come in for the end of the season.'

'Ah, "they went down to the sea in ships,"' he said quietly. 'Do many theatrical companies visit the place?'

'Unfortunately, very few,' replied the young man.

'Not well supported, perhaps; lacking appreciation for the drama: "various are the tastes of men."'

'I think it's from want of enterprise.'

'My dear sir, this would be one of no "great pith."'

'I wish, then, some one would try the speculation. I like to see a good play now and then;' here he offered Mr. Ainsworth a cigar.

'The drama,' said the manager slowly and with evident pride, 'is my profession.'

'You are, then, an—actor?'

'It is a fact, sir; moreover I am a manager.' He bowed, as if thanking the invisible audience for their timely applause before continuing. '"'Tis my vocation, Hal; 'tis no sin for a man to labour in his vocation," as the immortal playwright says.'

'Scarcely,' said the young man, wondering if his new acquaintance were quite sane.

'Allow me to present my card,' he said, handing one across the table.

The billiard-player read out the name, 'Mr. Alfred Algernon Ainsworth.' 'I believe I haven't a card about me, but my name is George Mortimer,' he replied, with a frank unceremonious manner, simple and winning.

'Delighted to have the pleasure of your acquaintance,' said the manager, with an almost overwhelming air. 'I may impart to you the information that I have taken the little theatre in this town.'

'Jolly glad to hear it; I wish you every success.'

'Thanks, many thanks; you see in me a man "cross'd with adversity," battling, sir, with the waves of a tempestuous life, who has sought in vain to win the "smiles of fickle Fortune."'

He paused, waiting for the imaginary applause from the invisible audience to subside before recommencing.

'James Shirley informs us "there is no armour against Fate;" and Alfred Algernon Ainsworth can prove the truth of his words. It has been my misfortune to fail in most of the grave transactions of life, notwithstanding the finely finished phrase of the late Lord Lytton's, declaring there is no such word in the bright lexicon of youth.'

'I suppose you must allow for poetic license,' put in Mortimer.

'True. My first effort at management was in the suburbs, where I met with "but varying success." You know, my dear sir, "'tis not in mortals to command success." My second venture was in a cathedral town in the North. There I was regarded as the "abomination of desolation." How little the histrionic talent we displayed was appreciated may be judged from the fact that "under the friendly shades of night" the members of my company fled from the reach of some vulgar though credulous creditors.'

'Upon my life, you bear your losses philosophically.'

'Sorrow is intrusive and impairs the faculties. I have learned by experience that "life has many ups and downs,"' he said, with a tone of sadness. Then he added more cheerfully, 'I have known "its many-coloured changes," and I hope to succeed here.'

'I think your coming is a capital idea.'

'And I trust it may turn me in some capital,' he said laughingly. 'But I fear, my dear sir, the night flies apace. You see, "time and the hour runs through the roughest day."'

'Stay,' said George, 'and we will have some brandy-and-soda, and then I'll get home.'

CHAPTER IV.

BEGINNING A NEW LIFE.

GEORGE MORTIMER was by profession a medical doctor. He had just attained the age of six-and-twenty when he succeeded his late uncle, good old Dr. Phestal, to the practice of Rockstrands, in which town the prosy gentleman had passed fifty years of his life 'universally esteemed,' as his mural tablet set forth.

The matrons, who formed no inconsiderable part of the population, and certainly the most remunerative to a medical man, were inclined to consider George Mortimer too young. But youth is a fault that mends daily; and the grown-up daughters of the Rockstrands matrons were in favour of him, and, when they could, overruled the maternal judgment; for the new doctor was an eligible man, who might one day be led bound by maiden charms to the hymeneal altar.

Moreover, he soon gave proof of his skill, and by degrees he slipped into the enjoyment of a comfortable practice.

His late uncle's wife, with whom he lived, was the bugbear of his domestic life. Melancholy and a tract society had long ago marked her for their own; her declared and only object in life was to rescue her fellow-creatures from the perils of perdition. She wrote and patiently distributed religious pamphlets without limit, and bemoaned the wickedness of mankind in general and her nephew in particular; for Mortimer was never seen beguiling his leisure time with the cheerful perusal of the *Rock* or any of Mrs. Phestal's literary compositions. Though 'Warning Words to the Weary Worldling,' or even 'Satan's Snares for Soiled Souls,' were frequently laid in his chamber candlestick, beneath his pillow, on his breakfast-tray, and between the pages of whatever book he was reading, he never employed them more profitably than in lighting a cigar.

He had lived in London all his life until he succeeded his uncle ; a place that Mrs. Phestal declared ' the broad road to destruction.'

' And by far the most pleasant place I know,' said George on one occasion.

' It is ever so to the unwary,' she answered, with a sigh.

A few days after he had met Mr. Ainsworth in the billiard-room, that gentleman had issued his bills, and posted them on every available space of dead wall.

Miss Barrington, they set forth, would appear—those latter words were repeated thrice at respectful distances—as Margaret Wentworth in *Henry Dunbar*, supported by a company carefully selected from the London theatres.

Before one of the most attractive of these bills, on which scarlet letters linked blue, and blue in turn linked yellow across an orange background, in general effect like topers seeing each other home, Beatrice and her father stood gazing admiringly.

' The manager is a man of creative genius ; he should have been an author,' said the old man, reading this fair specimen of Mr. Ainsworth's, where many adjectives and long quotations appeared.

' Here he comes,' said Beatrice ; ' and there is a stranger with him.'

Mr. Ainsworth came towards them with a jubilant air, talking loudly to a young man rather stout of stature and with a general appearance of bluffness. Not a magnificently wicked-looking dark man, nor a muscular Christian, physically a giant, intellectually an idiot, nor a soft-voiced golden-moustached creature ; but a man with an honest frank countenance. His mouth was a trifle too large,

his nose was of no particular type, but his handsome blue eyes looked you pleasantly in the face. He was plain of speech, tender of heart, practical, and just relieved from commonplace. Not the best-natured fellow in the world ; for in modern parlance that indicates a fool or a sot—a phrase meant to cover a multitude of omissionary sins. He was simply an English gentleman.

As the manager approached, he bowed low and waved his hand gracefully.

' Miss Beatrice Horatia Barrington'—the second name had just occurred to him at that moment —'permit me to introduce Dr. Mortimer, a gentleman possessing a keen appreciation of genius and the drama.'

Beatrice bowed ; George raised his hat, smiling at Mr. Ainsworth's mode of introduction.

' And this is her only parent ; she is the sole daughter of his home and heart. Dr. Mortimer, Mr. Barrington.'

Hats were lifted, bows exchanged ; the gentlemen were happy to make each other's acquaintance.

' Miss Barrington's name,' said the manager grandly, ' is euphonic. The first savours of royalty, being that of a gentle and interesting princess ; to the ears of the British public Horatia has a patriotic sound, recalling the memory of that brave but one-armed man, the hero of Trafalgar ; the surname is syllabic and musical. After all, there is a great deal in a name, notwithstanding the idea expressed to the contrary, and allied by our great poet to a charming simile.'

He paused, more for want of breath than words, and bowed to his invisible audience.

' Will not a rose smell just as sweet ?' said Mr. Barrington, speaking as if to himself.

' A man or woman with a name

common in our mouths as household words never succeeds,' continued Mr. Ainsworth. 'Who ever heard of a heroic Smith, a poetic Brown, a dramatic Jones? There is much, believe me, there is much significance in the fact of Fate sending children to parents with commonplace names.'

By joint consent they walked towards the town, Beatrice and Dr. Mortimer a little in advance.

'Your coming has created quite a sensation amongst us, Miss Barrington; we are all anxious to see you.'

'An anxiety easily satisfied.'

George was not quite sure she was pleased with his remark, and remained silent for some minutes.

'Rockstrands seems a charming place,' Beatrice said, by way of breaking the conversational ice. 'You must enjoy living here?'

'I cannot say I do; it's fearfully dull usually; its dulness, indeed, is my pet grievance.'

'Happy is the life that has no history,' she said, looking down; and George, glancing at her then, thought he had never seen a handsomer face.

'I suppose I am a needful machine in the proper place. I set a broken bone, keep down gout in some aristocratic toe, help the fever-stricken back to life if I can, and so repeat my duties over and over again.'

'Some one says no life wanders like an unfettered stream. There is a mill-wheel for the tiniest rivulet to turn. Do you believe it?'

'I wish I could. But we must all make the best we can of life once we are launched into it. Yet I often think that if at the starting we could get a glimpse of the future, how would it be with us?'

'Would it be well?' she asked carelessly.

They had reached the door of Beatrice's lodgings.

They looked in each other's face and smiled.

CHAPTER V.

SOCIETY *versus* LOVE.

IT was just an hour past noon on the day succeeding Lady Ariadne's 'at home.' Belgravia lay quiet in the shade of the midday sun. Many of the houses in the neighbouring squares showed signs of desertion. Shutters were closed, blinds drawn; an air of languidness and peace prevailed generally on this August day.

Mrs. Weston lingered late in town this season. Parliament was yet sitting; and though town was on the wing, society had not yet taken flight. On this morning she sat in the drawing-room of her small home near Belgrave-square, waiting the arrival of a visitor. Charlotte sat on a low couch by the fire, an open book on her knees; she turned the leaves listlessly, and leant her head on her hand, ever and anon thinking deeply.

This season was her third in society. Mrs. Weston had introduced her daughter to the *beau monde* with the determination of marrying her into the peerage. She made no allowances for possible affections of the heart; but had the Marquis of Mountibank, who was gouty, old, and *blasé*, proposed, every allowance would have been made for affections of the liver in calculating the probable period of his existence. Charlotte Weston was well trained. Whilst yet in the nursery, she could without a moment's hesitation name all eligible matrimonial parties, their revenues and expectations, with all the readiness of a charity-school girl jabbering a hymn.

Her face was indeed beautiful, fair and sweet, a little cold, perhaps, in repose, but most lovely when her deep violet-hued eyes smiled upon you and lit her face with ever-varying expressions. Her *début* marked a season in society; she ran the perilous gauntlet of criticism and came out unscathed; she was a success.

Her admirers were numerous; but the observant members of her sex remarked she never favoured very young men, nor younger sons, nor that numerous class of portionless nephews of peers, provided they were not heirs presumptive. Mrs. Weston was disappointed that at neither the close of her first or second season was she engaged.

The worldly matron had married early in life the Honourable Dignare Weston, eldest son of Lord Broton. The first disappointment of her wedded life was the birth of a daughter; a year afterwards her husband died of fever in India, sincerely regretted by his widow, who lost all chances of a title by his untimely demise. Lord Broton, with an utter disregard to her ambition, persisted in living till a month after his son's death, when the next heir succeeded, and married a contemporary beauty of Mrs. Weston's, whom she had cut in the first days of her wedded life.

Mrs. Weston never married again. Mrs. Frumage whispered she had never been asked. Her income was sufficient to float her in society; she lived up to it, and entertained great expectations of her daughter marrying 'handsomely,' as she termed it. Out of a vast number of matrimonial prizes, two men were looked on with particular favour by her watchful maternal eye: those were Lord Hillington, Baron of the United Kingdom and Ireland, and the Honourable Cecil Grayford, heir presumptive to the Earl of Rockstrands.

Mr. Grayford's income, at this period of his existence, barely sufficed for his expenses; he was handsome, universally popular, and clever: it was whispered he could make his mark as a politican if he chose, and there was no knowing what day he might inherit his uncle's title. Lord Rockstrand's principal property was unentailed, and had been handed down intact from generation to generation; the entailed lands were merely worth five thousand a year; the revenue of the other estates, which had been acquired and added to from century to century by the heads of the house, was estimated at sixty thousand per annum: without these the title was a mere empty bauble. It was whispered that the unentailed estates would never fall to Cecil Grayford's possession. It was a mere chance.

Miss Weston's second suitor, Lord Hillington, was a politician. His years numbered almost half a century; his rent-roll brought him thirty thousand pounds yearly. He was plain of person, and prosy. His speeches in the House, though excellent in themselves, were never reported; they had a soothing effect on many of the right honourable members, like a dose of chloral or a heavy sermon, and induced gentle slumbers. His talents were not destined to render him remarkable. *Punch* or his contemporaries never presented him in ludicrous mode to an amused public.

It was much easier to keep Lord Hillington from formal declarations than his younger and handsomer rival, being one of those elderly simple men, of an older school, to whom Love's ways are as fresh woods and pastures new.

Had Charlotte Weston been left to her inclinations, she would have taken Cecil Grayford for better or worse; there was something in him to which her whole being responded; with him she could have been happy, come weal or woe. But her mother had preached her feelings down. She owed a duty to herself and society, Mrs. Weston said; sentiment was dangerous, and never outlived experience of the world: love was all very well in romances; but in real life it should never be allowed to interfere with the prospects of a marriage into the peerage, or the chances of a handsome settlement.

Now that Charlotte believed she would be called upon to make a choice between inclinations and what her mother termed duty, she felt the task would prove no easy one. She did not love Cecil Grayford sufficiently to set all maternal maxims at defiance, yet could not bear to think her refusal would part them for ever; how could she tell him she did not love, or could not marry him?

The recollection came back to her of her cousin, Miss Arrant, who, thirty years ago, refused Jack Hardliver of the Guards, though very much in love with him, and waited and waited for a better offer that, alas, never came. Jack grew into a portly major, and became the father of a family, whilst his once fair love grew faded and angular, and developed a disposition for gossip and afternoon teas.

'Lord Rockstrands may die to-morrow, or next day,' said Mrs. Weston, breaking a prolonged silence, ' or he may go on living for years, as old people whose deaths are looked forward to frequently do; then they talk about some quarrel between him and Mr. Grayford's late father which the old man has never forgiven: that may prevent the unentailed estates falling to him.'

'That quarrel happened years ago; surely Lord Rockstrands

would not visit the sins of the father on his son!' answered Charlotte pleadingly.

'I cannot say; at all events you must keep him in love's bondage a little longer;' and Mrs. Weston smiled.

'Strange that the Earl lives so long.'

'Inconsiderate, under the present circumstances.'

As she spoke, a servant presented a card.

'Say Miss Weston is at home,' said the matron. 'My dear,' she added, ' if you feel any necessity for my presence, just drop your book on the floor. Be strong, Charlotte;' and so saying this exemplary mother vanished, closing the folding-doors behind her.

In another moment Cecil Grayford entered the drawing-room, smiling as he advanced to where Charlotte sat.

'I hope I have not interrupted your maiden meditations,' he said, when their first greetings were over.

'No. I was just reading a chapter from an insipid book — a French novel from the Grosvenor Library.'

'Containing, I suppose, the usual amount of love by moonlight, murder in a storm, with a mixture of passion and exotics, cruel parents, parted lovers, despair and anguish, followed by celestial happiness in the last chapter of the third volume?'

She laughed a little forcedly at this verbal picture—a sweet rippling laugh like music.

'That is not quite the author's programme in this book: the first volume is filled with the hero and heroine's love; it seems an indispensable ingredient in the composition of novels.'

'Being the most powerful passion.'

'The second tells how they marry, though poor as church mice, and how they suffer for their silliness.' She strove to speak lightly; it was the safeguard against the secret her heart held.

'Would you marry any one who loved you deeply and faithfully, if he were poor?'

He asked the question in a low earnest voice, fixing his dark eyes on her as if to read her thoughts. She looked away from him.

'No,' she said, struggling with herself. 'I believe I never could. I know I am weak and not heroic, and—and—I couldn't, I know I couldn't.' She strove to keep down her tears, and almost sobbed out the words, believing them to be false.

Looking up at him, she saw a hot flush on his cheeks.

'Would you not make some sacrifice? I will speak plainer: I came to tell you, if words can, how earnestly, how passionately I love you!'

'Mr. Grayford!'

A new light came into his eyes; he took her hand in his.

'Can you not love me in return?' he asked entreatingly.

'This is untimely, useless; it can only cause us pain.'

'Why is it useless, Charlotte? I shall do all that man can to make your life happy.'

What could she say? O, that there was no such thing in existence as society! that her mother would allow her to marry him!

'I—I cannot promise you anything,' she said. 'Let us speak no more about it.'

He felt her hand trembling, and saw the tears standing in her violet eyes. He rose and walked to the window, but a royal procession might have passed in the street below without attracting his notice. He had a strong will that could overcome many obstacles; he had never yet been baulked in his desires. His keenest wish in life was to marry Charlotte Weston; he

might have to bide his time, but he was as certain as he lived she would sooner or later become his wife.

'You must forgive me,' she said, without looking at him, 'if I have caused you pain.'

He came across the room quickly and sat by her; his lips were close to her face; she felt his hot breath on her cheek.

'Charlotte,' he said passionately, 'no man can ever love you better than I. Forget this wretched society. I will give up all things for you. Will you make no sacrifices? We will live abroad; we—'

'No,' she interrupted him, 'it can never be.'

She struggled to get out the words, as if they choked her. Had she followed her impulses, she would have thrown herself on his breast, and sobbed out her heart there.

'One word more: may I hope that some day you will change your mind? Let me look forward to it as a hope; have some heart,' he said the last words reproachfully. If he only knew how much heart she had! how she longed to tell him she was playing a hollow part at the dictation of another!

She was silent a moment, and he raised her hand to his lips; his hot kiss seemed to burn her like fire.

'I can give no promise,' she said, not daring to look at him. She stood up as she spoke, and the book resting on her knees fell to the ground.

Another instant, and Mrs. Weston entered the room, starting back with surprise at seeing Cecil there.

'Mr. Grayford!' she exclaimed, in melodramatic fashion.

He advanced to meet her, a cynical look coming into his eyes, the faintest smile of mockery playing on his lips.

'I have made an early call,' he said, coming to the point at once, 'in order to have a conversation with Miss Weston.' Looking round the room, he saw that Charlotte had gone.

'Indeed !' said the matron, with apparent astonishment.

'Yes; I have asked her to be my wife, and she refused.'

Each looked at the other intently. Greek had met Greek.

'You seem surprised,' he said somewhat bitterly.

'It was rashness.'

'May I ask why you think so ?'

'Mr. Grayford, let us understand each other,' she said, sitting down, and motioning him to a seat opposite. 'You are a man of the world; I may therefore avoid all sentiment.'

He did not speak, but bowed.

'My daughter has no dowry. If you married her, I believe it would be impossible for you to maintain her in the position she has been accustomed to. I speak plainly.'

'You do.' He felt the blood surging through his veins.

'Both of you belong to a society in which poverty is ranked worse than crime.'

'When I asked Miss Weston to marry me, I looked beyond the present. You know I must sooner or later succeed Lord Rockstrands.'

'His estates are not entailed.'

'Not all of them, but—'

'And if he pleases, he may will them to some stranger, or marry again. Older men than he have done so before.'

'That is scarcely probable,' he answered, with a nervous laugh, while his face paled at the words so carelessly spoken.

'Fortune is fickle,' said Mrs. Weston, remembering her past life, and sighing involuntarily.

'Then until my succession I cannot pretend to Miss Weston's hand ?'

'I will not contradict you.'

He stood up at once; she followed his example. Nothing more passed between them on the subject, and, smiling, they shook hands, each feeling a secret distrust of the other.

'I know,' said Grayford, as he walked towards his club, 'the girl would marry me if it were not for her mother. Curse the old hag !' He lit a cigar. 'She shall marry me yet, by ——!' he said half aloud.

'Halloo, Grayford !' said a voice behind him. 'There's a belief that men who speak aloud are mad— mere prejudice, I know. You like to commune with a sensible man; besides, you can afford to be considered eccentric now.' And Jack Hawksley took his arm, and walked on with him.

'Why now more than before ?'

'You have heard the news, haven't you ? I congratulate you, my boy.'

All the blood rushed to Grayford's head.

'For Heaven's sake, what do you mean ?'

'Your sudden prosperity has made you religious. By and by, you will become a respectable man, dull and decorous, and all that sort of thing; fellows like you always do. Well, old man, your uncle is dead—went off rather suddenly. The king is dead— long live the king !'

'If I had only known this an hour ago !' he said, when he had recovered his first surprise.

'Why? Have you been getting a bill done ?'

'No.'

'There are some telegrams waiting you at the club. I have just come from it, and saw you as I drove by; so I got out and came after you.'

Ten minutes afterwards and Cecil was in the club.

'My letters,' he said to the porter.

'Yes, sir—my lord, hem !' and the man actually looked perplexed.

There were two telegrams for him. One announced Lord Rockstrands had been seized with paralysis; the second announced his death.

Three hours more and Cecil stood beside the lifeless form of John, tenth Earl of Rockstrands.

[To be continued.]

SONG IN THE SUMMER SOUTH.

SWEET is the clime in which our pulses beat,
The noon, the sea, the sultry waves of wheat,
The mellow lights, and silence of the ground,
The summer world's siesta without sound.
    Perfumes of vines and spray,
        O'er tracts in bloom and bud,
    Come to us, and go their way,
        While full of ripeness seems the wood
    Cincturing our orchard-home ;
Cool as spring its frondage, and their fruit within their vernal dome
Flavorous of summer, red as sunset, fresh as morning foam.

The waters languish round the summer shore,
Lapsing into silence more and more ;
Far off the vivid quiet of the deep
Quivers in the bright dream of its sleep.
    So while the earth and air
        In tropic beauty glows ;
    While under clouds, as lilies fair,
        Life is a full-blown rose,—
    Sing, sweet friend, or read to me
Songs with the aroma of some golden-globed dark orange-tree
Exhaled in the strong sunshine glowing o'er the languid dark-blue sea.

                                    T. C. IRWIN.

METEORIC STONES.

By J. A. B. OLIVER.

———◆———

STRANGE as it may seem, it was not until the beginning of the present century that such a thing as a stone that had fallen from the air was believed to have an actual existence. Notwithstanding that many of the writers of antiquity mentioned the descent of stones to the earth, that the authors of the Middle Ages bore like testimony, that numerous persons had actually seen the phenomenon and examined the stones when found upon the ground, and that the recorded instances, ancient and modern, numbered more than one hundred and fifty, the *savants* of last century would have none of it; and the populace, taking their cue from those learned ones, laughed to scorn the unlucky men who countenanced or upheld such a palpable fiction. The first man of science who directed attention to the subject was the German philosopher, Chladni. In 1794 he published at Riga and Leipzig a tract upon the mass of native iron found by Dr. Pallas in Siberia, in which he maintained that the descent of that and similar bodies from the air was not beyond the bounds of probability. The appearance of Chladni's paper, and that of Howard in the *Philosophical Transactions* for 1802, together with the more convincing evidence afforded by the remarkable meteoric shower which occurred at L'Aigle in 1803, dispelled all doubt in the matter, and led to the appointment by the Institute of France of the celebrated Biot to examine on the spot the whole circumstances attending the L'Aigle phenomenon.

Specimens of the stones which fell on that occasion were analysed by Vanquelin and Thenard, and yielded the same result as an analysis by Howard of a stone that was found near Benares in December 1798. A striking similarity was also observed between this Benares stone and one that fell in Yorkshire in December 1795, weighing fifty-six pounds, and which was exhibited in London in 1796. All this placed beyond a doubt the authenticity, or at least the credibility, of the many recorded instances of stones falling from the atmosphere; and so we find Cuvier, in his report in 1809 on the progress of science during the preceding ten years, saying that this phenomenon, though mentioned both by the authors of antiquity and those of the Middle Ages, had only been established as a truth in physical science during that period by the conjectures of Chladni, the analyses of Howard, Vanquelin, and Langier, and the researches of Biot.

Before discussing the probable origin of meteoric stones, it may be well to say something about their composition and the phenomena which accompany their fall to the earth. Accounts of such phenomena are very numerous; but they must not be implicitly trusted. A man of science, accustomed to accurate observation, is not always on the spot when a meteor glides across the sky and bursts into a thousand fragments, and the spectacle is far too impressive not to strike a mere casual observer with surprise and wonder, and lead to gross exaggeration in recounting the circumstances. If divested of the vivid colouring with which ignorance too often embellishes such occurrences, many of the remarkable recitals about balls of fire the size of the moon, with tails of incalculable length, careering through the heavens and bursting into countless flaming fragments with a noise like thunder, would resolve themselves into narratives of by no means extraordinary appearances.

The meteorites in the British Museum are arranged thus: 1. aërolites, which are rocky masses composed principally of silicates with isolated particles of nickeliferous iron and troilite interspersed; 2. aërosiderites or siderites, masses of native iron containing phosphides of nickel and iron, troilite, and occasionally carbon; 3. siderolites, which partake of the character of both aërolites and siderites, being porous or spongy masses of nickeliferous iron with silicates in the cavities. Of these three classes the first is the commonest, the number of specimens possessed by the Museum being 211, the largest of which weighs 134 pounds. Of siderites there are 114 specimens in the collection, the largest weighing over three and a half tons; and of siderolites there are twelve specimens, the weight of the largest being nearly sixteen pounds.

The most famous meteoric stone mentioned in the ancient records is that which fell near Ægos Potamos, in Thrace, about the year in which Socrates was born. It is described by Plutarch in the life of Lysander, and also by the elder Pliny (book ii.), who says that it was to be seen in his time (that is, about five hundred years afterwards); that it was of a burnt colour, and that its fall was accompanied by a meteor. It has been described as of the size of two millstones, and equal in weight to a full wagon load. This stone is mentioned in the chronicle of the Parian Marbles. Livy states that a shower of stones fell on the Alban Mount, not far distant from Rome, in the reign of Tullus Hostilius (about 654 B.C.); but as Humboldt has pointed out, the historian probably refers to pumice ejected from that mountain, which was a volcano, and not wholly extinguished at the time. At Pessinus, in Galatia, the mother of the gods was worshipped under the form of a stone which was said to have fallen from heaven. In consequence of a treaty with Attalus, King of Pergamus, this stone was solemnly brought to Rome by Publius Scipio Nasica, about 204 B.C., and placed in the Temple of Cybile.

To come to more modern times, a remarkable aërolite fell on November 7, 1492, at Ensisheim, near Basle, in the presence of Maximilian I., King of the Romans. It weighed 2¾ cwt., and imbedded itself five feet in the ground. It was long venerated as a miraculous object, a portion of it being suspended by a chain near the door of the church. In 1510 more than one thousand stones are said to have fallen from the clouds near Milan; and Gassendi states that he saw a stone with an apparent diameter of four feet fall on an eminence in Provence. When examined it was found to be very hard, of a dark metallic colour, and fifty-nine pounds in weight. An immense meteoric mass was found by Dr. Pallas in 1776, on a mountain of slate near the river Jenesei, in Siberia. It weighed about 1400 pounds, was irregular in form, and of a cellular structure, the cells containing small granular pieces of the simple mineral olivine, so common in basalt. The iron was tough and malleable, but does not appear to have been of a uniform composition, as Howard found seventeen per cent of nickel, Klaproth and John a much smaller proportion, while the analysis of Langier yielded silica, magnesia, sulphur, and chrome. A tradition existed in the neighbourhood where this mass was found, that it had fallen from heaven, and it was accordingly held in veneration by the Tartars. It was subsequently removed to the town of Krasnojarsk by the inspector of iron mines there. Another vast meteorite was found in South America, in the jurisdiction of Santiago del Estero, about 500 miles north-west from Buenos Ayres. It was inspected by Don Rubi de Celis, who published a description of it, in the Spanish language, in the *Philosophical Transactions* for 1788. It lay in an immense plain of about 100 leagues in extent, half sunk in the ground. Its length was over seven feet, and its weight, estimating it by the specific gravity of iron, was more than thirteen tons. Analyses by Prout and Howard yielded ninety per cent of iron and ten of nickel. Specimens of this mass were sent to the Royal Society, and are now in the collection of the British Museum. In Brazil, about fifty leagues from Bahia, an enormous stone was found, the weight of which was estimated at 14,000 pounds. It contained, according to Dr. Wollaston, four per cent of nickel. Van Marum, in the *Haarlem Transactions*, describes a meteorite of about 177 pounds' weight which fell at the Cape of Good Hope, and is mentioned by Barrow, in his *Travels in Africa*, as an artificial production. A large portion of it was sent to the Haarlem Museum. A meteoric stone, which is in the Museum of Natural Sciences at Madrid, weighs 2¼ cwt. Another, that fell on Christmas-day 1869, at Mourzouk, is nearly a yard in diameter. The Caille aërolite, found in the Maritime Alps, and now in

the Paris Museum, weighs 12¼ cwt. At Santa Rosa (New Granada) one fell in April 1810, weighing 14¾ cwt.; and on the island of Lanaïà-Hawaï there is a meteorite six or seven yards in diameter, which fell at the beginning of the century, and is so firmly imbedded in the ground that it has resisted all the efforts made to raise it to the surface. A stone found at Charcas weighed more than 15¼ cwt. The most colossal meteorites (if the masses are of meteoric origin) yet known were discovered by Professor Nordenskjöld, in the year 1870, on the island of Diskö (Greenland). They were resting on basaltic rocks of the Miocene age. Their composition is peculiar, and has led some geologists to entertain the opinion that they were, perhaps, ejected by volcanoes at an early period of the earth's history. The largest mass weighs twenty-one tons. They were brought home in the year following their discovery by two Swedish war-vessels sent out for the purpose.

Of the manner in which meteorites fall to the earth we have many graphic accounts by eye-witnesses and others. A few of the more important may be interesting to those who have seen the phenomenon, and may serve to give those who are less fortunate an idea of the sight.

In the vicinity of Benares, about eight o'clock in the evening of the 19th of December 1798, a large ball of fire was observed in the heavens, which caused an illumination described as being equal to the brightest moonlight; and at the same time a noise like thunder was heard, followed by the sound of heavy bodies striking the ground. On examination it was found that the earth was newly torn up in places; and further search resulted in the discovery of peculiar stones, most of them buried to a depth of six inches in the ground. Specimens of these stones, some of which weighed two pounds, were sent to Sir Joseph Banks in London. The sky was perfectly serene when the meteor appeared—had been so for more than a week previously—and remained without a speck of cloud for many days after the occurrence.

The meteor which appeared in Normandy on the 26th of April 1803 was peculiar in many respects. It had not the 'ball of fire' aspect so frequently described, but rather resembled a small rectangular cloud, the vapour of which was scattered in all directions at each explosion. It was almost stationary, and must have been at a considerable elevation, as it appeared to the inhabitants of two villages situated more than a league distant from each other to be immediately overhead at the same time. It was seen at Caen, Falaise, Alençon, Verneuil, and Pont Andemer—places far distant from each other. The sound of the explosions, which resembled the firing of cannon and musketry, lasted for five or six minutes, and was followed by a long-continued noise like the beating of many drums. Then succeeded a hissing sound, and a vast number of stones fell to the ground. The space on which they fell formed an ellipse of two leagues and a half long, by one broad; the larger diameter being from south-east to north-west, the direction in which the meteor moved. The largest stones were found at the south-east end of the ellipse, and the smallest at the opposite extremity. Above two thousand were collected, varying in weight from two drams to seventeen pounds and a half. The sky, as in the preceding instance, was almost cloudless.

Flammarion describes the fall of a bolide which took place in the arrondissement of Casale, in Piedmont, on the 29th of February 1868. About half-past ten in the morning, the sky being rather dark, a loud detonation, similar to the discharge of a heavy piece of artillery, was heard, followed, after an interval of two seconds, by a double report. The sound was heard at a place twenty miles distant. It had hardly died away when a small irregular cloud of smoke was observed at a considerable height above the ground. Some spectators saw several spots like clouds, which disappeared nearly instantaneously. A long train of smoke marked the path of the descending mass. 'Some men at work in the fields saw several blocks fall through the air, and heard the noise which they made as they struck the ground. Every one whom it was possible to question on the subject was unanimous in affirming that there were a large number of these blocks, and that they must have occasioned a regular shower of aërolites of all sizes. Labourers at work felling trees in a wood three-quarters of a mile from Villeneuve, on the high-road from Casale to Vercelli, saw something like a hailstorm of grains of sand after these detonations, and a somewhat large fragment struck the hat that one of them was wearing.' Two aërolites were found upon the ground—one weighing 14¾ lbs. and the other 4¼ lbs.—and the fragment of a third, which had been shattered by falling upon a pavement.

Some large stones fell from a fire-ball at Ställdalen, in Sweden, on June 28th, 1876. The meteor equalled the full moon in size, and was visible over a large portion of middle Sweden. It was variously described by observers in different localities. To some it appeared as a pear-shaped mass of dazzling whiteness, and to others as a luminous streak of a violet hue. It was not visible at the place where the stones fell, but previous to their descent loud noises were heard. Eleven stones were found, spread over an oval space a mile and a quarter broad by five miles long, the largest weighing nearly thirty pounds. They fell with a comparatively small velocity, as one of them, eighteen pounds in weight, sunk only eight inches in the ground.

We shall now pass from the region of fact to that of speculation. It were needless, as well as impossible in a short article like this, to mention all the theories that have been offered by scientific men at various times to account for the fall of stones from the sky. The Greek philosophers held widely different opinions, and so do those of the present day. Until more unanimity is arrived at, we may rest assured that the true explanation is not yet found.

One of the oldest theories, and the one that is, perhaps, most consistent with known facts and laws, is that meteorites are bodies moving round the sun, which occasionally enter our atmosphere, and are either frittered into dust or reach the earth as aërolites. In other words, they are abnormally large fragments of comets. Small fragments are dissipated in the higher regions of the air by the intense heat produced by friction, and give rise to the phenomenon of shooting-stars. Larger pieces appear as fire-balls, and very large masses fall through the air in a state of combustion, which is not, however, sufficiently intense to consume their volume before reaching the ground. This idea of a celestial origin seems to have originated among the Greeks. Plutarch says : ' Falling stars are, according to the opinion of some physicists, not eruptions of the ethereal fire extinguished in the air immediately after its ignition, nor yet an inflammatory combus-

tion of the air, which is dissolved in large quantities in the upper regions of space ; but these meteors are rather a fall of celestial bodies, which, in consequence of a certain intermission in the rotatory force, and by the impulse of some irregular movement, have been hurled down not only to the inhabited portions of the earth, but also beyond it into the great ocean, where we cannot find them.' The views of Diogenes of Apollonia are expressed thus : ' Stars that are *invisible*, and consequently have no name, move in space together with those that are visible. These invisible stars frequently fall to the earth, and are extinguished, as the *stony star* which fell burning at Ægos Potamos.' Chladni, as the result of his investigations, advanced the opinion that meteors are bodies moving in space, being either accumulations of matter as originally created, or fragments separated from a larger mass of a similar nature. Sir H. Davy offered the same explanation in the *Philosophical Transactions* for 1817. These views, or rather a modification of them suited to our increased knowledge of cosmical ways and means, have their modern advocate in Professor H. A. Newton of Yale College.

In 1664, Paolo Maria Terzago, an Italian physicist, surmised that aërolites might be of selenic origin. Olbers, in 1795, without any knowledge of this conjecture, investigated the amount of initial tangential force that would be requisite to bring to the earth masses projected from the moon. Laplace, Biot, Brandes, and Poisson also took up the problem. Olbers, Brandes, and Chladni decided against the view of a selenic origin ; but Laplace seems to have inclined somewhat to that hypothesis. It was then believed that active volcanoes existed in the moon ; but that idea has been abandoned, and the lunar theory of aërolites with it. At the present time a number of eminent men who have studied the subject of meteorites think that they must have been ejected from volcanoes on some celestial body, probably the earth at a remote period of its physical history. This may be the true theory, but facts are wanted to confirm it, and until those are discovered it is not safe to pass judgment.

THE OLD LETTER.

CROUCHING over the fire with wan cheek and whitened hair,
And sad sunk eyes, on the embers fixed with a dull unseeing stare;
Crouching over the fire, the woman, worn and old,
With the flickering flame on the letter that trembles in her hold.

Outside, the sleet beats fast and thick on the uncurtained pane,
The wind sobs round the lonely house, as it sweeps the snow-clad plain;
Inside, the ghosts of joy, and hope, and fearless household mirth
Flit and whisper round the woman who sits beside the hearth.

Yet the magic spell of the letter has sent her fancies back,
Flying past all the tombstones that mark the past's long track,
Flying past change and sorrow, flying past wrong and ruth,
Till the heart beats fast, and the pulses thrill, to the passionate glow of
　　　　youth.

She stands once more where the roses their breeze-kissed petals shed,
And the tall laburnum dropped its gold over her golden head;
She hears the brother's tender jest, his boyish laughter rings,
As her gallant lover's letter to her eager clasp he brings.

The gray Australian grasses waves the bold boy's sleep;
Year after year Crimean snows above her soldier heap;
And the pretty fingers, where his ring still flashes in the light,
How worn and thin they show for all they hold the page so tight!

Ah, duller still her life will show, harder the task-work seem,
For that weak hour by fancy snatched for memory's golden dream!
Put by the letter, let it share thy slow and sure decay;
Patient and meek take up again the burden of the day.

SUSAN K. PHILLIPS.

SCEPTRE AND RING.

By B. H. BUXTON,

AUTHOR OF 'JENNIE OF "THE PRINCE'S,"' 'FROM THE WINGS,' ETC.

Part the Third.

CHAPTER I.

TWO PROPOSALS.

It is the morning after the Great Event, and the early spring sunshine falls gently on Diana Hartley's rich black hair and fair rounded cheek, as she lies idly back in a luxurious armchair in her drawing-room, which in every detail is indicative, not only of artistic taste, but of ease and comfort. It is a room that essentially bears the impress of its owner's daily presence and influence. On a fair-sized round table beside her chair lie the day's papers and the latest magazines, surrounding an ornamental pot full of delicate-tinted hyacinths in rich and fragrant bloom; big Japanese jars containing great fresh-looking ferns stand in the deep bow-window; whilst here and there, in dimmer corners, are bright groups of dainty pink tulips imbedded in baskets of moss, so green and moist that the sight of it carries one's mind irresistibly away into deep cool woodland nooks and glades 'far from the madding crowd.' A grand-piano stands open at one end of the room, some loose sheets of manuscript music-paper and a pencil on the stand betraying the fact that the mistress of this charming room has higher ambitions than simply to interpret other people's ideas. The day, though sunny, is ruffled by a light east wind that makes the blazing coals in the broad fireplace very grateful, as Madame Margherita seems to think, for she is seated on the soft hearthrug, apparently absorbed in watching the flames leap and glitter in the brilliant steel fender, though a book lies open on her lap.

Both ladies feel a slight embarrassment, and both feel somewhat aimless and uncertain what to do next. The Great Event, which for some weeks has filled the thoughts of both, is over and past. For more than a month it has been the one absorbing interest and occupation which has bound them together, and for a much longer period even than that it has given colour and interest to Diana's otherwise somewhat objectless life. The writing of her libretto amused her for many weeks, and kept her active mind fully and constantly occupied; subsequently there was the ever-recurring interest of having Campo Maestro's musical rendering of her ideas submitted to her; the criticising and arguing, the trying over, and everlasting rehearsals which never grew tedious to either of the authors. Finally, came the far greater interest of teaching Madame Margherita, and of watching her quick and intelligent development into a charming ideal Marguerite. To-day life looks tame and flat again, reminding one of the old simile of a ballroom the day after the dance, where the flowers are faded and drooping, and every corner, so recently full of warm and vivid life, silent and deserted. And then what should she do about Madame Margherita? The month's trial was up, the purpose for which she wanted her accomplished; what excuse could she make in the future to retain her companionship and still keep Patty and the baby in the country?

Margherita's thoughts were busy in the same direction. Ought she not at once to propose to leave her kind patroness's hospitable roof? Her heart bounded at the thought of having her child—her darling May —with her once more, in the close loving tie of daily companionship. But how should they live? What could she do to earn money beyond singing in the streets again? And she shrank from that now, she could not deny it; her heart sank within her as she recalled those terrible evenings, and the coarse words and light jokes that she had to take amidst the silver and copper she earned. With clasped hands and head bent low she pondered deeply over the difficulties before her, answering but briefly the few desultory remarks that Diana addressed to her.

Suddenly the garden-gate swung to with a sharp click, which was quickly followed by an impetuous knock at the front door. Diana laughed lightly.

'There is no mistaking our impulsive Campo's advent,' she said brightly. 'I am glad he has come to rouse us up.'

She welcomed the little man with both hands extended, whilst Margherita rose hastily from her lowly seat upon the hearthrug, heartily glad to get this reprieve from her perplexing thoughts. Campo Maestro lost no time in beating about the bush.

'Good-morning, Signora Diana; good-morning, Madame Marghe-rita, my child; it is vell, I find you here—both. I have sleep but leettel dis night, and I have come early for a consult serious!'

Margherita made some timid proposal to leave the room; but the vivacious musician, with whom it was mostly a case of thunder and lightning of a harmless kind, snapped at her instantly.

'Why for would you go? It is for la signorina that to speak it is necessary. It is now ze time for talk and consult,' he said, shaking that grizzled head of his, and screwing his face into so many wrinkles that the beady-black eyes almost disappeared.

Diana knew the little tyrant too well to attempt any contradiction : where professional interests were at stake the impresario tolerated no opposition; and besides she hoped his 'consult serious,' as he called it, might throw some light on the difficulties she had been considering all the morning; so she gaily drew a large lounge up to the crackling fire, and, begging the others to do the same, prepared to give her attention to Campo.

'I vill that you tell to me, *cara mia,*' the Italian begins, turning towards his young pupil, 'how is it vid you. Do you find you have zing so very perfeck dis last night ?'

'O no; indeed, indeed, signor, I bitterly felt my shortcomings, my want of experience and practice. I know you are going to reproach me, and I deserve it; for I have disappointed both you and dear Miss Hartley.' Madame Margherita speaks in tones of profound contrition ; and though too proud to sob aloud, she cannot restrain the tears that fill her eyes.

'To talk of reproaches is nonsense, child,' says Diana promptly ; 'you ought to know our dear master's blunt way of speaking better by this time than to take him at his word. You have certainly verified my assertion, and proved the strength of your dramatic instinct. Indeed, it would have been impossible for me, among all the amateurs I know, to find a single one who would have done justice to the difficult part of our heroine as you have done.'

' And for ze voice, ze soprano, it is there vid melody and force,' interrupts Maestro impatiently. 'But it is not cultivate; it has not practice; it is the voice of *ingénue* Margaret, not of Madame Margherita the prima donna, who has a grand experience.'

' It is quite evident to me, dear master,' says Miss Hartley, in that deferential voice of hers (which is the more flattering, perhaps, because so rarely used), 'that you have some plan to suggest, some scheme to propose, which will tend to further your pupil's improvement. She herself, you, and I also, ascertained by the public rehearsal last evening that, though her voice is full of happy promise, her execution by no means enables her to take up a tenable position as a professional singer at present. That being the case, it only remains for us to ask, What do you advise ?'

This is the question to which Campo, under all his seeming impatience, has been steadily and consistently leading up. It bears directly on that pet scheme of his to which his pupil's confidences anent her beggar - relative had already given a certain impetus. He had not lost that former opportunity; but had, on the contrary, urged on Miss Hartley the desirability of removing his pupil beyond the reach of any such disturbing influences.

'She has give up her child for ze sake of you and ze art,' suggested Campo. ' It is now for you to save her from future collision vid any such shameful relations as ze one who has complete upset her to-day.'

Diana assented, but saw no way of altering matters at that time. Now, however, Maestro made a much more definite proposal to her. He offered to go over to Paris the following week to find a suitable home for his pupil, and to make all the necessary arrangements for her studying there at the Conservatoire for three years.

Having delivered himself of this most weighty and unexpected proposition, the wily Italian bent low over the blazing fire, stretching out his short fingers, with their long-pointed nails, to the grateful warmth with evident relish, and leaving his two listeners to digest this new idea undisturbed.

Their feelings were most conflicting. Miss Hartley's rapid impulsive mind flew swiftly over the pros and cons of the situation. She would lose the daily companionship that had become so very pleasant to her; but under any circumstances could she retain that long? She had not forgotten the scene in the carriage during the drive to Richmond, though no mention of the matter had ever been made between them since. She knew well that under Madame Margherita's quiet exterior lay a deep passionate love for her child that made her count the hours that separated them; and she felt certain that she would not much longer consent to that separation now that the Great Event was over, and her obligation to Miss Hartley in some measure discharged. On the other hand, if she agreed to join in sending the girl to Paris to study, she would have the great interest of watching her progress in the art for which she had such considerable natural talent, the delightful amusement of running over to Paris now and again to see her, and the eventual glory and triumph of having been instrumental in unearthing this bright jewel when she shone before the great world, two or three years hence, as an acknowledged star and queen of song. She had already made up her mind to join hands with Campo Maestro in this matter; but Madame Margherita, what would she say?

The girl sat lost in thought, rapidly surveying the past, the present, and the future, the quick alternations of her feelings plainly depicted on her sensitive girlish face. At last she raised her head, to find Miss Hartley and Campo Maestro both eagerly watching her. She flushed painfully as she looked from one to the other.

'Well,' said Miss Hartley quickly, 'will you go, child?' and Campo knew that *she* at least had acceded to his proposition, and once more stretched out his hands placidly to the fire. The rest would follow, all in good time.

Madame Margherita rose to her feet, and toyed nervously with the book she still held in her hands.

'Dear Miss Hartley, dear master, my best of friends, what shall I say? Give me a little time to think; and—' she hesitated painfully, looking timidly from one to the other, 'and—baby May?'

'Had better stay wid ze good nurse in ze pritty Engleesh home,' growled Campo, tossing back his rough hair defiantly.

Madame Margherita drew herself up with quiet pride.

'I am very sorry; I would not for worlds seem ungrateful for your great kindness; but I *could not* live away from my child for three years,' she said, with touching dignity. 'She would forget me quite,' she added, with a nervous sob of pain at the very thought of such a terrible calamity.

Campo lifted his head quickly, with a peppery remark about 'ze 'rt,' which absorbed his whole be-

ing, upon his tongue; but Diana hastily interposed.

'Come and dine with us to-night, Campo *mio*,' she said; 'and then we can talk it over quietly. Sir Gilbert would be hurt if we decided on anything without consulting him; and he has been so warmly interested in Madame Margherita's progress, that it is but right we should ask his opinion about this new and somewhat startling project. But you like acts to follow thoughts as quickly as the thunder follows the lightning, dear master, don't you?' she added, laughing gaily, and at the same time laying her hand, with a kindly reassuring pressure that was very grateful to the girl, on Margherita's arm.

'If it is here before me, the thing that is best to do, I like to do it straight, quick, like a firework,' said the little man, with fierce excited gestures. 'Wid women it is talk and talk and talk.'

'And with you it is sing and sing and sing,' mimicked Diana mischievously. Then, suddenly becoming quite serious, she turned gently to the irate little man, and smoothed his ruffled feathers with a few words spoken in her sweetest and most deferential manner.

'Will you walk across the Park with me, signor, to Sir Gilbert's? On the way we can talk over the details of your most kind and generous proposal, which I shall then be better able to submit to Sir Gilbert, and afterwards our little nightingale shall hear everything about it, and we will let *you* have the result of all the talking in one word to-night, when you come to dine with us.'

When Margherita was left alone she paced the room backwards and forwards in feverish unrest, and longed intensely for baby May to soothe and divert the troubled current of her thoughts. Nothing should induce her to consent to going away without her child. If she might take baby, she would go, and work and slave morning, noon, and night in the hope of some day repaying her kind friends; but if she were on one side of the Channel and her darling on the other, her voice would die away in tears and lamentations whenever she tried to sing. She had just sunk down once more in her favourite position on the thick white hearth-rug, and determined to try and fix her thoughts on her book until Miss Hartley's return, when the drawing-room door was thrown open, and old Luke announced, in a very decided tone,

'Sir Conway Joy.'

The young girl sprang to her feet, and welcomed the new-comer with the natural timidity and reserve of a dependent in the absence of the rightful mistress of the house.

'Miss Hartley is out, Sir Conway. I thought Luke knew she had gone out; she will be sorry.'

'Forgive me, Madame Margherita. I knew Miss Hartley was out—Luke told me; but I thought you would permit me to inquire personally for your health, after the great fatigue of last night,' replied Sir Conway, looking with increased admiration at the sweet face, that appeared even fairer and fresher in the bright searching morning sunshine than it had done in the shaded light of the evening before.

Margherita thanked him in a few simple words. She was too much absorbed in the complications and difficulties of her own life in the past and present, too utterly without personal vanity, to have thought twice of Sir Conway's warmly-expressed admiration for her the evening before, or to appreciate the feeling which made him ask for her when he found Miss Hartley was out. She stands absently fidgeting with her book, without asking him to be seated, under the

evident impression that his visit is to Miss Hartley, and that he will leave again immediately. Her face is still flushed and troubled, showing very clear signs of recent agitation to Sir Conway's anxious eyes. He is quite at a loss what to do or say next under these circumstances. It had flashed upon him like a sudden inspiration that morning, as he took his solitary breakfast in his bachelor rooms in St. James's-street, that he might, without in any way violating the rules of polite society, pay a brief morning call on such an old and intimate friend as Diana, even though he was going to dine with her in the evening. He was quite determined to keep to his dinner engagement. He had found a hasty note from Miss Armstrong on his breakfast-table, reproaching him for breaking his engagement with her, and saying she should expect him to escort her to the De Veres'. She had evidently thought better of her determination to dine at The Cottage by some means or other with Conway, and was attempting instead to draw him back to his old allegiance to her. After settling in his own mind to call at The Cottage before lunch, he felt that he could afford to make some concession to Aurelia, and had sent her a note to the effect that he was sorry he could not break his dinner engagement now, but that he would try and join her at the De Veres' later in the evening. To pass the time until he could reasonably present himself in Regency-terrace he had gone for a walk round Hyde Park before turning his steps in the direction of South Kensington; and seeing neither the many fair horsewomen who galloped past him in the Row, nor the still fairer chestnut buds that were just beginning to glisten in the early spring sunshine, he beguiled his walk with speculations as to whether he should see Madame Margherita during his call at The Cottage, and if so what he would say to her, and how she would turn her calm clear eyes on him as she answered. But, as too often happens in life, the reality was totally unlike any of the many different ways of meeting that he had dreamed about. It had never occurred to him, in the first place, that Miss Hartley could be so cruel as to be out; and when first met by old Luke's 'Not at home, sir,' he had wavered and hesitated on the doorstep in a way rather to excite that old man's curiosity before asking almost timidly for Madame Margherita. And now that he was actually in her presence he seemed to have no pretext for remaining there; the innumerable remarks of a brilliant and original kind that he had expected to make to her had all fled he knew not whither, and only the most commonplace words suggested themselves to him.

'You look very tired,' he said, almost in a whisper.

The soft gentle tone was too much for the girl in her nervous unstrung state. Hot tears rose to her eyes and rolled helplessly down her fair round cheeks.

'You are not well, you are troubled,' he said, with eager boyish impetuosity. '*Do* let me help you if I can, if I may; it will give me greater happiness than I have known for a long time.'

She controlled herself by a sudden decided effort, and brushing away the tears, looked up at him with brave clear eyes.

'I am very sorry. I am not generally so weak and silly. Please forgive me! I have been a little troubled and perplexed to-day.'

'May I not try and help you?' he said, with winning deference and gentleness. 'I am young, I know; but I have been through great trouble, and know what it is. I lost my wife more than two years ago.'

Margherita looked up at him with a soft sympathy in her sweet gray eyes, and with sudden youthful impulse held out her hand silently. He took it in his warm firm clasp, and said hotly and hurriedly,

'Margherita, come and cheer my lonely life; be my sweet wife, and a mother to my little daughter. Forgive me, my darling!' he added still more rapidly, as she tried to draw her hand away, and gazed at him with startled eyes. 'Listen to me one minute; I love you so, Margherita! I loved you the first moment I saw you! I will make you so happy; you shall never know trouble or care that *I* can save you.'

She found breath at last, and drawing her hand decidedly from him, said quickly,

'I am very sorry; I believe you are good and kind, but I am married already; and I do not know—' she hesitated painfully—'that I am a widow. Good-bye; please tell no one,' and she was gone.

CHAPTER II.

EXILED FOR ART.

IT is Easter Sunday in Paris: a bright, warm, breezy day, with a cloudless sky overhead, and the busy hum of gay holiday life filling the streets below. Early mass is over. Troops of merry holiday-makers, in their fresh clean costumes and bright ribbons, are flocking to the railway-station or directing their way, in carriages or on foot, towards the Champs Elysées, and away under the grand Arc de Triomphe to the Bois de Boulogne, and so into the open country. The cafés are all astir; the quick waiters, in their white aprons, darting about amongst the little white-marble tables, on which stand picturesque baskets of tempting-looking rolls and loaves of all imaginable shapes and sizes. Near the Madeleine may be seen numerous homely - looking countrywomen, standing almost imbedded in flowers, some done up into bouquets, others in pots, shielded from the spring breezes by sheaths of dainty white paper. These flowers are bought eagerly by many of the passers-by, and carried into some church and laid as an offering on the chancel-steps, which duty done, and a devout ' Pater noster' repeated, the donor goes forth with a clear conscience to enjoy the rest of the day in the open air.

On Easter-day les Grandes Eaux always play at Versailles; and numerous trains, laden not only inside, but on the covered roofs, with gay throngs of people, are dragging their slow length out of the city towards those lovely gardens and grounds, dropping a few passengers, perhaps, at Saint Cloud, which had not yet had its beauty injured by the Prussian guns.

Under a tree in the Bois de Boulogne, but a little way removed from the main road, sat an unmistakable English trio, comfortably ensconced on a thick Scotch plaid which they had spread on the soft green grass. A fair young English girl, her plump laughing baby, and her maid, the latter of whom was so absorbed in staring at the numerous passers-by, the men in their white or blue blouses, the girls mostly in pretty coquettish aprons and caps, so different from the cheap finery her countrypeople don on all holiday occasions, that she paid but little heed to her small charge, who lay on her back kicking and crowing with delight as her mother tried to tickle her little fat neck with the long grasses that bent

their slender heads before the breeze within reach of her hand.

' It's a pretty sight, Miss Olga.'

' What is, Patty ?'

' All these people going off to enjoy theirselves in the sunshine. They look quite different-like from poor people, with their grand aprons and ribbons, and yet they don't seem as if they was trying to be fine ladies, like some of our poor folk at home. And they do seem that bright and merry it makes one glad-like just to see them trip along, looking so clean and fresh.'

' Wouldn't you like to wear a nice cap and apron too, Patty ?' asked Madame Margherita rather timidly.

Patty smiled broadly all over her homely honest face.

' Lor', Miss Olga, I should look so queer, with my red frizzy hair and my thick waist, not like those trim maids.'

' But they are not all " trim maids," Patty; some are middle-aged women, only their fresh clean caps and neat hair make them look trim and dapper.'

' Well, I would do anything or wear anything to please you, dear mistress,' said Patty, with another broad smile at the idea of herself walking out in a French cap and apron and no bonnet.

' I know you would, dear Patty,' said her mistress, laying her slim ungloved fingers affectionately on Patty's coarse hand, that showed the marks of many a hard day's toil, 'except when you forget,' she added mischievously. ' But seriously, Patty, I really wish you would try to give up calling me " Miss Olga;" some one will hear you one day, and perhaps recognise the peculiar name.'

A comical look of sorrowful penitence spread itself over Patty's face, succeeded by a most resolute determined air.

' I will,' she said, with intense earnestness; ' I'll learn to say "madame" as pat as any *parley-voo* of 'em all, you see if I don't. Madame—Madame Margherita. I'll go and practise it up and down under the trees yon. Come, my blessed lamb, come with Patty, and learn to talk French pretty, pretty; we'll pick a fine nosegay, and leave Madame Mamma to read her book nice and quiet, Mamzelle May;' and Patty laughed aloud, and tossed her baby-charge in delight at her own cleverness; and away the two went over the grass, Patty singing cheerily to the child, ' Madame Mamma, Mamzelle May! Madame Mamma, Mamzelle May !'

Left to herself, Margherita slightly shifted her position, so that she might command a full view of the child and her nurse, and took up her book. It was a somewhat tough treatise on the study of singing and the development of the human voice, lent to her by her new master at the Conservatoire, M. Valentino; and after knitting her white brow over a couple of pages of it, the demoralising influence of the sun and air, and the gay voices around, was too much for her, and she leant back against the tree and gave herself up to the full enjoyment of idle thoughts.

Her thoughts were not altogether pleasant, though. She was enjoying now a certain amount of peace and rest, happiness in the society of her child, and hope and interest in the study of the great art for which she had consented to exile herself from her own country, and from the neighbourhood where alone she could expect to hear any news of those connected with that phase of her life which had begun and ended before she ever saw Miss Hartley or entered the gates of The Cottage in Regency-terrace. But her mind was still troubled with doubts as to whether she had acted

rightly in leaving London for three years, thus losing for that time all chance of finding her poor wandering parent, whom she had so solemnly promised to take care of. Her sensitive conscience was at times very sore on this subject; and Patty's oft-repeated consolation that it was the father who turned her off, not she who deserted him, was not always successful.

Margherita had now been nearly three weeks in Paris with her faithful Patty and her baby May, but this was the first time they had ventured farther than the gardens of the Tuileries, near which, in the Rue Miroménil, her modest lodging was situated. On Good Friday they had wandered as far as Notre Dame, where Patty had gaped open-mouthed at the long candles burning as an offering before the shrines of dead relatives; at the sad-looking Sisters of Mercy, who stand holding out their money-boxes to all passers-by, accompanied by the monotonous chant, ' Pour les pauvres, pour les pauvres !' and above all at the solemn chapel, draped in black, where lay the effigy of the crucified Saviour, surrounded by watchers, and dimly illumined by tall wax-candles. The sight sent awe into Patty's soul for the time being, though, as soon as she was out again in the cheerful busy streets, she thought it was ' real Popish stuff.' But it made Margherita's heart ache painfully; she could hardly tell why; and even now she thought of that calm placid figure, resting so quietly after such agonies of torture, with deep pity and sadness in her soul. Only those who have suffered intensely themselves can feel this intensity of pity for the sufferings of others.

But on Easter-day the bright sunshine and general atmosphere of gaiety infected Margherita as well as every one else, and Patty had responded with delight to her mistress's proposal that they should take their lunch and try and find their way out of the city and into the suburbs.

'How *could* he think I would give up my darling, even for my art!' murmured Margherita, as she watched with loving eyes the merry play of Patty and the little one round and round the trees. 'What would life be to me without her? But he was very angry, very indignant;' and Margherita smiled to herself as she recalled the fiery looks of scorn the enthusiastic Italian cast on the mother who cared for her child more than she did for the glorious voice that Nature had given her. But Margherita had stood firm; she would not be separated from her child any longer.

Miss Hartley had returned from her walk with Campo to Sir Gilbert's in radiant spirits, full of enthusiasm for this new scheme from which Campo prophesied such glory and honour in the future; her impulsive mind leapt at once to the climax, without being in the least shadowed or damped by the interval that must elapse before that climax could become a present fact. She was going to set to work to write another libretto for a new operetta,—perhaps something more ambitious still, who could tell? She had met several people who had been present the evening before, and who had been enchanted with everything. She was fired with ambition; her brain was teeming with ideas, if she could only get time to reduce them to order. Her manner to Margherita was fascinating in its frank kindliness as she talked fully and freely to the girl of Campo Maestro's proposal.

'You need feel under no obligation to us, child,' she said, striking with her ready woman's wit straight at the root of Margherita's hesita-tion and uneasiness. 'You have been of immense service to us in helping to carry our operetta triumphantly through its first performance; and if only half dear enthusiastic old Maestro's prognostications are fulfilled, you will be able to ease your independent little soul in the future by repaying us any mere money expenses, if you prefer to. But you know, child, I am rich, and Sir Gilbert is richer still, and it is an immense interest and amusement to us to be privately hatching such a *rara avis* as we expect you to turn out. I shall run over to Paris occasionally and see how you are getting on, and I shall work as hard in London as you will in Paris. Cyril Clive shall come home to find me famous;' and she glanced up with a beaming face at the portrait of the bright boy Margherita loved for reminding her faintly of her own blue-eyed baby.

'How long will it be before he returns?' asked Margherita softly.

'Perhaps two or three years,' replied Diana sadly; 'but it *might* be much sooner, one can never be sure. I long to have him back. But now, my bonnie Margherita, you will consent to our plan? I may tell Campo that you will agree to his proposal?'

Margherita had been thinking deeply over her own position since she had been so startled by Sir Conway Joy's sudden proposal to her. If Miss Hartley heard of his offer to make her his wife, she would naturally urge her to secure at once such a safe and happy prospect, or to give some good and valid reason for refusing it. And that she could not do. She would tell *no one* the history of the past till she knew—and she set her little white teeth hard as she registered the resolve—whether she was a true wedded wife or not, and whether her husband was living or dead. Until that mystery was solved, and light cast on that dark hour of her life, the story of her brief love-time should remain a secret, should live and die with her—only suspected by her faithful Patty. If she went to Paris, she would be safely out of the way of this trouble at least; and she would be perfecting herself in a profession that would, in the future, make her and her child independent of all aid from others. If, on the other hand, she refused this generous proposal, what could she do? Her kind benefactress would be annoyed, and perhaps even disgusted with her, and refuse longer to befriend one so obstinate and foolish; and she could then only sink back again into the obscure poverty that would more effectually prevent her from finding and helping her father, or from ever learning anything more about those short blissful hours of her honeymoon, than any mere distance of land or sea. And so it came to pass that when Miss Hartley appealed to her so sweetly, and almost deferentially, for her decision on this momentous subject, she showed no hesitation, but, clasping her hands and leaning eagerly forward, exclaimed,

'Most gratefully, dear Miss Hartley; indeed, I do not at all know how to thank you and your good generous friends for their great kindness to me; some day, perhaps, I may be able to prove substantially how much I feel. But,' she added timidly, after a short pause, and looking half doubtfully at Diana—'but—'

'Your baby?' questioned Miss Hartley, coming to her rescue, but with the faintest suspicion of sharpness in her tone. 'Of course, your baby and Patty must go with you. Signor Campo must swallow that pill as best he can. He will not like it, poor little man,' she added, with a laugh.

Margherita flushed with delight at Diana's decided reply, and breathed a soft sigh of relief.

'Thanks, a thousand times!' she exclaimed warmly. 'Believe me, I shall study more earnestly and heartily if she is near me, so that I can always see and know for myself how she is. And you will let us live very inexpensively, dear Miss Hartley—in our old homely way.'

'Campo Maestro's idea was for you to go alone, and be placed in a *pension* or convent. I think,' said Diana, laughing gaily, 'we shall have to combat that notion, and make him find you a nice little flat in a good house. By the way, Luke told me Sir Conway Joy called whilst I was out, and saw you. Had he anything particular to say? Is he coming to dinner this evening, or has Miss Armstrong succeeded in making him dance attendance upon her?'

In spite of herself, the delicate colour mounted into Madame Margherita's face; but Miss Hartley's attention was at the moment distracted by the entrance of Luke with the afternoon tea, and before the old servant quitted the room again the young girl's conscious flush had died away.

'Sir Conway only stayed a few minutes,' she replied; 'he did not say anything about dinner.'

'Then I suppose he is coming,' said Miss Hartley; 'you had better go and lie down, child, you look very pale. I, too, will go and rest a while before I dress.'

A week from that time had seen all preliminaries settled; and less than a fortnight found the mother and child, and their stanch friend Patty, reunited in a modest little home on the third floor of a quiet respectable house in the Rue Miroménil.

At this point in her interesting retrospection Margherita suddenly became conscious of the entire cessation of Patty's boisterous 'peep-bo's,' and baby's answering screams of delight; and with a nervous start of terror she looked up, to find that the afternoon sun was slowly sinking westwards, casting long level shadows over the grass as his race neared its end, and that Patty was sitting placidly on the ground, absorbed in watching the 'funny French folk,' as she alliteratively called them, with tired baby May fast asleep on her lap.

Refreshed by her long rest in the open air, Margherita helped Patty to pack the still sleeping child in her little carriage, and the trio set off briskly on their return home, Patty enlivening the walk by her inexhaustible comments on all she saw and heard.

'Lor, Madam' Marg'rita, this looks like a Britisher coming right along in front of us. He ain't no parley-vooing Frenchified feller, I'll be bound!' she suddenly exclaimed.

Margherita, who was smiling happily down on the unconscious face of her little sleeping child, looked up quickly as Patty spoke, and found herself face to face with Sir Conway Joy.

In the first moment of surprise at meeting a familiar friendly face so unexpectedly in this strange land, she uttered an exclamation of pleasure, and held out her hand frankly to receive the eager grasp of Sir Conway. He was in a gray knickerbocker suit, with a white-straw hat on his head, a knapsack on his shoulders, and a stout walking-stick in his hand, evidently bound on a pedestrian excursion.

Margherita inquired eagerly for Miss Hartley and Campo Maestro, and expressed her surprise at seeing Sir Conway so far from home.

'I am going for a walking-tour,' he said simply and briefly. He did not tell her he had already wasted two days in Paris trying to meet her. 'Miss Hartley says you have forsworn all visitors until your studies are completed.'

'Yes,' replied Margherita, 'I must give all my time and attention to my work; I promised to do so if I might have my little girl with me.'

Her little girl! He started and looked hurriedly towards the little carriage which Patty had wheeled a few yards on.

'I am going away to recover myself,' he said, in a quiet manly way; adding gently, 'That is, Margherita, if you can give me no hope. Is there none—is it quite useless waiting?'

'Quite,' she said, raising her eyes to his face, full of tears, but with a steady light in them that left him no room to doubt her resolution.

CHAPTER III.

ALINE.

THE bright spring-time had deepened into hot summer sunshine more than once, and more than once had the glowing tints of autumn faded away before the cold shadow of winter, and still Madame Margherita was busily pursuing the even tenor of her life in the little Paris flat, walking daily with brisk light footsteps through the lively foreign streets from the Rue Miroménil to the Faubourg Montmartre to study at the Conservatoire. With unwearying patience and perseverance, she went through all the drudgery her master exacted from her before he allowed her to touch, scarce even to look at, the operas in which she one day hoped to take the title-rôle. M. Valentino, her master, differed in almost every way from Campo Maestro. Large in make and somewhat lazy in movement, he owned a calm placid face, and long sleek black hair which offered a most striking contrast to Campo's rough grizzly head and sharp rapidity of tongue and movement. He had his peculiarities too, which greatly amused Margherita in the early stages of her study. He always tuned his piano himself, and would very often commence a lesson by taking a tuning-fork out of his waistcoat-pocket, and sitting down deliberately to pull his piano to pieces.

'We cannot run the risk of any false notes, you know, my dear; that would never do. It is a saving of time in the end to start fair. Now begin: open your mouth well —wide—so; wider!' and he opened his own large mouth wider and wider, for his pupil to imitate. He maintained that the whole ground-work of good singing depended on your learning, in the beginning, to· open your mouth *properly*. But clever little Campo knew what he was about when he placed his favourite Margherita under M. Valentino's tuition. He was at the top of his profession in Paris, and could not only train her perfectly in her art, but secure her an engagement hereafter in the Paris Opera, if she in any degree fulfilled the expectations that Maestro had formed of her. All this he had impressed on Madame Margherita; and though sorely tempted to laugh during her first lesson, she controlled herself, and, gazing steadily at the flexible lips of M. Valentino, explicitly followed his directions, and was rewarded by his commendation.

'You have been carefully taught so far, child,' he said, nodding his head slowly; 'there's nothing to unlearn, which, I am sorry to say, is not often the case with my pupils; but there is a mountain of work before you yet. You must practise hard—several hours a day at intervals; don't overdo it. Chest strong?'

Margherita assured him her chest and lungs were invulnerable, and that she was not at all afraid of hard work, and loved singing above all things; whereupon he smiled benignly, and bowed her a most polite farewell.

Her home-life was quiet in the extreme, but peaceful and contented, disturbed only by occasional restless thoughts about her father, which she resolutely tried to put aside, with all other painful memories, until the time of her probation was at an end. Very soon after her unexpected meeting with Sir Conway Joy in the Bois de Boulogne, she had received a letter from Miss Hartley, telling her that Sir Conway had made her his *confidante* before leaving England.

'You foolish child,' she wrote, 'to refuse such a chance in life. And he is such a nice fellow too, good-hearted, high-minded, chivalrous, with a little motherless girl not much older than your baby May. He is far too good for Aurelia Armstrong. By the way, she is furious at his slipping off to Paris, and I should not be at all surprised if she made some excuse to follow him. But to return to our muttons: *why* did you refuse him? Is there no possibility of reconsidering your refusal? I know nothing of your early life; but I think, child, you might trust me.'

Margherita was devoutly thankful that this appeal was written, and not spoken face to face. It was easy in writing her reply to touch lightly only on what it was absolutely necessary to answer, and ignore all the rest entirely.

The first Christmas she was in Paris, Miss Hartley had come over for a week's dissipation; but Lady Furnival had accompanied her, and the two had kept up a whirl of driving and sight-seeing, so that Margherita had really seen but little of her kind patroness, and had easily escaped all private questioning. Sir Conway she had seen again for a few minutes one day in the Tuileries gardens. He was on his way back to England, and tried by his frank pleasant manner to disabuse her mind of all fear that he should distress her again by urging his suit.

'I shall run over occasionally, when I feel to be getting rusty down in my country home,' he said, as he bade her farewell. 'If you ever want the help of a true friend, do not forget that I would give much to be of service to you.'

One blazing July day, when the fierce rays of the sun were beating pitilessly on the white pavement of the streets, Margherita was returning home from the Conservatoire, and turned hastily, with a gasp of relief, into the cool, dark, spacious entrance of the house, on the third floor of which her present abode was situated. Seated at the foot of the stairs she found Patty, with baby May in her lap. The child's cool linen bonnet was thrown aside, and her fair soft curls were all tumbled over her flushed face as she rolled backwards and forwards in Patty's lap, trying to catch the great juicy red strawberries held laughingly just above her nose by a slim bright-faced young girl, whom Patty had once or twice mentioned to her mistress as living in the ground-floor rooms, and taking great notice of baby whenever they met.

Little May forgot the strawberries, and set up a shout of delight when she saw her mother; and the young girl turned, with a quick and graceful movement, to apologise for thus stopping the way.

'Forgive me, madame; your child is such a sweet merry little thing, I never can resist trying to make her laugh when I meet her. Papa says I am only a baby myself yet,'

she added, laughing merrily; 'so I mean to enjoy my infancy still, and laugh and play with any other nice baby I can find. You will not mind my playing with her?' she questioned, with the frank friendliness of a young girl who had nothing to conceal, and had never yet learnt to distrust any one. 'My name is Aline Urquhart, and we live in this house too. My father is an artist; I shall make him paint baby. You are Madame Margherita, I know,' she rattled on, 'and are studying singing. You have a lovely voice. I made papa go up and stand on the landing to hear you the other night, when you were singing some of Lucia's songs.'

She paused here, principally from want of breath. She was small and slight almost to a fault. But the agile grace and vivacity of her movements, and the sparkling intelligence of her extremely pretty face, redeemed her appearance from anything like insignificance. She looked more childish than she would otherwise have done from the fact of having her dark hair cut quite short, and curled thickly in soft rings all over her head; a scarlet ribbon flashed in and out amongst the curls, and was tied in a coquettish little bow on the top of her head. Over her cool white cambric gown she had a large useful holland apron, with a bib and big pockets, fantastically trimmed with narrow scarlet braid and edged with lace; and from under this screen, which reached to the edge of her dress, a pair of most minute scarlet shoes, with steel buckles and high heels, peeped forth.

Madame Margherita was delighted with the child's quaint artistic appearance and genial *bonhomie;* besides, her heart was taken by storm by the eager admiration, not of her singing, but of her child. What true mother's heart ever resisted *that* flattery? 'I shall make him paint her.' The phrase remained in her mind. How delightful to have a portrait of her sweet baby! Not a colourless scientifically-accurate photograph, but a warm living likeness in oils of the round white limbs, the bright curling hair, and laughing dimpled mouth. She smiled brightly at Aline as she answered,

'Baby seems quite at home with you.'

'O yes,' answered the girl, 'we often have a little game on the stairs here, or in the hall. I am very lonely sometimes when papa is out, and I am tired of practising my violin.'

'Do you play the violin?' asked Margherita, in great amazement.

'Ah, yes, I love my violin! I learn with M. Taupin. He says in a few years, if I practise *very* steadily, I may perhaps play in public. Are you going to sing in public, madame?' asked Aline, looking with her frank childish gaze straight into Madame Margherita's equally clear truthful eyes.

'Yes, I hope so, Mdlle. Urquhart. I hope to sing and earn money for baby, if I can sing well enough.'

'O madame, well enough! You sing like an angel straight from heaven. Not that I ever heard one,' said the lively girl, suddenly becoming serious. 'I don't know why we say such things without knowing a bit about it. Perhaps the angels sometimes sing out of tune as well as other people;' and she gazed thoughtfully for an instant across the cool dim hall out on to the hot street, where the blazing sun still beat mercilessly down on the few passers-by. Then suddenly returning to the lively manner that seemed more natural to her, she exclaimed,

'But do not call me Mdlle. Urquhart, madame; call me Aline.

Every one calls me Aline. Fancy, madame, if one day I could accompany your singing with my violin. Would it not be enchanting? But I am afraid I shall never play well enough for that,' she added sadly; 'it is such a difficult instrument, but I *do* love it.'

'Whatever made you learn the violin?' asked Margherita.

Aline laughed gaily.

'It must seem funny,' she said. 'Papa says a tambourine would suit my style better. He says I am rattle-pated. But I shall sober down before I can play well enough to appear in public; and I have always loved the violin ever since I was a child. I had a little toy-fiddle I used to play when I was only about five years old.'

'I *should* love to hear you play a tune on the fiddle, miss—I beg yer pardon, mamzelle,' said Patty suddenly, with a beaming smile.

'Should you? I will play for you directly. Would *you* care to hear me play, madame?' she added shyly, turning to Madame Margherita.

'I should like to hear you very much indeed,' replied Madame Margherita. 'I never heard a girl play the violin. Will you come to my room? It is on the third floor. We are not rich,' she added simply and proudly. 'We have to be very careful till I can sing well enough to make some money. Perhaps monsieur — perhaps your father would not like you to come.'

'O yes, he would not mind a bit!' replied Aline gaily. 'He is very glad when I am happy and busy with nice people.'

'Are we "nice people," do you think?' asked Margherita, laughing.

'Of course, any one can see that directly,' answered Aline decidedly. 'I will come up in a few minutes, when I have told old Julie, our old servant. We live here on the ground floor. *Au revoir*, madame;'

and she danced away lightly over the stone floor, and disappeared through a dark oak door that swung heavily to behind her.

This friendship with Aline Urquhart made a bright spot in the lives of the trio on the Troisième Etage. Her character was an odd mixture of the child and the woman. She would go with Patty and May into the gardens of the Tuileries, and laugh and play as carelessly and contentedly as any baby there; or she would sit and talk softly and tenderly to Madame Margherita, in the twilight, of her own life, of her dead mother, whom she and her father had laid to rest some three or four years ago in a little quiet graveyard amongst the Swiss mountains. After her mother's death she had gone to school for two or three years, to a secluded school kept by two high-minded simple-hearted gentlewomen in a retired village about ten miles from London, where she had been carefully taught and guarded, and which had been like another home to her. She had been with her father now for nearly a year. He thought it would be good for her to spend a little time in Paris, and study music properly, and become quite familiar with the language. In this way she used to prattle on about herself, having nothing to hide in her innocent childish life. But with natural tact and delicacy she abstained from asking any questions in return, or making the slightest attempt to learn from Margherita anything she did not herself volunteer to tell. She concluded at once that Madame Margherita was a widow, left badly off, with her little child to support. 'Isn't it sad, papa?' she said, when recounting her adventure to her father on the evening of her first visit to Madame Margherita. 'She is *so* lovely, and really does not look much older than I do, though she is tall and

stately; and she is a widow already, with a little child, such a sweetly pretty little girl. You must paint her, papa. And she has to earn money for them both as soon as she has finished her studies at the Conservatoire.'

It often puzzled Margherita to think where she had heard this peculiar name of Urquhart before, and how it was that it seemed in some indistinct way associated with that deep trouble of her life which she never spoke about to any one. She would think about it as she walked to her lessons, and as she returned from them; as she dressed in the morning, and as she undressed at night. Our memories seem, like wells, to have unending depths, in which we sometimes lose small facts, that only after days and days of patient groping we manage to grasp again and bring to the surface. So it was with Margherita: after many days of persistent searching in the recesses of her brain, it suddenly recurred to her that Urquhart was the name of the friend who owned that studio where the happiest hours of her life had been spent. Urquhart was the name on the telegram shown her by that hard and insolent housekeeper, on the dark dreary day of her life when she first heard that Cuthbert was gone. Having satisfied her mind on this point she was at rest. It could not be the same Urquhart, and if it was she could not do anything; but still it stirred her heart faintly, and made her encourage Aline's pleasant chatter the more. The name alone seemed some faint link with that happy time; though she knew it was best and wisest to put that time altogether aside, and keep her face steadily towards her child and her work. But the heart she was trying to steel against the past was destined to be stirred yet more deeply, and in a most unexpected manner.

One gloomy evening, late in autumn, when even Paris looked dull and uninteresting under the gray mantle that it seemed to have borrowed for the nonce from the English metropolis, Aline laid down the violin on which she had been diligently practising for more than an hour past, and tripped out from the *salon* into the kitchen beyond to amuse herself with Julie, or the cat, or anything else of an attractive nature that presented itself to her wandering fancy. But she found Julie intensely busy, gofering the elaborate frills of her own best cap and Aline's Sunday petticoat, and too anxious to talk.

'Go and play with your little baby-friend up-stairs, *ma petite*,' suggested the good-natured old woman.

'I do not like to go so often up-stairs, Julie; they may get tired of me, and it is past baby's bedtime.'

'Ask madame to come down with you a bit, then. Monsieur will not be home till late this evening, if he is gone into the woods painting autumn colours; he will stay and dine at the *auberge*.'

'She does not like coming to our rooms, I think, Julie; she is so shy and retiring. She has never come yet.'

'Ah, tell her to come and look at the sketch monsieur made yesterday of her little child. It is only just a slight sketch, I know; but it will delight her, or she is no mother.'

Almost before Julie had finished speaking Aline's swift feet were half-way up the stairs; and presently she returned with Madame Margherita, and led her to an easel on which stood the merest sketch of little May. But Mr. Urquhart had outlined it in a happy moment,

and the child's own sweet eyes laughed back at the mother from the canvas. Margherita clasped her hands in delight.

'O Aline, it is wonderful! He has caught her very soul. My little pet!'

Aline stood by trembling with delight. She was devoted to her father, and immensely proud of him; and as soon as Margherita could make up her mind to turn from the portrait of her little daughter, Aline began shyly drawing her attention to other pictures painted by her father's hand.

'Has he never painted you, Aline?' asked Margherita presently.

'O yes, madame, often. The most finished one is in his bed-chamber. But here are several old sketches done long ago;' and she pulled out a heavy brown portfolio from a dark corner, and opened it on the ground. It was too heavy to lift up to the table.

The two girls knelt beside it on the floor and turned the loose sketches over slowly, till they came to one on which Margherita's hand closed tightly as she leaned heavily forward. Her heart gave a wild leap upward, and then beat so loudly that she thought the girl at her side must hear it. At one bound her mind was back in the studio at Westminster, warm words of passionate love were in her ears, strong clasping arms supported her trembling frame. The room she was in seemed to vanish from her sight; Aline's voice, prattling on beside her, sounded far away as in a dream; her misty eyes could see nothing; her tingling frame could be conscious only of the fact that she was gazing on the face she had once so idolised, the picture of the father of her child.

[To be continued.]

LORDS AND LADIES.

Scene : Top of a drag at the 'Varsity Match.

'WELL, dear, this is charming ; so glad that I came ;
   So kind of Lord Ernest to give me a seat.
We couldn't be better for seeing the game,
   And watching a match is to me such a treat !
Let's see—it is Oxford that wears the light blue ?
   I'm *awfully* Oxford. What ! Cambridge is light ?
Well, then, I am Cambridge. Look, there's Mr. Pugh !
   I met him at Lady MacGillies' last night.
Do give me a card, for I must keep the score.
   O, thank you so much, you're quite awfully nice !
And now, if you won't think me too great a bore,
   You'll show me the way I'm to keep it. An ice ?
Well, really, I think I should like one, you know.
   O dear ! what's the matter ? Some poor fellow out ?
What *shall* I put down ? Do just look at them throw
   The ball to each other. What *are* they about ?
Another man in, and it's " over." O dear !
   The game can't be finished ? Ah, just so, I see ;
I haven't been keeping the score right, I fear.
   My card and the telegraph board don't agree ;
I'll keep it no more, it is getting too hot,
   And watching the people is much better fun.
O, thank you, Lord Ernest, just one apricot ;
   No, really, Lord Ernest, I mean it—just one.
I *will* take a little champagne. Look at that
   Young Noel and Ethel, he's clearly *épris ;*
And there goes Frank Gascoyne, he's got a new hat.
   Poor fellow ! I wish he had more £ *s. d.*
But as he is now, I could never afford
   To think of— What, really, the match is quite done !
I must say I haven't been very much bored,
   And O ! by the bye, tell me *which* side has won ?'

   She cannot distinguish a bat from a wicket,
   And that is the lady's idea of cricket.

SOMERVILLE GIBNEY.

THE MAGIC EMERALD.

By HENRY GEORGE MURRAY.

'Shadows to-night
Have struck more terror to the soul of Richard,
Than could the substance of ten thousand soldiers.'

I.

'THE magic emerald, did you say, Mr. Langton? Dear me, how very interesting!'

'Did you never hear of it before, Lady Matilda? I thought that everybody knew that old story.'

'O, one doesn't always hear things, you know. But tell me, what does the magic emerald do?'

Lady Matilda's companion, with a little sigh of resignation, settled his back more comfortably against the roots of the enormous oak under which he was lying. He was a long, lean, wrinkled man, with a skin burned, by long exposure to tropic suns, to the tint of the autumn leaves that lay about him. He would have been a noticeable figure anywhere, but he was particularly so amid his present surroundings. He was the kind of man one would have rather expected to meet in an Arabian desert or on the wilds of the Pampas than amid this quiet English landscape; and his dress, which was a compromise between civilised requirements and tropic ease, tended to increase the natural strangeness of his aspect.

Stephen Langton, like all men of any strength of character at all, had his friends and his enemies, and their estimates of him differed as much as people's estimates of their acquaintances do differ. But on one point they were unanimous: Langton was 'queer.' That verdict had been pronounced on him very early in life, and had stuck to him ever since. In the cradle, in the nursery, at school, he had differed from all other babies, from all other children, from all other schoolboys. His regimental companions in the 200th had accepted and confirmed the designation of his nurse and his schoolmates. He took no interest in any of the things in which the British subaltern most delighted. He did not bet, he never touched a card, he did not brag about his prowess with the fair sex. I suspect it was that last-mentioned trait that most exercised the minds of his messmates. What could you make of a fellow who seemed as anxious to avoid the blandishments of the prettiest girls of a garrison town as though they had been as faded and as dull as the lady whose commonplaces bored him to death on this glorious autumn afternoon? And Stephen Langton was worth a pretty girl's smile, and might have had his choice in most ballrooms. Independently of the advantages of a handsome face and figure, his expectations were thrice as great as those of any other man in the 200th. But Nelly Despard of Portsmouth, and Nelly Despard of Chatham, and other Nellys and Fannys innumerable, all of them pretty and some of them rich, retired in turn from the assault of that impregnable fortress. Stephen Langton was not a marrying man, and Sir Charles Grandison himself was not more ignorant of the verb 'to flirt.' He especially disliked any allusion to his martial achievements; and if he had left his regiment with the 'Rogue's March' in his ears, could not have been more unwilling to talk of his campaigning days. But he had done good service in his time, and in many a village on the wild north-western border of Hindostan the name of Langton Sahib, the 'Feringhee boy-devil,' is whispered to this day by white-haired men, who remember with what a rod of iron he ruled the district in the days of the rebellion.

But sombre as were the prevailing tints of his character, it had lights as well as shadows. Many a man who was louder-tongued in sympathy lacked the depths of real tenderness that lay under that hard exterior. It is a great tribute to the sterling worth of a man who makes but few friends when the few who know him most thoroughly are loudest in their praises. There were those who could tell of deeds of quiet heroic self-sacrifice done by this silent and sardonic man on sea and battle-field, for duty and for friendship's sake. Everybody knew at whose cost the children of poor Jack Naseby were being fed and educated, and how nobly the promise whispered in the ear of the dying comrade had been fulfilled. And when poor little Tompkins, the soap-boiler's son, came that awful cropper over the Derby, and saw nothing before him but to sell out and retire to an eternity of soap-boiling under the eyes of an indignant father, it was Langton who set him right, and tided him over that disastrous time. But still, in spite of such stories as these, of which his friends would tell you many, the ordinary verdict regarding Stephen Langton was that he was 'queer;' and the general impression he made on most people was the reverse of favourable.

On his accession to his fortune he had behaved in a fashion totally different from what had been ex-pected of him, and Langton Hall had never for a month together been empty of guests. His liberality in this respect did not arise from any modification of his own peculiarities, but was solely due to the influence of his sister, Miss Bertha Langton, to whom, report said, he was passionately attached. Report was right for once, and Bertha's word was law to her brother, who concentrated upon her all the affection that other men dissipate on the thousand and one objects to which he was utterly indifferent.

'The magic emerald,' said Stephen Langton, 'has been an heirloom in our family for the last four hundred years. Apart from its associations, it is a very valuable stone from its size and quality. It is said under certain circumstances to have the power of losing its tint, and becoming perfectly colourless.'

'What are those circumstances?' asked Lady Matilda.

'If its possessor is guilty of any great meanness or rascality, if he betrays a friend, or commits any really vile or wicked action, the emerald loses its colour, and when that happens it is the warning of certain punishment. The criminal may strive to avert the penalty; but it will come, in spite of all he may do.'

'And has that ever happened?'

'Never, since it has been in our family,' responded Langton. 'My forbears have either been exceptionally virtuous, or the emerald has lost its powers, or never possessed them.'

'O Mr. Langton, pray don't cast doubt on such a really charming story! So very romantic, so truly interesting. But, supposing that its possessor—you, for instance (though I'm sure, of course, that you wouldn't)—were to do something really dreadful, would the emerald never recover its colour?'

'Never, so long as it remained in my possession. But directly it became another man's property it would be as at present, and would remain so, until he did something awful, and so on.'

Lady Matilda made no remark in answer to her companion's last speech, and, indeed, seemed not to have heard it. She was looking intently between the bushes behind Langton, and, as he ceased to speak, she rose, in order to obtain a better view of the object on which her eyes were fixed. Langton turned, and gazed with a languid curiosity in the same direction. But suddenly he rose too, and stood beside his companion, with his teeth set fast, and his face paling beneath its ruddy bronze. Lady Matilda's face was white with ill-dissembled anger, and the hand which parted the leaves was agitated by an angry tremor.

A young man of twenty-two or three, light haired, fresh coloured, and looking exasperatingly cool and calm in the blazing sunlight which lit the open space about him, came lounging up the little hill on which stood the copse which hid the listeners from view. Beside him walked a girl, some few years his junior, attired in a dress of some diaphanous fabric, lit by ribbons of pale blue. Her summer-hat, decorated like her dress, she carried in her hand, and a thickly twisted coronet of leaves and flowers was in its place upon her lustrous hair. Ignorant of the scrutiny to which they were subjected, they came on until they were within twenty yards of their concealed watchers. Then, seized by a sudden faintness, the young man fell, limp and invertebrate, against a tree, uttering a hollow groan. The lady regarded him with a countenance whose gravity was contradicted by the laughter of her eyes. He raised his appealingly to her face, and groaned again.

'Well?' she asked.

He pressed his hand upon his heart, and gasped,

'The customary restorative.'

The girl looked about her, and then, believing herself unperceived, stooped over her exhausted companion and kissed him. He, with a sigh of relief, briskly recovered the perpendicular, and the pair disappeared from the view of the enraged Lady Matilda and her companion.

'Shameful!' gasped the angry lady. 'Shameful! Outrageous! How dare he?'

Langton made no answer, but tugged silently at his moustache.

'Mr. Langton,' panted Lady Matilda, 'I pray you to believe that I am no party to this disgraceful conduct on the part of my daughter.'

'Disgraceful!' repeated Langton, with an astonished lifting of the eyebrows. 'Why disgraceful? Perfectly natural, I should say.'

Lady Matilda glared at him as though doubtful of his sanity.

'Given,' continued her companion, 'a country house, a handsome young man, a pretty girl, time, place, and opportunity, surely the result should not surprise you.'

'But without consulting me—'

Langton broke in, with a calm impudence which completely bewildered his companion,

'Did you always ask your mamma's permission before—'

He did not complete his sentence, but eked out his meaning with a smile.

The lady, with an angry flirt of her parasol, turned from him and walked towards the distant Hall. He followed her.

'My dear Lady Matilda, pray don't take the matter so hardly. There is—isn't a better fellow in the whole world than Roderic Vane.'

'A penniless adventurer.'

'Permit me. Not an adventurer,

and not penniless. That he has a decent position is past dispute ; he is a gentleman, and has very good prospects.'

'A very good catch 'for a tradesman's daughter, no doubt,' answered the offended mother. 'But I had looked higher than a Government clerk for Elsie.'

Langton would have spoken again ; but she flashed round on him suddenly with undisguised rage in face and voice.

'Do *you* plead his cause, Mr. Langton ?'

'I do. If I may be permitted to say so, I shall regard it as a good match on both sides.'

She turned from him with a gesture and exclamation in which anger, disdain, and surprise were all expressed, and left him where he stood.

II.

STEPHEN LANGTON gained the solitude of his own room, and shut himself in, to fight out the great struggle of his life, and have his bitter hour unseen. The pride that had kept back any avowal of what he now knew to be a hopeless passion was too shallow a pretence to be kept up to himself. The agonies of such a mind are easier imagined than described, at least by such a pen as mine. There is no scrap of the proverbial wisdom which is truer than that one which teaches us that the stillest waters are ofttimes the deepest, and those passions that Stephen Langton so perseveringly cloaked in cynicism were wider and more real than any even of his closest intimates would have deemed them.

A knock came to his door, and, in answer to his query, the voice of his valet announced the advent of his dinner-hour. He bade the fellow begone savagely, and a

minute after cursed himself for his weakness.

'You ass !' he said, apostrophising his reflection in the mirror. 'Is this your philosophy ? Is this the result of the self-drilling of a lifetime, to make yourself the babble of your own servants'-hall, and the tool of such a match-making old harridan as *that*? What do you want with the girl, you wrinkled, crow's-footed, overgrown schoolboy ? What's the girl to you, or you to her ? What quality of body or brains or heart have you to win such a prize by ? What right have you to cast your ugly shadow on two lives ?'

A second knock came to the door as he finished this uncomplimentary harangue.

'Who's there ?' he asked.

'It is I,' answered a female voice. 'Is anything the matter, Stephen ?'

'No,' he answered, afraid to trust his voice to say more.

'John said he thought you were ill,' returned the voice.

'I am not ill,' returned Stephen. 'I shall be down to dinner presently.'

'Stephen, I am sure there is something the matter,' continued the voice, with feminine persistency.

Langton opened the door and confronted his visitor.

'What do you want ?' he asked ungraciously.

'What is the matter with you ?' reiterated this feminine Irish echo.

Stephen Langton was tall and dark, Bertha Langton was small and fair. Stephen was forty, and looked more ; Bertha was almost twenty-one, and looked less. They differed in a dozen other things, and yet were alike in some mysterious way. Where the likeness lay the most astute observer could never have determined ; but it existed, nevertheless.

'There's nothing the matter with me,' answered Langton. 'Can't you take an answer?'

'Don't talk to me in that way, Stephen,' answered the lady, in calm reproof. 'You'll only be sorry for it afterwards.'

Langton gave an uneasy growl; Bertha smiled.

'It's only business affairs, my dear. I've been bothered lately. Run away, like a good girl. I'll be at dinner directly.'

He turned away as he spoke, and walked towards his toilet-table. But before he reached it a pair of soft arms were round his neck, and his sister's cheek against his own.

He sat down, almost unmanned by this touch of womanly pity. The girl would have spoken; but there was such a look in the eyes he turned on her that she forbore. Presently he said, quite in his ordinary voice,

'You are the only creature who has my secret. Keep it, Bertha.'

She answered by a kiss, and left him.

Feeling strangely composed and quiet after his intense mental excitement, Stephen dressed and descended to dinner. His appearance was the signal for a general movement to table. Roderic Vane, he noticed, was ill at ease, and divided his furtive regards between Lady Matilda, who sat, prim and rigid, exactly opposite him, and her daughter Elsie, his companion of the afternoon, who had been established far down the table, with an insuperable barrier of two county members, their wives, and a clerical dignitary between them. Elsie was very pale, and sat out the dinner, eating nothing, and sending away her plate untouched after each course. There seemed to be a sense of constraint on all present; and conversation languished, in spite of the gallant efforts of Bertha, ably seconded by her brother.

'We were speaking this afternoon, Lady Matilda, of the magic emerald,' said Langton.

Lady Matilda remembered the conversation.

'That is the stone in the centre-piece of my sister's necklace.'

It was not a stone of extraordinary size, and would have shown but poorly in that respect beside some of its famous sisters. But its colour and brilliance were marvellous; and its water as pure as that of the famous treasure for love of which poor Isaac Levi went mad. Its mention gave a fillip to the conversation; and though Lady Matilda still maintained a stony silence, and Roderic and Elsie remained taciturn or monosyllabic, the rest of the guests found plenty to talk of regarding the histories and legends of famous jewels.

Dinner over, it was proposed by Bertha, and carried with acclamation, that tea should be partaken of in the garden, where the ladies accordingly repaired. During the after-dinner symposium, Langton noticed that Vane drank much more than his usual quantity of wine, swallowing glass after glass in rapid succession, and with a countenance of unaltered gloom. On rising to join the ladies, who could be seen wandering round the terraces of the garden, the young man took Langton's arm, and drew him away down a sequestered alley, which led into the park. The wide expanse of green stretched in one unbroken wave-like roll, until it met the over-arching blue. The birds, recovering from the languor of the day, were giving the preliminary trills of their evensong. It was such an evening as is made for lovers' confidences, —when not filtered through a third party. So thought Stephen Langton; but being fairly caught, he braced himself up for silent endurance.

'I must school myself,' he thought; 'and here is an opportunity for a lesson. What's the matter, Vane?' he asked aloud; 'I never saw you look so glum.'

'I never felt so glum before, Steve. I'm a gone coon.'

'Will you translate?'

'I'm in love.'

'For the first time?'

'Yes, to anything like this extent. Look here, Langton, I must tell somebody or burst. Let me tell you.'

Langton dropped his hand on the young man's shoulder.

'You young muff! As if I didn't know all about it!'

Vane stared; his companion smiled.

'Well, it saves me the trouble of telling you, and you the bore of listening. You're a good fellow, Langton, and you've been very kind to me. What would you advise me to do? Lady Matilda knows it, I swear. She cut me dead this afternoon, and Elsie came in to dinner looking like a ghost; so I suppose she has been having a bad quarter of an hour, too. You see, I'm only a younger son. The governor won't stand a penny more than three hundred a year, and I get another three from the office. I can't marry Elsie on that. Her mother won't hear of it. I suppose she's right. It's hard to ask a girl to give up a life of ease and comfort to live, and perhaps rear a family, on six hundred a year. If Lady Matilda were another sort of woman, she might make things straight for us. But that's past hoping for. I must give her up, old man, and get out of this. I've got enough coin to buy an axe, and get a passage to Canada; and I'll go out there and live it down. But it's hard lines,' he said, with a break in his voice. 'It's hard lines.'

'Keep up your heart, my boy,' returned Langton, touched by the young man's artless expressions of grief. 'It's bad; but might be worse. If the girl loves you, it won't matter to her if you have six hundred a year or sixty thousand. And if she doesn't mind, why should you? There are better chances on the cards than Canada, any way. Hang on and watch, that's my advice, since you ask it.'

One by one the guests wandered back to the Hall, and distributed themselves over the carpeted desert of the great drawing-room, while the ladies officiated at the piano. Miss Elsie, being warmly pressed to sing, begged to be excused; and Roderic, after several vain endeavours to get within conversation distance of his inamorata —each attempt being cleverly frustrated by Lady Matilda—wandered off to smoke a sadly contemplative cigar, and muse upon her manifold perfections and his own unworthiness.

Lady Matilda, buried in the downy depths of an armchair, her eyes apparently exploring vacancy, but in reality keenly watching the movements of Langton, waited with feline patience. She was too wise a woman to meddle actively in the matter and court another rebuff; but Langton's affectation of indifference had by no means blinded her to the true state of the case, and she hoped still. Elsie sat apart, beside the window, half in and half out of the flood of moonlight which partially lit the drawing-room. But Langton, with the exception of a few phrases, of course, did not trouble her with his conversation, and presently retired quietly, leaving Bertha at the piano.

He sat at the window of his room, and looked out over the moon-flooded park, past the thin ribbon of silver which marked the course of the river, past the rich-leaved trees that stood like islands of shadow in a sea of light. He was looking beyond them into his own future. He was calmer now, and could look at it quietly, in spite of the terrible gusts of passion that still shook him for a moment, and passed, leaving the calm deeper. So far he had done well, and was satisfied with himself upon the whole, as he had a right to be. The prime temptation of his life was overcome, and his passion had made him false neither to love nor friendship.

The calm beauty of the night seemed to draw him from the house out into the alley in which he had heard the confidences of the love-lorn Roderic. He could not pass the spot without something of a tremor. His hopes lay buried under that grassy mound, and a great wave of some nameless emotion, made up of love and sorrow and hopeless hope, rose in his soul. And before it sank again he saw before him something that sent the blood from his face—Roderic and Elsie, dimly visible in the shade at the turning of the alley. He slipped back into the darkness with a curse on his lips, and something very like a prayer in his heart. Some blind feeling that his trial was being made unnecessarily bitter crossed his mind. The voices reached him where he stood, too low for the words they uttered to be understood; and then another sound, unmistakable in the silence of the night, faint as it was. A white figure fluttered by him, lost in the shadow, and Vane's step went slowly crunching the grass in the distance.

Langton left the spot with hurried unequal steps, and walked rapidly across the park in the direction of the river. When he came to its banks he turned and walked with its current. Before he had gone a mile the sound of the

falling of distant waters met his ears, and presently he came to the spot at which the bed of the river suddenly made a sheer descent of some twenty feet. He stood at the brink, looking down at the foaming caldron into which the water rushed with roar and clang like the shouting of an army. Some vague thought that in that furious hell of warring waters he might find the peace denied to him elsewhere crossed him as he gazed. But Stephen Langton was not of the stuff whereof suicides are made. 'The coward's remedy,' he muttered, as he turned away. 'Not that! not that!'

He continued his stroll along the edge of the basin until his further progress was barred by the trees that ran to the edge, intertwined breast-high with bramble and brushwood, and which served to mark the bounds of his domain. Here, perforce, he turned and retraced his steps. What was the black shadow recumbent on the edge of the fall, on the very spot on which he had stood ten minutes before? He drew nearer to it with silent steps, something too hideous to be called a hope growing in his heart as he advanced. The figure moved, and he saw the moonlight full upon its face. It was Roderic Vane. With a shout that rang high above the tumult of the fall, he rushed down the bank. Vane was on his feet and met the shock.

'Langton! Good God, what are you doing?'

He had his arms about his victim, and resolutely thrust him back, foot by foot, until they stood upon the edge. With all the tenacity of despair the supple youngster clung about him, holding on with hands and teeth in a last hard struggle for dear life; but Langton loosed his grip, and drove him with a cruel blow over the brink. One stifled gurgling cry, and his body struck the water. The murderer knelt upon the turf, and looked down into the foam. Was it fancy, or did he indeed see the white face looking up at him through the surges? What matter? The appeal was voiceless, and could be heard by no man save himself.

The horror of the place was so strong upon him that he ran like a hunted hare across the park, straight for the house. He slipped in unperceived, and mounted the stairs. His dress was torn and disordered, and his cheek was bleeding. He must not be seen so. He hastily changed his dress, stanched the slight scratch, and then, pale but calm, descended to the drawing-room.

The guests were grouped in the centre of the room, evidently under the influence of some strong emotion of surprise or wonder. As he entered, his sister broke through them, and came towards him, her necklace in her hand.

'Stephen! look! My emerald! What does it mean?'

He looked and saw, colourless as his own haggard face, the jewel centrepiece. It was no fable, then, this old wife's story. The curse was come upon him. He fell back with outstretched hands, as if to ward off some palpable horror that threatened him.

The dreamer sprang to his feet, his eyes dazzled by the flood of light that inundated the room in which he sat, and glared out upon the scene before him—park and garden and river and sky flooded by the rosy morning light. A clear voice rang up from below:

> ' L'aurore s'allume,
>   L'ombre épaisse fuit,
> La rêve et la brume
>   Vont où va la nuit.

> Paupières et roses
>   S'ouvrent demi-closes,
> Du reveil des choses
>   On entend le bruit.'

He ran to the window, and looked eagerly down into the garden. His sister looked up at him, and waved him a good-morning salute with the dew-drenched flowers she held in her hand. The illusion of the dream was so strong upon him still, that he half believed the vision had been a waking reality, and his present state a dream. He slipped gently into his sister's room, and searched among her jewels with trembling fingers, until he came upon the emerald. It was unchanged, as steadfast in its glorious hue as his heart should be henceforth to the accomplishment of the task he had set himself.

'Dear Sir William,—On a certain occasion, which I would rather not specify, you told me that if it should ever be in your power to render me a service, you trusted I would afford you the opportunity. Permit me to request of you one favour, which I know you will the more readily grant, inasmuch as it will give you the chance of killing two birds with one stone, by doing two kindnesses in one.

'There is, employed in your department, a young gentleman of the name of Vane, in whom I take a great interest. His present salary, I hear, is three hundred a year. He is meditating the committal of that blunder which you and I have so happily avoided; but mamma is implacable. Can you do anything for him? He is a smart young fellow, well up to the duties of any post that a man of his age is likely to be intrusted with.—Permit me to solicit your good offices on his behalf, and believe me, yours most faithfully,

'STEPHEN LANGTON.'

A SYMPHONY IN RED.

By ARTHUR T. PASK.

THE Quartier Latin of London, year 1860!

The sickly sun-gleams of the first days of March stream over the housetops of Charlotte-street. In angular strips of light they show up the dirt-stained bricks and the blistered sashes of the window-frames. Yet the faint signs of coming spring are welcome. The street flower-girl, sallow and grimy of skin, stands directly in the rays, and smells her stock of forced violets as if they breathed a rich instead of a fading perfume. The Italian organ-man watches the light on the red chimney-pots, shows his white teeth, and plays with brisker hand; and the children, toe and heel, foot it more merrily on the dusty pavement.

A young man, pale of face and ill-dressed, comes out of one of the houses near by. He looks at the flower-girl, the children dancing, and the Italian, with not an appreciative but a critical gaze. He is an artist. According to his æsthetic code, he would not paint that scene for a fortune. He would not degrade his art by such a subject. Yet it *is* a subject, so he cannot help noticing it.

He walks down Charlotte-street into the Euston-road, makes for the Regent's Park, passes up the long avenue, and then turns off on to one of the paths leading to the left. He looks at the cold sunset growing into a warmer light. It plays on the backs of the soot-dyed sheep grazing on the slope. It colours the grass, gray and green

in the daylight, with now a half-golden, now a pinkish, now a crimson hue.

'I wish I could do something with that colour in it,' he says. Then he turns and looks at a form near by. On it is seated a woman, a handsome woman too. Cold clearly-cut features, with the exception of a rather full mouth.

'It is the third time she has been here,' he thinks to himself. 'It is rather strange; I should like to paint something Greek with her for a model. How she would fit in with that red ibis of mine and the robe I had made up from the Algerine silk!'

The pathway runs right in front of the form on which the woman is sitting. She is looking down at the grass before her. He loiters slowly along, still turning towards her. She raises her eyelids. Involuntarily he says, 'I beg your pardon!' and a blush rises to his cheek.

She answers with a perfectly collected voice, 'There is no need, or there is much need; you have looked the same way these three days.'

For a moment or so he does not answer. The silence is unbroken except by the tinkling of a distant sheep-bell and the harsh scream of a macaw from the Gardens near by. He is no young butterfly of the studios. He is only a quiet earnest worker at his art. In the presence of the woman he would have been entirely ill at ease, had it not been that her face had appealed to his artistic feeling, and *that* once aroused, he thought but little of circumstance or consequence.

'I was thinking,' he says, half stammering, 'I was thinking that I have not been able to get a sub: ject for the Academy, and that— pardon—your face at last solved the question.'

She looks up with a half-curl of her upper lip. The red tinge on her cheek may be the flush of anger or the glow of the rich rays of sunset. Then, at last, she answers, with a smile,

'What a wonderful thing that I should be such an inspiration ! But I am walking.' And then she adds, with a careless languor of in-difference, 'You may go with me as far as the avenue.'

They stroll up the winding gravel path. The cold wind creeps over the grass slopes and rustles her rich dress.

'Some of you artists are rather strange,' she continues. 'What sort of picture was it that made you fancy me for a model ?'

'It was a study of a Greek wo-man, with a red ibis, and a sunset background. You are the only person that I could paint it from.'

By this time they have reached the avenue. The woman stops, looks the artist straight in the face, and then laughs curiously.

'Suppose now I came to sit to you ?' then she turns and looks at the distant Gardens, growing dim and shapeless in the fast gathering twilight.

He answers instantly,

'I should be able to paint a good picture—the best I ever have done ;' and his voice is full of re-strained excitement.

'What is your name and ad-dress ?' she asks composedly.

'John Summers. I have not got a card. I live at 220 A Char-lotte-street.'

'I shall be there the day after to-morrow, at ten in the morning; now go.'

She does not even offer her hand, but walks away. He stands and watches her as she passes under the shadow of the trees. Soon she is lost in the dying light.

A park-keeper touches him on the shoulder. 'It is time to go out, the gates are being closed.'

The morning sun is streaming through the skylights of a large, almost bare, studio. Bare it ap-pears, for such a little is there of everything compared to the size of the room. On the walls are a few charcoal studies on gray paper, a few casts of fragments of classic friezes, and here and there a piece of pottery on a rough bracket. Yet in one corner, by the fireplace, there is a sort of attempt at luxury. On the models' throne, the great couch is a handsome piece of furni-ture. The rug is genuine Persian. On the small Indian table, covered with a strip of crimson Utrecht velvet, there are two pots, holding great bunches of jonquils.

Leaning against the mantelshelf is young John Summers. He has been reading a letter, which he now slowly tears up and throws into the fire.

'I am sorry,' he says to himself, 'but I shall not return home. I must do something for the Academy that will tell for good or bad. If she would only keep her promise, I could paint it in a fortnight. If she does not, I know that I cannot do anything else.' Then he moves to the canvas on his easel. 'That composition will be good enough.'

Even in the charcoal outline he has caught something of a likeness of the expected model—the clear-cut features, the somewhat hard, but perfectly graceful, lines of the figure. Yet, what is most curious, he has preserved the strange air of repulsion that there is about her. The eyes are looking steadily out of the canvas; but the head and shoulders are turning away, and all the drapery is running from the foreground. She is drawn as resting on a couch, with one arm hanging loosely down. At the back of the couch is an ibis perched upon a stand. He keeps looking intently at the canvas. There is a slight noise, and standing in the open doorway is the expectant model. She is very punctual. The old clock on the staircase outside is only finishing striking the hour.

'You see I have come,' she says; then she walks up to the study on the easel. 'I should think that would come out well. I suppose that is the dress you wish me to wear,' and she points to a red-silk robe hanging over a screen. 'Is that a dressing-room?' He nods assent. She turns towards a door, opens it, and enters, carrying the robe with her; the door is closed after her, and he is left alone. He takes up a piece of charcoal, again looks at the sketch, and makes a slight alteration. Then he walks to a small shelf and takes down a book. It is Goethe's *Affinities.* He turns over a few of the leaves, then presses the book to his under lip, and says, in a half-whisper,

'I wonder what the other fellows would think of all this. Yet somehow it seems to come quite naturally. She does not seem pleased to be here, neither do I feel so at her presence. She is a piece of my fate, perhaps, or I of hers. One can't tell why the seaweed floats away from the rocks and comes to the sand. Why she is here at all is strange. One thing is certain: I feel that I shall be sure to paint my picture now.'

She reënters the room. There can be no doubt about there being a chance to make a splendid study.

The hidden bands of the drapery half reveal, half conceal a splendid figure. The bare arms are perfect; the head is essentially Grecian.

'I am to use that couch?' she says, without the slightest tone of interest, much less of pleasure.

'Yes,' he answers, taking up a stick of charcoal.

She walks to the couch and lies down.

'You must have noticed the sketch very carefully,' he remarks, in a tone of surprise.

'I hardly looked at it.'

'Yet you have fallen into the exact pose I wanted. You must have sat before. I beg pardon. Of course, not as a professional model.'

'I have never but once sat for my portrait;' and her voice has no touch of sympathy, but only a cold languor.

He looks at the sketch, throws the piece of charcoal into the fireplace, and takes up his palette and brushes. In less than a quarter of an hour her face is on the canvas. In less than half an hour the red head of the ibis is painted in. She lies perfectly still. There is not the slightest movement, not the slightest sign of fatigue. After a time she moves up the arm that is hanging down, but soon lets it fall again. In silence he paints for over an hour and a half. Then he begins to be nervous. He attempts an alteration.

'We have finished for to-day,' she says quietly, and rises from the couch and walks to the dressing-room.

Quite mechanically he cleans his palette and brushes, and puts them away in a table-drawer.

She comes back again in her own dress—a handsome, fashionable woman, entirely different from the Greek priestess.

'It is like me,' she remarks quietly, as she looks at the canvas;

'but I did not know I had that expression.'

'I think so,' he answers, looking carefully at her.

She neither smiles nor appears confused.

'By the way,' she continues, in her cold even voice, 'do you ever go to the theatre?'

'Never,' he replies; 'it is not in my way. I neither care for it, nor yet can afford it.'

'Then do not go,' she answers. 'You are not of a curious nature?'

'I think not, excepting when I want anything for my work.'

'You do not notice many things either. You are not one, for instance, who would waste an hour in the Strand and Regent-street looking at the portraits in the photograph-shops?'

'I never did such a thing in my life;' and, almost forgetful of her, he half closes his eyes and thoughtfully scans his work.

'So much the better,' is the answer. 'Good-day. I must be going. Do not come down-stairs. I shall be here to-morrow about this time.'

She does not offer him her hand, but walks to the door and leaves him by the easel. In a minute he hears the street-door shut, followed by the dull sound of wheels.

The same night the young artist is trying to sleep in his small bedroom opening out of the studio. He has tried the usual experiments, and has utterly failed. He has counted the imaginary sheep jumping through the imaginary hedge. He has counted up to three or four hundred. He has tried to recite a page or two of 'The Deserted Village.' He hears the clock on the staircase strike one.

'I can't stand this,' he says aloud.

He gets up, lights his candle, and walks into the studio. The moonlight is streaming in so strong that even the light of the candle can only subdue it for a few feet around. He walks up to his easel and looks at the newly-commenced picture. As he moves his candle, it seems as if the waving light lent a life to the eyes of the face on the canvas. It seems as if the lips open in a half-sneering smile.

'It is a good study,' he says aloud; and, going back to his bed, falls fast asleep.

The same night there is a 'first-night' meeting at the Bolero. Mdlle. Verie is sitting next to the enterprising manager. She still wears her stage dress of Hélène.

'You are quietness itself,' says the enterprising manager. 'Are you musing o'er the mutability of human affairs? are you wrath with Grevin's notion of your costume? or are you studying mankind in general?'

'It is a good study,' she answers, and, with an unpleasant smile, puts down her glass.

'Ta-ta, Jorkins,' says a stout man, with a glass in his eye; 'it has just gone one, and I want to be off.'

This time the sunset light is glowing on the walls of the studio in Charlotte-street. The Greek priestess is still reclining on the couch in her red robe. The red ibis is still flaming in colour on his wooden perch.

The picture is almost finished.

'And what was that your friend said?' asks the amateur model.

'He said that it was rather odd how intensified the expression was becoming in the eyes here. He said, too, that he liked the title, "A Symphony in Red." He further wanted to know who my model was. I do not know myself,' the artist adds; 'so of course I could not tell him. I told him nothing—why should I?'

'Perhaps he was more interested in me than you are yourself;' and the model gives him a searching glance.

'You know quite differently. You know what an effect you have had upon me. You know that you must have altered the whole tenor of my life.'

'You do not mean to say you are in love with me?' says his visitor, raising herself on her arm.

He quietly puts down his palette and brushes on the table, and joins his hands behind his back.

'How can I tell what I am?' he answers, with a nervous tremor. 'Do you know that they expect me home to marry my cousin? I shall not do it. Why should I have burnt the little purse she gave me? Why, unless you have come to me as my fate! Why did I buy that wretched bird there that put me in mind of a study in red? Why did I meet you in the sunset? Why did you come here? We cannot go from all this, say what you will.'

'Have you that girl's portrait?' the model asks, but with no tone of interest.

He opens a drawer in the table, takes out a photograph, and hands it to her.

'A pleasant face,' she says, and lets it fall on the floor.

'And now,' he cries, 'tell me who you are!'

She only answers, 'Wait.'

She rises from the couch, walks to the small dressing-room, and, in a minute or two, comes back in her every-day costume.

'I shall write a note,' she says.

She sits down at the small table, and pens a few lines on a sheet of paper; this she folds up, wafers, and writes something on the outside. Then she places it in a small envelope, on which she writes again. On the mantelshelf is a small Indian vase. She walks up to it, and drops in the envelope. Then she turns, and looks him in the face.

'If I ask you,' she speaks, with a strange smile, 'you will not look at that envelope until the 1st of May, when the Academy opens? If you go to the address that is upon that envelope, you will see me. I have your promise?'

'You have,' he answers.

'And so you think—you do not know—you love me?' and her eyes are raised to his.

'I swear.'

She does not even blush. There is not the slightest sound of passion or of tenderness in her voice. Her lips part with no smile.

'You may kiss me once,' she says—'it will perhaps be for the last time—then I go.'

A mixed feeling of fear and delight comes over him. He takes her hand, and kisses her lips. She walks from him to the door. The red sunset is playing on her face, and her dark eyes flash the more brilliantly.

For the first time a tender yearning smile is on her lips.

Then she is gone.

The Academy is crammed to suffocation. The art-critics are scribbling away in their note-books. Around one small picture there is quite a crowd.

'A queer subject, "A Symphony in Red,"' says one critic, with a cool business-like look; 'very good, all the same: the fellow will make a name.'

A hansom cab rattles along Portland-place, then by the side of the Park, and turns into St. John's Wood. At the corner of the Ewbank-road a young man gets out. He has a refined face, yet something in his manner suggests an unaccustomed feeling of discomfort. A young Bohemian in a

Vigo-street coat. He pays the cabman, and then looks at an envelope that is in his hand : 'Madame Descluses, Fountain Villa.' He walks up the road, and stops before a door set in a high wall. He pulls at the heavy bell beside it, and the door is opened by a dark-faced middle-aged woman.

'Madame Descluses,' he says, offering the envelope.

'I am Madame Descluses,' the woman answers quietly. 'Come in, monsieur.'

She shuts the door behind them. He finds himself on a stone pathway which runs between a belt of evergreens up to a door which is wide open.

Two men are standing in front of it. One is a handsome, military-looking man, with a black moustache waxed at the points. The other has a sober professional look. He is saying,

'It is almost doubtful whether I ought to grant a certificate.'

The two men stare hard at the new-comer. Then they stand apart for him and his guide as they walk into the house.

They are in a large room, half hall, half conservatory. There is a trophy of Eastern arms, there are the antlers of a deer, and two great pots of azalea glowing in blossom. The artist looks down at the woman.

'Mr. Summers,' she says almost in a whisper, 'she said you were to see her.'

Then she opens the envelope. To his surprise she hands him the contents. He opens the sealed letter. The words within are :

'As to what you say to me, as to what you think of me, I know not how you are influenced. All I know is that we met. I could be happy with no one. She might be happy with you. Still, for certain, I know that I am weary, and am glad of the end. Be as happy as the world and yourself will let you. Adieu ! HENRIETTE VERIE.'

The young man looks up. What can it mean ? Madame Descluses is standing on the landing above the staircase. She beckons to him. He ascends the stairs. Is it the strong scent of the exotics in the hall below which produces a sickening faintness ? She turns the handle of a door and they enter. The blood-red sunset is streaming on something which is lying on a bed strewn with flowers. Madame Descluses walks stealthily to it, and uncovers a still set face.

The young man falls to the ground.

It is his model for 'A Symphony in Red,' which has brought him fame and fortune.

A SPIRIT WIFE.

By JESSIE SALE LLOYD,

AUTHOR OF 'THE HAZELHURST MYSTERY,' 'THE SILENT SHADOW,' ETC.

It was a love-match, at any rate upon the lady's side, when Laura Corthorn and John Heyland were married.

And not a bad thing for the gentleman either, from any point of view.

There was only one subject upon which they did not agree. She was a spiritualist, and he a disbeliever in everything supernatural; but surely it was easy enough for them to avoid that one topic, and upon all others their minds were in unison.

If Laura's affection was of a finer cast and nobler mould, so much the better for John Heyland. Every one thought him a very lucky fellow, and in truth he considered himself so too.

His wife was a few years older than himself, but she was a beautiful woman of a peculiar type, and she had a good fortune of her own, which she freely placed in her husband's hands with loving confidence. Still, perhaps, it would not have entered into John Heyland's head to have aspired to her hand had he not seen the love-light shine upon him from her soft dark eyes.

Laura's features were delicate, her hair like a glossy raven's wing, her eyes timid as a gazelle's, her clear olive-tinted complexion unlike that of our island-bred girls.

A sweet, over-anxious, loving face, ever varying in expression at a word, a look, from the man she loved; as sensitive to his touch as quicksilver to the influence of the atmosphere. She worshipped her husband, and to him she was very dear.

It was a happy year they spent together after their marriage, and then a son was born to them. They had looked forward to the birth of their child with great delight, not thinking of the sorrow it was to bring them; never once imagining that the spirit of the mother would pass away before that of the child had dawned into sense—that she would never hear him lisp her name.

They had not dreamed of such a possibility, yet it came upon them—not roughly, with no shock; but the mother never rallied after her boy was born, and sank very gently till she passed away.

After the first day or two she knew that it would be so, realising the truth with deepest sadness.

Ah, how could she bear to leave the husband she loved so well, and the new strange joy of motherhood?

Yet she had no choice in the matter. She must follow the pale hand of Death, who was beckoning her over the borderland. She lay, her few-days-old babe in her arms, with her eyes closed. A quiet footstep entered the room, and then hesitated. The eyes opened at once.

'I thought you were sleeping, my dearest,' said John Heyland kindly.

'No, dear, I am awake; I was thinking.'

'Thinking, love?'

'Yes; I was thinking how sad it is to leave you and our boy.'

There was a tone of agony in his voice as he answered her. He was a warm-hearted impulsive man, and she had never been so dear to him as now, when he was about to lose her.

'O my wife, I cannot part with you—I cannot! God will not be so hard as to take you from me.'

She smiled faintly.

'Death must come to us all some time, dear,' she said gently. 'If I had not so much to leave, I should say it is better to die young; but now—' she stopped, and tears started to her loving eyes, and dimmed them. 'I must die, John —I must die,' she faltered; 'and it is so hard.'

She placed her arms about his neck, and wept there; and sobs wrung the strong man's heart. She heard them, and for his sake grew calm.

'You are very young, dear,' she said after a pause. 'Some time hence you will marry again.'

'Hush, my wife, never; no one can ever fill your place.'

'You think so now,' she continued, in a dreamy voice; 'but you are strong and have a long life before you—you cannot be always alone. Yes, you will marry; but, dear, be careful in your choice, for our boy's sake. A stepmother is not always kind.'

Then, after another pause, an earnestness came into her eyes, a great tenderness shone out of them, and she looked at him fully.

She spoke in an eager voice, yet with some nervousness; for was she not going to enter upon that subject which, although sacred and solemn to her, he had always laughed at?

'John, you may not see me, for you do not believe; but I shall never be far away. In spirit I shall watch over you and our boy, night and day; and when you take another wife, I shall see; and if she does not make you both happy, I shall know no rest. Be careful how you choose, for my sake; remember, I shall know all.'

Her eyes closed, and she sank upon his breast fainting.

She did not rally again, although she lived many hours; once only she opened her eyes, and her lips moved.

He fancied they framed the word 'remember;' but he could not be sure. He leant down to listen, but there was no sound, not a breath to fan his cheek.

She lay smiling; her eyes were fixed upon him fondly; but she was dead!

'For so He giveth His beloved sleep.'

She was a good woman, and God had given her a peaceful end.

Three years after, a merry party were picnicking under the spreading trees of Bushey Park.

The chestnuts were white with bloom, the hawthorns were ready to blossom, the fountains were throwing their crystal jets into Diana's pool, the deer came close, asking for food with their soft brown eyes.

One of that party looked at them, and thought of a woman who was dead.

But there was another present whose sunny face soon recalled him from the past: a woman young and fair, with eyes like forget-me-nots in the morning dew; and for her he now lived, loving her with a passionate devotion which he had never known before.

The pleasure-seekers rose, shook themselves free from crumbs, threw the remnants of their feast to some clamouring gipsies, and paired off for a stroll.

'I want to go over to the Court

Gardens,' said Nellie Favell (for that was the name of the blue-eyed woman). 'See, I have filled my pocket with bread for the gold-fish and the swans. Will you take me over to feed them?' and she looked up into the manly face with a smile. 'They are all darlings,' she ran on; 'but the black ones with their red beaks are my especial pets, I think. You must tell me which you like best when we get to the Long Water.'

'But don't the swans eat the gold-fish?' asked her companion absently.

Nellie laughed a merry ringing laugh.

'No doubt they would, if they had the chance; but the gold-fish are not in the Long Water, they are in the pond, and you knew that quite well. The fact is you are not attending to a word I am saying. Tell me what you are thinking about, and if it is anything very important I will forgive you.'

They were passing along the paths where Henry's Queens had trod with beating hearts centuries before; where bluff King Hal had thought out his many love-stories; where he had decided upon the death of more than one fair wife, because his heart was set upon another woman; while the river ran on unheeding with its rush and foam. It ran on still, just as the King and his Queens had heard it; and two hearts were beating as theirs had throbbed all those years ago.

The old, old tale had been told in those regal gardens for hundreds of years, making or marring the life happiness of thousands; ay, and will be repeated there for hundreds more, if the world only lasts.

As Nellie Favell and her companion passed along, that tale was about to be told over again. Standing there by the fountain, with a sheen of golden living

movement at their feet, he told the blue-eyed woman of his love. She stood beside him, with her eyes fixed upon her bright-hued pensioners, not seeing them, mechanically dropping crumbs into the water.

'Why do you not answer me, dearest?' he asked. 'Will you not be my wife?'

'Do you know,' she said slowly, with an averted face, 'I have always said nothing should ever induce me to marry a widower?'

'Surely, Nellie, you would not be so cruel as to refuse me on that score. I cannot help having been married; but for your sake I would recall the past if it were in my power.'

It had been a still day, and the sun was shining upon the lovers; but as he spoke the wind passed over them with a sigh, and fled shivering among the leaves of the trees, while a full-blown rose dropped its sweet-scented petals in a shower.

He saw them fall.

The rose had been the favourite flower of a woman who was dead; and when they fell he remembered her.

'Did you love your first wife—I mean your wife—very much?' she asked.

(In thought she had already replaced her.)

'I believed so in former days; now I have learnt the contrary. I did not know what love was till I met you.'

'Poor wife!' said the girl, with a sad smile. 'She loved you, I suppose?'

'Yes, most truly.'

'Ah, it must be sad to care for any one very much without return!' And Nellie scattered crumbs yet again to the glittering bevy at her feet.

'Yes, it must be sad! Do not let it be my fate, Nellie.'

'Do you care so very much?' she asked, turning her blue eyes upon him earnestly, while her colour came and went. 'Would it pain you greatly if I said no?'

'Pain me! it would distress me beyond measure. What should I have left to live for?'

'You have your boy.'

'O yes, of course; but he could not fill my life.'

The sky was not overcast, yet the sun did not shine, and the wind quivered the trees like living suffering things.

'Nellie,' continued the lover passionately, 'why do you keep me in suspense? What is it you are thinking of? If you cannot return my love, tell me so plainly, and once for all, and I must bear it.'

'It is not that,' she answered gently; 'but I was questioning my own heart as to whether I could love your boy and be a mother to him, not in name only, but in very truth, so that he may never feel the need of a mother's love. Unless I could do this, I would not accept your offer, as I should fail in one of my chief duties.'

How the sun shone out as she said these words! And the wind passed from among the trees gently, and the lover was looking into the clear depths of the true blue eyes with exceeding fondness.

'I knew how beautiful you were, Nellie, and how much I loved you; but now I have learnt another thing—how good you are.'

'Nay,' she answered gently, 'I am far from good, or I should not rejoice that you have never loved before.'

'Are you glad at that, Nellie?' he cried triumphantly; 'then, my dear, you must love me.'

'Yes, I love you,' she answered, while the roses deepened on her cheeks.

'Then you will be my wife, dear,' he said joyfully, passing his hand within her arm, and drawing her towards him with the air of proprietorship. 'My Nellie, I am so happy!' he exclaimed, while the fish came to the surface and opened their mouths in wonder.

'I have not said yes,' answered the girl, with a smile.

'No; but you meant it, darling. You are too true a woman to make a fool of a man.' And looking into those eyes, he knew he was right.

There were others besides the gold-fish who were astonished. Some more of the picnic-party had wandered through the Palace gardens, and some were in the picture-gallery looking down upon the lovers.

'My goodness!' cried Mrs. Bryant; 'just look! I declare Mr. Heyland is proposing to Nellie, and—why, dear me, she must have accepted him, or she's not the girl to let him hold her arm like that; and yet she always declared nothing should ever induce her to marry a widower! O dear, what a funny world it is! People never appear to know their own minds! And it seems only the other day his poor wife died. One sees changes indeed!'

'It's three years, my dear,' meekly suggested Mr. Bryant, with a loyal attempt to 'stick up' for his friend.

'What if it's four?' demanded Mrs. Bryant snappishly; 'he was a broken-hearted widower, and said he should never get over it, and all that; and now he is going to marry again.'

'We don't know that he is,' suggested Mr. Bryant quietly.

'O, but we do know,' answered his wife. 'Do you think a friend of mine would allow such attentions if it were not the case?' And then turning to a lady who was keenly observing the young people, 'What do *you* think, Mrs. Grundy?'

'You're quite right, my dear. John Heyland will be married to Nellie Favell before many months are out; I have seen the attachment for some time.'

'Dear me, I never noticed anything; and Nellie's my friend. She might have told me about it, I think.'

'Ah, my dear, you don't know so much about the ways of the world as I do,' answered Mrs. Grundy, with dignity.

And John Heyland wandered on under the trees with the woman who was to become his wife, unspeakably happy.

Nellie Favell was Mrs. Bryant's guest, and Mrs. Bryant was of a most inquisitive turn of mind; therefore she was very loving and affectionate to Nellie upon the evening of that day, even to deserting her lord and master to share the girl's bed; and Nellie had told her all her love-story as she brushed out her gold-brown hair, and Mrs. Bryant had kissed her with many congratulations and expressions of goodwill. But Morpheus is more powerful even than Cupid. The lady, for whom those sweet day-dreams were past, soon got too drowsy to listen, and, turning her back to the happy maiden, closed her eyes to sleep, when all at once a blow or knock fell upon the bed, vibrating in its brasswork.

It aroused her suddenly, and somewhat crossly she addressed her young friend:

'Don't do that, Nellie.'

She, thinking Mrs. Bryant more than half asleep, and wondering herself at the sound, gave no reply, but lay still, with her eyelids closed.

Again the same unaccountable noise was heard.

This time Mrs. Bryant was really angry.

'Nellie,' she cried, 'don't do that; you will shake me out of bed.'

'I am not doing anything, indeed,' answered the girl.

'Yes, you are: you are holding up your arms, and letting them come down flop.'

'No, indeed, Mrs. Bryant dear; turn round, and you will see that my hands are under the clothes.'

Mrs. Bryant did turn round.

The moon was shining in at the window, and Nellie was plainly visible—a pretty picture of fair beauty, lying on her back, with her golden hair tossed upon her pillow, and her hands clasped together on her breast; and even while Mrs. Bryant was looking at her, the knock on the bed was repeated.

To add to her surprise, Nellie's eyes were turned away from her; apparently she was observing something with keen interest; but although Mrs. Bryant stared with all her power, nothing could she see. Nellie had sat up, still gazing in the same direction. At length the girl spoke:

'Will you strike a light?'

'Why, are you ill?'

'No; I am quite well.'

'Then I shall not strike a light. I am tired, and want to go to sleep. Do lie down and keep still.'

But Nellie gazed on.

'What on earth are you staring at?' demanded Mrs. Bryant. 'What a strange girl you are!'

'Nothing on earth,' answered Nellie, in a subdued voice. 'Still I should like a candle. It is by your side: will you light it, please?'

'Candle! nonsense! The light of the moon is enough for you to think of John Heyland by, and I am tired to death.'

Saying which, she turned somewhat abruptly from her young friend, and tried to go to sleep; but it was some time before she was able to do so, for Nellie's conduct puzzled her. She had never known the girl behave so oddly; for Nellie had got out of bed, and pulled back the window-curtains to their fullest extent, and had thoroughly searched the room, even looking under the bed.

Mrs. Bryant watched her furtively, half afraid. What did the girl mean by it? She had heard of people going suddenly out of their minds; had Nellie done so? If so, would she hurt her? Mrs. Bryant's heart beat fast; but when Nellie got quietly into bed again and lay quite still, the good woman felt more secure, and in time fell asleep; and, as the hours of night rolled on, Nellie followed her example.

The next morning, emboldened by the daylight, Mrs. Bryant questioned her friend about her strange behaviour on the previous night.

Nellie's face was grave. 'Well,' she said, 'I think it was John's first wife.'

'My dear, I did not know he had a second yet,' answered Mrs. Bryant, greatly enjoying her own joke.

'No, no, of course not,' said the girl, blushing hotly; 'but you know what I mean; I think I saw Mrs. Heyland last night.'

'Saw Mrs. Heyland last night!' echoed Mrs. Bryant, turning pale, while her blood curdled and made her skin into what people call 'chicken's flesh.' 'Saw Mrs. Heyland, Nellie! How can you say such awful things! it's really quite shocking!'

'It is rather solemn,' answered the girl softly, 'but I do not think it is shocking, and it is true.'

'That you saw her?' (with a shudder.)

'Yes; I believe so. You knew her; tell me what she was like, and I shall then know.'

'No, you tell me what you saw; that will be a far surer test, as you did not know poor Laura.'

'Very well,' answered Nellie quietly; 'I will tell you my story through. Like yourself, I was tired when we went to bed, but, unlike you, I was not sleepy. I closed my eyes, however, and lay thinking of John. I was very happy, and I was certainly not thinking of Mrs. Heyland. All at once there came a knock or thump upon the bed, which shook it and made it tremble, and you spoke to me, desiring me not to do it. I had *not* done it, but I thought you were half asleep and that you had. The knock was repeated, and you got cross with me. That time I became aware that the sound had not come from your side of the bed. I asked you to look at me, and convince yourself I was not moving; and then I turned my eyes the other way, strangely impelled to do so by an influence I could neither understand nor resist. By the bed stood a woman, and her eyes, which were large and dark, were fixed earnestly upon my face.'

'O Nellie, how frightened you must have been!'

'No, I was not afraid; it was a sweet beautiful face, sad and mournful, and full of love. At first I thought I must be asleep, so I sat up and looked at her as steadfastly as she gazed at me. She shrank back a little from the intensity of my regard, but she continued to gaze at me. I then asked you to light a candle, but you would not.'

'Why didn't you tell me what was the matter? I would have done it in a moment, unless I had been too much alarmed.'

'Yes, I thought you would be afraid; that was why I did not name it. Well, I had never before seen a spirit, and I thought it possible some one might be playing a trick; so, as you know, I searched the room, but, of course, no one was there, and I got back into bed.'

'Did she come any more?' asked Mrs. Bryant, trembling. 'Only fancy my going to sleep with a ghost in the room! O my dear, I shall never like this house any more!'

'No, she did not return.'

'You have not told me what she was like,' at length Mrs. Bryant remarked. 'I only hope you will describe her wrong.'

Nellie Favell looked dreamily before her as she replied, 'She was a short woman, slightly built, dark, with olive-tinted skin, soft wistful brown eyes, with, O, such a loving anxious look in them, a small straight nose, and a "cupidon" mouth. She was an unusual-looking woman, with masses of blue-black hair slightly waved.'

'Nellie, you must have known her—you must have seen her; you have described her exactly.'

'I have never seen her in life,' she answered, with quiet decision.

'Dear me—really it is dreadful! If Laura Heyland is to haunt you, how on earth are you to marry her husband?'

'I should not do so if such were the case; I should feel that she was trying to prevent my becoming his wife or her child's stepmother.'

'And if she does not come again?'

'I shall marry Mr. Heyland, and believe that she is willing I should do so.'

'Yours is a strange theory, Nellie, but it is well you can take the matter so quietly. It would have shaken my nerves. I never could have married him after last night.'

'Why?'

'O, I don't know; but I couldn't.'

'Then you wouldn't have much affection for him, I think.'

'Ah, well, it is fortunate you can see it in that light, Nellie.'

And Nellie kept her word; she did marry John Heyland, but not before she had told him of the apparition she had seen by her bedside on the night of her engagement. She had almost feared to broach the subject, but she need have felt no uneasiness about the matter.

John Heyland did not believe a word of it; he never had believed in spirits, and he never intended to do so; he even laughed at the idea of his dead wife's ghost.

'My dearest,' he said, 'you were over-excited, you saw your own white petticoat hanging on the door.'

'No, John,' she replied, 'you are wrong; the door was on the other side of the room; there was nothing which the most imaginative person could have converted into a figure.'

'Then, my dear, you were asleep, and dreaming. Don't ask me to believe otherwise, for, even to please you, I couldn't.'

Laura Heyland's spirit seemed content, for she never visited Nellie again, either before or after her marriage; but the second Mrs. Heyland did not forget the first, and was a gentle kindly mother to her boy, whom she grew to love as though he had been her own, treating him in every way, save one, like the children who were borne to her.

She talked often to him of his dead mother, and taught him to love and revere her memory. But she never let him feel the loss of a mother's love: that she gave him freely. And whenever she met her old friend Mrs. Bryant, she reminded her of the night which had followed her engagement, adding,

'You see my theory was right:

poor soul, she was willing I should fill her place.'

'Well, my dear, she could not have chosen a better successor; you have proved faithful to your trust. You have been a good wife to John, and a good mother to the boy.'

'I have done my best,' she replied, with her usual sweetness.

'And nothing could be better than that, Nellie,' said a cheery voice at the window, while John Heyland's happy face looked in. 'You two ladies always talk ghosts and treason when you get together. Ah, yes, you will never give up the point. You both saw it of course, or you both heard it, it's all the same. You back each other up. All I can say is, I am truly thankful my two wives get on so well together, for if poor Laura's ghost had only frowned, Nellie would have been lost to me for ever, wouldn't you, Nell?'

'John dear, I wish you wouldn't make a joke of it; it pains me,' she answered gently. 'Indeed, indeed I saw her. I cannot bear to hear you make fun of it.'

'Very well, dear,' he replied, with a good-tempered smile, 'I will be mum for ever; you may receive poor Laura's spirit whenever you like. She was a good woman, and if such a thing were possible as for her to return, she would do nothing but good to me and mine; of that I feel sure.'

THE TOWN OF THE BIG STRAND.

By EDMUND DOWNEY.

Two bold headlands, rising sheer from the blue Atlantic, mark the entrance to Tramore Bay. On the eastern headland stand two plain white towers, about fifty feet in height; and on the western promontory three pillars of similar build and similar hue. The summits of the eastern towers are crowned with neither lighthouse, flag, nor figure-head. A stranger in the land of Pat might at first be under the impression he was gazing upon two of the famous Round Towers of Ireland, transplanted and whitewashed by some whimsical archæologist. But, beyond rotundity of form, the Tramore structures differ in every material point from the mysterious Round Towers. They are not hollow, their circumference at the base is not greater than their circumference at the top, and the cuniform cap which protects the head of the Round Tower is absent. The pillars on the western headland, in addition to their numerical strength, have another advantage over their eastern neighbours, namely, the presence on the summit of the central pillar of a man of iron. This figure is called the 'Metalman,' and furnishes the title for the district which he 'rules as his demesne,' it being known as the Metalman Head. The Metalman's stature is about fourteen feet; but, standing at the base of this pedestal, he appears to be the ordinary height of a clothes-wearing animal. A curious and somewhat startling effect may be produced should you descend one of the paths which Nature has formed in the rugged cliffs. It is possible to descend far enough to cut off completely the view of the white pillar which supports the Metalman; and if, forgetful of the existence of the iron figure, you look up suddenly, you will be alarmed at discovering a man in seafaring attire warning you angrily off the premises. If your temperament is a nervous one, your first impulse will probably be to take a header into the Atlantic. The entrance to a wonderful cave, whose waters are as clear as crystal, lies in the cliffs beneath the Metalman; and with the aid of a small boat the cave can be easily explored. Close at hand is a natural waterspout, which has proved the grave for more than one adventurous explorer imbued with the spirit of the elder Pliny.

The *raison d'être* of the pillars on the eastern and western headlands is easily explained. Tramore Bay lies close to the harbour of Waterford, on the south coast of Ireland; and from the sea a stranger might easily confound the entrance to the dangerous bay with the entrance to the safe harbour. Therefore the pillars were erected in order that some distinguishing marks might exist for mariners. It will naturally suggest itself to many that, at the time when the distinguishing marks are most likely to be valuable—during a dark night or in a fog—they would most likely be invisible, and that a lighthouse would be the proper guiding star. But it is supposed that a lighthouse would only render confusion worse confounded; or it may be that economy has a good deal to do with the matter. At all events, no mariner trading round this coast should ignore the warning, in doggerel, which the Mettleman is said to chant during stormy weather:

'Keep off, good ship, keep off from me;
For I'm the Rock of Misery.'

The span from the western to the eastern headland is about three miles. This headland is called Brownstown, and its neighbourhood is seldom visited by the inhabitants of Tramore, chiefly because of the distance from the town. It would be impossible to reach Brownstown by land without travelling at least six or seven miles; and the difficulty of crossing a creek has to be encountered by the pedestrian about the middle of the journey. This creek, called Rhin-a-Shark—the river of the shark—flows into the bay, and forms the extreme eastern boundary of the Tramore Strand. A ferry is supposed to exist near the point where Rhin-a-Shark joins the sea; but I remember once, returning from Brownstown Head, I waited considerably over an hour at the eastern side of the creek, unable to discover either a ferry-boat or a ferryman, or anything resembling a ferryman. My patience being at last worn out, I tried to launch an old boat which lay bottom upwards on the sands. As soon as I had succeeded in turning the boat over on her keel, a sound struck faintly on my ears, and, looking inland, I saw a man standing at the door of a cottage about half a mile distant, shaking his arm vigorously. But I let him shake his arm, and continued my unholy work with renewed energy. Then the man disappeared; and when, after about a quarter of an hour's hard labour, I had succeeded in launching my barque, and was

industriously seeking for something in the shape of an oar, an elderly man of the sea came panting up, and roared,

'What are you about?'

'What is that to you?'

'Be the powers, I'll soon let you know, me fine fellow, what it is to me. Do you know that's *my* boat?'

'Well, I want to cross Rhin-a-Shark, and she will answer for want of a better.'

'Be me sowl, dhin yer *not* going to cross in her, I can tell you!'

'I'm not going to swim, at any rate.'

'None iv yer palaver for me. Lay go the boat at wance.'

'You're a nice hospitable lot down here. You pretend to have a ferry, and I'm going to cross. Just you try to stop me, and I'll give you a taste of this oar across the skull.'

We were about to have a fight for dear life; but several other fishermen-farmers had now arrived on the spot, and prudence warned me to be less Irish and more nice.

'Look here,' I said, 'I'm quite willing to pay you. How much do you want to ferry me over?'

'Half a sovereign. Divil a fraction less!'

'What! Half a sovereign for two minutes' work?'

'Come, fork out half a sovereign, or you can take the road round be the Back Sthrand—'tis only about five or six miles more that way, me bully.'

'I'd see you very much farther. I wouldn't give you as much as a penny now,' I replied, throwing down my oar, and proceeding towards the road inland.

The ferryman saw he was about to be foiled, so he cried after me,

'Half-a-crown?'

'No.'

'A shillin', dhin?'

'No.'

'Well, come, as yer a sthranger, begor, I'll do it for sixpence.'

'No, you won't.'

'Well, yer no gintleman, bad luck to you! For two pins I'd put the peelers on to you for thrying to do away wid me property, bad luck to yer impudence!'

Had the hospitable boatowner 'rowed me o'er the ferry,' I should have disembarked within twenty yards of one end of the Rabbit Burrow—a title given to a cluster of pyramidical hills of sand in which thousands of rabbits find a home. The 'geographical situation' of the Burrow is as follows: bounded on the north by the 'Back Strand;' on the south, by the 'Strand' itself; on the west (two or three miles distant), by the town of Tramore; and on the east, by Rhin-a-Shark. As the Back Strand, the Strand, and the town have yet to be visited, it is not likely a stranger to Tramore will derive from this description of 'the Burrow bounds' any information as to its whereabouts. However, a school-board geography adopts a similar method when describing the situation of a country, and surely a little school-board license may be claimed in the pages of a magazine. The Burrow is about a mile in length, and, perhaps, in some parts a quarter of a mile broad; so it may be seen that it covers a considerable area. It lies between the Back Strand and the Strand proper, and at high water is—to quote an ex-Member of the Lower House—'an island completely surrounded by water.' And standing on the summit of one of its many hills of sand, one is tempted to make another quotation, from the Laureate this time:

'On one side lay the ocean, and on one
Lay a great water.'

The heart of the Burrow is nearly three miles distant from the town of Tramore, and is sought less seldom than might be expected. You may travel all day through the Burrow, mounting with difficulty one side of the great hills, and sliding swiftly down the other side into a silent valley of sand, and hear no sound save the shrill notes of the curlew or seagull. It is with difficulty you can believe that half an hour's brisk walking would carry you into the busy, or rather (in the summer-time at least), the indolent haunts of men.

Zimmermann or St. John would have been delighted with the Burrow, and, with a copy of the *Essay on Solitude*, a good pipe, plenty of tobacco, and a hot July sun, I defy the efforts of Nature to produce a more soothing and luxurious spot than one of those valleys of sand. Murmurs and cool breezes from the ocean are wafted faintly towards you, lulling you with a delicious sense of calm. No sound of life is here save when a timid rabbit bounds along the sand for a few yards, to be lost to sight again before your rude voice has had time to alarm it. No vegetation seeks to flourish, except a few tufts of slender rush grass or some tiny blue flowers, which have a hard struggle for existence. You can stretch forth your hands and pick up many-hued shells, which for centuries have sheltered no crustacea. The sand is so soft that you sink into it as into a well-stuffed couch.

Reluctantly quitting the Burrow in a northern direction, you arrive at the Back Strand, a weary waste of waters when the tide is full, and an unprofitable-looking desert, half mud, half sand, at low water. In its bed myriads of cockles, mussels, and other minor shell-fish are discovered; and once or twice a year its level surface is utilised for horse-racing while the tide is out. A portion of the Back Strand

—how many acres I know not—was reclaimed about fifteen years ago, and is now under cultivation; but the cost of keeping out the waters has hitherto prevented capitalists from reclaiming a larger portion. A long low embankment, almost wide enough for a one-horsed vehicle to travel upon, marks the boundary of the cultivated slice.

The Strand proper is the lion of Tramore, and from it is derived the name of the pleasant watering-place, *tra more* being good Gaelic for 'big strand.' The 'yellow sands,' stretching in a slightly-curved line from the western corner of the bay to Rhin-a-Shark, a distance of over three miles, are, for the most part, as level as a lawn-tennis ground, and as firm under foot as a freshly-asphalted footpath. Wrecks are, unfortunately, no strangers to the strand. In 1813 the troop-ship Sea Horse, carrying soldiers and spoil from the Peninsula, found her grave there. All hands were lost, and the bodies ultimately recovered were buried at the entrance to the Rabbit Burrow, where a gravestone has been erected to their memory. It is said that many worthy dwellers in Tramore at that period discovered that digging in the sands for shell-fish was not nearly so profitable an occupation as digging for the doubloons which the ill-fated Sea Horse had carried from Spain. Sea *horses* appear to have a fancy for Tramore; for, about fifteen years ago, a barque named the Wild Horse was wrecked on the eastern side, and for months her big battered hull lay imbedded on the sands not a stone's throw from high-water mark. In this case, however, the crew was rescued. A few good ships driven into the Bay of Tramore have been saved from destruction in the Rhin-a-Shark creek, but the chances of finding a haven

there are very small indeed; and the large majority of vessels which a southerly gale sends inside Brownstown and Metalman Head have left their bones on the 'big strand' or the pitiless rocks.

Sea-bathing is, of course, Tramore's strong point. The western corner of the Strand is hallowed ground, being the ladies' bathing-place, and, as I am of the male persuasion, I dare not linger there. A little farther up the Strand the stronger sex disport themselves in the waters; but the men, as a rule, prefer the cliffs for clothes-divesting operations. The feminine bathing-machines are invariably structures of wood, and the male bathing-machines are invariably 'clothed in white samite' (or rather canvas), 'mystic, wonderful.' In the winter the machines are hauled up high and dry on the beach, or deposited in some place of shelter behind the Strand; but occasionally Father Neptune declares open war against them, and retires victorious, leaving a large field of killed and wounded behind him.

As your eye wanders round the western arm of the bay, the first object which attracts attention is a grassy slope running down to the edge of the cliff, which rises sheer at this point for about thirty or forty feet. This slope is the Doneraile Walk, and is the most frequented spot in Tramore. From its slope, which faces the south-east, a clear view of the greater part of the town and the country inland, as well as of the bay, the Strand, and the cliffs, can be obtained. The Doneraile is seldom overcrowded, except upon special occasions, such as when a military band is playing on the walk, or when a regatta is being held on the bay. For persons of a romantic disposition, there is no time so delicious for a lounge upon the Doneraile as during a clear moonlight night. They can watch the yellow moon stealing over Brownstown Head, and gradually ascend the sky, until a slender silver bar glittering in the waters reminds them it is high time they sought their pillows. If there is no moon the view is equally entrancing. Perhaps there is a shoal of mackerel in the bay, attended with a phosphorescent gleam which would almost rival the moon's reflection.

There are about half a dozen wooden seats on the Doneraile, but no one who can find a resting-place in the closely-cut grass would dream of occupying one of those seats. At the top of the slope is a narrow gravelled promenade, upon which, in the season, you can behold as many pretty feminine faces and figures as ever were beheld upon the same length and breadth of a promenade in any part of the globe.

Almost immediately behind the Doneraile, on the highest eminence in Tramore, the coastguard station is built—and an easy time of it the inhabitants of that station have! Smuggling is an almost unheard-of experiment in the district; and, barring an occasional practice with the gun, which is fixed on the edge of the Doneraile cliff, and some charming boating exercise, there is little to disturb the even tenor of the Tramore coastguardsman's way. If ever the Ministers of a bounteous Government—for reasons unknown to themselves—should think of paying me a compliment, I hope they will see their way to giving me the refusal of a coveted post— the Captaincy of Coastguards at Tramore.

Descending a steep road from the Doneraile, you arrive at the pier, a diminutive specimen of 'a projecting wharf or landing-place' (*vide* Nuttall). The pier is quite a modern structure, having been erected within the past ten years.

Its friendly arm affords a shelter for several small fishing-boats and pleasure-boats, and it is the only place in Tramore from which a craft of any description can find her way to the waters. The locality of the pier was formerly a beautiful cove, down the centre of which a narrow stream flowed; but most of its beauties departed with the advent of the engineer and the mason.

The next indentation which the sea makes on the western side of the cliffs is about a mile further, at Newtown Cove. Some years ago the only mode of approach along the coast to Newtown Cove was by means of a pathway at the extreme edge of the cliffs; but modern progress has established a carriage-road (little frequented, however, by horse or vehicle) over the ruins of the ancient path. From an æsthetic point of view the new road is scarcely an improvement on the former pathway; but no doubt it is a safer route, if a less romantic one.

Continuing your course along the cliffs from Newtown Cove for about a mile, you arrive at the Metalman Head, described in the opening of this paper. Beyond the Metalman lies the broad Atlantic, and, taking a sharp turn to the westward, the rugged coast-line can be seen for miles.

And now, having gone round the bay from headland to headland, it is time to take a peep at the town.

Tramore is situated about seven miles from the seaport of Waterford, with which it is connected by a single-line railway, and is built on the rising ground at the north-western side of the bay. Not being what one would term a fashionable watering-place—although it does claim to be the head-quarters of the two members of Parliament for the city of Waterford and of the present mayor of that ancient corporation—rents are very reasonable. Nor will hotel charges in Tramore at all alarm an economical visitor. The Great Hotel is a fine building, and ' to one who has been long in city pent' the prospect from its windows is worth a king's ransom.

The permanent residents have naturally endeavoured to secure the most charming dwelling-places; but there should be little commiseration felt for those who can find a vacant four walls on any of the terraces commanding a sea-view.

Tramore is almost destitute of buildings devoted to public amusement. There is one, certainly, called the Assembly Rooms, in which a ball is given once or twice a year; and I have a faint recollection of seeing a theatrical company and a diorama under its roof; but usually the building resembles the ancient temple of Janus during times of peace. Probably those who visit Tramore during the summer months are desirous simply of ' dreamful ease,' and have no zest for amusements other than those which mother Nature affords.

The Assembly Rooms stand at the top of a hill, at whose base is the railway terminus. Should you happen to scale over sixteen stone, I would not recommend frequent ascents of that hill. But it is a level prairie compared with another elevation which may be discovered a little further west, and known as Constitution Hill. The prevailing opinion is that this hill is so called because it would break down the constitution of the strongest man, if he were to attempt a daily climb —the sort of place Mr. Justice Hawkins would revel in.

During the season, which extends from June to September, Tramore is a favourite Sunday resort for pleasure-seekers from Waterford and the neighbouring counties. To the town of the Big Strand, on the Sabbath, excursion-trains carry crowds of visitors, occasionally attended with amateur brass bands, which do their level best to make the air hideous, if it is possible to make Tramore atmosphere hideous; but for the remainder of the week ' the air a solemn still-ness holds,' save when a military band invades the Doneraile Walk.

Tramore can boast of the absence of the elements of modern enlightenment, namely, gas in the streets and a newspaper (unless the existence of the *Waterford Mirror and Tramore Visitor* can be urged in refutation of this statement); so it may fairly claim an idyllic fla-vour denied to many watering-places of to-day.

STRAWBERRY LEAVES.

BY RICHARD DOWLING,

AUTHOR OF 'THE MYSTERY OF KILLARD,' 'THE WEIRD SISTERS,'
'UNDER ST. PAUL'S,' ETC.

Part the First.

THE DUKE OF LONGACRE.

CHAPTER XIX.

THE RESCUE.

WHEN the wave, which Cheyne had seen approaching, struck him, he was dashed violently against the rock behind him. Fortunately he had got round the corner of the opening. Had he happened to be in the gap, he would to a certainty have been hurled through it into the sheltered water inside the reef, and the chances are that, if he had been thus taken unawares, he would have been killed in that gap. Another thing, too, had been in his favour : the rock against which he had been thrown had a small cleft in it, and into this cleft he had been jambed by the force of the water. This fact prevented him from being knocked down and carried away.

Before another wave could strike him, he had extricated himself, and was ready to meet it. Crouching down in the recess, he bent his head, and received the full weight of the water on his crown. The moment the water fell he rose to his feet, and looked around. He was standing on a smooth piece of rock about level with the still water. On each side of him were irregular rocks, a man's height, resting on a bed of flat rock, not more than a few inches submerged in the intervals between the billows.

He looked up, and could now see the yacht forty or fifty yards off to the south-east of where he stood. He had not heard the cheer which went up from the crew when they caught sight of him, and guessed his mission. The crew did not see him until the wave which stunned him for a moment was upon him.

But while his strength was failing him, his object seemed as far from accomplishment as ever. He had now come to the end of the line, and he was still unable to reach the yacht. To venture among those low rocks out there, and face the waves, would be to court almost certain death. For it would be impossible for any one who, like him, knew absolutely nothing of the place, to move more than a couple of feet a minute, as it would be necessary for him to explore with his feet or hands every inch of the way he took, lest he should step into a hole. In case he attempted to run and missed his footing, and got into a hole, a wave would surely be upon him before he could recover himself, and then all would be lost.

All these thoughts passed through his mind with the rapidity of lightning. When he had done with them, he looked up at the yacht.

They had not been idle there. Already a man was out on the foremast-head with a coil of rope. The man waited for the next wave to pass; then, when he saw Cheyne stand up once more, he threw the coil. Fortunately the wind was almost fair for the rope, and it fell within two feet of Cheyne. In an instant it was in his hand. In a few minutes more it was bent to the line Cheyne had tied round his wrist. Then Cheyne loosed the line from his wrist; he had not done so before lest by some mistake or failure of his strength—which he found momentarily giving way—the shore-line might be carried away before the communication had been established.

Then he drew in the slack of the line from the yacht until he had fifty or sixty yards to spare. He wound the line twice round him, and seizing the yacht end of the line, plunged forward through the shallow water. The men on board the yacht drew in the slack of the line, so as to keep it taut without putting any strain upon him.

He heard a roller burst upon the weather-side of the reef, and plunged forward with all his remaining force to reach the yacht before it was upon him.

At that moment he swayed suddenly forward and disappeared from view. He had fallen into one of the holes he had feared to meet. As he did so, the tawny-headed monsters of the water dashed hissing in and swept over the pool in which he lay.

The conditions of this pool were very different from the low level waters in the gap. Here the lower water was almost wholly undisturbed laterally, for the water, the plain of rock in which the hole was, lay almost on a level with the still water, and the water in the pool was consequently almost undisturbed by the waves.

Cheyne rose in a few seconds close to the spot where he sank. The men in the yacht had hauled in the line softly when they saw him come to the surface, and thus they drew him across the hole. In a few seconds he was once more upright, and before another wave had time to reach him he had gained the yacht. Just as they hauled him up the side, the water rose and touched him once more. But this time it was powerless to hurt him, and with a cheer from those on board, he was drawn over the bulwark of the lee-side.

He was almost insensible. His shirt and drawers were torn into shreds, and beat in rags about him in the wind. He was bleeding from twenty wounds, not one of which, however, was dangerous. The line had chafed through his shirt at his waist, and a livid circle marked where it had tightened upon him. His left wrist was torn and discoloured by the later coil, and his hands, feet, and knees were covered with bruises and small cuts from his conflict in the narrow passage.

They had to support him as he stood, while they forced some brandy down his throat. Up from the forecastle they brought blankets, and wrapped them round him. It was some minutes before he had sufficiently recovered to speak.

In the mean time the sailors had not been idle.

Captain Drew was competent and energetic. He knew the yacht would not hold together very much longer, and that every second was of vital importance. Already the block had been lashed for the whip, the whip was rove, and the men on shore were now pulling in the whip by means of the line Cheyne had carried out.

When Cheyne was first carried up windward, both the Duke and the Marquis went up to him and thanked him cordially, and commended his valour. Then they saw he was not in a position to understand them, so they contented themselves with superintending the application of blankets and the administration of brandy, now and then lending a hand to support his drooping figure. All on the yacht saw he was a stranger. They had seen the attempt and failure of Bence. They had seen this other man, this strange man, strip and jump in with the rope; and then they had seen nothing of him until he emerged from that narrow opening in the rock and encounter the first wave. While he was swimming towards them unseen, they were not ignorant of his progress, for repeated signals from the men on shore kept them informed of the way he made.

At the moment Cheyne dived the Duke turned to the captain and asked him what he thought was the chance of success.

'Bence had tried, and Bence has failed,' answered Drew, with a shake of the head. There was no need to say more. The captain's opinion was plainly expressed by his words and manner. Bence had tried to swim out to the yacht with a rope, had failed, and there was no likelihood any other man would succeed.

But as time went on, and the men on the shore signalled by an outward gesture of the arms, as in swimming, and by then holding up an arm for each opening passed, the excitement on board the yacht became intense. The captain ordered a man to the masthead with a rope; he also ordered another man aloft to cut away the topmast, so as to lighten her above. For now he had begun to hope.

The reason why it was utterly impossible for a man to swim from the yacht to the shore was simple enough. In order to do so it would be necessary to cross that comparatively open space between the yacht and the narrow passage,

and to enter the passage with one's back to the source of danger. This alone was an enormous difficulty, added to the others already existing. But what prevented any member of the crew trying to swim ashore was the conviction that no human being could ever get through that passage with life. Bence had more than a local reputation as a swimmer, and any one could understand his trying to do what no other man would attempt.

When at last the signal came that Cheyne had reached the seventh passage, the excitement on board became intense. Only a few seconds had before elapsed between the signal that Bence had entered and the signal that he had failed. Now minutes went by, and the men on board saw that the men ashore had not begun to draw in the line or made any signal of recall. The eyes of every man were now fixed on the mouth of the passage.

'If he does it,' said the captain, 'he deserves a monument.'

'And he shall have it,' said the Duke.

No one had the least clue to what station in life Cheyne belonged. The sailors assumed he was a seafaring man of some kind, because he would have been a credit to their class. While bathing it is difficult to recognise in the water an acquaintance until you hear his voice. But although Cheyne was battered and ragged and marred, there was something about him which told the Duke of Shropshire that the man who had come to the rescue was not an ordinary sailor. You can always tell a sailor by his hands; and the Duke saw by this man's hands that he had not had any long dealing with ropes. The hand was small and powerful, but the knuckles were not abnormally developed, and the nails were smooth and fine.

The men both ashore and on board worked with a will. The whip had been hauled ashore, and the block of it made fast; and now they were hauling the hawser to the beach. Once the hawser was made fast to the anchor on the knoll, they could begin sending the men ashore.

Meanwhile men had been busy in the ship preparing the jackets for the warp. The hawser was new and strong. The whip was of unusual thickness, and, as time was the only thing which could now beat them, Captain Drew decided that two men should go at a time.

Two deep baskets were lashed to a short spar, and then firmly to one another top and bottom. The spar was then secured to two patent blocks, and these patent blocks were slipped in on the hawser and secured. All now was ready for the first two men to go ashore.

Meanwhile Cheyne had recovered to a great extent. He was now able to stand alone. They had brought him clothes, which he had put on, and although he began to feel cold and sick the stiffness of reaction had not yet set in.

Cheyne was standing with his right arm round a pump, his blood-stained face dropped into his blood-stained hand, and his eyes fixed on the man he had sworn to destroy. The Duke and the Marquis stood by the weather-rigging, anxiously watching the men at work on the baskets and hawser.

The captain stood at the lee-rigging, looking up at the men aloft. When all was ready, he crossed the deck and said to the Duke,

'Now, your grace, all is ready for you and his lordship.'

The Duke pointed his long lean finger at Cheyne and said,

'That man must go first.'

The captain drew back to the mast in surprise.

'But, your grace, I am afraid there is danger in delay.'

The water was at every wave bursting over the rocks to windward and rushing from aft along the deck, so that it was impossible to stand without holding on to something.

'There was danger for him when he swam with the rope. He and my son must go first. I will remain. My life is nearly done. If one is to die, let it be me.'

As the Duke said this the captain noticed a change come over the Marquis. His eyes closed, his knees bent under him, and he fell to the deck. He had fainted. The relief of knowing there was now a chance of all of them being saved had been too much, and his exhausted strength had broken down under the reaction.

The men carried the insensible man to the basket, and lashed him in it.

'You are to go with the Marquis,' said the captain to Cheyne.

'Go where?'

'Ashore in the sling. And here's a flask of brandy. His lordship has fainted. Give him some brandy as you are hauled ashore.'

Cheyne took the flask.

'Who says I am to go ashore the first trip?'

'His Grace the Duke.'

'But does he know why I have come here, and who I am?'

'No, I don't think so. But do not waste any more time. If we are to escape there must be no loss of time.'

'Of course not,' thought Cheyne. 'The Duke may not know who I am, or anything about me. How could he know me? I have not told my name to any one here. I thought it would be fine vengeance to come down here and kill this weakling. But would it not be a finer revenge to save him, and then, when he has recovered, declare who I am, and ask if it were likely I, who had risked my life to save him and his father from death, had written that book with an unworthy motive or could be the son of an unworthy mother? Yes, by all means, let him give what help he could.'

Without a moment's hesitation, he allowed himself to be hoisted up to the basket and secured.

The Marquis had not yet recovered. His head was drooping on his chest; his arms were hanging down lifelessly at his side. When Cheyne had got into the basket, and the men were lashing him, he supported the drooping head, and pressed the mouth of the flask against the white lips of the insensible man. They were above the reach of large bodies of water, but they were still deluged with heavy sheets of spray.

The gale not only continued to blow, but increased in fury. Every wave flung tons of water over the deck, and the difficulty of maintaining a position on it increased every minute.

The Duke was still standing by the weather rigging. With his right hand he hung on by a ratlin. Wave after wave poured tons of swishing water on the trembling deck. Already the seams of the planks on which the men stood began to gape, and when the water rushed up from the after end of the yacht and struck against the forecastle bulkhead below, it squirted up through the opening seams.

Twice had the Duke been forced from his hold and cast against the mast. He declined to be lashed. But he was no longer young, and his hold on the ratlin was not nearly as firm as it might be. The very smallness of the line, while it enabled him to grasp it round completely, tended to numb the hand. He felt cold and wretched.

The wind and wetting had begun to produce pains in his shoulder more intense than any he had felt before.

The signal had been given by the man at the masthead to the men on shore to haul in, and already the baskets had begun to glide away from the yacht when a shout of warning and terror came from the man at the masthead.

'On deck there, hold on for your lives!' shouted the man aloft.

The words were hardly out of his mouth when a huge wave, larger by far than any other which had struck the ill-fated yacht, burst upon her, and covered her with boiling torrents of tawny water, hissing foam, and swishing spray.

When the water cleared away two men were missing, a sailor and Reginald Francis Henry Cheyne, seventh Duke of Shropshire.

The men uttered a cry of dismay. Ropes were thrown and two lifebuoys, which were secured to the pump-case. But neither the sailor nor the Duke was ever again seen alive by any one on board that wreck. Before the nobleman, who left the Seabird as Marquis of Southwold, and Charles Augustus Cheyne reached the shore, the Duke of Shropshire had died, and George Temple Cheyne, late Marquis of Southwold, was eighth Duke of Shropshire and virtual owner of four hundred thousand a year, five princely residences, and of all the power and influence of the great house of Cheyne.

Next day the bodies of the Duke and the sailor were found in a little cove at the top of the bay, and hard by the two a book in three volumes, bound with a string which was cleaved and broken at the loose end. On opening these volumes they were found to be *The Duke of Fenwick*, a novel, by Charles Augustus Cheyne. The facts that the book had been found near the body of the dead nobleman, and that it was something to do with a duke, led the simple people who found it to believe that it had not only come ashore from the wreck, but that it was in some way or other connected with the person of the late Duke, so they sent it up to the Castle in the same carriage with the body.

In that same carriage, on the day before, the present Duke and the bruised and battered Cheyne had been driven from the place where they had landed to Silverview Castle, above Silver Bay, the residence of the Duke of Shropshire.

CHAPTER XX.

FAME.

THE little household in Knightsbridge, where Marion Durrant lived with her invalid aunt, Miss Traynor, did not breakfast early. It was very rarely the teapot found its way to the table until ten o'clock. Miss Traynor was one of those invalids who suffer from sleeplessness, together with other maladies, and it was often three, four, or five o'clock in the morning before she closed her eyes.

Miss Traynor was old-fashioned and kindly, with none of the irritability or exactingness of the invalid about her. She was often in great pain, but at such times she wished to be alone. She was never exacting or capricious. She always behaved in her own house as though she was a guest, as far as herself was concerned. She hated ringing bells for the servant, and tried to prevent Marion doing a number of little services which many women in health exact of those around them.

But she was most decidedly old-fashioned. She had a great num-

ber of settled notions, notions acquired long ago, and which nothing in the world could shake. All the eloquence or argument in the world would not move her on any subject she had settled in her mind twenty or thirty years ago. She had an antipathy to new theories, new places, new people. She was an enthusiastic admirer of Church and State. She considered all Liberals murderers and regicides at heart, not that she had even a dim idea what a Liberal was. Personally she would not have hurt the meanest of God's creatures, but she could have read with lively satisfaction that all the Liberals and Radicals had been drowned, provided all detail were omitted, and a bishop had something to do with the matter.

She looked on clergymen of the Church of England with the greatest respect, and she considered bishops infallible and impeccable. She did not put the least faith in missions to savages. She had a mean opinion of savages, and did not think them worth the trouble taken with them by pious folk of a certain way of thinking.

Her father before her had taken in the *Times*, and she took it in too; not that she read much of it, but that she thought every staid respectable house ought to have the *Times*; and that, after the Church and State, the *Times* was the most important institution in the country. She had no comprehensive notion of what the Church was, and her idea of the State was the *Court Circular*. But in what way the *Times* contributed to the welfare of the country, she had no conception whatever. She was always quite sure that whatever the *Times* said must infallibly be right. Any suggestion that, possibly, a conflict or difference of any kind could arise between these three, she would have treated with merciless scorn. There were the Church, State, and *Times;* and as long as they went on, England must continue to be the greatest, most pious, and most successful country under the sun.

After the Church, State, and *Times,* the institution which claimed her greatest respect was the Peerage of England. She would cheerfully have allowed art and commerce to die if we might only retain our old nobility. She had no social ambition for herself. She knew she was not of the metal peers are made of. If a lord had spoken to her, she would have felt he was doing something derogatory to his order. She was a firm believer in caste, and did not wish those above her to come down any more than she wished herself to go up.

'We ought all to keep in our own places, my dear,' she would say. 'It pleases Heaven that we shall be born in a certain state of life. If Heaven intended we should fill any other, there is no doubt we should have been born in that state. We ought not to try and change these things. We are not in our own hands, but in the hands of those Above. If a king is wanted, one is sent; if a lord is wanted, one is sent; and so on; and we ought not to try and alter these laws of Nature any more than any other laws of Nature.'

Upon being reminded that great generals and lawyers and statesmen are often made lords of, she would say,

'These, my dear, were intended by Nature to be lords; but there was no vacancy for them at the time. But you see, in the end, Nature found a vacancy, and they became lords. If a man is intended by Nature to be a lord, nothing in the world will keep him from being one.'

The morning after the wreck of

the yacht Seabird, Miss Traynor was later than usual for breakfast. She came down looking white and worn. She had been more sleepless than usual that night. But on mornings, after such nights, she was more gentle and considerate than at other times.

'How are you this morning, Marion?' she asked, as she kissed the girl and sank into her elbow-chair.

'Pretty well, aunt, only I slept badly. How are you? You look as if you had had one of your bad nights,' said Marion, as she began pouring out the tea.

'So I had, my child, so I had. I heard every hour till four, and I did not go to sleep even soon after that. What kept you awake?'

'O, I don't know, aunt,' said the girl wearily.

'Well, if you don't know, I do, Marion; and you are a little goose to fret about the matter. I know him, dear, better than you do.'

Marion smiled; as though any one, or all the world together, could know her Charlie as she knew him!

'And he's a noble-hearted splendid fellow any girl might rely on and be proud of.'

Marion pouted. As though any human being could be more proud of any other than she was of him!

'And, Marion, you ought not to be a goose, and go fidget your life out, because you have not heard from her for two or three days. Now if it were weeks or months you might have cause to be uneasy.'

Marion looked at her aunt in horror, as though it would be possible for her to live if she were months without hearing from him.

'You know very well, child, there is not a more loyal or gentle-minded man in all London.'

Marion looked down and smiled. As though any one knew anything of Charlie's gentle-mindedness compared with what she knew of it!

'I'll take another cup of tea, and I'll engage you hear from him before the week is out.'

'Before the week is out, aunt!' said Marion, speaking aloud for the first time on the subject. 'Before the week is out! If I don't hear before then, I shall *know* something dreadful has happened.'

'But I tell you you shall. I have a presentiment, a very strong presentiment, you will have a letter from him the morning after to-morrow, saying he is in town, and will be out to see you that afternoon.'

'But why could he not come out, aunt, if he was in London the night before, instead of writing?' Even talking of the chance of his being in London was so much better than thinking of him as far away.

'I did not say he would be in London the night before. Might he not post his letter in Wales, or Cornwall, or Scotland, or Ireland?'

'Yes; but then, aunt, he ought to be here as soon as his letter.'

'Now you are an impatient girl. Business might prevent his coming on by the mail. He might come by a late train. My presentiments are always right, or nearly always; and this is one of the very strongest I ever had in all my life.'

Marion shook her head in despair rather than incredulity. Whatever was the matter, Charlie might have written. What business had he anywhere? In the ordinary sense of the word, he had no business. What he had to with editors and proprietors of papers and publishers was all done in London, not in that hateful place to which he had gone, wherever it was.

She did not care for her breakfast that morning. She drank a cup of tea, ate a mouthful of dry bread, but left the eggs and bacon untouched.

Miss Traynor having done all she could to cheer her niece, and being one of those gentle natures which cannot endure the sight of unhappiness in others when she was powerless to lessen it, took up the *Times*, partly to try and distract herself, and partly to shut out from her eyes the painful sight of the young girl's saddened face.

The gale of the night and day before had been general in England, and London had got its share of it. But a whole gale on the coast never seems more than a stiff breeze in London. Nevertheless the gale of yesterday had not passed over London without inflicting injury; and among the other things it had done within the ten-mile radius was to fling a chimney-pot into the street just opposite Miss Traynor's front-door.

This had been a terrible event in the mind of Miss Traynor. She had been fascinated at the time, and anticipated nothing short of the destruction of her own house and of every one in it. She had eventually congratulated herself a dozen times on the fact that her will was made, and that Marion should have all she had the power to will, in complete forgetfulness that, according to her own theory, Marion would be included among the slain.

However, as afternoon passed into evening, the gale subsided, and Miss Traynor's apprehensions declined. But as she ceased to fear she began to feel an interest in the perils she had passed. Therefore when, this morning, she saw a column of the *Times* headed 'Yesterday's Gale,' it instantly attracted her interest, and settling her spectacles on her nose, she began to read.

'O dear!' she cried suddenly.

'What is it, aunt?' said Marion, with little interest.

'There has been a dreadful wreck of a yacht; and the owner of it, the great Duke of Shropshire, is drowned.'

'Good gracious!' said Marion, somewhat roused from the contemplation of her own unhappiness.'

The old woman read on, but did not say anything further.

Marion had raised her eyes in expectation of more news, and was now looking with awakened interest at her aunt.

Gradually Miss Traynor's face lengthened with astonishment. The mouth opened, the eyebrows went up, the eyes grew round, and the plump cheeks became almost hollow.

'What *is* it?' said Marion, now thoroughly alert.

At last Miss Traynor put down the paper, and looked speechlessly at her niece for a while.

'Aunt, *do* tell me what it is!'

'What did I say about your being proud?'

'I'm sure I don't think I'm very proud,' said the girl, in uneasy perplexity.

'Of him?'

'Of whom, aunt? Do tell me!'

'Of Charles?'

'Well, I'm sure I'm very proud of him. But what has he to do with the storm, and the wreck, and a duke, and the paper?' asked the girl almost piteously.

From her aunt's manner one might assume anything, so long as the thing was very violent and unusual.

'There, read for yourself!' cried the aunt, handing the paper across the table to her niece.

With sparkling eyes and trembling hands, Marion caught the paper and began to read.

The comment on the rescue wound up with these words:

'For endurance and gallantry we may search in vain for a case parallel to this of Mr. Charles Augustus Cheyne. He will receive the medal of the Royal Humane Society, as a matter of course. But in a case of this kind it is to be regretted that some even higher distinction cannot be awarded for endurance and courage inferior to nothing which has gained for a handful of our boldest soldiers the Victoria Cross.'

When Marion had finished reading, she put the paper down on the table before her, looked feebly at her aunt for a moment, and then fell fainting back in her chair.

CHAPTER XXI.

COINCIDENCES.

FOR a few days Edward Graham worked at his big canvas under Anerly Bridge. The weather was superb, the 'studio' as quiet as the top of Horeb, and the artist in the very best of spirits. He had already dead-coloured his work, and got in some of the most important shadows.

This cavernous chamber had many advantages for a painter. The light was of the coolest and softest. But few people and fewer vehicles passed over that bridge to disturb the quiet of the place. Owing to the moisture of the air, the rattling of wagons or carts did not cause any dirt or dust to fall from the roof.

Graham had not told any of the people at the Beagle or in the village that he was going to paint the scene under Anerly Bridge. The morning after the easel, canvas, and colours arrived he had arisen at four and carried them to the bridge, and got them over the parapet and under the arch without any one seeing them or him. He did not want to be haunted by village boys or idle men. He wanted to paint his picture, and to paint it in peace and quietness.

So every morning he arose before the village was stirring, walked to the bridge, and painted until breakfast-time. He waited until all the people were at breakfast, then went down the little glen as far as the church, got into the churchyard, and returned to the Beagle by the church-path and the main road. He had a simple dinner then at the inn, a pint of cider and a pipe under the portico, where he sat until all the village folk were once more at work. Then he went down to the church again, ascended the glen, and recommenced painting.

A more happy or peaceful time Graham never spent than those hours beneath Anerly Bridge. He was young, in full health, had enough money to keep himself comfortably, was by nature light of heart, and had made a good beginning of a picture which he firmly believed would establish his fame. Nothing could be more delightful than working away at his big canvas down there. No one in the town but Cheyne knew where he was or what he was doing; and even Cheyne had only a general notion that he was painting a landscape, nothing more. He should get back to town in a month or so with his great picture finished. He should not sell it for a while, not until he had it on the walls of the Academy anyway. He could live very well until next spring or summer without selling this; and he would put a big price on it, and send it to Burlington House. Suppose it got well hung, he would get his money for it, and a lot of press-notices besides. Cheyne could get him one or two press-notices, anyway.

The afternoon before the gale he had been at work on the sky. The sky was to be full of pure blue morning light, and across it were to float shining white clouds. All was to be calm and radiant; and somehow or another he did not like the look of the sky that after-noon. The colour aloft was thin and dragged out. There was also a disheartening chill in the air. He felt no disposition for work after dinner. This disinclination he attributed to having drank stout instead of cider for his dinner.

'It will never do,' he said to himself, 'to get any bile or stout into that sky. Champagne above and mareschino below are what this picture ought to be painted in. Stout is fit only for still-life and decorative work.'

Therefore, a couple of hours after dinner, he left his studio, and, descending by the glen, reached the churchyard, whence he returned to the village. It was too early for the village elders to assemble, and Graham did not know exactly what to do with his time. It was not inviting out of doors, so he went up to his room and cast about him to see if he could find any not too laborious occupation to fill up the time until he might go down and smoke a big pipe with the elders in the porch.

It was not easy to find any occupation in that room. It was perfectly satisfactory as a sleeping-chamber for a bachelor, but it afforded no means of amusement. Of course, Graham could smoke; but merely smoking was not enough to keep a young man employed for hours. Besides, Graham was such an inveterate smoker that a pipe was no more to him than a coat or a pair of boots. It went without saying.

At last he thought he would sit down, and, as he was going to paint the scene under Anerly Bridge, write out the story of Anerly Church told him by Stephen Goolby. Cheyne had not made any allusion to the coincidence between the name of the chief actors in that story and his own.

He wrote on for a long time, telling the story as plainly and as tersely as he could. It was close on six before he had finished, and then he was obliged to leave a blank for the names of the man and woman who had been married. He knew the man's surname was Cheyne, but could not recall the Christian name of the man, or either the Christian name or surname of the woman.

As soon as he heard voices in the porch, he went down, and, having called for cider and a long pipe, joined in the conversation. Gradually he worked it round to Stephen Goolby's favourite story, and got the old man to tell him the names once more.

' If you like,' said Stephen, ' you are welcome to come down and see the entry yourself.'

'O no, thank you,! I only asked out of curiosity,' said Graham.

Soon after that the evening turned suddenly cool, and from cool to cold. The men took their measures and pipes and tobacco into the comfortable front parlour, whence, at an early hour, Cheyne retired to his room.

Here he took up the story, and having found out the blanks for the names, wrote them in. It was not until he had written in the names, and was reading them over, that another coincidence struck him. Not only were the surnames of the man married thirty-five years ago and his literary friend the same, but the Christian names were also identical. Both men were Charles Augustus Cheyne.

This seemed to Graham a most remarkable circumstance; and when he remembered that Cheyne never spoke of his father and mother except when he could not help it, and that he was now about thirty-four years of age, and that this marriage took place thirty-five years ago, he was more than surprised—he was interested. He made up his mind to keep the story by him until he got back to London, and then work gradually round Cheyne until he got him to tell all he knew of his own history. Then, if there seemed to be any likelihood of this story fitting to the real history of Cheyne, he would give him the manuscript; and if not, he would destroy it.

He went to bed, and slept soundly, so soundly he never heard the gale that tore across the land from the north-east, and smote the fore front of the forest, and beat back the unvailing trees, and thrust the corn flat upon the earth, and winnowed the weakly leaves out of the roaring woods, and hauled great curtains of cloud swiftly across the distracted heavens, and held back the current of the persistent river, and defied the wings of the strongest birds, and beat a level pathway where the young saplings stood.

He slept unusually long that morning. It was six when he awoke. As soon as he knew of the storm, he dressed himself hastily, and walked as quickly as the wind would let him to the bridge.

Here his worst fears were realised. The archway had acted as a funnel, and focussed the wind coming down the glen. The canvas was not to be seen; the easel had been flung half-way through the bridge, and smashed. The colour-box, with all the colours out, had been blown out of the vault, and lay in the foreground below.

He swore at the wind and at himself for his folly in leaving the canvas there. Then he started in pursuit of the fugitive picture.

He found it, face down, in a shallow pool, just under the church. He pulled it out of the water, and placed it flat upon the ground. He then stood back from it a few feet, saw it was all cut and torn; jumped on it half a dozen times; rolled it up carefully; carried it back to the bridge; and, having emptied the bottle of turpentine over it, succeeded, after many efforts, in lighting a match, and setting it on fire.

Then he sat down on his camp-stool—the storm had spared that—and watched the unlucky canvas blaze in the sheltered place he had thrown it.

'If I had only a fiddle now, and could play it, I'd be a kind of modern Nero. But I haven't a fiddle, and if I had I couldn't play it; so, upon the whole, I think I had better get out of this place.'

He rose and went back to the inn. All that day nothing was thought of or talked of but the storm. By night the wind died away. Next morning arose bright and serene. He had made up his mind to stay at Anerly no longer. He would not paint that landscape. He would not try to recover the wreck of that easel. He would not gather up the scattered contents of his colour-box. The place had served him a scurvy trick, and he would leave it without any other recognition of its existence than that of paying what he owed at the Beagle. He would get back to town at once. Be it ever so humble, there was no place like town.

At breakfast he called for his bill and paid it.

The London morning papers did not reach Anerly until ten o'clock. Breakfast had softened Graham's mind towards the village. He no longer called down fire and brimstone from heaven on the unlucky place. After all, the wind, which had only been, like himself, a visitor, was more to blame than the place. It was a horrid thing to get to London in the early afternoon, the horrible practical dinner-eating business - rushing afternoon. No. He would wait until the shades of eve were falling fast, and then he'd

through a Devon village pass, bearing a banner, with the sensible device, 'Nearest railway-station where I can book for London?' In the mean time he would sit under the porch, have some cider and a pipe, and look at the London paper, which had just come.

Having been a severe sufferer from the storm, Graham naturally turned to the account of it. The first thing that caught his eye was 'Gallant Rescue of a Yacht's Crew.' The report did not consist of more than two dozen lines, but it contained all the important elements of the story, and wound up by saying that Mr. Charles Augustus Cheyne was now the guest of his Grace the new Duke of Shropshire. In the early part of the paragraph it spoke of Mr. Cheyne as being the author of the late and very successful novel, *The Duke of Fenwick*, so that no doubt could exist in Graham's mind as to the individuality of the hero.

'In the fact that Cheyne's name is the same as that of the man mysteriously married here thirty-five years ago, and that the name is the same as that of the Duke of Shropshire, and that Cheyne is at Silverview now, there is more than mere coincidence, and I cannot do better than send off my manuscript to Cheyne to-night.'

So he put the sheets into an envelope, with a note, and posted them at the railway-station on his way up to town.

———

CHAPTER XXII.

THIRTY-FIVE YEARS AFTER.

MRS. MANSFIELD still lived at Wyechester, and in the same house as she had spent the early days of her widowhood. With the disappearance and disgrace of her daughter, she had closed her heart against the world. She had provided, in a mechanical way, for her grandson, and she kept herself informed of his whereabouts and his doings. Otherwise she lived a blind narrow life of rigid devotion and unscrupulous severity.

From the day the baby-boy and the packet arrived from Brussels, she had never broken the seal of that packet. For thirty-five years it had lain where she had that day placed it in her desk. The brown paper in which it had been wrapped was now rotten, and might be shaken asunder.

Why should she open it? Her daughter had run away with a man, and had not, in her first letter, said she was married. What was the good of looking through those papers? If it contained any statements in favour of that wretched girl, these statements were, beyond all doubt, lies. Nothing in the world could clear her daughter's name or mitigate the disgrace of her conduct.

Mrs. Mansfield took in the *Wyechester Independent.* She did not read the general news as a rule. But the *Independent*, as became the only daily paper in a town whose sole claim upon distinction was that it had a cathedral and a bishop, devoted much of its space to local and general religious topics. The religious news and comments she always read.

That morning after the storm, the *Wyechester Independent* had a long account of the storm and of the wreck of the Seabird, the death of the Duke of Shropshire, and of the heroic conduct of ' Mr. Charles Augustus Cheyne, a gentleman who has recently won his spurs in the field of literature, and whose latest achievement fills all England this day with wonder and admiration, and of whom the people of Wyechester are naturally proud, as he owes his parentage on one side to this city.'

What, Wyechester proud of her grandson, of the child of her unhappy daughter! Wyechester, the pious cathedral-town of Wyechester, proud of him she had always looked upon as a disgrace! It was unkind, ungenerous, unmanly of the author of that article to thus even distantly hint at the disgraceful past. It was not necessary or decent for the writer of that article to unearth a long-buried scandal. It was an outrage on the living and the dead. The man who wrote it was a low creature, and ought to be scouted from all decent society; that is, indeed, if ever he had been in decent society.

While the old woman was giving full scope to her anger, there was a knock at the door. A gentleman desired to see Mrs. Mansfield; a gentleman who gave the name of Friston. Mrs. Mansfield did not know any gentleman of that name, but the servant might show him in.

A stout little man entered the room, and bowed to Mrs. Mansfield, and said briskly,

' Mrs. Mansfield, I believe?'

' Yes, sir, I am Mrs. Mansfield,' she said, with great coldness and repelling precision.

He took no notice of her manner.

' My name is Friston, madam.'

' And to what, Mr.—er—eh—Friston, do I owe the honour of this visit? I have no recollection of having seen you before, sir,' she said frigidly.

' You are right, my dear madam.'

The old woman drew herself back at the unwarrantable freedom of this man calling her ' my dear madam.'

The visitor took no notice—in fact, did not observe her manner. He went on:

' We have never met before; and you owe my visit to the flattering fact that you have a grandson, whose name is now a household word in all England.'

'Sir!' she said, rising angrily.

He did not see her anger.

'I have come, my dear madam, to know if you will be good enough to furnish me with additional particulars about your grandson, about his youth, and so on—in short, a brief biography. I represent the *Wyechester Independent* and one of the most influential metropolitan dailies. Any facts you will be good enough to give me will not, you may be certain, suffer in my hands. I will do the best I can to make them light and readable. Any anecdote of your grandson's prowess as, say, a boxer or a cricketer, while a boy, would be peculiarly acceptable, particularly if there was a touch of magnanimity about it. One of the fruits of my long experience is that nothing appeals so universally to the British public as magnanimous muscle.'

The old woman stood pale and without the power of speech while he made this long harangue. When he paused she raised her arm, and, pointing with a long thin yellow finger at the door, said huskily,

'Go, sir, go at once!' She could say no more.

He bounded to his feet in amazement. He had no intention to hurt or offend. Nothing was farther from his thoughts. He had been simply heedless, full of his own mind, unobservant.

'I am sure I beg your pardon,' he said, in a tone of sincere apology. 'I had no intention of causing you any annoyance. I thought you might like to make the *Independent* and the *Metropolitan Vindicator* the medium—'

'Go, sir, go! You are committing an outrage. Go!'

'Believe me, madam,' he began, backing towards the door.

'I do not want to hear any more. Go, sir!'

'But, my dear madam, you must allow me to explain—'

'If you do not leave at once I shall send my servant for the police!'

The reporter had reached the door by this time, and, as Mrs. Mansfield ceased speaking, he bowed and retired, comforting himself with the assurance that she was mad.

When she was alone she sank down and covered her face with her hands, too much exhausted to think.

For upwards of an hour she did not move; then she took away her hands from before her face, arose, and, with resolute step, crossed the room to where her desk stood on a small table in the pier. With resolute hands she opened the desk, and took out that old bundle which had been sent to her by her dying child by the same messenger that had brought the boy five-and-thirty years ago.

Yes, she would destroy this hateful relic of disgrace and dishonour. She would burn it down to the last atom. Nothing of it, nothing of that perfidious daughter, should survive.

She sat down and broke the seals, and cut the mouldering cord, and released what was inside. This proved to be a large leather pocket-book.

The first thing that met her eye was the copy of a certificate of marriage between Charles Augustus Cheyne and Harriet Mansfield at Anerly Church. She searched in the pocket-book and found a small sealed packet, bearing, in a man's writing, these words, 'Not to be opened for three years.' The date was the same as that on the copy of the marriage-certificate.

With trembling hands the old

woman cut the silk and broke the seal. She found nothing but a letter on an old-fashioned sheet of letter-paper, which, on its right-hand corner, bore a coronet surrounded by strawberry leaves.

END OF PART L.

[To be continued.]

SUMMER'S SECRETS.

SWALLOW, tell me ere thou goest
　　O'er the ocean blue ;
Swallow, tell me all thou knowest,
　　All she told to you ;
Tell me, was it love that lit her
Eyes when thou didst see them glitter,
Listening to thy trembling twitter ?
　　Swallow, tell me true.

Cruel swallow, still coquetting,
　　Flitting to and fro,
How canst thou have joy in fretting,
　　Torturing me so ?
Ah, thou couldst not be so cruel,
Swallow, if you only knew well
How thy flitting fans the fuel
　　Of my burning woe.

Ocean, ere you grow imperious,
　　Tell me, I implore,
All her secret words mysterious
　　Whispered by thy shore,
When she, pausing, would resume her
Thoughtful meditative humour,
Hearkening something in the rumour
　　Of thy ceaseless roar.

Many secrets since thou glided
　　First beneath the sun
In thy bosom have subsided :
　　All I ask is one ;

Proud to be with that one gifted,
On thy billows gently lifted,
Well thou knowest where it drifted
    When its voyage done.

Into thy recesses, pressing
    Deep her mouth and nose,
Oft she whispered, love confessing,
    O too happy rose !
Nay, deny not, for the gushing
Of the fountain of her blushing,
All thy pallid petals flushing,
    Thy connivance shows.

Rose, thou art no honest martyr,
    For thou didst presume
For her secret's truth to barter
    Thine unstaid perfume ;
Wilful, wily, wizard flower,
Yield thy talisman of power,
Ere thy comrades of the bower
    Mourn thy latest bloom.

Wind, with sympathetic fingers
    Passing through her hair ;
Wind, with cooling palm that lingers
    On her forehead fair ;
At thy touch of love she'd heave a
Sigh, and thou wouldst then receive a
Soft injunction swift to leave a
    Message : tell me where ?

Fairy good of summer breezes,
    While thy powers last,
Ere the winter demon teases
    Sailors with its blast,
Waft my bark of Hope, though frail it
Seem, and teach me how to sail it,
Lest a doubt-struck waif I wail it ;
    Guide me—ah, 'tis past !

T. G.

LOVED AND LOST.

By Mrs. ADOLPHE SMITH.

THEY walked along in silence together. They could hear the gay voices of the people of their party in the distance; a snatch of song reached them now and then, and seemed, to their troubled minds, like a discord. Darkness was gathering quickly around them; shadows were creeping up among the trees, the long branches looked like black arms stretching into the softer blackness of the leaves, and, here and there, there was a break and a glimpse of the gray evening sky.

'How dark it is!' murmured Mary Temple.

'Does the darkness make you nervous?' asked her companion.

'No,' she answered shortly; 'but it reminds me that it is getting late, and that we must not keep so far behind our friends. I wonder they have not waited for us.'

'They have not missed us,' rejoined her companion; 'and they would not be anxious about you if they did, since you are with me, and they know what old friends we are. But we will hasten on, and overtake them, if you like.'

She did not answer, but accelerated her pace, and walked so fast at last that her companion had some difficulty in keeping up with her; but presently she stopped short.

'You must be tired; won't you rest a little?' he pleaded.

'No, Richard,' she said quickly; 'I must not rest here in the forest alone with you. It would not be right of me. I ought not to have lingered behind our friends; but I had no idea how late it was,

and the darkness came on so quickly. And now, you see, they are not within hearing evidently; for we cannot distinguish their voices any longer.'

It was true. The sounds of laughter and of singing had died away, and, listen intensely as they might, they could hear nothing beyond the nameless sounds of the forest itself—the indescribable whir and rustle and flutter of the woods at night.

'It was very inconsiderate of them to hasten on without waiting for us,' murmured Mary Temple, standing perfectly still, and speaking in a low voice. 'But the best thing to be done now is to hasten on after them.'

'I am afraid you will be exhausted if you walk long at such a rate,' said Richard, as they resumed their hurried pace.

On they went, the shadows creeping closer, the strange weird sounds increasing around them, the trees growing blacker, the sky growing darker, and over everything the soft white mist rising and spreading itself out like a huge pall.

'Why, Dick, I do believe I see a glowworm!' exclaimed Mary Temple suddenly, in a voice as different from that in which she had spoken before as sorrow is different from joy, as tears are different from smiles.

The man's heart beat almost to suffocation as he heard the old familiar name, but he controlled himself sufficiently to answer briskly and naturally.

'Haven't you seen them before?'

he said. 'There are numbers in the forest, I believe.'

'Don't you remember how we used to hunt for them in the wood and in the hedges at home?' said Mary, speaking still in the altered voice—such a bright, sweet, gay voice it was. 'And you used to play tricks upon me, and make me run all down the garden at night to see them; and, of course, when I got there none were to seen. And we never found any out in the wood in those days, did we? I wonder why that was, Dick?'

'I daresay because those little Kentish woods are, as a rule, so overrun with people that the glow-worms are all taken. You know, there is nothing delights a Cockney so much,' answered Richard Lovel.

'What a tease you were then!' continued Mary Temple; 'what a worry you were to me! Do you remember persuading me to climb up the ladder into the old oak-tree down the garden, when I was a child; and, directly I had got up, you scampered down the ladder as fast as you could, and ran away with it, leaving me literally "up a tree;" and you would not bring the ladder back until the dinner-bell had rung, and I was scolded for being late? Then that time when I went on a visit to your home; and the night you were to come back from boarding-school, your father and brothers insisted on hiding me in the cupboard in the schoolroom. Then when you came into the room, I heard them tell you that a present had come for you during the week; and you said it was not true, and that they were trying to "take you in;" and you were such a long time before you would come and open the cupboard; and you were so angry when you did open it and found it was "only Moll" inside. Poor Dick! you were thoroughly disappointed then, were you not?'

And she laughed heartily at the recollection, and Lovel tried to laugh too.

'However, I suppose in the wild life you have led abroad,' she continued presently, 'you have forgotten all those little incidents of childhood; but I have passed such a quiet time that I have been apt to go over all those pleasant merry days again and again.'

'The wild life you speak of has not made me forget a single small event,' said Lovel, in a low voice. 'Through all my adventures and peril in South America, I never forgot you. The thought of "little Moll" was my guiding-star; it kept me from harm many a time; it fired my spirit; and when sometimes we were in any danger, I used to say to myself that I *must* make a proud figure, for, if I did, I should like "little Moll" to hear a good account of my end. When I awoke one night and found myself in a room hedged in with fire on every side—you heard of it, you told me this morning—I swear to you that my first thought was, O, if I could only let "little Moll" know how I have loved her since I was a boy!'

'Hush, hush!' whispered Mary, her voice trembling as she whispered, 'You must not say this to me now; it is terribly wrong for you to say anything of the kind to me, and for me to listen.'

'Am I to go away from you then, still bearing all the load of my disappointment and sorrow?' said Lovel bitterly. 'May I not have the miserable satisfaction of knowing that some one knows of my trouble? Will you deny me that?'

'But nothing you can say can mend matters,' Mary expostulated; 'in fact, everything is tending to make matters worse. See, how late it is; and although we are hurrying on so fast, we do not seem to be getting any nearer. If I do not reach home soon after our party go through the village, they will grow anxious about me; and I myself am getting more nervous every moment.'

'Moll,' he said passionately, 'I am going to leave this place to-morrow, and I do not believe you will ever see me again! I came home only a month ago, and went down to Fairfield to find you, and there they told me the bitter truth. I bore it, however, and I determined to come and take a look at you in your Hampshire home before going away again. I reached your village last night. I broke in upon you this morning. I have spent the day with you; and when all your merry friends called upon you and asked you to join in their evening stroll in the forest, I must confess that I was anxious to accompany you. I did not think of saying a word of this to you then, but I only felt that it would be comparative happiness to walk beside you, to see you, to know you were near, without being forced by the exigencies of society and conventionality to laugh and joke and talk platitudes. I have been through hardships of a kind that would make your woman's heart bleed. I have lain out in the open, night after night, in the vast solitude of those magnificent American prairies. I have been, I can say literally, through fire and water; and I went through it all with a light heart—with a happy heart even. I thought of you day after day, morning after morning, night after night, and an indefinable instinct seemed to tell me that my "little Moll," as I had so often called you, was really mine, that she loved me in her heart, that she would not have forgotten me. If I had known the truth I should never have come back to England; you would never have heard of me

again, Moll; and perhaps it would have been better so.'

'O, hush, Dick!' she said again faintly, and clasping her hands tightly together as if in agony. 'All these things you are saying sink into my heart, and make me cold at the thought of what I have done.'

He was silent for a few moments; and presently they emerged from under the trees into an open plain, dotted here and there with masses of bush and fern, and bounded on all sides by vast plantations of pine and beech and ash trees. As they stepped out from the underwood they came into comparative light, and they could see the dim outline of each other's face, and see the gentle undulation of the land in front of them.

Mary looked about her in dismay.

'I don't remember crossing this place as we came from home,' she said.

But Lovel did not answer her remark. He stopped short in front of her, and, seizing her hands to prevent her walking on, he said, his voice faltering with emotion,

'Moll, you must and shall hear me and answer me. Considering all that you have done for me, considering how you have spoilt the rest of my life, it is only fair that you should at least let me speak to you. You say it is wrong in you to listen to me. It may be so; but the principal wrong, the foundation of all wrong, is in the feeling itself, which lies at my heart, and which, right or wrong, will lie there as long as I live, I fancy. You knew what I felt. If you did not know it before, you have, must have, known it to-day; you must have seen it in my face. Is it not as bad, as wrong, for you to know that I love you as to hear my poor weak words?'

He paused for a reply; but she

only shivered and breathed a deep sigh.

'You know why I left home,' he continued passionately—'because my father married again and put a frivolous flippant woman in my dear dead mother's place. I had always been a wild fellow, they said; and I went out to America to work off my wildness, determined to fall on my feet somehow while I was there; and then to come back to you, Moll, to tell you how I had loved you ever since those boyish days when I used to save up my pocket-money to buy you presents—simple trifling presents they were, but they came from my young heart. I did not seek to bind you by any promise. It seemed to me unfair to attempt to tie you to a worthless fellow, such as I was, without home or prospects, and for whom you might have to wait years; but at the bottom of my heart there was a firm belief in you, a hope that you had understood me, and that you would feel the instinct that I felt, the natural ineradicable love that springs from perfect communion of souls. I should have laughed at the idea of making you promise me anything; it seemed to me that you must have felt all I felt, and that I should find you waiting for me on my return, and should only have to say, "Moll darling, I have come back to you!" and take you to my arms for ever. Did you understand nothing of all this, then? Was I entirely mistaken? Did those pretty smiles and glances of yours mean nothing? Have I deceived myself throughout?'

By this time Mary had disengaged her hands, and had covered her face with them.

'Answer me, Moll!' Lovel cried. 'Did you not guess that I loved you—did you not know it?'

'I used to fancy you did,' she answered, with something like a sob stopping her every now and then; 'but when you were so long away, and I heard nothing of you, I came to think at last that it had been only a boyish liking, that it was merely because we had grown up together as playmates. Then my father and mother fell into such sudden difficulties, as you have been told; and in all their trials and troubles Mr. Temple was so good and kind; he helped them in so many ways; and at last, when my father, on his deathbed, told me that our faithful friend wanted me to be his wife, when my father told me how contented and happy he should die if I only consented—how could I refuse? You had been away so long, and you had never said a word to me of love, and I did not know that you had not forgotten me. And so my dear father died in peace, and I was married to Mr. Temple. I have not been unhappy with him; he has been so good to me always; he has trusted me so fully, and has tried to please me in every way. I have attempted, in return, to be a good wife to him. I have resolutely put aside all my old hopes and dreams, and have—'

'Your *hopes*, Moll! Did you say your *hopes?*' said Lovel passionately.

'Yes; they were hopes—once!' she answered.

'So you loved me, Moll, after all!' he cried. 'Tell me that you did love me? Answer me, if only for the sake of the happy years we passed together as children; give me that shred of consolation; tell me that you did love me?'

'I never knew myself how much until this morning,' she replied simply.

He caught her hands in his and pressed his lips upon them as if he were beside himself, and she heard him muttering some impassioned words as if he were hardly conscious of what he was saying. She submitted; she let him kiss her hands, and press them tightly in his. It seemed to her like a dream, from which she would awake presently and find herself in her sunny home in the picturesque New Forest village.

'You are shivering. Are you cold, my darling?' were the words that roused her at last.

She put her hands to her ears wildly, as if to shut out the sound of the words.

'You must not say that to me, Dick,' she said. 'You must not say any more to me; but take me home as quickly as possible. I I am cold—and ill—and miserable. Let us walk on.'

And she started forward with a rapid and determined step, as if resolved that there should be no more conversation. Her mind was in a whirl, and above all her self-reproaches the tender tone of that word of endearment was ever recurring. She was no longer overwhelmed by anxiety as to the concern of her husband and her friends. Those feelings had been entirely dispelled by the emotions of the last few moments, by Lovel's passionate words, by her own sensations of utter hopeless misery; and if she longed to be at home, it was that she might shut herself up and think over the incidents of the day undisturbed. And then she remembered that he had said he should be gone to-morrow; he had said that she would not see him again, and she felt instinctively that it was true. What should she do to-morrow, and the day after to-morrow, and on all the days through which she would have to live? How could she ever be happy again? How could she ever even appear to be happy in her quiet home? Hitherto she had had no excessive feeling one way or the other. She had not been

very happy, and she certainly had not been very unhappy; but this one day had altered everything. From the moment in that morning when her old friend and playmate had come to her in her garden, sent by her husband to give her a welcome surprise, she had felt as if she were a different person. She had dropped all the flowers that she had picked, and had stood before him unable to speak; and, at the first sound of his voice, she had burst into tears. That she had afterwards attempted to account for by saying that he reminded her of her home, her dead parents, her childhood.

What should she do? she asked herself over and over again. How should she live on? She knew now that her heart had been with Dick all along, and she felt that those girlish hopes and dreams of hers, those undefined thoughts and scruples which had made her delay her marriage to the utmost limit, were all for him.

They had nearly crossed the plain, when Mary turned round to Lovel, who had been walking silently beside her, and, stopping suddenly, said,

'I do not remember crossing this broad expanse of land, do you?'

'To speak frankly, I do not,' answered Lovel. 'But there are conditions of mind in which field and forest are much alike, and I must own that I was not observing the beauties of Nature as I came along. I certainly do not remember this plain, however.'

Mary looked about her in dismay. Everything appeared unfamiliar. She was convinced that they had never passed that sombre line of pine-trees that stood out against the sky on the summit of the easy hill they were climbing.

'We must turn back,' she said decisively. 'We have missed our

way; and all we can do is to retrace our steps until we get into
the right road.'

'But are you sure of this?' said
Lovel. 'It seems to me that it
will be terribly difficult to retrace
our footsteps under the trees, to
say nothing of finding the path we
have missed. Do you not know
what part of the forest this is?
Do you not know in what direction
we are going? I feel very unwilling to go back beneath the
trees; it is so damp there; and
you might be cold, in spite of the
fact that it is August. See how
misty it all is.'

'I must go back through the
cold and the mist and the damp,
however,' said Mary; and back
they went, resolutely, walking side
by side, in utter silence.

'Dick, this is dreadful!' Mary
exclaimed at last. 'I do not
know where we are, or where we
are going, and the forest is bewildering. I heard Mr. Temple
say that he lost himself in it once
for hours at night; but I could
not believe he was not trying to
frighten me. Now I can understand it. Still, I think we are
going in the right direction; yet,
after all, the trees did not seem so
thick or the grass and ferns so
high.'

'What will your friends do?'
asked Lovel. 'Will they start off
to find you, do you think? What
will Mr. Temple do?'

'I daresay he will guess what
has happened, and will wait at
home for me, for some time at least,'
answered Mary. 'I have often
heard him speak of the folly of
searching-parties starting too soon.
Then they will all tell him that you
are with me; and he trusts me so
fully that he will fear nothing.'

'There is one thing that I will
make you do,' said Lovel; 'and
that is, rest yourself a little while.
You will be ill after all this fatigue.'

Mary thought, too, that she
should be ill; but she said nothing.

'If you will consent to rest a few
moments,' Lovel continued, 'I
will make up a fire here. This
furze will burn splendidly; and I
have some matches in my pocket.'

'That will be capital,' said
Mary brightly; 'and if any of
them come back to look for us,
the light of the fire will attract
them.'

Quick as thought he made a
pile of furze and fern and dried
leaves, and set fire to it. The
flames did not grow rapidly, because of the damp; but Mary
drew near gratefully, and held her
slender hands towards the burning
pile.

'How cheerful it looks!' she
said, as Lovel banked it up on all
sides. 'I suppose you have often
made a fire like this before? Just
think how delighted we should
have been at this adventure if we
had been children.'

He laughed, and sighed too,
and stood still beside her, looking
with melancholy eyes at the crackling leaves and branches.

Mary glanced round with something like awe; the trees seemed
bigger and blacker than ever; innumerable shadows appeared to
be grouped in the background;
it looked as if every inch of the
ground was moving in a ghastly
ghostly fashion; and, as she raised
her eyes to the canopy of leaves
and boughs over her head, she fancied she saw endless varieties of
faces and forms peering down at
her, the faces laughing maliciously,
the long arms pointing to her.
With a beating throbbing heart,
she turned quickly to her companion, and putting her hand on
his arm, said hurriedly,

'I am almost frightened, Dick;
the trees are so full of shadows!'

'You need not be frightened;

I will take care of you,' he answered; and he drew her cold trembling hand within his arm, and held it firmly.

She let him do it. She dared not trust herself to remonstrate; and they stood together, her arm in his, her hand in his, in the light of the fire, afraid to speak to each other, afraid to look at each other. Suddenly, in the dead silence—a silence so intense that they almost seemed to hear each other's heart beating—there arose a far, far distant sound. It was so faint that though they both heard it they both thought it was fancy. They listened, and heard it again, and presently again—a little more distinct this time.

' Did you hear that sound, Dick?' asked Mary, raising her eyes to his face. ' What does it sound like to you? Is it not singing? Hark! There! It is more distinct now! Yes, it *is* singing! They are coming to look for us. They are singing " O hills and vales of pleasure." '

With a bitter cry, he threw his arms round her and clasped her to him.

' My little Moll, they are coming to take you from me!' he murmured, as he bent his head over the pale fair face on his shoulder.

The sound of the gay singing came nearer and nearer, and presently there was a loud ' Halloo!' that echoed round and round them.

' God only knows why this agony should have been reserved for me,' said Lovel, speaking in a low quick voice. ' It will serve some purpose of His, I must suppose. I cannot see why I should not have been allowed to have you for my very own; but I can only try to believe there is some reason. No one, however, can control one's thoughts and hopes; and in that world to which we are going, in that life that follows after death, surely we shall meet there at last, and I shall

hold out my arms to you, and be free to clasp you in them for ever!'

' Dick, this is worse than death!' she said faintly.

' They are calling again. I must answer. Kiss me once, my little Moll, if only for the sake of our happy childhood, for the sake of my long love, of my wasted hopes! Kiss me once!' he said passionately. And she raised her white face and kissed him.

' Halloo!' cried Lovel, walking hurriedly in the direction where the sounds of music had come; and ' Halloo!' rang through the woods around; and in a few moments he was surrounded by the boisterously merry party of young people.

' Where is Mrs. Temple?' was the cry.

' She is still crouching by the fire I made for her,' answered Lovel, speaking as unconcernedly as he could. ' You see we lost our way; of course, I knew nothing about it; and Mrs. Temple has been nervous and cold. She ought to get home as soon as possible. To tell you the truth,' he added, almost confidentially to one of the party, ' I am exceedingly glad that you have come up; for you will be able to see her home, and I wanted to go on to the next village, from which it will be easier to reach the station to-morrow morning. It is a matter of life and death to me to catch that first train.'

Hereupon one of the young men volunteered to show him ' a bit of the way,' and Lovel started off, determined to find his road across the forest in some way, and to leave England and end his life on the other side of the Atlantic.

In the general confusion and laughter and acclamations of Mary's friends, no one noticed Lovel's curiously abrupt departure. The young man who had volunteered walked about half a mile with him, and did not find him particularly unentertaining.

As for Mary, her friends took her home; and as they were afraid, from her excessive cold, that the damp had given her a touch of that ague and fever often consequent upon exposure in the evening mists of the forest, they did not tease her with questions or jocularities, but left her to her own miserable and remorseful thoughts.

In a letter Lovel received some months later, in America, from his brother in England, the following passage occurred:

'You will be sorry to hear that poor Mary Temple—Mary Vane that was, you know—is dead. It appears that she caught a cold, some time in the summer, by walking in the forest at night, and she never recovered from the effects of it. She had a bad attack of fever, and regularly wasted and pined away. What a blow this would have been to you when you were a boy!'

SONG OF PLENTY.

I COME with the sunshine, I lurk in the shadow;
    I come with the soft warm rain;
I nurture the richness of upland and meadow;
    I nourish and ripen the grain.
The south wind's my henchman, the blue sky's my banner,
    And Earth is the darling I love;
At noontide I waft scented breezes to fan her,
    And I brood her at night like a dove.

Bright hope, in the spring-time, with blossoms I cherish;
    The summer with roses I crown;
And to autumn give cheer, that the poor may not perish,
    When the snow-clouds of winter sweep down.
In vineyard and cornfield with welcome I'm greeted,—
    Where joyous are laughter and song;
And hearts warm and thankful, for blessings repeated,
    Soft vespers at nightfall prolong.

I love to give more than the reapers can gather,
    When harvest-time gladdens the land;
That the rich may remember, when thanking 'our Father,'
    To leave for the poor gleaner's hand.
I joy in the fulness of orchard and garden,
    With fruit hanging ripe in the air;—
So spreading my bounty, that no heart may harden,
    And none be left out of my care.

THOMAS EARP.

END OF VOL. XXVIII.

LONDON : ROBSON AND SONS, PRINTERS, PANCRAS ROAD, N.W.

CPSIA information can be obtained at www.ICGtesting.com
Printed in the USA
LVOW03s0108220214

374705LV00017BA/684/P